STARS OF SOUL AND RHYTHM & BLUES

STARS OF
SOUL AND
RHYTHM & BLUES

TOP RECORDING ARTISTS AND SHOWSTOPPING PERFORMERS, FROM MEMPHIS AND MOTOWN TO NOW

LEE HILDEBRAND

BILLBOARD BOOKS
An imprint of Watson-Guptill Publications/New York

Edited by Tad Lathrop
Senior Editor: Paul Lukas
Book and Cover Design: Bob Fillie, Graphiti Graphics
Cover Illustration: Charles Burns
Production Manager: Hector Campbell

First published 1994 by Billboard Books, an imprint of Watson-Guptill
Publications, a division of BPI Communications, Inc., 1515 Broadway,
New York, NY 10036.

Library of Congress Cataloging-in-Publication Data
Hildebrand, Lee.
   Stars of soul and rhythm & blues : top recording artists and
showstopping performers, from Memphis and Motown to now / Lee
Hildebrand.
      p.   cm. — (Billboard hitmakers series)
   Includes discographies and index.
   ISBN 0-8230-7633-4
   1. Soul music-0Bio-bibliography. 2. Rhythm and blues music—Bio
-bibliography. I. Title. II. Series.
ML102.S65H55 1994
782.42'1643'0922—dc20
   [B]   94-27594

Manufactured in the United States of America

First Printing, 1994

1 2 3 4 5 6 7 8 9 / 99 98 97 96 95 94

To the memories of Mike Leadbitter, Mark Edmund, and Troyce Key

CONTENTS

About "Billboard Hitmakers" ix

Preface x

Acknowledgments xii

JOHNNY ACE 1

ASHFORD AND SIMPSON 2

ATLANTIC STARR 3

ANITA BAKER 4

LaVERN BAKER 6

HANK BALLARD AND THE MIDNIGHTERS 7

THE BAR-KAYS 8

ARCHIE BELL AND THE DRELLS 10

WILLIAM BELL 12

REGINA BELLE 13

GEORGE BENSON 14

BROOK BENTON 15

CHUCK BERRY 17

BOBBY BLAND 18

BOOKER T. AND THE MG'S 20

BOYZ II MEN 21

BOBBY BROWN 23

CHARLES BROWN 25

JAMES BROWN 26

ROY BROWN 28

RUTH BROWN 29

PEABO BRYSON 31

SOLOMON BURKE 32

JERRY BUTLER 33

CAMEO 34

MARIAH CAREY 36

CLARENCE CARTER 38

GENE CHANDLER 39

RAY CHARLES 40

THE CHI-LITES 42

CHIC 43

GEORGE CLINTON 45

THE CLOVERS 47

THE COASTERS 48

NATALIE COLE 49

CON FUNK SHUN 50

SAM COOKE 52

ROBERT CRAY 54

TYRONE DAVIS 55

DeBARGE 56

THE DELFONICS 58

THE DELLS 59

BO DIDDLEY 61

FATS DOMINO 62

LEE DORSEY 63

THE DRAMATICS 65

THE DRIFTERS 67

EARTH, WIND AND FIRE 68

THE EMOTIONS 70

EN VOGUE 71

BETTY EVERETT	73	KC AND THE SUNSHINE BAND	120
THE 5 ROYALES	74	CHAKA KHAN	121
ROBERTA FLACK	76	BEN E. KING	123
THE FLAMINGOS	77	KING CURTIS	124
EDDIE FLOYD	78	GLADYS KNIGHT AND THE PIPS	126
THE FOUR TOPS	80	KOOL AND THE GANG	128
ARETHA FRANKLIN	81	PATTI LABELLE	130
THE GAP BAND	83	DENISE LASALLE	131
MARVIN GAYE	85	LeVERT	132
LARRY GRAHAM	86	JOE LIGGINS	134
AL GREEN	88	LITTLE ANTHONY AND THE IMPERIALS	135
ROY HAMILTON	89	LITTLE MILTON	137
WYNONIE HARRIS	91	LITTLE RICHARD	138
DONNY HATHAWAY	92	NELLIE LUTCHER	140
ISAAC HAYES	93	FRANKIE LYMON AND THE TEENAGERS	141
Z. Z. HILL	95	THE MANHATTANS	143
HOT CHOCOLATE	96	THE MARVELETTES	144
WHITNEY HOUSTON	97	CURTIS MAYFIELD	145
IVORY JOE HUNTER	99	PERCY MAYFIELD	147
THE INTRUDERS	100	MAZE FEATURING FRANKIE BEVERLY	148
THE ISLEY BROTHERS	101	VAN McCOY	150
BULL MOOSE JACKSON	103	CLYDE McPHATTER	151
FREDDIE JACKSON	104	AMOS MILBURN	152
JANET JACKSON	105	STEPHANIE MILLS	153
MICHAEL JACKSON	107	ROY MILTON	155
MILLIE JACKSON	108	THE MOMENTS	156
THE JACKSONS	110	THE MOONGLOWS	158
ETTA JAMES	111	MELBA MOORE	160
RICK JAMES	113	THE NEVILLE BROTHERS	161
LITTLE WILLIE JOHN	114	NEW EDITION	163
BUDDY JOHNSON	116	THE OHIO PLAYERS	165
QUINCY JONES	117	THE O'JAYS	166
LOUIS JORDAN	118	THE ORIOLES	168

JEFFREY OSBORNE	169	DONNA SUMMER	220
JOHNNY OTIS	170	THE SYLVERS	221
RAY PARKER, JR.	171	JOHNNIE TAYLOR	222
PEACHES AND HERB	173	THE TEMPTATIONS	223
ANN PEEBLES	174	TAMMI TERRELL	225
TEDDY PENDERGRASS	176	JOE TEX	227
ESTHER PHILLIPS	177	CARLA THOMAS	229
WILSON PICKETT	178	RUFUS THOMAS	230
THE PLATTERS	180	THE THREE DEGREES	232
THE POINTER SISTERS	181	THE TIME	233
BILLY PRESTON	183	TONY TONI TONÉ	234
LLOYD PRICE	185	JOE TURNER	235
PRINCE	186	TINA TURNER	237
THE RAVENS	188	LUTHER VANDROSS	239
LOU RAWLS	189	JR. WALKER AND THE ALL STARS	240
OTIS REDDING	190	WAR	241
MARTHA REEVES AND THE VANDELLAS	192	BILLY WARD AND HIS DOMINOES	243
LIONEL RICHIE	194	DIONNE WARWICK	244
SMOKEY ROBINSON	195	DINAH WASHINGTON	246
ROSE ROYCE	197	MARY WELLS	247
DIANA ROSS	199	THE WHISPERS	249
SADE	201	BARRY WHITE	250
SAM AND DAVE	202	DENIECE WILLIAMS	252
SHALAMAR	203	CHUCK WILLIS	253
THE SHIRELLES	205	JACKIE WILSON	254
JOE SIMON	207	BILL WITHERS	256
SISTER SLEDGE	208	BOBBY WOMACK	257
PERCY SLEDGE	210	STEVIE WONDER	258
SLY AND THE FAMILY STONE	211	BETTY WRIGHT	260
THE SPINNERS	213	ZAPP AND ROGER	261
THE STAPLE SINGERS	214		
EDWIN STARR	216	Index	264
CANDI STATON	217	Photo Credits	288
THE STYLISTICS	219	About the Author	288

ABOUT "BILLBOARD HITMAKERS"

Billboard is the home of the pop charts. For a century, those charts have chronicled the hit songs and albums that have come to represent the pinnacle of commercial achievement in the music industry.

But the charts are not the whole story. Of key importance both in and outside the industry are the artists — the rock and roll bands, soul singers, country musicians, and pop icons who produce the vast body of work from which chart successes emerge.

Billboard Hitmakers is about those artists.

The Hitmakers series presents a broad overview of popular music, with separate volumes devoted to such subject areas as Pioneers of Rock and Roll, Singer-Songwriters, Rhythm and Blues, and Country and Western. Each Hitmakers volume is designed to be enjoyed as a separate reference work dedicated to a distinct segment of the pop spectrum, but the books also complement and reinforce each other. Just as the music scene is constantly changing and growing, the Hitmakers series will expand as new volumes covering new subject areas are published. Taken together, the Billboard Hitmakers series adds up to a growing library of information on pop music's prime movers — with a unique Billboard slant.

Each book explores its topic in depth and detail via individual artist profiles arranged alphabetically, with the artists selected for inclusion on the basis of their commercial and/or aesthetic impact on the music scene — including, of course, their history of Billboard chart activity.

The artist profiles themselves provide more than just raw chart data, however. Along with biographical facts and career highlights, each profile gives a sense of the artist's impact, offers insights about the music, and places the subject in the grand musical scheme of things. Artists are viewed not as isolated entities but as contributors to an ever-changing soundscape, drawing music from the past, adding to it in the present, and passing it on to musicians of the future. The volumes in the Billboard Hitmakers series chronicle this ongoing evolution, providing a history of popular music as seen from the perspective of the artists who created it.

In addition, each Hitmakers profile lists the artist's significant songs and albums. Titles are chosen first from the top of the Billboard charts and are listed chronologically, along with the name of the record's label, its year of release, and its peak chart position. In cases where a profiled artist has no top 40 hits, the titles listed are those generally regarded as the artist's best or most significant recordings.

With rock and roll now moving toward the half-century mark and the originators of blues, gospel, country, and jazz slipping into history, popular music is steadily maturing. Its present-day boundaries encompass an intricate latticework of known genres, nascent movements, as-yet-unlabeled trends, and one-person sonic revolutions. Our intent with the Billboard Hitmakers series is to identify the major players within these diverse yet interrelated musical worlds and present their fascinating stories. And if the books also translate into print some of the musical pleasure these hitmakers have given us over the years, so much the better.

PREFACE

. . . .

Chronicled herein are the recordings and careers of 180 of the top R&B and soul artists of the past 50 years, from, if you will, Charles Brown and Roy Brown through Ruth Brown and James Brown to Bobby Brown.

But first, some definitions are needed.

Rhythm and blues, although not officially named until 1949 (more on that in a moment), is a style of African-American popular music that began to take shape during and just after World War II. With the big-band swing era coming to an end, many young jazz musicians turned to bop, a new approach to improvisation that swung so fast and furiously that most people found it undanceable.

This development coincided with the mass migration of black people from the South to work in northern defense industries. They brought with them rural blues, which began to fuse with riff-based remnants of big-band jazz and led to an alternative to bop that was both highly danceable and hugely popular.

As rhythm and blues, largely unknown outside the black community in its original form, began to permeate mainstream popular music in the United States and around the world under the guise of "rock and roll," a new musical sub-genre evolved during the mid- to late 1950s that borrowed liberally from the music of the African-American church. The vocal techniques, chord progressions, and call-and-response patterns of gospel merged with the blues underpinning of older R&B forms, giving birth to "soul."

With rock and roll having opened up the door for the acceptance of black popular music styles by top 40 radio, soul music too became universally popular, as evidenced by the impact of Motown records in the 1960s.

But for every soul artist who became a pop icon, there were countless others for whom the crossover door was seldom, if ever, opened. The main focus of this book is on R&B and soul artists who achieved popularity primarily among African-American record buyers, as measured by *Billboard* magazine's R&B charts. A secondary consideration is their crossover appeal to the larger pop market.

Speaking of crossover, the definitions of R&B and soul in this book allow for the inclusion of artists who had some crossover appeal in other musical genres, although their main field of activity was R&B. Therefore, such blues artists as Charles Brown, Joe Turner, and Bobby Bland, whose styles overlap into R&B or soul, are included, while "straight" blues artists like T-Bone Walker, B.B. King, and Muddy Waters are not. Likewise, such "jazz" artists as Lionel Hampton and Count Basie and such primarily "pop" artists as Nat "King" Cole, Johnny Mathis, and the Fifth Dimension are excluded, even though each had a number of R&B chart hits. And while rap is a vital expression of African-American musical culture, it too falls outside the parameters of the book.

Most of the artists here scored more than 10 entries on the *Billboard* R&B top 40 singles charts, although a few had not as many chart hits but are nevertheless included because their impact cannot be judged by numbers alone.

Some words are needed here about the historical confusion about what to call African-American popular music. I prefer "black pop," though other tags come in handy when referring to specific sub-genres. The first label that the record industry invented for black pop, back in the 1920s, was "race," as in "music for the race." "The race" was then used by the NAACP and many in the black bourgeoisie to denote pride, much as "la raza" was later used among Mexican Americans. But by the 1940s, "race" had fallen from favor and, indeed, taken on a pejorative taint. The music trade journals began searching for a more appropriate label. In 1949, Jerry Wexler, then a staff writer at *Billboard* and later a guiding force behind the soul music explosion at Atlantic Records, coined the term "rhythm and blues."

As the gospel influence became more pronounced in black pop during the 1960s, many people began calling it "soul," a term first employed in secular music to characterize the blues- and gospel-rooted jazz of such musicians as Cannonball Adderley, Milt Jackson, Les McCann, Horace Silver, Jimmy Smith, and Bobby Timmons. "Soul" became *Billboard*'s official designation in 1969 and remained in general use until the early 1980s, when such newer trends as funk and rap became increasingly prevalent.

Beginning with the issue dated June 26, 1982, *Billboard* settled on "black," which seemed right on target, except to many programmers of black-oriented radio stations. Realizing that non-blacks constitute a sizable portion of their listenership and not wanting to alienate those listeners or advertisers interested in reaching beyond the black market, they began calling the music "urban contemporary." On October 27, 1990, however, *Billboard* changed the designation of its black pop singles and albums charts to "R&B." Today, that term is again in wide use—among artists, industry people, and fans alike—as a handy moniker for African-American popular music in all its glorious stylistic permutations.

The evolution of the *Billboard* chart names has reflected the confusion. The magazine debuted its black chart on October 24, 1942, calling it "Harlem Hit Parade." That title was retained until February 8, 1945, when the outdated label "race" was applied. From June 15, 1949, until the belated arrival of "soul" on August 8, 1969, the journal fluctuated between the terms "Rhythm & Blues" and "R&B."

Throughout the text of this book, in order to simplify things, "R&B" is used to denote the *Billboard* black pop charts, even when referring to those that predated Wexler's coinage. Positions cited encompass records that showed up on *Billboard*'s charts from October 24, 1942, through the end of 1993.

To further confuse the name-game matter in retrospect, *Billboard* also published several different black pop charts for a time. From 1945 until 1957, there was a "Most Played in Juke Boxes" chart, along with the main "Best Selling" or "Best Sellers" list. And from 1955 until 1958, a "Most Played by Jockeys" chart also existed. (*Billboard* published no R&B charts at all from November 30, 1963, until January 23, 1965, a significant time in the expansion of the music's popularity.) Citations in the text of chart positions for records that appeared during those periods refer to the highest one attained on any of the two or three charts.

Major hits by R&B artists that appeared in the magazine's pop top 40 are mentioned in the text. A maximum of 10 albums and/or songs are listed in the discographies accompanying each artist's profile; the artist's total number of additional top 40 recordings, if any, is noted as well. Pop chart positions, where applicable, follow the R&B positions, thereby offering a barometer of the inroads made, if any, by specific R&B recordings into the larger pop mainstream. It is interesting to note that the crossover trend was more frequent during the mid-1940s than one might expect and that it declined by the late 1940s, picked up again in the mid-1950s, and dropped off during the mid-1970s. Such odd vacillation merits thorough statistical and sociological study.

LEE HILDEBRAND
Oakland, California
June 1994

ACKNOWLEDGMENTS

All uncredited quotes found in this book are from the author's interviews, except for a few that are from record company bios. I'm indebted to the following artists for having granted me interviews over the years: Nikolas Ashford, Anita Baker, George Benson, Frankie Beverly, Bobby Bland, Leroy "Sugarfoot" Bonner, Charles Brown, James Brown, Roy Brown, Ruth Brown, Solomon Burke, Jerry Butler, George Clinton, Michael Cooper, Robert Cray, the Dramatics, the Emotions, Betty Everett, Harvey Fuqua, Little Anthony Gourdine, Al Green, Millie Jackson, Etta James, Maxine Jones, Chaka Khan, King Curtis, Denise LaSalle, Little Milton, Little Richard, Nellie Lutcher, Curtis Mayfield, Percy Mayfield, Thomas McElroy, Clyde McPhatter, New Edition, Johnny Otis, Wilson Pickett, Lou Rawls, Lionel Richie, Smokey Robinson, Joe Simon, Valerie Simpson, the Spinners, Roebuck Staples, Johnnie Taylor, Joe Tex, Rufus Thomas, Willie Mae Thornton, Roger Troutman, Jr. Walker, Mary Wells, the Whispers, Bobby Womack, and Betty Wright.

I am especially grateful to my friends Opal Nations, Joel Selvin, and Willie Collins for sharing their knowledge and files. Work of the following journalists, authors, and annotators was also consulted: John Abbey, Barry Alfonso, Clive Anderson, Jay Anthony, Al Aronowitz, Whitney Balliett, Lacy J. Banks, G. Fitz Bartley, Sandy Stert Benjamin, Jonas Bernholm, David Bianco, Stu Blank, Rob Bowman, Fred Bronson, John Broven, Cleveland Brown, Geoff Brown, Geoffrey F. Brown, David Browne, Scott Poulson Bryant, Debby Bull, Tony Burke, Walter Price Burrell, John Calendo, Bill Carpenter, D. Michael Cheers, Georgia Christgau, Dick Clark, Sue Cassidy Clark, Stanley Crouch, Tony Cummings, Bill Dahl, Jim Dawson, Sharon Davis, Dave Dexter, Jr., Jancee Dunn, Philip H. Ennis, Leonard Feather, Kim Field, Ben Fong-Torres, William V. Francis, Jr., Michael Freedberg, Paul Freeman, Roger Friedman, Robert Gallagher, Phyl Garland, Bob Garbutt, Carl Gayle, Nelson George, Gary Giddins, Charlie Gillett, Marv Goldberg, Michael Goldberg, Richard Goldblatt, Leslie Gourse, Bob Greene, Paul Grein, Peter A. Grendysa, Phil Groia, Steve Guarnori, Peter Guralnick, Jimmy Gutterman, Denise Hall, Lionel Hampton, Jeff Hannusah, Barry Hansen, Michael Haralambos, Phil Hardy, Spider Harrison, Anthony Heilbut, Nat Hentoff, John Hersey, Norbert Hess, Chester Higgins, Robert Hilburn, Dave Hill, Randal C. Hill, David Hinckley, Gerri Hirsey, Stephen Holden, Bill Holdship, Barney Hoskyns, Eddie Huffman, Dennis Hunt, Bruce Huston, Wayne Jancik, Connie Johnson, Karen Jones, Mike Joyce, Neal Karlen, Larry Kelp, Ronald E. Kisner, Cub Koda, Dave Laing, Gene Lees, Keri Leigh, Ed Levine, Alan Light, Kurt Loder, Michelle Lomax, Bob Lucas, Michael Lydon, Dave Marsh, Joe McEwen, David McGee, Bill Millar, Judith Moore, Dan Morgenstern, Frederick Douglas Murphy, Charles Sharr Murray, Ken Murray, Sonia Murray, David Nathan, Dan Nooger, Amy O'Neal, Jim O'Neal, Robert Palmer, Jeffrey Peisch, Dave Penny, Don Piper, Leonard Pitts, Jr., Bruce Pollock, Stephen C. Propes, Robert Pruter, Vicki Jo Radovsky, Rosetta Reitz, David Ritz, Wayne Robbins, Margaret Robin, Richard Robinson, Charles E. Rogers, Steve Roeser, Diana Ross, Mark Rowland, Greg Rule, Randy Russi, Leo Sacks, Charles L. Sanders, Greg Sandow, Robert Santelli, Jack Sbarbori, Ken Settle, Doug Seroff, Arnold Shaw, Don Shewey, Merrill Shindler, Davitt Sigerson, Raymona Gordy Singleton, David Smallwood, Joe Smith, Terri Sutton, Michael J. Sweeney, J. Randy Taraborelli, Carla Thomas, Eliot Tiegel, J. H. Thompkins, Ray Topping, Nick Toshes, Lee Underwood, Billy Vera, Gary von Tersch, Barry Walters, Jay Warner, Tony Watson, Harry Weinger, Lindsay Wesker, Joel Whitburn, Charles White, Cliff White, Jan White, Timothy White, Valerie Wilmer, Russ Wilson, Stephen Winding, Karen Winner, and Doris G. Worsham.

Much thanks to Tad Lathrop for his guidance, patience, thoughtful editing, and diligent fact checking.

Many thanks to my mother-in-law, Bessie McCants.

And special thanks to Frank Weimann and Randy Pitts.

JOHNNY ACE

Johnny Ace (b. John Marshall Alexander, Jr., June 9, 1929, Memphis) was the first tragic figure of the rhythm and blues era. At the height of his brief career, on Christmas 1954, the young singer-pianist was felled by a bullet from his own .22 pistol during a backstage game of Russian roulette.

One of 10 children of Reverend John and Mrs. John Alexander, Sr., he showed little interest in music as a child other than singing in the choir at his father's church. In 1947, after a stateside stint in the Navy and a scrape with the law in Mississippi, he took up guitar, then piano, and two years later was backing fledgling blues singer-guitarist B. B. King. Dubbed the Beale Streeters, King's band also included tenor saxophonist Billy Adolph Duncan, drummer Earl Forrest, and warm-up singer Bobby Bland.

By early 1952, with King's recording career beginning to skyrocket, the bluesman turned the Beale Streeters over to Alexander, Jr. The band was booked by WDIA program director James Mattis to do a recording session for his new Duke record label at the radio station's Memphis studio. Bland was the intended vocalist but was unable to memorize the lyrics to the songs he'd been given. A reluctant Alexander, Jr., substituted, singing a number hastily penned by himself and Mattis that was based loosely on "So Long," an earlier hit for pop bandleader Russ Morgan, then R&B vocalist Ruth Brown. "My Song" marked the recording debut of Johnny Ace, a name Mattis had thought up for his new vocalist. It was the first of the singer's three number one R&B hits.

Although Ace could jump the blues like the rest of his Beale Street cohorts, the melancholy "My Song," a ballad rendered in a soothing, somewhat breathy baritone akin to that of Charles Brown, set the style Ace would take for the remainder of his short stay in the limelight. Such subsequent hits as "Cross My Heart," "The Clock," "Saving My Love for You," "Please Forgive Me," and "Pledging My Love" (some featuring the vibraharp of Johnny Otis) betrayed a similarly pensive, often forelorn quality that was especially attractive to teenagers.

Ace toured widely, usually headlining package shows with such blues artists as Bland, Little Junior Parker, and Willie Mae "Big Mama" Thornton (whose original version of "Hound Dog" was cut at the same August 1953 Los Angeles session that produced "Please Forgive Me"). He was a major R&B attraction yet suffered from stage fright, prompting a *Variety* reviewer to describe a 1953 performance at Harlem's Apollo Theater as "too stiff and wooden." Ace's shy stage demeanor was in sharp contrast to a frequent recklessness offstage that included treating a cheap pistol he'd purchased in Tampa, according to bandleader Johnny Board, "like a toy."

On Christmas night 1954, during the intermission of a show at Houston's City Auditorium that was promoted by Don Robey (who'd wrestled control of Duke Records from Mattis the previous year), Ace was pointing the gun at people in the dressing room. This angered Thornton, who was also on the program, particularly after he'd spun the cylinder (containing one round), placed it to his girlfriend's head, and pulled the trigger.

"Why don't you put it to your own head?" Thornton allegedly told Ace. He did. The gun fired, and his body slumped to the floor, his brains oozing out of his right temple and his processed hair, in Thornton's words, standing "straight out like porcupine quills."

"Pledging My Love," released just days before his death, became Ace's swan song and biggest hit, reaching the top of the R&B chart within a month. It was also his first crossover hit, peaking at number 17 on the pop chart, the same position achieved the following month by pop star Theresa Brewer's cover version of the Don Robey–Fats Washington composition. A spate of tribute records also followed, including Varetta Dillard's "Johnny Has Gone" (complete with a record company press release falsely claiming she had been Ace's girlfriend), Johnny Fuller's "Johnny Ace's Last Letter," and Johnny Moore's "Why, Johnny, Why?"

Some of Ace's hit songs were later recorded by such artists as Aretha Franklin, the Impressions, Elvis Presley, and Luther Vandross. His blues ballad

---

TOP SONGS

MY SONG (Duke, '52, *1 R&B*)

CROSS MY HEART (Duke, '53, *3 R&B*)

THE CLOCK (Duke, '53, *1 R&B*)

SAVING MY LOVE FOR YOU (Duke, '53, *2 R&B*)

PLEASE FORGIVE ME (Duke, '54, *6 R&B*)

NEVER LET ME GO (Duke, '54, *9 R&B*)

PLEDGING MY LOVE (Duke, '55, *1 R&B, 17 Pop*)

ANYMORE (Duke, '55, *7 R&B*)

style also had a profound influence on the Louisiana "swamp rock" sound associated with singers like Rod Bernard, Jimmy Clanton, and Jivin' Gene. And, in 1981, Paul Simon composed "The Late Great Johnny Ace," drawing a parallel between Ace's death and that of John Lennon.

ASHFORD AND SIMPSON

Nickolas Ashford (b. May 4, 1943, Fairfield, South Carolina) and Valerie Simpson (b. Aug. 26, 1948, New York) are soul music's most successful songwriting, producing, and singing couple. Although the two began working together in 1964, they didn't marry until nine and a half years later.

"It just hit us that we were in love and kind of inseparable," Ashford said in 1982. "We had been friends for such a long time. There was obviously something underneath the relationship, but we had a fear that it might destroy what we had built up as friends and working partners. But, as they say, true love will emerge, and eventually it did. It was just one of those things that happened when we were out one evening."

They met at Harlem's White Rock Baptist Church, where Simpson was singing and playing piano for a gospel group called the Followers. Ashford had recently relocated to New York from Michigan to pursue a career as a jazz dancer. Times were so tough, however, that he spent some nights sleeping in parks. Looking for a free meal, he came to the church. He soon joined Simpson in the choir, and they began writing songs together—first gospel, then secular. She composed the music, he the lyrics—a pattern they've followed throughout their professional partnership.

They recorded three duet singles for the Glover label between 1964 and '65 but put performing on hold to focus on composing. Signed as staff writers to Scepter/Wand Records, they wrote material for Maxine Brown, Chuck Jackson, and the Shirelles.

Ashford and Simpson

TOP ALBUMS

Is It Still Good to Ya (Warner Bros., '78, 20)
Stay Free (Warner Bros., '79, 23)
Solid (Capitol, '85, 29)

Additional Top 40 Albums: 1

TOP SONGS

It Seems to Hang On (Warner Bros., '78, 2 R&B)
Found a Cure (Warner Bros., '79, 2 R&B, 36 Pop)
Love Don't Make It Right (Warner Bros., '80, 6 R&B)
Street Corner (Warner Bros., '83, 9 R&B)
Outta the World (Capitol, '85, 4 R&B)
Count Your Blessings (Capitol, '86, 4 R&B)
I'll Be There for You (Capitol, '89, 2 R&B)

Additional Top 40 R&B Songs: 2

The team's reputation was solidified in 1966 when Ray Charles took "Let's Go Get Stoned," a number they'd written with former Ikette Joshie Jo Armstead, to the top of the R&B chart.

Motown took notice and signed Ashford and Simpson to its Jobete publishing wing. During their six-year association with the Detroit company, the pair penned and, in most cases, produced such hits as "Ain't No Mountain High Enough," "Your Precious Love," "Ain't Nothing Like the Real Thing" for Marvin Gaye and Tammi Terrell, and "Reach Out and Touch (Somebody's Hand)," a reprise of "Ain't No Mountain High Enough," and "Remember" for Diana Ross.

Simpson recorded two solo albums in 1972 for Motown's Tamla subsidiary that, while critically acclaimed, were commercial bombs. She and Ashford then cut an album of duets, but Motown refused to issue it, causing the couple to jump ship in 1973 to Warner Bros., where their career as a self-produced singing team gradually built momentum. They struck gold with the fifth album, 1977's *Send It,* containing the hit disco single "Don't Cost You Nothin'." After scoring three more top 10 hits at Warner Bros., they moved to Capitol, for whom they had their biggest hit, the 1984 R&B Number One "Solid."

The team continued to write and/or produce other artists, their greatest successes being the Dynamic Superiors' "Shoe Shoe Shine," Quincy Jones's "Stuff Like That" (on which they, along with Chaka Khan, sang), Khan's "I'm Every Woman" (later a hit for Whitney Houston), and Stephanie Mills's "Keep Away Girls." They also produced albums for Diana Ross, Gladys Knight and the Pips, and Valerie's brother Ray Simpson (later lead singer of the Village People).

As performers, Ashford and Simpson are a study in contrasts. He is thin and statuesque, she diminutive and slightly rounded. When singing together, he takes the higher part, soaring in a reedy soprano to her full-bodied alto. When soloing, she is the stronger singer, her phrasing rich in fluid gospel technique. Ashford, though moving back and forth between a pinched falsetto and a naturally coarse baritone, has limited range in each voice.

Like the theme of togetherness that runs through so many of their songs, Ashford and Simpson function in harmony when speaking, often completing each other's sentences by adding to the thought, rather than interrupting. On stage, they work together like two lovebirds, displaying an outward affection and sensuality perfectly in sync with the elegant romanticism of their material.

ATLANTIC STARR

Throughout Atlantic Starr's career as one of the most successful self-contained soul groups of the '80s, leaders David, Wayne, and Jonathan Lewis strived for stylistic versatility. Initially inspired by Sly and the Family Stone, the band offered three or four alternating lead singers and gospel-style harmony in a mix of horn-fueled, rock-imbued dance-floor burners and amorous, candy-coated ballads. But as hard as the Lewis brothers tried to vary the musical menu with their mostly self-composed material, the record-buying public kept selecting the group's soft, sweet songs, particularly those that featured a succession of female leads: Sharon Bryant (1975–83), Barbara Weathers (1984–88), Porscha Martin (1989–90), and Rachel Oliver (1991).

Atlantic Starr was organized in 1975 from the personnel of three competing bands in the Westchester County, New York, towns of White Plains and Greenburgh. The nucleus—trombonist-percussionist Jonathan Lewis, flutist-percussionist Joseph Phillips, trumpeter Bill Sudderth III, bassist Cliff Archer, and drummer-vocalist Porter Carroll, Jr.—came from a

TOP ALBUMS

BRILLIANCE (A&M, '82, *18*)
AS THE BAND TURNS (A&M, '86, *17*)
ALL IN THE NAME OF LOVE (Warner Bros., '87, *18*)

TOP SONGS

CIRCLES (A&M, '82, *2 R&B, 38 Pop*)
TOUCH A FOUR LEAF CLOVER (A&M, '83, *4 R&B*)
SECRET LOVERS (A&M, '85, *4 R&B, 3 Pop*)
IF YOUR HEART ISN'T IN IT (A&M, '86, *4 R&B*)
ALWAYS (Warner Bros., '87, *1 R&B, 1 Pop*)
MY FIRST LOVE (Warner Bros., '89, *1 R&B*)
MASTERPIECE (Warner Bros., '92, *3 R&B, 3 Pop*)

Additional Top 40 R&B Songs: 13

group, formed in 1970, called Newban. Jonathan's younger brothers, keyboardist-singer Wayne and guitarist-singer David, were members of Unchained Youth, while Sharon Bryant sang with Exact Change (which cut an unsuccessful single for United Artists). All had attended the same high school.

The octet soon relocated to Los Angeles and, after adding saxophonist Damon Rentie, signed with A&M. (Manager Earl S. Cole, Jr., had compiled an alphabetical list of record companies. The A&R department at ABC was out to lunch, but he was luckier at A&M.) Teamed with Philadelphia producer Bobby Eli, the group enjoyed moderate success with its first single, 1978's brassy, disco-flavored "Stand Up" (number 16 R&B) but didn't begin to break big until its third album, 1981's *Radiant*. Produced by Commodores mentor James Anthony Carmichael, the disc included the medium-tempo ballad "When Love Calls," a number five R&B chart single. Led by Bryant in a smoky, seductive alto voice that recalled Chaka Khan's, the David and Wayne Lewis–penned tune set the tone for the group's future hits.

After two more hit singles featuring Bryant, 1982's uptempo "Circles" and the next year's "Touch a Four Leaf Clover," she left Atlantic Starr, married former Change percussionist Rick Gallway, worked as a session vocalist, and emerged as a soloist in 1989 with the number two R&B single, "Let's Go," on Wing Records.

While touring in the South, the group had met Greensboro, North Carolina, singer Barbara Weath-

ers and planned to produce her as a solo artist. When the vacancy occurred, she became Atlantic Starr's new distaff lead. Her smooth, honey-toned alto alternated with David Lewis's soaring Marvin Gaye–like tenor on the gentle 1985 ballad, "Secret Lovers"; placing at number four on *Billboard*'s R&B chart and number three on the pop list, it became the group's first crossover hit. It was taken from *As the Band Turns*, the first album by the band to be produced by David and Wayne Lewis themselves, as well as the first to sport a newly compressed, synthesized lineup: the horn section, bassist, and drummer had been dropped, with the three Lewis brothers now playing keyboards and Joseph Phillips beating the traps when live drums, instead of a machine, were required.

Jumping to Warner Bros. in 1987, Atlantic Starr scored its biggest hit with "Always," a love song composed by all three Lewis brothers in 1982 that was rejected at the time by producer Carmichael. The first single from the album *All in the Name of Love*, the Weathers-led "Always," topped both the R&B and pop charts.

Weathers, however, soon departed for a solo career, and her spot was filled by Porscha Martin. While the Atlanta-born vocalist was featured on 1989's *We're Movin' Up*, the album's hit single, "My First Love," served as a showcase for Wayne Lewis's warm, emotive baritone. Martin's stay was brief; by the band's next album, 1991's *Love Crazy*, yet another attractive young southerner had been recruited: North Carolina native and former Miss Black America Rachel Oliver. "Masterpiece," a Kenny Nolan–penned track from the album, gave Alantic Starr another crossover hit the following year.

ANITA BAKER

Between 1983 and 1990, Anita Baker (b. Dec. 20, 1957, Toledo, Ohio) took the art of soul singing to a new level of sophistication through a series of four albums containing what she has described as "fireside love songs." Combining a knowledge of jazz phrasing with the earthy emotionalism of her gospel upbringing, the diminutive (four-foot-eleven-inch) vocalist used her nearly four-octave range to create a uniquely elastic style filled with deep, rounded low notes; soaring soprano sustains; cascading slurs; and swooping melismas.

British critic Barney Hoskyns, in his 1991 book *From a Whisper to a Scream: The Great Voices in Popular Music*, observed that "the whole mode of her singing, her articulation and 'expression,' is that of an instrument, half alto saxophone, perhaps, and half trumpet, and she plays the instrument with the same controlled abandon as any great jazzman.... [S]he clamps her vowels so tightly that one feels only a steady stream of shapes folding into each other, gliding and sliding through songs as though entranced and magnetized by something outside itself."

Baker, who had only two months of formal vocal training, said that she developed her style unconsciously; yet in a 1983 interview she was able to partially analyze her unusual technique. "To get the most out of certain vowels," she explained, "I have to say them a certain way. If I'm singing a very low note, the closed tones like the 'oohs' come out a lot better, so I may take an open syllable and close it in order to get the most out of the note. That's why my phrasing is sometimes a lot different than someone else's may be.

"And the higher tones—if I'm using my head voice, then also closed tones work a lot better for me to get up into the sopranos. If I'm using my chest voice for the higher ranges, I'll use an open note. I may take a word that ends on a closed syllable and open it up at the end so I can get that note out of there. It's real weird, but I do what I do in order to get the notes out when I feel 'em."

Anita Baker

TOP ALBUMS

RAPTURE (Elektra, '86, *11*)
GIVING YOU THE BEST THAT I GOT (Elektra, '88, *1*)
COMPOSITIONS (Elektra, '90, *5*)

TOP SONGS

ANGEL (Beverly Glen, '83, *5 R&B*)
SWEET LOVE (Elektra, '86, *2 R&B, 8 Pop*)
NO ONE IN THE WORLD (Elektra, '87, *5 R&B*)
GIVING YOU THE BEST THAT I GOT (Elektra, '88, *1 R&B, 3 Pop*)
JUST BECAUSE (Elektra, '88, *1 R&B*)
LET ME INTO LOVE (Elektra, '89, *4 R&B*)
TALK TO ME (Elektra, '90, *3 R&B*)

Additional Top 40 R&B Songs: 8

The granddaughter of a barnstorming minister, Baker was raised in Detroit by an aunt and uncle. Her early influences included soul singers Stevie Wonder, Aretha Franklin, Gladys Knight, Mavis Staples, and gospel queen Mahalia Jackson, whose "big, round tones" Baker especially admired. She later became a fan of such jazz vocalists as Nancy Wilson, Sarah Vaughan, Eddie Jefferson, and Al Jarreau, but never sang jazz in clubs. "I was into sweatin', playin' tambourine, and jumpin' around on stage," she said. (After her rise to stardom, Elektra recorded her performing a set of standards at the Montreux Jazz Festival with an all-star jazz group led by keyboardist George Duke, but it was never issued.)

In 1978, Baker joined a ten-piece club band called Chapter 8. While appearing at the Total Experience in Los Angeles, the group was signed to Ariola Records by label executive Otis Smith and recorded one album for the company that was little noticed, except for the Baker-led single "Ready for Your Love," which checked in at a modest number 38 on

Billboard's R&B chart in 1979. Chapter 8 soon dissolved, and Baker headed back to Detroit, where she worked as a receptionist at a law firm until 1982, when Smith, now running his own Beverly Glen label, called.

The Songstress, Baker's debut album, was issued in March of 1983. Decidedly different from anything else being heard on black radio at the time, the Patrick Moten–Otis Smith–produced disc was slow in taking off, but it gradually caught the ears of many upwardly mobile young African-American adults who listened to "quiet storm"–formatted stations. By year's end, the album's second single, "Angel," had peaked at number five on the R&B chart.

This brief glimpse of success was followed by over two years of inactivity on record, during which time Smith attempted to block Baker from signing with another label. She emerged victorious in March of 1986 as executive producer of her Elektra Records debut, *Rapture.* With all but one of its eight tracks produced by her old friend, former Chapter 8 co-leader Michael J. Powell, the album yielding four top 10 R&B hits, including "Sweet Love" and "No One in the World," and established Baker as a major star.

Baker briefly returned to her gospel roots in 1987 as guest vocalist with the Winans on the number 15 R&B Qwest single "Ain't No Need to Worry," then continued her working relationship with Powell for the next year's *Giving You the Best That I Got.* The sumptuous album, containing the Number One R&B, number three pop title track, as well as the Number One R&B "Just Because," proved to be the singer's best effort, going to the top of the album chart. The follow-up, a 1990 set of Powell-produced Baker originals titled *Compositions,* was comparatively less successful, but it did rise to number five on the list of best-selling albums. Elektra reissued her first album, *The Songstress,* on compact disc in 1991.

LaVERN BAKER

The first woman R&B singer to become a star of the nascent rock and roll genre, LaVern Baker (b. Delores LaVern Baker, Nov. 11, 1929, Chicago) entered the music business with blues in her blood. Her brassy, often raucous style, once described by a *Billboard* reviewer as "full-throated, vibrant belting with a sexy tease," owed much to her aunt, Merline Johnson, a blues singer who recorded prolifically during the 1930s as "the Yas Yas Girl." And the legendary Memphis Minnie was a distant cousin.

Having sung in church as a child, Baker made her professional debut in 1947 at Chicago's Club De Lisa with Fletcher Henderson's band. Dubbed "Little Miss Sharecropper" and wearing a patchwork sack dress, she presented a comic stage act inspired by Little Miss Cornshucks, a popular blues singer of the period. Henderson recommended Baker to Columbia Records, which cut a session but kept it in the can. Her first issued records were as Little Miss Sharecropper with bandleader Eddie "Sugarman" Penigar for RCA Victor in 1949. Two years later, she appeared as "Bea Baker" on both Columbia and Okeh and under the Sharecropper moniker on National. In 1952, she joined pianist Todd Rhodes's band, with which she recorded for King. None of these early sides was a hit, though some, especially 1951's "I Want a Lavendar Cadillac" with Maurice King and the Wolverines on Okeh, betrayed hints of the comic timing she would use to such winning effect on her novelty hits of the mid-'50s.

Before going on the road with Rhodes, Baker was based at Detroit's Flame Show Bar, where she is said to have influenced Johnnie Ray, a white singer who would soon become a major pop star with his blues-inflected delivery. The club's booker, Al Greene, became Baker's manager, and, in 1953, he took her to Atlantic Records. While her first single for the New York company, a torchy, gospel-drenched blues ballad titled "Soul on Fire," failed to generate much action, the third cemented her role as "the High Priestess of Rock and Roll."

Originally intended as the flip side of the blues ballad "Tomorrow Night," the Winfield Scott–penned "Tweedlee Dee"—a catchy, if trite, Latin-tinged ditty that Baker hated and continues to—captured the imagination of the emerging rock and roll market as no Atlantic release had before. It went to number four R&B and number 14 pop, though a cover version by pop singer Georgia Gibbs that faithfully copied the arrangement of Baker's original topped the pop chart. Incensed, Baker lobbied Congress to enact a law protecting musical arrangements. The law failed to pass, but Baker maintained a sense of humor about the situation, once quipping that, when flying, she'd take out insurance in Gibbs's name so "she'd be covered in case something happened to me."

As she recorded more novelty numbers, including "Bop-Ting-A-Ling," "Tra La La" (covered less successfully by Gibbs), "Jim Dandy," and "Jim Dandy Got Married," Baker was embraced by the rock and roll world. Disc jockey Alan Freed, who popularized the term, regularly featured her in his all-star rock and roll stage shows, as well as in two of his low-budget motion pictures, *Mister Rock and Roll* and *Rock, Rock, Rock.*

The singer's biggest hit, 1958's "I Cried a Tear," saw her returning to her earlier church-hewn blues ballad approach, while at the same time foreshadowing the coming soul era. Also that year, she recorded the critically acclaimed jazz album, *LaVern Baker Sings Bessie Smith.* Following 1961's "Saved," a lively gospel send-up penned and produced by Jerry Leiber and Mike Stoller, and the next year's revival of Ma Rainey's "See See Rider," Baker's days on the charts were limited. She left Atlantic in 1964 and signed with Brunswick, for whom she had one minor hit, "Think Twice," a duet with Jackie Wilson.

While on a 1969 tour of Asia, which included USO dates in Vietnam, the vocalist became ill while appearing at the Playboy Club in Hong Kong and was hospitalized in the Philippines. She remained in that country for the next two decades, performing and serving as entertainment director at the U.S. Navy base at Subic Bay.

Baker finally returned to the United States in 1988 to take part in Atlantic's 40th anniversary celebration at Madison Square Garden and, two years later, spent nine months as the star of the hit Broadway musical *Black and Blue,* having replaced former Atlantic labelmate Ruth Brown in that role. Since her homecoming, Baker has recorded albums for Rhino and DRG and contributed songs to the soundtracks of *Shag: The Movie, Dick Tracy,* and *A Rage in Harlem.* She was inducted into the Rock and Roll Hall of Fame in 1991.

HANK BALLARD AND THE MIDNIGHTERS

No group in history has spawned more answer records than the Midnighters, led by the soaring, emotion-wrought voice of Hank Ballard (b. Henry Bernard Ballard, Nov. 18, 1936, Detroit). The Detroit-based group launched two popular music crazes. The Midnighters' 1954 recording of the salacious Ballard-penned "Work with Me Annie," a Number One R&B hit that also managed to penetrate the pop charts in spite of being banned by many radio stations, led to such successful responses as Etta James's "The Wallflower" (also known as "Roll with Me Henry"), Georgia Gibbs's sanitized "Dance with Me Henry," and a string of related hits by the Midnighters themselves. And in 1959 Ballard and the group recorded "The Twist," which, thanks to Chubby Checker's cover of the next year, kicked off an international dance mania that was further fueled by countless tunes with "twist" in their titles.

The Midnighters began their career as the Royals. Organized in late 1950 or early '51 by Henry Booth and Charles Sutton, the original lineup is said to have also included Levi Stubbs (later of the Four Tops) and Jackie Wilson. By 1952, when bandleader Johnny Otis discovered the group at the Paradise Theater in Detroit and recommended it to Federal Records producer Ralph Bass, the personnel comprised lead singers Booth and Sutton, harmony vocalists Lawson Smith and Sonny Woods, and guitarist Alonzo Tucker. Booth led the Royals' first waxing, the Otis doo wop composition "Every Beat of My Heart" (later a smash for Gladys Knight and the Pips).

The Royals' initial style was smooth, owing much to Sonny Til and the Orioles. It changed radically when Ballard, who'd grown up singing in church in Bessemer, Alabama, replaced Smith in 1953. Inspired by the Dominoes' Clyde McPhatter, the 16-

TOP SONGS

TWEEDLEE DEE (Atlantic, '55, 4 R&B, 14 Pop)

BOP-TING-A-LING (Atlantic, '55, 3 R&B)

PLAY IT FAIR (Atlantic, '55, 2 R&B)

STILL (Atlantic, '56, 2 R&B)

I CAN'T LOVE YOU ENOUGH (Atlantic, '56, 7 R&B, 22 Pop)

JIM DANDY (Atlantic, '56, 1 R&B, 17 Pop)

JIM DANDY GOT MARRIED (Atlantic, '57, 7 R&B)

I CRIED A TEAR (Atlantic, '58, 2 R&B, 6 Pop)

I WAITED TOO LONG (Atlantic, '59, 5 R&B, 33 Pop)

Additional Top 40 R&B Hits: 11

of the gospel-drenched Ballard ballad "Teardrops on Your Letter."

While "Teardrops" rose to number four on the R&B chart with minimal pop response, the flip also generated some action, peaking at number 16 R&B during its initial round on the charts. "American Bandstand" host Dick Clark was so enamored of the tune that he had Ernest Evans rerecord it. Dubbed "Chubby Checker" by Clark's wife, the Philadelphia singer took "The Twist" to the top of the pop chart twice, in 1960 and again two years later. Checker's version was so close to the original that Ballard, upon first hearing it on the radio, thought it was his own.

Rather than being set back by the cover, Ballard and the Midnighters benefited. By the middle of 1960, they had three simultaneous hits in the pop top 40: "Finger Poppin' Time," "Let's Go, Let's Go, Let's Go," and their original version of "The Twist." And Ballard came up with other dance-oriented hits for the group, including "The Hoochie Coochi Coo," "The Continental Walk," "The Float," and "The Switch-A-Roo," but chart action dried up after 1961 and group members began to defect.

By the late '60s, Ballard was working as a single, often with James Brown's revue, and he had two minor Brown-produced R&B hits: 1968's "How You Gonna Get Respect (If You Haven't Cut Your Process Yet?" and 1972's "From the Love Side." After a long hiatus from performing, the singer returned in the mid-'80s with a new set of Midnighters, first female, then male. In 1990, Ballard was inducted into the Rock and Roll Hall of Fame.

THE BAR-KAYS

It wasn't the musical abilities of several members of a youthful Memphis soul band called the River Arrows that first caught the attention of the great Otis Redding. The Big O simply liked the way they shined his shoes. They worked at a barbershop across the street from Stax-Volt Records, and Redding, noting their interest in music, invited them to hang out at the studio and watch him record.

As it turned out, Redding became even more impressed by their instrumental prowess than by the way they popped rags. And so were the members of the company's rhythm section—keybordists Booker T. Jones and Isaac Hayes, guitarist Steve Cropper,

---

TOP SONGS

GET IT (The Royals, Federal, '53, 6 R&B)

WORK WITH ME ANNIE (The Midnighters, Federal, '54, 1 R&B, 22 Pop)

SEXY WAYS (The Midnighters, Federal, '54, 2 R&B)

ANNIE HAD A BABY (The Midnighters, Federal, '54, 1 R&B, 23 Pop)

TEARDROPS ON YOUR LETTER (King, '59, 4 R&B)

FINGER POPPIN' TIME (King, '60, 2 R&B, 7 Pop)

THE TWIST (King, '60, 6 R&B, 28 Pop)

LET'S GO, LET'S GO, LET'S GO (King '60, 1 R&B, 6 Pop)

THE HOOCHIE COOCHIE COO (King, '61, 3 R&B, 27 Pop)

THE SWITCH-A-ROO (King, '61, 3 R&B, 26 Pop)

Additional Top 40 R&B Songs: 10

---

year-old former Ford assembly line worker became lead singer, bringing to the group a hard gospel edge and a suitcase full of rhythm-charged, frequently raunchy songs, beginning with 1953's "Get It."

As "Work with Me Annie" was gaining momentum in early 1954, the Royals changed their name to the Midnighters to avoid confusion with the Five Royales, another hard, gospel-styled R&B group. "Annie" and its answers kept the Midnighters going strong for a year and a half, after which they experienced a respite from the charts that lasted three and a half years. Personnel fluctuated during this period, with Smith returning to replace Sutton, Norman Thrasher replacing Woods, and guitarist Cal Green replacing Arthur Porter, who'd earlier taken Tucker's place. Federal Records seemed to be placing its faith in a new group, James Brown and the Famous Flames, which modeled its torrid style, to a great degree, on that of the Midnighters.

In 1958, Ballard wrote "The Twist," an uptempo 12-bar blues that used a melody he'd lifted from the group's flop of the previous year, "Is Your Love for Real?" which he had in turn borrowed from McPhatter and the Drifters' 1955 hit "What'Cha Gonna Do?" Unhappy at Federal, Ballard took the new tune to Vee-Jay, which cut it but didn't release it. Then King, Federal's parent label, picked up the group's option and recorded "The Twist," the first record to place Ballard's name on the label in front of the group's. It was issued, however, as the B side bassist Duck Dunn, and drummer Al Jackson, Jr.—who took them under their wing and began grooming them to be the firm's second-string house band.

The River Arrows—bassist James Alexander, trumpeter Ben Cauley, saxophonist Phalon Jones, guitarist Jimmy King, organist Ronnie Caldwell, and drummer Carl Cunningham—were dubbed the Bar-Kays (after the Mar-Keys, the Stax-Volt house band consisting of Booker T. and the MG's plus the Memphis Horns) and scored the instrumental smash of the summer of 1967 with their first Volt single, "Soul Finger." Redding took them on the road as his backup band. Then, on December 10th of that year, Redding's private plane crashed into an icy lake near Madison, Wisconsin. Four of the Bar-Kays perished with him.

Alexander and Cauley, who were not on the flight, wasted no time in putting a new band together. By 1970, with Booker T. having already left Stax and Cropper about to quit, the new Bar-Kays were the first-string house band at Stax. Their tight, funky sound became the backbone of countless releases by

the company, including sides by the Staple Singers, Albert King, Carla Thomas, Johnnie Taylor, William Bell, the Emotions, and especially Isaac Hayes, to whose groundbreaking *Hot Buttered Soul* and *Shaft* albums they contributed.

On their own, the post-crash Bar-Kays continued recording for the Volt label through 1975, although only one single, 1971's number 10 R&B "Son of Shaft," managed to crack the charts. Personnel changed often during this period. Cauley was replaced by Carl Allen, leaving Alexander at the helm. Saxophonist Harvey Henderson was a constant. Other members included guitarists Michael Toles, Vernon Burch, Barry Wilkins, and Lloyd Smith; keyboardists Ronnie Gordon and Winston Stewart; and drummers Roy Cunningham, Willie Hall, Alvin Hunter, and Michael Beard.

With the addition in 1970 of vocalist Larry Dodson, the Bar-Kays evolved from being a primarily instrumental band to a self-contained unit in the tradition of Sly and the Family Stone, and they helped to pioneer a genre, initially called "black rock," that

The Bar-Kays

soon became known as "funk." Dressed eccentrically—several members donned blonde wigs and Dodson frequently appeared on stage with a live boa constrictor around his neck—they played louder than traditional soul bands and added heavy doses of rock guitar. Dodson's snarling vocal delivery, influenced by Sly Stone, in turn influenced such other singers as Leroy "Sugarfoot" Bonner of the Ohio Players, Lionel Richie of the Commodores, and Larry Blackmon of Cameo.

For their Volt releases, the group had worked most often with producer Allen Jones, and they continued that relationship after signing with Mercury Records in 1976. The group, now comprising Alexander, Allen, Henderson, Stewart, Smith, Beard, and Dodson, quickly moved from being an influential opening act on the black concert circuit to headline status, beginning with that year's number five R&B "Shake Your Rump to the Funk" from the album *Too Hot to Stop*. It was the first of the unstoppable band's nine top 10 R&B hits over the next 11 years, all on Mercury except for 1978's "Holy Ghost," a previously unissued track that Stax's new owner, Fantasy Records, found in the vault. By 1980, the group consisted of 10 members, with trombonist Frank Thompson, second keyboardist Mark Bynum, and percussionist Sherman Guy having joined the previous lineup.

The Bar-Kays' bass-driven party sound became

more electronic during the 1980s, reflecting the influence of Prince. By 1987, following the death of producer Jones, only Henderson, Stewart, and Dodson remained. Two years later, this trio cut the Bar-Kays' final Mercury album, *Animal,* on which the band's early hero, Sly Stone, made a guest apperance. A revival of interest in funk during 1993 found Mercury issuing the *Best of the Bar-Kays* CD in its "Funk Essentials" series, as well as a new recording by the group on the Zoo Entertainment label.

ARCHIE BELL AND THE DRELLS

Singer Archie Bell (b. Sept. 1, 1944, Henderson, Texas) was stationed with the U.S. Army in West Germany when his first and biggest hit, "Tighten Up," hit the top of both the R&B and pop charts in the spring of 1968. He and his vocal group, the Drells, had recorded the tune a year earlier (while he was on leave after basic training) as the B side of a 45 on the obscure Ovide label in Houston that was subsequently leased to Atlantic Records. The Drells sang little on the dance ditty, other than to incessantly repeat its title over a hypnotic uptempo groove supplied by the TSU Tornadoes, a popular frat band from Texas State University, featuring the choked, choppy chording of guitarist Will Thomas and the propulsive bass line of Tanny Busby. What had begun as a throwaway flip side suddenly thrust Archie Bell and the Drells into the spotlight, even though the leader wasn't around to fully savor the success.

"The first time I heard the record played," Bell recalled to J. H. Tompkins in 1990, "I was sitting at a table with some Army buddies. There was music playing on Armed Forces Radio, and one guy said, 'Hey, check out this jam. This is pretty good.' So I listened and realized that it was me. I told him, and then everyone started saying, 'That's not you, Bell.' When they finally began to believe it, they wanted to hang around me all the time."

Raised in Houston, Bell sang in church as a child and, by age 11, was belting the blues in local clubs. He joined his first group, Little Pop and the Fireballs, while in junior high school, then formed the Drells with friends Huey "Billy" Butler, James Wise, and Willie Parnell. Fashioning their high harmonies after

---

TOP ALBUM

INJOY (Mercury, '79, *35*)

TOP SONGS

SOUL FINGER (Volt, '67, *3 R&B, 17 Pop*)
SHAKE YOUR RUMP TO THE FUNK (Mercury, '76, *5 R&B, 23 Pop*)
TOO HOT TO STOP (PT. 1) (Mercury, '77, *8 R&B*)
HOLY GHOST (Stax, '78, *9 R&B*)
MOVE YOUR BOOGIE BODY (Mercury, '79, *3 R&B*)
BOOGIE BODY LAND (Mercury, '80, *7 R&B*)
HIT AND RUN (Mercury, '81, *5 R&B*)
DO IT (LET ME SEE YOU SHAKE) (Mercury, '82, *9 R&B*)
FREAKSHOW ON THE DANCE FLOOR (Mercury, '84, *2 R&B*)

Additional Top 40 R&B Songs: 16

those of the Impressions, the Drells won over 20 talent contests at Phyllis Wheatley High School before catching the attention of Houston disc jockey Skipper Lee Frazier, who first recorded them for his Ovide label in 1967. "Dog Eat Dog," backed with "Tighten Up," was their second release.

As "Tighten Up" was gaining momentum and offers for live performances began pouring in, the Drells hired Joe Cross to do Bell's solo part on the record, which consisted of little more than declaring that they were from Houston, Texas, and "we don't only sing, we dance just as good as we want." The leader, however, was able to get several passes that allowed him to fly home to do some shows with the group as well as travel to Philadelphia to hastily record new sides, now with producer-songwriters Kenny Gamble and Leon Huff.

The group's next hit, "I Can't Stop Dancing," capitalized on the "Tighten Up" formula, albeit with more melodic content and professional polish, as did such follow-ups as "Do the Choo Choo" and "There's Gonna Be a Showdown." Those three

TOP SONGS

TIGHTEN UP (Atlantic, '68, *1 R&B, 1 Pop*)
I CAN'T STOP DANCING (Atlantic, '68, *5 R&B, 9 Pop*)
DO THE CHOO CHOO (Atlantic, '68, *17 R&B*)
THERE'S GONNA BE A SHOWDOWN (Atlantic, '69, *6 R&B, 21 Pop*)
GIRL YOU'RE TOO YOUNG (Atlantic, '69, *13 R&B*)
DANCING TO YOUR MUSIC (Glades, '73, *11 R&B*)
LET'S GROOVE (PART 1) (TSOP, '76, *7 R&B*)

Additional Top 40 R&B Songs: 7

Gamble-Huff productions also allowed Bell to showcase his elastic, if rather raspy, vocal chops to a much greater degree. But by the time of Bell's Army discharge in April 1969, big hits had pretty much dried up for the Drells, now including Archie's younger brother Lee, who served as the fast-stepping group's main choreographer. In England, however, one of

Archie Bell and the Drells

the Drells' Atlantic album tracks, "Here I Go Again," became a top 20 pop hit in 1972.

Unhappy at Atlantic, the Drells moved to Henry Stone's Glades label in Miami the following year and were sent to Muscle Shoals, Alabama, to record "I Could Dance All Night" with producer Phillip Mitchell. By 1975, they were back in Philadelphia, at Gamble and Huff's TSOP label, for which they cut their last top 10 R&B hit, the disco-styled "Let's Groove," the next year. The group had, in some ways, anticipated disco, but it was unable to further ride the crest of the craze. By 1981, the Drells had broken up, and Archie was recording as a soloist for the Becket label. He continues to perform with pick-up bands and sometimes with old members of the Drells, mostly in the Carolinas, where "beach beat" dancers never stopped shagging to the group's music.

WILLIAM BELL

William Bell

The fact that "You Don't Miss Your Water" by William Bell (b. William Yarborough, July 16, 1939, Memphis) reached only as high as number 95 on *Billboard*'s pop chart and didn't even appear on the R&B list is deceptive. The 1961 record, one of the first to appear on Jim Stewart and Estelle Axton's fledgling Stax label, was a massive hit in much of the southern United States and in some other regions. Penned by Bell and produced by Chips Moman, the slow waltz's distinctive combination of black gospel and white country elements signaled the stylistic direction the Memphis-based company, in particular, and southern soul music, in general, would take for the remainder of the decade.

As a child, William so closely resembled his grandmother, whose name was Belle, that he was given Bell as a nickname, and it stuck. He grew up in Memphis, and he sang in a Baptist church for which a young Booker T. Jones, later his closest associate at Stax, played organ.

In high school, Bell formed a vocal group called the Del-Rios that won a talent contest, which led to one recording for Lester Bihari's Meteor label in 1956. Both sides of the single "Alone on a Rainy Night" b/w "Lizzie" were composed by Bell. Future Stax labelmate Rufus Thomas's band, the Bearcats, supplied the instrumental backing. While the record received little attention outside Memphis, it led to steady work for the group over the next four years

with the bands of Ben Branch, Gene "Bowlegs" Miller, Willie Mitchell, and Phineas Newborn, Sr.

Bell was enrolled in junior college with his sights set on becoming a doctor when Moman approaching him about recording for Stax. "You Don't Miss Your Water" and its follow-up, "Any Other Way," generated enough work for the singer that he put his studies on temporary hold. Then the Army called, removing Bell from the Memphis music scene for two years.

He returned to Stax upon his discharge to find himself lost amid an artist roster that had grown to include Otis Redding, Booker T. and the MG's, the Mad Lads, and Sam and Dave, as well as earlier signees Rufus and Carla Thomas. Not one to be easily discouraged, the singer began working closely with Jones, and together they came up with the aptly titled "Everybody Loves a Winner," crooned by Bell in a resonant low tenor over a cushion of strings and Jones's Floyd Cramer–like piano fills. A number 18 R&B hit, it marked the start of a prolific songwriting partnership between Bell and Jones that yielded such other Bell hits as "Everyday Will Be Like a Holiday" (a perennial Christmas favorite), "A Tribute to a King" (in memory of Otis Redding), "Private Number" (a duet with Judy Clay that had been intended initally for Redding and Carla Thomas), and "I Forgot to Be Your Lover," as well as the blues standard "Born Under a Bad Sign," originally recorded by Albert King.

Bell became increasingly disenchanted with Stax following Jones's 1969 departure, but he tried his best to maintain a positive outlook and stayed on board almost until the company's demise four years later. In the meantime, however, he had moved to Atlanta and started his own record label, Peachtree, for which he produced singles for such artists as soul singer Mitty Collier and blues guitarist Johnny Jones. He also studied acting at Atlanta's Theatre Academy of Dramatic Arts and appeared as Stanley Kowalski in a production of *A Streetcar Named Desire*.

Ironically, after 14 years of service at Stax, Bell finally found the smash he'd been striving for—at another record company. "Tryin' to Love Two," written by the singer and co-produced with Atlanta jazz pianist Paul Mitchell, was issued in late 1976 by Mercury Records and went all the way to Number One on the R&B chart and number 10 pop. A medium-tempo tale about the hazards of two-timing, the tune set Bell's cool vocals against an underpinning of strings and woodwinds and a hypnotically loping bass line. Two Mercury albums followed—but no more substantial hits. He again turned to producing others, including Jackie Moore, whose 1978 Bell and Mitchell–produced "Personally," while only a minor R&B hit, was revived successfully four years later by pop singer Karla Bonoff.

After one album for Kat Family, Bell formed his own Wilbe label in 1985 and recorded himself and

former Stax artist Eddie Floyd, among others. The veteran vocalist is a board member of the Atlanta chapter of the National Academy of Recording Arts and Sciences (NARAS). Although his own tastes remain rather traditional, he helped to convince the organization to include a rap music category in its annual Grammy Awards.

REGINA BELLE

Vocalist Regina Belle didn't take Vaughn Harper seriously at first. The disc jockey, of New York's popular "quiet storm" station WBLS, had approached the young singer backstage following a 1985 concert at Rutgers University starring Mtume and Lisa Lisa and Cult Jam. Belle, a soloist with the school's jazz ensemble, had opened the show with a stirring rendition of "the black national anthem," James Weldon Johnson's "Lift Every Voice and Sing." Harper had asked her to phone him. She didn't.

He remained persistent. Before the year was out, Harper had recommended her to the Manhattans, and she spent the next two years on the road with the veteran stand-up soul vocal group. She made her recording debut, a duet with Manhattans lead Gerald Alston, on the group's 1976 Bobby Womack–produced Columbia single, "Where Did We Go Wrong?" By the following year, Belle had her own contract with the company.

Both of Belle's parents were gospel singers; her mother was a soprano in the choir at Friendship Baptist Church in Englewood, New Jersey, while her father led and sang baritone with a group called the Belle-Tones. Initially inspired by gospel singers Shirley Caesar and Inez Andrews of the Caravans, Regina also became interested in the Temptations and other soul artists at an early age. Her folks were disappointed at her turn toward secular music but nevertheless encouraged her musical pursuits. She played trombone, baritone horn, and tuba in her school band and later mastered steel drums. After making her public singing debut at age 12 with a treatment of the Emotions' "Don't Ask My Neighbors," she began performing at fashion shows and weddings, eventually joining a group called Private Property. While still in high school, she received a scholarship to the preparatory department at the Manhattan School of Music, where she studied

TOP SONGS

SHARE WHAT YOU GOT (Stax, '66, *27 R&B*)

NEVER LIKE THIS BEFORE (Stax, '66, *29 R&B*)

EVERYBODY LOVES A WINNER (Stax, '67, *18 R&B*)

A TRIBUTE TO A KING (Stax, '68, *16 R&B*)

PRIVATE NUMBER (Judy Clay and William Bell, Stax, '68, *17 R&B*)

I FORGOT TO BE YOUR LOVER (Stax, '68, *10 R&B*)

LOVIN' ON BORROWED TIME (Stax, '73, *22 R&B*)

TRYIN' TO LOVE TWO (Mercury, '76, *1 R&B, 10 Pop*)

EASY LOVIN' OUT (HARD GOIN' DOWN) (Mercury, '77, *30 R&B*)

Additional Top 40 R&B Songs: 3

opera and breath control under Inge Wolfe. After graduation, she enrolled at Rutgers and continued her musical development there with William Butler Fielder, Horace Young, and noted jazz pianist Kenny Barron.

By the release of her debut album, 1987's *All by Myself,* Belle was a seasoned professional who combined her gospel, soul (the late Donny Hathaway was a major inspiration), and more recent jazz influences (including Billie Holiday and John Coltrane) into a sophisticated ballad approach. Her wide range, richness of tone, and elastic, jazz-informed phrasing at times brought to mind Anita Baker, a comparison heightened by the fact that Baker cohort Michael J. Powell produced four of the album's nine selections.

It was producer Nick Martinelli, however, who gave Belle her first two hit singles, "Show Me the Way" and "So Many Tears." In that same year, Belle teamed with duet-ballad king Peabo Bryson (an association that would bear greater fruit five years down the road) for "Without You," a song, produced by Powell and Sir Grant, from the soundtrack of *Leonard, Part 6.* Two years later she joined with former Kool and the Gang lead James "J. T." Taylor on the Narada Michael Walden–produced "All I Want Is Forever" from the motion picture *Tap.*

Belle's follow-up album, 1989's *Stay with Me,* yielded four top 10 R&B hit singles, two of which went to Number One: the Walden-produced "Baby Come to Me" and the Martinelli-produced "Make It

Like It Was" (penned by Carvin Winans of the Winans gospel group). "Baby Come to Me" was followed immediately at the top of the R&B chart by "You Are My Everything," a Columbia single by the vocal trio Surface on which Belle subtly echoed Bernard Jackson's lead. She also made an uncredited cameo appearance that year on a track from the Manhattan's *Sweet Talk* album on the Valley Vue label.

A hiatus from recording that lasted over three years was broken at the end of 1992 when Belle again locked her voice with Bryson's to render the lilting title song from the animated Disney motion picture *Aladdin.* Whereas none of her previous records had managed to make it to the pop top 40, the Walden-produced "A Whole New World (Aladdin's Theme)" went right to the top, although it stalled at number 21 on the R&B chart. The song was featured in her third album, 1993's *Passion,* which also included the hit R&B ballad "If I Could," produced by former Walden-associate-turned–Mariah Carey alchemist Walter Afanasieff.

GEORGE BENSON

A devout Jehovah's Witness, George Benson (b. Mar. 22, 1943, Pittsburgh) isn't bothered that few people recognize his smiling face when he goes door to door with copies of *The Watchtower* and *Awake* magazines, but it does get under his skin that many fans of his vocal hits don't know he plays guitar. Although he had begun his recording career as a singer, it was as a self-taught jazz guitarist of astonishing technical prowess that he first achieved international acclaim during the mid-1960s.

At age 10, billed as "Little Georgie Benson," he cut a rhythm and blues song titled "She Makes Me Mad" for RCA Victor in 1953. The public wasn't mad about it, however, and like his 1959 recording for the Amy label as lead vocalist of a Pittsburgh doo wop group called the Altairs, it flopped. Benson then began concentrating on guitar, an instrument he'd first taken up at around age nine after having strummed a ukulele for two years. Among his influences were Charlie Christian, Django Reinhardt, Hank Garland, Grant Green, and Wes Montgomery.

While passing through Pittsburgh in 1962, organist Jack McDuff spotted the 19-year-old picker and

TOP SONGS

SHOW ME THE WAY (Columbia, '87, *2 R&B*)

SO MANY TEARS (Columbia, '87, *11 R&B*)

WITHOUT YOU (Peabo Bryson and Regina Belle, Elektra, '87, *14 R&B*)

ALL I WANT IS FOREVER (James "J. T." Taylor and Regina Belle, Epic, '89, *2 R&B*)

BABY COME TO ME (Columbia, '89, *1 R&B*)

MAKE IT LIKE IT WAS (Columbia, '89, *1 R&B*)

WHAT GOES AROUND (Columbia, '90, *3 R&B*)

THIS IS LOVE (Columbia, '90, *7 R&B*)

A WHOLE NEW WORLD (ALADDIN'S THEME) (Peabo Bryson and Regina Belle, Columbia, '92, *21 R&B, 1 Pop*)

IF I COULD (Columbia, '93, *9 R&B*)

Additional Top 40 R&B Songs: 1

TOP ALBUMS

BREEZIN' (Warner Bros., '76, *1*)
IN FLIGHT (Warner Bros., '77, *9*)
WEEKEND IN L.A. (Warner Bros., '78, *5*)
LIVIN' INSIDE YOUR LOVE (Warner Bros., '79, *7*)
GIVE ME THE NIGHT (Warner Bros., '80, *3*)

Additional Top 40 Albums: 2

TOP SONGS

THIS MASQUERADE (Warner Bros., '76, *3 R&B,
10 Pop*)
THE GREATEST LOVE OF ALL (Warner Bros., '77,
2 R&B, 24 Pop)
ON BROADWAY (Warner Bros., '78, *2 R&B, 7 Pop*)
GIVE ME THE NIGHT (Warner Bros., '80, *1 R&B,
4 Pop*)
TURN YOUR LOVE AROUND (Warner Bros., '81,
1 R&B, 5 Pop)

Additional Top 40 R&B Songs: 15

took him on the road. Over the next three years, Benson recorded a string of bluesy, straight-ahead jazz albums with McDuff's quartet for the Prestige label. Leaving the organist at the end of 1965, the guitarist formed his own combo and was signed to Columbia Records by legendary producer John Hammond. Between 1967 and 1985, Benson worked with producer Creed Taylor, principal architect of the pop-tinged "crossover jazz" sound, first at Verve, then A&M, and finally at Taylor's own CTI label. Taylor found in Benson an ideal instrumentalist to carry down the same light-jazz path he'd successfully taken Wes Montgomery on during the two years prior to that guitarist's untimely death in 1968. Many of Benson's albums with Taylor were strong sellers in the limited jazz market, and some included vocal selections, though none of those were to the guitarist's liking. He also contributed his fluid, fast-fingered guitar to numerous sessions by CTI's other artists, including Hank Crawford, Joe Farrell, Freddie Hubbard, and Esther Phillips.

Warner Bros. staff producer Tommy LiPuma had long admired Benson as a guitarist and singer and jumped at the opportunity to collaborate with him when the artist joined the company in late 1985. "Breezin'," the title cut of his 1976 debut album for the label, was an instrumental previously recorded

by its composer, Bobby Womack, with fellow guitarist Gabor Szabo. Benson's version generated some airplay beyond the usual jazz stations, but it was the album's one vocal track, a romantic revamp of Leon Russell's "This Masquerade," that captured huge mainstream attention, rising to number three on *Billboard*'s R&B chart and number 10 pop and earning a Grammy Award for Best Record of the Year.

The next year's follow-up, *In Flight,* featured four vocal selections, including the number two R&B, number 24 pop hit single "The Greatest Love of All" (an inspirational Michael Masser–Linda Creed ballad that Whitney Houston took to the top of the pop chart nine years later). From then on, vocals became the focus of Benson's albums, although he played on all of them, frequently scat singing along with his rapid-fire solos.

If Benson's clear, ringing tenor voice recalled that of the late Donny Hathaway on "This Masquerade," "The Greatest Love of All," 1978's "On Broadway" (from the live, double-disc *Weekend in L.A.* album), and 1979's "Love Ballad," he affected a grittier, Stevie Wonder–inspired tone for his two uptempo Number One R&B hits: 1980's Quincy Jones–produced "Give Me the Night" and the next year's Jay Graydon–produced "Turn Your Love Around." The singer attributes this chameleon-like tonal range to his doo wop days. "I used to be an imitator," he said in 1985. "I could do perfect imitations of Smokey Robinson, Jackie Wilson, and Sam Cooke."

As his popularity as a pop and R&B artist dipped during the mid-1980s, Benson began refocusing on his jazz roots. Besides lending his blistering bebop guitar attack to albums by such old friends as Dexter Gordon, Jimmy Smith, and Stanley Turrentine, he recorded two jazz albums for Warner Bros.: 1989's *Tenderly,* with a trio featuring pianist McCoy Tyner, and the next year's *Big Boss Band* with the Frank Foster–led remnants of the late Count Basie's orchestra. Both, however, were primarily vocal affairs.

BROOK BENTON

A steady outpouring of R&B and pop hits by Brook Benton (b. Benjamin Franklin Peay, Sept. 19, 1931, Camden, South Carolina) for Mercury Records between 1959 and '61, in which producer Clyde Otis wedded the singer's deep, melisma-dripping gospel baritone to a bed of swirling Belford Hendricks–arranged strings, did much to anticipate the coming of soul music. The majority of those songs were composed by Benton himself (although sometimes under the pseudonym "Willie Dixon," not to be confused with the Chicago blues songwriter of the same name), often in tandem with Otis.

Benton's big break at Mercury was preceeded by more than a decade of struggle in New York, where he pushed a handcart around the city's garment district for a period. The son of a Baptist choir director,

---

TOP ALBUM

BROOK BENTON TODAY (Cotillion, '70, 27)

Additional Top 40 Albums: 1

TOP SONGS

IT'S JUST A MATTER OF TIME (Mercury, '59, *1 R&B, 3 Pop*)
THANK YOU PRETTY BABY (Mercury, '59, *1 R&B, 16 Pop*)
SO MANY WAYS (Mercury, '59, *1 R&B, 6 Pop*)
BABY (YOU'VE GOT WHAT IT TAKES) (Dinah Washington
    and Brook Benton, Mercury, '60, *1 R&B, 5 Pop*)
A ROCKIN' GOOD WAY (TO MESS AROUND AND FALL IN LOVE)
    (Dinah Washington and Brook Benton, Mercury, '60,
    1 R&B, 7 Pop)
KIDDIO (Mercury, '60, *1 R&B, 7 Pop*)
THE BOLL WEEVIL SONG (Mercury, '61, *2 R&B, 2 Pop*)
HOTEL HAPPINESS (Mercury, '62, *2 R&B, 3 Pop*)
RAINY NIGHT IN GEORGIA (Cotillion, '70, *1 R&B, 4 Pop*)

Additional Top 40 R&B Singles: 21

---

he had performed around South Carolina with the Camden Jubilee Singers before coming to New York in 1948 to join Bill Langford's Langfordaires, a gospel group that cut two singles for Columbia the following year. Benton sang with the Jersalem Stars in 1951 before renewing his relationship with Langford in an edition of the world-famous Golden Gate Quartet.

By 1955, when he waxed his first secular sides for Columbia's Okeh subsidiary, Ben Peay was singing lead for a pop group called the Sandmen and had, at the company's suggestion, changed his name to Brook Benton. The company felt, he explained in a 1978 interview with David Smallwood of *Jet* maga-

zine, that "pretty soon somebody is going to pronounce it 'pee' and somebody is gonna get the giggles." Besides recording two Okeh singles of their own, the Sandmen backed blues balladeer Chuck Willis on his 1955 Okeh release, "I Can Tell."

Benton moved to Columbia's Epic label as a soloist in 1956 and recorded "The Wall," his first collaboration with Clyde Otis. The two continued working together at RCA's Vik label in 1958, but the singer was still unable to break through with a hit of his own. He instead recorded countless demos for others, two of which, both written by Benton and Otis, resulted in major 1958 hits: Nat "King" Cole's number two R&B, number five pop "Looking Back" on Capitol and Clyde McPhatter's Number One R&B, number six pop "A Lover's Question" on Atlantic.

Benton signed with Mercury in 1959. Otis was then on the firm's staff, having become the first African-American to head the A&R department of a major label. It was not, however, at Otis's insistence that his friend came to join the company but rather at that of Nat Goodman, manager of the Diamonds, who was strongly impressed with the way Benton had sung on the demo of "The Stroll" (an Otis composition that had given the Canadian vocal group a number five R&B, number four pop hit on Mercury the previous year). The combination of Benton and arranger Belford Hendricks, who was able to fulfill the singer's dream of putting "full strings behind a voice like mine singing blues or sacred-styled songs," gave Benton a smash with his initial Mercury release, the Number One R&B, number three pop ballad "It's Just a Matter of Time." The Benton-Otis-Hendricks sound resulted in 10 more top 10 R&B and half that many top 10 pop hits over the next two years, including two deliciously clever, partially ad-libbed uptempo Benton duets with Mercury labelmate Dinah Washington: "Baby (You've Got What It Takes)" and "A Rockin' Good Way (To Mess Around and Fall in Love)."

In 1962, Benton began working with Mercury staffer Shelby Singleton in Nashville, where he recorded hits like "Hotel Happiness" and "I Got What It Takes" that presaged the later country-soul work of such artists as Joe Simon and Joe Tex. Benton's luck began to run out in 1963, however, and after two years of modest sales at Mercury, he switched to RCA Victor and then to Reprise, with even more meager results.

His fortunes improved after he signed with Atlantic's new Cotillion label in 1968. Placed under the creative control of producer-arranger Arif Mardin, the singer was again sent south, first to Muscle Shoals, Alabama, where he applied his deep pipes to a haunting rendition of Toussaint McCall's "Nothing Can Take the Place of You" (number 11 R&B in 1969), then to Miami to record "Rainy Night in Georgia," a Tony Joe White tune that took Benton back to the top of the R&B chart in 1970. Guitarist Cornell Dupree's gently cascading chords, Billy Carter's wispy organ, and Toots Thielmans' lonesome harmonica combined with Benton's deliberately lazy vocal delivery to give the song an intensely melancholy ambience. It would, however, be the singer's last major hit.

Benton jumped from label to label—Brut, Stax, All Platinum— during the 1970s, finding little success. That changed when he was reunited with Otis in 1979 on the Olde World label, where they had a minor hit with a disco-styled treatment of White's "Makin' Love Is Good for You." Benton continued touring, often in Europe, until shortly before his death, on May 9, 1988, of complications from spinal meningitis.

CHUCK BERRY

I f Elvis Presley was the "king" of rock and roll, Chuck Berry (b. Charles Edward Anderson Berry, Oct. 18, 1926, St. Louis, Missouri) was its most influential stylist and articulate spokesperson, boldly proclaiming the arrival of this raucous new music in such clearly enunciated blues-based anthems as "Roll Over Beethoven" and "Rock and Roll Music." Although he was nearly 30 by the time he began making records, in 1955 for Chess Records, he delineated the joys and frustrations of teenage life in America through a series of brilliantly crafted upbeat compositions, including "School Day," "Sweet Little Sixteen," and "Almost Grown." His raw, rhythmically propulsive guitar style—part blues, part country—had a profound impact on countless white rock musicians of the 1960s, especially the Beach Boys, the Beatles, the Rolling Stones, and Creedence Clearwater Revival, as well as numer-

ous country artists. Curiously, his influence on black music itself was less lasting.

As a child in St. Louis, Berry played piano and dabbled in poetry, eventually taking up guitar and developing a style based on those of pioneering electric blues guitarist T-Bone Walker and Carl Hogan of Louis Jordan's seminal jump blues combo, the Tympany Five. After the first of his three scrapes with the law, which found him serving three years of a 10-year prison sentence for auto theft, Berry worked for a period on the General Motors Fisher Body plant assembly line, then as a hairdresser. In 1952, he joined pianist Johnnie Johnson and drummer Ebby Harding to form a trio at the Cosmopolitan Club in East St. Louis, Illinois, where, over the next three years, they performed a mixture of jazz, jump blues, ballads, soft blues of the Charles Brown variety, and an occasional hillbilly number.

Traveling to Chicago in 1955, Berry encountered bluesman Muddy Waters, who put him in touch with Chess Records head Leonard Chess. Berry returned a week later with a hastily recorded demo containing four songs, one of which was the country hoedown evergreen "Ida Red." Retitled "Maybellene," and with a new set of Berry lyrics, the lively two-beat tune skyrocked to the top of *Billboard*'s R&B chart, staying in that position for 11 weeks. Perhaps more importantly, it rose to number five on the pop chart, becoming the first rock platter by an African-American artist to achieve such success during a time when white cover versions of R&B songs were still the rule.

The unprecedented crossover success of "Maybellene" was greatly abetted by Alan Freed, to whom Chess had given a third of the song's composer credit, even though the influential New York deejay had nothing to do with its creation. Berry became a featured performer at Freed's stage shows and duck-walked his way across the screen in three of the disc jockey's low-budget films: 1956's *Rock, Rock, Rock,* 1957's *Mister Rock and Roll,* and 1959's *Go, Johnny, Go* (its titled taken from the hook of the 1958 Berry hit "Johnny B. Goode"). Berry also became a popular attraction on Dick Clark's "American Bandstand."

Berry's career when into a slump in 1959, when he was charged with having brought a 14-year-old prostitute across state lines to work as a hat checker at a nightclub he'd opened outside St. Louis. After serving two years in federal prison, he emerged a bitter man. The 1964 "British invasion" of his musical disciples did, however, reactivate interest in his music, and he found himself back on the pop charts that year with three new songs: the number 23 "Nadine," the number 10 "No Particular Place to Go," and the number 14 "You Never Can Tell." (*Billboard* published no R&B charts that year.)

The singer left Chess for Mercury Records in 1966 but had no more hits until he returned to Chess and scored in 1972 with his live-in-England recording of "My Ding-a-Ling," a silly double-entendre ditty that he claimed writer's credit for, though it was actually an adaptation of the Dave Bartholomew tune "Toy Bell." The record topped the pop chart but, reflecting Berry's declining popularity in the black community, failed to crack the R&B top 40.

Berry cut his final studio album for Atlantic in 1979, the year he was brought up on income tax evasion charges. While serving a 102-day prison term, he began work on *Chuck Berry: The Autobiography.* The book was published in 1987 and coincided with the release of the Terry Hadford–directed motion picture documentary *Chuck Berry: Hail! Hail! Rock 'n' Roll,* featuring guest appearances by Rolling Stones guitarist Keith Richards (the film's musical director), Eric Clapton, Linda Ronstadt, Robert Cray, Etta James, and the late John Lennon's son Julian, as well as Berry's longtime piano partner, Johnnie Johnson. A soundtrack album was issued on MCA.

Bobby Bland

TOP ALBUM

THE CHUCK BERRY LONDON SESSIONS (Chess, '72, 8)

Additional Top 40 Albums: 2

TOP SONGS

MAYBELLENE (Chess, '55, 1 R&B, 5 Pop)

THIRTY DAYS (Chess, '55, 2 R&B)

ROLL OVER BEETHOVEN (Chess, '56, 2 R&B, 29 Pop)

TOO MUCH MONKEY BUSINESS (Chess, '56, 4 R&B)

SCHOOL DAY (Chess, '57, 1 R&B, 3 Pop)

ROCK AND ROLL MUSIC (Chess, '57, 6 R&B, 8 Pop)

SWEET LITTLE SIXTEEN (Chess, '58, R&B, 2 Pop)

JOHNNY B. GOODE (Chess, '58, 2 R&B, 8 Pop)

ALMOST GROWN (Chess, '59, 3 R&B, 32 Pop)

Additional Top 40 R&B Songs: 9

BOBBY BLAND

Although Bobby Bland (b. Robert Calvin Bland, Jan. 27, 1930, Rosemark, Tennessee) is usually classified as a blues singer, his distinctive combination of urban blues and gospel vocal techniques more accurately places him in a category some have called "soul-blues." Along with Little Willie John, Bland was a pioneer of this style during the mid- to late 1950s. In Bland's case, he drew the inspiration for his alternately intense and mellow baritone vocal approach from B. B. King (his frequent performing partner for over four decades), Roy Brown, and Dixie Hummingbirds lead Ira Tucker.

Raised in Rosemark, a small cotton town outside Memphis, Bland worked in the fields before moving to Memphis in 1947 and joining the Miniatures, a gospel quartet patterned on the Pilgrim Travelers. In 1950, he hooked up with the Beale Streeters, a confederation of local Memphis bluesmen, under King's leadership, that also included vocalist Rosco Gordon and pianist Johnny Ace. Bland and Gordon served as warm-up acts for their leader, with Bland doubling as King's chauffeur.

Bland cut his first record with producer Sam Phillips for Chess in 1951 and appeared the next year on Modern, backed by pianist Ike Turner's band. The singer signed with local deejay David Mattis's Duke label later in 1952 and found a spot on fast-rising labelmate Ace's touring revue. Bland's fledgling career was interrupted at the end of that year when the Army called, an ordeal chronicled in 1953's "Army Blues," recorded while he was on leave. While the vocalist was stationed in Japan, Houston promoter Don Robey took control of Duke Records, thus continuing a chain of contractual obligations for Bland that lasted until 1985, as Duke was sold to ABC-Dunhill in 1973 and ABC to MCA in 1979.

Upon his discharge, Bland began recording for Robey in Houston in 1955 and was placed under the creative guidance of trumpeter-arranger Joe Scott, who helped to shape the singer's style over the next few years. Bland's approach became less imitative of King's, his declarative midrange punctuated by piercing falsetto screams and deep, throaty squalls; the style reached fruition with his first national hit, 1957's "Farther Up the Road."

Bland toured the country incessantly as part of a package show billed as "Blues Consolidated," headlined by Duke blues star Little Junior Parker and featuring Joe Scott's orchestra, from 1955 until 1962, by which time his popularity had eclipsed Parker's through a steady string of hits, including "Little Boy Blue," "I'll Take Care of You," "Don't Cry No More," and "Turn on Your Love Light." Bland took Scott's brassy, jazz-imbued band with him when he left Parker.

Throughout his peak of popularity in the 1960s, Bland alternated on disc between such straight blues as 1962's "Stormy Monday Blues" (a revival of T-Bone Walker's "Call It Stormy Monday" that featured the brilliant guitar work of longtime Bland sideman Wayne Bennett) and gospel-tinged soul numbers like the 1967 Willie Mitchell–produced "A Touch of the Blues." Bland and Robey had a heavy falling out in 1968, and with the boss no longer handling Bland's bookings and personal finances, the singer's career plummeted. He spent two months in jail for failure to pay alimony, lost his band to Johnnie Taylor, and stopped recording, although Duke continued to issue songs it had in the can.

Bland returned to the fold in 1972. "I decided that my best bet would be to go back, because I had heard certain threats," he said 11 years later. "It seemed safer to go back." He resumed recording for Duke that year and, by the next, had managed to rehire much of the old band. After Duke was sold to ABC-Dunhill, the mainstream company paired the vocalist with producer Steve Barri and attempted, with modest results, to break Bland with the elusive pop audience. Two live albums with B. B. King fared better, the camaraderie between the two blues titans easily overcoming the sessions' obvious lack of preparation.

After a series of Al Bell–produced albums for ABC and MCA during the late 1970s and early '80s, on which arranger Monk Higgins kept recycling the same brass, woodwind, and string riffs, Bland broke his contractual chains and joined Malaco Records in 1985. The Jackson, Mississippi, firm issued a more thoughtfully crafted succession of Bland albums aimed at the now middle-aged, working-class African-American audience that had always formed his fan base. The roaring high and low ends of his voice had been chiseled away by the wear and tear of too many one-nighters on the so-called chitlin circuit, but "the lion of the blues," as critic Michele Lomax once dubbed him, kept on purring blues and soul ballads in his timeless baritone.

TOP ALBUM

CALL ON ME (Duke, '63, *11*)

TOP SONGS

FARTHER UP THE ROAD (Bobby "Blue" Bland, Duke, '57, *1 R&B*)

I'LL TAKE CARE OF YOU (Duke, '59, *2 R&B*)

I PITY THE FOOL (Duke, '61, *1 R&B*)

DON'T CRY NO MORE (Duke, '61, *2 R&B*)

TURN ON YOUR LOVE LIGHT (Duke, '62, *2 R&B, 28 Pop*)

THAT'S THE WAY LOVE IS (Duke, '63, *1 R&B*)

THESE HANDS (SMALL BUT MIGHTY) (Duke, 65, *4 R&B*)

THIS TIME I'M GONE FOR GOOD (Dunhill, '73, *5 R&B*)

I WOULDN'T TREAT A DOG (THE WAY YOU TREATED ME) (Dunhill, '74, *3 R&B*)

Additional Top 40 R&B Songs: 41

BOOKER T. AND THE MG'S

Stax Records, originally known as Satellite, had been in existence for three years and had scored only two top 10 R&B and pop hits when four musicians came together in 1962 at the Memphis company's converted movie theater studio to cut an off-the-cuff instrumental blues shuffle titled "Green Onions." Intended as a B side filler, it gave Stax its first Number One R&B charter (number three pop). The session also brought together for the first time three of the key players who would define the label's sound for the remainder of the decade.

They were dubbed Booker T., after their young African-American organist, Booker T. Jones (b. Nov. 12, 1944, Memphis), and the MG's, which either stood for "Memphis group" or was the name of a sports car, depending on which version of the story one chooses to believe. Included in the quartet was the white guitarist Steve Cropper (b. Oct. 21, 1942, Willow Springs, Missouri), who, as a member of the Mar-Keys, had given the company its second hit, 1971's number two R&B, number three pop "Last Night." Rounding out the band were two black veterans of the Memphis music scene: drummer Al

Jackson, Jr. (b. November 27, 1934, Memphis), and bassist Lewis Steinberg.

With Donald "Duck" Dunn (b. Nov. 24, 1941, Memphis), the Mar-Keys' white bassist, taking over for Steinberg in 1964, Booker T. and the MG's cut hit after hit through 1971, not only for themselves, but for virtually every vocalist on the Stax roster. As a unit and individually, they played on, produced, and composed hits for Otis Redding, Carla Thomas, Rufus Thomas, William Bell, Eddie Floyd, Johnnie Taylor, Sam and Dave, Albert King, Isaac Hayes, the Emotions, and, on an Atlantic Records–sponsored visit to Memphis, Wilson Pickett.

Jones's clean, mellow-toned organ swells; Cropper's razor-sharp, alternating lead and rhythm guitar parts; Dunn's steady, loping bass lines; and Jackson's rock-solid, slightly delayed backbeat became the backbone of the Stax sound. They were not virtuosos but musicians who tightly interlocked to complement each other with subtle perfection and to enhance the singers they accompanied with a special empathy. Although they often worked in the studio from 10 A.M. until after midnight, six or even seven days a week, they treated each song as a unique entity, bouncing ideas off of each other until they had the final take just right.

Booker T. himself was not present for some of the MG's' mid-'60s sessions—Isaac Hayes filled in on

Booker T. and The MG's

organ for the group's second hit, 1965's "Boot-Leg"—as he was away much of the time studying music at Indiana University. Back in Memphis, he began applying some of the advanced theory he'd learned to the group's instrumentals, especially 1968's key-changing "Hang 'Em High" (which, curiously, went to number nine on *Billboard*'s pop chart, while placing only as high as 35 on the magazine's R&B list), as well as to the sessions he supervised for Eddie Floyd and other Stax vocalists.

After 1969's "Time Is Tight," Booker T. and the MG's began to come apart. Jones moved to California that year, and the combo only reunited for occasional sessions, all outside Memphis. Following their last hit, 1971's jazzy "Melting Pot," Cropper left Stax and set up shop across town at Trans Maximus Sound Studios, where, among other things, he produced and played on an album by an MG's sound-alike group called Washrag, billing himself as "Captain Guitar" to avoid contractual hassles with Stax. With Dunn and Jackson still on board and Carson Whitsett and Bobby Manuel replacing Jones and Cropper, the MG's made a final album for Stax in 1973 that proved unsuccessful.

Booker T. remained quite successful during the 1970s as a producer, his largest trophies being singer-songwriter Bill Withers's number six R&B, number three pop "Ain't No Sunshine" in 1971 and country star Willie Nelson's 1978 triple-platinum *Stardust* LP. Cropper went on to produce such artists as Harry Nilsson, the Temptations, and Tower of Power.

Dunn and Jackson remained at Stax, although the drummer moonlighted with old friend Willie Mitchell at Hi Records, where he played on and co-wrote many of Al Green's hits, including "Let's Stay Together" and "I'm Still in Love with You," until his murder in 1975.

With former Bar-Kay Willie Hall on drums, Booker T. and the MG's reunited in 1977 to tour and record an album for Asylum. Cropper and Dunn did several stints with the Blues Brothers before reuniting with Jones in 1992 to play in the rhythm section for Bob Dylan's all-star 30th anniversary concert celebration. In '93, they toured as rock singer Neil Young's backup band and cut a new Booker T. and the MG's album for Columbia.

BOYZ II MEN

I f the "doo-hop" explosion of the early 1990s, which combined neo–doo wop singing with hip-hop beats, produced many youthful groups whose harmonies were sometimes off-key and who sported "gangsta" looks and lyrics, Boyz II Men stood out from much of the pack. Comprising Michael "Bass" McCary, Nathan "Alex Vander-pool" Morris, Wanya "Squirt" Morris (no relation), and Shawn "Slim" Stockman, the Philadelphia four-some led the "new jack" harmony sweepstakes with a jazz-tinged, perfectly pitched vocal blend and a clean-cut preppie image, scoring six top 10 R&B hits in 1991 and '92, two of them performed entirely a cappella.

The Boyz, all from middle-class families, came together in 1988 at the Philadelphia High School for the Creative and Performing Arts. Besides soul music, they were greatly inspired by Take 6, a Seventh Day Adventist a cappella sextet noted for its innovative fusion of quartet gospel and intricate Hi-Lo's–like jazz harmonies. In March 1989, after having sung together only a few months, they managed to sneak backstage at a New Edition concert, where they did an impromptu a cappella audition for Michael Bivens. Impressed with what he heard, the New Edition member gave the Boyz his phone number. He soon left New Edition and, besides forming Bell Biv DeVoe with two of his cohorts from the group, launched his own management and production company. Of the artists signed to Biv Entertainment, including the preteen singing group Another Bad Creation and rapper M. C. Brains, Boyz II Men proved the most successful.

Cooleyhighharmony, the group's 1991 debut album, took its title from *Cooley High,* a 1975

TOP SONGS

GREEN ONIONS (Stax, '62, *1 R&B, 3 Pop*)
BOOT-LEG (Stax, '65, *10 R&B*)
MY SWEET POTATO (Stax, '66, *18 R&B*)
HIP HUG-HER (Stax, '67, *6 R&B, 37 Pop*)
GROOVIN' (Stax, '67, *10 R&B, 21 Pop*)
SOUL-LIMBO (Stax, '68, *7 R&B, 17 Pop*)
HANG 'EM HIGH (Stax, '68, *35 R&B, 9 Pop*)
TIME IS TIGHT (Stax, '69, *7 R&B, 6 Pop*)
MELTING POT (Stax, '71, *21 R&B*)

Additional Top 40 R&B Songs: 1

Boyz II Men

motion picture by Michael Schults that, despite its Chicago setting, featured a soundtrack of Motown oldies, most of them recorded in Detroit. The Motown album's first single, an uptempo slice of new jack swing produced by Dallas Austin and co-authored by Austin, Bivens, and group members Nathan Morris and Shawn Stockman, was titled "Motownphilly." "We grew up on the Motown sound and the Philadelphia sound, like the Blue Notes and the O'Jays," Wanya Morris explained to Alan Light in a 1992 *Rolling Stone* interview. "We're trying to connect the two."

The second single was an a cappella rendition of "It's So Hard to Say Goodbye," a ballad penned by Freddie Perren and Christine Yarian and originally performed by former Spinners lead G. C. Cameron on the *Cooley High* soundtrack. While Cameron's 1975 version had gone only as high as number 38 on *Billboard*'s R&B chart, the tune gave the Boyz a

Number One R&B, number two pop hit. *Cooley-highharmony* yielded two more hit ballads—"Uhh Ahh," written by Nathan and Wanya Morris with Bivens, and the Nathan Morris composition Please Don't Go"—both featuring remarkably mature bass monologues by the then-20-year-old Michael McCary.

After spending the first half of 1992 as a supporting act for rapidly fading rap star Hammer, the Boyz made chart history with their fifth single. "End of the Road," a haunting love lament written and produced by Antonio "L. A." Reid, Kenneth "Baby-face" Edmonds, and Daryl Simmons for the soundtrack of the Eddie Murphy comedy *Boomerang*, topped *Billboard*'s pop singles chart for 13 weeks, breaking a previous rock-era record of 11 weeks set in 1956 by Elvis Presley's double-sided single, "Don't Be Cruel" b/w "Hound Dog." For a follow-up, taken from "The Jacksons: An American

TOP ALBUMS

COOLEYHIGHHARMONY (Motown, '91, 3)
CHRISTMAS INTERPRETATIONS (Motown, '93, 19)

TOP SONGS

MOTOWNPHILLY (Motown, '91, 4 R&B, 3 Pop)
IT'S SO HARD TO SAY GOODBYE TO YESTERDAY
    (Motown, '91, 1 R&B, 3 Pop)
UHH AHH (Motown, '91, 1 R&B, 16 Pop)
PLEASE DON'T GO (Motown, '92, 8 R&B)
END OF THE ROAD (Motown, '92, 1 R&B, 1 Pop)
IN THE STILL OF THE NIGHT (I'LL REMEMBER)
    (Motown, '92, 4 R&B, 3 Pop)

Dream," a four-hour, Motown-produced ABC-TV dramatic miniseries about the Jackson 5 in which the Boyz had a cameo role, they returned to a cappella to do a remake of the Five Satins' 1956 doo wop classic, "In the Still of the Night (I'll Remember)."

With one multi-platinum album and six hit singles behind them, Boyz II Men were re-signed to Motown during the summer of 1993 for a reported eight-figure amount. The new contract called for seven albums, the first of which arrived in plenty of time for the holidays. Largely produced by the group itself, *Christmas Interpretations* found the quartet applying its distinctively layered harmonies to eight original seasonal selections, as well as to an unaccompanied reading of "Silent Night."

BOBBY BROWN

Although Bobby Barrisford Brown (b. Feb. 5, 1969, Boston) wasn't the principal lead vocalist of New Edition, a role assigned to the slightly older Ralph Tresvant, he was, to many of the teenage quintet's pubescent female fans, its sexiest member. They were shocked in 1985 when the then-16-year-old heartthrob, who had enjoyed three Number One R&B hits with New Edition, suddenly quit the group to embark on a solo career. His debut single, "Girlfriend," written by members of a Sacramento, California, group called Collage, was at the top of *Billboard*'s R&B chart by the end of 1986, but the album *King of Stage* failed to live up to its title, and the next single, "Girl Next Door," produced by Larry Blackmon of Cameo, peaked at a disappointing number 31 R&B. Word at the time was that Brown had made a big mistake by leaving his Boston singing buddies.

MCA Records placed the singer with two of the hottest young production teams in the business—Antonio "L. A." Reid and Kenneth "Babyface" Edmonds (collectively known as La'Face) along with Gene Griffin and Teddy Riley—for his follow-up album, 1988's *Don't Be Cruel*. The company expected that the disc would do well, as did Brown's manager, who booked him on a year-long tour as an opening act for New Edition.

But no one had anticipated *Don't Be Cruel*'s massive crossover appeal. Before the year was out, it was the Number One album in the land and had yielded two Number One R&B singles: the La'Face-produced title track and the Griffin-produced "My Prerogative"—the former also topping the pop chart. Three more smashes from the album—"Roni," "Every Little Step," and "Rock Wit'cha," all produced by La'Face—came in 1989. While still stuck in his supporting slot on the tour, Brown emerged as the king of new jack swing, a style that fused traditional soul elements with electronic hip-hop beats. Singing in a grainy tenor, he had become a brash, ultra-macho R&B superstar, the likes of which hadn't been seen since Teddy Pendergrass's heyday a decade earlier.

The second youngest of the eight children of a construction worker and his school-teaching wife, Brown grew up in the Orchard Park projects of Boston's Roxbury district. He ran with a gang and was a petty thief until, at age 11, he resolved to straighten up after the stabbing death of his best friend. He began singing with his basketball partner Michael Bivens, and together they recruited Ricky Bell, Ralph Tresvant, and Ronnie DeVoe to form New Edition. Brown was the youngest member.

The group hit the top of the R&B chart with its first single, 1983's Maurice Starr–produced "Candy Girl" on the Streetwise label, and they signed with MCA the following year. Despite New Edition's ongoing success, Brown was becoming frustrated by the group's financial arrangement with its management as well as by its bubblegum-soul musical direction. "It wasn't my sound," he told Barry Michael Cooper in a 1988 interview with *Spin* magazine. "I wanted to come out hard, with the street in full effect."

Following his phenomenal 1988–89 *Don't Be Cruel* breakthrough, as well as the Number One

Bobby Brown

R&B La'Face-produced "On Our Own" from the *Ghostbusters II* soundtrack and an album of new mixes of previously issued material titled *Dance! ...Ya Know It!*, Brown disappeared from records for three years (with the exception of a one-track guest appearance on a 1991 remix album by Bell Biv DeVoe, the group that remained after New Edition's dissolution two years prior). In the interim, he moved from Los Angeles to Atlanta, set up a production company (eventually producing *B. Brown Posse*, a 1993 MCA album of various up-and-coming singers and rappers), and became romantically involved with superstar vocalist Whitney Houston, five years his senior. Their July 1992 wedding was much publicized, as was the March 1993 birth of their first child, Bobbi Kristina Brown.

Mr. and Mrs. Brown sang a duet, the Teddy Riley–produced "Something in Common," on *Humpin' Around,* Bobby's long-awaited third album. The 1992 disc also reunited him with La'Face, collaborator Daryl Simmons having been added to the original duo of Reid and Edmonds. *Humpin' Around* went to number two on *Billboard*'s album chart and contained four top 10 R&B singles, three of which also made the pop top 10.

"I consider myself a hip-hop/new jack artist," the singer said in a 1992 interview with Scott Poulson-Bryant of *Vibe* magazine. "My music is basically R&B. It's street music. The pop community accepts it, but I'm not making music for a race. I make music for everybody."

TOP ALBUMS

DON'T BE CRUEL (MCA, '88, *1*)
HUMPIN' AROUND (MCA, '92, *2*)

Additonal Top 40 Albums: 1

TOP SONGS

GIRLFRIEND (MCA, '86, *1 R&B*)
DON'T BE CRUEL (MCA, '88, *1 R&B, 8 Pop*)
MY PREROGATIVE (MCA, '88, *1 R&B, 1 Pop*)
RONI (MCA, '88, *2 R&B, 3 Pop*)
EVERY LITTLE STEP (MCA, '89, *1 R&B, 3 Pop*)
ON OUR OWN (MCA, '89, *1 R&B, 2 Pop*)
ROCK WIT'CHA (MCA, '89, *3 R&B, 7 Pop*)
HUMPIN' AROUND (MCA, '92, *1 R&B, 3 Pop*)

Additional Top 40 R&B Songs: 4

CHARLES BROWN

Singer-pianist Charles Brown (b. Sept. 13, 1922, Texas City, Texas) is one of the major stylists in the history of rhythm and blues. His many hit recordings, including "Drifting Blues," "Merry Christmas Baby," "Trouble Blues," and "Black Night," made him one of the most popular blues artists of the mid-1940s to early '50s, and his sophisticated, jazz-informed piano approach and wispy baritone vocal delivery had a profound impact on such later stars as Ray Charles, Amos Milburn, Floyd Dixon, Fats Domino, Johnny Ace, and Chuck Berry.

Raised by his grandparents, Brown studied classical piano as a child and would pump the pedals of the family's player piano, paying close attention to the piano-roll notes of jazzmen Art Tatum and Fats Waller as they flew across the keyboard. (He later incorporated into his own style the percussively hammered two-handed chords heard on those rolls.) Other important influences included Texas blues singer-pianist Ivory Joe Hunter, Kansas City jazz pianist Mary Lou Williams, and two soft-toned pop vocalists: Phea Terrell of Andy Kirk's big band and Helen O'Connell of Jimmy Dorsey's orchestra.

Brown earned a B.A. in chemistry at Prairie View College and taught high school for a period before landing a civil service job as a junior chemist at an Arkansas facility that manufactured mustard gas. Moving to California in 1943, he began to pursue a career as a professional musician, first in Berkeley and San Francisco. After winning an amateur contest at the Lincoln Theater in Los Angeles in 1944 with a repertoire of classical and boogie woogie instrumentals, he was approached by guitarist Johnny Moore, who was looking for a singer-pianist in order to form a group patterned after the then-popular King Cole Trio, in which Johnny's brother Oscar played guitar.

Like Nat Cole's group, Johnny Moore's Three Blazers, featuring Charles Brown, initially entertained white audiences with a mixture of pop tunes, jazz, boogies, and an occasional blues. Their early recordings, beginning in 1945 for the Exclusive and Atlas labels, reflected this eclecticism. But it was 1946's "Drifting Blues" for Philo Records (on which drummer Johnny Otis joined the trio) that caught on big with black record buyers and marked the direction Brown's career would take.

The group scored hit after blues hit through 1948, at which point Brown left to form his own trio continuing in that musical vein. He remained a

Charles Brown

major record seller and attraction on the black theater circuit until 1952, when problems with the musicians' union and the I.R.S., coupled with his unwillingness to adapt his gentle musical approach to the rapidly emerging rock and roll style, began to derail his career.

For the next three and a half decades, Brown existed on the periphery of show business, recording sporadically and performing in small clubs with often inadequate pickup bands, even abandoning the piano for a long period in favor of an organ. He became a largely forgotten figure, remembered only at Christmastime, when his two oft-covered seasonal hits, "Merry Christmas Baby" (first recorded for Exclusive in 1947 with the Three Blazers) and "Please Come Home for Christmas" (issued in 1960 by King Records, and Brown's only chart hit after 1952), filled the airwaves from coast to coast.

"If the kids today never hear about you any other time of the year, they know that at Christmastime they're gonna hear Charles Brown," he said in 1984. "At least I have that going for me, along with Bing Crosby."

"I had some beautiful days," he added. "I bought Cadillacs and I had limousines. Listen, the world doesn't owe me nothin', 'cause I had it. Now I have a little peace and quiet for myself and I can enjoy the little things I wanna do."

Brown was living at a senior citizens' home in Berkeley, practicing Ravel and Debussy every morning before leaving his modest studio apartment to play the horses at a local track (a lifelong obsession first chronicled in his 1946 Aladdin recording of "Race Track Blues" with the Three Blazers). His semiretirement was interrupted in 1989 when bluesy rock singer Bonnie Raitt asked him to tour as her opening act. A contract with Rounder's Bullseye Blues label followed, and Brown formed a combo of seasoned professionals capable of maneuvering his music's complex chord progressions and subtle swing. He quickly became a star attraction at festivals and first-class jazz clubs around the world.

TOP SONGS

Johnny Moore's Three Blazers:
DRIFTING BLUES (Philo, '46, 2 R&B)
SUNNY ROAD (Exclusive, '46, 4 R&B)
SO LONG (Modern Music, '46, 4 R&B)
NEW ORLEANS BLUES (Exculsive, '47, 2 R&B)
MERRY CHRISTMAS BABY (Exclusive, '47, 3 R&B)
Charles Brown:
GET YOURSELF ANOTHER FOOL (Charles Brown Trio, Aladdin, '49, 4 R&B)
TROUBLE BLUES (Charles Brown Trio, Aladdin, '49, 1 R&B)
IN THE EVENING WHEN THE SUN GOES DOWN (Aladdin, '49, 4 R&B)
BLACK NIGHT (Aladdin, '51, 1 R&B)
SEVEN LONG DAYS (Aladdin, '51, 2 R&B)

Additional Top 40 R&B Songs: 15

JAMES BROWN

Over a 32-year period, from 1956 to 1988, James Brown (b. James Joe Brown, Jr., probably May 5, 1933, Barnwell, South Carolina) amassed an amazing total of 98 entries on *Billboard*'s top 40 R&B singles chart, a record unsurpassed by any other artist. Seventeen of them reached Number One, a feat topped only by Stevie Wonder and Louis Jordan and equalled only by Aretha Franklin.

Brown's rise from juvenile delinquent to Soul Brother Number One is among the great modern-day American success stories. The only child of a poor backwoods family, he was sent to Augusta, Georgia, at age five to live at an aunt's brothel. He earned his keep by running errands for soldiers at nearby Camp Gordon, entertaining them with his buckdancing and enticing them into his aunt's establishment. Singing gospel music and playing piano, drums, and guitar served as an emotional outlet for the young Brown. A junior high school dropout, he spent three years in reform school for petty theft, during which time he resolved to make something of himself.

Paroled in 1952, Brown settled in Toccoa, Georgia, and joined the Gospel Starlighters, a quartet led by Bobby Byrd. Theirs was a raw southern gospel style inspired by Julius Cheeks and the Sensational Nightingales and Reverend Reuben Willingham and the Swanee Quintet. Eventually, however, the Starlighters evolved into a rhythm and blues outfit. They were originally known as the Avons, then as the Flames.

In November 1955, while based in Macon, Georgia, the Flames cut a demonstration record at radio station WIBB of an original tune titled "Please, Please, Please." While passing through Atlanta, record producer Ralph Bass heard the demo and was so impressed with Brown's impassioned lead and the group's hard harmonies that he immediately drove to Macon and signed them to King Records, a Cincinnati company for which two of the Flames' favorite groups, the Midnighters and the 5 Royales, were recording. A session was held in Ohio the following week. Released on King's Federal label two months later, in March 1956, "Please, Please, Please" reached number five on *Billboard*'s R&B chart.

Brown's boyhood dream of escaping poverty was

not immediately realized, however. Although he and the Flames continued to make records for Federal, it would be nearly three years before they again hit the national charts. "Try Me," produced by Andy Gibson, hit big during the winter of 1958–59, giving the group its first Number One R&B record and enabling Brown to hire a steady backup band. Through grueling rehearsals and barnstorming one-nighters, Brown developed the band into the hottest R&B unit in the land. His musicians' precision timing was geared to accent every bloodcurdling

---

TOP ALBUM

LIVE AT THE APOLLO (King, '63, 2)

Additional Top 40 Albums: 14

TOP SONGS

James Brown and the Famous Flames:
PAPA'S GOT A BRAND NEW BAG (PART I) (King, '65, 1 R&B, 8 Pop)
I GOT YOU (I FEEL GOOD) (King, '65, 1 R&B, 3 Pop)
IT'S A MAN'S MAN'S MAN'S WORLD (King, '66, 1 R&B, 8 Pop)
COLD SWEAT (PART 1) (King, '67, 1 R&B, 7 Pop)
I GOT THE FEELIN' (King, '68, 1 R&B, 6 Pop)

James Brown:
SAY IT LOUD—I'M BLACK AND I'M PROUD (PART 1) (King, '68, 1 R&B, 10 Pop)
MOTHER POPCORN (YOU GOT TO HAVE A MOTHER FOR ME) (PART 1)
   (King, '69, 1 R&B, 11 Pop)
SUPER BAD (PART 1 & PART 2) (King, '70, 1 R&B, 13 Pop)
GET ON THE GOOD FOOT (PART 1) (Polydor, '72, 1 R&B, 18 Pop)

Additional Top 40 R&B Songs: 89

---

scream, every flying split, every knee drop, every one-legged skate, and every shimmy of Brown's stunning array of acrobatics, which by now had become the visual trademark of the group's stage act.

While he continued scoring hit singles during the early 1960s, now issued on the King label, Brown came up with the idea that if the hysteria he was generating in person could be captured on an album, people who hadn't seen him yet could at least hear and feel the excitement of him screaming and hollering till his back got soaking wet. King Records was convinced that such an album wouldn't sell, so Brown put up his own money to record a performance at the Apollo Theater in October 1962. Released nearly a year later, *Live at the Apollo* went to number two on *Billboard*'s album chart, an

unprecedented feat for a live R&B album. Radio stations played it with a frequency formerly reserved for singles, and attendance at Brown's concerts mushroomed.

Brown scored his first top 10 pop single in 1965 with "Papa's Got a Brand New Bag," and the hits kept on coming for the next decade, one after another at an unheard-of rate. He gradually phased out the Flames, and the gospel and blues structures of his early records gave way to open-ended vamps that emphasized his rhythmically riveting sandpaper vocals and the complex funk syncopations of his band. His innovations during this period had a profound influence on popular music styles around the world, including funk, rock, Afro-pop, and, eventually, rap. In charge of his own productions, he also produced hits for such singing members of his revue as Bobby Byrd and Lynn Collins and for his band, the J.B.'s.

Brown's popularity began to wane after 1976's number four R&B "Get Up Offa That Thing" on Polydor. He would not have another top 10 record until 1985's Dan Hartman–produced "Living in America" on the Scotti Bros. label took him to number four pop and number 10 R&B. His last major charter was 1988's number two R&B "I'm Real," but he found himself back in trouble with the law before the year was out. Having allegedly been under the influence of PCP, a powerful mind-altering drug, he was arrested after a wild car chase through South Carolina and Georgia, tried, and sentenced to six years in prison.

After being paroled in 1991, Brown resumed recording for Scotti Bros. Although he had no further hits, his status as "the Godfather of Soul" remained undiminished. Indeed, he had picked up a new generation of fans who'd become familiar with his funk grooves through their frequent use as samples on rap records. Already a member of the Rock and Roll Hall of Fame, Brown added to his collection of accolades when he received a special lifetime achievement Grammy Award in 1992.

Roy Brown

ROY BROWN

Vocalist-songwriter Roy Brown (b. Sept. 10. 1925, New Orleans) never intended to be a blues singer, having begun his career as a Bing Crosby imitator. Developed by accident, Brown's semi-operatic, precisely enunciated approach to the blues—rooted rhythmically in the blues shouter tradition, yet infused with a wailing falsetto derived from his Baptist upbringing—was unique and made him one of the top-selling African-American recording artists between 1948 and '51, with 13 of his sides from that period hitting *Billboard*'s R&B top 10. If his peak of popularity was brief, Brown's style had a lasting impact on those of such other blues artists as B. B. King and Bobby Bland, as well as on pioneering soul man Jackie Wilson. Some critics have argued, not without merit, that Brown was the first soul singer.

Brown was raised in Eunice, Louisiana, by his mother, church choir director and organist True Love Brown. At age 13, he organized the Rookie Four, a gospel quartet for which he began composing songs. ("The same style I'm using singing the blues," he said in 1970, "I did when I was singing spirituals.") Losing his mother when he was 14, Brown finished high school in Houston, then hoboed to California in 1942 to become a boxer. A welterweight, he won 16 of 18 professional matches before quitting the game, having found that the sight of blood nauseated him. In 1945, he entered an amateur contest at the Million Dollar Theater in Los Angeles and took home the $60 first prize with his renditions of "San Antonio Rose" (a western swing tune by Bob Wills, popularized by Crosby) and "Jingle, Jangle, Jingle" (a hit for novelty bandleader Kay Kyser).

After a period in Shreveport, Louisiana, Brown formed a band in Galveston, Texas, called the Mellodeers. He continued to specialize in pop songs, leaving the blues numbers to trumpet player Wilbert Brown. One of those was an uptempo Roy Brown composition titled "Good Rockin' Tonight." During a radio broadcast over Galveston station KGBC, Wilbert became ill just as the announcer was introducing "Good Rockin'." "I started to sing," Roy recalled, "not singing—I was shouting."

Back in New Orleans in 1947, Brown tried to interest Wynonie Harris, the leading blues shouter of the day, in "Good Rockin'," but was rebuffed. He then took it to another top blues artist, singer-pianist Cecil Gant, who was so impressed that he called Jules Braun of DeLuxe Records in Linden, New Jersey, in the middle of the night and had Brown sing it over the phone. Braun arrived in the Crescent City three days later and recorded Brown.

His recording of "Good Rockin' " rose to number 13 on *Billboard*'s R&B chart in June 1948, its sales undercut by a cover version on King Records by none other than Wynonie Harris, which went to Number One. (Elvis Presley's 1954 treatment of the tune was more faithful to Brown's original than Harris's had been.) Brown's follow-up, "Long About Midnight," became a chart topper and solidified the singer's three-year run on the R&B best-seller lists. During the spring of 1949, he had three records simultaneously in the R&B top 15, including a reissue of "Good Rockin'," which reached number 11 in its second round.

His releases alternated between jump blues like "Rockin' at Midnight" and such tortured slow blues as the autobiographical "Hard Luck Blues." All

Brown's DeLuxe hits were original compositions. "I make up a story, and I play the part of all the people in it," he explained. "You tell the story, and you have to feel it. This is why I wail and cry when I'm singing slow tunes, and I get happy when I'm shouting."

Following the sale of DeLuxe to Syd Nathan's larger King operation in Cincinnati, Brown's records began appearing on the King label after 1951, but none were hits. His luck changed briefly in 1957 when New Orleans songwriter-arranger-producer Dave Bartholomew signed him to Imperial Records. Brown's cover of the Buddy Knox rockabilly hit "Party Doll" went to number 13 on the R&B chart, while his treatment of the producer's "Let the Four Winds Blow" (later repopularized by Fats Domino) reached number five R&B and number 29 pop.

The vocalist recorded sporadically during the 1960s, for such labels as Home of the Blues (with Willie Mitchell's band), DRA, Connie, Mobile, Bluesway, Gert, Summit, and Tru-Love. Settling in Los Angeles in 1961, he spent much of the decade helping his wife with her catering business and, for a period, sold encyclopedias door to door.

An appearance with the Johnny Otis Show at the 1970 Monterey Jazz Festival rekindled his interest in performing, and he launched his own Friendship label. Brown's 1971 Friendship recording of his own "Love for Sale" sold so well in some regions that Mercury licensed it for national distribution. He continued appearing at clubs and festivals in the U.S. and Europe until his death on May 25, 1981.

TOP SONGS

LONG ABOUT MIDNIGHT (DeLuxe, '48, *1 R&B*)
'FORE DAY IN THE MORNING (DeLuxe, '49, *6 R&B*)
RAINY WEATHER BLUES (DeLuxe, '49, *5 R&B*)
ROCKIN' AT MIDNIGHT (DeLuxe, '49, *2 R&B*)
BOOGIE AT MIDNIGHT (DeLuxe, '49, *3 R&B*)
HARD LUCK BLUES (DeLuxe, '50, *1 R&B*)
LOVE DON'T LOVE NOBODY (DeLuxe, '50, *2 R&B*)
CADILLAC BABY (DeLuxe, '50, *6 R&B*)
BAR ROOM BLUES (DeLuxe, '51, *6 R&B*)
LET THE FOUR WINDS BLOW (Imperial, '57, *5 R&B*)

Additional Top 40 R&B Songs: 7

RUTH BROWN

Known alternately as "Miss Rhythm" and "the girl with the tear in her voice," vocalist Ruth Brown (b. Ruth Weston, Jan. 30, 1928, Portsmouth, Virginia) was the top-selling black female recording artist in America between 1951 and '54. A series of rocking blues numbers she made at Atlantic Records during that period, including "5-10-15 Hours" and "(Mama) He Treats Your Daughter Mean," did much to set the stage for the coming of rock and roll, though her initial stardom began to fade following its advent.

The eldest of seven children, she began singing at Portsmouth's Emmanuel African Methodist Episcopal Church, where her father was the choir director. Initially inspired to sing jazz by Billie Holiday, Dinah Washington, and Sarah Vaughan, she ran away from home, much to her father's dismay, to go on the road with singer-trumpeter Jimmy Brown, whom she soon married.

Ruth was singing at the Frolic Show Bar in Detroit in 1946 when she was spotted by bandleader Lucky Millinder. Although he already had two vocalists in his orchestra, Annisteen Allen and Bull Moose Jackson, Millinder added Brown to the aggregation but fired her a month later for having fetched some drinks for musicians in the band during an engagement. As an afterthought, he told her she couldn't sing.

Stranded in Washington, D.C., she landed a gig at the Crystal Caverns—a club operated by Cab Calloway's sister Blanche—in order to raise enough money for her bus fare back to Portsmouth. Patrons, however, were taken with Brown's unique blue note–dripping delivery of ballads, and she stayed on, Miss Calloway becoming her manager. One night, Duke Ellington and disc jockey Willis Conover came into the club. Impressed by what he heard, Conover phoned two friends in New York, Herb Abramson and Ahmet Ertegun, who were in the process of launching a new record label called Atlantic.

En route to New York for her Atlantic audition, as well as for a debut at the Apollo Theater, Brown (and Calloway) were injured in an auto accident. Her leg mangled, Brown was hospitalized for nine months. Finally, on May 25, 1949, she stood on crutches to record the Russ Morgan ballad "So Long," backed by an all-star jazz band led by guitarist Eddie Condon. An immediate sensation, going to number six on *Billboard*'s R&B chart, "So Long" became Atlantic's second major hit, after Stick McGhee's "Drinkin' Wine, Spo-Dee-O-Dee," and established Brown as a national star.

More blues-tinged ballads followed, but it was 1950's "Teardrops from My Eyes," an uptempo blues by Atlantic house writer Rudy Toombs, that set Brown's stylistic course for the remainder of the decade. It was the first fast tune that Brown recorded, and during the session her voice cracked to produce a squeal-like sound. Co-producer Abramson liked what he heard, calling it a "tear," and it became a Brown trademark. "Teardrops" skyrocketed to Number One on the R&B chart, and later that year, pop song belter Frankie Laine, then known as "Mr. Rhythm," dubbed her "Miss Rhythm."

After four more Number One R&B hits through 1954, Brown's reign on the charts began to slip, though she had several more successful records, including 1957's number six R&B, number 25 pop, Jerry Leiber and Mike Stoller–produced "Lucky Lips," into the rock and roll era. She kept a relatively low profile during the 1960s, performing ballads and jazz on the Playboy Club circuit and recording for Philips and Solid State (for whom she made a remarkable, though little-noticed album with the Thad Jones–Mel Lewis big band) before retiring to raise her two sons.

The singer finally reemerged in 1976—as an actress—to play the role of Mahalia Jackson in *Selma,* a Los Angeles musical theater production by comedian Redd Foxx. She then moved to Las Vegas, where she sang at Circus Circus and acted in plays. Television producer Norman Lear spotted her in one

Ruth Brown

TOP SONGS

So Long (Atlantic, '49, *4 R&B*)

Teardrops from My Eyes (Atlantic, '50, *1 R&B*)

I'll Wait for You (Atlantic, '51, *3 R&B*)

5-10-15 Hours (Atlantic, '52, *1 R&B*)

Daddy Daddy (Atlantic, '52, *3 R&B*)

(Mama) He Treats Your Daughter Mean
    (Atlantic, '53, *1 R&B, 23 Pop*)

Wild Wild Young Men (Atlantic, '53, *3 R&B*)

Oh What a Dream (Atlantic, '54, *1 R&B*)

Mambo Baby (Atlantic, '54, *1 R&B*)

I Wanna Do More (Atlantic, '55, *3 R&B*)

Additional Top 40 R&B Songs: 14

of those and, impressed with her natural comedic timing, cast her as Leona in the popular sitcom "Hello, Larry." Other acting roles followed, including parts in the TV series "Checkin' In" and in the motion pictures *Under the Rainbow* and *Hairspray.*

Brown made her Broadway debut in 1989 as the star of *Black and Blue,* which won her a Tony Award for Best Performance by a Leading Actress in a Musical. She had signed with Fantasy Records the previous year, and her second album for the company, a 1989 set of blues and jazz standards titled *Blues on Broadway,* earned her a Grammy for Best Jazz Vocalist.

PEABO BRYSON

Crossing over from the R&B to the pop chart is not uncommon for many African-American artists, but what happened to veteran soul crooner Peabo Bryson (b. Robert Peabo Bryson, Apr. 13, 1951, Greenville, South Carolina) in early 1993 was unprecedented: he found records on which he appeared topping four different *Billboard* charts simultaneously. "A Whole New World (Aladdin's Theme)," a duet with Regina Belle from the soundtrack of the animated Disney motion picture *Aladdin,* was Number One on both the pop and adult contemporary charts. *Breathless,* an album by soprano saxophonist Kenny G containing a Bryson vocal on the track "By the Time This Night Is Over," led the contemporary jazz list. And a recreation of Rodgers and Hammerstein's *The King and I,* featuring "We Kiss in a Shadow," a Bryson duet with Miss Saigon star Leah Salonga, sat atop the classical crossover chart. While none of those three records cracked the R&B top 10, the Atlanta-based vocalist was no stranger to that chart either, having scored 10 entries between 1978 and '91.

Raised on a farm in Mauldin, South Carolina, Bryson was one of four children of a churchgoing family, and his religious training would later become manifest in the deeply spiritual quality of much of his music. At age 12, he won a talent contest with his rendition of a song by Sam Cooke, who, along with Jackie Wilson, Ray Charles, and the Drifters, he has cited as an early influence. After singing around Greensville with Al Freeman and the Upsetters, Bryson joined Moses Dillard and the Tex-Town Display in 1988. Besides touring internationally, including dates in the Caribbean and Vietnam, the group also recorded unsuccessfully for Curtom in Chicago and Bang in Atlanta during the singer's five-year tenure. Run by Eddie Briscoe and Ilene Berns (widow of label founder Bert Berns), Bang Records took a special interest in Bryson and encouraged his development as a producer and songwriter.

As featured vocalist with studio musician Michael Zager's Moon Band, Bryson made his R&B chart debut in 1976 with the number 25 "Do It with Feeling" on Bang. A self-produced solo album, simply titled *Peabo,* followed later that year on Bang's new Bullet label, yielding three top 40 R&B singles: "Underground Music" b/w "It's Just a Matter of Time," "Just Another Day," and "I Can Make It Better." The title of the latter song was prophetic; if his Bullet recordings showed an artist still in search of a style, Bryson had settled into the role of romantic balladeer, singing in a clear, ringing tenor much like that of Donny Hathaway, by the time he signed with Capitol in 1978. Bryson's popularity began to take off that year with such mildly erotic ballads as the number six R&B "Reaching for the Sky" and the number 13 R&B "Feel the Fire," both cut in Chicago and co-produced by Bryson and veteran arranger Richard Evans.

TOP ALBUM

BORN TO LOVE (Peabo Bryson/Roberta Flack, Capitol, '83, 25)

Additional Top 40 Albums: 2

TOP SONGS

REACHING FOR THE SKY (Capitol, '78, 6 *R&B*)
I'M SO INTO YOU (Capitol, '78, 8 *R&B*)
GIMME SOME TIME (Natalie Cole and Peabo Bryson, Capitol, '79, 8 *R&B*)
LET THE FEELING FLOW (Capitol, '81, 6 *R&B*)
TONIGHT, I CELEBRATE MY LOVE (Peabo Bryson/Roberta Flack, Capitol, '83, 5 *R&B, 16 Pop*)
IF EVER YOU'RE IN MY ARMS AGAIN (Elektra, '84, 6 *R&B, 10 Pop*)
SHOW AND TELL (Capitol, '89, 1 *R&B*)
ALL MY LOVE (Capitol, '89, 6 *R&B*)
CAN YOU STOP THE RAIN (Columbia, '91, 1 *R&B*)

Additional Top 40 R&B Songs: 23

The vocalist's tonal similarity to Hathaway, who had recorded a series of hit duets with Roberta Flack prior to his suicide in 1979, did not escape the notice of Capitol and other companies. Capitol paired Bryson with Natalie Cole in 1979 for the number eight R&B hit "Gimme Some Time." The following year, Atlantic teamed him with Flack herself for the number 13 R&B charter, "Make the World Stand Still," their professional relationship culminating in 1983's number 25 Capitol album *Born to Love,* which contained the number five R&B, number 16 pop single, "Tonight, I Celebrate My Love." Also in 1981, Bryson played musical chairs with Melissa Manchester on Arista's number 35 R&B "Lovers After All."

Duets remained a Bryson trademark and included two with Regina Belle—1987's number 14 R&B "Without You" on Elektra and 1992's Number One pop, number 21 R&B "A Whole New World (Aladdin's Theme)" on Columbia—in addition to 1992's number nine pop "Beauty and the Beast" (also from a Disney film) with Celine Dion on Epic and that year's *The King and I* meeting with Leah Salonga.

Bryson continued having solo hits throughout the 1980s and early '90s. Moving from Capitol to Elektra in 1985, then back to Capitol in 1988, he scored his first Number One R&B chart single the following year with a version of "Show and Tell," a Jerry Fuller composition, originally recorded by Johnny Mathis, that had given Al Wilson a Number One pop hit 14 years earlier. By 1991, Bryson was at Columbia Records, for which he cut the Number One R&B "Can You Stop the Rain," maintaining his image as the consummate, clean-cut soul balladeer, while expanding his artistic horizons through a growing variety of other musical projects.

SOLOMON BURKE

Dubbed "the Wonder Boy Preacher" as a child and "the King of Rock and Soul" at the height of his popularity during the 1960s, the Bishop Dr. Solomon Burke (b. 1936, Philadelphia) never strayed far from his gospel roots during a prolific career spanning four decades. An influence on such other singers as Otis Redding and Mick Jagger, he has always informed his material, spiritual or secular, with a vast array of churchy tones and inflections, from soft purrs and graceful melisma-dripping glides to semi-operatic sustains reminiscent of Roy Hamilton and bone-crushing Little Richard–like rasps. Singing with crystalline diction, he works mostly within a baritone range but drops frequently to a resonant bass or leaps upward to a vibrato-shivering tenor, all with the greatest of ease.

Burke began his recording career as a gospel singer at Apollo Records in 1955, switching to rhythm and blues two years later. Like Sam Cooke, who made a similar career move during the same period, he was criticized in church circles for crossing the fence. Yet, by 1961, when his decade-long string of hits began at Atlantic Records, the term "soul" had come into vogue to describe the type of gospel-imbued pop music that he and Cooke were performing.

"My elders at the church would not let me be an R&B singer," he said in 1991, "but they approved the word 'soul,' which opened the doors for me to sing the blues or to sing about love, to sing about sex, to sing about hurt and pain, more than just singing about 'To Thee,' 'You'll Never Walk Alone,' or 'You Can Run, But You Can't Hide.' " (The latter tune, recorded by Burke for Apollo, was written by former heavyweight boxing champ Joe Louis.)

A preacher at age nine, Burke came to head a nonsectarian denomination called Solomon's Temple: The House of God for All People, which he claims was founded by his grandmother during the 1920s in anticipation of his birth. (By 1986, he said, the church had 40,000 members at 161 branches in the U.S., Canada, and Jamaica.) His first records were of the quasi-religous "inspirational" genre popularized by Roy Hamilton's Number One R&B 1954 hit, "You'll Never Walk Alone." After the commercial failure of his first secular singles for Apollo in 1957, he retired from performing for a period to study mortuary science and, after receiving a doctorate in the trade, went to work at his aunt's Philadelphia funeral parlor. He returned to recording in 1959 for the obscure Singular label. A year later, Jerry Wexler signed him to Atlantic.

Burke scored his first hit in 1961 with "Just Out of Reach (Of My Two Open Arms)," a previous country hit for both Faron Young and T. Texas Tyler that *Billboard* editor Paul Ackerman had suggested to producer Wexler. While not the first country tune to be covered by an African-American artist, Burke's number seven R&B, number 24 pop rendition of "Just Out of Reach" predated a successful series of similar country-soul ballads begun a few months later by Ray Charles. The follow-up, 1962's number five "Cry to Me," was written and co-produced by Bert Berns and featured Burke rhythmically stuttering the word "cry," a device that would later become a trademark of Otis Redding's style. Berns continued to supervise many of Burke's recordings over the next three years, including the Berns-Burke-Wexler composition "Everybody Needs Somebody to Love," a minor pop hit for Burke in 1964 (*Billboard* published no R&B charts that year) that soon became a staple of the Rolling Stones' repertoire.

Leaving Atlantic in 1968, the singer signed with Bell Records the following year and scored with a soul version of Creedence Clearwater Revival's then-recent rock hit, "Proud Mary." He jumped from label to label during the 1970s, including MGM, ABC, Chess, and Amherst. Burke returned to gospel music in the early 1980s, recording two albums for Savoy, then cutting two retro-soul albums for Rounder that had rock critics raving.

He launched his motion-picture acting career in 1986, playing a doctor of oils, incense, and herbs in *The Big Easy,* and later co-starred in three Italian films. Tending to his church duties, three funeral parlors and 21 children and 14 grandchildren also kept Burke off the music scene much of the time, though he occasionally ventured out to appear at clubs and blues festivals and made albums, including 1993's *Soul of the Blues* on the Black Top label.

"Sometimes as I minister," he explained, "I can't get the message out all the way to my parishioners as quick as I can in an auditorium to 10,000 people who want to hear 'If You Need Me' or 'Everybody Needs Somebody to Love.' They can relate to that. And when you come in with the truth, and you come in with the love and the courage and the faith and incorporate it all together, it works."

JERRY BUTLER

Known for his cool, confident demeanor, on and off stage, Jerry Butler (b. Dec. 8, 1939, Sunflower, Mississippi) was dubbed "the Ice Man" in 1964 by Philadelphia disc jockey Georgie Woods. Yet Butler's resonant bedroom baritone voice, its slightly frayed edges melting with choked emotion, has been the epitome of warmth throughout a prolific recording career that began in 1958 and peaked during his brilliant if brief association with producers Kenny Gamble and Leon Huff in the late 1960s.

The Butler family settled in Chicago when Jerry was three. There, he sang several church choirs before spending three years with the Northern Jubilee Gospel Singers, a teenage quartet that included singer-guitarist Curtis Mayfield. Studying restaurant management at Chicago's Washburne Trade School, Butler helped to pay his tuition by singing with a local doo wop group called the Quails.

In 1957, three members of a Chattanooga group called the Roosters—Arthur and Richard Brooks and Sam Gooden—moved to Chicago and recruited Butler, who in turn brought Mayfield into the flock. The following year, after a couple of unsuccessful auditions for Vee-Jay Records, the Roosters were given an opportunity to record by label executive Ewart Abner. The April session, supervised by Calvin Carter, included "For Your Precious Love," a haunting gospel-imbued ballad written by lead singer Butler with the Brooks brothers. The song, credited to "Jerry Butler and the Impressions," first appeared on Vee-Jay's short-lived Falcon subsidiary, then on Abner, and finally on Vee-Jay itself, making a strong impression on *Billboard*'s charts by rising to number three R&B and number 11 pop.

After a disappointing follow-up, the number 29 R&B "Come Back My Love," Butler left the group to pursue a solo career. Mayfield soon followed him, spending a year on the road as Butler's guitarist

TOP SONGS

JUST OUT OF REACH (OF MY TWO OPEN ARMS) (Atlantic, '61, 7 R&B, 24 Pop)

CRY TO ME (Atlantic, '62, 5 R&B)

IF YOU NEED ME (Atlantic, '63, 2 R&B, 37 Pop)

YOU'RE GOOD FOR ME (Atlantic, '63, 8 R&B)

GOT TO GET YOU OFF MY MIND (Atlantic, '65, 1 R&B, 22 Pop)

TONIGHT'S THE NIGHT (Atlantic, '65, 2 R&B, 28 Pop)

TAKE ME (JUST AS I AM) (Atlantic, '67, 11 R&B)

PROUD MARY (Bell, '69, 15 R&B)

LOVE'S STREET AND FOOL'S ROAD (MGM, '72, 13 R&B)

MIDNIGHT AND YOU (ABC, '74, 14 R&B)

Additional Top 40 R&B Songs: 9

TOP ALBUM

The Ice Man Cometh (Mercury, '69, 29)

TOP SONGS

For Your Precious Love (Jerry Butler and the Impressions,
Abner, '58, *3 R&B, 11 Pop*)
He Will Break Your Heart (Vee-Jay, '60, *1 R&B, 7 Pop*)
Never Give You Up (Mercury, '68, *4 R&B, 20 Pop*)
Hey, Western Union Man (Mercury, '68, *1 R&B, 16 Pop*)
Only the Strong Survive (Mercury, '69, *1 R&B, 4 Pop*)
Moody Woman (Mercury, '69, *3 R&B, 24 Pop*)
What's the Use of Breaking Up (Mercury, '69, *4 R&B, 20 Pop*)
Ain't Understanding Mellow (Mercury, '71, *3 R&B, 21 Pop*)
One Night Affair (Mercury, '72, *6 R&B*)

Additional Top 40 R&B Songs: 34

Several ventures with staff producers Luchi De Jesus and Jerry Ross yielded moderately appealing results before the vocalist was placed in the creative hands of Philadelphia's up-and-coming Kenny Gamble and Leon Huff. This association gave Butler six consecutive top 10 R&B hits during 1968 and '69: "Never Give You Up," "Hey, Western Union Man," "Are You Happy," "Only the Strong Survive," "Moody Woman," and "What's the Use of Breaking Up." All were Gamble-Huff-Butler compositions, and their lavishly orchestrated, rhythmically driving sound signaled the arrival of the Philly soul style that would permeate popular music during the next decade.

Butler was left to swim on his own after Gamble and Huff broke up with Mercury at the start of 1970. He remained at the company until 1974, producing himself most of the time, but managed to hit the R&B top 10 only four more times. After establishing a songwriting workshop in Chicago that launched the writing-producing team of Charles Jackson and Marvin Yancy (later of Natalie Cole fame), he signed in 1976 with Motown (then being run by Ewart Abner), where he scored his final top 10 hit, 1977's number seven R&B "I Wanna Do It with You." By the next year, he had joined Gamble and Huff at their own Philadelphia International label, even though, as he said five years later, "After you get a divorce, it ain't always good to get remarried."

The singer continued performing (and did a 1983 reunion tour with Mayfield and the Impressions) and recording sporadically for small labels, but he increasingly turned to nonmusical interests. He owned a beer distributorship for a period, then entered politics, and, in 1986, was elected Cook County Commissioner for Chicago's Second Ward.

before rejoining the Impressions. Mayfield also contributed significantly, as composer, guitarist, and harmony vocalist, to his friend's first three major solo hits, all on Vee-Jay: 1960's Number One R&B, number nine pop "He Will Break Your Heart" (co-written with Butler and Carter); 1961's number 10 R&B, number 27 pop "Find Another Girl" (co-written with Butler); and the same year's number eight R&B, number 25 pop "I'm Telling You" (penned by Mayfield alone).

Although he had returned to the old group, Mayfield continued supplying material to Butler, including "Need to Belong," "A Woman with Soul," and "I've Been Trying" (the latter two later popularized by the Impressions), but the singer's greatest successes during the remainder of his tenure at Vee-Jay were middle-of-the-road tunes picked by Carter from outside sources: 1962's number 14 R&B, number 11 pop "Moon River" (by Johnny Mercer and Henry Mancini); that year's number 18 R&B, number 20 pop "Make It Easy on Yourself" (by Burt Bacharach and Hal David); and 1964's number five pop duet with Betty Everett on the French song "Let It Be Me." Butler penned a few himself, including 1964's now-standard "I Stand Accused" (a collaboration with his guitar-playing younger brother Billy), and also teamed up with Otis Redding to write that singer's 1965 Volt hit, "I've Been Loving You Too Long (To Stop Now)."

Following Vee-Jay's 1966 demise, Butler joined Chicago's more firmly established Mercury label.

CAMEO

Throughout a recording career that produced 15 albums in 15 years, the funk band Cameo managed to be simultaneously experimental and commercial. The group, varying in size from 13 to 3 members, adopted, then abandoned, new musical fashions with each release—including disco grooves, heavy-metal guitar flights, surging horn riffs and solos, new wave synthesizer splashes, Afro-Latin and electronic percussion touches, and rap interludes—all the while maintaining a fat, undulating bass-and-drums bottom that served as its signature. Wacky one minute, serious the next, Cameo created a body of music that made listeners think while shaking their rumps to the funk.

Cameo was the brainchild of New York City drummer, bassist, and singer Larry Blackmon. As a boy, he attended shows at the Apollo Theater in Harlem and not only became entranced by such performers as James Brown, Otis Redding, and Cannonball Adderley but was fascinated by the lighting and other visual aspects of the productions. Jimi Hendrix was another early hero. Blackmon studied at New York's prestigious Juilliard School of Music for a period and played drums in a succession of local bands, including East Coast, the Mighty Gees, Concrete Wall, and the New York City Players. The latter group, which included keyboardist Gregory Johnson, evolved into Cameo.

Signed to the Chocolate City label, a division of Casablanca, Cameo cut its first single, "Find My Way," in 1976. Blackmon was literally finding his way in the studio, having become the group's producer when the record company failed to furnish one. "I didn't even know what a producer was," he explained five years later. "The guy asked us who

was the producer, and all the guys pointed to me." Blackmon has been Cameo's record producer, as well as its principal songwriter and vocalist, drummer, and sometime bassist, ever since. (In addition, during the next decade, he put his interest in the theatrical side of musical performance to good use as the producer of a series of imaginative videos for the group.)

While the band's debut release failed to draw much attention beyond New York discos, "Rigor Mortus," a single from the 1977 album *Cardiac Arrest,* rose to number 33 on *Billboard*'s R&B chart and brought Cameo's career to life. Blackmon promptly quit his day job as a tailor and took the group on the road, opening shows across the country for such acts as the O'Jays, the Bar-Kays, and Parliament-Funkadelic. The personnel at this point consisted of Blackmon, Johnson, singer-percussionist Tomi Jenkins, trumpeter Nathan Leftenant, saxophonist Arnett Leftenant, guitarist Eric Duram, bassist Gary Dow, and falsetto vocalist Wayne Cooper. Cameo recorded three more albums during the next two years and toured incessantly, building a loyal fan base through its lively, creatively choreographed shows and finally hitting the R&B top 10 in the summer of 1979 with the number three "I Just Want to Be" from the fourth album, *Secret Omen.*

Having achieved headlining status, Cameo performed an average of four concert dates a week during 1980, when it played to an estimated 1.6 million

Cameo

people and lugged 40 tons of lighting, sound, and stage equipment on three semis across 100,000 miles. By 1981, the year of the number three R&B single "Freaky Dancin'," the group had expanded to a dozen members. Duram and Dow had been replaced by guitarist Anthony Lockett and bassist Aaron Mills. Other new Cameo appearances were trombonist Jeryl Bright, keyboardist Thomas Campbell, guitarist-vocalist Charlie Singleton, drummers Damon Mendes and Vince Wilburn, and singer Stephen Moore.

The economic burden of carrying such a large entourage forced Blackmon to pare the group down to five—himself, Johnson, Jenkins, Nathan Leftenant, and Singleton—in 1982. He'd already moved the band and his production company, still known as New York City Players, to Atlanta, where he established his own Polygram-distributed label, Atlanta Artists, which issued the new wave–influenced *Alligator Woman* album in 1982. Charter member Johnson was gone by the next year's *Style* album.

The risqué, rap-imbued title track of *She's Strange* gave Cameo its first R&B chart topper in 1984. This synthesis of funk and hip-hop styles culminated in 1986's Number One R&B, number six pop "Word Up," the biggest hit of the band's career. By that time, Cameo comprised only three members—Blackmon, Jenkins, and Leftenant (now singing instead of playing trumpet)—with guest musicians hired to round out the sessions. Jazz trumpet icon Miles Davis, uncle of former Cameo drum-

mer Vince Wilburn, turned up on one track of the 1988 album *Machismo*.

Cameo's Atlanta Artists singles continued to place in the R&B top 10 through 1990's number five "I Want It Now," but the group vanished from the charts entirely after the meager showing of the number 38 R&B "Close Quarters" later that year. A new edition, consisting of Blackmon, Jenkins, Singleton, Mills, and drummer-keyboardist Kevin Kendricks, emerged in 1982 with *Emotional Violence* on Warner Bros. Although Blackmon declared at the time that "funk is an art form, and Cameo is about bringing that art form front and center," the album had little commercial impact.

MARIAH CAREY

Mariah Carey (b. Mar. 27, 1970) knew by the time she was three that she wanted to be a professional singer. By her 24th birthday, with less than four years behind her as a recording artist, she had hit the top of *Billboard*'s pop singles chart eight times and sold over 25 million records worldwide.

The superstar vocalist is the youngest of the three children of Afro-Venezualan aeronautical engineer Alfred Carey and the former Patricia Hickey. Mariah was raised by her Irish-American mother, a vocal coach and former mezzo-soprano with the New York City Opera. Around the house, Mariah constantly mimicked her mom's singing. She also memorized many of the commercial jingles she heard on television as well as records by Aretha Franklin ("the perfect singer," she once stated) and Stevie Wonder. The late Minnie Riperton, whose stratospheric coloratura sustains Mariah would take to new heights, was another important influence.

At 14, with financial assistance from her older brother, Carey started cutting demo tapes at studios near her Long Island home. She also formed a songwriting partnership with drummer-keyboardist Ben Margulies; six of the songs they composed together when she was 16, including "Vision of Love," would eventually surface on her debut album. Leaving home at 17, she scuffled for a year, working an assortment of odd jobs, including checking coats and hats, waiting tables, and sweeping up hair at a beauty salon, while continuing to make demos and do background vocals.

TOP ALBUM

WORD UP! (Atlanta Artists, '86, 8)

Additional Top 40 Albums: 3

TOP SONGS

I JUST WANT TO BE (Chocolate City, '79, 3 *R&B*)
FREAKY DANCIN' (Chocolate City, '81, 3 *R&B*)
SHE'S STRANGE (Atlanta Artists, '84, 1 *R&B*)
ATTACK ME (Atlanta Artists, '85, 3 *R&B*)
SINGLE LIFE (Atlanta Artists, '85, 2 *R&B*)
WORD UP (Atlanta Artists, '86, 1 *R&B*, 6 *Pop*)
CANDY (Atlanta Artists, '86, 1 *R&B*, 21 *Pop*)
BACK AND FORTH (Atlanta Artists, '87, 3 *R&B*)
YOU MAKE ME WORK (Atlanta Artists, '88, 4 *R&B*)

Additional Top 40 R&B Songs: 17

Mariah Carey

One of the artists for whom she was contributing harmony was Latino pop-soul singer Brenda K. Starr, and through Starr, one of Carey's tapes ended up in the hands of Tommy Mottola, president of Sony Music Entertainment. Bowled over by the young singer's five-octave range and remarkably mature, melisma-dripping delivery, as well as by the quality of her songs, Mottola phoned her, promptly signed her to Columbia Records and, in June 1993, married her.

Released in May 1990, her self-titled debut album rose to Number One on the *Billboard* album chart and yielded four consecutive Number One pop singles: the torchy, gospel-imbued "Vision of Love," produced by Rhett Lawrence; the sensual ballad "Love Takes Time," produced by Narada Michael Walden associate Walter Afanasieff; the churchy, uptempo "Someday," produced by Ric Wake; and the heart-breaking "I Don't Want to Cry," produced by Walden. (The first two also topped the R&B chart.) Carey co-composed all four, the first three with Margulies, the last with Walden. The fledgling diva received two 1990 Grammy Awards—for Best Pop Vocal Performance, Female (for "Vision of Love"), and Best New Artist—as well as three "Soul Train" Awards.

For her second album, *Emotions*, released in September 1991, Carey served as co-producer and co-writer of every track. Its first single, the upbeat title song (produced and written with David Cole and Robert Clivilles of C + C Music Factory), went to Number One on the pop chart, while the next two, the lush "Can't Let Go" (produced and written with Afanasieff) and the autobiographical, house music-styled "Make It Happen" (with Cole and Clivilles), peaked at numbers two and five respectively.

Carey had failed to capitalize on the success of her recording by touring, and talk began to circulate that she was merely a studio creation. This was dispelled with the May 20, 1992, telecast of "MTV Unplugged," on which she performed live with a 27-member aggregation of musicians and singers. A set of seven songs from the show, titled *MTV Unplugged EP*, followed. Besides new renditions of five of her previous hits, as well as "If It's Over" (her

TOP ALBUMS

MARIAH CAREY (Columbia, '90, *1*)
EMOTIONS (Columbia, '91, *4*)
MTV UNPLUGGED EP (Columbia, '92, *3*)
MUSIC BOX (Columbia, '93, *1*)

TOP SONGS

VISION OF LOVE (Columbia, '90, *1 R&B, 1 Pop*)
LOVE TAKES TIME (Columbia, '90, *1 R&B, 1 Pop*)
I DON'T WANNA CRY (Columbia, '91, *2 R&B, 1 Pop*)
EMOTIONS (Columbia, '91, *1 R&B, 1 Pop*)
CAN'T LET GO (Columbia, '91, *2 R&B, 1 Pop*)
DREAMLOVER (Columbia, '93, *2 R&B, 1 Pop*)

Additional Top 40 R&B Songs: 4

songwriting collaboration with Carole King from *Emotions*), it included a heartfelt duet with backup singer Trey Lorenz on the Jackson 5's 1970 hit "I'll Be There." Issued as a single, "I'll Be There" became Carey's sixth pop chart topper and led to Lorenz's own 1992 album for Epic, which included the number five R&B, number 19 pop hit "Something to Hold," written by Lorenz, Carey, and Afanasieff and produced by Afanasieff and Carey.

Music Box, released in August 1993, rose to the top of the album chart by year's end, its first two singles, the medium-tempo, new jack swing ballad "Dreamlover" (penned by Carey and Dave Hall and produced by the two with Afanasieff) and the self-affirming ballad "Hero" (written and produced by Carey and Afanasieff), both going Number One pop. In November of that year, she launched her first tour, a six-city swing through the U.S. Tickets to the tall (5' 9") soul singer's date at New York's Madison Square Garden sold out in less than an hour.

CLARENCE CARTER

There was always a hint of lasciviousness in the blues-drenched southern soul music of singer, pianist, guitarist, and songwriter Clarence Carter (b. Jan. 4, 1936, Montgomery, Alabama), especially when he punctuated his folksy baritone vocals with sly, gutteral chuckles. Working in Muscle Shoals, Alabama, with producer Rick Hall,

Carter created a string of often humorous hits during the late 1960s and early '70s that focused on the cheating side of romance.

As a boy, inspired by the recordings of fellow blind musician Ray Charles, Carter taught himself to play piano and, by listening to records by such blues artists as John Lee Hooker, Lightnin' Hopkins, and Jimmy Reed, the guitar. He attended the Alabama School for the Blind at Tuskegee, then enrolled at Alabama State College in Montgomery, where he learned to read, write, and arrange music in braille. He intended to become a teacher, but after graduating with a bachelor's degree in music, he teamed up with blind singer Calvin Scott, an association that lasted five and a half years.

Billed as Clarence and Calvin, Carter's deep, gruff tones contrasting with Scott's high, wailing gospel tenor, they made their first recordings for Bill Lowry's Fairlane label in Atlanta around 1962. Three more followed, one as by "the C & C Boys," on Don Robey's Houston-based Duke Records between 1963 and '65. None charted. Later in 1965, the duo went to Fame Studios in Muscle Shoals and paid for a session themselves. The song, a Carter-Scott composition titled "Step by Step," ended up on the Atco label, but it too was a flop. Scott left the team the following year after being seriously injured in an auto accident, eventually reemerging with limited success as a solo artist.

Fame Studios owner Rick Hall had been strongly impressed by Carter and, in late 1966, began producing the singer. Carter's first release on the Atlantic-distributed Fame label, the original composition "Tell Daddy," reached number 35 on the *Billboard* R&B chart. (Two years later, Hall produced the song for Etta James; her version on the Checker label, titled "Tell Mama," became a number 10 R&B, number 23 pop hit.)

After one more single on Fame, 1967's number 38 R&B "Thread the Needle," Carter began appearing on Atlantic itself, though still being produced by Hall. His third release for the company, "Slip Away," took him into the top 10 on both the R&B and pop charts and established him as a major club attraction. He formed his own band and began featuring former gospel singer Candi Staton. Landing her a contract with Fame, he co-wrote her first hit, 1969's number nine R&B "I'd Rather Be an Old Man's Sweetheart (Than a Young Man's Fool)," as well as the next year's number 13 R&B "I'm Just a Prisoner (Of Your Good Lovin')." Clarence and

Candi, who recorded one obscure duet for Atlantic, were wed in August 1970, although the marriage lasted only a few years.

Six more top 10 R&B hits followed "Slip Away," culminating in 1970's "Patches." The biggest record of Carter's career, this Ronald Dunbar–General Johnson composition, previously recorded on an Invictus album by Johnson's Chairmen of the Board, was atypical of Carter's earlier output. The maudlin story song, on which Carter alternated between talking and singing, became a number two R&B, number four pop hit.

Carter never cracked the top 10 or the pop top 40 again. Dropped by Atlantic at the end of 1971, he reemerged on Fame, now being distributed by United Artists, and continued working with Hall through 1973. The singer had become interested in producing records himself and produced a few for his new band vocalist, ex-gospel singer Margie Alexander, including 1971's haunting though little-known "Can I Be Your Main Thing" on Atlantic and 1974's "Keep on Searching," a minor R&B hit that appeared on his own short-lived, Stax-distributed Future Stars label.

By the mid-1970s, Carter was based in Atlanta and producing his own records for ABC. He also appeared on the Venture label in 1981 but didn't find much success again until the mid-'80s, when he formed his own Ichiban-distributed Big C label, reverted to his blues roots, and cut a string of hilarious, blatantly sexual sides, including a risqué revamp of Tampa Red's "Love Me with a Feeling" and his own "Grandpa Can't Fly His Kite ('Cause Grandma Won't Give Him No Tail)." His biggest seller of this period was the catchy, self-penned 1986 soul ditty "Strokin'," a nationwide jukebox favorite that received little airplay due to its mildly pornographic lyric content. Although no longer a major star, Carter had become the new king of the time-honored, underground "party record" tradition.

GENE CHANDLER

Although he had been a recording artist for under a year, Eugene Dixon (b. July 6, 1937, Chicago) found himself faced with having to make a major career decision during the frigid Windy City winter of 1961–62. He'd cut two records during one session with the Dukays—a doo wop group comprising himself, Shirley Jones, James Lowe, Earl Edwards, and Ben Broyles—that were simultaneously starting to attract national attention. One was "Night Owl," the group's second release on the New York–based Nat label. The other, "Duke of Earl," was issued by Chicago's Vee-Jay Records; in order to avoid a legal dispute with Nat, the company listed the artist as "Gene Chandler." Would Dixon stick with his South Side buddies in the Dukays, or would he become Chandler, a name he and producer Carl Davis had picked because both were fans of Hollywood matinee idol Jeff Chandler?

The singer chose to take his chances on "Duke of Earl," a tune that had begun as a warm-up vocal exercise for the Dukays, and become Gene Chandler. He soon discovered he'd made the wisest choice. Although "Night Owl" is now considered to be one of the last classics of R&B's doo wop period, it proved to be only a minor pop hit at the time and never even entered the national R&B chart. "Duke of Earl," however, shot to Number One on both charts, establishing Chandler as a big-name attraction.

While the Dukays struggled on without him, recording a few more sides for Vee-Jay and Jerry-O before disbanding, their former lead singer played the "Duke of Earl" role to the hilt, making public appearances decked out in tuxedo, top hat, cape, cane, and monocle. On the follow-up single, "Walk On with the Duke," and his debut album, Vee-Jay temporarily dropped the Chandler name and billed him simply as the "Duke of Earl."

Chandler's second hit, 1963's "Rainbow," was originally intended as the B side of "You Threw a Lucky Punch," an answer to Mary Wells's "You

TOP SONGS

SLIP AWAY (Atlantic, '68, 2 R&B, 6 Pop)

TOO WEAK TO FIGHT (Atlantic, '68, 3 R&B, 13 Pop)

SNATCHING IT BACK (Atlantic, '69, 4 R&B, 31 Pop)

THE FEELING IS RIGHT (Atlantic, '69, 9 R&B)

DOIN' OUR THING (Atlantic, '69, 9 R&B)

I CAN'T LEAVE YOUR LOVE ALONE (Atlantic, '70, 6 R&B)

PATCHES (Atlantic, '70, 2 R&B, 4 Pop)

IT'S ALL IN YOUR MIND (Atlantic, '70, 13 R&B)

THE COURT ROOM (Atlantic, '71, 12 R&B)

I'M THE MIDNIGHT SPECIAL (Fame, '73, 15 R&B)

Additional Top 40 R&B Songs: 9

Beat Me to the Punch." Disc jockeys, however, turned the record over, and the stark, gospel-imbued Curtis Mayfield composition, rendered by Chandler in a thin though heart-wrenching tenor over a dirge-like tempo, became the singer's signature song. He revived it with greater success two years later on the Constellation label as "Rainbow '65," recorded in front of an effusive audience at Chicago's Regal Theater, and again years later on Chi-Sound as "Rainbow '80," but with limited commercial results.

After a string of other collaborations with producer Davis and songwriter Mayfield at Vee-Jay, then Constellation, including "Man's Temptation," "Just Be True," "You Can't Hurt Me No More," "Nothing Can Stop Me," and "Good Times," Chandler entered into an unusual contractual arrangement. Between 1966 and 1969, he alternated releases between Checker and Brunswick, with Davis producing his songs for both labels. Itching to become a producer himself, Chandler purchased the failing St. Louis–based Bamboo Records, moved the company to Chicago, and amassed a roster of some two dozen artists, including Lee Charles, the Profiles, and the Voice Masters. His most successful Bamboo act was the Mississippi singing duo of Mel and Tim, who had a number three R&B, number 10 pop hit in 1969 with the Chandler-produced "Backfield in Motion."

Chandler joined Mercury Records in 1970, scoring his first R&B Top 10 hit in three years with "Groovy Situation" and cutting a duet album with fellow Chicago soul singer Jerry Butler that included an inspired song about prostitution titled "Ten and Two (Take This Woman Off the Corner)." Mercury set Chandler up with his second custom label, Mr.

Chand, for which he produced Simtec and Wylie's "Gotta Get over the Hump," a number 29 R&B chart entry in 1971. Also that year, he produced the Sisters Love's number 20 R&B single "Are You Lonely?" for A&M.

Leaving Mercury, Chandler recorded for Mayfield's Curtom label in 1973, but he soon found himself without a contract. His life hit bottom when, in December 1976, he was convicted of selling 388 grams of heroin with a street value of $30,000. Carl Davis, his original producer, came to the rescue. By the time Chandler had finished his four-month jail term, he was serving as a vice president of Davis's new Chi-Sound label and was back on the charts as an artist with "Get Down." Penned by former Voice Master Jerry Thompson, this throbbing 1978 slice of heavily synthesized disco, atypical of the ballad work that had been the singer's trademark, took Chandler into the top five on the *Billboard* R&B chart for the first time in 12 years.

He continued recording for Chi-Sound until 1982, then turned up briefly on Salsoul and FastFire, but was never again able to reclaim his title as one of soul music's royal figures.

RAY CHARLES

R ay Charles (b. Ray Charles Robinson, Sept. 23, 1930, Albany, Georgia) is a towering figure in 20th-century music, having achieved mass popularity with an ingenious synthesis of blues, gospel, jazz, country, and Tin Pan Alley traditions. The variety and vitality of his output—especially during the period beginning in 1955, when he had his first major R&B hit with "I've Got a Woman," through his 1960 breakthrough into the pop mainstream with "Georgia on My Mind," and ending in 1964 with the breakup of his first big band—have been staggering and permanently affected the course of popular music. While he charted little new musical territory after the mid-1960s, he had clearly demonstrated that the diverse strains of American music, though divided by ethnic, regional, and class distinctions, were all parts of a common cultural heritage.

Charles began playing piano at age four and later learned alto saxophone. Having contracted glaucoma at six, he was soon totally blind. His father died when he was ten, his mother five years later. He

---

TOP SONGS

DUKE OF EARL (Vee-Jay, '62, *1 R&B, 1 Pop*)

RAINBOW (Vee-Jay, '63, *11 R&B*)

NOTHING CAN STOP ME (Constellation, '65, *3 R&B, 18 Pop*)

RAINBOW '65 (PART 1) (Constellation, '65, *2 R&B*)

I FOOLED YOU THIS TIME (Checker, '66, *3 R&B*)

TO BE A LOVER (Checker, '67, *9 R&B*)

GROOVY SITUATION (Mercury, '70, *8 R&B, 12 Pop*)

YOU'RE A LADY (Mercury, '71, *14 R&B*)

GET DOWN (Chi-Sound, '78, *3 R&B*)

Additional Top 40 R&B Songs: 15

Ray Charles

following year, Charles continued recording for the company, which had been renamed Swingtime, still copying Cole and Brown and even using guitarists Oscar Moore (formerly of Cole's group) and Johnny Moore (of the Three Blazers) on some sessions. Two of Charles's Swingtime singles became R&B hits: 1951's Brown-styled "Baby Let Me Hold Your Hand" (number five) and 1952's rawer, jumping "Kiss Me Baby" (number eight). Charles also toured as pianist and musical director for blues singer-guitarist Lowell Fulson, Swingtime's biggest star, between 1950 and '52 and began honing his skills as an arranger, developing a way of voicing Fulson's small horn section so that it sounded larger than it actually was.

Atlantic Records purchased Charles's Swingtime contract in 1952. While his early sides for the New York label remained largely derivative, his own sound began to emerge after he formed his own band in Dallas in 1954. It included saxophonist David "Fathead" Newman, whose bop-tinged alto and tenor solos would be a feature of many Charles hits over the next decade. Inspired by gospel music— especially the recordings of the two Chicago-based groups Alex Bradford and the Bradford Specials and Albertina Walker's Caravans (featuring James Cleveland)—Charles mixed the chord structures, call-and-response patterns, and emotional urgency of gospel with the blues to create such ground-breaking 1955–56 R&B hits as "I've Got a Woman" (his first Number One record), "A Fool for You," "Drown in My Own Tears," and "Hallelujah I Love Her So."

Atlantic encouraged its blooming star's bold eclecticism. Besides the proto-soul singles, including his first major crossover hit, 1959's torrid "What'd I Say," Charles recorded several sets of straight-ahead instrumental jazz, an album of pop and blues standards with big band and strings (1959's *The Genius of Ray Charles*), and his first experiment with country music, a 1959 version of Hank Snow's "I'm Movin' On," complete with pedal steel guitar.

Charles's pop appeal was cemented when he jumped ship to ABC-Paramount in 1960 and expanded his seven-member band by 10. A haunting rendition of Hoagy Carmichael's "Georgia on My Mind" gave Charles his first Number One pop hit (number three R&B) later that year, and in 1962 he released *Modern Sounds in Country and Western Music*, the first of two best-selling albums of his unique interpretations of country standards. He also formed his own ABC-distributed Tangerine label

studied classical piano and clarinet at St. Augustine's School for the Deaf and Blind in Orlando, Florida, but left following his mother's death to join a dance band in Jacksonville. In 1947, after a period in Tampa, Charles moved to Seattle and formed the McSon Trio with guitarist Gosady McGee and bassist Milt Garred. The group patterned its style after two popular groups of the day—the King Cole Trio and Johnny Moore's Three Blazers—with Charles's smooth vocal and piano approach alternating between those of Nat Cole from the former and Charles Brown of the latter.

The trio's first recording, "Confession Blues," cut in Seattle in 1949 for Jack Lauderdale's Los Angeles–based Downbeat label, reached number two on *Billboard*'s R&B chart. Moving to Los Angeles the and began producing some of his musical heroes, including Percy Mayfield (composer of Charles's 1961 smash, "Hit the Road Jack"), Lula Reed (whose 1952 recording of "I'll Drown in My Tears" he had transformed into "Drown in My Own Tears"), and Louis Jordan, as well as his backup vocal group, the Raeletts.

Although he remained an icon of the entertainment world, Charles's popularity on records declined after his number nine R&B, number nine pop cover of the Beatles' "Yesterday" in 1967. He recorded for his own Crossover label in the mid-1970s then briefly rejoined Atlantic before signing with Columbia, for whom he made several albums of straight-up country music during the '80s. Renewing his longtime relationship with early Seattle associate Quincy Jones, Charles took part in the producer's 1985 Number One R&B and pop all-star USA for Africa recording of "We Are the World" on Columbia. Four years later he sang a duet with Chaka Khan on Jones's Number One R&B, number 18 pop hit, "I'll Be Good to You" on Qwest.

TOP ALBUM

MODERN SOUNDS IN COUNTRY AND WESTERN MUSIC (ABC-Paramount, '62, 1)

Additional Top 40 Albums: 14

TOP SONGS

DROWN IN MY OWN TEARS (Atlantic, '56, 1 R&B)

WHAT'D I SAY (PART 1) (Atlantic, '59, 1 R&B, 6 Pop)

ONE MINT JULEP (Impulse, '61, 1 R&B, 8 Pop)

HIT THE ROAD JACK (ABC-Paramount, '61, 1 R&B, 1 Pop)

UNCHAIN MY HEART (ABC-Paramount, '61, 1 R&B, 9 Pop)

I CAN'T STOP LOVING YOU (ABC-Paramount, '62, 1 R&B, 1 Pop)

YOU ARE MY SUNSHINE (ABC-Paramount, '62, 1 R&B, 7 Pop)

LET'S GO GET STONED (ABC/TRC, '66, 1 R&B, 31 Pop)

I'LL BE GOOD TO YOU (Quincy Jones featuring Ray Charles and Chaka Khan, Qwest, '89, 1 R&B, 18 Pop)

Additional Top 40 R&B Hits: 63

THE CHI-LITES

In an era when most stand-up soul vocal groups took a macho stance, the Chi-Lites offered a refreshing alternative. The Chicago quartet projected an image of vulnerability during its 1971–74 heyday on the charts, thanks to lead singer, songwriter, and producer Eugene Record's innocent, candy-cane falsetto and pathos-drenched ballads, including "Have You Seen Her," "Oh Girl," "A Letter to Myself," Homely Girl," and "Toby." The forlorn quality of much of the Chi-Lites' material was further heightened by their smooth, ethereal harmonies and Record's meticulously crafted, high-gloss productions.

The group, originally a quintet, formed around 1961 from the remnants of two South Side units. Record (b. 1940, Chicago), tenor Robert "Squirrel" Lester (b. 1942, McComb, Mississippi), and bass Clarence Johnson had sung with the Chanteurs, and baritone Marshall Thompson, Jr. (b. 1941, Chicago) and bass Creadel "Red" Jones (b. 1939, St. Louis) with the Desideros. Each group had recorded with limited success, the Chanteurs for Renee, Vee-Jay, and Mercury, the Desideros for Renee only. Thompson, son of noted jazz drummer Marshall Thompson, Sr., and a gifted drummer himself, became the new group's leader, while Record wrote most of the songs. They called themselves the Hi-Lites.

After they made their debut single, 1963's "I'm So Jealous" on the obscure Daran label, Johnson left the group. The Hi-Lites then affixed a C to the front of their name in order to avoid legal action from another act calling itself the Hi-Lites. Now known as Marshall and the Chi-Lites, the group scuffled for several years, its members at one point living together in a single room, sleeping in shifts. Record drove a cab, while Thompson earned his living as house drummer at the Regal Theater, where he backed some of the leading soul artists of the period. Through those contacts, Thompson was able to keep the Chi-Lites on record. Between 1965 and 1968, they jumped from label to label—Blue Rock, Ja-Wes, Dakar, Revue—before landing at Brunswick, where they soon hit the jackpot.

Brunswick's business offices were in New York, but its A&R department, headed by Carl Davis, was located in Chicago. There, Record began to blossom as a songwriter and eventually as a producer. A number of tunes written in whole or in part by

Record made the charts between 1968 and '70, including Barbara Acklin's number three R&B, number 15 pop "Love Makes a Woman"; Young-Holt Unlimited's number three R&B and pop "Soulful Strut" (both on Brunswick); Betty Everett's number three R&B, number 26 pop "There'll Come a Time" (on Uni); and Otis Leavill's number 19 R&B "Love Uprising" (on Dakar). And, in 1969, the Chi-Lites themselves scored their first chart entry, the number 10 R&B "Give It Away."

While most of the Chi-Lites' early sides had been ballads, they switched direction in 1971 with "(For God's Sake) Give More Power to the People" and its follow-up, "We Are Neighbors," both being uptempo funk numbers inspired by the Temptations' "Psychedelic Shack," albeit with politically militant messages. Beginning with that year's haunting "Have You Seen Her," Record perfected the "neoclassical" ballad style—based on gently loping rhythm tracks recorded by himself (on keyboards, guitar, and bass) and drummer Quinton Joseph, then lushly orchestrated—that gave the Chi-Lites a brief spell of crossover success. That song went to Number One on the R&B chart and number three pop, and the next release, "Oh Girl," featuring the lonesome harmonica of Cy Touff, soared to the top of both lists.

Record's productions became increasingly experimental, and he began collaborating with country songwriter Stan McKenny to create 1973's "My Heart Just Keeps on Breakin' " (an ingenious fusion of soul and country music, complete with hoedown fiddle, that proved too bold for either radio format to appreciate or embrace) and 1974's more typical "Homely Girl."

Jones left the group in 1973, followed three years later by Record. Without their creative front man, the Chi-Lites floundered as they moved from Brunswick to Mercury, back to Brunswick, then to Inphasion. Record's three Warner Bros. solo albums also met with minimal acceptance. In 1980, the old quartet came back together to record for Carl Davis's new Chi-Sound label, then they went to Larc, where they scored their final top 10 R&B hit with 1973's funk-styled "Bottom's Up." Jones quit again, but the group continued as a trio at Private I Records.

By 1990, when the Chi-Lites cut an album for Ichiban, Record too was gone, replaced by Anthony Watson. Record's old songs lived on that year, however, with "Have You Seen Her" successfully revamped by rapper M. C. Hammer and "Oh Girl" by British pop vocalist Paul Young.

TOP ALBUMS

(FOR GOD'S SAKE) GIVE MORE POWER TO THE
  PEOPLE (Brunswick, '71, *12*)
A LONELY MAN (Brunswick, '72, *5*)

TOP SONGS

(FOR GOD'S SAKE) GIVE MORE POWER TO THE PEOPLE
  (Brunswick, '71, *4 R&B, 26 Pop*)
HAVE YOU SEEN HER (Brunswick, '71, *1 R&B,
  3 Pop*)
OH GIRL (Brunswick, '72, *1 R&B, 1 Pop*)
A LETTER TO MYSELF (Brunswick, '73, *3 R&B,
  33 Pop*)
STONED OUT OF MY MIND (Brunswick, '73, *2 R&B,
  30 Pop*)
HOMELY GIRL (Brunswick, '74, *3 R&B*)
TOBY (Brunswick, '74, *7 R&B*)
BOTTOM'S UP (Larc, '83, *7 R&B*)

Additional Top 40 R&B Songs: 20

CHIC

The self-consciously swank style that guitarist Nile Rodgers, Jr. (b. Sept. 19, 1952, New York) and bassist Bernard Edwards (b. Oct. 31, 1952, Greenville, North Carolina) fashioned for their group Chic took disco music to a new level of sophistication during the late 1970s and set the stage for the partners' individual careers as leading pop producers of the following decade. The pair created a string of nostalgia-laced international dance hits for Chic in which their catchy melodies were set to simple vocal chants and riffing strings over the hypnotic rhythmic foundation of Rodgers' choked guitar syncopations, Edwards' undulating bass lines, and drummer Tony Thompson's four-on-the-floor grooves. Two of their songs—1978's "Le Freak" (the biggest selling single in the history of Atlantic Records) and the next year's "Good Times"—topped the *Billboard* R&B and pop charts.

Rodgers and Edwards initially hated disco. The son of a Greenwich Village jazz drummer, Rodgers studied theory at the Manhattan School of Music and jazz guitar with noted instructor Ted Dunbar. While playing in the house band at the Apollo Theater and touring with a road show from "Sesame Street," Rodgers dreamed of becoming a rock guitar star. Edwards, who settled in New York City at age 10, played saxophone before switching to electric bass at 15. James Jamerson, Sr., the bassist on most of Motown's hits of the 1960s, was an early inspiration.

The two musicians first worked together in the Big Apple Band, an instrumental group that toured with the proto-disco vocal quartet New York City (which scored a number 14, number 17 pop hit in 1973 with the Thom Bell–produced "I'm Doin' Fine Now" on Chelsea Records) between 1972 and '75. After New York City broke up, Rodgers and Edwards considered forming a punk-rock band. "But," Edwards told Geoff Brown of England's *Black Music* magazine, "we were intelligent enough to realize that punk was even more alienating than R&B and that disco was the new thing that everybody was into."

They began writing and recording disco songs, all of which met with record company rejection until a New York club deejay began playing a tape of "Dance, Dance, Dance (Yowsah, Yowsah, Yowsah)" during the summer of 1977. Combining rhythms suited to the Hustle, a disco dance craze of the period, with images inspired by Depression-era

dance marathon scenes from the motion picture *They Shoot Horses, Don't They?*, the song was soon issued by Atlantic and gave Chic a number six hit on both the R&B and pop charts. Besides the leaders, the record featured lead vocalist Norma Jean Wright and drummer Thompson.

With Alfa Anderson replacing Wright (who went on to a short-lived solo career), Chic enjoyed its greatest successes during 1978 and '79. Many critics dismissed Chic's hit records as thoughtless party music, but established rock and fledgling rap artists were paying close attention, especially to Edwards's innovative bass patterns on "Good Times." The song served as the foundation for both the Sugarhill Gang's pioneering 1979 hip-hop record "Rapper's Delight" (number four R&B, number 36 pop) and Queen's 1980 "Another One Bites the Dust" (number two R&B, Number One pop).

While Chic's run on the top 10 ended with 1980's "Rebels Are We" and the group itself broke up three years later, Rodgers and Edwards found themselves much in demand as producers for other artists. They gave Sister Sledge two Number One R&B hits in 1979—"He's the Greatest Dancer" and "We Are Family"—and the next year produced *Diana*, the biggest album of Diana Ross's long and storied career, including the Number One R&B and pop single "Upside Down."

Rodgers and Edwards both issued solo albums during the 1980s, but their greatest post-Chic achievements were as producers. Rodgers's credits included Debbie Harry, David Bowie ("Let's Dance"), Madonna ("Like a Virgin"), Mick Jagger, Sheena Easton, the Thompson Twins, Jeff Beck, Duran Duran, the Vaughan Brothers (Jimmie and Stevie Ray), and the *Coming to America* soundtrack. With Beck, Robert Plant, and Jimmy Page, Rodgers was also a member of the Honeydrippers rock group. Like his former partner, Edwards was part of another short-lived all-star rock band, Power Station, and produced hits for such artists as Robert Palmer ("Addicted to Love"), Jody Watley ("Don't You Want Me"), and Rod Stewart ("Crazy About Her").

The duo reunited in 1991 to record *Chic-ism*, but the Warner Bros. album was a commercial failure. "I don't think there'll be any more Chic records," Rodgers later told Michael Freedberg of the *San Francisco Bay Guardian*. "I realize times change, but I'm not going to....I wish there was still an audience for the kind of music we make."

TOP ALBUMS

CHIC (Atlantic, '78, 27)
C'EST CHIC (Atlantic, '78, 4)
RISQUE (Atlantic, '79, 5)

Additional Top 40 Albums: 1

TOP SONGS

DANCE, DANCE, DANCE (Yowsah, Yowsah, Yowsah) (Atlantic, '77, 6 R&B, 6 Pop)
EVERYBODY DANCE (Atlantic, '78, 12 R&B, 38 Pop)
LE FREAK (Atlantic, '78, 1 R&B, 1 Pop)
I WANT YOUR LOVE (Atlantic, '79, 5 R&B, 7 Pop)
GOOD TIMES (Atlantic, '79, 1 R&B, 1 Pop)
REBELS ARE WE (Atlantic, '80, 8 R&B)
SOUP FOR ONE (Mirage, '82, 14 R&B)

Additional Top 40 R&B Songs: 2

GEORGE CLINTON

Singer, songwriter, bandleader, and P-Funk referee George Clinton (b. July 22, 1941, Kannapolis, North Carolina) did not invent funk, but he gave the genre new definitions. The sounds and sights he unleashed during the 1970s with his group, known concurrently as Parliament and Funkadelic, went beyond music. His was an assault on the psyches of African-American youth, a conscious attempt to break down inhibitions and taboos through fun and fantasy. "We don't care if we are cute or sound good, as long as we make 'em think about somethin'," he said in 1977.

His influences included the music of James Brown, the Beatles, and Sly Stone; the no-holds-barred humor of Richard Pryor; and the psychedelic utopian movements of the 1960s, and he drew them all together through science fiction, nursery rhymes, and street-corner jive into a mind-boggling soul theater of the absurd. By the end of the 1970s, he had succeeded, to a large degree, in placing one nation under his hypnotic, consciousness-raising groove.

Raised 50 miles from Winston-Salem, North Carolina, Clinton moved with his family to Newark, New Jersey, in 1956. He worked there as a barber and, inspired by Frankie Lymon and the Teenagers, formed a doo wop group with friends. Known as the Parliaments, they made their recording debut in 1959 with "Poor Boy" b/w "Party Boys" on the Apt label and later that year cut "Lonely Island" b/w "You Make Me Wanna Cry" for Flipp. Neither 45 met with much success.

The Parliaments settled in Detroit during the 1960s. Clinton signed on as a staff writer at Jobete, and the group recorded some unreleased material for Motown, the publishing firm's parent company. They did see one release on the Golden World label, but it remains even more obscure than their first two singles. Things finally broke in 1967 when the Parliaments (vocalists Clinton, Raymond Davis, Calvin Simon, Clarence "Fuzzy" Haskins, and Grady Thomas) and their backing band (organist Mickey Atkins, lead guitarist Eddie Hazel, rhythm guitarist

Lucius Tawl Ross, bassist Billy Nelson, and drummer Ramon "Tiki" Fulwood) recorded for another Motor City label. The Clinton-penned-and-produced "(I Wanna) Testify," the group's first Revilot single, not only gave them their first national hit but hinted that psychedelia was creeping into the leader's brain. That influence became even more pronounced in the group's five subsequent singles—four on Revilot, one on Atco.

Legal hassles resulted in Clinton losing rights to the Parliaments' name, but he wasted no time in signing a contract with the Detroit-based Westbound label for his singers and players under a new name—

TOP ALBUMS

MOTHERSHIP CONNECTION (Parliament, Casablanca, '76, 13)
FUNKENTELECHY VS. THE PLACEBO SYNDROME (Parliament, Casablanca, '78, 13)
ONE NATION UNDER A GROOVE (Funkadelic, Warner Bros., '78, 16)
UNCLE JAM WANTS YOU (Funkadelic, Warner Bros., '79, 18)

Additional Top 40 Albums: 3

TOP SONGS

(I WANNA) TESTIFY (The Parliaments, Revilot, '67, 3 R&B, 20 Pop)
FLASH LIGHT (Parliament, Casablanca, '78, 1 R&B, 16 Pop)
ONE NATION UNDER A GROOVE—PART 1 (Funkadelic, Warner Bros., '78, 1 R&B, 28 Pop)
AQUA BOOGIE (A PSYCHOALPHADISCOBETABIOAQUADOLOOP) (Parliament, Casablanca, '78, 1 R&B)
(NOT JUST) KNEE DEEP (Funkadelic, Warner Bros., '79, 1 R&B)
ATOMIC DOG (Capitol, '83, 1 R&B)

Additional Top 40 R&B Songs: 25

Funkadelic. While recording for Westbound as Funkadelic, the group signed in 1970 with Invictus Records—as Parliament. Several personnel changes took place during the early 1970s, the most notable being the replacement of keyboardist Atkins by Bernie Worrell, whose often eerie organ work combined elements of Sun Ra, Bach, and soap opera specialist George Wright. The group's other significant new instrumentalist was Eddie Hazel, whose sputtering, acidic guitar lines were part Jimi Hendrix, part his own invention.

Clinton launched one of the most bizarre shows ever staged by a musical group. Singing lead, nearly naked and bewigged in blonde, he fronted the attack. His compatriots were just as outrageously garbed—

George Clinton

in diapers, stars-and-striped loincloths, leopard-skin leotards, and the like. Through their records and concerts, Parliament-Funkadelic steadily built a cult following until, in 1978 (with Parliament's recordings being issued on Casablanca and Funkadelic's on Warner Bros.), they fractured the mass consciousness with the R&B chart-topping hits "Flash Light," "One Nation Under a Groove," and "Aqua Boogie (A Psychoalphadiscobetabioaquadoloop)." Clinton also produced several satellite groups during the late '70s: the Brides of Funkenstein, Parlet, Fred Wesley and the Horny Horns, and the most successful, former James Brown bassist Bootsy Collins's Rubber Band, which scored 11 top 40 R&B hit singles on Warner Bros. between 1976 and '82, including 1978's Number One R&B "Bootzilla."

In 1982, having lost the rights to the names Parliament and Funkadelic, Clinton formed the short-lived P-Funk All Stars with Sly Stone and recorded two singles with the group for his own Hump label. He then signed as a solo artist with Capitol, scoring a Number One R&B hit in 1983 with "Atomic Dog." While it proved to be his last major hit, his grooves and crazed sensibility continued to inform popular music, especially hip-hop, where his old beats were sampled more often than those of any other artist aside from James Brown. He became a godfather figure to a new generation of admirers, including Dr. Dre, Humpty Hump, Ice Cube, MC Breed, Yo-Yo, and (from the Red Hot Chili Peppers) Anthony Kiedis and Flea, all of whom made guest appearances on Clinton's 1993 Paisley Park album, *Hey Man ...Smell My Finger.*

THE CLOVERS

Much has been made of how cover records by pop singers Georgia Gibbs and Pat Boone cut into the respective record sales of R&B artists LaVern Baker and Little Richard. Yet, when Elvis Presley finally opened pop radio's floodgates to rock in 1956, Baker and Richard were beneficiaries, and their white imitators eventually faded from favor.

The Clovers, the most popular R&B vocal group of the early 1950s, were not as fortunate. They too were victims of covers, both during their heyday and well after. But their record company also misjudged the tastes of the new marketplace. Just as the ears of

white America were readying for the hard R&B sounds from which rock was derived, the Clovers made a shift to the softer pop style of their Washington, D.C., beginnings, thus starting a slow slide into chart oblivion.

The group that became the Clovers was organized in 1946 as a trio at Washington's Armstrong High School. By 1949, the lineup consisted of charter member Harold Lucas (baritone) plus John "Buddy" Bailey (lead), Matthew McQuater (tenor), and Harold Winley (bass). For good luck, they dubbed themselves "The Four Clovers." Classically trained guitarist Bill Harris soon became their accompanyist. Lou Krefetz, a Baltimore record store owner, signed on as their manager and took them to the tiny Rainbow label in New York, for which they waxed their first record, 1950's pop-styled "Yes Sir, That's My Baby."

Dissatisfied with the dismal sales of the group's debut, Keifetz contacted New York's Atlantic Records, a fast-rising force in the emerging R&B market. Company co-owner Ahmet Ertegun was not especially enamored of the Clovers' repertoire, consisting of pop material associated with the Ink Spots, Orioles, Ravens, and Charioteers, but was sufficiently impressed with their vocal abilities to sign them. To get the 'blacker' sound he wanted out of the group, he began writing songs, crediting himself as "A. Nugetre," spelling his last name backwards.

"Don't You Know I Love You," the group's initial Atlantic release, rose to Number One on the *Billboard* R&B chart, becoming the first of seven Ertegun-penned Clovers hits to place in the top three between 1951 and '54. For the tune, a medium-tempo shuffle based on gospel chord changes, Ertegun and co-producer Herb Abramson had coaxed a bluesy performance out of lead tenor Bailey and backed the group with a socking rhythm section that played a loping bass pattern inspired by Ertegun's idol, Chicago blues and boogie pianist Jimmy Yancey. It was also the first vocal group hit to include a tenor saxophone solo, courtesy of Atlantic artist Frank "Cole Slaw" Cully.

While the Clovers continued to ride the charts with "Fool, Fool, Fool," "Middle of the Night," "Ting-A-Ling," "Hey, Miss Fannie," "Good Lovin'," "Lovey Dovey" (all composed by Ertegun); "One Mint Julep," "Crawlin'" (both by Rudy Toombs); and "I Played the Fool" (by Lee Magid), the fusion of blues, gospel, and African-American pop harmony they created with Ertegun and, in many cases, arranger Jesse Stone formed the basis of the "Atlantic sound" of the 1950s and had a marked influence on such other groups as the Dominoes, the Midnighters, and the Drifters. Pop radio was not yet ready for R&B, however, as the Clovers saw "Ting-A-Ling" covered by Kay Starr and "One Mint Julep" by both Louis Prima and Buddy Morrow. (Morrow rendered the song as an instrumental, as did Ray Charles, who took it to the top of the R&B chart in 1961).

Drafted into the Army in 1953, Bailey was replaced by Charlie White, who gave the group an even bluesier sound for "Good Lovin' " and "Lovey Dovey." He, in turn, was replaced in 1954 by Billy Mitchell, who stayed on as second lead upon Bailey's return later that year. But the Clovers' days as consistent hitmakers were over. Their 1956 recording of "Love, Love, Love" placed at number four R&B and was their first to penetrate the pop chart, where it was forced to compete with a cover by the Diamonds, a white Canadian group. Now working under producers Ertegun and Jerry Wexler, the Clovers adopted the smoother sounds of "Blue Velvet" and "Devil or Angel," songs that would find greater fame a few years later in the hands of pop singers Bobby Vinton and Bobby Vee respectively.

Leaving Atlantic in 1957, the group cut an album of popular standards for manager Krefetz's Popular label then signed with United Artists, for which their 1959 recording of "Love Potion No. 9," written and produced by Jerry Leiber and Mike Stoller in the fashion of their hits for the Coasters, placed at number 23 on both the R&B and pop charts. (A 1965 version by Liverpool's Searchers was far more suc-

cessful.) After returning to Atlantic in 1961 for one non-hit, the Clovers split into rival groups, one led by Bailey, the other by Lucas, that recorded a series of obscure singles into the late 1960s.

THE COASTERS

The Coasters were, in the words of critic Dave Marsh, "the funniest group in rock and roll history." No other rhythm and blues act of the 1950s better captured the rebellious spirit of teenaged America, with the possible exception of Chuck Berry. The versatile southern California vocal quartet served as a sounding board for the brilliant musical vignettes of lyricist Jerry Leiber and tunesmith Mike Stoller, delivering such three-minute slices of social satire as "Yakety Yak" and "Charlie Brown" with punch lines perfectly timed for optimum comic effect. "If rock 'n' roll had produced nothing but the Coasters and Leiber and Stoller," author Arnold Shaw stated in *The Rockin' '50s,* "it would still have commanded attention as the sound embodiment of a time and generation. They reflected the world of the young with understanding, good humor, and social insight. This was rock 'n' roll at its best—ebullient, energizing, entertaining, expressive and danceable."

The Coasters evolved from a group, formed in 1947 and comprising Ty Terrell and brothers Billy and Roy Richards, called the A Sharp Trio. They were spotted at the Barrelhouse Club in Los Angeles by bandleader Johnny Otis, who added bass singer Bobby Nunn to the lineup and rechristened them the Bluebirds, then the Robins. Between 1949 and '54, the Robins recorded prolifically, for such labels as Aladdin, Savoy, Recorded in Hollywood, Modern, and RCA Victor, hitting the top of the R&B chart in 1950 with Savoy's "Double Crossing Blues" on which they were joined vocally by Little Esther Phillips and backed by the Otis band. Their first association with Leiber and Stoller came with 1951's "That's What the Good Book Says" on Modern, followed by 1953's "Ten Days in Prison" on RCA, the first tune in which the group adopted character parts inspired by Leiber's interest in such radio dramas as "The Shadow," "Gangbusters," and "Amos 'n' Andy."

With profits from their first major hit, 1953's "Hound Dog" by blues belter Willie Mae "Big

---

TOP SONGS

Don't You Know I Love You (Atlantic, '51, 1 R&B)

Fool, Fool, Fool (Atlantic, '51, 1 R&B)

One Mint Julep (Atlantic, '52, 2 R&B)

Ting-A-Ling (Atlantic, '52, 1 R&B)

Hey, Miss Fannie (Atlantic, '52, 2 R&B)

I Played the Fool (Atlantic, '52, 3 R&B)

Crawlin' (Atlantic, '53, 3 R&B)

Good Lovin' (Atlantic, '53, 2 R&B)

Lovey Dovey (Atlantic, '54 , 2 R&B)

Devil or Angel (Atlantic, '56, 3 R&B)

Additional Top 40 R&B Songs: 11

TOP SONGS

DOWN IN MEXICO (Atco, '56, 8 R&B)

ONE KISS LED TO ANOTHER (Atco, '56, 11 R&B)

SEARCHIN' (Atco, '57, 1 R&B, 3 Pop)

YOUNG BLOOD (Atco, '57, 2 R&B, 8 Pop)

YAKETY YAK (Atco, '58, 1 R&B, 1 Pop)

CHARLIE BROWN (Atco, '59, 2 R&B, 2 Pop)

POISON IVY (Atco, '59, 1 R&B, 7 Pop)

WAKE ME, SHAKE ME (Atco '60, 14 R&B)

LITTLE EGYPT (YING-YANG) (Atco, '61, 16 R&B, 23 Pop)

Additional Top 40 R&B Songs: 2

Mama" Thornton on Peacock, Leiber and Stoller launched Spark Records in 1954. At their own label, the songwriting-producing team perfected their sitcom approach with the Robins (now featuring lead singer Carl Gardner) on such tunes as "Riot in Cell Block #9" (with bass singer Richard Berry subbing for Nunn), "Framed" (containing an element of protest against racism), and "Smokey Joe's Cafe." Those sides were strong sellers in southern California, but not nationally, due to the company's limited distribution.

"Smokey Joe's Cafe" sparked the interest of Atlantic Records, which not only purchased the Spark catalog, but signed Leiber and Stoller to an unprecedented contract as independent producers. Reissued on Atlantic's new Atco subsidiary, the song rose to number 10 on *Billboard*'s R&B chart. There was a hitch, however. Several members of the group didn't want to be with the New York company and organized a new group of Robins to record for manager Gene Norman's Whippet label that quickly sunk into obscurity. Gardner and Nunn chose to remain with Leiber and Stoller and Atco and recruited singers Leon Hughes and Billy Guy, along with guitarist Adolph Jacobs, to become the Coasters.

Between 1956 and '61, the Coasters cut a nearly unbroken string of hits (all written and produced by Leiber and Stoller, excepting 1960's Billy Guy–penned "Wake Me, Shake Me") as well as provided backing for LaVern Baker on her 1967 Atlantic hit "Jim Dandy Got Married" and for Bobby Hendricks on his 1958 Sue hit "Itchy Twitchy Feeling." Beginning with the double-sided 1957 single "Searchin' " b/w "Young Blood," the Coasters were also consistent favorites on the pop charts. Hughes was replaced by Obie Jessie, then Cornell Gunter, in 1957, and Nunn by Will "Dub" Jones, the comic bass voice of 1959's "Charlie Brown." Gunter left two years later, his place taken by former Cadillacs lead Earl "Speedo" Carroll.

The Coasters had no more top 40 hits, on either the R&B or pop charts, after 1961. They were dropped by Atco four years later, then recorded briefly for Lloyd Price's Turntable label before being reunited in 1966 with Leiber and Stoller at Columbia's Date subsidiary, for which they recorded such non-hit numbers as "Soul Pad," "Down Home Girl," and the original version of "D. W. Washburn," later a hit for the Monkees.

Various editions of the Coasters have toured the oldies circuit since the late 1960s, including one led by Gardner, another by Guy and Jones, and three others by Nunn, Gunter, and Hughes. Nunn died of a heart attack in 1986, a year before the Coasters' induction into the Rock and Roll Hall of Fame. Gunter was murdered in Las Vegas three years later.

NATALIE COLE

Throughout her rocky career, vocalist Natalie Cole (b. Feb. 6, 1950, Los Angeles) found herself caught between two abiding musical influences: the jazzy yet conservative pop music of her father, Nat "King" Cole, and the more emotionally overt, gospel-fueled soul of Aretha Franklin. The latter supplied her ticket to soul-diva status during the mid-to-late 1970s, while the former firmly ushered her into the pop mainstream in the early '90s.

"The fact that I am Nat 'King' Cole's daughter will be an ever-present thing," she told Fredrick Douglas Murphy in a 1975 interview with *Black Stars* magazine. "I don't even want to touch his style with a ten-foot pole, unless I am sure I can do it right. Maybe in 10 years there will be something in the wings for me, to do the kind of things that my father used to do. But right now, I have to be Natalie."

Cole had made her public singing debut at age 11, as part of her dad's show at the Greek Theater in Los Angeles. A decade later, while attending the University of Massachusetts at Amherst, she was studying psychology and dreaming of opening a clinic for disadvantaged children. Then, a top 40 band at the school recruited her as its vocalist, and she became a popular attraction around campus with her covers of

TOP ALBUMS

UNPREDICTABLE (Capitol, '77, *8*)
UNFORGETTABLE WITH LOVE (Elektra, '91, *1*)

Additional Top 40 Albums: 5

TOP SONGS

THIS WILL BE (Capitol, '75, *1 R&B, 6 Pop*)
INSEPARABLE (Capitol, '75, *1 R&B, 32 Pop*)
SOPHISTICATED LADY (SHE'S A DIFFERENT LADY)
    (Capitol, '76, *1 R&B, 25 Pop*)
I'VE GOT LOVE ON MY MIND (Capitol, '77, *1 R&B,
    5 Pop*)
OUR LOVE (Capitol, '77, *1 R&B, 10 Pop*)
JUMP START (Manhattan, '87, *2 R&B, 13 Pop*)
I LIVE FOR YOUR LOVE (Manhattan, '87, *4 R&B,
    13 Pop*)
MISS YOU LIKE CRAZY (EMI, '89, *1 R&B, 7 Pop*)

Additional Top 40 R&B Songs: 19

tunes by Jefferson Airplane, Janis Joplin, and other rock artists. She soon developed a more subdued supper club act and toured the lounge circuit before hooking up in 1974 with the Chicago songwriting-producing team of Rev. Marvin Yancy and Charles Jackson.

Yancy and Jackson had already enjoyed R&B chart success as producers and members of the Independents, a vocal quintet that hit the top of the *Billboard* R&B chart in 1973 with "Leaving Me" on the Wand label. Pianist Yancy was a stylistic disciple of Chicago gospel great Jessy Dixon, while Jackson was the younger brother of Rev. Jesse Jackson. Both men were Baptists, and they proceeded to infuse Cole's singing with an intense gospel edge. Yancy also baptized the former Episcopalian at his church. "I believe that this has a great deal to do with the way I sound now," she told Murphy.

Signed to Capitol Records (her father's old label), Cole scored Number One R&B hits with her first three singles—"This Will Be," "Inseparable," and "Sophisticated Lady (She's a Different Lady)"—all written and produced by Yancy and Jackson and featuring Yancy's churchy piano. In spite of her success, many observers charged that Cole sounded too much like Aretha Franklin, to which she countered, "We don't do the same things vocally, but I do think we have the same feeling."

Cole and Yancy had wed in 1975, but by 1980 their marriage—and her career—had begun to unravel. She had become severely addicted to cocaine. Capitol dropped her in 1982, and by year's end, Maria Cole was granted legal conservatorship of her daughter's rapidly dwindling estate. Mrs. Cole's court petition had charged that Natalie was "unable to properly provide for her personal needs for physical health, food, clothing, or shelter."

Cole completed a six-month rehabilitation in late 1983, but her career comeback was a slow process. Albums for the Epic and Modern labels flopped. Finally, in 1987, she was signed to EMI-Manhattan Records and scored three hit singles—the appropriately titled "Jump Start" (produced by Reggie Calloway of Midnight Star) and "I Live for Your Love" and a cover of Bruce Springsteen's "Pink Cadillac" (both produced by Dennis Lambert)—off *Everlasting,* her first album for the company. And, in 1989, the year she married former Rufus drummer Andre Fisher (he'd produced two cuts on *Everlasting*), she topped the R&B chart for the first time in nearly a dozen years with the Michael Masser–produced ballad, "Miss You Like Crazy."

Cole had gradually shed her Aretha Franklin trappings during the 1980s and, in 1991, released the record her fans had long anticipated: a set of songs associated with the late Nat "King" Cole. *Unforgettable with Love,* a lavishly crafted Elektra album featuring "Unforgettable" (a David Foster–produced duet with her dad created through studio wizardry), rose to the top of *Billboard*'s album chart and solidly established the singer as a favorite of older record buyers. The follow-up, 1993's *Take a Look,* took a similarly conservative course but was far less successful. Its title track, a poignant Clyde Otis–penned plea for racial tolerance, found Cole revamping a tune first recorded by Franklin nearly 30 years earlier.

CON FUNK SHUN

Con Funk Shun was the biggest thing to have come out of Vallejo, California, since Sly Stone. Sporting the hook-filled compositions and alternating lead vocals of Michael Cooper and Felton Pilate II, high background harmonies, brassy riffs, jazzy horn and organ solos, molten rock guitar licks, and a fat, funky backbeat, the seven-man band

Con Funk Shun

scored four gold albums and eight top 10 R&B singles during its 1976–86 association with Mercury Records.

"Our music is high-energy pop rhythm and blues," Pilate said in a 1977 interview with Doris Worsham of the *Oakland Tribune*. "It's a cross between Kool and the Gang and Chicago." The group had an even more diverse range of other influences, included the Archies, Bachman-Turner Overdrive, the Bar-Kays, the Beach Boys, Brick, James Brown, Mandrill, Wes Montgomery, and San Francisco–Oakland Bay Area heroes Sly and the Family Stone and Tower of Power.

Formed in 1968 by guitarist Cooper and drummer Louis McCall, classmates at Vallejo High School, the group was originally known as Project Soul. Within a year, the co-founders had brought on board trombonist-trumpeter-keyboardist Pilate, trumpeter Karl Fuller, saxophonist-flutist Paul Harrell, keyboardist Danny Thomas, and bassist Cedric Martin—a lineup that would remain constant for over a decade and a half. All of the members sang. The Soul Children, a two-man, two-woman vocal group that recorded for Stax Records in Memphis, passed through the Bay Area in 1971 and recruited Project Soul as their road band. Cooper, Pilate, and company relocated to Memphis the following year and also began providing backing for Rufus Thomas, then beginning his third decade as an R&B

hitmaker. On August 20, 1972, the band accompanied both Thomas and the Soul Children at the marathon Seventh Annual Watts Summer Festival, the results of which appeared on disc and motion picture as *Wattstax/The Living Word*.

After being dropped by the Soul Children, Project Soul remained in Memphis and began searching for a record deal and a new name. Signing with Fretone, a new label run by former Stax co-owner Estelle

---

TOP ALBUMS

LOVESHINE (Mercury, '78, 32)
SPIRIT OF LOVE (Mercury, '80, 30)

TOP SONGS

FFUN (Mercury, '77, *1 R&B, 23 Pop*)
SHAKE AND DANCE WITH ME (Mercury, '78, *5 R&B*)
CHASE ME (Mercury, '79, *4 R&B*)
GOT TO BE ENOUGH (Mercury, '80, *8 R&B*)
TOO TIGHT (Mercury, '80, *8 R&B, 40 Pop*)
BABY, I'M HOOKED (RIGHT INTO YOUR LOVE)
    (Mercury, '83, *5 R&B*)
ELECTRIC LADY (Mercury, '85, *4 R&B*)
BURNIN' LOVE (Mercury, '86, *8 R&B*)

Additional Top 40 R&B Songs: 9

Axton, the group became Con Funk Shun, a tag taken from the title of an obscure song by the Nite-Liters. Two singles, including an imaginative booty-bumpin' rendition of Bob Dylan's "Mr. Tambourine Man," appeared on Fretone and led to a contract with Mercury, which issued Con Funk Shun's first album, produced by veteran Memphis engineer Ron Capone, in 1976. *Secrets,* the follow-up album, was produced by Earth, Wind and Fire associate Skip Scarborough and yielded the 1977 Number One R&B, number 23 pop "Ffun," an uptempo Cooper party song that was modeled in part on "Dazz," a Number One R&B hit the previous year by the "disco-jazz" Atlanta band Brick.

"Ffun" kicked off Con Funk Shun's nine-year run on the R&B top 40, but only one subsequent single, 1980's "Too Tight," managed to make the pop top 40, despite the consciously pop sound of many of the group's creations. The band, back in Vallejo since 1979, began producing its own records.

In an attempt to broaden Con Funk Shun's pop appeal, Mercury brought in arranger Eumir Deodato to produce 1983's *Fever* album, but he failed to generate the same crossover magic he had worked for the label's Kool and the Gang, although the single "Baby, I'm Hooked (Right into Your Love)" did give the band another top five R&B hit. Maurice Starr, the Svengali behind New Edition, was recruited for 1985's *Electric Lady,* which produced a number four R&B single of the same title, but little pop interest. Pilate had dropped out by that time. The rest of the group called it quits in February 1987.

After working for six months as a Solano County deputy sheriff, Cooper launched a solo recording career at Warner Bros. and scored a number three R&B charter with 1987's "To Prove My Love," the first of his seven R&B top 40 entries through 1992. Pilate had set up a studio in the basement of his Vallejo home, and he began producing up-and-coming singers and rappers from the area, including Oakland's M. C. Hammer. Hired as Hammer's musical director, Pilate co-produced 1990's Number One *Please Hammer Don't Hurt 'Em,* the biggest selling rap album of all time.

On New Year's Eve, 1993, following Mercury's issuance of *The Best of Con Funk Shun* in its "Funk Essentials" series and a general revival of interest in funk, the group staged a reunion concert in Oakland. "Music is so electronic now," Cooper said at the time, "so the only place to really go is back to the basics—back to live music."

Sam Cooke

SAM COOKE

Sam Cooke (b. Sam Cook, Jan. 22, 1931, Clarksdale, Mississippi) was arguably the most influential of all soul singers. Since his tragic death in 1964, elements of Cooke's unique style have continued to reverberate through pop, rock, soul, blues, gospel, reggae, and even bluegrass music.

"He's got to be the best singer that ever lived, bar none," producer Jerry Wexler told author Gerri Hirshey. "Modulation, shading, dynamics, progression, emotion, every essential quality—he had it all."

The son of Rev. Charles S. Cook, Sr., and Annie May Cook, Sam moved to Chicago with his family at age two and, as a boy, sang with his brothers Charles, Jr., and L. C. and sisters Mary and Hattie in a gospel group called the Singing Children. At age 15, while attending Wendell Phillips High School, he became lead singer of the Highway Q.C.'s, a teenage gospel quartet that served as sort of a little league version of the famous Texas-bred, Chicago-based Soul Stirrers, who featured the soaring, sometimes sweet, sometimes gritty tenor voice of R. H. Harris. The Soul Stirrers were then recording for Specialty

Records in Hollywood. When Harris quit at the end of 1951, Cooke was recruited to take his place. He could sound uncannily like his predecessor at the beginning of his six-year association with the group, yet he was no mere Harris imitator. Cooke's effortlessly floating vocal manner, marked by graceful rhythmic and melodic invention, became increasingly pronounced as he settled into his role as the Soul Stirrers' star lead. He also developed quickly as a songwriter, contributing such gospel hits as "Be with Me Jesus" and "Touch the Hem of His Garment" to the group's repertoire.

Cooke's decidedly different vocal style and youthful good looks made him a star on the gospel circuit. They also began to draw the attention of secular music producers. The singer initially passed on offers to "jump the fence," but he relented at the end of 1956 by recording his first pop song, "Lovable" (modeled on the Soul Stirrers' earlier "Wonderful"), for Specialty producer Bumps Blackwell. Because Cooke was still a member of the gospel group, the company attempted to disguise his identity by issuing the single as being by "Dale Cook."

Specialty owner Art Rupe was not pleased with Cooke's new direction. A dispute developed during 1957, resulting in the vocalist's release from his contract. The settlement also enabled Blackwell to take some of the demos he'd been working on, including "You Send Me," across town to Keen Records. As "You Send Me" climbed the charts, eventually topping the *Billboard* R&B and pop lists, Specialty took another demo still in its possession, "I'll Come Running Back to You," which had originally featured just Cooke and his guitar, and overdubbed it with a band and vocal group. The result also topped the R&B chart.

Between 1957 and '65, Cooke scored 30 top 40 pop hits and 31 on the R&B chart. He composed the overwhelming majority himself, although he occasionally credited them to others, including brother L. C. and childhood sweetheart and future wife Barbara Campbell.

After two years at Keen, Cooke signed with RCA Victor in 1959. While most of his sessions for the company were credited to producers Hugo Peretti and Luigi Creaturo, the singer and arranger-guitarist Rene Hall took creative control of many, especially for the singles. Cooke's early RCA albums were geared toward a middle-of-the-road audience and contained such tepid material as "Secret Love" and "Arrivederci, Roma," but the singles were pure soul music with universal pop appeal.

Cooke was an astute businessman. With manager J. W. Alexander (formerly of the Pilgrim Travelers gospel quartet), Cooke formed Kags Music in 1958 and became one of the first R&B artists to control the publishing rights to his own compositions. Two years later, the partners launched SAR Records; initially started to record the post-Cooke Soul Stirrers, the label soon assembled an R&B roster that included such Cooke-produced artists as Johnnie Morisette, Johnnie Taylor, the Sims Twins, the Valentinos (the Womack Brothers), Billy Preston, and Mel Carter.

Cooke's career came to an abrupt end on December 11, 1964, when he was shot to death by the manager of a cheap Los Angeles motel during a scuffle surrounding an alleged rape attempt by the singer on a young woman he'd picked up at a restaurant.

Although the hard-socking "Shake" was his biggest posthumous hit, its flip side, the haunting "A Change Is Gonna Come," was viewed by many as his real swan song. Cooke's memory lived on, in the voices of Otis Redding, Rod Stewart, Al Green, and countless more whose styles he so profoundly influenced, and in the many compositions that have been rendered hits by others again and again.

TOP ALBUM

SAM COOKE (Keen, '58, 16)

Additional Top 40 Albums: 3

TOP SONGS

YOU SEND ME (Keen, '57, 1 R&B, 1 Pop)

I'LL COME RUNNING BACK TO YOU (Specialty, '57, 1 R&B, 18 Pop)

WONDERFUL WORLD (Keen, '60, 2 R&B, 12 Pop)

CHAIN GANG (RCA Victor, '60, 2 R&B, 2 Pop)

TWISTIN' THE NIGHT AWAY (RCA Victor, '62, 1 R&B, 9 Pop)

BRING IT ON HOME TO ME (RCA Victor, '62, 2 R&B, 13 Pop)

NOTHING CAN CHANGE THIS LOVE (RCA Victor, '62, 2 R&B, 12 Pop)

ANOTHER SATURDAY NIGHT (RCA Victor, '63, 1 R&B, 10 Pop)

SHAKE (RCA Victor, '65, 2 R&B, 7 Pop)

Additional Top 40 R&B Songs: 21

ROBERT CRAY

It was Halloween night 1977 when two Eugene, Oregon–based blues bands, one led by guitarist Robert Cray, the other by harmonica player Curtis Salgado, were sharing a bill at a local hotel. Actor John Belushi, in town to film *Animal House,* dropped by the show and was so taken with their music that it soon became the basis of his Blues Brothers act with fellow comedian Dan Aykroyd on "Saturday Night Live," a hit album, and then the movie *The Blues Brothers.*

Cray, who'd been leading his band since 1974, was offered a part in two scenes of *Animal House,* playing bass with a fictional R&B band called Otis Day and the Knights. Salgado, whose band merged with Cray's shortly after the film was made, provided the direct inspiration for the Blues Brothers' routine. Belushi and Aykroyd copied his exuberant stage manner, right down to his dark glasses and lower-lip goatee, and he supplied them with vintage blues material from his record collection, some of which subsequently appeared on the Blues Brothers' first album.

While the Blues Brothers became stars of stage, screen, and radio, the Cray band faded back into relative obscurity, playing a series of one-nighters for the next eight years at small clubs up and down the West Coast. The group, comprising Cray, Salgado, bassist Richard Cousins, and drummer Dave Olson, saw the release of its debut album, *Who's Been Talkin'* on the Tomato label, in 1980, but few noticed and the company went backrupt shortly thereafter. Salgado soon dropped out, and Cray's incisive tenor vocals and nimble, brittle-toned guitar picking became the band's primary focus.

In 1983, veteran blues songwriter-producers Bruce Bromberg and Dennis Walker, who'd produced the first album, formed HighTone Records with partner Larry Sloven to issue the second Cray album, *Bad Influence,* by which time he had developed a modern, sophisticated approach that owed as much to Memphis soul as it did to the blues. He composed most of the material in collaboration with his producers.

Cray's second HighTone album, 1985's *False Accusations,* began his breakthrough into the main-

stream. It became a hit in England, where Mick Jagger and other rock stars turned out to see the band perform, and *Newsweek* hailed it as one of the top 10 pop albums of the year. HighTone received offers for Cray's next release from a dozen major labels and settled on PolyGram, which issued 1986's *Strong Persuader* under the Mercury/HighTone logo. The first of five Cray albums to feature trumpeter-trombonist Wayne Jackson and tenor saxophonist Andrew Love—known collectively as the Memphis Horns, they were the same men who'd played on the old Otis Redding, Eddie Floyd, Johnnie Taylor, Little Milton, O. V. Wright, Otis Clay, and Al Green records that Cray so deeply adored—it rose to number 13 on the *Billboard* album chart, the first blues album to have cracked the top 20 since Bobby Bland's *Call on Me* in 1963. Writing in the *New York Times,* Samuel G. Freedman called Cray "the best young hope in a genre constantly worried that it has terminal illness." Of *Strong Persuader,* the typically modest Cray said at the time, "It's not any different from what Little Milton and Bobby Bland did a long time ago."

The son of an Army career man, Cray spent his youth living in Alabama, Georgia, Virginia, Pennsylvania, Indiana, California, and Germany before his family finally settled in Tacoma, Washington. Raised on the blues and soul of Ray Charles, Sam Cooke, and Bobby Bland, as well as the gospel music of such quartets as the Soul Stirrers and the Five Blind Boys of Mississippi, he studied piano before taking up the guitar. He led a rock band in Tacoma for a period but soon became enamored of the blues of such guitarists as Magic Sam, Buddy Guy, Hubert Sumlin, and Albert Collins.

Although he never repeated the success of *Strong Persuader,* Cray remained an international concert attraction and continued recording for Mercury and working with Walker after the producer's split with Bromberg and HighTone in 1990. *Shame and a Sin,* his 1993 release, was a self-produced back-to-the-blues affair, however.

Cray made his first recorded guest appearance in 1985 with Albert Collins and Johnny Copeland on the Grammy-winning *Showdown!* on Alligator Records and went on to contribute to albums by Tina Turner, Chuck Berry, Katie Webster, Eric Clapton, John Lee Hooker, and B. B. King, among others.

TOP ALBUMS

STRONG PERSUADER
  (Mercury/HighTone, '86, 13)
DON'T BE AFRAID OF THE DARK
  (Mercury/HighTone, '88, 32)

TYRONE DAVIS

Throughout his decade and a half as one of R&B's steadiest hitmakers, Tyrone Davis (b. May 4, 1938, Greenville, Mississippi) seldom varied his musical approach. If his range—somewhere between low tenor and baritone—is narrow and his tone is slightly hoarse, he has used his vocal limitations to great advantage. His phrasing is the essence of relaxation—he stretches his lines in cool detachment over loping Chicago soul grooves—and his inflections have a deep, breathy quality that oozes sincerity and sensuality.

"Other male singers envy Tyrone's consistent control of the only two pitches he throws," Mike Freedberg commented in a 1977 *Soul* magazine review. "His patient ballads, sung close to the mike with Tyrone practically tonguing the listener's ear, are the wonder of more formalistic baritones such as Teddy Pendergrass and Johnnie Taylor, while Tyrone's high-stepping advice songs, agonizing and full of fight, guide folks through love as if it were dangerous waters and thus get over plenty of message without sounding militant."

Although he has recorded few blues songs during his prolific career, Davis is considered a blues singer by some fans. Raised by his father in Saginaw, Michigan, he settled in Chicago in 1959 and quickly affixed himself to that city's thriving blues scene. Between day jobs, including washing cars and working at a steel mill, he served as a valet and chauffeur for blues singer-guitarist Freddie King. Davis, like his friend Otis Clay, was greatly encouraged by fellow Windy City vocalist Harold Burrage and, in 1965, made his recording debut with the Burrage-penned "Suffer" on the local Four Brothers label, which billed him as "Tyrone the Wonder Boy."

After two more minor Chicago hits on Four Brothers, Davis turned up on ABC for one 1968 single then signed with Carl Davis's new Dakar label, where he was placed in the creative hands of producer-arranger Willie Henderson. The topside of the singer's first Dakar release, "A Woman Needs to Be Loved," was, like some of his earlier recordings, a bluesy ballad rendered in a manner similar to that of

Tyrone Davis

his idol, Bobby Bland. The record appeared to be going nowhere until a Houston disc jockey known as Wild Child began playing the medium-tempo flip, "Can I Change My Mind." Davis moaned the confessional Barry Despenza–Carl Wolfolk composition at an almost lazy pace that, when set against the pronounced, quite busy bass lines of session player Bernard Reed, created an uncanny mood of tension. "Can I Change My Mind," which topped *Billboard*'s R&B chart in February 1969 and crossed over to number five pop, set a stylistic pattern that Davis continued to mine successfully into the 1980s.

Putting together a tight, brassy band along the lines of Bobby Bland's, Davis hit the road and became a hero of the so-called chitlin circuit, where he attracted a loyal corps of mostly female working-class fans. Although two of his early Dakar hits, "Can I Change My Mind" and 1970's "Turn Back the Hands of Time," had placed in the pop top five, he remained largely unknown to white listeners. By 1975, Davis had become effectively ghettoized by pop top 40 radio, which considered his music "too black" for white tastes. That year's "Turning Point," written and produced by Leo Graham and again featuring Reed's undulating bass, hit the Number One slot on the *Billboard* R&B chart yet didn't even place on the magazine's Hot 100 list because top 40 stations wouldn't touch it. It was the first Number One R&B hit of the 1970s not to make the Hot 100, a trend that would become increasingly prevalent during the remainder of the decade.

The association between Davis and Graham, which had begun when Graham co-wrote the singer's 1971 number 10 R&B hit, "Could I Forget You," reached fruition with "Turning Point," the quintessential recorded performance of Davis's career. Their professional relationship proved lasting. Leaving Dakar in 1976, Davis signed with Columbia, where three of his Graham-produced songs—"Give It Up (Turn It Loose)," "This I Swear," and "In the Mood"—managed to become top 10 hits despite the onslaught of disco. The team scored one last top 10 R&B entry in 1982 with "Are You Serious" on the Highrise label, and they continued making records together, at Ocean-Front Records, Future, and finally Ichiban, into the 1990s.

DeBARGE

The 10 offspring of Robert Louis DeBarge and the former Etterlene Abney stood out from other children in their native Grand Rapids, Michigan. The handsome products of a white father and black mother, they were the frequent targets of both disdain and curiosity. But they found solice at Bethel Pentecostal Church, where one uncle served as pastor, another as choir director. It was there that they developed their formidable vocal and instrumental talents.

Two DeBarge brothers—Bobby and Tommy—were the first to break away from gospel music. As members of Switch, they caught the ears of Jermaine Jackson, former Jackson 5 member and son-in-law of Berry Gordy, Jr., and signed with Motown Records. Switch racked up five top 40 R&B hits on the Gordy label between 1978 and '80. Back in Grand Rapids, four other siblings—Etterlene (better known as "Bunny"), Mark, Eldra ("El" for short), and James—had formed a gospel group. All sang, with Mark doubling on trumpet and saxophone and El and James playing keyboards. The DeBarges, as they were first known, soon switched to secular music and, through Jackson, auditioned for Mr. Gordy. Sensing the opportunity to groom another youthful group along the lines the Jackson 5, his great find of a decade earlier, the Motown boss signed the quartet in 1979.

The DeBarges, the group's first album, was produced by brother Bobby and issued in 1981 on the Gordy label, but it failed to attract much attention.

TOP SONGS

CAN I CHANGE MY MIND (Dakar, '68, *1 R&B, 5 Pop*)

IS IT SOMETHING YOU'VE GOT (Dakar, '69, *5 R&B, 34 Pop*)

TURN BACK THE HANDS OF TIME (Dakar, '70, *1 R&B, 3 Pop*)

I HAD IT ALL THE TIME (Dakar, '72, *5 R&B*)

WITHOUT YOU IN MY LIFE (Dakar, '73, *5 R&B*)

TURNING POINT (Dakar, '75, *1 R&B*)

GIVE IT UP (TURN IT LOOSE) (Columbia, '76, *2 R&B, 38 Pop*)

THIS I SWEAR (Columbia, '77, *6 R&B*)

IN THE MOOD (Columbia, '79, *6 R&B*)

ARE YOU SERIOUS (Highrise, '82, *3 R&B*)

Additional Top 40 R&B Songs: 24

DeBarge

By the 1982 release of the next album, *All This Love,* singing and bass-playing brother Randy had been added to the lineup, now simply known as DeBarge. While all five contributed songs and all but Mark sang leads, El (b. June 4, 1961) was clearly emerging as the group's star. He co-produced the album with Berry's niece Iris Gordy, and his clear, ringing tenor voice, which some likened to that of Michael Jackson, was featured on the set's two hit singles, "I Like It" (written by Randy and El) and the self-penned title track (which included a flamenco-style guitar solo by Jose Feliciano). El was placed in complete control of production of the third DeBarge album, 1983's *In a Special Way,* which contained the group's first Number One R&B charter, a romantic ballad titled "Time Will Reveal."

A variety of outside producers were brought in for 1985's *Rhythm of the Night.* Inspired by Lionel Richie's recent smash, "All Night Long (All Night)," the uptempo title track was produced by Richard Perry and written by Diane Warren for the Berry

Gordy, Jr., motion picture *The Last Dragon* (in which the group also appeared) and gave DeBarge its biggest hit. El returned to his trademark teen-heart-breaking ballad form for the disc's other hit single, "Who's Holding Donna Now."

If the next single, 1985's "The Heart Is Not So Smart," made it only as high as number 29 on the R&B chart, it was clear from the billing on the label—"El DeBarge with DeBarge"—that Motown was grooming the group's heartthrob for a solo career. Sure enough, El emerged the following year with his eponymous solo debut album. Curiously, the singer did not write, produce, or play on any of the tracks. The glossy, uptempo "Who's Johnny," written and produced by Peter Wolf for the sound-track of the film *Short Circuit,* took El to the top of the R&B chart and to number three pop. The fol-low-up single, "Love Always," a romantic ballad written and produced by Burt Bacharach and Carol Bayer Sager, became a number seven R&B charter. Younger brother Chico DeBarge also turned up in

1986 with a solo album on Motown, which yielded the number seven R&B hit, "Talk to Me."

The group DeBarge, reconstituted to comprise Bobby, Randy, Mark, and James, reemerged in 1987 with an album on Striped Horse, a short-lived label run by former Motown executive Barney Ales. Sales were disappointing, and the album's title, *Bad Boys,* proved to be prophetic. Bobby and Chico were arrested and convicted in 1988 for cocaine trafficking. (James had earlier stirred up controversy when his brief 1984 marriage to Janet Jackson ended in annulment.) The group's clean-cut image had been severely undermined, and no more recordings followed.

El continued to record sporadically, however. His second Gordy album produced only one hit, 1989's number eight R&B "Real Love," after which he signed with Warner Bros. He co-produced many of the tracks on 1991's *In the Storm* with Maurice White, but the number that got the most attention was "After the Dance," on which he was featured with Fourplay, an all-star crossover jazz quartet. A year earlier, El joined fellow vocalists Al B. Sure!, James Ingram, and Barry White on "The Secret Garden," a seductive Quincy Jones creation that topped the R&B chart.

TOP ALBUMS

All This Love (Gordy, '83, 24)
Rhythm of the Night (Gordy, '85, 19)
El DeBarge (El DeBarge, Gordy, '86, 24)

Additional Top 40 Albums: 1

TOP SONGS

I Like It (Gordy, '82, 2 R&B, 31 Pop)
Time Will Reveal (Gordy, '83, 1 R&B, 18 Pop)
Rhythm of the Night (Gordy, '85, 1 R&B, 3 Pop)
Who's Holding Donna Now (Gordy, '85, 2 R&B, 6 Pop)
Who's Johnny (El Debarge, Gordy, '86, 1 R&B, 3 Pop)
The Secret Garden (Quincy Jones featuring Al B. Sure!, James Ingram, El DeBarge, and Barry White, Qwest, '90, 1 R&B, 31 Pop)
After the Dance (Fourplay featuring El DeBarge, Warner Bros., '91, 2 R&B)

Additional Top 40 R&B Songs: 10

THE DELFONICS

Although the Delfonics' run on the R&B and pop top 10 lasted just two years, the innovative symphonic soul sound that arranger Thom Bell created for the high-harmony Philadelphia trio had a pronounced effect on subsequent vocal groups, the Stylistics and Blue Magic in particular. Between 1968 and '70, the Delfonics scored a string of sugar-sweet Bell-produced hits that gushed with swirling strings, foreboding bassoons, calming oboes and muted flugelhorns, triumphant French horns, and booming timpani, all anchored by the tightly locking rhythm section (guitarists Norman Harris and Roland Chambers, bassist Ronnie Baker, drummer Earl Young, and vibraharpist Vince Montana) that would become a trademark of the "Sound of Philadelphia" during the 1970s.

British author Tony Cummings commented that "Bell had taken a vocal group whose deft harmonic blend focused around a breathy high tenor lead and developed orchestrations that gave sophisticated embellishment to the vocal mood of trembling romanticism. Without jarring, he managed to combine the seeming contradiction of a black vocal style in a lavish orchestral setting."

Influenced by Little Anthony and the Imperials and Frankie Lymon and the Teenagers, lead tenor William Hart (b. Jan. 17, 1945, Washington, D.C.), his baritone-singing brother Wilbert Hart (b. Oct. 19, 1947, Washington, D.C.), second tenor Richard Daniels, and bass Ricky Johnson called themselves the Four Gents when they came together in 1964 at Philadelphia's Overbrook High School. Johnson soon dropped out to become a minister, leaving the group as a trio known as the Orphonics.

In 1966, Stan Watson, a onetime member of the Dell-Vikings, became their manager, changed their name to the Delfonics, and took them to Cameo Records, where Thom Bell was working as a pianist for Chubby Checker and trying to persuade the company to let him try his hand at producing. Watson gave Bell the opportunity, but Cameo passed on his first effort, the Delfonics' "He Don't Really Love You," so Watson sold it to the tiny MoonShot label. The record did so well in and around Philadelphia that Cameo opted to release the group's second single, 1967's "You've Been Untrue," but the company soon went belly up. Meanwhile, having received his draft notice, Daniels left the group at this point and was replaced by Randy Cain (b. May 2, 1945, Philadelphia).

Watson then formed his own Philly Groove label and secured national distribution through Bell Records. The Delfonics scored with the debut for the new label, 1968's "La -La -Means I Love You," a song inspired by the babble of William Hart's young son. It was the first of a string of six top 40 hits, all written by Hart and Bell and produced by Watson and Bell, and all featuring Hart's ethereal high tenor. It wasn't a falsetto, the singer insisted, but rather his natural voice.

When Bell left Philly Groove in 1970 to join the hot producing team of Kenny Gamble and Leon Huff at Philadelphia International Records, Watson and the Delfonics struggled on without him. But as much as they tried to emulate his now-signature sound, even using his brother Tony Bell to arrange some sessions, their chart momentum began to slip. "Over and Over," released in 1971, was the group's only post–Thom Bell offering to crack the R&B top 10. Cain left the trio in 1971 and was replaced by Major Harris (b. Feb. 9, 1947, Richmond, Virginia), a veteran of the Jarmels and the Teenagers who'd also recorded as a soloist for Okeh. Harris, however, had to wait until after leaving the group and going solo again to have a major hit, 1975's Number One R&B, number five pop "Love Won't Let You Wait."

As Bell's star ascended with hit productions for such artists as the Stylistics, Ronnie Dyson, New York City, Dionne Warwick, and especially the Spinners, the Delfonics sunk to the lower reaches of the charts, 1974's number 26 R&B "I Told You So" being their last top 40 entry. Leaving Philly Groove that year, they had little luck during a brief stay at Curtom Records and have not been heard from on vinyl since.

THE DELLS

The Dells had bounced back and forth between two Chicago record companies, Chess and Vee-Jay, for 13 years and scored only two national R&B chart hits when, in 1966, Chess decided to give the vocal quintet from nearby Harvey, Illinois, a third change. Lead baritone Marvin Junior (b. Jan. 31, 1936), lead tenor Johnny Carter (b. June, 2, 1934), second tenor Verne Allison (b. June 22, 1936), baritone Michael McGill (b. Feb. 17, 1937), and bass Chuck Barksdale (b. Jan. 11, 1935) had spent the earlier part of the decade in relative obscurity. They had toured as a backup group for Dinah Washington, opened shows for Ray Charles, and lent their top-to-bottom harmonies to countless recording sessions (including Barbara Lewis's Number One R&B, number three pop smash, "Hello Stranger"). But during their third round at Chess, the Dells came up with an uncanny fusion of doo wop and contempoary soul that resulted in a total of 22 top 40 R&B hits between 1967 and '74, all issued on the company's Cadet label.

The veteran group, whose personnel has remained unchanged since 1962, possesses one of the richest, most distinctive vocal blends in the pop music business. Carter, a former member of the Flamingos, takes the first lead on many of the tunes, crooning in a gossamer tenor or chirping in high, forceful falsetto tones reminiscent of Claude Jeter of the Swan Silvertones gospel quartet. Carter then turns the reins over to Junior, who booms in with his raspy, urgent baritone, while the others, anchored by Barksdale's resonant bass, create a full-bodied web of harmony into which Carter injects soaring, wordless strands. This finely crafted tension-release formula is perhaps best exemplified by the Dells' biggest hit, 1968's "Stay in My Corner" on Cadet, an elongated, tour de force treatment of a tune they'd recorded less successfully for Vee-Jay three years earlier.

TOP SONGS

LA - LA - MEANS I LOVE YOU (Philly Groove, '68, *2 R&B, 4 Pop*)

BREAK YOUR PROMISE (Philly Groove, '68, *12 R&B, 35 Pop*)

YOU GOT YOURS AND I'LL GET MINE (Philly Groove, '69, *6 R&B, 40 Pop*)

DIDN'T I (BLOW YOUR MIND THIS TIME) (Philly Groove, '70, *3 R&B, 10 Pop*)

TRYING TO MAKE A FOOL OF ME (Philly Groove, '70, *8 R&B, 40 Pop*)

WHEN YOU GET RIGHT DOWN TO IT (Philly Groove, '70, *12 R&B*)

OVER AND OVER (Philly Groove, '71, *9 R&B*)

WALK RIGHT UP TO THE SUN (Philly Groove, '71, *13 R&B*)

Additional Top 40 R&B Songs: 6

Initially known as the El-Rays, the group was organized in 1952 by five friends from Harvey's Thornton Township High School—Junior, Allison, McGill, Barksdale, and original lead tenor Johnny Funches—plus McGill's brother Lucius. After honing their harmonies at a local ice cream parlor and on street corners, the El-Rays cut a single the following year for Checker (a Chess subsidiary). Titled "Darling I Know," it went nowhere. Two years later, minus Lucius McGill, they began recording for Vee-Jay as the Dells. Their third release for the company, the Funches-led "Oh, What a Nite," became a national number four R&B hits and an enduring doo wop classic that the group successfully revived 13 years later, taking it all the way to the top of the *Billboard* R&B chart.

In 1958, while they were enroute to an engagement in Philadelphia, the A frame of the Dells' station wagon snapped, resulting in an accident that left McGill seriously injured. The group disbanded for nearly two years. A new edition emerged in 1960, with Johnny Carter in Funches's place. They toured and recorded with Dinah Washington for a period, then broke up again. Carter and Barksdale remained with Washington, while the other members resumed recording for Vee-Jay, with Dallas Taylor of the

Danderliers singing lead on 1962's "Swingin' Teens." Later that year, the entire group came back together to record for Argo (another Chess label), cutting four singles before returning to Vee-Jay in 1964 and recording three, including the original version of "Stay in My Corner," a number 23 R&B charter that became the group's first hit in nine years.

During their stint with Washington, the Dells had been tutored by Curt Stewart, a vocal coach who expanded their already full approach to harmony to include more complex jazz voicings reminiscent of the Hi-Lo's. It was this intricate blend, combined with the group's doo wop roots, that producer Bobby Miller and arranger Charles Stepney utilized during the late 1960s to revitalize the Dells' career with a series of lavishly orchestrated R&B and pop hits, including the new "Stay in My Corner," "Always Together," "I Can Sing a Rainbow/Love Is Blue" and the revamped "Oh, What a Night."

By 1973, the Dells were working in Detroit with Don Davis, who produced that year's "Give Your Baby a Standing Ovation," but their days as top 10 R&B hitmakers soon ended. They continued their association with Davis at Mercury in 1975 then jumped to ABC in 1978, 20th Century in 1980 (with

The Dells

TOP ALBUM

THERE IS (Cadet, '68, 29)

TOP SONGS

OH WHAT A NITE (Vee-Jay, '56, 4 R&B)
STAY IN MY CORNER (Cadet, '68, 1 R&B, 10 Pop)
ALWAYS TOGETHER (Cadet, '68, 3 R&B, 18 Pop)
I CAN SING A RAINBOW/LOVE IS BLUE (Cadet, '69, 5 R&B, 22 Pop)
OH, WHAT A NIGHT (Cadet, '69, 1 R&B, 10 Pop)
OPEN YOUR HEART (Cadet, '70, 5 R&B)
THE LOVE WE HAD (STAYS ON MY MIND) (Cadet, '71, 8 R&B, 30 Pop)
GIVE YOUR BABY A STANDING OVATION (Cadet, '73, 3 R&B, 34 Pop)
I MISS YOU (Cadet, '73, 8 R&B)

Additional Top 40 R&B Songs: 25

producers Carl Davis and Eugene Record, they made a third version of "Stay in My Corner"), Private I in 1984 (with producers Charles Jackson and Marvin Yancy), Veteran in 1988, and Urgent! in 1989. The group scored a number 13 R&B hit in 1991 with "A Heart Is a House for Love" on Virgin, from the soundtrack of the motion picture *The Five Heartbeats,* and recorded an album the following year with producers Kenny Gamble and Leon Huff for their Philadalphia International label.

BO DIDDLEY

Singer, guitarist, and songwriter Bo Diddley (b. Ellas Bates, Dec. 30, 1928, McComb, Mississippi) likes to be introduced as "the man who put the rock in rock and roll." If that claim is rather overblown, he was unique among first-generation rock stars, having fashioned, however subliminally, a rhythmically propulsive style of R&B that drew on a vast reservoir of African-American folk culture and has remained his trademark. His stage name, given to him when he was a child, derives from the diddley bow, a homemade one-string guitar of African origin, although he never played one. The "shave and a haircut, two bits" beat of "Bo Diddley," his 1955 debut record, came from the hambone, a type of body percussion often used by black children to accompany their rhymed games, and the lyrics of that record were not unlike those ring songs, although he claims never to have played them. Other African-American folk elements that Diddley brought into the pop mainstream included the "shout" rhythmic patterns of the sanctified church and the playful verbal insults of the streets, variously known as signifying, "the dozens," or, during the hip-hop era, "dissing."

The boy Diddley spent his first seven years in Mississippi before being adopted by his mother's first cousin, Gussie McDaniel (whose last name he assumed), and moving to Chicago's South Side. He studied classical violin under Professor O. W. Fredrick at Ebenezer Baptist Church and would later employ some of the techniques he learned on that instrument to his unorthodox guitar approach, marked by choppy, muted strokes. His sister Lucille gave him a guitar when he was 13, but he soon built his own—the first in a series of odd-shaped, often rectangular, instruments he would strap on throughout his career—while studying carpentry at Foster Vocational School. His early guitar influences included bluesmen John Lee Hooker and Muddy Waters.

While training to be a boxer, the teenaged Diddley began playing along Chicago's Maxwell Street as a member of the Hipsters, a trio that also included vocalist Samuel Daniel and washtub bassist Roosevelt Jackson. With the addition of maracas player Jerome Green and harmonica blower Billy Boy Arnold, the group became known as the Langley Avenue Jive Cats. Green became an important contributor to the emerging Bo Diddley sound, his maraca beats giving it a "jungle" flavor and his vocal interjections adding to the humor of Diddley's frequently boastful songs.

In 1955, Diddley took a demo of an original song titled "Uncle John" to the local Vee-Jay label, but executive Ewart Abner was unimpressed. Across the street at Chess Records, owners Phil and Leonard Chess had the opposite reaction and signed the musician. They suggested, however, that he change the name of the song to that of his own moniker. Released on the Checker label, "Bo Diddley" by Bo Diddley shot to the top of *Billboard*'s R&B chart, while "I'm a Man," the Muddy Waters–styled flip side, also received heavy airplay. The hambone beat entered the international pop music vernacular and went on to serve through the years as the basis of numerous other hits, including the Crickets' "Not Fade Away," Johnny Otis's "Willie and the Hand Jive," Shirley Ellis's "The Clapping Song (Clap Pat Clap Slap)," the Who's "Magic Bus," and U2's "Desire."

For his next hit, 1955's "Diddley Daddy," he employed a loping shuffle rhythm and the vocal backing of the Moonglows; he then returned to the hambone for the following year's Willie Dixon–penned "Pretty Thing." "Say Man," an exchange of spoken insults between Diddley and Green delivered over a Latinized shout beat, reached number three on the R&B chart and number 20 pop in 1959. It was Diddley's greatest success in the white marketplace, although his influence on white rock music in decades to come would be immense. Among the artists who would use his songs, rhythms, and raw, overdriven guitar attack to great advantage were the Rolling Stones (Mick Jagger was inspired by Green to play the maracas), the Who, the Pretty Things (a British group that named itself after one of Diddley's hits), Ronnie Hawkins, the Doors, Bruce Springsteen, Elvis Costello, George Thorogood, and the Smiths.

Although he stopped having hits after 1967's soul-tinged "Oh Baby," Diddley remained a godfather-like figure to many young rockers, including the Clash, who had him open several dates on their 1979 U.S. tour. He served as a sheriff in Los Lucas, New Mexico, during part of the 1970s, made his acting debut in the 1983 Dan Aykroyd–Eddie Murphy comedy *Trading Places,* and joined Los Lobos on their rerecording of his song "Who Do You Love?" for the soundtrack of the 1987 motion picture *La*

Bamba. Also in 1987, Diddley was among the first group of artists inducted into the Rock and Roll Hall of Fame.

FATS DOMINO

Singer, pianist, and songwriter Fats Domino (b. Antoine Domino, Feb. 26, 1928, New Orleans) was the most successful rhythm and blues recording artist of the 1950s. Between 1950 and 1961, he amassed an amazing 40 top 10 *Billboard* R&B chart entries, all on the Imperial label, most written by himself with producer-arranger Dave Bartholomew. Nine of Domino's records reached Number One R&B, collectively holding down that position for a total of 51 weeks. He was also the most successful crossover artist of that era, with 10 of his songs making the pop top 10. He is credited with having sold 65 million records, a score topped during rock's first decade only by Elvis Presley.

The endearing quality of Domino's voice, a distinctively slurred, Creole-tinged baritone, and the bounce of his boogie, two-beat, and triplet piano accompaniment had universal appeal, as did the simplicity of his songs. "Our secret was to keep it plain," Bartholomew told *New York Daily News* critic David Hinckley in 1991. "In a sense, we were doing nursery rhymes: 'You made me cry/When you said goodbye' [the opening lines of "Ain't That a Shame"]. We didn't want to go over people's heads. I've always kept the commercial side in mind."

The youngest of nine children, Domino was schooled in the art of New Orleans–style piano, a style marked by rolling bass patterns and treble arpeggios, by his brother-in-law, jazz pianist Harrison Verrett. Later influences included three Texas-born, piano-playing rhythm and blues pioneers: Charles Brown, Amos Milburn, and especially Little Willie Littlefield, whose use of steady triplet chords in the right hand would become a Domino trademark. Having quit school at age 14 and married his childhood sweetheart, Rose Mary, three years later, Domino worked in a factory by day and performed at local honky tonks by night. In 1949, while appearing at the Hideaway Club with bandleader Billy Diamond, who dubbed him "Fats," Domino was approached by trumpeter Bartholomew, then in search of artists to record for Lew Chudd's Los Angeles–based Imperial label.

TOP SONGS

Bo Diddley (Checker, '55, 1 R&B)

Diddley Daddy (Checker, '55, 11 R&B)

Pretty Thing (Checker, '56, 4 R&B)

I'm Sorry (Checker, '59, 17 R&B)

Crackin' Up (Checker, '59, 14 R&B)

Say Man (Checker, '59, 3 R&B, 20 Pop)

Say Man, Back Again (Checker, '59, 23 R&B)

Road Runner (Checker, '60, 20 R&B)

You Can't Judge a Book by Its Cover (Checker, '62, 21 R&B)

Oh Baby (Checker, '67, 17 R&B)

Additional Top 40 R&B Songs: 1

"The Fat Man," a Domino-Bartholomew adaptation of "Junker's Blues," which fellow Crescent City singer-pianist Champion Jack Dupree had recorded for Okeh in 1941, was Domino's first release and reached number two on the *Billboard* R&B chart in early 1950. After a tour with Bartholomew's band headlined by Imperial labelmate Jewel King, Domino formed his own group with the assistance of his brother-in-law. Verrett also offered an important business tip: ask the record company for royalties rather than accept the then-common practice of being paid a lump sum per session. That advice enabled Domino to continue enjoying "the fat life" he'd sung about on his first recording, even after the hits stopped coming in the mid-1960s.

Using a combination of musicians from his own and Bartholomew's band—including tenor saxophonists Lee Allen, Herb Hardesty, and Alvin "Red" Tyler; guitarists Ernest McLean and Walter "Papoose" Nelson; and drummers Cornelius Coleman and Earl Palmer—for his Imperial sessions, Domino was a consistent R&B hitmaker during the early 1950s, hitting the top of the chart for the first time with the slow blues "Goin' Home" in 1952. His second Number One R&B hit was 1955's "Ain't It a Shame"; although Pat Boone's tame cover version went to the top of the pop chart, Domino's original made it to number 10 pop, launching his rapid assent to pop stardom.

From 1956 through '63, he was a fixture on both the R&B and pop charts, not only with such songwriting collaborations with Bartholomew as "I'm in Love Again," "Blue Monday," "I'm Walkin'," "Valley of Tears, "Whole Lotta Loving," and "Walking to New Orleans" but also with unique renditions of old standards like "My Blue Heaven," "When My Dreamboat Comes Home," and, his biggest hit, "Blueberry Hill."

Upon the sale of Imperial to Liberty in 1963, Domino switched over to ABC-Paramount Records, but his new company's attempt to increase the singer's pop appeal by "sweetening" his records with such devices as strings and female choruses backfired. Domino fared even less well at Mercury in 1965 and, after an unsuccessful 1967 reunion with Bartholomew on their own Broadmoor label, signed the following year with Reprise, for whom he cut an album with producer Richard Perry that included two Beatles songs.

Domino recorded little after leaving Reprise in 1970, except for an occasional live album, a country song on the soundtrack of the 1980 Clint Eastwood comedy *Any Which Way You Can,* and a collaboration with Cajun fiddler Doug Kershaw on a 1985 cover version of the Rockin' Sidney zydeco hit, "My Toot Toot." He continued to tour, however, delighting fans around the world with his oldies and invariably ending the show by using his belly to push the piano across the stage.

TOP ALBUM

Rock and Rollin' with Fats Domino (Imperial, '57, 17)

Additional Top 40 Albums: 2

TOP SONGS

Goin' Home (Imperial, '52, 1 R&B, 30 Pop)
Ain't It a Shame (Imperial, '55, 1 R&B, 10 Pop)
All by Myself (Imperial, '55, 1 R&B)
Poor Me (Imperial, '55, 1 R&B)
I'm in Love Again (Imperial, '56, 1 R&B, 3 Pop)
Blueberry Hill (Imperial, '56, 1 R&B, 2 Pop)
Blue Monday (Imperial, '56, 1 R&B, 5 Pop)
I'm Walkin' (Imperial, '57, 1 R&B, 4 Pop)
I Want to Walk You Home (Imperial, '59, 1 R&B, 8 Pop)

Additional Top 40 R&B Songs: 50

LEE DORSEY

Although New Orleans pianist-arranger Allen Toussaint composed and/or produced numerous hits for such artists as Ernie K-Doe, Al Hirt, Herb Alpert, LaBelle, and Glen Campbell, he saved many of his best songs for auto body and fender repairman Lee Dorsey (b. Irving Lee Dorsey, Dec. 24, 1926, New Orleans). The diminutive singer, whose dry, somewhat nasal vocal delivery overflowed with infectious humor and rhythmic vitality, scored hits during the 1960s with such Toussaint-penned-and-produced numbers as "Ride Your Pony," "Get Out of My Life, Woman," and "Working in a Coal Mine" and also cut the original versions of such Toussaint classics as "Yes We Can," "Sneakin' Sally Thru the Alley," "Freedom for the Stallion," and "Night People."

TOP SONGS

YA YA (Fury, '61, *1 R&B, 7 Pop*)

DO-RE-MI (Fury, '62, *22 R&B, 27 Pop*)

RIDE YOUR PONY (Amy, '65, *7 R&B, 28 Pop*)

GET OUT OF MY LIFE, WOMAN (Amy, '66, *5 R&B*)

WORKING IN A COAL MINE (Amy, '66, *5 R&B, 8 Pop*)

HOLY COW (Amy, '66, *10 R&B, 23 Pop*)

GO-GO GIRL (Amy, '67, *31 R&B*)

EVERYTHING I DO GOHN BE FUNKY (FROM NOW ON) (Amy, '69, *33 R&B*)

"If a smile had a sound," Toussaint once stated, "it would be the sound of Lee Dorsey's voice. It's no wonder that he inspired so many of my favorite songs: songs that, if not for him, I would never have written."

A childhood friend of Fats Domino, Dorsey left the Crescent City with his family at age 10 and settled in Portland, Oregon, where he developed a fondness for country music. After serving as a gunner on a Navy destroyer in the Pacific during World War II, he pursued a career as "Kid Chocolate," a lightweight boxer with an unbroken string of wins, before returning to New Orleans in 1955 and getting a job at a body shop.

He loved to sing while hammering out dents and one day caught the attention of Reynauld Richards, a local talent scout who had come to get his car fixed. Richards took Dorsey to Cosimo Matassa's studio, where the singer cut his first record, the self-composed "Rock, Pretty Baby," issued in 1957 on the Rex label. A moderate hit around town, it led to a second recording two years later—Dorsey's "Lottie Mo," backed with Toussaint's "Lover of Love"—produced by the pianist for the Valiant label. The record's local success inspired Toussaint to decide to focus on writing and producing from then on, rather than on trying to earn his living as a piano player in clubs. It was picked up by ABC-Paramount, and while it did not chart nationally, it earned Dorsey a spot on Dick Clark's "American Bandstand." Perhaps more importantly, it caught the ears of record promotion man Marshall Sehorn, who felt the singer had great potential due to his tonal similarity to Ray Charles.

Through Sehorn, Dorsey signed with Bobby Robinson's Harlem-based Fury Records. Toussaint was unavailable for the singer's debut Fury session due to contractual ties to another company, so Marcel Richardson substituted, giving the band a similar rhumba boogie piano flavor. The song, "Ya Ya," inspired by an off-color children's game song and sanitized by Dorsey for mass consumption, gave the vocalist a massive hit in 1961 that topped *Billboard*'s R&B chart and reached number seven on the pop chart. Toussaint returned to play on "Do-Re-Mi," a moderately successful follow-up written by Earl King, but he was soon inducted into the Army. Dorsey and Sehorn floundered on Fury, Mercury, and Constellation until Toussaint returned to New Orleans in 1965.

"Ride Your Pony," written by Toussaint and produced by him and Sehorn, marked the beginning of a two-year string of top 10 R&B dance hits for Dorsey on the Amy label and led to a formal business partnership between Toussaint and Sehorn that lasted two decades. With those recordings, on which the pianist often sang call-and-response parts to Dorsey's leads, Toussaint developed the syncopated rhythm

Lee Dorsey

style, rooted in second-line street parade beats, that became synonymous with New Orleans funk, especially in the later Toussaint and Sehorn-produced instrumental hits of the Meters, who also backed Dorsey on 1969's "Everything I Do Gohn Be Funky (From Now On)" and the following year's "Yes We Can" (later the debut hit for the Pointer Sisters).

Dorsey returned to body shop work during the 1970s, his two brilliant albums of that decade— 1970's *Yes We Can* on Polydor and 1978's *Night People* on ABC—being largely overlooked, except by a devoted cult of rock fans and musicians. That cult included Southside Johnny and the Asbury Dukes, who featured him on their first album in 1976, and the influential British punk band the Clash, which invited him to be the opening act on its 1980 U.S. tour. Such diverse artists as the Band, Devo, the Judds, John Lennon, Little Feat, and Robert Palmer recorded songs originally made by Dorsey, but he died in relative obscurity, of emphysema, on December 1, 1986.

THE DRAMATICS

It's probably a good thing success didn't come overnight to the Dramatics. So many other Detroit groups of the 1960s made it to the top quickly, only to be broken apart by ego conflicts. Although they had their share of dissension and trouble, the Dramatics took their time, polished their harmony and choreography, and became one of the biggest soul vocal groups of the 1970s, scoring nine top 10 R&B hits between 1971 and '80.

Originally known as the Dynamics, the group was formed in 1962 when 13-year-old tenor Ron Banks, a student at Detroit's Cleveland Junior High School, hooked up with second tenor Larry Reed, baritone Robert Ellington, and bass Arthur Phillips, all from Pershing High School, to enter a talent contest. After Larry "Squirrel" Demps, Elbert Wilkins, and Roderick Davis had replaced Reed, Ellington, and Phillips, the quartet was discovered while performing at Mr. Kelly's in Detroit and signed to the local Wingate label. Although it didn't make it beyond Detroit, the Dramatics' first single, a bright Temptations-styled number titled "Inky Dinky Wang Dan Doo," displayed the top-to-bottom harmony that has become one of their trademarks.

Another Dramatics' calling card has been their

fast-paced choreography. Davis explained the origins to author John Hersey for his 1968 best-seller, *The Algiers Motel Incident:* "One time in 1965 we were watching a group called the Contours do a show, and we saw the M.C. call out the names of the guys in the group, and each one came out sliding and jumping up on the opposite sidewall and came back doing splits. This gave us the idea for our routine, and we've used it ever since."

The Dramatics' first (although minor) national hit, "All Because of You," had just dropped off the *Billboard* R&B chart when they checked into Detroit's Algiers Motel on July 23, 1967, following a concert appearance with George Clinton's Parliaments. Massive riots had broken out in the ghetto, and the group sought refuge. Two days later, their valet and two other motel guests were mysteriously murdered, allegedly by police.

The group survived the tragedy, but hard times set in, and Davis left. He was replaced by Willie Ford, and a fifth member, lead baritone William "Weegee" Howard, was added. "We were all determined to make it," Howard recalled, "although we didn't know if we ever would."

Detroit producer Don Davis came to their rescue in 1968 and signed the group to Stax-Volt Records in Memphis. The first Volt single, "Your Love Was Strange," flopped, and the Dramatics were dropped by the company, only to be re-signed two years later

---

TOP ALBUM

WHATCHA SEE IS WHATCHA GET (Volt, 72, 20)

Additional Top 40 Albums: 1

TOP SONGS

WHATCHA SEE IS WHATCHA GET (Volt, '71, *3 R&B, 9 Pop*)

IN THE RAIN (Volt, '72, *1 R&B, 5 Pop*)

HEY YOU! GET OFF MY MOUNTAIN (Volt, '73, *5 R&B*)

ME AND MRS. JONES (ABC, '75, *4 R&B*)

YOU'RE FOOLING YOU (ABC, '75, *10 R&B*)

BE MY GIRL (ABC, '76, *3 R&B*)

I CAN'T GET OVER YOU (ABC, '77, *9 R&B*)

SHAKE IT WELL (ABC, '77, *4 R&B*)

WELCOME HOME (MCA, '80, *9 R&B*)

Additional Top 40 R&B Songs: 14

when Davis put them in the creative hands of his associate, songwriter-producer Tony Hester. The Hester sound, which showcased the group's multi-lead vocals, immediately took the Dramatics to the top. The lively "Whatcha See Is Whatcha Get" gave them their first gold single, and the album of the same title yielded "In the Rain," a melancholy ballad that went Number One R&B and number five pop. An eight-month cross-country tour with James Brown helped to solidify a fervent following for the group. Howard and Wilkins left the fold in 1972 to form a splinter group, and for the next four years, two sets of Dramatics toured the concert circuit. The Howard-Wilkins group, which also included Dupree Sims and Isaac Reed, signed with Mainstream Records but had only a minor hit, 1975's number 26 R&B "No Rebate on Love." The other set changed its billing to "Ron Banks and the Dramatics," and with L. J. Reynolds and Lenny Mayes having filled the vacancies, continued having hits on Volt, Cadet, ABC, and MCA.

When Reynolds and Demps quit in 1980, Craig Jones was hired, and the Dramatics were again a quartet. After the 1983 Capitol album *New Dimensions,* the group disbanded. Banks launched a solo career at Columbia, following Howard and Reynolds, who had already done solo albums for Cotillion and Capitol respectively. Three years later, however, Banks, Reynolds, Howard, Mayes, and Ford got back together to make a reunion album for Fantasy. All but Howard decided to stick together, and with new member Steve Boyd, they recorded two albums for the reactivated Volt label, a division of Fantasy.

In 1993, the Dramatics contributed their full-bodied harmonies to "Doggy Doggy World," a track on *Doggystyle,* the Number One album debut by controversial rapper Snoop Doggy Dog.

The Dramatics

THE DRIFTERS

Few vocal groups racked up as many hits over such a long period of time as the Drifters. Between 1953 and 1967, they scored a remarkable 29 entries on the *Billboard* top 40 R&B chart and 15 on the pop top 40. Then, after a period in which their U.S. itinerary had been relegated to the oldies circuit, they suddenly became high-profile in England, where they had 11 top 40 hits between 1972 and '76.

During their 23 years of chart success, the Drifters had even more members than they did hits. Personnel shifted constantly, and, indeed, the group that recorded between 1953 and '58 was entirely different from the one that recorded from 1958 on, both in style and membership. At least a dozen lead singers were featured over the long stretch, the most notable being Clyde McPhatter, Johnny Moore, Ben E. King, and Rudy Lewis. And to add to the confusion, numerous groups have toured under the Drifters' banner since the 1960s.

The Drifters' story began in early 1953 when McPhatter, whose soaring gospel tenor had led Billy Ward's Dominoes through three years of R&B chart success, left the former group and was signed to Atlantic Records with a mandate to build a new group around himself. He recruited four men from the Mount Lebanon Singers, a Harlem gospel group with which he had sung before becoming a Domino. This aggregation did one session for Atlantic, but the results were deemed too raw and kept in the can for a period. McPhatter then hired four other former gospel singers—tenors Bill Pinkney and Andrew Thrasher, baritone Gerhart Thrasher, and bass Willie Ferbie—although Ferbie soon dropped out and Pinkney took over the vocal bottom. This lineup topped the R&B chart with "Money Honey," the Drifters' first release, followed by five more R&B top 10 hits. ("Lucille," a 1954 release that reached number seven, was by the rejected Mount Lebanon edition.)

By the time the group's last McPhatter-led hit, 1955's "What'Cha Gonna Do," was issued, he had left to begin a successful solo career and was replaced temporarily by David Baughan (from the earlier Mount Lebanon lineup) before Johnny Moore came aboard. The Cleveland vocalist led on many of the group's songs, including 1956's Number One R&B "Adorable," until the Army called the

next year. His place was taken by Bobby Hendricks, later of "Itchy Twitchy Feeling" fame.

While fixtures on the R&B chart, the Drifters' records had seldom penetrated the pop market, a situation that changed radically in 1958, when manager George Treadwell fired the entire group during an engagement at Harlem's Apollo Theater and hired the Crowns, an obscure local act on the same show, to become the new Drifters. Comprising lead Ben E. King plus Charlie Thomas, James "Poppa" Clark, Doc Green, and Elsbury Hobbs, this edition worked at Atlantic with producers Jerry Leiber and Mike Stoller to create a lavishly orchestrated, often Latin-tinged style that had instant pop and R&B appeal and would greatly influence the direction of soul music during the 1960s, especially the work of producers Phil Spector, Burt Bacharach, and Bert Berns (all of whom worked on Drifters sessions), and the Motown sound in general.

After contributing his soothing lead tenor to such massive crossover hits as "There Goes My Baby" and "Save the Last Dance for Me," King opted for a solo career and was replaced by Rudy Lewis, the emotive lead on 1961's "Some Kind of Wonderful" (number six R&B, number 32 pop), 1962's "Up on the Roof" (number four R&B, number five pop), and 1963's "On Broadway" (number seven R&B, number nine pop). Johnny Moore had rejoined the

---

TOP ALBUM

UNDER THE BOARDWALK (Atlantic, '64, *40*)

TOP SONGS

Clyde McPhatter and the Drifters:
MONEY HONEY (Atlantic, '53, *1 R&B*)
SUCH A NIGHT (Atlantic, '54, *2 R&B*)

The Drifters featuring Clyde McPhatter:
HONEY LOVE (Atlantic, '54, *1 R&B, 21 Pop*)
WHITE CHRISTMAS (Atlantic, '54, *2 R&B*)
WHAT'CHA GONNA DO (Atlantic, '55, *2 R&B*)

The Drifters:
ADORABLE (Atlantic, '55, *1 R&B*)
THERE GOES MY BABY (Atlantic, '59, *1 R&B, 2 Pop*)
DANCE WITH ME (Atlantic, '59, *2 R&B, 15 Pop*)
SAVE THE LAST DANCE FOR ME (Atlantic, '60, *1 R&B, 1 Pop*)

Additional Top 40 R&B Songs: 20

group by 1963, and, after Lewis's death the following year, he became lead singer again, debuting on the Berns-produced "Under the Boardwalk," the group's last top 10 pop hit in the U.S.

Moore remained at the helm as other members left, but Atlantic was unable to keep the group in the upper reaches of the charts. After trying several different producers, the company dropped the Drifters in 1971. The next year, however, British Atlantic reissued "Saturday Night at the Movies," a modestly successful Drifters song from eight years earlier, and it became a hit. Taking notice, Bell Records signed the group (now composed of Moore, Bill Fredericks, Grant Kitchings, and Butch Leake), hooked it up with pop producers Roger Cook and Roger Greenway, and scored with such top 10 U.K. hits as "Kissin' in the Back Row at the Movies," "There Goes My First Love," and "You're More Than Number One in My Little Red Book." Another set of Drifters, led by Charlie Thomas, also recorded in England during this period, for EMI International, but with far less luck.

EARTH, WIND
AND FIRE

In 1970, after four years as an ace Chicago studio drummer and three more on the road with crossover jazz pianist Ramsey Lewis, Maurice White (b. Dec. 19, 1941, Memphis) conceived of his own group, a large, boldly eclectic unit that would bring together elements of soul, jazz, rock, gospel, and African music; deliver uplifting, often mystical messages; and, hopefully, appeal to audiences of all races. Five years later, after opening engagements for everyone from Uriah Heep and Santana to Weather Report and Parliament-Funkadelic, White's Earth, Wind and Fire emerged as a major concert headliner. Over the next six years, they remained African-American music's greatest crossover success story.

White, often working in tandem with former Chess staff arranger Charles Stepney, fashioned tunes around individual members' musical personalities. He used a five-man horn section to achieve big band–like textures, voicing the blaring trumpets on top to enhance the excitement, into which as many as eight vocalists would weave wordless horn-like lines. In concert, White would sometimes step from

behind his timbales and continue beating with his sticks as if there were still drums before him, the band matching his silent thrashings beat for beat. He was no longer playing the drums: he was playing Earth, Wind and Fire.

While White is also a vocalist of considerable ability, Philip Bailey was the band's singing star, whether sailing in falsetto duet with the leader on "That's the Way of the World" or wailing on his own on "Reasons." Other significant members during EW&F's heyday included guitarist Al McKay, keyboardist Larry Dunn, trombonist Louis Satterfield, saxophonists Don Myrick and Andrew Woolfolk, and Maurice's two brothers, bassist Verdine and drummer Fred.

The group's concerts were theatrical spectacles that included magic acts created by Doug Henning and David Copperfield. At one point in the show, White would cover five members with red sheets as they sat in a row of chairs, then pull off the sheets one by one. Presto!—everybody was gone, only to turn up seconds later locked in a clear plastic cage atop a pyramid-shaped platform at the back of the stage.

A doctor's son, White sang gospel music and took up the traps in Memphis before settling in Chicago at age 16. While studying at the Chicago Conservatory of Music, he began doing studio work, beginning with Betty Everett's 1963 Vee-Jay hit, "You're No Good." Over the next four years, he lent his deft touch to countless sessions, including records by Fontella Bass, Chuck Berry, Buddy Guy, John Lee Hooker, Howlin' Wolf, the Impressions, Etta James, Ramsey Lewis, Billy Stewart, Sonny Stitt, Muddy Waters, and Jackie Wilson, that provided an eclectic grounding for his future pursuits. A week spent subbing for Elvin Jones in John Coltrane's group, as well as a trip to Egypt as a member of the Ramsey Lewis Trio, whetted the drummer's interest in metaphysical philosophy. Also while working with Lewis, White began featuring the kalimba, a hand-held African thumb piano that would become his trademark.

White's first group, the Salty Dogs, formed in 1969, evolved into Earth, Wind and Fire. The original 10-member edition cut two wildly experimental albums for Warner Bros. in 1971 then regrouped as an octet and signed with Columbia. EW&F had grown to 16 members by 1974, the year they scored their first top 10 R&B hits: "Mighty Mighty" and "Kalimba Story." The next year, they recorded the

Earth, Wind and Fire

soundtrack for and appeared in the low-budget motion picture *That's the Way of the World*. The film bombed, but EW&F's career exploded, with an album of the same name going to Number One and the single "Shining Star" doing likewise on both the R&B and pop charts. Too busy to record a follow-up album, the band issued a two-disc set of concert performances titled *Gratitude* that also shot to Number One, while its studio-made single, "Sing a Song," toppped the R&B chart.

White, who formed his own Kalimba Productions and, eventually, the Columbia-distributed ARC label, became much in demand as a producer. Among his credits between 1976 and '86 were hits by Ramsey Lewis, the Emotions, Deniece Williams, Jennifer Holliday, Barbra Streisand, and Neil Diamond.

EW&F broke up in 1983. White recorded a solo vocal album in 1985 that included his number six R&B revamp of the old Ben E. King hit "Stand by Me." Bailey also launched a solo career, as both a pop and gospel artist, achieving his greatest success with "Easy Lover," a 1984 number three R&B, number two pop duet with Phil Collins. White and Bailey reorganized EW&F in 1987 and hit the top of the R&B chart for the last time with "System of Survival" from the album *Touch the World*. After the

relative failure of 1989's *Heritage,* in which they attempted to update their sound with guest appearences by the Boys and rapper M. C. Hammer, EW&F returned to Warner Bros., where their album *Millennium* appeared in 1993 on the Reprise label.

TOP ALBUMS

THAT'S THE WAY OF THE WORLD (Columbia, '75, *1*)
GRATITUDE (Columbia, '75, *1*)

Additional Top 40 Albums: 12

TOP SONGS

SHINING STAR (Columbia, '75, *1 R&B, 1 Pop*)
SING A SONG (Columbia, '75, *1 R&B, 5 Pop*)
GETAWAY (Columbia, '76, *1 R&B, 12 Pop*)
SERPENTINE FIRE (Columbia, '77, *1 R&B, 13 Pop*)
GOT TO GET YOU INTO MY LIFE (Columbia, '78, *1 R&B, 9 Pop*)
SEPTEMBER (ARC, '78, *1 R&B, 8 Pop*)
LET'S GROOVE (ARC, '81, *1 R&B, 3 Pop*)
SYSTEM OF SURVIVAL (Columbia, '87, *1 R&B*)

Additional Top 40 R&B Songs: 30

The Emotions

THE EMOTIONS

The Emotions were the most popular female vocal group of the 1970s, not just because they were young, gifted, and irresistibly cute but also because their style was decidedly different from that of any other. Their harmony was sweet and fluffy, like cotton candy without being saccharine. It simultaneously evoked the innocence of youth and the sensuality of womanhood. Like other family groups, from the Boswell Sisters and the Mills Brothers to the Staple Singers and the Bee Gees, sisters Sheila, Wanda, and Jeanette Hutchinson achieved an uncanny vocal blend that is the result of shared genes and a lifetime of singing together.

The Hutchinsons were in their mid-teens when Pervis Staples, who'd left his family group to pursue the business side of music, brought them to the attention of Stax-Volt Records. Yet they'd been honing their harmony for over a decade, with their father serving as vocal coach. Based on Chicago's South Side, Joe Hutchinson, Sr., was a member of the Wings of Heaven during the 1950s. At home, he began trying out vocal arrangements for the quartet

with Sheila, Wanda, and Jeanette, then aged three, four, and five. Sheila sang leads on the slower selections, Wanda on the faster ones, a pattern they followed throughout their career.

Besides schooling them in traditional gospel quartet sounds, their father also had them experimenting with Four Freshman–styled modern jazz harmonies. "We began to develop our ear for harmony," Jeanette remembered. "When the Wings of Heaven would go to church to sing those songs, we'd be in the back singing along, and a lot of people would look back at us."

Joe, Sr., soon abandoned the quartet and formed the Hutchinson Sunbeams, consisting of the girls plus himself as lead singer and guitarist. They performed on gospel programs around Chicago with the likes of Mahalia Jackson and the Staple Singers during the late 1950s and early '60s. Beginning in 1962, the group recorded for such Chicago labels as Onederful! and Tollie under various names, including Heavenly Sunbeams and Three Ribbons and a Bow. (Papa Joe was the beau.) Switching to secular music in 1967, they became the Emotions and signed with the local Twin Stacks label, scoring several hits around their hometown. With their father serving in an advisory capacity, the group jumped from Twin Stacks to Stax.

The Memphis company assigned the hitmaking team of Isaac Hayes and David Porter to produce the Emotions. The trio's first release on the firm's Volt subsidiary, a Sheila Hutchinson ballad titled "So I Can Love You," was quite unlike anything Stax had recorded. The soft-soul song featured the sisters' velvety, gospel-tinged harmonies backed by a infectiously loping beat and Hayes's appropriately wispy organ fills. Going to number three on the *Billboard* R&B chart in 1969, it was the biggest hit of the group's six-year association with Stax. After Hayes ascended to superstar status, the Emotions were bounced around between various staff producers. Although they had a total of nine top 40 R&B hits at Stax, the material was uneven.

Jeanette left the Emotions in 1970 to get married and was replaced for four years by cousin Theresa Davis. Jeanette returned to the fold for two years but left again in 1976 and was replaced by younger sister Pamela. By 1979, they were a quintet consisting of Jeanette, Wanda, Sheila, and brother Joe, Jr., who played guitar and occasionally sang.

After Stax went belly up, the Emotions were contracted by Earth, Wind and Fire leader Maurice White, who had once played with them when they were the Sunbeams. White signed the group to Kalimba Productions, and a string of uptempo disco-flavored hits followed, including the double-sided "Flowers"/"I Don't Want to Lose Your Love" and

the Number One R&B and pop ""Best of My Love." While members of Earth, Wind and Fire played on those songs, the whole group teamed up with the Emotions for 1979's "Boogie Wonderland." Leaving White's ARC label in 1981, the group resurfaced three years later with several minor hits on Red Label. An album for Motown in 1985, by which time Pamela had been replaced by Adrianne Harris, yielded no chart action, and the Emotions disbanded shortly thereafter.

EN VOGUE

Terry Ellis, Cindy Herron, Maxine Jones, and Dawn Robinson barely knew one another before 1988. San Francisco native Herron was working as an actress in Los Angeles. Ellis lived in Houston, where she first met Herron at an audition for Olympic athlete Carl Lewis's band. Jones and Robinson both lived in Oakland and had sung together only at an impromptu jam session at a local hair salon where Jones worked and Robinson was a customer.

When the four women, all then in their mid-20s, showed up at an audition for Denzil Foster and Thomas McElroy, the hitmaking Oakland record production and songwriting team known for its previous work with Timex Social Club, Club Nouveau, Tony! Toni! Toné!, and Michael Cooper, it was quickly apparent that the singers had a harmony mix so special it was like they'd been born to sing together. Initially dubbed U-4, then Vogue, they ended up contributing to *FM2*, a 1989 Atlantic album by Foster-McElroy. "I think we were really fortunate and lucky to get four women whose voices fit the way theirs did," McElroy stated. "It was kind of like God's blessing."

"I say it's divine order," added group member Jones. "Before we came together, I had a problem blending with different people. For some reason, when we got together for the audition, it worked. My voice fit right in with theirs. I guess we all have the same tone qualities in our voices. Something's alike there." Renamed En Vogue and signed to Atlantic, the four saw their debut single, 1990's "Hold On," become a Number One R&B, number two pop hit. The group's strong blend—polished, yet with a raw gospel edge—was evident from the opening bars of "Hold On," a medium-tempo number by

---

TOP ALBUMS

REJOICE (Columbia, '77, 7)
SUNBEAM (Columbia, '78, *40*)

TOP SONGS

SO I CAN LOVE YOU (Volt, '69, *3 R&B, 39 Pop*)
SHOW ME HOW (Volt, '71, *13 R&B*)
FLOWERS (Columbia, '77, *16 R&B*)
I DON'T WANT TO LOSE YOUR LOVE (Columbia, '77, *13 R&B*)
BEST OF MY LOVE (Columbia, '77, *1 R&B, 1 Pop*)
DON'T ASK MY NEIGHBORS (Columbia, '77, *7 R&B*)
SMILE (Columbia, '78, *6 R&B*)
BOOGIE WONDERLAND (Earth, Wind and Fire with the Emotions, ARC, '79, *2 R&B, 6 Pop*)

Additional Top 40 R&B Songs: 11

EnVogue

TOP ALBUMS

BORN TO SING (Atlantic, '90, *21*)
FUNKY DIVAS (EastWest, '92, *8*)

TOP SONGS

HOLD ON (Atlantic, '90, *1 R&B, 2 Pop*)
LIES (Atlantic, '90, *1 R&B, 38 Pop*)
YOU DON'T HAVE TO WORRY (Atlantic, '90, *1 R&B*)
DON'T GO (Atlantic, '91, *3 R&B*)
MY LOVIN' (YOU'RE NEVER GONNA GET IT)
    (EastWest, '92, *1 R&B, 2 Pop*)
GIVING HIM SOMETHING HE CAN FEEL (EastWest,
    '92, *1 R&B, 6 Pop*)
GIVE IT UP, TURN IT LOOSE (EastWest, '92,
    16 R&B, 15 Pop)
RUNAWAY LOVE (En Vogue featuring FMOB,
    EastWest, '93, *15 R&B*)

Additional Top 40 R&B Songs: 2

the quartet and producers Foster and McElroy, which began with a brief a cappella rendition of Smokey Robinson's "Who's Loving You."

The pairing of "Who's Loving You" and "Hold On" was an accident. Foster had suggested "Who's Loving You" as a practice song for the singers. "We just wanted to work up the harmonies," Jones explained. "The little bit that you hear on the record is as far as we had gotten." Following it on the practice tape was a hip-hop rhythm that McElroy had been experimenting with on a drum machine. When Foster heard the two fragments juxtaposed, he, his partner, and the women set about composing "Hold On" to fit the drum beat.

A cappella singing quickly became an En Vogue trademark and launched a widespread revival of unaccompanied harmony in African-American popular music. At the 1991 *Billboard* Awards ceremony, where "Hold On" was named Best R&B Single of the previous year, the group sang its "thank you" to the melody of the hit, instead of giving a speech. And at Lakers and Warriors basketball games, En Vogue delivered elaborately arranged renditions of the national anthem.

"Hold On" was included in the group's first album, 1991's *Born to Sing,* which contained two other Number One R&B hits: "Lies" and "Don't Go." En Vogue's huge success led to a renewed inter-

est in female vocal groups, and such others as SWV (Sisters with Voices) and Jade followed in their footsteps.

Funky Divas, the group's sophomore album release, issued in 1992 on Atlantic's subsidiary EastWest label, gave the women two more R&B chart-toppers: the fast, funky Foster-McElroy composition "My Lovin' (You're Never Gonna Get It)" and a remake of "Giving Him Something He Can Feel," a churchy Curtis Mayfield ballad that Aretha Franklin had taken to Number One on the R&B chart 12 years earlier. The disc's third single, a bold, rock-imbued Foster-McElroy song titled "Free Your Mind," didn't fare as well. Intended as a missive against racial prejudice, it was largely rejected by black consumers and went only as high as number 23 on the R&B chart. It did much better on the pop chart, however, peaking a number eight.

En Vogue's success as the most popular female vocal group of the early 1990s drew frequent comparisons to that of Diana Ross and the Supremes during the '60s. While flattered, Jones pointed out that, unlike the Supremes, all four members of En Vogue take turns singing lead. "When the Supremes were out," she added, "they were like the sophisticated girl group of the time. I think they paved the way for us to be able to do what we're doing now."

BETTY EVERETT

Throughout a professional singing career that spanned 22 years, Betty Everett (b. Nov. 23, 1939, Greenwood, Mississippi) was torn between the morality of her strict religious upbringing and the sometimes saucy messages of the secular songs that made her one of the most popular soul singers of the 1960s. "I didn't really want to sing the blues," she recalled. "My parents never wanted me to—never did and still don't."

Everett sang and played piano as a child at her hometown's Jones Chapel Baptist Church and, by age 14, was also playing for two other local congregations. Three years later, however, she fell in love with a blues singer who was passing through the area and followed him to Chicago. She then joined Muddy Waters' blues band but, due to stage fright, left after a week-long engagement in Cleveland. Back in Chicago, she hooked up with West Side blues guitarist Magic Sam, who took her to Cobra Records.

TOP SONGS

THE SHOOP SHOOP SONG (IT'S IN HIS KISS) (Vee-Jay,
 '64, 6 *Pop*)

LET IT BE ME (Betty Everett and Jerry Butler,
 Vee-Jay, '64, 5 *Pop*)

THERE'LL COME A TIME (Uni, '69, 17 *R&B*)

I CAN'T SAY NO TO YOU (Uni, '69, 29 *R&B*)

IT'S BEEN A LONG TIME (Uni, '69, 17 *R&B*)

I GOT TO TELL SOMEBODY (Fantasy, '70, 22 *R&B*)

AIN'T NOTHING GONNA CHANGE ME (Fantasy, '71,
 32 *R&B*)

SWEET DAN (Fantasy, '74, 38 *R&B*)

Working with bassist-producer Willie Dixon, the singer waxed three singles for the company in 1958 and '59 on which she was backed by such prominent blues players as Little Brother Montgomery, Ike Turner, and Wayne Bennett. Turner was so taken with her voice that he brought her to St. Louis to join his band, but her stay was brief, due to her dismay at the loose morality of Turner and his musicians.

Still singing jump blues and gospel-flavored blues ballads, Everett recorded for Chicago's obscure C.J. label in 1960 before moving in a more modern soul direction the following year at manager Leo Austell's Renee Records. Her Monk Higgins–produced Renee recording of "Your Love Is Important to Me" became a hit in Chicago and was picked up by the larger One-derful! label. Everett's local success was noted by Vee-Jay producer Calvin Carter, who signed her in 1963.

Carter took his new artist down a pop path, choosing material for her by a series of New York songwriters. With the Dells providing foot stomps, Clint Ballard, Jr.'s "You're No Good" gave the vocalist her first national chart entry, although it rose only as high as number 51 on the *Billboard* pop chart, its popularity in the 1963 R&B market masked by the fact that the magazine was not publishing an R&B chart during that period. (The song was revived 12 years later by Linda Ronstadt, who took it to Number One pop.) Everett scored her biggest solo success in 1964 with Rudy Clark's "The Shoop Shoop Song (It's in His Kiss)," a pop ditty of the then-popular Brill Building "girl group" genre on which she was joined vocally by the Opals.

A duet with Vee-Jay labelmate Jerry Butler, a romantic reprise of the Everly Brothers' earlier hit "Let It Be Me," gave Everett her only other top 10

pop single. A follow-up with Butler, the Charlie Chaplin chestnut "Smile," sold moderately well, but subsequent solo Vee-Jay sides by Everett failed to chart, despite material from Gerry Goffin and Carole King and from Nick Ashford, Valerie Simpson, and Joshie Jo Armstread. Following Vee-Jay's demise, Everett went to ABC-Paramount and cut four 45s (including another Ashford-Simpson-Armstead offering), none of which charted.

Renewing her association with manager Austell, the vocalist signed with MCA's Uni subsidiary in 1968 and scored her biggest R&B chart hit, "There'll Come a Time," a bluesy, gospel-flavored ballad penned by Eugene Record of the Chi-Lites and Floyd Smith. After two more R&B charters at Uni, she moved in 1970 to Fantasy Records, where she was reunited with producer Carter. Two plaintively sung singles, "I Got to Tell Somebody" and "Ain't Nothing Gonna Change Me," both arranged by Donny Hathaway, were moderate sellers, after which Fantasy paired her with Memphis hitmaker Willie Mitchell for two that proved to be total flops. She returned to the R&B top 40 for the last time in 1974 with the sizzling "Sweet Dan," a number written and produced by blues-and-funk man Johnny "Guitar" Watson that, she said at the time, was "a little too involved with sex, as far as I'm concerned." And, she complained, "I don't believe in using God's name in the blues."

Everett continued cutting singles for Sound Stage 7, United Artists, and 20th Century Fox, alternating between producers Austell and Carter, but retired from the music business in 1980, frustrated by lack of sales and by the fact that no company would allow her to record an album of the gospel music that had become increasingly close to her heart.

THE 5 ROYALES

While many, perhaps most, male rhythm and blues vocal groups trace their stylistic roots to gospel quartets, none injected more raw church passion into their music than the 5 Royales (pronounced with the emphasis on "-ales"). In fact, the Winston-Salem, North Carolina–based quintet began in gospel and made the switch from spiritual to secular, in the midst of a single 1951 session for Apollo Records, by simply altering the lyrics to one of the religious numbers in its repertoire.

The 5 Royales had only one strong year on the R&B charts—1953, during which two of their songs held down the Number One position for a total of eight weeks—yet their impact on the development of soul music was profound. Their urgent, unpolished vocal delivery, along with that of Hank Ballard's Midnighters, was a major influence on James Brown and the Famous Flames. And Steve Cropper, Stax session musician and member of Booker T. and the MG's during the 1960s, modeled his razor-edged, alternating rhythm and lead guitar attack on that of the Royales' Lowman Pauling, Jr.

Originally known as the Royal Sons Quintet, the group was formed in Winston-Salem in 1938 and included brothers Lowman, Clarence, and Curtis Pauling, whose father, Lowman Pauling, Sr., had been a West Virginia coal miner who also sang and played guitar with a gospel quartet. Touring as far north as Ohio, the group at first specialized in jubilee numbers by the Golden Gate Quartet before adding more modern gospel material associated with the Soul Stirrers and the Dixie Hummingbirds. By the time the Royal Sons began recording, in 1951 for Apollo, Clarence and Curtis had dropped out, although Clarence reemerged during the 1960s as "Clarence Paul" at Motown Records, where he served as assistant A&R director, composed such

The 5 Royales

TOP SONGS

BABY, DON'T DO IT (Apollo, '53, 1 R&B)
HELP ME SOMEBODY (Apollo, '53, 1 R&B)
CRAZY, CRAZY, CRAZY (Apollo, '53, 5 R&B)
TOO MUCH LOVIN' (Apollo, 53, 4 R&B)
I DO (Apollo, '54, 6 R&B)
TEARS OF JOY (King, '57, 9 R&B)
THINK (King, '57, 9 R&B)

hits as "Fingertips" and "Hitch Hike," and guided the early career of Stevie Wonder.

Group personnel for the Royal Sons' debut recording, cut in an auditorium at Winston-Salem State Teachers College, consisted of John Tanner (lead), Obadiah Carter and Jimmy Moore (tenor-baritones), Otto Jeffries and William Samuels (baritone-bassos), and Lowman Pauling, Jr. (basso and guitar). After the release of their first single, "Bedside of a Neighbor," the Royal Sons (with Jeffries and Samuels out and Johnny Holmes in) were brought to New York for a session that yielded the gospel "Come over Here" and the secular "Too Much of a Little Bit." Apollo issued both, dubbing the group the Royals for the R&B single but soon affixing "5" to the name, then adding an "e," to avoid confusion with another set of Royals, the Detroit group that later became Hank Ballard and the Midnighters.

With Eugene Tanner replacing Holmes and splitting passion-filled vocal chores with older brother John, the 5 Royales did big business for Apollo during 1953, placing four top five R&B chart hits, starting with the Number One "Baby, Don't Do It," a gospel-drenched eight-bar blues rocker penned, like most of the group's material, by the prolific Pauling. On the Apollo sides, his stinging blues guitar sound was often buried in the backing by tenor saxophonist Charlie "Little Jazz" Ferguson's combo, but it became increasingly pronounced after the group followed Apollo executive Carl LeBow to King Records in 1954.

The group's fortunes at King proved to be spotty, however. After a three-year hitless period, the Royales returned to the R&B charts in 1957 with "Tears of Joy" and "Think." Also that year, they recorded "Dedicated to the

One I Love," a ballad credited to Pauling and producer Ralph Bass that is said to have been inspired by former Royal Son William Samuels's "I Don't Want to Know," which he had written and recorded earlier with another Winston-Salem R&B group, the Casanovas. Although "Dedicated to the One I Love" was a major seller in some regions, the song did not make the national charts until it was revived by the Shirelles in 1959 and again by the Mamas and the Papas in 1966. After James Brown scored in 1960 with Pauling's "Think" (the first of three times he would successfully cover the tune), the guitarist quit the group to strike out on his own as "El Pauling."

Between 1960 and '65, Pauling recorded with the Royalation and with the Exciters, for Federal and Savoy respectively, and returned to the 5 Royales for singles on Home of the Blues, Vee-Jay, ABC-Paramount (all produced by Willie Mitchell); Todd, King, Smash (produced by James Brown); and White Cliffs, none of which were successful. By 1966, the group had ceased to exist, and its members retired from the music business—all except Pauling. He toured for a period with Brown, Ben E. King, and Sam and Dave but was working as a night watchman in New York when he died in 1973, a largely forgotten man. Eighteen years later, the city of Winston-Salem named a street after the 5 Royales, and James Brown was still waxing ecstatic about Lowman Pauling, Jr.

ROBERTA FLACK

By the end of 1971, Roberta Flack (b. Feb. 10, 1939, Asheville, North Carolina) had recorded three critically acclaimed Atlantic albums. Each contained a smattering of protest tunes and a larger amount of gentle ballads sung in velvety alto tones at the kind of dirge-like tempo associated with such jazz cult favorites as Little Jimmy Scott and Shirley Horn. Flack's own cult had become nationwide, especially among jazz fans and college students, and she had begun to attract some mainstream attention when "You've Got a Friend," a duet with former Howard University classmate Donny Hathaway, reached number eight on the Billboard R&B chart earlier that year, though their treatment of the Carole King composition was undercut in the pop market by James Taylor's concurrent version.

First Take, Flack's 1969 debut album, had included a haunting reading of "The First Time Ever I Saw Your Face," a tender ballad penned by Scottish folksinger Ewan MacColl. It turned up nearly three years later on the soundtrack of Clint Eastwood's blockbuster suspense thriller, Play Misty for Me. Atlantic paired the song down by 66 seconds from its original length of five minutes, 21 seconds, and issued it as a single. The record rose to number four on the R&B chart and Number One pop during the spring of 1972, and the three-year old album also became a chart topper. "The First Time Ever I Saw Your Face" won Grammy Awards for Record of the Year and Song of the Year and established Flack as a major star.

As a child in Richmond and Arlington, Virginia, Flack was a quick learner. She was already in the second grade by age five. At 13, she replaced her mother as organist at Arlington's African Methodist Episcopal Zion Church and, at 15, graduated high school and began attending Howard on a music scholarship. She earned a bachelor's degree in music education after only three years of study and went on to teach for eight years in public schools, first in Farmville, North Carolina, then in Washington, D.C.

By the mid-1960s, the classically trained pianist was working as an accompanist to strolling opera singers at a D.C. restaurant and, during intermissions, singing and playing a mixture of folk, pop, and jazz songs. Jazz pianist Les McCann was so impressed by her performance at a benefit for the Inner City Ghetto Children's Library Fund that he became her manager and arranged for an audition with Atlantic producer Joel Dorn, at which she rendered 42 songs from her club repertoire, including "The First Time Ever I Saw Your Face," in the space of three hours.

The belated success of that song was quickly followed by a third single from the Roberta Flack and Donny Hathaway album. "Where Is the Love," written by Ralph McDonald and William Slater and produced by Dorn, became a Number One R&B, number five pop hit, while Flack's next solo single, 1973's Dorn-produced "Killing Me Softly with His Song" (written by Norman Gimble and Charles Fox), went to number two R&B and Number One pop and, like her first hit, won Grammys for Record of the Year and Song of the Year. In 1974, the vocalist found herself at the top of both charts with "Feel Like Makin' Love," a song by her frequent associate, early-'60s pop singing star Eugene McDaniels. She produced the record herself, using the thinly veiled pseudonym "Rubina Flake."

After a three-year hiatus from recording, Flack returned in 1978 with the Number One R&B, number two pop "The Closer I Get to You." Written by Reggie Lucas and James Mtume, then members of her band, it was her first duet with Hathaway in six years. He was ill at the time and had to make a trip from the hospital to do the session. A year later, while the two singers were working on an album, eventually released in 1980 as *Roberta Flack with Donny Hathaway,* he ended his life by jumping from the 15th floor of a New York hotel.

During the early 1980s, Flack recorded a series of duets with Hathaway sound-alike Peabo Bryson, the biggest being 1983's number five R&B, number 16 pop "Tonight, I Celebrate My Love" on Capitol. Flack made no further recordings until 1988, when she re-signed with Atlantic and cut "Oasis," an African-flavored composition and production by Luther Vandross cohort and former Miles Davis bassist Marcus Miller. The single became a Number

One R&B hit, although it failed to make a pop showing. Flack returned to the pop chart for the first time in seven years with 1991's "Set the Night to Music," a duet with reggae vocalist Maxi Priest. It climbed to number six but didn't crack the R&B top 40.

THE FLAMINGOS

The Flamingos were unlike any other vocal group, their intricate close harmonies as pristine as freshly polished glass. Rather than having been brought up in the African-American Christian church, as had so many other R&B singers, four of the five original Flamingos were black Jews, members of Chicago's Church of God and Saints of Christ, a denomination that combines elements of Judaism, Christian Pentacostalism, and black nationalism. "Our harmonies were different because we dealt with a lot of minor chords, which is how Jewish music is written," Nate Nelson, one of the group's several non-Jewish lead vocalists, told interviewer Wayne Jones.

Originally known as the Swallows, the group was formed around 1949 by cousins Jacob "Jake" Carey (b. Sept. 9, 1926, Pulaski, Virginia) and Ezekiel "Zeke" Carey (b. Jan. 24, 1933, Bluefield, West Virginia) and Chicago-born cousins Johnny Carter and Paul Wilson—all members of the black Jewish congregation—plus non-Jew Earl Lewis. As the Five Flamingos, they began performing at house parties in and around Chicago before graduating to talent contests.

With the Mississippi-born Sollie McElroy having replaced Lewis in 1951, they were soon appearing in nightclubs and, in 1953, signed with record distributor Art Sheridan's Chance label, for which they cut six singles over the next year and a half. While their Chance repertoire included an assortment of blues and jump tunes, their ballads were what attracted the most local attention, especially 1953's "Golden Teardrops," on which Carter's surreal high falsetto hovered over McElroy's forlorn low tenor to achieve one of the most haunting sounds in the annals of black harmony.

A class act, vocally and visually (their choreography is said to have influenced both the Four Tops and the Temptations), the Flamingos hooked up with the powerful Associated Booking Company, which sent

TOP ALBUMS

FIRST TAKE (Atlantic, '72, *1*)

KILLING ME SOFTLY (Atlantic, '73, *3*)

ROBERTA FLACK & DONNY HATHAWAY (Atlantic, '80, *3*)

Additional Top 40 Albums: 6

TOP SONGS

THE FIRST TIME EVER I SAW YOUR FACE (Atlantic, '72, *4 R&B, 1 Pop*)

WHERE IS THE LOVE (Roberta Flack and Donny Hathaway, Atlantic, '72, *1 R&B, 5 Pop*)

KILLING ME SOFTLY WITH HIS SONG (Atlantic, '73, *2 R&B, 1 Pop*)

FEEL LIKE MAKIN' LOVE (Atlantic, '74, *1 Pop*)

THE CLOSER I GET TO YOU (Roberta Flack with Donny Hathaway, Atlantic, '78, *1 R&B, 2 Pop*)

TONIGHT, I CELEBRATE MY LOVE (Peabo Bryson/Roberta Flack, Capitol, '83, *5 R&B, 16 Pop*)

OASIS (Atlantic, '88, *1 R&B*)

Additional Top 40 R&B Songs: 13

TOP SONGS

I'LL BE HOME (Checker, '56, 5 R&B)

A KISS FROM YOUR LIPS (Checker, '56, 12 R&B)

LOVERS NEVER SAY GOODBYE (End, '59, 25 R&B)

I ONLY HAVE EYES FOR YOU (End, '59, 3 R&B,
    11 Pop)

NOBODY LOVES ME LIKE YOU (End, '60, 23 R&B,
    30 Pop)

MIO AMORE (End, '60, 27 R&B)

THE BOOGALOO PARTY (Philips, '66, 22 R&B)

BUFFALO SOLDIER (Polydor, '70, 28 R&B)

them on tours with the Lionel Hampton and Duke Ellington orchestras in 1953 and '54. Still, the group was unable to score on record outside Chicago while at Chance and, in 1954 and '55, at Chicago disc jockey Al Benson's Parrot label. McElroy left the quintet, his lead role taken by the Chicago-born Nate Nelson. The Flamingos' fortunes changed, however, when they appeared in January 1956 with "I'll Be Home" on Checker. The sweetly harmonized, Nelson-led ballad gave the group its first national hit, peaking at number five on *Billboard*'s R&B chart, although Pat Boone stole most of the action with his number four pop cover version.

Just as their efforts were paying off, Zeke Carey and Johnny Carter were drafted in 1956 and the Flamingos disbanded for a period. (Discharged two years later, Carey returned to the group, while Carter worked as a plastering contractor for a year before joining the Dells, of which he remains a key member.) A reorganized group, based in New York and comprising Jake Carey, Nelson, Wilson, and Pittsburgh-born singer Tommy Hunt, signed with Decca but had virtually no success during 1957.

With Zeke Carey back in the fold and the addition of Baltimore singer-guitarist Terry Johnson, the Flamingos moved to George Goldner's End label the next year. Their fourth single for the company, 1959's "I Only Have Eyes for You," became their biggest hit, reaching number three on the R&B chart and number 11 pop. The love ballad, with words by Al Dubin and music by Harry Warren, had a long history. It was introduced by Dick Powell and Ruby Keeler in the 1934 motion picture *Dames*, became a major pop hit that year for both Ben Selvin and Eddy Duchin, and was subsequently recorded by Doris

Day and Gordon MacRae, among others. In the Flamingos' hands, with Johnson's falsetto floating lightly around Nelson's coolly emoting lead tenor as the rest of the group chanted "do-wop-sho-wop," it was transformed into one of the true classics of the doo wop genre.

The Flamingos stayed with End Records through 1962, gradually updating their sound to reflect changes in black popular music, especially those of Sam Cooke (they recorded his composition "Nobody Loves Me Like You" in 1960) and the Drifters, but were unable to come up with another smash. Hunt left the group in 1961 to go solo and had a number five R&B hit that year with "Human" on Scepter. After one release on Roulette, the Flamingos moved to Philips, where they enjoyed modest success in 1966 with an unlikely dance number titled "The Boogaloo Party" that later became a dance-club favorite in northern England. The group's last chart entry was 1970's "Buffalo Soldier," a homage to black cavalry troops of the 1880s, on Polydor.

Group personnel continued to fluctuate—Nelson had left to work briefly as a soloist before joining the Platters in 1966—but the Carey cousins kept the Flamingos active as they continued to record, mostly for their own Ronze label. Zeke remained at the helm following Jake's death in the early 1990s.

EDDIE FLOYD

Singer-songwriter Eddie Floyd (b. June 25, 1935, Montgomery, Alabama) is best remembered for his 1966 smash, "Knock on Wood," a Number One R&B chart hit. Co-written with Stax guitarist-producer Steve Cropper, the hard-punching number has been one of the most durable and frequently covered tunes of the 1960s. Like "In the Midnight Hour," "Respect, "Tell Mama," and "Soul Man," it has come to epitomize what sock-it-to-me southern soul music was all about.

The vocalist has been making records since 1956, but it was during the nine years he spent in Memphis as a member of the Stax-Volt crew that he enjoyed his greatest success, not only as a recording artist but as the composer of tunes for such others as Wilson Pickett, Otis Redding, Carla Thomas, and the Emotions, his old buddy Pickett's 1966 Number One R&B charter "634-5789 (Soulsville, U.S.A.)" being biggest. Nicknamed "Greentree" because of his six-foot-one-inch stature, Floyd scored 10 top 40 R&B hits while at Stax. With the exception of his uptempo treatment of Sam Cooke's "Bring It on Home to Me," Floyd had a hand in writing all of them.

Originally inspired by Cooke, Chuck Willis, and Johnny Ace, Floyd honed his singing and songwriting skills as a member of the Falcons. The Detroit vocal group was organized in 1955 by Floyd and Bob Manardo, who were then working together in a jewelry store. Between 1956 and 1962, the Falcons chalked up a dizzying discography of records for such labels as Lu Pine, Mercury, Silhouette, Kudo, Flick, Unart, Contra, Chess, Anna, United Artists, and Atlantic. Although Floyd frequently sang lead, other members were featured on the group's two biggest hits: Joe Stubbs (brother of the Four Tops' Levi Stubbs) on 1959's number two R&B, number 17 pop "You're So Fine" on Unart and Wilson Pickett on 1962's number six R&B "I Found a Love" on Lu Pine.

While still a member of the Falcons, Floyd began cutting demos of his own songs for his uncle Robert West's Lu Pine Productions in Detroit as well as recording his first sides as a solo artist. (At one Lu Pine session, he was backed by a female vocal group called the Primettes, later to become the Supremes.) Following the success of the Falcons' "I Found a Love," Pickett left for New York to record for Lloyd Price's Double L label, while Floyd moved to Washington, D.C., and recorded three singles for the Safice label. A business partnership between Floyd, Chester Simmons (Marvin Gaye's former singing partner in the Rainbows and the Moonglows), and influential disc jockey Al Bell (whose actual last name was Isbell), Safice derived its name from the three men's initials.

When Bell was hired in the fall of 1965 as Stax Records' first black executive, Floyd followed him to Memphis. The singer's first Stax release didn't fare especially well, but its title, "Things Get Better," was prophetic. The follow-up, "Knock on Wood"—with its unforgettable line, "it's like thunder, lightnin', the way you love me is frightnin' "—had been written with Redding in mind, but company boss Jim Stewart insisted Floyd cut it himself.

Although he never had another hit as big as "Knock on Wood," the singer came close twice two years later with "I've Never Found a Girl (To Love Me Like You Do)" and "Bring It on Home to Me." The former tune, co-written with Bell and Booker T.

Jones, contained another galvanizing line—"just like fire shut up in my bones"—this time lifted from Jeremiah 20:9 in the Old Testament. Floyd never cracked the top 10 again, but he stayed with Stax until it closed its doors in 1976, recording not only in Memphis but also in Los Angeles, Muscle Shoals, Detroit, and even Kingston, Jamaica.

Throughout his career at Stax, Floyd maintained a riveting rhythmic authority and a keen ear for wordplay. Many of his songs were collaborations with Cropper, who was also Redding's partner-in-pen. Even after Cropper had resigned his staff position at the company and quit the MG's, he continued to write and produce with Floyd at Stax, as did Booker T. himself.

Floyd's compositions betray the dual influence of Cooke and Redding. "To me," he told Britain's *Black Music* magazine in 1974, "they were really like one person. Their songs had a feeling, a special feeling, and the lyrics were simple. A lot of times, when I write, I think about them and how they would probably write certain lyrics or melody."

After Stax, Floyd attempted to ride the disco wave during brief spells at Malaco and Mercury and then disappeared from vinyl for a decade. He reemerged in 1988 with an album on onetime Stax labelmate William Bell's Wilbe label and, during the early 1990s, was reunited with Cropper and former Stax bassist Duck Dunn to tour and record as part of the Blues Brothers Band. Eddie Floyd was again knocking on wood.

TOP SONGS

KNOCK ON WOOD (Stax, '66, *1 R&B, 28 Pop*)

RAISE YOUR HAND (Stax, '67, *16 R&B*)

LOVE IS A DOGGONE GOOD THING (Stax, '67, *30 R&B*)

ON A SATURDAY NIGHT (Stax, '67, *22 R&B*)

I'VE NEVER FOUND A GIRL (TO LOVE ME LIKE YOU DO) (Stax, '68, *2 R&B, 40 Pop*)

BRING IT ON HOME TO ME (Stax, '68, *4 R&B, 17 Pop*)

DON'T TELL YOUR MAMA (WHERE YOU'VE BEEN) (Stax, '69, *18 R&B*)

WHY IS THE WINE SWEETER (ON THE OTHER SIDE) (Stax, '69, *30 R&B*)

CALIFORNIA GIRL (Stax, '70, *11 R&B*)

THE BEST YEARS OF MY LIFE (Stax, '70, *29 R&B*)

THE FOUR TOPS
• •

The Four Tops enjoy the singular distinction among vocal groups of having maintained consistent personnel longer than any other—since their inception in 1954. Lead vocalist Levi Stubbs and his boyhood friends Renaldo "Obie" Benson, Abdul "Duke" Fakir, and Lawrence Payton, all Detroit natives, first harmonized together at a friend's birthday party. They called themselves the Four Aims. Upon signing two years later with Chicago's Chess label, for which they cut their first record, "Could It Be You" b/w "Kiss Me Baby," they were rechristened the Four Tops in order to avoid confusion with the Ames Brothers. It would be another eight years, however, until they had a hit.

Although tight harmonies have always been their trademark, the early Four Tops' music was decidedly different from that of their later R&B and pop hits. The group specialized in jazz-imbued pop standards and spent much time on the hotel circuit, from the resorts of New York's Catskill Mountains to Las Vegas casinos, sometimes providing backing vocals for such artists as Brook Benton, Billy Eckstine, and Della Reese. They joined Columbia Records in 1970,

along with Detroit associate Aretha Franklin, but their one 45 for the company, "Ain't That Love," went nowhere, as did a 1962 rendition of "Pennies from Heaven" for Riverside.

Berry Gordy, Jr., who had first approached the group several years earlier, finally brought the quartet into his growing Motown stable in 1963 and the next year issued *Breaking Through* on his short-lived Jazz Workshop label. (The album failed to break anywhere, even on jazz stations.) The company also used the foursome to add harmonies on some of its sessions. Among them were the Supremes' 1963 recording of "When the Lovelight Starts Shining Through His Eyes," a number 23 pop charter written and produced by Brian Holland, Lamont Dozier, and Eddie Holland, and a little-known single from the same year, "What Goes Up Must Come Down," issued as by Holland and Dozier with the Four Tops and the Andantes.

Gordy then transferred the Four Tops to the Motown label and placed them in the hands of Holland, Dozier, and Holland. Those three penned and produced the Tops' debut Motown single, 1964's "Baby I Need Your Loving," which firmly placed the group in the soul camp and rose to number 11 on the *Billboard* pop chart. (The trade publication ran no

TOP ALBUM

THE FOUR TOPS GREATEST HITS (Motown, '67, 4)

Additional Top 40 Albums: 7

TOP SONGS

I CAN'T HELP MYSELF (Motown, '65, *1 R&B, 1 Pop*)

IT'S THE SAME OLD SONG (Motown, '65, *2 R&B, 5 Pop*)

REACH OUT, I'LL BE THERE (Motown, '66, *1 R&B, 1 Pop*)

STANDING IN THE SHADOWS OF LOVE (Motown, '66, *2 R&B, 6 Pop*)

STILL WATER (LOVE) (Motown, '70, *4 R&B, 11 Pop*)

AIN'T NO WOMAN (LIKE THE ONE I'VE GOT) (Dunhill, '73, *2 R&B, 4 Pop*)

ONE CHAIN DON'T MAKE NO PRISON (Dunhill, '74, *3 R&B*)

WHEN SHE WAS MY GIRL (Casablanca, '81, *1 R&B, 11 Pop*)

Additional Top 40 R&B Songs: 35

R&B lists during that period.) The quartet's association with the production trio yielded seven top 10 R&B hits, of which 1965's "I Can't Help Myself" (often identified by its opening line, "Sugar pie, honey bunch") and 1966's "Reach Out, I'll Be There" both reached the peak of the R&B and pop charts. The others were "It's the Same Old Song," "Shake Me, Wake Me (When It's Over)," "Standing in the Shadows of Love," "Bernadette," and "7 Rooms of Gloom."

More so than any others on the Detroit firm's creative staff—even Smokey Robinson—Holland, Dozier, and Holland created the quintessential Motown sound by crafting deceptively simple songs with instantly memorable hooks and unorthodox chord structures and wedding them to throbbing beats and full orchestral instrumentation. Their three-minute soul symphonies managed to take the gospel-rooted sounds of black America to unprecedented levels of universal acceptance and yet retain enough ghetto grit to still appeal to the music's core audience. That H-D-H could simultaneously fashion chart-busters for the soft, sensual voice of the Supremes' Diana Ross and for the gruff, church-hewn shout of Four Tops baritone Levi Stubbs was further evidence of their ingenuity.

The Four Tops' hit streak ended with the departure of H-D-H from Motown in late 1967. The group finally returned to the R&B top 10 with four hits in 1970 and '71, including the Frank Wilson–written-and-produced "Still Water (Love)" and a collaboration with the Supremes on the old Ike and Tina Turner number "River Deep—Mountain High." Joining ABC-Dunhill in 1972, the quartet scored seven top 10 R&B entries over the next four years, the most successful being 1972's "Ain't No Woman (Like the One I've Got)," produced by Steve Barri and written by Dennis Lambert and Brian Porter.

A move to Casablanca Records brought the Four Tops back to the top of the R&B chart for the first time in 15 years with 1981's David Wolfert–produced "When She Was My Girl." Two years later, they were again at Motown, where two of their singles made the R&B top 40. By the late 1980s, the Tops were recording for Arista, making their last chart appearance at number 31 R&B in 1988 with "If Ever a Love There Was," a vocal meeting with one-time Columbia labelmate Aretha Franklin.

ARETHA FRANKLIN

Aretha Franklin (b. Mar. 25, 1942, Memphis) reigns as the all-time Queen of Soul. Her R&B hitmaking record is unequaled by any other woman: 89 top 40 entries between 1960 and 1992, 17 of which reached Number One. What has made her so paramount is a flawless vocal technique, marked by a four-octave range and fantastic breath control that enables her, in the words of a 1969 *Time* magazine cover story, "to spin out long phrases that curl sinuously around the beat and dangle tantalizingly from blue notes," coupled with a raw emotional urgency derived from her gospel upbringing.

The eldest of the three daughters of the Reverend C. L. Franklin, she spent her youth on the gospel highway. When not singing at his home base, Detroit's 4,500-member New Bethel Baptist Church, she traveled with him across the country, from sanctuary to auditorium, soaking up such influences as Clara Ward of the Ward Singers and Sam Cooke of the Soul Stirrers along the way. Rev. Franklin was the most popular preacher in black America, commanding as much as $4,000 per sermon, and she and her sisters Carolyn and Erma made their recording debut singing behind him on two 78s, issued in 1951

Aretha Franklin

without sacrificing any of the spiritual passion. The disc yielded two top 10 R&B hits—"Today I Sing the Blues" and "Won't Be Long," both sporting her own churchy piano accompaniment—but neither single made the pop chart. The company soon got other ideas and, over the course of nine more albums in five years, attempted to subdue her sound for middle-of-the-road pop appeal. The usually string-laden results were disappointing commercially and, for the most part, artistically, with only four more of her Columbia singles (two of them issued after she'd left the label) making the R&B top 40 and none cracking its pop counterpart.

The downward spiral of Franklin's career changed radically after her 1967 signing to Atlantic Records. Producer Jerry Wexler, who'd admired her work since the 1950s, took her to Muscle Shoals, Alabama, the scene of then-recent R&B chart-toppers by Percy Sledge and Wilson Pickett. Working at Rick Hall's Fame Studios with a rhythm section that included organist Spooner Oldham, guitarist Jimmy Johnson, and drummer Roger Hawkins, Franklin applied her voice and piano with a vengeance to the gospel-tinged Ronnie Shannon ballad "I Never Loved a Man (The Way I Loved You)." The song shot to Number One on the *Billboard* R&B chart and to number nine pop, kicking off a string of top 10 R&B hits for Franklin that remained nearly unbroken for a decade.

"I Never Loved a Man" was, however, the only tune she completed in Muscle Shoals. The session was abruptly canceled following a racial confrontation between the black Ted White, her husband and manager at the time, and Hall and his musicians, all of whom where white. For the next three years, Wexler flew the core of the Muscle Shoals band to New York to play on such Franklin classics as "Respect" (a reworking of an earlier Otis Redding hit that became her only single ever to top both the R&B and pop charts), "Baby I Love You," "A Natural Woman (You Make Me Feel Like)," "Chain of Fools," "(Sweet Sweet Baby) Since You've Been Gone," "Think," "The House That Jack Built," and "Share Your Love with Me."

Franklin kept working with Wexler, usually using New York–based musicians, through 1974, and she went on to score Number One R&B singles, though less consistently, with such other producers as Quincy Jones ("Angel"), Curtis Mayfield ("Something He Can Feel"), and Marvin Hamlisch and Carole Bayer Sager ("Break It to Me Gently")

on the Gotham label. Five years later, Aretha saw the release of her first solo record, the emotion-searing "Never Grow Old," on the tiny Detroit-based JVB label; it and its follow-up, "Precious Lord," were picked up for national consumption by Checker in Chicago and subsequently appeared on the album *The Gospel Soul of Aretha Franklin*. Even after crossing the fence to pop music, the singer occasionally returned to her roots, recording the albums *Amazing Grace* for Atlantic in 1972 and *One Lord, One Faith, One Baptism* for Arista in 1987.

Producer John Hammond, who had years earlier launched the recording careers of Billie Holiday and Count Basie (and would later do the same for Bob Dylan and Bruce Springsteen), sensed something special about the teenaged gospel singer and, in 1960, signed her to Columbia Records. For *Aretha,* her first album on the label, he paired his new discovery with gospel-imbued jazz pianist Ray Bryant's combo and managed to fit her into a secular setting

TOP ALBUM

I NEVER LOVED A MAN THE WAY I LOVED YOU
(Atlantic, '67, 2)

Additional Top 40 Albums: 20

TOP SONGS

I NEVER LOVED A MAN (THE WAY I LOVED YOU)
(Atlantic, '67, 1 R&B, 9 Pop)
RESPECT (Atlantic, '67, 1 R&B, 1 Pop)
CHAIN OF FOOLS (Atlantic, '67, 1 R&B, 2 Pop)
(SWEET SWEET BABY) SINCE YOU'VE BEEN GONE
(Atlantic, '68, 1 R&B, 5 Pop)
SHARE YOUR LOVE WITH ME (Atlantic, '69, 1 R&B,
13 Pop)
SPANISH HARLEM (Atlantic, '71, 1 R&B, 2 Pop)
SOMETHING HE CAN FEEL (Atlantic, '76, 1 R&B,
28 Pop)
JUMP TO IT (Arista, '82, 1 R&B, 24 Pop)
FREEWAY OF LOVE (Arista, '85, 1 R&B, 3 Pop)

Additional Top 40 R&B Songs: 71

throughout the decade. Since 1980, she has been with Arista Records, where she scored three R&B chart toppers—1982's "Jump to It" and 1983's "Get It Right" (both written and produced by Luther Vandross) along with 1985's "Freeway of Love" (written and produced by Narada Michael Walden)—as well as "I Knew You Were Waiting (For Me)," a 1987 number five R&B duet with George Michael that became the second Number One pop hit of the soul diva's prolific career.

THE GAP BAND

T he cowboy attire—broad-brimmed hats and tasseled leather vests and boots, all white—favored by brothers Ronnie, Charlie, and Robert Wilson, who comprised the core of the Gap Band, befit their Tulsa, Oklahoma, upbringing. Yet there was nothing western about their music—a perky, good-humored brand of funk that gave the group 13 top 10 R&B hits between 1979 and 1990.

The sons of a Pentacostal preacher, the Wilson brothers broke into music as members of their church choir, which was directed by their mother.

Older brother Ronnie, who doubled on trumpet and keyboards, formed the group in 1969, initially calling it the Greenwood, Archer, and Pine Band after the main arteries in Tulsa's black business district. The name was later shortened to G.A.P. Band, then, due to a printing error on a poster, to Gap Band. At one point, the personnel included guitar virtuoso Tuck Andress, later to achieve recognition in the jazz world as half of Tuck and Patti. Lead vocalist and keyboardist Charlie, the next oldest, joined in 1973, followed two years later by the youngest, bassist Robert, by which time they were being employed as a backing band for rock star Leon Russell, also an Oklahoma native.

If *Magician's Holiday,* the Gap Band's first album, issued in 1975 on Russell and his partner Denny Cordell's Shelter label, failed to garner much attention, two years of touring with Russell exposed the brothers to mass audiences, especially when they opened shows for the Rolling Stones and Kansas. It also provided them with opportunities to work with other artists, Charlie contributing to albums by Mary McCreary (Russell's wife), D. J. Rogers, and Billy Preston and Robert to some Ike Turner tracks that were never released. Then, in 1977, Russell dropped the group.

"I thought my life had ended," Charlie recalled in a 1982 interview with Dennis Hunt of the *Los Angeles Times.* "There I was in the big time and all of a sudden, it was back to bologna, cheese and crackers. I had a taste of that glitter life, and I liked it. I didn't want it to end."

Through former Shelter artist D. J. Rogers, the group quickly landed a deal with Tattoo Records, but its one album for the RCA-distributed label yielded only two minor R&B hits, neither of which broke into the top 40. The Gap Band, made up of 14 members at the time, was struggling to survive—until Lonnie Simmons came to the rescue. The former Dallas businessman had parlayed a Los Angeles clothing store and two night clubs into a successful recording studio, called Total Experience after one of the clubs (and eventually spinning off a record label of the same name), and signed the group. He pared it down to the three brothers—they would hire sidemen to complete the band for live dates—and got them a contract with Mercury Records.

Produced by Simmons, as all of their records would be over the next seven years, *The Gap Band I,* the brothers' 1979 debut Mercury album, gave them a number four R&B single, "Shake," which was a hilarious, disco-styled take on the public's "booty" fixation of the period. Four subsequent albums, their titles following in Roman numerical order, went gold (two achieving platinum sales) and yielded major R&B hits, including "I Don't Believe You Want to Get Up and Dance (Oops, Up Side Your Head)," the Number One "Burn Rubber (Why You Wanna Hurt Me)," "Yearning for Your Love," the Number One "Early in the Morning," "You Dropped a Bomb on Me," "Outstanding," and "Party Freak," though none of these singles made a similar impression in the pop market. Stevie Wonder had become a fan, inviting the brothers to play on his 1980 *Hotter than July* album and returning the favor three years later by guesting on *Gap Band V—Jammin'*.

After two more years of continued success, especially with 1984's "Beep a Freak" and 1986's "Going in Circles" (a remake of the Friends of Distinction's hit of 17 years earlier, it was a rare ballad hit for the Gap Band), the group called it quits in 1986. Charlie worked for a period as a sideman and

TOP ALBUM

GAP BAND IV (Total Experience, '82, 14)

Additional Top 40 Albums: 2

TOP SONGS

SHAKE (Mercury, '79, 4 R&B)
BURN RUBBER (WHY YOU WANNA HURT ME) (Mercury, '80, 1 R&B)
EARLY IN THE MORNING (Total Experience, '82, 1 R&B)
YOU DROPPED A BOMB ON ME (Total Experience, '82, 2 R&B, 31 Pop)
OUTSTANDING (Total Experience, '82, 2 R&B)
PARTY TRAIN (Total Experience, '83, 3 R&B)
BEEP A FREAK (Total Experience, '86, 2 R&B)
GOING IN CIRCLES (Total Experience, '86, 2 R&B)
ALL OF MY LOVE (Capitol, '89, 1 R&B)

Additional Top 40 R&B Songs: 15

The Gap Band

songwriter for the Eurythmics, getting back together with Ronnie and Robert in 1988 to perform the title track for the blaxploitation spoof *I'm Gonna Git You Sucka,* which was issued on Arista. They then signed with Capitol. Although their one album for the company, 1989's *Round Trip,* produced by Ronnie and Charlie, generated the group's third R&B chart topper, "All of My Love," the album was the Gap Band's last. Charlie reemerged in 1992 with *You Turn My Life Around,* a moderately successful solo album on the MCA-distributed Bon Ami label. By the next year, however, the Gap Band was back in the saddle again—riding the funk revival circuit.

MARVIN GAYE

Marvin Gaye

Marvin Gaye (b. Marvin Pentz Gay, Jr., Apr. 2, 1939, Washington, D.C.) was a rebel. As a youth, he resisted the tyrannical rules of his Apostolic minister father and received severe beatings in return. As an artist, he struggled to free himself from the assembly line–like process imposed at Motown Records. The vocalist won the latter battle, boldly declaring his creative independence with the 1971 concept album *What's Going On* to become what critic Stanley Crouch called "the most brilliant and complex thinker in contemporary black popular music." He ended up the loser in the former conflict, being shot to death by his dad on April 1, 1984, while trying to stop Marvin, Sr., from beating Marvin, Jr.'s long-suffering mother.

Singing in a strong, flexible voice that sailed effortlessly from a low, gritty tenor to clear, angelic falsetto tones, Gaye scored 33 top 10 R&B singles between 1962 and 1985, 13 of which reached Number One. Eighteen also made the pop top 10. Six albums—*What's Going On* (1971), *Let's Get It On* (1973), *Marvin Gaye Live!* (1974), *I Want You* (1976), *Marvin Gaye Live at the London Palladium* (1977), and *Midnight Love* (1982)—placed in the top 10.

Gaye began singing in church at age three and soon learned to play organ, piano, guitar, and drums. At 15, he was a member of a doo wop group called the Rainbows and, after a brief Air Force stint, formed the Marquees, with whom he cut his first record, the Bo Diddley–produced "Wyatt Earp," for the Okeh label in 1957. A year later, Harvey Fuqua recruited the Marquees to become a new edition of

his group the Moonglows, and with them, Gaye was featured on the 1959 Chess recording "Mama Loochie." The record went nowhere, and the Moonglows disbanded. Fuqua moved to Detroit to work as a promotion man for Anna Records, run by Gwen Gordy and named after her sister. Harvey and Gwen married and launched the Harvey and Tri-Phi labels, using Gaye as a drummer on many sessions, including the Spinners' number five R&B hit "That's What Girls Are Made For" in 1961. Gaye married Anna Gordy that year.

He also worked as a drummer and background singer at the rapidly rising Motown operation, run by Gwen and Anna's brother Berry. Gaye's first solo single, the Mickey Stevenson–produced "Let Your Conscience Be Your Guide," was issued in May 1961 but attracted little attention. The vocalist hit pay dirt with his fourth 45, 1962's number eight R&B "Stubborn Kind of Fellow," produced by Stevenson and penned by Stevenson, Gaye, and Gwen Gordy. Numerous solo hits followed during the 1960s, including "Hitch Hike," "Pride and Joy,"

TOP ALBUM

LET'S GET IT ON (Tamla, '73, 2)

Additional Top 40 Albums: 10

TOP SONGS

AIN'T THAT PECULIAR (Tamla, '65, *1 R&B, 8 Pop*)

I HEARD IT THROUGH THE GRAPEVINE (Tamla, '68, *1 R&B, 1 Pop*)

TOO BUSY THINKING ABOUT MY BABY (Tamla, '69, *1 R&B, 4 Pop*)

WHAT'S GOING ON (Tamla, '71, *1 R&B, 2 Pop*)

MERCY MERCY ME (THE ECOLOGY) (Tamla, '71, *1 R&B, 4 Pop*)

INNER CITY BLUES (MAKE ME WANNA HOLLER) (Tamla, '71, *1 R&B, 9 Pop*)

LET'S GET IT ON (Tamla, '73, *1 R&B, 1 Pop*)

GOT TO GIVE IT UP (PART 1) (Tamla, '77, *1 R&B, 1 Pop*)

SEXUAL HEALING (Columbia, '82, *1 R&B, 3 Pop*)

Additional Top 40 R&B Songs: 44

"Can I Get a Witness," "You're a Wonderful One," "Try It Baby," "How Sweet It Is (To Be Loved by You)," "I'll Be Doggone" (the first Gaye single to top the R&B chart), "Ain't That Peculiar," "One More Heartache," "I Heard It Through the Grapevine" (the first to hit Number One on both the R&B and pop charts), "Too Busy Thinking About My Baby," and "That's the Way Love Is."

As Motown's leading sex symbol, Gaye was paired with Mary Wells for 1964's number 17 pop "What's the Matter with You Baby," then with Kim Weston for 1967's number four R&B "It Takes Two." The duet concept didn't reach full fruition, however, until he was teamed in 1967 with Tammi Terrell, with whom he had six R&B top 10 charters, including "Ain't Nothing Like the Real Thing" and "You're All I Need to Get By," both of which topped the R&B chart in 1968. Nearly four years after Terrell's tragic 1970 death, Gaye recorded an album with Diana Ross, but it was unable to recapture the old Marvin-and-Tammi magic.

The vocalist had been working with such top Motown producers as Holland, Dozier, and Holland; Smokey Robinson; Harvey Fugua and Johnny Bristol; Norman Whitfield; and Ashford and Simpson, but he longed to be a producer himself. He was

given that opportunity in 1969 and '70, writing and producing two hits—the Number One R&B "Baby I'm for Real" and the number four R&B "The Bells"—for the Originals. Then came the self-produced album *What's Going On,* on which he used multitracked vocals and commented on burning political issues. It yielded the Number One R&B singles "What's Going On," "Mercy Mercy Me (The Ecology)," and "Inner City Blues (Make Me Wanna Holler)." The 1973 sexual tour de force *Let's Get It On* became Gaye's biggest selling album. His music then grew increasingly experimental and the hits less frequent. Of his later Motown output, only 1976's "I Want You" and the next year's "Got to Give It Up" managed to crack the R&B top 10, though both singles reached Number One.

Having chronicled his bitter divorce from Anna Gordy in the 1979 double-disc album *Here, My Dear,* Gaye was free from Berry Gordy, Jr.'s company and sister by 1982. With Fuqua, who had broken with Motown and Gwen Gordy much earlier, providing creative assistance, the singer reemerged at Columbia Records with *Midnight Love;* another treatise on sexuality, it spawned the Number One R&B, number three pop single "Sexual Healing." The song proved to be Gaye's last major hit, until 1985's posthumously issued number two R&B "Sanctified Lady."

LARRY GRAHAM

Innovation is sometimes the child of necessity, as it was in the case of electric bassist Larry Graham, Jr. (b. Aug. 14, 1946, Beaumont, Texas). The percussive plucking and thumping approach to the instrument that Graham unleashed on the world during his 1966–72 stint as a key member of Sly and the Family Stone began to permeate popular music during the 1970s. As Graham continued popping the bass with his own post-Sly band, Graham Central Station, his style became a major component of other groups, from funk and rock to disco and jazz fusion.

Graham, who played with his mother's combo as a teenager, developed the unorthodox technique after the trio lost its drummer. "The style I play is a result of not having a drummer and trying to play the bass and keep the rhythm at the same time," he explained in a 1974 interview with Frederick Douglas Murphy of *Black Stars* magazine. "This accounts for the rhythmic thumping sound—it's like overplaying. You try to compensate for what is missing."

Singer-pianist Dell Graham, who'd come from Texas to Oakland, California, when Larry was two and recorded with bluesman Lowell Fulson for the Swingtime label during the early 1950s, was a cocktail lounge performer who specialized in often risqué jump blues and jazz tunes. She greatly encouraged her son's development as an entertainer, sending him to dance classes when he was five and starting him on piano lessons when he was eight. By the time he joined her group, he'd also learned the guitar and had organized his own rock and roll band, the Losers, as well as worked with another unit called the Five Riffs. With the Dell Graham Trio, he sang pop ballads and, at first, played guitar while simultaneously pumping the bass pedals of an organ, until the organ broke and he switched to bass.

Sly Stone, then a San Francisco disc jockey and record producer, heard Graham with the trio in 1966 and recruited him for his new band. Sly and the Family Stone went on to revolutionize black popular music, with Graham holding down the low end, both as a bassist and singer, the rich bass-baritone range of his three-and-a-half-octave voice serving as a foil to the leader's raspy tenor.

In 1972, Graham became interested in producing Hot Chocolate, a Bay Area club band (not to be confused with the same-named British group) that featured the gospel-hewn leads of Tyler, Texas–born singer Patryce "Chocolate" Banks. The bassist had no thoughts of leaving the Family Stone, but by year's end he and Sly had a falling out. Graham soon joined Hot Chocolate and renamed it Graham Central Station. The group, comprising Graham, Banks, guitarist David Vega, drummer Willie Sparks, and keyboardists Hershall Kennedy (who doubled on trumpet) and Robert Sam, saw the 1973 release on Warner Bros. of its eponymous debut album, from which came the top 10 R&B single "Can You Handle It?" The leader wrote the majority of the material and arranged all of it, as would be his practice on the group's six subsequent albums.

The third album, 1975's *Ain't No 'Bout-a-Doubt It,* left little question in the minds of Warner Bros. executives that they'd made the right decision in taking on Graham Central Station as the label's first funk act. The disc gave the company its first gold album by a black group, as well as its first Number One R&B charter in "Your Love." The song, based on the triplet patterns of Sly's 1969 hit "Hot Fun in

TOP ALBUMS

AIN'T NO 'BOUT-A-DOUBT IT (Graham Central Station, Warner Bros., '75, 22)
ONE IN A MILLION YOU (Warner Bros., '80, 26)

TOP SONGS

Graham Central Station:
CAN YOU HANDLE IT? (Warner Bros., '74, 9 R&B)
YOUR LOVE (Warner Bros., '75, 1 R&B, 38 Pop)
THE JAM (Warner Bros., '76, 15 R&B)
LOVE (Warner Bros., '76, 14 R&B)
NOW DO-U-WANTA DANCE (Warner Bros., '77, 10 R&B)

Larry Graham:
ONE IN A MILLION YOU (Warner Bros., '80, 1 R&B, 9 Pop)
WHEN WE GET MARRIED (Warner Bros., '80, 9 R&B)
JUST BE MY LADY (Warner Bros., '81, 4 R&B)

Additional Top 40 R&B Songs: 9

Larry Graham

the Summertime," found Graham exploring the high falsetto end of his elastic pipes.

Doubt began to set in, however, as the group largely failed to keep up with its funk and disco competition, except for 1977's "Now Do-U-Wanta Dance," a slice of molten funk that featured the bassist using a synthesizer device to talk through his instrument. Personnel had begun to change a year earlier, with Banks and Sparks being replaced by Gail Muldrow and Gaylord Birch. Graham had married the band's hairdresser in 1975; after she converted him to the Jehovah's Witness faith, his lyrics became increasingly preachy. Tina Graham herself joined in 1978, replacing Muldrow, but the band soon dissolved.

Larry surprised many of his fans, other than those who remembered his treatment of "Let Me Hear It from You" on Sly's first album, by reemerging in 1980 as a romantic bass-baritone balladeer with "One in a Million You," a Number One R&B hit composed by Sam Dees. The singer continued in that mold, scoring again that year with "When We Get Married" (a cover of an earlier hit for both the Dreamlovers and the Intruders) and the following with the self-composed "Just Be My Lady," before he was dropped by Warner Bros. in 1985. Little else was heard thereafter on record, except for an occasional Graham guest appearance on albums by such artists as Fox Fire and Aretha Franklin.

AL GREEN

At the peak of his popularity in the mid-1970s as soul music's major sex symbol, singer-songwriter Al Green (b. Apr. 13, 1946, Forrest City, Arkansas) found himself at a crossroad, trapped between the physical passion of his hit songs and the spiritual yearning of his newfound religious conviction. The object of his desire became increasingly ambiguous in the lyrics of such hits as 1974's "Sha-La-La (Makes Me Happy)" and 1975's "L-O-V-E (Love)." By the next year, he was proselytizing during his pop performances, much to the consternation of his adoring female fans. The battle between flesh and spirit was resolved in 1977 when he recorded "Belle," telling the song's distaff subject that, while it was her that he wanted, it was God that he really needed. The single was the vocalist's last top 10 R&B hit, bringing to an end a seven-year

Al Green

streak of best-sellers, after which he went on to become a successful gospel artist.

Gospel music, of course, was at the core of Green's unearthly R&B style. Influenced by the melismatic crooning of Sam Cooke and the piercing falsetto of the Swan Silvertones' Claude Jeter, Green redefined the art of soul singing. He soared into the stratosphere one second, groaned low the next, and tossed in squeals, stammers, whispers, laughs, and other often unintelligible asides. It was as if he was carrying on a conversation with an inner voice, an effect heightened through his and producer Willie Mitchell's inspired use of overdubbing to create, in the words of critic Barney Hoskyns, "parallel voices, nudging, prodding, commentating, [that] played off against each other like reflections in a hall of mirrors."

One of nine children raised 40 miles from Memphis, Al sang gospel music with his brothers William, Walter, and Robert. They toured the southern gospel circuit with their father, bassist Robert Green, and, after the family's move to Grand Rapids, Michigan, in 1959, appeared throughout the Midwest. Al's stint with the Green Brothers ended when his father caught him listening to a Jackie Wilson record. Booted out of the quartet, Al formed a secular group called the Creations. Renamed Al Greene and the Soul Mates, the new outfit cut its first record, "Back Up Train," in 1967 for the local Hot Line Music Journal label. The single was picked up for national distibution by Bell Records and reached number five on the *Billboard* R&B chart.

Subsequent Hot Line singles and an album, which pictured a then-pudgy Green leaning out of a loco-motive window, failed to generate much interest, and the group broke up. He began touring on his own and, at one 1968 gig in Midland, Texas, was spotted by Willie Mitchell. The bandleader and pro-ducer invited the struggling singer to come to Mem-phis to record for Hi Records. Green's early Hi singles, including a 1968 cover of the Beatles' "I Want to Hold You Hand," revealed artist and pro-ducer searching for a sound. The first to attract widespread attention was 1970's "I Can't Get Next to You," a bluesy revamp of the Temptations' hit of a year earlier that gave Green a number 11 R&B charter. After a second foray into blues territory with Roosevelt Sykes's "Driving Wheel" didn't do the same trick, Green turned to his softer side for 1971's "Tired of Being Alone," which rose to number seven R&B and number 11 pop.

Having found a winning formula, Green and Mitchell refined it, beginning with "Let's Stay Together," a Number One R&B and pop smash in early 1972. The minor-key song was composed by Green, Mitchell, and, moonlighting from Stax Records, drummer Al Jackson, Jr. Supported by the low rumble of the Hodges brothers—organist Charles, guitarist Teenie, and bassist Leroy—and the tightly interlocking drums of Howard Grimes and Jackson; a light cushion of strings, subtly punching riffs by the Memphis Horns; and the cooing vocal harmonies of Rhodes, Chalmers, and Rhodes, Green's elastic tenor sailed with effortless abandon. The 1972 album *I'm Still in Love with You* solidified the singer's crossover success, spawning three huge singles—the title track, "Look What You Done for Me," and "You Ought to Be with Me"—as well as "Love and Happiness," a song that was not issued at the time as a single but became the one with which Green is most frequently identified.

Having experienced a religious reawakening in 1973, Green began searching his soul in public. He became an ordained minister three years later and opened his own church, the Full Gospel Tabernacle, in Memphis. Breaking with Mitchell but remaining at Hi, he produced 1977's *The Belle Album* himself and, in 1980, signed with Myrrah, a Christian label in Waco, Texas, before moving to A&M four years later. His gospel albums, containing a mixture of tra-ditional hymns and gospel songs, self-penned reli-gious odes, and inspirational pop tunes, were warmly embraced by some segments of the gospel community, though others were skeptical of the for-mer soul man. He had a number nine pop hit in 1988 with "Put a Little Love in Your Heart," a duet with rock singer Annie Lennox. By the next year, when he reentered the R&B chart for the first time in a dozen years with the number 15 single "As Long As We're Together," Green was again straddling the fence, interjecting some of his old soul hits into his gospel performances.

TOP ALBUM
....

I'M STILL IN LOVE WITH YOU (Hi, '72, 4)

Additional Top 40 Albums: 7

TOP SONGS
....

LET'S STAY TOGETHER (Hi, '71, *1 R&B, 1 Pop*)
LOOK WHAT YOU DONE FOR ME (Hi, '72, *2 R&B, 4 Pop*)
I'M STILL IN LOVE WITH YOU (Hi, '72, *1 R&B, 3 Pop*)
YOU OUGHT TO BE WITH ME (Hi, '72, *1 R&B, 3 Pop*)
HERE I AM (COME AND TAKE ME) (Hi, '73, *2 R&B, 10 Pop*)
LIVIN' FOR YOU (Hi, '73, *2 R&B, 19 Pop*)
SHA-LA-LA (MAKES ME HAPPY) (Hi, '74, *2 R&B, 7 Pop*)
L-O-V-E (LOVE) (Hi, '75, *1 R&B, 13 Pop*)
FULL OF FIRE (Hi, '75, *1 R&B, 28 Pop*)

Additional Top 40 R&B Songs: 17

ROY HAMILTON
....

Roy Hamilton (b. Apr. 16, 1929, Leesburg, Georgia) is most commonly associated with such easy-listening mid-'50s pop ballads as "You'll Never Walk Alone" and "Unchained Melody," his two Number One R&B hits, on which his huge voice was swathed in a lush blanket of strings and woodwinds. To dismiss him as merely a middle-of-the-road crooner, however, would be to overlook the gospel shout that rang through his near-operatic baritone and to ignore the impact he had on the development of rock and soul. Singers who were strongly influenced by Hamilton include Elvis Presley, Solomon Burke, Ed Townsend, and the Righteous Brothers' Bill Medley.

"My style," Hamilton stated, "is 50 percent gospel, 30 percent popular, 20 percent semi-classical."

Hamilton began singing in church choirs when he was six. At 14, he moved with his family to Jersey City, New Jersey, where he became a star soloist at Central Baptist Church. He studied art at Lincoln High School and classical singing with J. Martin Rolls and, for a period, was an amateur heavyweight boxer. He sang for five years with Jersey City's Searchlight Gospel Singers before switching to secular music and being discovered at a local nightclub by Bill Cook. The disc jockey and aspiring songwriter landed Hamilton a contract at Epic Records and guided his career until the early 1960s. (Cook later tried to get gospel singer Sam Cooke to go pop. Although he was unsuccessful at the time, Cook ended up as the composer of Cooke's second pop hit, "I'll Come Running Back to You.")

"You'll Never Walk Alone," written by Richard Rodgers and Oscar Hammerstein II for their 1945 Broadway musical *Carousel*, had been Hamilton's signature song, one that he performed often at Apollo Theater amateur contests, although he is said to have lost each time because he would go flat during the final bars. There was nothing off-pitch about his 1954 Epic recording of the quasi-religious anthem, however, and it took him to the top of *Billboard*'s R&B chart and enjoyed some pop crossover success. "I'm Gonna Sit Right Down and Cry," the single's

bluesy, medium-tempo flip side, penned by former Ravens pianist-arranger Howard Biggs, didn't go unnoticed. Two years later, on his first album, Elvis Presley included a version that owed much to Hamilton's.

"If I Loved You" (also from *Carousel*), "Ebb Tide" (a Carl Sigman–Robert Maxwell composition later revived by the Righteous Brothers), and "Hurt" (a Jimmie Crane–Al Jacobs ballad that was introduced by Hamilton and later covered successfully by Timi Yuro) followed, all making the R&B top 10 during 1954. The next year gave Hamilton the biggest hit of his career, "Unchained Melody." Written by Hy Zaret and Alex North for the Warner Bros. motion picture *Unchained*, it proved to be the most popular song of 1955, thanks to three competing versions, all hugely successful. Les Baxter's instrumental treatment on Capitol topped the pop chart, while Hamilton's reading on Epic placed at Number One R&B and number six pop, and fellow black baritone Al Hibbler's Decca rendition also went to Number One R&B, as well as to number three pop. (Ten years later, the Righteous Brothers scored with it at number six R&B and number four pop.)

Hamilton had become one of the most popular singers in America, but stardom began to take its toll. Reportedly suffering from exhaustion, he retired from performing in 1956. For his comeback two years later, he switched direction with "Don't Let Go." The number two R&B, number 13 pop rocker, authored by veteran jazz and R&B tunesmith Jesse Stone, drew on the call-and-response patterns of Hamilton's gospel upbringing and also reflected, ironically, the influence of Presley (as had Jackie Wilson's slightly earlier "Reet Petite"). A similar formula was applied for the singer's final hit, the Bill Cook–penned "You Can Have Her," a number six R&B, number 12 pop charter in 1961.

After cutting 16 albums for Epic, Hamilton moved on to MGM, then RCA. His career floundered during the 1960s, in spite of help from such top producers as Bert Berns and Jerry Leiber and Mike Stoller. By decade's end, he was recording in Memphis for producer Chips Moman's AGP label, for which he waxed stunning versions of the James Carr hit "The Dark End of the Street" and Conway Twitty's "It's Only Make Believe." Presley, at Moman's tiny American Studio to cut what would become two career-rejuvenating albums, stood watching during his idol's early 1969 sessions. But for Hamilton, there

---

TOP SONGS

You'll Never Walk Alone (Epic, '54, *1 R&B, 21 Pop*)

If I Loved You (Epic, '54, *4 R&B, 26 Pop*)

Ebb Tide (Epic, '54, *5 R&B, 30 Pop*)

Hurt (Epic, '54, *8 R&B*)

Unchained Melody (Epic, '55, *1 R&B, 6 Pop*)

Forgive This Fool (Epic, '55, *10 R&B*)

So Long (Epic, '57, *14 R&B*)

Don't Let Go (Epic, '58, *2 R&B, 13 Pop*)

I Need Your Lovin' (Epic, '59, *14 R&B*)

You Can Have Her (Epic, '61, *6 R&B, 12 Pop*)

---

would be no comeback. Within months, on July 10, 1969, he was dead of a stroke.

WYNONIE HARRIS

Wynonie Harris (b. Aug. 24, 1915, Omaha, Nebraska) lived the life he boasted about in his songs, most of them dealing with alcohol or sex. The hard-drinkin', hard-lovin', hard-shoutin' "Mr. Blues," as he was billed, was one of the biggest stars of the early days of rhythm and blues. Although his career didn't survived into the rock and roll era, he proclaimed its coming in such raucous hits as "Good Rockin' Tonight" and "All She Wants to Do Is Rock," neither of which were about dancing.

"Good Rockin' Tonight," a 1948 version of an uptempo blues he'd turned down a year earlier when its creator, Roy Brown, initially offered it to him at Foster's Rainbow Room in New Orleans, was Harris's first Number One hit under his own name. (He'd had an R&B chart topper three years earlier, as vocalist with Lucky Millinder's big band.) The tune was recorded again in 1954, by Elvis Presley, at his second session for Sun Records. But if the up-and-coming hillbilly cat's version was more faithful to Brown's original than to Harris's cover, Presley copied more than a few tricks from Harris's hip-shaking, arm-flailing stage act.

"I knew that I had to be different if I was going to make any 'bread' singing the blues," Harris explained in "Women Won't Let Me Alone," a self-penned 1954 article for *Tan* magazine. "The woods are full of blues singers—some good, some great, and some who stink. I wanted to be the greatest of them all. Since I don't play piano or guitar, I had to work out a new approach.

"Long before, I knew that if the women were with me, I was homefree. I started snarling at 'em, upsetting them, sneering at them and doing anything I could think of to get them mad at me. I was operating on the theory that no woman really likes a 'nice, conservative' kind of fellow. What most of them want deep down in their hearts is an outright hellion, a rascal."

Luther and Nellie Harris wanted their only son to become a doctor, and, to that end, he spent two years as a pre-med student at Omaha's Creighton University. To help cover his tuition, Harris began working as a dancer at local clubs and soon found that he liked the night life better than school. He also took up drums during the mid-1930s and led his own combo for a period before heading out in 1940 to Los Angeles, where he was hired as a dancer, emcee, and blues singer at the Club Alabam.

Strongly influenced by Kansas City blues shouters Joe Turner and Jimmy Rushing, as well as by T-Bone Walker and Rubberlegs Williams, Harris was spotted in 1944 at Chicago's Rhumboogie Club by popular swing bandleader Lucky Millinder. Harris's husky baritone was featured on Millinder's Decca recording of "Hurry, Hurry," a minor hit in 1944, and again on the following year's "Who Threw the Whiskey in the Well?" That 78 not only went to the top of the R&B chart but also placed at number seven on the pop list. For his vocal services, Harris had been paid the standard $37.50 session fee. Realizing that his fortunes lay elsewhere, he soon struck out on his own.

Between 1945 and 1947, Harris discs appeared on a variety of labels. For his first solo single, "Around the Clock" on Philo, he was supported by an all-star jazz combo led by drummer Johnny Otis. It was a hit in some regions but failed to chart nationally, due to stiff competition from cover versions by Jimmy Rushing on Excelsior (also with an Otis band) and Willie Bryant on Apollo. Harris himself then turned up on Apollo and hit the charts twice in 1946, with "Wynonie's Blues" (backed by tenor sax star Illinois Jacquet's group) and "Playful Baby." After other sides for Lionel Hampton's Hamp-Tone label, Bullet, and Aladdin, the singer signed an exclusive contract with King Records in Cincinnati.

TOP SONGS

WYNONIE'S BLUES (Apollo, '46, *3 R&B*)
PLAYFUL BABY (Apollo, '46, *2 R&B*)
GOOD ROCKIN' TONIGHT (King, '48, *1 R&B*)
DRINKIN' WINE SPO-DEE-O-DEE (King, '49, *4 R&B*)
ALL SHE WANTS TO DO IS ROCK (King, '49, *1 R&B*)
SITTIN' ON IT ALL THE TIME (King, '50, *3 R&B*)
I LIKE MY BABY'S PUDDING (King, '50, *5 R&B*)
GOOD MORNING JUDGE (King, '50, *6 R&B*)
BLOODSHOT EYES (King, '51, *6 R&B*)
LOVIN' MACHINE (King, '52, *5 R&B*)

Additional Top 40 R&B Songs: 5

Whereas Harris's earlier recordings had featured him as one voice among several instrumental jazz soloists, the King sessions placed him in the spotlight and matched his vocal bluster with hard-riffing accompaniment more in tune with the emerging rhythm and blues sound, beginning with "Good Rockin' Tonight," where hand claps accentuated the backbeat. Among his other hits for the company were "Drinkin' Wine Spo-Dee-O-Dee" (a cover of Stix McGhee's number two R&B song), "All She Wants to Do Is Rock," "Bloodshot Eyes" (a cover of Hank Penny's number four country hit), and "Lovin' Machine." With proceeds from his records and personal appearances, the singer purchased a large English manor–type home in St. Albans, Long Island, New York.

Harris remained at King until 1954, but he had stopped having hits two years earlier. Singles for Atco in 1956 and Roulette in 1960 failed to rejuvenate his career. He owned a bar on Long Island until 1963 and then moved back to Los Angeles, where he worked as a bartender until his death from cancer on June 14, 1969.

DONNY HATHAWAY

Donny Hathaway

Singer, pianist, songwriter, and arranger Donny Hathaway (b. Oct. 1, 1945, Chicago) received his greatest public acclaim for a series of duets with onetime Howard University classmate Roberta Flack, including the two R&B chart toppers "Where Is the Love" and "The Closer I Get to You." His success as a solo artist was more modest, though 1972's *Donny Hathaway Live*, recorded at New York's Bitter End, reached number 18 on the *Billboard* album chart. The emotionally troubled artist's influence, especially as a vocalist, exceeded his popularity, however. He introduced into the African-American pop mainstream a vocal tonality, derived from gospel music and ringing with bell-like clarity, that would greatly affect the styles of such other tenors as George Benson, Peabo Bryson, Jeffrey Osborne, Luther Vandross, Freddie Jackson, and even Stevie Wonder.

Raised in St. Louis by his grandmother, gospel singer-guitarist Martha Crumwell, Hathaway began touring with her at age three, billed as "Donny Pitts, the World's Youngest Gospel Singer," accompanying himself on ukulele. He took classical piano lessons as a child, mastering the works of Bach, Greig, and Handel, and idolized Liberace. While still in high school, where he was a wrestling champion, he began studying music theory at Washington University in St. Louis. In 1963, he enrolled at Howard University in Washington, D.C., on a fine arts scholarship and, while there, formed a jazz trio with fellow student Ric Powell, playing for the first time outside the church.

Hathaway dropped out of college after three years and returned to his native Chicago, where he maintained a busy schedule over the next four years as a pianist, songwriter, arranger, and/or producer for such artists as the Impressions, the Five Stairsteps, Jerry Butler, Carla Thomas (another old Howard cohort), Pop Staples, jazz bandleader Woody Herman, and gospel singer Albertina Walker. Hathaway made his first recorded vocal appearance in 1969 with "I Thank You Baby," a duet with June Conquest on Curtis Mayfield's Curtom label that became a minor R&B hit.

At the recommendation of saxophonist King Curtis, Hathaway was signed to Atlantic Records in

1970. *Everything Is Everything,* his Atco debut album, co-produced with Ric Powell, featured Hathaway's soaring vocals over his rippling electric piano accompaniment and surging horn charts, bringing together his gospel, classical, jazz, and pop influences to create a brilliant, seamless pastiche. "The Ghetto (Part 1)," a largely instrumental track from the disc, became a number 23 R&B hit. "This Christmas," another 1970 single, didn't chart, but became a perennial holiday favorite (and was revived by the Whispers, with new lyrics, as "A Song for Donny" following the singer's tragic 1979 demise).

Company vice president Jerry Wexler took partial charge of the next album, 1971's *Donny Hathaway,* but it wasn't until the singer started working later that year with Flack, who'd been including his tunes on her own albums since 1969, that his voice began reaching a mass audience. *Roberta Flack and Donny Hathaway,* the only complete album the two made together, contained three hit singles, the biggest being the Number One R&B, number five pop "Where Is the Love."

Following his hit live album, Hathaway recorded 1983's vaguely autobiographical *Extensions of a Man,* from which the number 16 R&B single "Love, Love, Love" was drawn. It was his last solo album, aside from another live set, issued postumously in 1980. After singing the theme for the television sitcom "Maude" and playing electric piano on a couple of Aretha Franklin albums, depression won the upper hand and Hathaway disappeared from sight, spending the next few years in and out of mental hospitals.

Hathaway resurfaced in 1978 with "The Closer I Get to You," another Number One R&B hit duet with Flack, as well as with the number 17 R&B solo single "You Were Meant for Me." The next year, while the two singers were working on what was intended as their second album together, Hathaway ended his life by plunging from a 15th floor window of New York City's Essex House hotel. His body was taken to St. Louis, where the funeral was officiated by the reverends Jesse Jackson and Cleophus Robinson and attended by such friends as Flack and Stevie Wonder. Two completed tracks from the ill-fated duet session—"You Are My Heaven" and "Back Together Again"—became R&B hits in 1980.

Vocalist Lalah Hathaway, the eldest of the late musician's two daughters, emerged as a recording artist in 1990, scoring a number three R&B charter with the Virgin single "Heaven Knows."

TOP ALBUMS

Donny Hathaway Live (Atco, '72, *18*)
Roberta Flack & Donny Hathaway (Atlantic, '72, *3*)

Additional Top 40 Albums: 1

TOP SONGS

Roberta Flack and Donny Hathaway:
You've Got a Friend (Atlantic, '71, *8 R&B, 29 Pop*)
Where Is the Love (Atlantic, '72, *1 R&B, .5 Pop*)

Donny Hathaway:
I Love You More Than You'll Ever Know (Atco, '73, *20 R&B*)
Love, Love, Love (Atco, '73, *16 R&B*)
You Were Meant for Me (Atco, '78, *17 R&B*)

Roberta Flack with Donny Hathaway:
The Closer I Get to You (Atlantic, '78, *1 R&B, 2 Pop*)
You Are My Heaven (Atlantic, '80, *8 R&B*)
Back Together Again (Atlantic, '80, *18 R&B*)

Additional Top 40 R&B Songs: 4

ISAAC HAYES

Dubbed "Black Moses" at the height of his popularity, singer, pianist, songwriter, arranger, and producer Isaac Hayes (b. Aug. 20, 1942, Covington, Tennessee) revolutionized soul music, leading it out of the era of the three-minute single into two new areas: the symphonically orchestrated "concept" album with extended cuts and the black motion picture soundtrack. His second album, *Hot Buttered Soul,* issued on Stax Records' Enterprise label in 1969, contained only four tracks, with one, "By the Time I Get to Phoenix," running a full 18 minutes. The album became the first for the Memphis company to go gold. Hayes's fourth album, the soundtrack from the 1971 motion picture *Shaft,* hit Number One, and "Theme from Shaft" earned him an Academy Award for Best Original Song. That success opened the doors for such other soulmeisters as Curtis Mayfield and Norman Whitfield to write for the screen.

Isaac Hayes

Hayes was born on a farm 30 miles north of Memphis. While still an infant, his mother died, and his father deserted Isaac and his older sister, who were left to be raised by their sharecropping grandparents. He moved to Memphis with his grandparents when he was seven. Then his grandfather died, and, at age 10, Isaac suddenly became the man of the house. As a teenager, he juggled school and work schedules and learned to play piano and saxophone.

Originally a Brook Benton imitator, Hayes cut his first single, "Laura We're on Our Last Round," for Memphis producer Chips Moman in 1962 and, the following year, played piano on a Stax record titled "Boot-Leg" by baritone saxophonist Floyd Newman. Hayes was soon recruited by the company as a keyboard player, initially to fill in for Booker T. Jones, who was often away at college, and he began contributing to sessions by such artists as Otis Redding, Rufus Thomas, the Astors, and even Booker T. and the M.G.'s, as well as recording his own instrumental single, "Blue Groove," issued in 1965 as by "Sir Isaac and the Do-Dads." More importantly, he started collaborating as a songwiter and producer with David Porter to create hits for Carla Thomas ("B-A-B-Y"), Mable John ("Your Good Thing"), Johnnie Taylor ("I Got to Love Somebody's

Baby"), and particularly Sam and Dave. The Sam Moore–David Prater singing duo joined with the Hayes-Porter team to cut hit after hit between 1966 and '68, including "You Don't Know Like I Know," "Hold On! I'm Comin'," "You Got Me Hummin'," "When Something Is Wrong with My Baby," "Soul Man," and "I Thank You."

His first album, 1967's *Presenting Isaac Hayes*, was a low-budget, jazz-imbued affair recorded on the spur of the moment following a Christmas party with only bass and drums accompanying his piano and voice. The second, 1969's *Hot Buttered Soul*, offered something altogether different: a husky, very masculine baritone rapping and crooning intimately against a massive backdrop of strings and horns from the Memphis Symphony and the solid grooves of the Bar-Kays. Fans who weren't satisfied by the three-minute version of Jim Webb's "By the Time I Get to Phoenix" that was issued on a 45 rushed to buy the album, which also included an equally sensuous 12-minute reading of Burt Bacharach and Hal David's "Walk on By," adorned with a compelling fuzz-toned guitar riff.

Other hit albums followed—*The Isaac Hayes Movement* (featuring "I Stand Accused"), *To Be Continued*, the two-disc *Shaft*, and *Black Moses* (the poster cover, which depicted Hayes in a long, hooded robe standing on a river bank with arms outstretched, unfolded in the shape of a cross three feet wide and four feet tall)—as well as a successful 1971

TOP ALBUMS

Hot Buttered Soul (Enterprise, '69, *8*)
The Isaac Hayes Movement (Enterprise, '70, *8*)
To Be Continued (Enterprise, '70, *11*)
Shaft (Enterprise, '71, *1*)
Black Moses (Enterprise, '71, *10*)

Additional Top 40 Albums: 4

TOP SONGS

Never Can Say Goodbye (Enterprise, '71, *5 R&B, 22 Pop*)
Theme from Shaft (Enterprise, '71, *2 R&B, 1 Pop*)
Do Your Thing (Enterprise, '72, *3 R&B, 30 Pop*)
Joy—Part 1 (Enterprise, '73, *7 R&B, 30 Pop*)
Ike's Rap (Columbia, '86, *9 R&B*)

Additional Top 40 R&B Songs: 15

cover of the Jackson 5's then-recent "Never Can Say Goodbye." Hayes became soul music's first super-hero, a young black man who had risen from poverty to prove he could do everything musical: sing, play (keyboards, vibes, alto sax), produce, compose, arrange, and score motion pictures. He also launched an acting career in 1974, appearing in (as well as scoring) *Truck Turner* and *Three Tough Guys* and becoming a semi-regular on NBC-TV's "Rockford Files."

In 1975, Hayes signed with ABC, which set him up with his own Hot Buttered Soul label. *Chocolate Chip,* his first album under the new alliance, went gold. By 1976, however, he was $6 million in debt and declared bankruptcy. He moved to Polydor in 1978 and struck gold again with the following year's *Don't Let Go* album. Hayes continued to focus on acting, including a featured role in the 1981 motion picture *Escape from New York,* before reemerging on Columbia Records in 1986 with "Ike's Rap," his first top 10 R&B single in a dozen years. His last chart entry was 1992's number 29 R&B "Dark and Lovely (You over There)" on A&M, a duet with Barry White, an artist who, ironically, had risen to fame during the mid-1970s with an adaptation of Hayes's earlier bedroom baritone/orchestral soul innovations.

Z. Z. HILL

Until Arzell Hill (b. Sept. 30, 1935, Naples, Texas) recorded *Down Home*—the biggest-selling blues album of the 1980s until Robert Cray's breakthrough—for Jackson, Mississippi's Malaco label in 1982, his main claim to fame was that the Texas boogie-rock band ZZ Top had borrowed the initials of his stage name. Z. Z. Hill was just another journeyman trapped in the lower intestines of the so-called chitlin circuit, a poor man's Bobby Bland who had spent 18 years traveling the backroads between Texas and California, singing soul ballads and an occasional blues with whatever house band that happened to be on hand for a particular engagement. His gritty voice, handsome face and a handful of moderate R&B hits earned him a small following, but he was never able to carve out a real niche for himself in the music world.

Down Home, the singer's second Malaco album,

radically altered that course. It stayed on the *Billboard* R&B album chart for 93 weeks, peaking at number 17, and yielded the single "Cheating in the Next Room," a soul ballad written by George Jackson that reached number 19 on the R&B singles chart. But it was another Jackson-penned track, "Down Home Blues," that captured the imagination of radio programmers and the public. Though not issued as a single, the medium-tempo song, built around a bass-heavy Jimmy Reed rhythm pattern, was the first blues to receive substantial airplay on black radio in over a decade. It became the blues anthem of the 1980s.

Hill was suddenly a headline attraction. Singing a mixture of blues and soul in a low tenor that incorporated elements of Bobby Bland's roar, Otis Redding's tenderness, O. V. Wright's tortured cry, Johnnie Taylor's elegance, and Little Johnny Taylor's rawness, he put together a tight, brassy band and started earning big money. "In six months," he told *Billboard* columnist Nelson George in 1983, "I was making $10,000 or more [a night], depending on the city....In some cases I've got as much as $15,000."

Initially inspired by Sam Cooke, Hill began singing in church and later with a gospel group called the Spiritual Five. In 1963, after working as a truck driver for a Dallas grocery chain, he moved to San Diego to join his older brother Matt, an aspiring record producer. Z. Z.'s first record, a self-composed blues with a bouncy New Orleans R&B beat titled "You Were Wrong," was issued that year on Matt Hill's M.H. label. Although it reached only the bottom position on *Billboard*'s Hot 100 (the magazine published no R&B charts that year), it was a strong enough seller to attract the attention of the Bihari brothers' Kent label in Los Angeles. Between 1964 and '68, the vocalist cut 15 singles for Kent—mostly soul songs produced and arranged by Maxwell Davis. Some, including such original numbers as "You Don't Love Me" and "Someone to Love Me" and a cover of Willie West's Allen Toussaint–penned "Greatest Love," were regional hits, particularly in California, Texas, and Alabama, but none charted nationally, excepting a rerelease of "Someone to Love Me," retitled "I Need Someone (To Love Me)," after Hill had left the label.

The years 1969 through '72 found the singer jumping from label to label: Atlantic, Quinivy, Mankind, and his brother's Hill and Audrey labels. "Don't Let Me Pay for His Mistakes," a slow blues released in 1971 on Audrey, launched a series of biting Hill commentaries on the subject of adultery and gave him his first national R&B charter. Also in 1971, the Nashville-based Mankind label issued *The Brand New Z.Z. Hill,* a Swamp Dogg–produced album that yielded three moderate hit singles. Through Hill Records, United Artists signed the singer in 1972 and scored several moderate hits, including the Toussaint-produced "I Keep on Lovin' You" and the Lamont Dozier–produced "I Created a Monster." After a brief, unsuccessful stay at MHR (yet another Matt Hill label), Z. Z. joined the Columbia roster in 1977. His first single for the company, the soul ballad "Love Is So Good When You're Stealing It," produced by Bert DeCoteaux, became the highest charting 45 of the singer's career, peaking at number 15 R&B.

Signing with Malaco in 1980, Hill began working with house producers Tommy Couch and Wolf Stephenson. The first album, simply titled *Z. Z. Hill,* failed to generate much notice, but after the success of *Down Home,* sales seemed unstoppable. The third, 1982's *The Rhythm and the Blues* (featuring the Denise LaSalle–penned blues "Someone Else Is Steppin' In"), spent 51 weeks on the R&B album chart, as did the next year's *I'm a Blues Man.* His brief spell in the spotlight was cut short, however, when he slipped in the driveway of his Dallas home. Two weeks later, on April 27, 1984, Hill died when a blood clot from his broken leg traveled to his heart.

TOP SONGS

DON'T MAKE ME PAY FOR HIS MISTAKES (Hill, '71, *17 R&B*)

I NEED SOMEONE (TO LOVE ME) (Kent, '71, *30 R&B*)

CHOKIN' KIND (Mankind, '71, *30 R&B*)

SECOND CHANCE (Mankind, '72, *39 R&B*)

IT AIN'T NO USE (Mankind, '72, *34 R&B*)

AIN'T NOTHING YOU CAN DO (Hill/United Artists, '73, *37 R&B*)

I KEEP ON LOVIN' YOU (Hill/United Artists, '74, *39 R&B*)

I CREATED A MONSTER (Hill/United Artists, '75, *40 R&B*)

LOVE IS SO GOOD WHEN YOU'RE STEALING IT (Columbia, '77, *15 R&B*)

CHEATING IN THE NEXT ROOM (Malaco, '82, *19 R&B*)

HOT CHOCOLATE

With its unique combination of American soul, British pop, and rock and Caribbean influences, as well as hook-filled songs that often dealt with controversial subjects, the London-based Hot Chocolate scored a dozen top 10 hits in England between 1970 and 1983, all produced by Mickie Most and issued there on his RAK label. Also a favorite in Europe, the multiracial group enjoyed a briefer spell of success in the U.S. during the disco era.

Hot Chocolate was the creation of vocalist Errol Brown (b. Nov. 12, 1948, Kingston, Jamaica) and bassist Tony Wilson (b. Oct. 8, 1947, Trinidad), who began working together as songwriters in the late 1960s. Brown, who sang in church as a child, came to England at age 10 and, after college, worked as a clerical officer for the British government. Wilson played guitar with the Flames and the Trinidad All-Stars before being sent to England by his father in 1961 to study to be a dental technician; instead, he began playing around London with a variety of club bands. In late 1969, the two approached John Lennon with the idea of recording a reggae version of "Give Peace a Chance." Although Brown and Wilson had not yet formed a band, their treatment of the Lennon song was issued in 1970 on the Beatles' Apple label as by "Hot Chocolate." It was not a hit, but later that year, Apple artist Mary Hopkin saw top 20 U.K. chart action with the Brown-Wilson composition "Think About the Children."

When Apple showed no further interest, the duo took some of their tunes to Mickie Most, a producer known for his hits for such artists as Herman's Hermits, the Yardbirds, and Donovan. Following the moderate U.K. success of Herman's Hermits' recording of Brown and Wilson's "Bet Yer Life," Most signed the duo to RAK. Having organized a band that included keyboardist Larry Ferguson (b. Apr. 14, 1948, Nassau, Bahamas) and percussionist Patrick Olive (b. Mar. 22, 1947, Grenada), they hit the British top 10 in the late summer of 1970 with their first RAK single, "Love Is Life." By year's end, Harvey Hinsley (b. Jan. 19, 1948, Northampton, England), a guitarist who'd played on "Bet Yer Life," had become a permanent member of Hot Chocolate. The long-term lineup was completed in 1973 by Tony Conner (b. Apr. 6, 1947, Romford, Essex, England), who replaced original drummer Ian King.

While Herman's Hermits, along with such other RAK artists as Julie Felix and April Wine, continued having hits with Brown-Wilson songs, it was Hot Chocolate itself that proved the most consistent hitmaker. RAK released several of the group's singles in the U.S., but none attracted much interest. In 1973, however, a biting Hot Chocolate song about interracial romance titled "Brother Louie" was covered by the New York rock group Stories. Omitting the original record's spoken references to "honky" and "spook," the Stories took "Brother Louie" to the top of the U.S. pop chart.

Hot Chocolate finally broke into the American market in 1975 with "Emma," a number eight pop charter issued domestically on the Atlantic-distributed Big Tree label. An impassioned lament of a girlfriend's suicide, "Emma" featured Brown's tortured, warbling tenor and Hinsley's metallic guitar over a bottom-heavy, medium-tempo groove inspired by Willie Mitchell's productions for Al Green. The throbbing backbeat—played on tom toms and bass drum—was even more pronounced on the group's next two Big Tree singles—"Disco Queen" and "You Sexy Thing"—and caught on with disco dancers. Hot Chocolate's biggest U.S. hit, "You Sexy Thing," was, in the words of *Village Voice* critic Georgia Christgau, a "response to the empty clichés about sexual freedom and one-night stands that were becoming a staple of disco and pop in 1975."

Wilson left the band in 1976 to begin a solo career at Bearsville Records that yielded no hits on either side of the Atlantic. The rest of Hot Chocolate, with Olive switching from congas to bass, continued on successfully, garnering two more U.S. charters—1977's "So You Win Again" (a Russ Ballard com-

position) on Big Tree and the next year's "Every 1's a Winner" (written by Brown) on Infinity—and many more at home. The group never fully captured the imagination of American listeners, perhaps because it waited until 1983 to tour the states, in support of its EMI America album *Mystery*—which contained the top 10 U.K. hits "Girl Crazy" and "It Started with a Kiss" of the previous year. By that time, however, Hot Chocolate had lost its earlier U.S. momentum, and the album bombed. After the British success of a 1987 remix of "You Sexy Thing," Brown departed for a solo career at Warner Bros. Records.

WHITNEY HOUSTON

While Whitney Houston (b. Aug. 9, 1963, East Orange, New Jersey) traveled the time-honored route from Baptist choir to pop stardom, hers is far from the typical rags-to-riches story. The daughter of legendary background singer Cissy Houston and first cousin of Dionne Warwick, she already had a pedigree of talent when Arista Records signed her in 1983.

In January 1985, a month before the release of her eponymous debut album, the company let it be known that Houston was the singer to watch that year by mailing to the media a beach towel–sized calendar-poster of the swimsuit-clad former fashion model. Arista might just as well have sent out a long-term appointment book, with a picture of the tall, willowy vocalist on every page. Indeed, she quickly became popular music's paramount diva, accumulating three Number One albums and nine pop chart-topping singles between 1985 and '92. Her biggest song, 1992's "I Will Always Love You," made *Billboard* chart history by holding down the pop singles pinnacle for a record 14 weeks.

Word was out on Whitney even before Arista president Clive Davis took her under his wing. In a 1982 *Village Voice* review of a Cissy Houston club performance, critic Don Shewey focused on two songs that featured her then-18-year-old daughter, commenting, "She sang in long, unfussy lines, building slowly and holding off forever a gorgeous vibrato she deployed very sparingly and only after throwing in a few blocky gospel phrases almost as a surprise...she didn't wring the tunes dry or scrape them clean or anything like that—no violence, no

TOP ALBUMS

10 GREATEST HITS (Big Tree, '77)
EVERY 1'S A WINNER (Infinity, '79, *31*)

TOP SONGS

EMMA (Big Tree, '75, *8 Pop*)
DISCO QUEEN (Big Tree, '75, *40 R&B, 28 Pop*)
YOU SEXY THING (Big Tree, '75, *6 R&B, 3 Pop*)
SO YOU WIN AGAIN (Big Tree, '77, *31 Pop*)
EVERY 1'S A WINNER (Infinity, '78, *7 R&B, 6 Pop*)

Whitney Houston

overkill. The widest open note was controlled and clear as the hum she produced by holding the word 'time' with her lips closed; every note there was wanted. These are the best habits for a young singer to have."

The youngest of the three children of John Houston and the former Emily "Cissy" Drinkard, Whitney was surrounded by music as a child. At age four, she began attending recording sessions, watching her mother, a member of the Sweet Inspirations, sing behind such artists as Aretha Franklin and Wilson Pickett. Around the house, young Whitney sang along with records by Franklin, her early idol, and, at 11, made her solo debut with the junior choir at Newark's New Hope Baptist Church, where her mother has long served as minister of music. At 15, Whitney became part of Cissy's club act, at first doing background vocals, eventually sharing the spotlight. She began working as a model in 1981 and graced the covers and pages of such magazines as *Seventeen, Glamour,* and *Cosmopolitan.* She also contributed to sessions by Chaka Khan, Paul Jabara, Lou Rawls, and Material (soloing on a track of the avant-garde jazz-funk group's 1982 Elektra album, *One Down*) before catching the ear of Clive Davis.

The vocalist's first chart appearance occurred in 1984 with "Hold On," a duet with Teddy Pendergrass on the Asylum label that reached number five R&B, and she joined Jermaine Jackson the following year for one track on his debut album for Arista. Her own *Whitney Houston* became the best-selling debut album of all time by a solo performer, topping the album chart for 14 weeks and yielding five hit singles: "You Give Good Love" (produced by Kashif), "Saving All My Love for You" (Michael Masser), "Thinking About You" (Kashif), "How Will I Know" (Narada Michael Walden), and "Greatest Love of All" (Masser). Her sophomore album, 1987's *Whitney,* set another precedent by becoming the first album by a female artist ever to debut at Number One. Its hits included "I Wanna Dance with Somebody (Who Loves Me)," "So Emotional," and "Where Do the Broken Hearts Go" (all

TOP ALBUMS

WHITNEY HOUSTON (Arista, '85, *1*)
WHITNEY (Arista, '87, *1*)
I'M YOUR BABY TONIGHT (Arista, '90, *3*)
THE BODYGUARD (Arista, '92, *1*)

TOP SONGS

YOU GIVE GOOD LOVE (Arista, '85, *1 R&B, 3 Pop*)
SAVING ALL MY LOVE FOR YOU (Arista, '85, *1 R&B, 1 Pop*)
HOW WILL I KNOW (Arista, '85, *1 R&B, 1 Pop*)
I'M YOUR BABY TONIGHT (Arista, '90, *1 R&B, 1 Pop*)
ALL THE MAN THAT I WANTED (Arista, '90, *1 R&B, 1 Pop*)
I WILL ALWAYS LOVE YOU (Arista, '92, *1 R&B, 1 Pop*)

Additional Top 40 R&B Songs: 16

produced by Walden), and "Didn't We Almost Have It All" (Kashif).

If 1990's *I'm Your Baby Tonight* failed to top the album chart, it included two Number One R&B and pop singles: the title track (produced by Antonio "L. A." Reid and Kenny "Babyface" Edmonds) and "All the Man That I Needed" (Walden). Houston, who married new jack singing star Bobby Brown in 1992, saw her megastardom solidified at the end of that year when she made her motion picture debut co-starring with Kevin Costner in *The Bodyguard,* a Warner Bros. film that grossed a reported $411 million worldwide. The Arista soundtrack album featured six Houston performances, including the David Foster–produced "I Will Always Love You." The ballad, a Number One country hit 18 years earlier for its composer, Dolly Parton, was the tour de force of Houston's career. Following a long, entirely a cappella introduction, she filled the song with flawlessly executed gospel melismas, sustains, and a remarkable key modulation. While some rock critics scoffed, the public couldn't get enough of this masterpiece. The album sold over 24 million copies.

Other Houston recordings include her stunning rendition of "The Star Spangled Banner" (number 20 pop) from the 1991 Super Bowl game and featured guest appearances with BeBe and CeCe Winans in 1988, Aretha Franklin in 1989 (the number five R&B "It Isn't, It Wasn't, It Ain't Never Gonna Be"), and Dionne Warwick in 1993.

IVORY JOE HUNTER
• • • • • • • • • • •

R aised on blues, jazz, country, and church music, singer-pianist Ivory Joe Hunter (b. Oct. 10, 1914, Kirbyville, Texas) utilized all four elements during a recording career that spanned 41 years. While his first commercial sides were straight blues and boogies, he soon developed a sentimental pop ballad approach, influenced equally by blues and country, that became his signature and made him one of the early stars of rhythm and blues. Hunter's many compositions in that vein, including "Waiting in Vain," "Guess Who," "I Almost Lost My Mind," "I Need You So," and "Since I Met You Baby," not only gave him hits in his own right but

supplied a rich repertoire for other artists to mine down through the years. Among those who covered his songs were Pat Boone, Theresa Brewer, Ruth Brown, Solomon Burke, Nat "King" Cole, Freddy Fender, Eddie Fisher, the Five Keys, Connie Francis, B. B. King, the McGuire Sisters, Elvis Presley, and Ted Taylor.

Hunter's father was a preacher and guitarist, his mother a spiritual singer. Joe studied classical piano as a child in Port Arthur, Texas, and was greatly inspired by seeing Duke Ellington and Fats Waller in movies. Both parents died when he was 11, causing him to drop out of school and pursue music to help support himself and his 14 siblings. In 1933, on a trip to Weirgate, Texas, folklorist Alan Lomax recorded Hunter's barrelhouse rendition of "Stagolee" for the Library of Congress. The pianist settled in Houston in 1936 and led his own band for five years at the Uptown Theater. Its personnel included future jazz saxophone stars Arnett Cobb and Illinois Jacquet, as well as sousaphonist Eddie Williams, later a member of Johnny Moore's Three Blazers. And, for a period, he had his own radio program on Beaumont radio station KFDM.

In 1942, Hunter moved to Oakland and became a popular attraction at Slim Jenkins and other local supper clubs. Three years later, he formed his own record label, Ivory Records, and recorded "Blues at Sunrise." Curiously, he did not play piano on the song, but was accompanied instead by guitarist Johnny Moore's trio featuring Charles Brown (a pianist Hunter had strongly influenced back in Texas) and bassist Eddie Williams. The record attracted the attention of Los Angeles songwriter Leon Rene, who issued it for national consumption on his Exclusive label. "Blues at Sunrise" reached number three on the *Billboard* R&B chart, giving Hunter the first of his 17 top 10 R&B hits.

In partnership with disc jockey Don Hambly of Berkeley station KRE, Hunter launched the Pacific label in 1946 and cut a string of blues and boogies over the next three years, with "Pretty Mama Blues" hitting the top of the chart in 1948. By that time, however, he had signed with King Records in Cincinnati, where his trademark ballad approach first emerged on the 1949 hit "Guess Who." Besides Hunter's melancholy baritone voice and elegant piano, the record featured alto saxophonist Russell Procope, violinist Ray Nance, and other members of the Duke Ellington Orchestra. Backed by a band that included saxophonists Eddie "Cleanhead" Vinson and Eddie "Lockjaw" Davis, Hunter scored again that year with a cover of Jennie Lou Carson's "Jealous Heart," the first of many country songs he would record over the years.

Signing with MGM, Hunter enjoyed a massive 1950 hit with "I Almost Lost My Mind." Capitol Records had Nat Cole record a version that reached number seven R&B and number 26 pop, but the original won out in the R&B market, holding fast at Number One. (Pat Boone triumphed in the end, however, taking the tune to the top of the pop chart in 1956.) Hunter had three more hits at MGM in 1950, then disappeared from the charts, finally reemerging at Atlantic Records in 1955. His biggest seller for the New York company was 1956's "Since I Met You Baby" (his only pop top 40 entry), followed by the next year's "Empty Arms," written by country artist Leon Payne.

After scoring a minor pop charter in 1959 with a rendition of country singer Bill Anderson's "City Lights" on the Dot label, Hunter's hit streak ended. He continued recording, with little success, for a number of companies, including Golddisc, Capitol, Vee-Jay, Smash, Stax, Goldwax, Teardrop, Sound Stage 7, and Epic. He also became a frequent performer at the Grand Ole Opry and made a memorable appearance with the Johnny Otis Show at the 1970 Monterey Jazz Festival. Stricken by lung cancer, Hunter was saluted by country stars George Jones, Tammy Wynette, and Sonny James and soul star Isaac Hayes at a 1974 benefit concert in Nashville. He died in Memphis on November 8, 1974. His last album, issued that year by Paramount Records, was titled *I've Always Been Country*.

TOP SONGS

BLUES AT SUNRISE (Exclusive, '45, 3 R&B)
PRETTY MAMA BLUES (Pacific, '48, 1 R&B)
WAITING IN VAIN (King, '49, 5 R&B)
GUESS WHO (King, '49, 2 R&B)
JEALOUS HEART (King, '49, 2 R&B)
I ALMOST LOST MY MIND (MGM, '50, 1 R&B)
I QUIT MY PRETTY MAMA (King, '50, 4 R&B)
I NEED YOU SO (MGM, '50, 1 R&B)
SINCE I MET YOU BABY (Atlantic, '56, 1 R&B, 12 Pop)
EMPTY ARMS (Atlantic, '57, 2 R&B)

Additional Top 40 R&B Songs: 11

THE INTRUDERS

The Intruders had a knack for turning novel metaphors into solid R&B hits. Beginning with their first crossover smash, 1968's "Cowboys to Girls," the Philadelphia foursome moved on to baseball, medicine, scouting, and horse racing with "(Love Is Like a) Baseball Game," "Give Her a Transplant," "I'm Girl Scoutin'," and "(Win, Place or Show) She's a Winner," all written and produced by Kenny Gamble and Leon Huff and released on their Gamble label.

Heightening the teen angst of those and other Intruders' songs was lead singer Sam "Little Sonny" Brown's slightly adenoidal, decidedly off-pitch, and, in the words of British critic Tony Cummings, "bizarre bleating" style. Eugene "Bird" Daughtery, Robert "Big Sonny" Edwards, and Phil Terry wove intricate neo–doo wop harmonies behind Brown, while Huff's churchy piano, Vince Montana's chiming vibraharp, Earl Young's dramatic drums, and a string-and-woodwind orchestra (usually arranged by Bobby Martin) supplied lush cushioning.

"We were singing ballads with a little bit of the old doo wop sound, but with a kind of slickness in the production that the public wanted," Terry told Cummings. This was the cornerstone of what would become known as the Sound of Philadelphia, for it was with the Intruders, the first act signed by Gamble and Huff when they formed their partnership in 1965, that the producers developed a refreshing new approach to popular music that was at the heart of countless hits for such other artists as Jerry Butler, the O'Jays, and Harold Melvin and the Blue Notes.

The four Intruders grew up near one another on Philadelphia's rough North Side—"We were just hoodlum kids," Terry once stated—and began singing on street corners around 1960. A year later, they made their first record—"I'm Sold on You" b/w "Come Home Soon" on the Gowan label—a two-sided hit around Philly. In 1964, they cut a second single, produced by Leroy Lovett and issued on Musicor. Leon Huff played piano on the record. He had met Kenny Gamble that year at a session for Cameo Records that produced a minor hit called "The 81" by Candy and the Kisses. The two quickly formed a working relationship and, in 1965, with backing from local clothing manufacturer Ben Krass, launched Excel Records. The Intruders' "Gonna Be Strong" was their initial release.

Due to a theatened suit by another company with the same name, Excel became Gamble Records in 1966. Its debut release was the Intruders' "(We'll Be) United," a number 14 R&B charter in *Billboard* that gave the Intruders and their fledgling producers their first national hit. Four more top 40 R&B songs followed—"Devil with Angel's Smile," "Together," "Baby, I'm Lonely," and "A Love That's Real"—before the Intruders hit the top of the R&B chart (and number six pop) with "Cowboys to Girls" in 1968. It was followed by the number four R&B "(Love Is Like a) Baseball Game," after which the group experienced a two-year absence from the R&B top 10.

The Intruders returned in 1970 with the number eight R&B "When We Get Married," a cover of a song that had been a number 10 pop charter nine years earlier for Philadelphia's Dreamlovers. With Brown's yearning lead backed by the other members' bell-like harmonies, it was one of the group's loveliest performances. Brown himself soon got married and left the fold for a brief period. He was temporarily replaced by Bobby Starr for "I'm Girl Scoutin'," which scored the group a number 16 R&B chart entry in 1971.

The group's next two big hits—1972's "(Win, Place or Show) She's a Winner" and 1973's "I'll Always Love My Mama"—were prototypes of the emerging disco sound. Fueled by Earl Young's throbbing "four-on-the-floor" bass-drum beat, they became dance-floor favorites. The quartet easily could have continued to ride the disco bandwagon,

but they instead returned to ballad form for the follow-up, the plaintive "I Wanna Know Your Name." It was the Intruders' last top 10 R&B chart entry. They were transferred to Gamble and Huff's new label, TSOP (the Sound of Philadelphia) in 1974 but disappeared after the disappointing sales of several singles, including a remake of the Carpenters' 1971 hit "Rainy Days and Sundays."

THE ISLEY BROTHERS

During a recording career that has spanned nearly 40 years, the Isley Brothers—originally a vocal trio comprising Cincinnati-born siblings O'Kelly, Jr. (b. Dec. 25, 1937), Rudolph (b. May 21, 1941), and lead singer Ronald (b. May 21, 1941)—managed to keep their records on the charts by changing with the musical times. In the 1960s, they were a show-stopping stand-up act on the soul circuit that jumped from label to label, working with such songwriter-producers as Bert Berns and Holland, Dozier, and Holland. The Isleys refashioned their style during the next decade, producing mostly original material for their own T-Neck label, and, with the addition of younger brothers Ernie on guitar and drums and Marvin on bass, plus Rudolph's brother-in-law Chris Jasper on keyboards, creating a brand of molten, rock-tinged funk that transformed them into an arena-headlining band.

The sons of O'Kelly Isley, Sr., and the former Sallye Bernice Bell, Kelly (as O'Kelly, Jr., was known), Rudolph, Ronald, and younger brother Vernon (who died in 1954) began singing gospel music as children, with their mother supplying piano accompaniment. In 1956, the remaining three caught a Greyhound to New York City. Their first record, "Angels Cried" b/w "Cow Jumped over the Moon," was issued in 1957 on the Teenage label. The group started turning heads with its energetic stage act at such leading black theaters as the Apollo in Harlem, the Uptown in Philadelphia, the Royal in Baltimore, and the Howard in Washington, D.C. The Isleys recorded for George Goldner in 1958, and four singles appeared on his Cindy, Gone, and Mark-X labels, all produced by Richard Barrett, none much more successful than their first.

Their break came in 1959 when they signed with RCA Victor Records and were placed with producers Hugo Peretti and Luigi Creatore. The two-part

---

TOP SONGS

(WE'LL BE) UNITED (Gamble, '66, *14 R&B*)

TOGETHER (Gamble, '67, *9 R&B*)

COWBOYS TO GIRLS (Gamble, '68, *1 R&B, 6 Pop*)

(LOVE IS LIKE A) BASEBALL GAME (Gamble, '68, *4 R&B, 26 Pop*)

SLOW DRAG (Gamble, '68, *12 R&B*)

SAD GIRL (Gamble, '69, *14 R&B*)

WHEN WE GET MARRIED (Gamble, '70, *8 R&B*)

(WIN, PLACE OR SHOW) SHE'S A WINNER (Gamble, '72, *12 R&B*)

I'LL ALWAYS LOVE MY MAMA (PART 1) (Gamble, '73, *6 R&B, 36 Pop*)

I WANNA KNOW YOUR NAME (Gamble, '73, *9 R&B*)

Additional Top 40 R&B Songs: 12

The Isley Brothers

United Artists, where their 1963–64 releases failed to generate much notice. They launched their own label, T-Neck (distributed by Atlantic and named for their place of residence, Teaneck, New Jersey), in 1964 with the self-produced "Testify," which featured a screaming solo by Jimi Hendrix, their guitarist at the time. It flopped, as did their next three T-Neck productions, issued on the Atlantic label.

The brothers' fortunes improved temporarily after joining Motown. "This Old Heart of Mine (Is Weak for You)," written and produced by Brian Holland, Lamont Dozier, and Eddie Holland and released on the Tamla label, was a number six R&B, number 12 pop hit in 1966, but none of their subsequent singles for the label managed to crack the R&B top 10 or the pop top 40. In 1969, they reactivated T-Neck and had a Number One R&B, number two pop hit with "It's Your Thing," a funk tune on which younger brother Ernie played bass. They maintained a consistent presence on the charts for the next 14 years with their T-Neck releases, at first distributed by Buddah and, beginning in 1973, by CBS. During the Buddah period, they scored not only with such originals as "I Turned You On," "Lay-Away," and "Pop That Thing" but also with inventive reworkings of rock songs like Stephen Stills's

---

TOP ALBUM

THE HEAT IS ON (T-Neck, '75, *1*)

Additional Top 40 Albums: 11

TOP SONGS

TWIST AND SHOUT (Wand, '62, *2 R&B, 17 Pop*)

IT'S YOUR THING (T-Neck, '69, *1 R&B, 2 Pop*)

LOVE THE ONE YOU'RE WITH (T-Neck, '71, *3 R&B, 18 Pop*)

THAT LADY (PART 1) (T-Neck, '73, *2 R&B, 6 Pop*)

FIGHT THE POWER PART 1 (T-Neck, '75, *1 R&B, 4 Pop*)

THE PRIDE (PART 1) (T-Neck, '77, *1 R&B*)

TAKE ME TO THE NEXT PHASE (PART 1) (T-Neck, '78, *1 R&B*)

I WANNA BE WITH YOU (PART 1) (T-Neck, '79, *1 R&B*)

DON'T SAY GOODNIGHT (IT'S TIME FOR LOVE) (PARTS 1 & 2) (T-Neck, '80, *1 R&B, 39 Pop*)

Additional Top 40 R&B Songs: 42

"Shout," derived from a wild call-and-response gospel vamp that they used to conclude their stage rendition of Jackie Wilson's "Lonely Teardrops," was a minor pop hit in 1960 and quickly became a staple in the repertoires of other groups, including Joey Dee and the Starlighters, whose 1962 version on Roulette was a number six pop charter.

The trio had little luck at Atlantic in 1961. They then moved to Wand Records, where a 1962 treatment of the Latin-flavored Bert Berns–Phil Medley tune "Twist and Shout," originally recorded for Atlantic by the Top Tones, became a number two R&B, number 17 pop hit. (The Beatles revived the song again two years later, taking it to number two on the pop chart.) The brothers then turned up on

"Love the One You're With" and Bob Dylan's "Lay Lady Lay."

The group's initial CBS-distributed album, *3 + 3,* announced the official arrival of Ernie and Marvin Isley and Chris Jasper. It was the first of 10 albums to go gold for the sextet, of which three—1977's *Go for Your Guns,* 1978's *Showdown,* and 1980's *Go All the Way*—also went platinum. With Ronald's soaring gospel tenor in the forefront and Ernie providing blistering Hendrix-inspired guitar parts, the group enjoyed one hit song after another, most of them six-way writing collaborations, a notable exception being a 1974 cover of Seals and Crofts' "Summer Breeze."

Ernie, Chris, and Marvin broke away in 1984 to form Isley, Jasper, Isley and had an R&B chart topper with the next year's "Caravan of Love" on the CBS Associated label. The original trio joined Warner Bros. in 1985, but Kelly died of a heart attack in 1986 and Rudolph left three years later to become a preacher. Besides continuing to score hits under the group banner, the biggest being 1987's "Smooth Sailin' Tonight" and 1989's "Spend the Night" (both number three R&B), Ronald teamed up with Rod Stewart for a number 10 pop remake of "This Old Heart of Mine" and with future wife Angela Winbush on the number 10 R&B "Lay Your Troubles Down" (both in 1990). In 1993, the Isley Brothers, comprising Ronald, Ernie, and Marvin, signed with Elektra, for which Ernie had recorded a solo album three years prior.

BULL MOOSE JACKSON

A small man whose bespectacled, owl-shaped face hardly matched the seductiveness of his warm, resonant baritone voice, Bull Moose Jackson (b. Benjamin Clarence Jackson, 1919, Cleveland, Ohio) was an unlikely hero of R&B's formative period. Yet it was former big-band jazzmen like Jackson who occupied the front ranks of this emerging musical genre. Alternating between smoothly crooned love ballads and jumping, often risqué blues and novelty numbers, the singer-saxophonist and his combo, the Buffalo Bearcats, chocked up eight top 10 R&B hits between 1946 and '49.

Jackson was a child soloist with the junior choir at Avery African Methodist Episcopal Church in his native Cleveland and, at age six, began playing violin in his elementary school's orchestra. He later played saxophone in the band at Central High School, where he teamed up with trumpeter Freddie Webster (later an important influence on Miles Davis) to form a jazz group called the Harlem Hotshots.

After a period in Buffalo, where he worked with several dance bands, Jackson returned to Cleveland and was discovered there in 1943 by bandleader Lucky Millinder. A fat-toned tenor saxophonist of the Coleman Hawkins school, Jackson replaced Lucky Thompson in Millinder's popular jazz orchestra and remained with the aggregation through 1947. Besides contributing to Millinder's Decca recording of "Shorty's Got to Go," a number four R&B charter in 1946, Jackson played alto saxophone on an all-star 1945 session for Capitol Records led by drummer Big Sid Catlett.

Although Millinder was an exclusive Decca recording artist, he began moonlighting at Syd Nathan's new Cincinnati operation, Queen Records. Backed by the Millinder band, Jackson made his solo debut on Queen in 1945 with "Bull Moose Jackson Blues" and scored big the next year with the comical, self-penned number four R&B "I Know Who Threw the Whiskey in the Well," an answer to "Who Threw the Whiskey in the Well," a major R&B and pop hit in 1945 by the Millinder orchestra featuring blues shouter Wynonie Harris.

After cutting a few sides for Irving Feld's Superdisc label later in 1946, Jackson joined Nathan's King Records roster and enjoyed the greatest hit of his career, 1947's "I Love You, Yes I Do." The sentimental ballad, written by Millinder trumpeter-arranger Henry Glover (with "Sally Nix," a Nathan pseudonym, receiving co-credit) and rendered in a Billy Eckstine–like baritone, not only reached the top of the R&B list but also made a strong impression with white consumers, peaking at number 21 on the pop chart. The song's success allowed Jackson to strike out on his own, and he organized the Buffalo Bearcats, outfitting them in loud uniforms and fur hats. The septet became a huge dance hall draw, especially in the deep South, where both blacks and whites flocked to see them perform.

Jackson remained with King through 1954, and his recorded output there was wonderfully diverse,

TOP SONGS

I KNOW WHO THREW THE WHISKEY IN THE WELL
(Queen, '46, 4 R&B)
I LOVE YOU, YES I DO (King, '47, 1 R&B, 21 Pop)
SNEAKY PETE (King, '48, 10 R&B)
ALL MY LOVE BELONGS TO YOU (King, '48, 3 R&B)
I WANT A BOWLEGGED WOMAN (King, '48, 5 R&B)
I CAN'T GO ON WITHOUT YOU (King, '48, 1 R&B)
DON'T ASK ME WHY (King, '49, 12 R&B)
LITTLE GIRL, DON'T CRY (King, '49, 2 R&B)
WHY DON'T YOU HAUL OFF AND LOVE ME?
(King, '49, 2 R&B)
I LOVE YOU YES I DO (Seven Arts, '61, 10 R&B)

Additional Top 40 R&B Songs: 2

ranging from such love songs as "All My Love Belongs to You," "I Can't Go On Without You," and "Little Girl, Don't Cry" to slow blues, jump blues, and raucous covers of country tunes like Wayne Raney's "Why Don't You Haul Off and Love Me" and Moon Mullican's "Cherokee Boogie (Eh-Oh-Aleena)." (Raney and Mullican were both King artists, and Nathan and staff producer Glover encouraged the company's white and black artists to record tunes from each other's repertoires.) Jackson's 1948 recording of "I Want a Bowlegged Woman" became a classic of double entendre, as did 1952's "Big Ten Inch Record," which didn't chart but was a jukebox favorite.

After 1949's "Why Don't You Haul Off and Love Me," Jackson was absent from the charts for a dozen years. He signed with Marterry, a short-lived Chess subsidiary, in 1956 and then recorded for Encino and Warwick before reentering the R&B chart at number 10 with a 1961 revival of "I Love You, Yes I Do" on Seven Arts. By that time, however, he had gotten into the catering business. He settled in Washington, D.C., in 1963 and went to work as a waiter at the Smithsonian Institution. Forming a trio, he began playing occasional engagements at the national museum as well as private parties, weddings, and bar mitzvahs in the area. In 1974, Jackson appeared in a film titled *Sincerely the Blues* and, three years later, joined trumpeter Buck Clayton's jazz combo for a swing through France, North Africa, and the Middle East. Before his death in 1989, he worked and recorded with a Pittsburgh band called the Flashcats.

FREDDIE JACKSON

Critics have not always been kind to Freddie Jackson (b. Oct. 2, 1956, New York). British author Barney Hoskyns, for instance, dismissed the Harlem-bred tenor's melisma-dripping style as "ornate, ultra-mannered" and "really a rococo perversion of the Vandross voice." Yet of all the romantic soul balladeers who emerged during the 1980s in the wake of Luther Vandross's huge success, Jackson came out the clear winner among African-American record buyers. While Jackson never achieved the crossover appeal of Vandross, he racked up ten R&B chart toppers between 1985 and '91, compared to Vandross's seven from 1981 to '92.

"They can write all kinds of nice and even nasty things about you in this business, some true and some not," the singer said in a 1989 interview with Charles E. Rogers of *Black Beat* magazine, "but what's really important is that I'm recognized as someone who gave his all to his art, someone who cared about making people happy through it."

Although he didn't become famous until his 28th year, Jackson was almost born on stage. His mother, a gospel singer, was in the midst of a performance when she went into labor. "Luckily," he explained in 1987 to *Playboy* writer Merrill Shindler, "there was a hospital just around the corner from the concert hall." Besides soaking up gospel and soul sounds at the Apollo Theater, the young Jackson attended and became a star soloist at Harlem's White Rock Baptist Church, the scene of an earlier fruitful meeting between Nickolas Ashford and Valerie Simpson. At the church, he formed a lasting friendship with Paul Laurence Jones, a pianist who'd been trained by Simpson. As "Paul Laurence," Jones later produced Jackson's breakthough single, 1985's "Rock Me Tonight (For Old Time's Sake)," as well as four more of the singer's Number One R&B hits.

Turning down an opportunity to attend New York's celebrated High School for the Performing Arts, Jackson enrolled in business school and learned to type 100 words per minute. After graduation, he worked by day as a clerk-typist at a bank and at night as lead vocalist of the Laurence Jones Ensemble. He moved to California in 1981 to join Mystic Merlin, a band that combined music and magic. Although the group had earlier seen moderate success on Capitol Records, its one album featuring Jackson, *Mr. Magician,* went unnoticed, apparently even by company executives who, when the vocalist signed as a solo artist three year later, were unaware that he had been on the label previously.

After his brief stint with Mystic Merlin failed to do the trick, Jackson returned to New York to sing in cabarets, record reference tracks for other singers, and tour as a background singer with Harry Belafonte, Angela Bofill, and others. One of Jackson's 1982 club dates, where his repertoire included some Luther Vandross songs, was attended by Capitol artist Melba Moore, who was so impressed that she introduced him to her management firm, Hush Productions. Besides working as a background singer for Moore and fellow Hush artist Lilo Thomas, Jackson reunited with Laurence to compose Moore's 1983 number 14 R&B chart single, "Keepin' My Lover Satisfied."

Hush placed Jackson's debut album, *Rock Me Tonight,* with Capitol. It was a sensation, rising to number 10 on the *Billboard* album chart and yielding two consecutive Number One R&B singles: the Laurence-penned-and-produced title track (reminiscent of Marvin Gaye's "Let's Get It On") and "You Are My Lady," written and produced by Moore's musical director, the Juilliard-trained Barry J. Eastmond. The former song stayed at Number One for six weeks and ranked as the top R&B song of 1985 on *Billboard*'s year-end chart, while the latter reached number 12 on the pop list, six points higher than its predecessor, giving the singer the greatest crossover showing of his career.

Although Jackson worked with other producers at Capitol, all of his R&B chart toppers were done with either Laurence or Eastmond, with the exception of "A Little Bit More," a 1986 Gene McFadden–produced duet with Moore. That song was knocked off the R&B pinnacle by Jackson's solo recording of "Tasty Love," a Laurence-Jackson composition, making him the first artist to replace himself in that position since Dinah Washington had 26 years earlier.

Jackson was the quintessential soul love man of the middle and late 1980s, applying his strong, elastic pipes to one slow or medium tempo ballad after another, seldom failing to crack the R&B top 10. If, like the late Marvin Gaye, he seemed a bit uncomfortable with the role onstage, he played it to the hilt on record, with such overtly erotic songs as "Nice 'n' Slow," "Love Me Down," and "Do Me Again."

In 1993, Jackson signed with RCA, a label that had turned down *Rock Me Tonight* eight years earlier.

JANET JACKSON

Singer-actress Janet Dameta Jackson (b. May 16, 1966, Gary, Indiana) literally grew up before the eyes of the world. The youngest of the nine children of Joe and Katherine Jackson, she made her stage debut at age seven, doing a sassy impression of Mae West during a show at the MGM Grand Hotel in Las Vegas starring her famous brothers, the Jackson 5. At 11, Janet became a regular on the Norman Lear TV sitcom "Good Times," playing the role of the precocious Penny Gordon for two seasons, before moving on to parts in "A New Kind of Family," "Diff'rent Strokes," and "Fame." At her father's insistance, she turned to recording, cutting two teen-oriented albums for A&M in 1982 and '84 with a hodgepodge of producers. Her singing was tentitive, however, and the results were only moderately successful. "Young Love," her first single, charted at number two R&B, while 1984's "Don't Stand Another Chance" reached number nine. Neither song cracked the pop top 40.

Even if Janet had little faith in her abilities as a vocalist, her dad had great expectations. "If Janet listens to me and works a little harder, she'll be as big

TOP ALBUM

ROCK ME TONIGHT (Capitol, '85, *10*)

Additional Top 40 Albums: 1

TOP SONGS

ROCK ME TONIGHT (FOR OLD TIMES' SAKE) (Capitol, '85, *1 R&B, 18 Pop*)
YOU ARE MY LADY (Capitol, '85, *1 R&B, 12 Pop*)
TASTY LOVE (Capitol, '86, *1 R&B*)
HAVE YOU EVER LOVED SOMEBODY (Capitol, '86, *1 R&B*)
JAM TONIGHT (Capitol, '87, *1 R&B, 32 Pop*)
NICE 'N' SLOW (Capitol, '88, *1 R&B*)
HEY LOVER (Capitol, '88, *1 R&B*)
LOVE ME DOWN (Capitol, '90, *1 R&B*)
DO ME AGAIN (Capitol, '91, *1 R&B*)

Additional Top 40 R&B Songs: 14

as Michael," Joe Jackson told *Spin* magazine. His prediction was almost on target, although it proved to be streetwise producer-songwriters James "Jimmy Jam" Harris III and Terry Lewis, both formerly of the group the Time, who shepherded Janet's transformation from chubby cherub to mature, confident artist.

After a marriage to James DeBarge, of the singing group DeBarge, that lasted less than a year and ended in annulment, Janet left the sheltered environment of her parents' Encino, California, mansion to spend six weeks of 1965 in Minneapolis working on an album with Jam and Lewis. Rather than simply being handed a set of songs to record, as she had in the past, the singer was given creative input, with the pair translating ideas taken from her conversations with them into songs and giving them slamming techno-funk underpinnings. Released in the spring of 1986, *Control* was the then-19-year-old entertainer's declaration of independence as a woman firmly in control of her own destiny. It vaulted to Number One on *Billboard*'s album chart and spawned six Number One singles. "What Have You Done for Me Lately," "Nasty," "Control," "Let's Wait Awhile" (which became an anthem of teenage sexual abstinence), and "The Pleasure Principle" (written and produced by former Time member Monte Moir) all topped the R&B chart, while "When I Think of You" stalled at number two R&B but reached Number One pop.

The *Control* album, especially the track "Nasty," was instrumental in introducing a syncopated, hip-

Janet Jackson

hop-inspired dance rhythm that became known as "new jack swing" and quickly permeated black popular music. The singer's aggressive new stance also served as a model for other female vocalists, including Paula Abdul. (After choreographing several of the videos for *Control,* the dancer emerged as a hugely popular vocalist in the Janet mold.) Janet herself refrained from touring in support of the smash album and stayed out of the studio for three years, other than to lend her wispy mezzo tones to trumpeter (and A&M co-owner) Herb Alpert's "Diamonds," a Number One R&B, number five pop charter in 1987.

The singer finally returned to Jam and Lewis's Flyte Tyme Studios to cut 1989's *Janet Jackson's Rhythm Nation 1814* (the date being an obscure reference to the year Francis Scott Key wrote "The Star-Spangled Banner"), her fourth and final album for A&M. Inspired by television news stories about crime, drugs, injustice, and illiteracy, the Number One album offered an optimistic vision and yielded four R&B and/or pop chart-topping singles: "Miss

TOP ALBUMS

CONTROL (A&M, '86, *1*)
JANET JACKSON'S RHYTHM NATION 1814
    (A&M, '89, *1*)
JANET. (Virgin, '93, *1*)

TOP SONGS

WHAT HAVE YOU DONE FOR ME LATELY (A&M,
    '86, *1 R&B, 4 Pop*)
NASTY (A&M, '86, *1 R&B, 3 Pop*)
LET'S WAIT AWHILE (A&M, '87, *1 R&B, 2 Pop*)
MISS YOU MUCH (A&M, '89, *1 R&B, 1 Pop*)
RHYTHM NATION (A&M, '89, *1 R&B, 2 Pop*)
ESCAPADE (A&M, '90, 1 R&B, *1 Pop*)
THAT'S THE WAY LOVE IS (Virgin, '93, *1 R&B, 1 Pop*)

Additional Top 40 R&B Songs: 12

You So Much," "Rhythm Nation," "Escapade," "Black Cat" (produced by Janet with another ex-Time musician, Jellybean Johnson), and "Love Will Never Do (Without You)." Janet toured for the first time in 1990, her elaborately staged arena concerts attracting capacity crowds and receiving mixed reviews.

Critical opinion remained divided on Janet when she reemerged with 93's *janet.*, her first release under a reported million contract with Virgin Records. Many hailed the rather experimental album, on which she shared production credits with Jam and Lewis, as a masterpiece, while one called it "a mess." The public embraced this bold celebration of her sexuality, taking *janet* to Number One. The first single, "That's the Way Love Goes," went to the top of both the R&B and pop charts. The ultra-erotic "If" peaked at number three R&B and number seven pop, and a third single, "Again," reached number seven R&B and Number One pop.

Before embarking on a successful 1993 world tour, the now-svelte singer starred in the hit John Singleton film romance *Poetic Justice* and posed for the cover of *Rolling Stone,* her bare breasts covered by the hands of Rene Elizondo, her longtime boyfriend. Janet Jackson had indeed grown up.

MICHAEL JACKSON

Although Stevie Wonder holds down the all-time record for being the individual with the most Number One singles on the *Billboard* R&B chart—19 in all—Michael Jackson (b. Aug. 29, 1958, Gary, Indiana) nearly matches that count if his six Number One R&B entries as lead vocalist of the Jackson 5 are combined with his dozen as a solo artist. But while the extraordinary singer and dancer raked in the hits, selling over 110 million records worldwide during the 1980s alone, controversy continually swelled around him. His chameleon-like facial alterations and his bizarre personal behavior—some real, some alleged, some the figments of his own publicity-seeking imagination—became regular fodder for the tabloids and eventually the nightly news.

When the Jackson 5 made their national television debut, on October 18, 1969, on ABC's "The Hollywood Palace," host Diana Ross, ignoring the cue card, introduced the group as "Michael Jackson and the Jackson 5." Joe Jackson, the brothers' father and manager, fumed backstage. He didn't want his second youngest son singled out for special recognition. Yet from the beginning it was clear that Michael, the quintet's singing and dancing dynamo, was somebody very special.

Michael made his performing debut with the group at age five and was greatly influenced by such R&B stars as James Brown and Jackie Wilson, both of whom combined song and dance in their stunning stage acts. After two years of smash hits with the Jackson 5, Michael became the first of the brood to cut a solo album. *Got to Be There,* issued in Jaunary 1972, charted at number 14 and contained three hit singles: the number four R&B and pop title track, the number two R&B and pop updating of the 1958 Bobby Day classic "Rockin' Robin," and the number two R&B, number 16 pop "I Wanna Be Where You Are." The second album, 1972's *Ben,* rose to number five with the help of only one single, the title cut, a sentimental ballad about a bond between a boy and a rat. The song not only hinted at the singer's ongoing passion for animals but gave him the first of his 12 pop chart toppers. (The song peaked at number five on the R&B list.) Each of Michael's first two solo albums sold a respectable 350,000. The next two solo efforts, 1974's *Music and Me* and 1975's *Forever, Michael,* were less well received, selling under 100,000 units apiece.

In 1978, Michael co-starred with Diana Ross in Sidney Lumet's motion picture adaptation of the Broadway musical *The Wiz,* with Quincy Jones serving as musical director. "Ease on Down the Road," a duet with Ross from the MCA soundtrack album, became a number 17 R&B hit, while Michael's solo single "You Can't Win" failed to crack the top 40. During the film's production, however, Michael let it be known that he was looking for a producer for his next solo album. Jones volunteered. The result was 1979's *Off the Wall,* the Epic album that launched Michael's ascent to mega-stardom. Selling six-million copies, it generated three top 10 R&B singles: "Don't Stop 'Til You Get Enough," "Rock with You," and the title track.

The Jones-produced follow-up, 1983's *Thriller,* set an all-time record, selling some 40 million copies worldwide, over 20 million in the U.S. alone. Four top 10 R&B singles resulted: "Billie Jean," "Beat It," "Wanna Be Startin' Somethin'," and the title song. Also in 1983, Michael performed two duets with Paul McCartney: the Number One R&B, number two pop "The Girl Is Mine" and the number two R&B, Number One pop "Say Say Say." The following year, Michael purchased the ATV Music catalog for $45.7 million. Among the publishing company's holdings were most of McCartney and John Lennon's compositions for the Beatles, as well as tunes by Little Richard and numerous other blues, soul, rock, and gospel artists.

The singer's third Epic album, 1987's *Bad*, co-produced by Jones and Jackson, sold seven million in the U.S and became the first LP ever to spawn five chart-topping singles: "I Just Can't Stop Loving You," "Bad," "The Way You Make Me Feel," "Man in the Mirror" (all Number One R&B and pop), and "Dirty Diana" (number five R&B, Number One pop). A world tour, launched in Tokyo on September 12, 1987, and covering 15 countries, grossed over $125 million at the box office.

Having renegotiated his contract with Sony Music, Epic's parent company, for an unprecedented $65 million, Michael revamped his sound for 1991's *Dangerous* album, bringing in new jack swingmeister Teddy Riley for most of the selections. The disc debuted at Number One and contained the number three R&B, Number One pop "Black or White" (produced by Jackson and Bill Bottrell) and the Number One R&B, number three pop "Remember the Time."

On August 24, 1993, while in Asia on the first leg

of an international tour, Michael became embroiled in the most serious controversy of his life. News broke that Los Angeles County authorities were investigating accusations that the entertainer had sexually molested a 13-year-old boy. While no criminal charges were filed, the child's father slapped the superstar with a civil suit. Michael maintained his innocence but eventually settled the case out of court, a move that led to widespread speculation about the future of his career.

MILLIE JACKSON

While vocalist Denise LaSalle began her career as a writer of fiction for black confessional magazines, soul music's other queen of rap, Millie Jackson (b. Mildred Jackson, July 15, 1944, Thompson, Georgia) got her start in the entertainment business as a teenage model for some of the same publications. "I did the story thing in photos in magazines like *Bronze Thrills, Jive, Tan* …posing under captions that said, 'My father made me marry this old man,' and there's a picture of me sitting on a bed in a negligee with an old man whose hand is on my knee," she recalled in a 1980 interview with Frederick Douglas Murphy of *Black Stars* magazine, which had earlier been known as *Tan*. "Then on the cover of another magazine, I'm wearing shorts and swinging a baseball bat under the title 'I had to fight for my man.' "

Millie the model would eventually employ similar plots in her music. She was a rapper before there was a musical genre called rap. Her type of rap consisted of saucy monologues tossed into her throaty renditions of southern, country-tinged soul ballads. The first to gain notice appeared in the middle of her tour de force revamp of Luther Ingram's "(If Loving You Is Wrong) I Don't Want to Be Right" from the 1974 concept album *Caught Up*, volume one in a trilogy of discs on which she explored the complexities of a love triangle, alternating between the roles of wife and mistress. "The sweetest thing about the whole situation," she proclaimed about being in love with a married man, "is the fact that, when you go to the laudromat, you don't have to wash nobody's funky drawers but your own." That punch line created a sensation, helping to make *Caught Up* the biggest selling album of Jackson's career. It was also a precursor to more outrageous, increasingly salacious

---

TOP ALBUMS

OFF THE WALL (Epic, '79, 3)
THRILLER (Epic, '82, 1)
BAD (Epic, '87, 1)
DANGEROUS (Epic, '91, 1)

Additional Top 40 Albums: 2

TOP SONGS

DON'T STOP 'TIL YOU GET ENOUGH (Epic, '79,
    1 R&B, 1 Pop)
ROCK WITH YOU (Epic, '79, 1 R&B, 1 Pop)
BILLIE JEAN (Epic, '83, 1 R&B, 1 Pop)
BAD (Epic, '87, 1 R&B, 1 Pop)
THE WAY YOU MAKE ME FEEL (Epic, '87, 1 R&B,
    1 Pop)
REMEMBER THE TIME (Epic, '92, 1 R&B, 3 Pop)

Additional Top 40 R&B Songs: 26

Millie Jackson

Sam Cooke, Jackson returned to New York and got a job at Kimberly Knitwear, where she worked as an assistant supervisor in the shipping department.

Through songwriter Billy Nichols, the singer was introduced to producer Don French and signed to MGM Records, for whom she cut one unsuccessful single, "A Little Bit of Something," in 1969. Two years later, she was recording for the new Polydor-distributed Spring label, with which she would remain through the mid-1980s. "A Child of God," a ballad penned by Jackson and French, was Jackson's debut single for the company and rose to number 22 on the *Billboard* R&B chart. She held onto her day job, however, until the top 10 R&B success of the following year's Raeford Gerald–produced "Ask Me What You Want" convinced her that becoming a full-time entertainer was worth the risk.

In 1973, the singer scored her biggest hit single, a medium-tempo Phillip Mitchell–penned deep soul ballad titled "Hurts So Good" that was included on the soundtrack of the motion picture *Cleopatra Jones*. Recorded in Muscle Shoals, Alabama, the number four R&B, number 24 pop song marked the beginning of Jackson's long-term association with producer Brad Shapiro. They worked together (with Jackson as co-producer) for a decade, initially in Muscle Shoals, later in Nashville. Jackson also produced the vocal group Facts of Life, whose 1976

things to come, most of them unplayable on the radio.

"When I started singing, if you didn't have one of those very high voices, you weren't considered a singer," Jackson said in 1981. "I always sounded like the fellas. I found they liked my talkin' better than the singin', so I developed the rap."

Jackson, who credits Gladys Knight and Otis Redding as influences, never intended to be a singer. It happened on a dare, in 1964, when some of her friends coaxed her to get on stage during an amateur show at the Palms Cafe in Harlem. She went over so well that she was soon booked at the Club Zanzibar in Hoboken, New Jersey, and at the 521 Club in Brooklyn. Following a year and a half on the road as a background vocalist for L. C. Cooke, brother of

---

TOP ALBUMS

Caught Up (Spring, '74, *21*)
Feelin' Bitchy (Spring, '77, *34*)

TOP SONGS

Ask Me What You Want (Spring, '72, *4 R&B, 27 Pop*)
My Man, A Sweet Man (Spring, '72, *7 R&B*)
Hurts So Good (Spring, '73, *3 R&B, 24 Pop*)
How Do You Feel the Morning After (Spring, '74, *11 R&B*)
If You're Not Back in Love by Monday (Spring, '77, *5 R&B*)
All the Way Lover (Spring, '78, *12 R&B*)
Hot! Wild! Unrestricted! Crazy Love (Jive, '86, *9 R&B*)
Love Is a Dangerous Game (Jive, '87, *6 R&B*)

Additional Top 40 R&B Songs: 15

recording of "Sometimes" on the Kayvette label became a number three R&B hit.

Jackson herself had only three more top 10 R&B singles after "Hurts So Good": 1977's "If You're Not Back in Love by Monday," 1986's "Hot! Wild! Unrestricted! Crazy Love," and 1987's "Love Is a Dangerous Game," the latter two issued on the Jive label, live versions of which were included on the self-produced 1989 album *Back to the S—t*, its cover depicting Jackson grimacing as she sat, her panties around her ankles, on a commode. Much of her material, laced with profanity and dealing with such subjects as interracial romance and oral sex, had become too bold for radio, but albums and personal appearances geared toward working-class African-American adults remained her bread and butter.

THE JACKSONS

The nine Gary, Indiana-born offspring of Joseph Jackson and the former Katherine Scruce—Maureen Reilette "Rebbie" Jackson (b. May 29, 1950), Sigmund Esco "Jackie" Jackson (b. May 4, 1951), Toriano Adaryal "Tito" Jackson (b. Oct. 15, 1953), Jermaine La Jaune Jackson (b. Dec. 11, 1954), La Toya Yvonne Jackson (b. May 16, 1956), Marlon David Jackson (b. Mar. 12, 1957), Michael Joseph Jackson (b. Aug. 29, 1958), Steven Randall "Randy" Jackson (b. Oct. 19, 1961), and Janet Dameta Jackson (b. May 16, 1966)—have been a prolific lot. All received an early education in show business from their father, a crane operator at U.S. Steel and former rhythm and blues guitarist, with the exception of the oldest, Rebbie, who didn't begin performing until she was in her mid-20s.

The family singing group began in the early 1960s as a trio comprising Jackie, Tito, and Jermaine. By 1964, Marlon and Michael had joined. The quintet became known first as the Ripples and Waves Plus Michael, then as the Jackson Brothers, and finally as the Jackson 5. The group won local talent contests and began appearing at Mr. Lucky's, a Gary nightclub, as well as at small venues in nearby Chicago. The Jackson 5 cut their first record, "Bad Boy," in 1968 for the Gary-based Steeltown label. It became a minor regional hit, and engagements followed at the Regal in Chicago, the Apollo in New York, and other leading black theaters and clubs throughout the Midwest and East. Among the established artists who witnessed the youngsters' amazingly energetic act were Gladys Knight and Bobby Taylor, both of whom recorded for Motown.

Berry Gordy, Jr., head of the thriving Detroit firm, learned of the Jackson 5 through Knight and Taylor and signed them on March 11, 1969. He soon moved the brothers and their father to Los Angeles, where the company was in the process of relocating. While the others were put up in cheap motels, Michael stayed at the home of Diana Ross, who was falsely credited by Motown's publicity department with having discovered the group.

The Jackson 5's first Motown single, "I Want

The Jacksons

TOP ALBUMS

ABC (The Jackson 5, Motown, '70, 4)
THIRD ALBUM (The Jackson 5, Motown, '70, 4)
VICTORY (The Jacksons, Epic, '84, 4)

Additional Top 40 Albums: 11

TOP SONGS

The Jackson 5:
I WANT YOU BACK (Motown, '69, *1 R&B, 1 Pop*)
ABC (Motown, '70, *1 R&B, 1 Pop*)
THE LOVE YOU SAVE (Motown, '70, *1 R&B, 1 Pop*)
I'LL BE THERE (Motown, '70, *1 R&B, 1 Pop*)
NEVER CAN SAY GOODBYE (Motown, '71, *1 R&B,
    2 Pop*)
DANCING MACHINE (Motown, '74, *1 R&B, 2 Pop*)

The Jacksons:
HEARTBREAK HOTEL (Epic, '80, *2 R&B, 22 Pop*)

Additional Top 40 R&B Songs: 26

You Back," issued in October 1969 and featuring 11-year-old Michael's wondrously flexible, remarkably mature lead vocals, topped the *Billboard* R&B and pop charts and made the brothers international superstars. The song was written and produced by Freddie Perren, Fonze Mizell, and Deke Richards, with Gordy sharing a quarter of the credits, as were the group's next two Number One R&B and pop hits, "ABC" and "The Love You Save," both released in 1970. Later that year, the Jacksons repeated the same two-chart feat with the Hal Davis–produced ballad "I'll Be There." Davis also produced the group's only other R&B chart toppers, 1971's "Never Can Say Goodbye" and 1974's "Dancing Machine," both of which stalled at number two pop.

Motown, while still recording the Jackson 5 as a unit, began making solo records by Michael, Jackie, and Jermaine. Michael hit number four on both charts with his debut solo single, 1971's "Got to Be There," and Jermaine scored at number three R&B and number nine pop with his second 45, a 1972 remake of the Shep and the Limelights doo wop classic "Daddy's Home." No singles were issued from Jackie's only solo album, an unsuccessful 1972 affair.

By 1975, Rebbie, La Toya, Randy, and Janet had become part of the stage act, now known as the Jackson 5 Revue. In a quest for more artistic freedom, the Jackson 5 left Motown for Epic the following year—all except Jermaine. Having been married to Berry Gordy's daughter Hazel since 1973, he elected to stay behind as a solo artist and was replaced in the core quintet's lineup by Randy. Motown also held claim to the Jackson 5 name. Thereafter, the group was billed as the Jacksons.

At Epic, the group cut two albums with Philadelphia producers Kenny Gamble and Leon Huff, 1976's *The Jacksons* and 1977's *Goin' Places,* followed by the self-produced *Destiny* in 1978 and *Triumph* in 1980. The Jacksons' biggest post-Motown singles were "Enjoy Yourself," "Lovely One," and "Heartbreak Hotel," each of which reached number two R&B. As Michael's solo career skyrocketed, they disbanded, but the group reunited (with Jermaine back in the fold) for 1984's *Victory* album and a tour of the same title. Without Michael and Marlon, the remaining brothers made the final Jacksons album, 1989's *2300 Jackson Street,* containing the number four R&B single "Nothing (That Compares 2 U)."

Aside from Michael and Janet, Jermaine has been the most successful solo artist from the family, having garnered 20 top 40 R&B singles between 1972 and '92, including two R&B chart toppers: 1980's Stevie Wonder–produced "Let's Get Serious" on Motown and 1989's "Don't Take It Personal" on Arista. Rebbie had four top 40 R&B entries, the biggest being 1984's number four "Centipede," a Columbia single written and produced by Michael. Marlon had one, 1987's number two R&B "Don't Go" on Capitol, and Randy, with his band Randy and the Gypsys, hit number 16 R&B in 1990 with "Love You Honey" on A&M. La Toya, who eventually became estranged from the rest of the family, had four, none of which cracked the top 20.

ETTA JAMES

Applying her powerhouse contralto voice with alternating toughness and tenderness to rock and roll, down-home blues, uptown jazz ballads, stomping soul, and even country tunes, always with great emotional urgency, Etta James (b. Jamesetta Hawkins, Jan. 25, 1938) has produced a remarkably varied body of music since her first appearance on disc in 1955. Chess Records billed her as the "Queen of Soul" during the early 1960s, and for that brief period, she was—scoring nine entries in the R&B top 10 between 1960 and '63. Heroin addiction soon took its toll on her career, though she continued to record prolifically, score occasional hits, and win the praise of critics.

The illegitimate child of an Italian father and a teenaged African-American mother, James was raised in Los Angeles by her grandparents. She sang at St. Paul Baptist Church, where she was inspired by choir directors J. Earle Hines and Cora Martin. (Bluesman Johnny "Guitar" Watson was an important later influence.) At 11, she moved to San Francisco to join her mother, Dorothy Hawkins.

"She was a night person," James said. "She was always into something that she wasn't supposed to be into. She was never there when I got off from school, so I could pretty much do what I wanted to do. I was considered incorrigible—you know, running around with tattoos on my arm, drinking, smoking weed."

One thing that James's mother, a jazz fan, was strict about was her daughter's musical tastes. "Don't listen to that gutbucket blues," James recalled her saying. But around the corner, at her friend Sugar Pie DeSanto's house, James was able to listen to and sing the type of rhythm and blues that she and other young people of her generation so adored. (James and DeSanto toured as a duo during the mid-1960s and recorded two singles together.)

In 1954, when she was 15, James and two friends auditioned for Johnny Otis at a San Francisco hotel. They'd worked up a response to the Midnighters' then-popular hit "Work with Me Annie," calling it "Roll with Me Henry." The bandleader was so impressed with the song and James's mature lead vocals that he offered to take her to Los Angeles to record the next day. When he asked her if she was 18, she lied. He then sent her home to get permission from her mother, who was in jail at the time. James forged the signature.

With Richard Berry contributing the bass voice,

Etta James

TOP SONGS

THE WALLFLOWER (Modern, '55, *1 R&B*)

GOOD ROCKIN' DADDY (Modern, '55, *6 R&B*)

ALL I COULD DO WAS CRY (Argo, '60, *2 R&B, 33 Pop*)

IF I CAN'T HAVE YOU (Etta & Harvey, Chess, '60, *6 R&B*)

MY DEAREST DARLING (Argo, '60, *5 R&B, 34 Pop*)

AT LAST (Argo, '61, *2 R&B*)

TRUST IN ME (Argo, '61, *4 R&B, 30 Pop*)

DON'T CRY, BABY (Argo, '61, *6 R&B, 39 Pop*)

SOMETHING'S GOT A HOLD ON ME (Argo, '62, *4 R&B, 37 Pop*)

STOP THE WEDDING (Argo, '62, *6 R&B, 34 Pop*)

Additional Top 40 R&B Songs: 12

James's Otis-produced recording of "Roll with Me Henry," which appeared on the Modern label under the title "The Wallflower," became a Number One R&B smash, while a less racy rendition by Georgia Gibbs titled "Dance with Me Henry" topped the pop chart. A follow-up,"Good Rockin' Daddy," also did well, after which James dropped off the charts for nearly five years, although she continued to tour, for a time with zydeco accordionist Clifton Chenier's band.

Through Moonglows leader Harvey Fuqua, her boyfriend at the time, James signed with Chess Records in 1960 and remained with the Chicago company for 16 years, with releases appearing on the firm's Argo, Chess, and Cadet labels. Her first four years with Chess were the most successful and yielded such hits as the ballads "All I Could Do Was Cry," "My Dearest Darling," "At Last," and "Trust in Me" (all featuring the sumptuous yet bluesy string arrangements of Riley Hampton) and the rocking, gospel-styled "Something's Got a Hold on Me." After a three-year sales slump, James returned strong in 1967 with the number 10 R&B "Tell Mama," written by Clarence Carter and produced in Muscle Shoals, Alabama, by Rick Hall. Peaking at number 23 on the pop chart, it was her greatest success among whites but her last top 10 R&B entry.

Finally kicking her drug habit in the mid-1970s and then leaving Chess, James hopped from label to label, including Warner Bros. (with producer Jerry Wexler), T-Electric (with Allen Toussaint), Fantasy (where she was paired with Eddie "Cleanhead" Vinson in 1986 for two brilliant jazz albums), Island

(with former Muscle Shoals keyboardist Barry Beckett producing), Elektra (again with Wexler), and Private Music (which issued a John Snyder–produced 1994 set of tunes associated with Billie Holiday).

Although James has no trouble getting bookings at major blues and jazz festivals and clubs around the world and winning critical raves for her post-Chess output, the eclecticism of her music has made it difficult for radio programmers and record rackers to categorize. "I wanna show that gospel, country, blues, rhythm and blues, jazz, and rock and roll are all really just one thing," she stated. "Those are the American music and that is the American culture."

RICK JAMES

As a juvenile delinquent and aspiring musician, Rick James (b. James Ambrose Johnson, Jr., Feb. 1, 1948, Buffalo, New York) dreamed of one day being affiliated with Motown Records. He did, in fact, get his wish three times. During the mid-1960s, when he called himself Ricky James Matthews, the singer, bassist, and songwriter was a member of the Mynah Birds; the Toronto-based folk-rock group, which also included future star Neil Young, cut one album for the company, but it was never issued. By 1969, he was back at Motown, as a staff songwriter, but the association was brief and garnered only one moderate hit, "Malinda," a number 16 R&B charter for Bobby Taylor and the Vancouvers. He returned in 1978 as solo artist Rick James with *Come Get It!,* an album on Motown's Gordy label that launched his 10-year run on the R&B charts as the self-described King of Punk Funk.

James Johnson often tried to distance himself from his alter-ego, the sex-charged, dope-smoking performer Rick James. "I'm just tired of hearing people think Rick James is this freak...this crazy kind of manic person," he told Leonard Pitts, Jr., in a 1981 *Los Angeles Herald Examiner* interview. "In a way he is, but in a way he's not. I mean, that's just Rick James. People don't understand that Rick James is a character...who was created by me...for me. I play him very well. But there's two different people." The hedonism James projected on records and in concert caught up with Johnson in the end, however.

Like his mother, numbers runner Mabel Gladden Johnson, the young James frequently found himself in trouble with the law. He ran away to New York

TOP ALBUM

STREET SONGS (Gordy, '81, 3)

Additional Top 40 Albums: 5

TOP SONGS

YOU AND I (Gordy, '78, *1 R&B, 13 Pop*)

MARY JANE (Gordy, '78, *3 R&B*)

GIVE IT TO ME BABY (Gordy, '81, *1 R&B, 40 Pop*)

SUPER FREAK (PART 1) (Gordy, '81, *3 R&B, 16 Pop*)

STANDING ON THE TOP—PART 1 (The Temptations
featuring Rick James, Gordy, '82, *6 R&B*)

DANCE WIT' ME—PART 1 (Gordy, '82, *3 R&B*)

COLD BLOODED (Gordy, '83, *1 R&B, 40 Pop*)

GLOW (Gordy, '83, *5 R&B*)

LOOSEY'S RAP (Rick James featuring Roxanne
Shante, Reprise, '88, *1 R&B*)

Additional Top 40 R&B Songs: 14

City at age seven in his first attempt to to secure a recording contract. Back home in Buffalo, he stole vehicles, even a city bus, "because," he told *Us* magazine in 1981, "it was big and there were keys in it." Lying about his age, James enlisted in the U.S. Naval Reserve at 15, went AWOL, and fled to Canada, where he joined the Mynah Birds. Besides James and Neil Young, the band included Young's future Buffalo Springfield bandmate Bruce Palmer and Goldy McJohn, later of Steppenwolf.

After his late-'60s songwriting stint at Motown, James played in a variety of bands, including White Cane, with which he recorded an album in 1972 for MGM's Lion label. Two years later, he turned up as a solo artist with "My Mama," a self-penned-and-produced single on A&M that sounded like a cross between Buffalo Springfield and Sly and the Family Stone. Bitten by the funk bug, James took his next project to Motown, which signed him an artist and producer. *Come Get It!,* his 1978 album debut on the Gordy label, went gold and spawned two hit singles: the disco-flavored "You and I" (its lyrics filled with double entendres) and the funkier "Mary Jane" (a euphemism for marijuana). A Number One R&B charter, "You and I" placed at number 13 pop, his greatest success with white record buyers. Throughout his career, James bemoaned the fact that rock audiences were not more open to his strongly rock-imbued brand of funk.

Two 1979 albums—*Bustin' Out of L Seven* ("L7" equalling "square") and *Fire It Up*—were comparatively less successful, and, by year's end, he was hospitalized for hepatitis. Asserting that he'd cleaned up his lifestyle, James reemerged in 1981 with *Street Songs,* his first and only platinum album. It featured a guest appearence by the Temptations, as well as rock artists Grace Slick and John McFee, and contained the hits "Give It to Me Baby" and "Super Freak." Touring with his 10-member Stone City Band and vocalist Teena Marie (whose 1979 number eight R&B hit "I'm a Sucker for Your Love" he had produced), James presented an elaborate show that included eight-foot-high reefer-shaped pillars and a skit in which two prostitutes and their pimp kicked a policeman unmercifully. And, during performances, James would fire up a fat joint and dare any cop in the arena to arrest him.

James continued writing and producing hits, not only for himself but also for his female backup group, the Mary Jane Girls (1985's number seven R&B "In My House"), and comedian-turned-vocalist Eddie Murphy (1985's number eight R&B, number two pop "Party All the Time"), through 1986, but he was dropped by Motown the following year. He then signed with Reprise, where he had the 1988 R&B chart topper "Loosey's Rap," featuring rapper Roxanne Shante. Two years later, he saw M. C. Hammer use "Super Freak" as the foundation for the rap smash "U Can't Touch This."

James's life hit rock bottom in 1991, when he was arrested for holding one woman against her will and forcing another to engage in sex with his girlfriend during a six-day crack binge. At the time of the crime, according to his defense attorney, James had a $10,000-a-week cocaine habit. Instead of prison, the musician was sent in 1994 to the California Rehabilitation Center.

LITTLE WILLIE JOHN

Little Willie John (b. William Edgar John, Nov. 17, 1937, Camden, Arkansas) grew up fast and died young. The diminutive vocalist scored his first hit at age 17 and succumbed in a Washington State penitentiary at 30. Like the legendary Mississippi delta bluesman Robert Johnson, the former gospel singer is rumored to have made a pact with the devil, reaped the rewards, and eventually paid the price.

As intense on stage and in the studio as he was bellicose in his personal life, John left behind a galvanizing body of work from a recording career that spanned only nine years (1954–63), including the original version of the now-standard "Fever." He was, James Brown once stated, "a soul singer before anyone thought to call it that."

John's elastic, emotion-searing tenor voice emitted, in the words of author Barney Hoskyns, "a bizarrely magnetic sound, this sharp, slightly hoarse adolescent wail, with notes flattened at random and words chewed with delinquent disdain. He erupts out of the smooth flow of '50s melisma with a raw, frayed angst, at once doo-wop shrill and jazz-weary, cynically young and sempiternally withered."

The youngest child of Mertis and church pianist Lillian John, Willie moved from Arkansas to Detroit in 1942 when his father got a job on the Dodge assembly line. As a boy, he sang in a gospel quartet called the United Four that included his sister Mable John, who would later become the first solo female vocalist to record for Motown before going on score a number six R&B hit in 1966 with "Your Good Thing (Is About to End)" on Stax and join the Raeletts. Willie began slipping out of his bedroom window at night to sing in clubs and, by age 11, was a regular performer at the Book-Cadillac Hotel. Jazz musicians, including Count Basie, Duke Ellington, and Dizzy Gillespie, took a liking to him, and in 1951 he participated in a talent contest at Detroit's Paradise Theater that was attended by Johnny Otis. The bandleader recommended three acts he heard that evening—John, Jackie Wilson, and the Royals—to Syd Nathan of King Records in Cincinnati. Nathan passed on the two solo singers, but signed the Royals, who, after adding lead vocalist Hank Ballard, became known as the Midnighters.

John cut his first record, "Mommy What Happened to the Christmas Tree?," in 1954 for the obscure Prize label. He spent much of that year on the road with R&B bandleader Paul Williams, of "The Hucklebuck" fame, but was fired because of his wild antics. Stranded in New York City, the singer found his way to the branch office of King Records and auditioned for producer Henry Glover. John was signed on the spot and the next day recorded a cover version of Titus Turner's "All Around the World." John's sassy reading of the song quickly ecliped Turner's original, peaking at number five on the *Billboard* R&B chart. (Retitled "Grits Ain't Groceries," the tune became a number 13 R&B charter for Little Milton in 1969.) The next John release—"Need Your Love So Bad," backed with the Rudy Toombs blues "Home at Last"—was a double-sided hit.

The teenaged vocalist enjoyed the biggest record of his career with 1956's Number One R&B, number 24 pop "Fever," penned by Otis Blackwell and Eddie Cooley (and successfully revived by Peggy Lee two years later). More hits followed until 1961, including "Talk to Me, Talk to Me," "Let Them Talk," and "Heartbreak (It's Hurtin' Me)," but John had become increasingly reckless, squandering his money, then borrowing from others. (Falsely claiming that his mother had died, he is said to have conned Sam Cooke out of $5,000.) By the time King dropped him in 1963, his life had entered a downward spiral of drinking, gambling, and violence.

John was arrested in August 1964 for attacking a man with a broken beer bottle at a Miami club. He jumped bail and, two months later, stabbed a railroad worker to death following an argument at a Seattle speakeasy. Convicted of manslaughter, John began serving his eight-to-20-year sentence in July 1966 at Washington State Penitentiary at Walla Walla. He died there on May 27, 1968. Prison officials gave the cause as pneumonia, although there was speculation that it was the result of a severe beating.

Funeral services were held in Detroit, with Rev. C. L. Franklin delivering the eulogy and his daughter Aretha singing. In attendance were James Brown, Joe Tex, William Bell, Eddie Floyd, and Sam and Dave. Brown, who had once been John's opening act, recorded a tribute album later that year titled *Thinking of Little Willie John and a Few Nice Things*.

TOP SONGS

ALL AROUND THE WORLD (King, '55, 5 R&B)

NEED YOUR LOVE SO BAD (King, '56, 5 R&B)

HOME AT LAST (King, '56, 6 R&B)

FEVER (King, '56, 1 R&B, 24 Pop)

LETTER FROM MY DARLING (King, '56, 10 R&B)

TALK TO ME, TALK TO ME (King, '58, 5 R&B, 20 Pop)

LET THEM TALK (King, '59, 11 R&B)

HEARTBREAK (IT'S HURTIN' ME) (King, '60, 11 R&B, 38 Pop)

SLEEP (King, '60, 10 R&B, 13 Pop)

TAKE MY LOVE (I WANT TO GIVE IT ALL TO YOU) (King, '61, 5 R&B)

Additional Top 40 R&B Songs: 7

BUDDY JOHNSON

Big band jazz was one of the major antecedents of rhythm and blues. The orchestras of Count Basie, Tiny Bradshaw, Lionel Hampton, Erskine Hawkins, and Lucky Millinder were important links between the two genres, and all enjoyed hits into the R&B era. Yet none provided as vital a bridge between the two as did that of Buddy Johnson (b. Woodrow Wilson Johnson, Jan. 10, 1915, Darlington, South Carolina). The pianist, songwriter, and arranger, whose recording career spanned from 1939 into the early '60s, not only anticipated R&B with such blues-based World War II–era compositions as "Please Mr. Johnson" and "Since I Fell for You" but also eventually embraced the new form, as the titles of such late '50s tunes as "Rock On" and "Go Ahead and Rock" declared.

Johnson, who took up the piano at age four, was greatly inspired by the big bands of Basie, Cab Calloway, Duke Ellington, Fletcher Henderson, Earl Hines, Andy Kirk, and Chick Webb. Settling in New York City in 1938, Johnson toured Europe the following year with a Cotton Club revue and ended up in Berlin on the eve of World War II. Forced to make a hasty departure with the aid of the U.S. Consulate, he left behind most of his personal belongings, including a pile of original scores. These were found at the end of hostilities in the rubble of a bombed-out building and returned to him by American occupation forces.

Back in New York, he was spotted at a Greenwich Village club by a scout for Decca Records and signed to a short-term contract. His first 78, the self-penned "Stop Pretending (So Hip You See)," featuring vocals by Johnson and the Mack Sisters, became a hit in 1940, as did a cover version by the Ink Spots, also on Decca. He scored again in 1941 with his blues ballad "Please Mr. Johnson," on which his sister Ella Johnson (b. June 22, 1939, Darlington, South Carolina) made her recording debut. She served as his female vocalist for the remainder of his career and was featured on such later hits as "When My Man Comes Home," "That's the Stuff You Gotta Watch," "Since I Fell for You," "I Don't Care Who Knows," "Hittin' on Me," and "Bring It Home to Me." ("Since I Fell for You," the quintessential Buddy Johnson blues ballad, originally recorded in 1945, gave pianist Paul Gayten and His Trio, featuring vocalist Annie Laurie, a number three R&B, number 20 pop hit two years later, and singer Lenny Welch had a number four pop charter with it in 1963.) Critic Leonard Feather wrote in *The Encyclopedia of Jazz* that Ella "is one of the great individualists of modern blues singing; the combination of her laconic style and her brother's ingenious arrangements and lyrics is unique and delightful."

The success of Buddy's first two hits led to a long-term Decca contract and enabled him to enlarge his band. Nine pieces in 1942, it expanded to 16 within two years. While Buddy sang on such uptempo material as 1943's "Let's Beat Out Some Love" and the next year's "Fine Brown Frame" (later covered successfully by Nellie Lutcher), the romantic leads went to Warren Evans, the voice on 1943's "Baby Don't You Cry." Evans was replaced at the end of that year by Arthur Prysock, whose resonant bass-baritone pipes were featured on the Johnson hits "They All Say I'm the Biggest Fool" and "Because." Prysock remained with the band until its Decca contract expired in 1952; he then launched a prolific solo career.

While Johnson dabbled in "serious" music, performing his *Piano Concerto* and *Southland Suite* at Carnegie Hall in September 1948, his forte was dance music, and he toured incessantly, playing at dance halls, theaters, and nightclubs in the North as well as auditoriums and tobacco barns in the deep South. A poll of ballroom operators and dance promoters, conducted in 1949 by the *Pittsburgh Courier*, named him and his band "Kings of the One-Nighter Circuit." In 1950 alone, they traveled

TOP SONGS

LET'S BEAT OUT SOME LOVE (Decca, '43, 2 *R&B*)

BABY DON'T YOU CRY (Decca, '43, 3 *R&B*)

WHEN MY MAN COMES HOME (Decca, '44, 1 *R&B*, 23 *Pop*)

THAT'S THE STUFF YOU GOTTA WATCH (Decca, '45, 2 *R&B*, 14 *Pop*)

THEY ALL SAY I'M THE BIGGEST FOOL (Decca, '46, 5 *R&B*)

I DON'T CARE WHO KNOWS (Decca, '49, 11 *R&B*)

BECAUSE, PTS. 1 & 2 (Decca, '50, 8 *R&B*)

HITTIN' ON ME (Mercury, '53, 6 *R&B*)

I'M JUST YOUR FOOL (Mercury, '54, 6 *R&B*)

BRING IT HOME TO ME (Mercury, '56, 9 *R&B*)

Additional Top 40 R&B Songs: 4

28,500 miles, mixing extended engagements with a total of 133 one-night stands, this at a time when many other big bands had scaled down in size or gone out of business altogether.

He cut back the size of the orchestra during the early 1950s, augmenting it with studio players for his 1953–58 Mercury sides. By adapting his style to the harder beat of rock and roll, Johnson was able to maintain a strong presence on the R&B charts through 1957, when he scored his last hit with the number 13 "Rock On." After a 1959 album for Roulette and a single for Old Town a few years later, Buddy and Ella retired. He spent his last years tending to family and church affairs, dying of a brain tumor on February 9, 1977, at his sister's home.

QUINCY JONES

The unparalleled success of Quincy Delight Jones, Jr. (b. Mar. 14, 1933, Chicago) can be attributed to his remarkable instinct for bringing together just the right tunes, arrangements, vocalists, instrumentalists, and engineers to fit particular projects. In his four and a half decades as a producer, arranger, and recording artist in his own right, Jones has covered most of the bases of American vernacular music, from bebop and pop to soul and hip-hop. In the process, he collected over two dozen Grammy Awards, a feat topped only by Chicago Symphony conductor Georg Solti.

Raised on Chicago's South Side, where he began playing piano as a child, Jones moved with his family to Bremerton, Washington, when he was 10. He sang in a gospel quartet for a period and began playing trumpet professionally with Bumps Blackwell's band in 1948 after settling in Seattle. He received early pointers in the art of arranging from a young Ray Charles and trumpet tips from Count Basie sideman Clark Terry. Jones won a music scholarship to Boston's Schillinger House in 1951, but he dropped out before the year was out to join Lionel Hampton's orchestra.

Jones moved to New York City in 1953 and became much in demand as a free-lance arranger. His handsomely crafted charts were featured by a wide variety of artists during the 1950s, including Cannonball Adderley, LaVern Baker, Count Basie, Clifford Brown, Ray Charles, the Crew Cuts, Tommy Dorsey, Louis Jordan, Johnny Mathis,

James Moody, Oscar Pettiford, Sarah Vaughan, Dinah Washington, and Chuck Willis. Jones recorded *This Is How I Feel About Jazz,* the first in a series of all-star big band albums, for ABC-Paramount in 1956 and also served that year as musical director for Dizzy Gillespie before relocating to Paris, where he spent 18 months as a producer for the Barclay label and studied composition with Nadia Boulanger. Back in the U.S. in 1959, he earned his first Grammy nomination for his arrangement of Ray Charles's "Let the Good Times Roll" and launched his own short-lived big band.

He was hired in 1961 as A&R director for Mercury Records and was eventually appointed a vice president of the company, becoming the first African American to hold such a position at a major label. His greatest commercial achievements at the label were as producer of singer Lesley Gore, including her Number One pop "It's My Party" in 1963 and the next year's number two pop "You Don't Own Me." He also cut his own big band albums for Mercury and continued to write charts for such jazz-oriented vocalists as Tony Bennett, Billy Eckstine, Peggy Lee, and Frank Sinatra. Jones won his first Grammy in 1963 for an arrangement of "I Can't Stop Loving You" by Basie. After the success of his score for the 1965 Sidney Lumet film *The Pawnbroker,* Jones moved to Hollywood, where he composed music for over 30 motion pictures through 1971 as well as for such television series as "I Spy," "Ironside," "The Bill Cosby Show," and "Sanford and Son."

Signing with A&M Records in 1969, Jones began to refocus on his career as an artist and scored a hit in 1974 with *Body Heat,* an album that fused jazz and soul and introduced the songs "Everything Must Change" and "If I Ever Lose This Heaven." The next year's *Mellow Madness* featured guitarist George Johnson and his bass-playing brother Louis; Jones went on to produce four albums by the Brothers Johnson, which included three Number One R&B singles: 1976's "I'll Be Good to You," 1977's "Strawberry Letter 23," and 1980's "Stomp." He scored music for the celebrated 1977 television series "Roots" and, the next year, had his first Number One R&B hit as an artist with "Stuff Like That," featuring vocals by Chaka Khan and Ashford and Simpson. Also in 1978, he was reunited with Lumet for the motion picture adaptation of the Broadway musical *The Wiz.* Michael Jackson, who co-starred in the film with Diana Ross, was then in search of a record producer. Jones offered his services.

Jones proceeded to turn the former child singing star into the "King of Pop" with three huge albums: 1979's *Off the Wall*, 1982's *Thriller*, and 1987's *Bad*. *Thriller* sold some 40 million copies, earned eight Grammys, and became the biggest album of all time. Other Jones production credits include Rufus and Chaka Khan's Number One R&B "Do You Know What You Feel" in 1979, George Benson's Number One R&B "Give Me the Night" in 1980, Patti Austin and James Ingram's Number One pop "Baby, Come to Me" in 1982, and the Number One R&B and pop "We Are the World" by the all-star USA for Africa aggregation in 1985.

After launching his own Qwest label in 1981 and producing albums for Austin, Ingram, Sinatra, Lena Horne, and Ernie Watts, Jones finally got around to recording his own album for the label in 1989: *Back on the Block*, sporting a star-studded cast of jazz, soul, gospel, and rap artists and introducing pre-teen vocalist Tevin Campbell. It yielded three Number One R&B hits. A motion picture biography and book, both titled *Listen Up: The Lives of Quincy Jones*, appeared the next year. Jones's business horizons had already expanded to motion pictures in 1985 when he co-produced *The Color Purple* and to television in 1990 when he served as executive producer of the series "The Fresh Prince of Bel Air." He returned to his jazz roots in 1991 to collaborate with Miles Davis; their album *Live at Montreux*, released two years later, topped the jazz chart and earned Jones yet another Grammy.

LOUIS JORDAN

Singer-saxophonist Louis Jordan (b. July 8, 1908, Brinkley, Arkansas) was a pioneer: the pivotal figure in the development of what would become known as rhythm and blues, as well as the father of an audio-visual form that evolved into the music video. Backed by a riff-based shuffle-boogie combo called the Tympany Five, he was the biggest African-American recording artist of the 1940s, having garnered a total of 18 Number One entries on the *Billboard* R&B chart between 1942 and 1950, a score later surpassed by Stevie Wonder. His biggest seller, 1946's "Choo Choo Ch'Boogie," held down the top R&B slot for 18 weeks, an accomplishment equalled only by Joe Liggins's "The Honeydripper" of a year earlier, while "Ain't Nobody Here But Us Chickens," issued a few months later, stayed in that position for 17. And as popular as he was among black people, Jordan's mostly uptempo, humor-laced blues songs also had strong appeal to white listeners, with eight of his Decca 78s crossing over into the pop top 10.

Writing in the *New York Times,* on the eve of the 1992 Broadway opening of *Five Guys Named Moe,* a hit musical theater production based on the Arkansas entertainer's music, Michael Lydon observed that "the Jordan formula had a lasting influence on pop music. After the big bands, while be-bop combos took jazz further toward instrumental virtuosity, his arrangements created a setting for the story told by the vocal. His success with this uninhibited small-group style became an inspiration for Chuck Berry, Fats Domino, Bo Diddley, Little Richard, and through them, for the rock-and-roll generations that have followed." Among others profoundly influenced by Jordan were Ray Charles, B. B. King, Bill Haley, and James Brown.

An only child, Jordan received clarinet lessons from his bandmaster father at the age of seven and

TOP ALBUMS

BODY HEAT (A&M, '74, 6)
MELLOW MADNESS (A&M, '75, 16)
SOUNDS ...AND STUFF LIKE THAT!! (A&M, '78, 15)
THE DUDE (A&M, '81, 10)
BACK ON THE BLOCK (Qwest, '89, 9)

Additional Top 40 Albums: 1

TOP SONGS

STUFF LIKE THAT (A&M, '78, 1 R&B, 21 Pop)
ONE HUNDRED WAYS (Quincy Jones featuring James Ingram, A&M, '81, 10 R&B, 14 Pop)
I'LL BE GOOD TO YOU (Quincy Jones featuring Ray Charles and Chaka Khan, Qwest, '89, 1 R&B, 18 Pop)
THE SECRET GARDEN (SWEET SEDUCTION SUITE) (Quincy Jones featuring Al B. Sure!, James Ingram, El DeBarge, and Barry White, Qwest, '90, 1 R&B, 31 Pop)
TOMORROW (A BETTER YOU, A BETTER ME) (Quincy Jones featuring Tevin Campbell, Qwest, '90, 1 R&B)

Additional Top 40 R&B Songs: 7

TOP SONGS

G.I. JIVE (Decca, '44, *1 R&B, 1 Pop*)

CALDONIA (Decca, '45, *1 R&B, 6 Pop*)

BUZZ ME (Decca, '46, *1 R&B, 9 Pop*)

STONE COLD DEAD IN THE MARKET (HE HAD IT COMING) (Decca, '46, *1 R&B, 7 Pop*)

CHOO CHOO CH'BOOGIE (Decca, '46, *1 R&B, 7 Pop*)

AIN'T NOBODY HERE BUT US CHICKENS (Decca, '46, *1 R&B, 6 Pop*)

JACK, YOU'RE DEAD (Decca, '47, *1 R&B, 21 Pop*)

BOOGIE WOOGIE BLUE PLATE (Decca, '47, *1 R&B, 21 Pop*)

SATURDAY NIGHT FISH FRY (PART 1) (Decca, '49, *1 R&B, 21 Pop*)

BLUE LIGHT BOOGIE—PARTS 1 & 2 (Decca, '50, *1 R&B*)

Additional Top 40 R&B Songs: 47

Jordan followed it with "I'm Gonna Leave You on the Outskirts of Town." Later in 1942, Jordan topped the R&B chart for the first time with "What's the Use of Getting Sober," while its flip side, "The Chicks I Pick Are Slender and Tender and Tall," reached number 10. Many later 78s were also two-sided charters, including "G.I. Jive" b/w "Is You Is or Is You Ain't My Baby," "Mop Mop" b/w "You Can't Get That No More," "Caldonia" b/w "Somebody Done Changed the Lock on My Door," "Buzz Me" b/w "Reconversion Blues," "Beware" b/w "Don't Let the Sun Catch You Cryin'," and "Ain't Nobody Here But Us Chickens" b/w "Let the Good Times Roll." Dubbed "King of the Jukeboxes," Jordan held down the top slot on *Billboard*'s R&B chart for a total of 101 weeks between 1942 and 1950.

At the suggestion of his manager, Berle Adams, the entertainer made a 20-minute motion picture to promote his 1945 song "Caldonia" (which was

Louis Jordan

quickly mastered the C-melody and other members of the saxophone family, with the alto eventually becoming his main horn. As a teenager, he spent summers on the road with the Rabbit Foot Minstrels tent show and, after two years at Arkansas Baptist College, became a full-time musician. He moved to Philadelphia in 1930 and worked with the bands of Charlie Gaines and Kaiser Marshall, among others, before settling in New York City and joining drummer Chick Webb's orchestra in 1936. During his two years with Webb, Jordan played soprano and alto and also sang on three of the band's Decca sides. (Ella Fitzgerald was Webb's star vocalist at the time.)

Leaving Webb in 1938, the saxophonist formed a sextet that appeared at Elk's Rendezvous cabaret in Harlem. The combo, billed as "Louis Jordan's Elks Rendezvous Band," cut its first record for Decca later that year. By the next release, however, it was called "Louis Jordan and His Tympany Five," and the name stuck, even though the group would vary in size over the years. After 30 unsuccessful releases for Decca, Jordan struck with the double-sided hit "Knock Me a Kiss" b/w "I'm Gonna Move to the Outskirts of Town." His rendition of "Outskirts," a slow blues first recorded in 1936 by its composer, Casey Bill Weldon, became one of the most popular "race" records of 1942 and spawned successful covers by Big Bill Broonzy (who'd played guitar on Weldon's original), Jimmie Lunceford, and Count Basie.

written by Jordan, but credited to Felice Moore, his wife). It was the first film to be built around a song, rather than a group, and helped to make "Caldonia" a Number One R&B, number six pop hit. A year later, he did a one-hour film to accompany the release of the tune "Beware." Jordan also appeared in several full-length movies, including 1944's *Follow the Boys* and *Shout Sister Shout.*

Jordan had no more chart hits after 1951's number five R&B "Weak Minded Blues" and was dropped by Decca three years later. Ironically, at around the time of his departure, his old producer, Milt Gabler, began applying Jordan's jump blues approach to Decca recordings by Bill Haley and the Comets, formerly a country group. The hugely successful result was labeled "rock and roll." Jordan himself continued performing and recorded sporadically, for such labels as Aladdin, X, VIK, Warwick, Tangerine, Pzazz, and Blues Spectrum, until his death from a heart attack on February 4, 1975.

KC AND THE SUNSHINE BAND

Dismissed as "disco fluff" by some, as "bubblegum funk" by others, the ebullient dance music crafted by singer-keyboardist Harry Wayne "KC" Casey (b. Jan. 31, 1951, Hialeah, Florida) and his songwriting-producing partner, bass player Richard Finch (b. Jan. 25, 1954, Indianapolis, Indiana), for KC and the Sunshine Band made their Florida-based group one of the most consistent R&B crossover acts of the 1970s. Inspired by Motown soul and the junkanoo music of the Bahamas, the band delivered disco with an undulating bottom and a distinctive tropical twist. The simplicity of Casey and Finch's sing-songy compositions was intentional, as was the incessant repetition of the songs' titles in the lyrics, which they felt would cause consumers to know exactly what record to ask for.

Raised in a Pentecostal environment, Casey began writing songs when he was 12 and, at 16, sang with a band called Five Doors Down. He worked in a record store for a period, then was hired as a warehouseman at veteran record man Henry Stone's Tone Distributors in Hialeah, a suburb of Miami. After finishing his duties processing returned records, he would hang out at the studio around the

back of the building where records were actually being created. Stone's TK Productions, with a bevy of labels, including Alston, Cat, and Dade, was the hub of R&B recording activity in the Miami area and home to such singers as Clarence Reid and Betty Wright. Both took a liking to Casey, and Wright invited him to be an opening act at some of her gigs as well as sing backgrounds on her sessions.

Finch also started in the Tone stock room, but his knack for electronics soon led to work in the studio. He and Casey eventually began writing together and, with two members of Wright's band, guitarist Jerome Smith and drummer Robert Johnson, plus Havana-born percussionist Fermin Goytisolo and the husband-wife singing team of George and Gwen McCrae, recorded "Blow Your Whistle" in 1973. The song, influenced by the whistles and drums of a junkanoo group they'd heard at Reid's wedding reception, was the first single to be issued on the new TK label and became a number 27 R&B hit. The band's second, 1974's "Sound Your Funky Horn," did slightly better, rising to number 21.

That might have been the makeshift studio group's last record if George McCrae's voice hadn't ended up on a crudely made Casey-Finch demo of a song called "Rock Your Baby." The catchy ditty, propelled by Finch's bouncing bass, became a smash during the summer of 1974, topping the R&B and pop charts in the U.S., going Number One in England, and establishing Casey and Finch as certified hitmakers. As the McCrae record was keeping dance floors filled around the globe, KC and the Sunshine band found "Queen of Clubs," a track from their debut album, issued as a single on the Jayboy label in the U.K., where it became a top 10 hit. Also in 1974, Casey and Finch wrote and produced Betty Wright's number 15 R&B U.S. single, "Where Is the Love."

KC and the Sunshine Band's five-year run on the American top 10 kicked off in 1975 with their eponymous second album, which yielded two Number One R&B and pop singles in a row: "Get Down Tonight" and "That's the Way (I Like It)." Built around Casey, Finch, Smith, and Johnson, the band began touring, adding as many as seven extra players and singers for specific trips.

The hits continued through the middle of 1977, after which the band experienced a dry spell. In response to a widespread backlash against dance music, epitomized by the slogan "Disco sucks," the group responded with the funkier "Do You Wanna

Go Party," a number eight R&B single in 1979. The next, a cover of Frederick Knight's "I Betcha Didn't Know That," was the group's last R&B chart entry, peaking at number 25, but the flip side, "Please Don't Go," a rare ballad performance by Casey, became a pop chart topper.

The demise of disco led to the bankruptcy of TK Productions and the breakup of KC and the Sunshine Band. As a duet partner with Miami singer Teri DeSario, Casey scored a number 20 R&B, number two pop hit with a 1980 remake for the Casablanca label of Barbara Mason's "Yes, I'm Ready." He then signed with Epic and cut two albums under the Sunshine Band banner and one under his own name. In 1982, while he was recovering from serious injuries sustained in a head-on car crash near his Hialeah home, Epic came out with *All in a Night's Work,* his second band album for the label. It met with disinterest in the U.S., but the Irish branch of the company issued a track from it titled "Give It Up." The tune was so well received in Ireland that Epic issued it in England, where it became a Number One hit in 1983. The home office was insufficiently impressed to release it as a single domestically, so Casey bought back the master and put it out on his own Meca label. Reaching number 19 pop in the U.S. during the spring of 1984, "Give It Up" proved to be KC and the Sunshine's chart swan song.

TOP ALBUMS

KC AND THE SUNSHINE BAND (TK, '75, *4*)
PART 3 (TK, '76, *13*)

Additional Top 40 Albums: 1

TOP SONGS

SOUND YOUR FUNKY HORN (TK, '74, *21 R&B*)
GET DOWN TONIGHT (TK, '75, *1 R&B, 1 Pop*)
THAT'S THE WAY (I LIKE IT) (TK, '75, *1 R&B,
   1 Pop*)
(SHAKE, SHAKE, SHAKE) SHAKE YOUR BOOTY (TK,
   '76, *1 R&B, 1 Pop*)
I LIKE TO DO IT (TK, '76, *4 R&B, 37 Pop*)
I'M YOUR BOOGIE MAN (TK, '77, *3 R&B, 1 Pop*)
KEEP IT COMIN' LOVE (TK, '77, *1 R&B, 2 Pop*)
DO YOU WANNA PARTY (TK, '79, *8 R&B*)

Additional Top 40 R&B Songs: 7

CHAKA KHAN

Over a two-decade career that yielded nine Number One R&B hits, Chaka Khan (b. Yvette Marie Stevens, Mar. 23, 1953, Great Lakes Naval Training Center, Illinois) evolved from being a flamboyant black "chick" singer in a predominantly white soul band into an uncompromising diva who often chose to follow her own creative muse rather than bend to commercial trends. "I never think in terms of 'Will this be a hit?' " she said in 1988. "If I'm doing a song, I sing it because I love the song and feel some affinity for it. Money's not important. I have to sing. I must."

Raised in Chicago's Hyde Park district, the oldest child of a military man and his office-clerk wife, Khan was a rebellious youngster who was kicked out of a Catholic junior high and two public high schools. She formed her first group, the Crystalettes, at age 11. As a teenager, she became involved in the Black Power movement, adopted the name "Chaka" (an African term for "fire warrior"), and was briefly married to Assan Khan. She sang with several local groups, including Shades of Black, Lock and Chain, Lyfe, and Baby Huey and the Babysitters, before replacing Paulette McWilliams in Rufus. Formerly called Ask Rufus, after the name of an advice column in *Mechanics Illustrated* magazine, the group then consisted of keyboardists Kevin Murphy and Ron Stockert, guitarist Al Ciner, bassist Denny Belfield, and drummer Andre Fischer. Murphy and Cincer had been members of the American Breed, a Chicago rock band that scored at number five pop in 1967 with "Bend Me, Shape Me."

The McWilliams edition of Rufus had recorded one unsuccessful single for Epic in 1970. With Khan at the helm, the group was signed to ABC Records, but the eponymous Bob Monaco–produced first album, released in January 1963, also attracted little attention. Rufus spent a rough year and a half on the road. Promoters sometimes ran off with the money and, in one case, the band's equipment. In Kansas, the group was denied gas and restaurant service because of Khan's race. (Fischer, the other African-American member, was light enough to pass for white.) One person who did notice the album, however, was Stevie Wonder, who was impressed with Khan's torrid, throaty treatment of his "Maybe My Baby." During sessions for the next Rufus album, the prophetically titled *Rags to Rufus,* Wonder

Chaka Khan

TOP ALBUM

RAGS TO RUFUS (Rufus featuring Chaka Khan, ABC, '74, 4)

Additional Top 40 Albums: 8

TOP SONGS

YOU GOT THE LOVE (Rufus featuring Chaka Khan, ABC, '74, *1 R&B, 11 Pop*)

SWEET THING (Rufus featuring Chaka Khan, ABC, '75, *1 R&B, 5 Pop*)

AT MIDNIGHT (MY LOVE WILL LIFT YOU UP) (Rufus featuring Chaka Khan, ABC, '77, *1 R&B, 30 Pop*)

I'M EVERY WOMAN (Warner Bros., '78, *1 R&B, 21 Pop*)

DO YOU LOVE WHAT YOU FEEL (Rufus and Chaka Khan, MCA, '79, *1 R&B, 30 Pop*)

WHAT 'CHA GONNA DO FOR ME (Warner Bros, '81, *1 R&B*)

AIN'T NOBODY (Rufus and Chaka Khan, Warner Bros., '83, *1 R&B, 22 Pop*)

I FEEL FOR YOU (Warner Bros., '84, *1 R&B, 3 Pop*)

I'LL BE GOOD TO YOU (Quincy Jones featuring Ray Charles and Chaka Khan, Qwest, '89, *1 R&B, 18 Pop*)

Additional Top 40 Songs: 27

dropped in and offered the group "Tell Me Something Good."

The Wonder composition gave Rufus its first major hit. Peaking at number three on both the R&B and pop charts, it would be the band's greatest pop success, although four Number One R&B charters followed through 1983, beginning with "You Got the Love," a tune by Khan and Ray Parker, Jr., from *Rags to Rufus*. Personnel fluctuated during the 1970s, with David "Hawk" Wolinski, Tony Maiden, Bobby Watson, and John Robinson replacing Stockert, Ciner, Belfield, and Fischer, respectively. Khan cut a total of nine albums with Rufus, contributing frequently incendiary leads, as well as innovative background parts, before ending her relationship with the band in 1983. Most were produced or co-produced by the group itself, with the notable exception of 1979's *Masterjam* by Quincy Jones. Khan had two years earlier lent her voice to the producer's Number One R&B hit "Stuff Like That," and during the *Masterjam* sessions, Jones invited group members Wolinski, Watson, and Robinson to play on Michael Jackson's *Off the Wall* album.

While still a member of Rufus, Khan signed with Warner Bros. in 1978 as a solo artist and selected veteran producer-arranger Arif Mardin to work with her. The Ashford and Simpson composition "I'm Every Woman," from the solo debut album *Chaka*, was the first of her three Number One R&B solo hits, the biggest being her 1984 rendition of Prince's "I Feel for You." With rapper Grandmaster Melle Mel percussively repeating her name at the beginning and Wonder adding a harmonica solo, this techno-funk masterpiece became the vocalist's signature song, although she disliked it at the time because Warner Bros. had forced her and Mardin to come up with something commercial after three and a half years of relative failures. Mardin had been giving Khan free reign to explore her creative instincts, and she had started delving into jazz, including a 1982 rendition of Dizzy Gillespie's "A Night in Tunisia" on which she was joined by the bop trumpeter. Her boldest album was 1988's *C.K.*, which sported a cast including Wonder, Prince, Miles Davis, Bobby McFerrin, and George Benson.

Khan was also involved in many other projects, including albums by Benson, Joni Mitchell, Ry Cooder, Rick Wakeman, Robert Palmer (arranging and singing the backgrounds on 1986's Number One pop "Addicted to Love"), Stevie Winwood, David Bowie, and Quincy Jones (joining Ray Charles on the producer's 1989 Number One R&B "I'll Be Good to You") and soundtracks for "Miami Vice" and the motion pictures *White Knights* and *Krush Groove*. She recorded her only complete album of jazz standards, 1982's *Echoes of an Era*, as part of the group that included Freddie Hubbard, Joe Henderson, and Chick Corea. In 1993, Khan joined Whitney Houston for a remake of "I'm Every Woman" from *The Bodyguard*, that year's biggest selling album.

BEN E. KING

Despite long absences from the charts, singer Ben E. King (b. Benjamin Earl Nelson, Sept. 23, 1938, Henderson, North Carolina) managed to place records in the pop top 10 over a 27-year period. The remarkable elasticity of his voice, capable of soaring in a smooth, Sam Cooke–like gospel tenor or bearing down in a grittier baritone reminiscent of Solomon Burke's, was a record producer's dream and won King the favor of both soul and pop fans.

King began singing in a North Carolina church choir at age six and moved to New York City with his family shortly thereafter. His teenage years were spent harmonizing with street-corner doo wop groups, including the Four B's, which took its name from members Ben, Billy, Billy, and Bobby. (Ben eventually married Betty, sister of Bobby and one Billy.) He dropped out of high school to help out at his father's restaurant, where, in 1956, he was spotted by Lover Patterson, manager of the Five Crowns, a local group that had been recording with little success since 1952. King was featured on several of the Crowns' later singles, including 1958's "I'll Kiss and Make Up" on the R&B label. The Crowns' fortunes changed the next year when they appeared as an opening act at the Apollo Theater. George Tread-

well, manager of the Drifters, had just fired his famous group and hastily recruited the Crowns to become the new Drifters.

The King-led Drifters' first release, 1959's melancholy "There Goes My Baby," written by King, Treadwell, and Patterson and produced by Jerry Leiber and Mike Stoller, became a Number One R&B, number two pop smash. The Atlantic single, with King straining to reach the top of his tenor range and the group singing in a different key from the brooding strings and noticeably out-of-tune timpani, sounded like two different records being played at the same time, yet the unorthodox effect proved hypnotic. Its Latin-tinged beat also set the tone for subsequent Drifters hits, as well as for King's early solo efforts. King sang lead on only 10 other Drifters songs, five of which—"Dance with Me," "This Magic Moment," "Lonely Winds," "Save the Last Dance for Me," and "I Count the Tears"—made the R&B top 10.

By the time "Save the Last Dance for Me," the only record by either the Drifters or King to top both the R&B and pop charts, was released in late 1960, King had left the group. He remained with Atlantic, on the Atco subsidiary, but his first two singles—"Brace Yourself" and a duet with LaVern Baker titled "How Often"—were flops. He scuffled for a period, supported by his librarian wife, until his next

---

TOP ALBUMS

SUPERNATURAL (Atlantic, '75, 39)
BENNY AND US (Average White Band & Ben E. King, Atlantic, '77, 33)

TOP SONGS

SPANISH HARLEM (Atco, '61, 15 R&B, 10 Pop)
STAND BY ME (Atco, '61, 1 R&B, 4 Pop)
AMOR (Atco, '61, 10 R&B, 18 Pop)
DON'T PLAY THAT SONG (YOU LIED) (Atco, '62, 2 R&B, 11 Pop)
I (WHO HAVE NOTHING) (Atco, '63, 16 R&B, 29 Pop)
SEVEN LETTERS (Atco, '65, 11 R&B)
SUPERNATURAL THING—PART 1 (Atlantic, '75, 1 R&B, 5 Pop)
DO IT IN THE NAME OF LOVE (Atlantic, '75, 4 R&B)

Additional Top 40 R&B Songs: 11

Ben E. King

Records. The vocalist remained active on the lounge circuit, both in the U.S. and Europe. Ertegun caught his act at a Miami club in 1975 and re-signed him to Atlantic. His first single under the new contract, the disco-styled "Supernatural Thing," written by Patrick Grant and Gwen Guthrie and produced by Bert DeCoteaux and Tony Silvester, became a Number One R&B, number five pop hit, giving the singer his first top 10 entry in 13 years. A second hit, "Do It in the Name of Love," was followed in 1977 by a successful album collaboration with the Average White Band. King left the label again in 1981.

In 1986, "Stand by Me" inspired and was featured in the hit Rob Reiner–directed motion picture of the same title. King's 1961 single was reissued and reentered the pop chart, peaking at number nine. A year later, after being used in a Levi's commercial in England, it became a Number One hit in that country. The renewed interest led to a contract with Manhattan Records, for which King recorded an album in 1987 that utilized such producers as Mick Jones of Foreigner, ex-Led Zeppelin member John Paul Jones, and Lamont Dozier. By 1992, King was recording for Ichiban in Atlanta.

KING CURTIS

Tenor saxophone solos were indispensable to rhythm and blues records during the mid-1950s, and Sam "the Man" Taylor ruled the roost in New York City. Producers were often forced to schedule their sessions around Taylor's busy itinerary, until, in 1955, veteran songwriter-arranger Jesse Stone spotted a new kid in town at a Manhattan beer tavern. King Curtis (b. Curtis Ousley, Feb. 7, 1934, Fort Worth, Texas) made his New York recording debut the next day at a Stone session for RCA Victor and within three years had supplanted Taylor as the city's tenor man of choice.

The King Curtis sound burst all over the national airwaves during 1958, via his concise, declarative, thoughtfully sculpted statements on such hits as Chuck Willis's "What Am I Living For," the Coasters' "Yakety Yak" (his sputtering solo on that tune serving as the model for Nashville session player Boots Randolph's later "yakety sax" style), Bobby Darin's "Splish Splash," Clyde McPhatter's "A Lover's Question," and LaVern Baker's "I Cried a Tear," all for Atlantic Records. Working as a free-

solo single for Atco, "Spanish Harlem," produced by Leiber and Stoller and penned by Leiber and Phil Spector, became a number 15 R&B, number 10 pop hit at the beginning of 1961. (Aretha Franklin had a Number One R&B charter with the song a decade later.) The next release, the self-composed "Stand by Me," soared to the top of the R&B chart and firmly cemented King's solo standing. It became his signature song and was successfully revived over the years by such diverse artists as Spyder Turner, John Lennon, and Mickey Gilley. Other hits followed, including 1962's "Don't Play That Song (You Lied)" (written by King, using his wife's name, with Atlantic boss Ahmet Ertegun, it was also later taken to Number One R&B by Franklin) and another King original, 1965's country-flavored "Seven Letters." Subsequent Atco releases were less successful.

Ending an 11-year relationship with Atlantic, King switched to former Atlantic promotion man Larry Maxwell's Maxwell label, where he recorded the brilliant, boldly experimental album *Rough Edges* with producer Bob Crewe in 1970. It generated little interest, as did a later album for Mandala lance studio musician, he remained top tenor until his death in 1971, contributing to recordings by such diverse artists as the McGuire Sisters, Connie Francis, Nat "King" Cole, Brook Benton, Buddy Holly (for whom he composed the song "Reminiscing"), Waylon Jennings, Sammy Turner, Oliver Nelson, Roosevelt Sykes, Andy Williams, the Shirelles, Sam Cooke, Soupy Sales, Wilson Pickett, Herbie Mann, the Rascals, Eric Clapton, the Allman Brothers, Esther Phillips, Champion Jack Dupree, Donny Hathaway, John Lennon, and Aretha Franklin. The saxophonist also scored a number of instrumental hits of his own, including "Soul Twist," "Soul Serenade," "Memphis Soul Stew," and "Ode to Billie Joe."

Curtis, whose father was a sanctified church guitarist, was raised in Mansfield, Texas, a small town outside Fort Worth. He played bass drum in a junior high school band and then took up baritone horn. Inspired by Louis Jordan, he began playing alto saxophone in 1945 and quickly mastered the tenor and baritone saxophones. As a teenager, he worked in

King Curtis

TOP ALBUMS

KING CURTIS PLAYS THE GREAT MEMPHIS HITS (Atco, '67)
LIVE AT FILLMORE WEST (Atco, '71)

TOP SONGS

SOUL TWIST (King Curtis and the Noble Knights, Enjoy, '62, *1 R&B, 17 Pop*)
SOMETHING ON YOUR MIND (Atco, '67, *31 R&B*)
MEMPHIS SOUL STEW (Atco, '67, *6 R&B, 33 Pop*)
ODE TO BILLIE JOE (The Kingpins, Atco, '67, *6 R&B, 28 Pop*)
INSTANT GROOVE (King Curtis and the Kingpins, Atco, '69, *35 R&B*)

the Dallas–Fort Worth area with such visiting blues stars as Charles Brown, Wynonie Harris, and Amos Milburn. Later influences included Lester Young and especially Gene Ammons.

"I remember a teacher I'd had telling me that it didn't matter how many notes you played," Curtis told Nat Hentoff in 1960. "The point was to play the ones you pick clearly and to make them sound the way you heard them in your mind. Ammons did that, besides he played with much spontaneity and drive."

Curtis cut his first record, "Korea, Korea," in Texas with vocalist Bob Kent's band for the Par label in 1952 before a two-week road tour with Lionel Hampton's orchestra took him to New York. He stayed for a month, went back home, then returned for good in 1954. He led a trio for a period that included pianist Horace Silver and studied harmony, theory, and saxophone technique under noted instructors Garvin Bushell and Joe Napoleon before studio demands began consuming his time. Early King Curtis instrumentals appeared on such labels as Gem, Groove, Apollo, Crown, and Atco, and between 1960 and '62, he recorded a series of albums under his own name for Prestige, including two straight-ahead jazz dates with trumpeter Nat Adderley and a blues disc on which he sang and played alto sax and guitar.

When he wasn't in the studio, Curtis led a tight club combo composed of some of New York's finest, including former Fats Waller guitarist Al Casey. It was with that group, dubbed "the Noble Knights" for the occasion, that he recorded his biggest hit,

1962's Number One R&B, number 17 pop "Soul Twist" on Bobby Robinson's Enjoy label. Curtis then signed with Capitol, for whom he made the oft-covered original "Soul Serenade" in 1964. He returned to Atco for the remainder of his career, recording a series of singles and albums with his group, sometimes known as the Kingpins, as well as working as a sideman and producing such artists as Ben E. King, Freddie King, Roberta Flack, Delaney and Bonnie, Sam Moore, and Donny Hathaway. Having assembled a crack band that included guitarist Cornell Dupree, bassist Jerry Jemmott, and drummer Bernard Purdie, the saxophonist served as Aretha Franklin's musical director during the last year and a half of his life. He was stabbed to death in front of his Manhattan brownstone by a drug addict on August 13, 1971.

GLADYS KNIGHT AND THE PIPS

With the Pips' smooth, intricate harmonies curling around dusky alto leads that tempered the rawness of her gospel upbringing with sensual restraint, Gladys Knight (b. May 28, 1944, Atlanta, Georgia) scored 29 singles in the R&B top 10 between 1961 and 1988, 10 of them rising to Number One. Being members of the same family was a key factor in keeping Knight and the Pips together as a unit for nearly four decades—from 1952 till 1990.

Knight, whose parents had been members of the renowned Wings Over Jordan gospel choir, began singing at age four at Atlanta's Mount Mariah Baptist Church. At five, she was touring the South with the Morris Brown Choir, and two years later, she traveled to New York to appear on "The Original Amateur Hour," a network television program hosted by Ted Mack. She won the $2,000 first prize with a rendition of the Nat "King" Cole hit "Too Young." A year later, on September 4, 1952, at her brother Merald "Bubba" Knight's 10th birthday party, Gladys, Bubba, and their sister Brenda, along with cousin William Guest and his sister Elenor, harmonized together for the first time. The quintet continued singing, doing gospel as the Fountainaires and secular tunes as the Pips, so named because another cousin, James "Pip" Woods, was serving as manager.

Backed by Maurice King's band, the Pips cut their first record, "Whistle My Love," for Brunswick in 1957. Although the record flopped, working with the veteran Detroit musician gave the group invaluable lessons in harmony and choreography. Brenda and Elenor left in 1959 to attend college and were replaced by Knight's cousins Edward Patten and Langston George. While appearing at the Builder's Club in their hometown, the group made its second single, a primitively recorded treatment of the Johnny Otis tune "Every Beat of My Heart" (first recorded in 1952 by the Royals), for club owner Clifford Hunter and partner Tommy Brown's Huntom label. The record caught the ears of Marshall Sehorn, promotion director for Bobby Robinson's Fury label in New York. Signed to Fury and renamed Gladys Knight and the Pips, the quintet rerecorded the doo wop ballad. At about the same time, the Huntom single was licensed to Vee-Jay. On May 29, 1961, both versions entered the *Billboard* R&B chart. The Pips' record on Vee-Jay rose to Number One (and to number six on the pop chart), while Gladys Knight and the Pips' newer, better recorded Fury rendition stalled at number 15 R&B.

TOP ALBUM

IMAGINATION (Buddah, '73, 9)

Additional Top 40 Albums: 7

TOP SONGS

EVERY BEAT OF MY HEART (The Pips, Vee-Jay, '61,
    1 R&B, 6 Pop)
I HEARD IT THROUGH THE GRAPEVINE (Soul, '67,
    1 R&B, 2 Pop)
IF I WERE YOUR WOMAN (Soul, '70, 1 R&B, 9 Pop)
NEITHER ONE OF US (WANTS TO BE THE FIRST TO
    SAY GOODBYE) (Soul, '73, 1 R&B, 2 Pop)
MIDNIGHT TRAIN TO GEORGIA (Buddah, '73,
    1 R&B, 1 Pop)
I'VE GOT TO USE MY IMAGINATION (Buddah, '73,
    1 R&B, 4 Pop)
BEST THING THAT EVER HAPPENED TO ME (Buddah,
    '74, 1 R&B, 3 Pop)
I FEEL A SONG (IN MY HEART) (Buddah, '74,
    1 R&B, 21 Pop)
LOVE OVERBOARD (MCA, '87, 1 R&B, 13 Pop)

Additional Top 40 R&B Songs: 40

Gladys Knight and the Pips

"Letter Full of Tears," the third Fury release, went to number three R&B and number 19 pop, after which Knight and company experienced a six-year slump in sales, with 1964's number 38 pop "Giving Up," penned and produced by Van McCoy, being the only top 40 entry. George left the fold in 1962, followed by Knight herself. After marrying and having the first of her three children, she returned in 1964.

Noted for their polished club act, Knight and the three remaining Pips signed with Motown in 1966 and, between 1967 and 1973, enjoyed a dozen top 10 R&B hits on the firm's Soul subsidiary, including the original 1967 recording of "I Heard It Through the Grapevine." However, one week after their last of three Soul label chart toppers, a 1973 treatment of country songwriter Jim Weatherly's "Neither One of Us (Wants to Be the First to Say Goodbye)," had reached the peak, they said goodbye to Motown. Moving to Buddah, their first album for the company, 1973's *Imagination,* became the biggest of their career and spawned three Number One R&B singles, including the Weatherly compositions "Midnight Train to Georgia" (the group's only Number One pop hit) and "Best Thing That Ever Happened to Me."

Other big records followed at Buddah, among them the number two R&B, number five pop "On and On" from Curtis Mayfield's *Claudine* motion picture soundtrack in 1974. Knight made a serious miscalculation two years later, sinking much of her own money into the film *Pipe Dreams,* produced by then-husband Barry Hankerson and starring herself and Hankerson. It went up in smoke at the box office, leaving the singer deeply in debt. A complex web of lawsuits then flew between the group, Motown, Buddah, and Columbia Records, resulting in an injunction that barred Knight and the Pips from recording together, although they continued to appear as a unit in concert. The Pips' two Casablanca albums met with little success, as did Knight's 1979 solo album for Columbia.

Knight and the group were reunited on record at Columbia in 1980. They had sporadic hits throughout the decade, including 1983's Number One R&B "Save the Overtime (For Me)" on Columbia and 1987's Number One R&B "Love Overboard" on MCA. Knight resumed her acting career in 1985 as costar with Flip Wilson of the television sitcom "Charlie & Co." In that same year, she took part in Dionne Warwick's Number One R&B and pop all-star AIDS-research benefit anthem "That's What Friends Are For." Knight and the Pips broke up in 1990. She emerged the next year with the solo MCA recording "Men," a number two R&B hit.

KOOL AND
THE GANG

With punchy, jazz-informed horn lines arranged by musical director, tenor saxophonist, and keyboardist Khalis Bayyan (b. Ronald Bell, Nov. 1, 1951, Youngstown, Ohio) over often complex chord changes and the buoyant bass of brother Robert "Kool" Bell (b. Oct. 8, 1950, Youngstown, Ohio), Kool and the Gang created a style of upbeat, basically instrumental funk that filled dance floors during the 1970s. It was, however, a precursor to a lighter pop approach, featuring the silky tenor voice of James "J. T." Taylor (b. Aug. 16, 1953, South Carolina), that made the New Jersey–based band one of the most consistent crossover attractions of the following decade.

During their 20-year recording career, Kool and the Gang raked in a total of 25 top 10 entries in the R&B singles chart, 12 of which also made the pop top 10. The prolific group cut over two dozen albums, three of them—1980's *Celebrate!*, 1981's *Something Special*, and 1984's *Emergency*—going platinum. Their biggest hit, 1980's Number One R&B and pop "Celebration," became the victory anthem of the early 1980s. Inspired by the creation

story in the Holy Qur'an, the Khalis Bayyan composition greeted American hostages upon their arrival home from Iran on January 26, 1981, and also served as the theme song for that year's Superbowl game and for the Oakland A's.

The Bell brothers, whose father was a professional boxer and jazz devotee, moved to Jersey City in 1961. All of the group's original members—Robert, Khalis, trumpeter Robert Mickens, saxophonist-flutist Dennis Thomas, keyboardist Rickey Westfield, and drummer George Brown—attended that city's Lincoln High School, with the exception of guitarist Claydes Smith. Initially an African percussion ensemble, they evolved into the Jazziacs in 1966 after Robert Bell taught himself to play bass. Early influences included John Coltrane, Miles Davis, Rahsaan Ronald Kirk, Babatunde Olatunji, Mongo Santamaria, and Horace Silver. Jazzmen Pharoah Sanders, Leon Thomas, and McCoy Tyner would sometimes sit in with the band at early local club engagements.

The Jazziacs' musical course began to change in 1988 when they became part of the New Jersey–based Soultown Revue and had to learn current soul hits in order to accompany the troupe's singers. It was also a conscious commercial decision.

"We had to get into that funky thing because we have to live," Thomas explained in 1974. "We had to make sure our jazz roots didn't overpower the

TOP ALBUM

Celebrate! (De-Lite, '80, *10*)

Additional Top 40 Albums: 7

TOP SONGS

HOLLYWOOD SWINGING (De-Lite, '74, *1 R&B, 6 Pop*)
HIGHER PLANE (De-Lite, '74, *1 R&B, 37 Pop*)
SPIRIT OF THE BOOGIE (De-Lite, '75, *1 R&B, 35 Pop*)
LADIES NIGHT (De-Lite, '79, *1 R&B, 8 Pop*)
CELEBRATION (De-Lite, '80, *1 R&B, 1 Pop*)
TAKE MY HEART (YOU CAN HAVE IT IF YOU WANT IT) (De-Lite, '81, *1 R&B, 17 Pop*)
JOANNA (De-Lite, '83, *1 R&B, 2 Pop*)
FRESH (De-Lite, '85, *1 R&B, 9 Pop*)
CHERISH (De-Lite, '85, *1 R&B, 2 Pop*)

Additional Top 40 R&B Songs: 33

funk. This way it is more acceptable to the kids, and they are the ones who buy most of our records."

Renamed the New Dimensions, then Kool and the Flames, and finally Kool and the Gang, the septet signed with former King Records producer Gene Redd's obscure Redd Coach Records in 1969 and recorded the single "Kool and the Gang." After being picked up by the slightly larger New York–based De-Lite label, the instrumental song became a number 19 R&B hit.

More moderate R&B charters, many incorporating group vocal chants into the band's lively party sound, followed through 1973, when Kool and company broke into the R&B top 10 at number five with "Funky Stuff," after which the album *Wild and Peaceful* yielded two crossover smashes: the number two R&B, number four pop "Jungle Boogie" and the Number One R&B, number six pop "Hollywood Swinging." As disco took firm hold of pop music between 1976 and '78, however, the group's chart action slipped, although one of its tunes, 1976's "Open Sesame," turned up a year and a half later on the soundtrack of *Saturday Night Fever,* the biggest album of the disco boom.

Rethinking their musical strategy, the Gang brought vocalist Taylor into the fold in 1978 and began working with Eumir Deodato, a producer who shared their fondness for jazz but also had a keen pop sensibility. The group members' songwriting abilities, Deodato's high-gloss production style, and distribution by Polygram spawned immediate results in the form of 1979's Number One R&B, number eight pop "Ladies Night." Deodato dropped out of the picture in 1981, leaving Bayyan and the group, along with engineer Jim Bonnefond, in charge of production, but crossover hits kept coming through 1987. Yet even as Kool and the Gang's releases continued to rate high on both charts, the group's increasingly subdued direction, as exemplified by such songs as "Joanna" and "Cherish," led to a backlash among many African-American consumers. By the mid-1980s, Taylor estimated, black attendance at the Gang's concerts had dropped to 10 percent.

Taylor left the band in 1988, cut three albums for MCA, and scored twice in the R&B top 20, with "All I Want Is Forever," a number two R&B duet with Regina Belle in 1989, and 1991's number 13 R&B single "Long Hot Summer Night." The post-Taylor Gang was less successful, with 1989's number 27 "Raindrops" being their last R&B top 40 appearance.

Kool and The Gang

PATTI LaBELLE

The Blue Belles—Patti LaBelle (b. Patricia Louise Holt, May 4, 1944, Philadelphia), Cindy Birdsong (b. Dec. 15, 1939, Camden, New Jersey), Sarah Dash (b. May 24, 1942, Trenton, New Jersey), Nona Hendryx (b. Aug. 18, 1945, Trenton)—had their first hit with 1962's number 13 R&B, number 15 pop "I Sold My Heart to the Junkman." The single, issued on the Philadelphia-based Newtown label, was not performed, as the credit claimed, by the Blue Belles, but rather by the Starlets, a Chicago group that featured lead singer Maxine Lightner. It seems that after Newtown had recorded the Starlets, the company discovered that the group was signed to another label—thus the name switch.

"I Sold My Heart to the Junkman" nevertheless served to launch the career of the Blue Belles, which had been formed a year earlier when LaBelle and Birdsong, who'd been singing around Philadelphia with the Ordettes, joined forces with Dash and Hendryx of the Del Capris from nearby Trenton.

They were soon actually recording for Newtown, scoring at number 14 R&B with 1963's "Down the Aisle (Wedding Song)," then for Parkway and Atlantic, both with limited success. (Birdsong dropped out in 1967 to replace Florence Ballard in the Supremes.) Until 1987, when the group hit the top of the R&B and pop charts with "Lady Marmalade" following an image makeover and a name change to Labelle, "Junkman" stood as the group's biggest hit.

The trio's metamorphosis began in 1970 when producer Vicki Wickham whisked Patti, Sarah, and Nona away to London, became their manager, and encouraged them to write their own material. "In one blow Labelle swept away the conventional 'three-girl group' image and established a whole new direction for black girls in rock," Wickham stated two years later. "Here were three dynamite girls, all with good lead voices, with good gospel backgrounds, having sung their way through 10 years of other people's hits and standards, suddenly singing out-and-out contemporary rock, but still retaining all their blackness and individuality. It was outrageous."

Labelle (from left): Nona Hendryx,
Patti LaBelle, and Sara Dash.

TOP ALBUMS

NIGHTBIRDS (Labelle, Epic, '75, 7)
WINNER IN YOU (MCA, '86, 1)

Additional Top 40 Albums: 1

TOP SONGS

LADY MARMALADE (Labelle, Epic, '74, 1 R&B, 1 Pop)
IF ONLY YOU KNEW (Philadelphia International, '83,
   1 R&B)
LOVE HAS FINALLY COME AT LAST (Bobby Womack
   and Patti LaBelle, Beverly Glen, '84, 3 R&B)
NEW ATTITUDE (MCA, '85, 3 R&B, 17 Pop)
ON MY OWN (Patti LaBelle and Michael
   McDonald, MCA, '86, 1 R&B, 1 Pop)
FEELS LIKE ANOTHER ONE (MCA, '91, 3 R&B)
SOMEBODY LOVES YOU BABY (YOU KNOW WHO IT IS)
   (MCA, '91, 4 R&B)
WHEN YOU'VE BEEN BLESSED (FEELS LIKE HEAVEN)
   (MCA, '92, 4 R&B)

Additional Top 40 R&B Songs: 18

Signed to Track Records in the U.K. and Warner Bros. in the U.S., the revamped trio emerged in 1971 with the album *Labelle* and toured that year with the Who. After singing backgrounds on *Gonna Take a Miracle,* Laura Nyro's 1971 Columbia album of girl-group classics, Labelle recorded two more for Warner Bros. and one for RCA Victor. The albums, featuring Patti's soaring leads and Nona's distinctive, sometimes topical compositions, attracted a dedicated cult following, but the group's popularity didn't cross into the mainstream until it switched to Epic in 1974 and cut the album *Nightbirds* in New Orleans with producer Allen Toussaint. Although half of the tunes were penned by Nona, it was a Bob Crewe–Kenny Nolan song about a hooker, "Lady Marmalade," that took Labelle to the top.

With futuristic costumes and fever-pitched stage routines, Labelle became a huge concert draw. The trio cut two more albums for Epic before disbanding in 1977 due to artistic differences. Sarah went on to modest success as a disco artist. Nona enjoyed slightly more with her forays into rock and avant-garde funk, including collaborations with Talking Heads, Material, Defunkt, and Cameo, and had her biggest post-Labelle hit with 1987's number five R&B, Dan Hartman–produced "Why Should I Cry?" on EMI

America. Patti took the middle road and eventually became a major soul diva, scoring a dozen top 10 R&B hits between 1983 and 1992, compared to the two—"Lady Marmalade" and "What Can I Do for You?," both from *Nightbirds*—by her former group during its entire 15-year career.

Patti's early solo albums for Epic yielded no substantial hits, but after moving to the Philadelphia International label, she struck the top of the R&B chart with the 1983 Kenny Gamble–Dexter Wansel–produced ballad "If Only You Knew." Joining MCA in 1985, she toned down her histrionic vocal attack a bit and hit the R&B top five twice in a row with the singles "New Attitude" and "Stir It Up," both from the *Beverly Hills Cop* film soundtrack. The following year's *Winner in You* album became her greatest commercial success, rising to Number One on the *Billboard* album chart and spawning the Number One R&B and pop single "On My Own," a duet with Michael McDonald written and produced by Burt Bacharach and Carol Bayer Sager. In 1991, Patti, Sarah, and Nona were reunited for "Release Yourself," a Hendryx-penned track from Patti's album *Burnin'*.

DENISE LaSALLE

Although soul and blues singer-songwriter Denise LaSalle (b. Denise Craig, July 16, 1939, LeFlore County, Mississippi) had only modest success in her first career as a writer of "confessional" fiction stories for such magazines as *Tan* and *True Confessions,* she managed to turn similar, often salacious plots into a series of hit tunes, among them "Trapped by a Thing Called Love," "Now Run and Tell That," "What It Takes to Get a Good Woman (That's What It Takes to Keep Her)," "Married, But Not to Each Other," "Lady in the Streets," and "Your Husband Is Cheating on Us." One of the first African-American women to produce her own records, she also wrote and supervised sides for the Sequins (1970's number 34 R&B "Hey Romeo") and Bill Coday (1971's number 14 R&B "Get Your Lie Straight").

"During the first part of my career," she explained, "I found that it was questionable whether or not you could make it as an artist unless you did things that you didn't wanna do. For instance, I don't feel like I have to sleep with anybody to make it. I'm just not that kind. So what I decided to do was try to be my own producer and see if I have any talent."

LaSalle, who moved from Belzoni, Mississippi, to Chicago in 1955, began performing 10 years later in local clubs with blues singer Billy "the Kid" Emerson. Her first record, "A Love Reputation," appeared on Emerson's Tarpon label in 1967 and was picked up for national distribution for Chess. She formed Crajon Productions with future husband Bill Jones in 1969 and began working in Memphis with arrangers Willie Mitchell and Gene "Bowlegs" Miller and the Hi Rhythm Section (soon to be made famous via Al Green) on sessions by the Sequins, Coday, and herself.

The Sequins' records were issued on Gold Star, Coday's on Crajon and Fantasy, and LaSalle's on Westbound. Her Westbound recording of "Trapped by a Thing Called Love," a loping, triplet-based soul shuffle arranged by Mitchell, shot to the top of the *Billboard* R&B chart in the fall of 1971 and peaked at number 13 pop, her greatest crossover success in the U.S. She continued making hits in Memphis for Westbound through 1976's number 16 R&B "Married, But Not to Each Other" (quickly covered by Barbara Mandrell, who took it to number three on the country chart). Then she switched to ABC, where she had one last top 40 R&B charter with 1977's number 10 "Love Me Right." She and James Wolf (her current husband) settled in Jackson, Tennessee, that year and started a radio station.

TOP ALBUMS

TRAPPED BY A THING CALLED LOVE (Westbound, '71)
A LADY IN THE STREET (Malaco, '83)
STILL TRAPPED (Malaco, '90)

TOP SONGS

TRAPPED BY A THING CALLED LOVE (Westbound, '71,
    1 R&B, 13 Pop)
NOW RUN AND TELL THAT (Westbound, '72, *3 R&B*)
MAN SIZED JOB (Westbound, '72, *4 R&B*)
WHAT IT TAKES TO GET A GOOD WOMAN
    (THAT'S WHAT IT'S GONNA TAKE TO KEEP HER)
    (Westbound, '73, *31 R&B*)
MARRIED, BUT NOT TO EACH OTHER (Westbound,
    '76, *16 R&B*)
LOVE ME RIGHT (ABC, '77, *10 R&B*)

LaSalle didn't weather the disco storm well at ABC or later at MCA. "I tried to sell disco, but the deejays wouldn't play it," she explained. "They said, 'That's not Denise LaSalle.'" Then, in 1983, she reemerged at Malaco Records in Jackson, Mississippi, with the album *A Lady in the Street,* a mixture of southern soul and urban blues, including a version of the Z.Z. Hill hit "Down Home Blues." Her rendition contained a sassy monologue that made it too hot for most radio stations to play, but patrons of black working-class bars across the country kept dropping quarters into jukeboxes to hear it, and attendance at her live engagements mushroomed. Blues and sexually suggestive monologues became LaSalle's forte. She started composing and cutting 12-bar tunes of her own, of which 1984's "Someone Else Is Steppin' In" was also recorded by Hill and went on to become something of a blues and jazz standard.

In 1985, LaSalle entered the "Toot Toot" sweepstakes. Louisiana zydeco singer-accordionist Rockin' Sidney had recorded a catchy self-penned ditty called "My Toot Toot" for the regional Maison de Soul label that became a national jukebox favorite and a number 19 country hit. New Orleans soul singer Jean Knight (of "Mr. Big Stuff" fame) made a cover version that Malaco attempted to acquire. When Atlantic got it instead, Malaco had LaSalle do a cover (renamed "My Tu-Tu" to make it sound more spicy) of Knight's cover. Knight's recording beat out LaSalle's on black radio in the U.S., but LaSalle won the international competition at the time. Issued in other parts of the world on Epic with the original title, hers placed in the top 10 in both England and Germany. The song was still making the rounds as late as 1989, when the Colombian group Sonora Dinamita had a cumbia version titled "Mi Cucu" that became a smash in Mexico and much of the Spanish-speaking Americas.

LeVERT

Bloodline, the 1986 major label album debut by LeVert, was aptly titled, as two members of the Cleveland, Ohio, trio—vocalist Gerald Levert (b. July 13, 1966) and singer-percussionist Sean Levert (b. Sept. 28, 1968)—are sons of Eddie Levert, lead singer of the O'Jays, one of the most venerable of all soul vocal groups. Singer-key-

Levert

boardist Marc Gordon (b. Sept. 8, 1964), their friend since elementary school, is the third member. Between 1986 and 1993, LeVert scored a dozen top 10 R&B singles, five of which went to Number One. Gerald also had two R&B chart-toppers as a solo artist, and he and Marc emerged as one of the most in-demand songwriting-producing teams in the business.

Eddie Levert wasn't too keen about Gerald following in his footsteps, but he offered encouragement nonetheless and allowed him to travel with the O'Jays during summer vacations from school. Eddie bought the nine-year-old Gerald a piano and advised him to write his own songs, something the O'Jays were seldom allowed to do during the peak of their popularity in the 1970s. Within a year, Gerald was composing and was soon joined by Marc, with whom he began working in the Levert family's basement studio. They graduated from two-track to eight-track and eventually persuaded Sean to join them in forming a group.

After LeVert's demos were rejected by several major labels, the trio signed with the tiny Tempre label in Philadelphia, the city where the O'Jays' greatest hits had been made. *I Get Hot,* LeVert's first album, produced by Philly soul veteran Dexter

Wansel, was issued in 1985 and contained a song titled "I'm Still" that became a hit in Baltimore and attracted some national attention, including the interest of Atlantic Records. After they joined Atlantic the following year, LeVert's *Bloodline* album, produced by Keg Johnson and Wilmer Ranglin, spawned the Number One R&B single "(Pop, Pop, Pop, Pop) Goes My Mind," written by Gerald and Marc.

The two produced most of the group's next album, 1987's *The Big Throwdown,* but its biggest single, the Number One R&B, number five pop "Casanova" (LeVert's only significant crossover hit), was penned and produced by Reggie Calloway of Midnight Star. They were in full control of their next Number One R&B single, 1988's "Addicted to You" (co-written by Gerald and Marc with Eddie Levert), from the soundtrack of the hit comedy *Coming to America* starring Eddie Murphy, as well as of the 1989 album *Just Coolin'.*

Because of the trio's romantic style and the uncanny vocal similarity of lead singer Gerald's declarative low tenor to that of his dad, LeVert often drew comparisons to the O'Jays. But with *Just Coolin',* the young group took a more contemporary musical stance, one that completely embraced the hip-hop–inspired beats of the new jack swing movement. "This is our first attempt at doing some of the harder-edged funk stuff that the young people listen to," Gerald said at the time. The title track, featuring a rap interlude by Heavy D., became LeVert's fourth Number One R&B hit.

Gerald and Marc's Tervel Productions had already begun applying the LeVert sound to others, producing two top five R&B hits—"That's What Love Is" by Miki Howard (in duet with Gerald) and "Mamacita" by Troop—in 1988. Working together or separately, Gerald and Marc went on to write and/or produce material for such artists as the O'Jays (with whom they frequently toured), Stephanie Mills, Jennifer Holliday, Millie Jackson, James Ingram, Anita Baker, Eugene Wilde, the Rude Boys, Geoff McBride, Christopher Williams, Sweet Obsession, and Chuckii Booker. And they branched into artist management, bringing the Rude Boys and Men at Large under the Tervel wing.

LeVert's 1990 album *Rope a Dope Style* yielded the Number One R&B hit "Baby I'm Ready," after which Gerald recorded the 1991 solo album *Private Line,* its title track and the cut "Baby Hold on to Me" (a duet with his dad) both becoming R&B chart-toppers. The trio's sixth album, 1993's *For Real Tho',* was their first for Atlantic not to produce a Number One hit, but it did contain the number five R&B "ABC-123." In 1994, Eddie, Sean, and Marc were on the road again as an opening act for the O'Jays.

Joe Liggins

JOE LIGGINS

When former Led Zeppelin vocalist Robert Plant and an all-star group of British and American rock musicians recorded a mini-album of rhythm and blues standards in 1984, they intended it as a tribute to some of the artists who first inspired them. They named the group the Honeydrippers, after a popular jump blues band of the 1940s led by pianist-singer Joe Liggins (b. 1915, Guthrie, Oklahoma). The album, titled *The Honeydrippers, Volume 1,* and the single, a remake of Phil Phillips's 1959 Louisiana swamp-pop hit "Sea of Love," turned out to be huge hits

Liggins himself wasn't particularly thrilled about it, however. "It's a name I thought up and used for 40 years," he said at the time. Since the new Honeydrippers' album didn't include a version of "The Honeydripper," Liggins's self-penned 1945 smash, he couldn't even complain all the way to the bank.

The term *honeydripper* refers to a man who's popular with women. Liggins said he was first dubbed that in 1942 when he was playing piano with Sammy Franklin and the California Rhythm

---

TOP ALBUM

The Big Throwdown (Atlantic, '87, 32)

TOP SONGS

(Pop, Pop, Pop, Pop) Goes My Mind (Atlantic, '86, 1 *R&B*)

Casanova (Atlantic, '87, 1 *R&B, 5 Pop*)

My Forever Love (Atlantic, '87, 2 *R&B*)

Sweet Sensation (Atlantic, '88, 4 *R&B*)

Addicted to Your Love (Atco, '88, 1 *R&B*)

Pull Over (Atlantic, '88, 2 *R&B*)

Just Coolin' (LeVert featuring Heavy D., Atlantic, '89, 1 *R&B*)

All Season (Atlantic, '91, 4 *R&B*)

Baby I'm Ready (Atlantic, '91, 1 *R&B*)

Additional Top 40 R&B Songs: 9

Rascals at Billy Berg's Swing Club in Hollywood. "The drummer in the band said, 'He's dripping a lot of honey around. You're a honeydripper,' " Liggins recalled. "That was the first time I ever heard that."

Liggins was not, however, the first musician to use the moniker professionally. Blues singer-pianist Roosevelt Sykes was billed as the Honey Dripper on labels of many of his Decca 78s during the 1930s and recorded a tune by that title in 1936. Sykes began calling his band the Honeydrippers in 1943, a year before Liggins organized his own combo, but Sykes never enjoyed Liggins's mass popularity and didn't use the group name on record labels until 1951.

Liggins was strongly influenced by the Duke Ellington records he heard as a youth in Oklahoma. He played piano in church and trumpet, tuba, and mellophone in school bands and wrote his first arrangement at age 12. Shortly thereafter, he moved with his family to San Diego.

He composed "The Honeydripper" in 1942, intending it to fit the Texas Hop, a dance craze of the period. He tried submitting it to Jimmie Lunceford, but the orchestra leader, Liggins explained, "said the beat was too unusual and didn't fit the band's style." After organizing his own band, he recorded the tune in 1945 as a two-part 78 for the Los Angeles–based Exclusive label, one of the first independent record companies to have emerged at the end of World War II. The number, featuring the band members chanting over Liggins's loping shuffle piano and two furiously riffing saxophones, became that year's biggest-selling R&B record, topping the *Billboard* R&B chart for 18 weeks and crossing over to number 13 pop.

Because of Exclusive's initially limited distribution, Liggins's recording was slow in taking off. He recalled that Pullman porters would buy copies in Los Angeles for $1.05 apiece, take them to Chicago, and resell them for $10. And established companies cashed in on the song's popularity. Columbia had Cab Calloway cut it, Lunceford recorded it for Decca, and Sykes even made a version for Bluebird. All three covers placed on *Billboard*'s charts, but Liggins's original outsold them all. He collected songwriter's royalties on all renditions.

More hits followed, including "Got a Right to Cry" later in 1945 ("It was so popular with whites," he stated, "that stores like Sears-Roebuck had to stock a so-called race record"), "Tayna" in 1946, and "The Darktown Strutters' Ball" in 1948. After the collapse of Exclusive Records, Liggins joined his younger brother, blues singer-guitarist Jimmy Liggins, at Specialty Records in 1949 and had the next year's biggest R&B record, "Pink Champagne."

Joe Liggins and His Honeydrippers—who, along with Louis Jordan and His Tympany Five and Roy Milton and His Solid Senders, were a seminal influence on R&B combos of the 1950s—stopped touring in 1952. Tired of the road, he settled down with his wife and son in Compton, California. He left Specialty in 1954 and went on to record with little success for Mercury, Aladdin, and Blues Spectrum. Liggins and his band, including longtime saxophonist Little Willie Jackson, continued performing around six dates a month, mostly in southern California, until the leader's death on July 26, 1987.

TOP SONGS

The Honeydripper (Exclusive, '45, *1 R&B, 13 Pop*)
Left a Good Deal in Mobile (Exclusive, '45, *2 R&B*)
Got a Right to Cry (Exclusive, '45, *2 R&B, 12 Pop*)
Tanya (Exclusive, '46, *3 R&B*)
Blow Mr. Jackson (Exclusive, '47, *3 R&B*)
Sweet Georgia Brown (Exclusive, '48, *7 R&B*)
The Darktown Strutters' Ball (Exclusive, '48, *8 R&B*)
Rag Mop (Specialty, '50, *4 R&B*)
Pink Champagne (Specialty, '50, *1 R&B, 30 Pop*)
Little Joe's Boogie (Specialty, '51, *5 R&B*)

Additional Top 40 R&B Songs: 4

LITTLE ANTHONY
AND THE IMPERIALS

Anthony Gourdine (b. Jan. 8, 1940, New York), the spectacular lead falsetto of the Imperials, was shocked when, during the summer of 1958, he heard WINS disc jockey Alan Freed introduce the group's new record as being by "Little Anthony and the Imperials." The artist credit on the End 45 had simply read "the Imperials," and after all, Gourdine was hardly little, standing 5' 8 1/2". The New York City deejay was so influential that the record company started using that designation on subsequent pressings of the song. The singer learned to live with it, especially as the doo wop ballad climbed the *Billboard* charts to number two R&B and number four pop.

The son of jazz saxophonist Thomas Gourdine and his gospel-singing wife Elizabeth, Anthony grew up in Brooklyn admiring such artists as Nat "King" Cole, George Shearing, and the Flamingos. While attending Boys High School, he formed a quartet with friends William Dockery, William Delk, and William Bracy. Known as the DuPonts, they cut their first record, "You," for the Winley label in 1955. It generated little interest, but the next single, 1957's "Prove It Tonight" on Royal Roost, got the DuPonts an opening slot on Freed's all-star Easter rock and roll show at the New York Paramount Theater.

Gourdine left the DuPonts in 1957 and formed the Chesters with first tenor Tracy Lord, second tenor Ernest Wright, Jr., baritone Clarence Collins, and basso Glouster "Nate" Rogers. The new group, with Keith Williams temporarily replacing Collins, cut the Gourdine-penned "The Fires Burn No More" for Apollo in 1958, but heavy New York airplay by Freed failed to ignite sparks elsewhere in the country. The Chesters, with Collins back in, were signed by songwriter-producer Richard Barrett to George Goldner's End label later that year. Renamed the Imperials, they scored immediately with the sentimental Sylvester Bradford–Al Lewis ballad "Tears on My Pillow." After two more charters on End, 1959's "So Much" and the next year's "Shimmy, Shimmy, Ko-Ko-Bop," the group left the label in 1961, and Gourdine and the Imperials soon parted ways. He made two solo singles for Roulette, while the group cut one record for Carlton and two for Newtime. None were successful.

Gourdine rejoined forces with the Imperials, by now comprising Wright, Collins, and Sammy Strain (earlier with the Chips and the Fantastics, later with the O'Jays), in 1963. Signed to Don Costa's United Artists–distributed DCP label, they began working with songwriter-producer Teddy Randazzo on a series of melodramatic ballads that took them away from doo wop into a sophisticated soul sound. Gourdine, in the words of British author Barney Hoskyns, "wailed over strings and tympani with unbridled teen angst, keeping the high tenor-falsetto sob of Clyde [McPhatter] and Jackie [Wilson] alive in a new, massively orchestrated context." The group's association with Randazzo yielded such hits as 1964's number 15 pop "I'm on the Outside (Looking In)" (*Billboard* published no R&B chart at that time) and the number 22 R&B, number six pop "Goin' Out of My Head" and the number three R&B, number 10 pop "Hurt So Bad," both in 1965. "Goin' Out of My Head" was successfully revived by the Lettermen in 1968, while "Hurt So Bad" became a hit for the Lettermen in 1969 and for Linda Ronstadt in 1980.

Little Anthony and the Imperials were transferred to United Artists' Veep label in 1966 and three years later to United Artists proper, where they had a minor 1969 hit with a remake of the Five Keys' "Out of Sight, Out of Mind." A 1971–72 association with Janus Records proved unfruitful, after which they began working with Thom Bell at the Avco label. It seemed an ideal match, as Gourdine had been a major influence on the falsetto leads of two other Bell-produced groups, William Hart of the Delfonics and Russell Thompkins, Jr., of the Stylistics, yet the 1974 Bell-produced Imperials single, "I'm Falling in Love with You," managed to rise only as high as number 25 on the R&B chart. Gourdine soon split up with the group, while the Collins-led edition of the Imperials had a number 17 hit in England with 1977's "Who's Gonna Love Me" on the Power Exchange label.

Gourdine experienced a religious reawakening and recorded an album of contemporary Christian songs, produced by fellow born-again singer B. J. Thomas, for the Songbird label in 1980, but he otherwise continued to work the oldies circuit, as well as Las Vegas lounges. In 1987 he made a guest appearance with New Edition on a revamp of "Tears on My Pillow" for MCA. After an 18-year hiatus, Gourdine, Strain, Wright, and Collins were reunited for a 1992 concert in New York and at the 40th

TOP SONGS

TEARS ON MY PILLOW (End, '58, 2 R&B, 4 Pop)

SO MUCH (End, '59, 24 R&B)

SHIMMY, SHIMMY, KO-KO-BOP (End, '60, 14 R&B, 24 Pop)

GOIN' OUT OF MY HEAD (DCP, '65, 22 R&B, 6 Pop)

HURT SO BAD (DCP, '65, 3 R&B, 10 Pop)

TAKE ME BACK (DCP, '65, 15 R&B, 16 Pop)

I MISS YOU SO (DCP, '65, 23 R&B, 34 Pop)

OUT OF SIGHT, OUT OF MIND (United Artists, '69, 38 R&B)

HELP ME FIND A WAY (TO SAY I LOVE YOU) (United Artists, '70, 32 R&B)

I'M FALLING IN LOVE WITH YOU (Avco, '74, 25 R&B)

anniversary of "American Bandstand." By the following year, they were touring again as a unit.

LITTLE MILTON

Little Milton

Lines between blues and soul, drawn mainly by white critics and fans, became blurred by the early 1990s as the blues receded further and further from the pop mainstream. Soul singers like Otis Clay and Ann Peebles, who wouldn't have been booked by most blues festivals a decade earlier, were suddenly in demand for such events, as well as being recorded by blues labels. But many African Americans had been less prone to such stylistic compartmentalization, as evidenced by the acceptance of such artists as Tyrone Davis and Joe Simon, neither of whom ever specialized in blues, into the blues cannon.

Singer-guitarist Little Milton Campbell (b. Sept. 7, 1934, Inverness, Mississippi) began his recording career in 1953 at Sun Records in Memphis as a B. B. King–inspired bluesman. During the late 1950s and early '60s at the Bobbin label in East St. Louis, he fell under the soul-blues spell of Bobby Bland. By 1965, however, Milton was at Checker in Chicago and developed a more personal style under the guidance of producer Billy Davis. That year's Number One R&B "We're Gonna Make It," its lyrics in sync with the civil rights sentiments of the period, placed Milton squarely in the soul camp, as did the number four R&B follow-up, "Who's Cheatin' Who." From that point on, he alternated between soul selections and hard-core blues,

often brilliantly fusing the two, on releases for Checker, Stax, Glades, Golden Ear, MCA, and Malaco.

Raised in Greenwood, Mississippi, Milton was tagged "Little" because his dad was known as "Big" Milton. Taking up guitar when he was 12, Little Milton left home three years later to play in the bands of Eddie Cusic, Sonny Boy Williamson, and Willie Love. Ike Turner arranged for him to audition for Sun Records owner Sam Phillips in 1953, and Milton's first record, "If You Love Me Baby," was issued the following year. It garnered little interest, as did a second Sun release. He recorded another single for the Memphis-based Meteor label in 1957 and then moved to East St. Louis, where he signed with Bobbin Records under the auspices of saxophonist-bandleader Oliver Sain.

Moderate sales of Milton's Bobbin sides, especially 1958's "I'm a Lonely Man," attracted the

TOP SONGS

SO MEAN TO ME (Checker, '62, *14 R&B*)

WE'RE GONNA MAKE IT (Checker, '65, *1 R&B, 25 Pop*)

WHO'S CHEATING WHO? (Checker, '65, *4 R&B*)

FEEL SO BAD (Checker, '67, *7 R&B*)

GRITS AIN'T GROCERIES (ALL AROUND THE WORLD) (Checker, '69, *13 R&B*)

JUST A LITTLE BIT (Checker, '69, *13 R&B*)

LET'S GET TOGETHER (Checker, '69, *13 R&B*)

IF WALLS COULD TALK (Checker, '69, *10 R&B*)

BABY I LOVE YOU (Checker, '70, *10 R&B*)

THAT'S WHAT LOVE WILL MAKE YOU DO (Stax, '72, *9 R&B*)

Additional Top 40 R&B Songs: 9

attention of Leonard Chess, who signed him to Checker in 1961. (Chess later acquired the services of Milton's piano player, Fontella Bass, who, as a vocalist, scored at Number One R&B and number four pop in 1965 with "Rescue Me.") Milton's first Checker hit, 1962's "So Mean to Me," borrowed heavily from Bobby Bland's "I Pity the Fool," while his second, 1965's "Blind Man," was a direct cover of a tune from a Bland album.

Working with producers Davis, Gene Barge, and/or Calvin Carter, Milton had 10 top 40 R&B hits between 1965 and 1971. Most were in the soul vein, and few featured his incisive guitar work, a notable exception being 1967's number seven R&B "Feel So Bad" from the album *Little Milton Sings Big Blues*. His guitar became more prominent after a switch to Stax in 1971. His biggest seller for the Memphis company was the following year's number nine R&B "That's What Love Will Make You Do," an original composition produced by Don Davis on which Milton introduced his innovative "muffle-picking" technique. Other highlights of his four-year association with Stax include the jukebox favorites "Walking the Back Streets and Crying," "Little Bluebird," and "Tin Pan Alley."

After Stax folded, Milton jumped from label to label with uneven results before landing at Malaco in 1984 and making a series of handsomely crafted albums with producers Tommy Couch and Wolf Stephenson. He was still blurring the lines between blues and soul, but his audience remained overwhelmingly African American. Unlike B. B. King and, to a lesser degree, Bobby Bland, Little Milton never achieved significant crossover appeal.

LITTLE RICHARD

Little Richard (b. Richard Wayne Penniman, Dec. 5, 1932, Macon, Georgia) has always craved attention—and gotten it. As a boy, the third of the 13 children of Bud and Leva Mae Penniman, he once defecated in a shoe box, wrapped it, presented it as a birthday present to an old woman in the neighborhood, and waited around the corner to listen for her shriek. During the mid-1950s, as a rock and roll idol to rebellious youth, he shocked adults with his fierce vocals, incessantly pounding piano, flamboyant appearance, and wild stage antics. And during two later periods as an evangelist

---

TOP ALBUM

HERE'S LITTLE RICHARD (Specialty, '57, 13)

TOP SONGS

TUTTI-FRUTTI (Specialty, '55, 2 R&B, 17 Pop)
LONG TALL SALLY (Specialty, '56, 1 R&B, 6 Pop)
SLIPPIN' AND SLIDIN' (PEEPIN' AND HIDIN') (Specialty, '56, 2 R&B, 33 Pop)
RIP IT UP (Specialty, '56, 1 R&B, 17 Pop)
LUCILLE (Specialty, '57, 1 R&B, 21 Pop)
SEND ME SOME LOVIN' (Specialty, '57, 3 R&B)
JENNY, JENNY (Specialty, '57, 2 R&B, 10 Pop)
KEEP A KNOCKIN' (Specialty, '57, 2 R&B, 8 Pop)
GOOD GOLLY, MISS MOLLY (Specialty, '58, 4 R&B, 10 Pop)

Additional Top 40 R&B Songs: 11

---

on the Seventh Day Adventist revival circuit, he titillated congregations with lurid tales of drugs and orgies.

The self-proclaimed King of Rock and Roll received the greatest attention for the incendiary music he created during his initial 25-month stay at Specialty Records. Producer Bumps Blackwell took him to New Orleans in September 1955 to cut his first session for the Hollywood-based company. Teaming him with some of the town's top R&B studio musicians, Blackwell succeeded in bringing out an intensity in Richard that his earlier records had only hinted at. The result was "Tutti-Frutti," a masterpiece of musical abandon on which the singer whooped and hollered over the band's pile-driving beat, his raspy, melisma-dripping tenor at times soaring into short, ringing falsetto cries that betrayed the influence of gospel singer Marion Williams. And, at the entrance to Lee Allen's booting saxophone solo, Richard let out a torrid scream of ecstasy that became his trademark.

"Tutti-Frutti" shot to number two on the *Billboard* R&B chart and to number 17 pop in early 1956. The next release, "Long Tall Sally," went to Number One R&B and number six pop. Pat Boone made tepid cover versions of both tunes, but while Boone's "Tutti-Frutti" rose to number 12 pop, his treatment of "Long Tall Sally" fell two notches short of Richard's pop mark. Richard scored 16 more top 15 R&B hits at Specialty, two of which also made

Little Richard

the pop top 10, and he appeared in the films *Don't Knock the Rock, The Girl Can't Help It,* and *Mister Rock 'n' Roll,* but in late 1957 he shocked his fans and business associates by suddenly quitting show business and enrolling at Oakwood College, a Seventh Day Adventist school in Huntsville, Alabama.

The product of a strict religious upbringing, Richard was torn throughout his life between devotion and debauchery. After being kicked out of the house at age 13 because of his homosexuality, he appeared at the Tick Tock Club in Macon before going on the road with various medicine and minstrel shows, sometimes performing in drag or in blackface. By 1951, he was in Atlanta, where he began emulating not only the vocal style of Billy Wright but also the local blues singer's high, processed pompadour and use of makeup and mascara.

Through Atlanta disc jockey Zenas Sears, Richard made his first record, "Taxi Blues" b/w

"Every Hour," in 1951 for RCA Victor. It was no more successful than its three follow-ups, after which he recorded two singles for Peacock in Houston in 1953 as the lead singer of the Tempo Toppers and two more later that year for the same label as a soloist backed by the Johnny Otis band. The results of the sessions with Otis were not released until Richard had become a star at Specialty.

After dropping rock and Specialty, Richard made religious recordings for such labels as End, Mercury, and Atlantic, but the music was quite subdued because of the Seventh Day Adventists' abhorrence of anything rhythmic. In 1960, however, as a favor to his former sidemen, the Upsetters, he cut four rocking sides with the band for the Little Star label but appeared uncredited.

In October 1962, Richard traveled to England for what he thought was to be a gospel tour only to discover that Sam Cooke was his opening act. "He had the people screaming," Richard said of Cooke. The crowd booed the headliner when he followed with a set of hymns and spirituals, accompanied only by teenage organist Billy Preston. Richard couldn't stand it. "They wanted me to sing rock and roll," he recalled, "so I came back out and we did rock and tore the house down."

Richard recorded secular music with sporadic success for Specialty, Vee-Jay, Modern, Okeh (a series of marvelous 1966–67 soul sessions with producer Larry Williams), Brunswick, Reprise, Green Mountain, Manticore, Mainstream, and K-Tel between 1964 and 1976. He soon returned to religion, made a gospel album for Word Records, and spent much of the next decade railing against rock, drugs, homosexuality, masturbation, and the feminist movement.

Finally breaking with the Seventh Day Adventists and beginning a flirtation with Judaism (which also observes the Sabbath from sundown Friday to sundown Saturday and has similar dietary laws), Richard rocked out once again with the 1986 MCA single "Great Gosh A'Mighty!" from the motion picture comedy *Down and Out in Beverly Hills,* in which he made his acting debut. He became a fixture on television talk shows and commercials and made occasional recordings, including a little-noticed 1986 album for Warner Bros. and the best-selling 1992 children's album *Shake It All About* for Disney.

NELLIE LUTCHER

Singer-pianist Nellie Lutcher (b. Oct. 15, 1915, Lake Charles, Louisiana) somehow slipped through the cracks of American music history. Although she was the biggest-selling black female recording artist of 1947 and '48, there is no mention of her in most reference books on jazz and R&B, perhaps because her unique style doesn't fit handily into either category.

She considers herself a jazz artist, yet her romping, Earl Hines–inspired piano style is often dismissed as "primitive" by jazz aficionados. Her quirky contralto vocal manner is harder to characterize, and she is at a loss to describe it herself.

The *New Yorker*'s Whitney Balliett, one of the few jazz critics to have written at length about Lutcher, has said that "she is a master of dynamics: whispers and shouts and crooning continually sur-

prise one another. Like Joe Turner, she uses words to hang melody on, and what she sings is often unintelligible. She steadily garnishes her melodic flow with squeaks, falsetto, mock-operatic arias, yodels, and patches of talking."

The eldest of Isaac and Susie Lutcher's 16 children, Nellie began playing piano at age eight for the New Sunlight Baptist Church in Lake Charles. As a teenager, she joined her bass-playing father in Clarence Hart's Imperial Jazz Band, a group that included jazz trumpet pioneer Bunk Johnson and that also accompanied Ma Rainey, "the Mother of the Blues," when she came through Lake Charles without her pianist.

Lutcher moved to Los Angeles in 1935 and began developing her vocal style in local clubs. In 1947, she followed her younger brother Joe, a jump blues saxophonist, to Capitol Records. Her first recording, the self-composed "Hurry On Down," was an immediate sensation, as were such releases as the original "He's a Real Gone Guy" and a rendition of Buddy Johnson's "Fine Brown Frame."

"Some stations wouldn't even play 'Hurry On Down' because they considered that risqué," she recalled. "In today's market, of course, nobody thinks anything of it. It's really just a novelty song that may be a little suggestive, but compared to many of these things that are being done today, my God, it's almost a hymn."

Along with Louis Jordan, the Ink Spots, the Mills Brothers, and Nat "King" Cole (Lutcher and Cole shared the same manager, Carlos Gastel, and record-

---

TOP SONGS

HURRY ON DOWN (Capitol, '47, *2 R&B, 20 Pop*)

HE'S A REAL GONE GUY (Capitol, '47, *2 R&B, 15 Pop*)

THE SONG IS ENDED (BUT THE MELODY LINGERS ON) (Capitol, '48, *3 R&B, 23 Pop*)

DO YOU OR DON'T YOU LOVE ME (Capitol, '47, *9 R&B*)

FINE BROWN FRAME (Capitol, '48, *2 R&B, 21 Pop*)

COME AND GET IT HONEY (Capitol, '48, *6 R&B*)

COOL WATER (Capitol, '48, *7 R&B*)

ALEXANDER'S RAGTIME BAND (Capitol, '48, *13 R&B*)

I WISH I WAS IN WALLA WALLA (Capitol, '49, *13 R&B*)

FOR YOU, MY LOVE (Nat King Cole Trio with Nellie Lutcher, Capitol, '50, *8 R&B*)

Additional Top 40 R&B Songs: 1

ed the duet "For You, My Love" in 1950), she was one of the few black recording stars of the 1940s who was popular among both blacks and whites, with four of her songs crossing over from the R&B to the pop charts. "The rest of the people were considered 'race' artists," she explained. "At that time, most of the clubs I played where white places."

After sales of her Capitol recordings declined in the early 1950s, Lutcher moved to the Decca, Okeh, Liberty, and Imperial labels with little success. "I got a little disturbed by certain things in the business, and at that time, rock was coming into the picture," she said. "I was asked if I would do some rock, even some of my big hits in rock and roll style. I said, 'No, I would not.' Some big artists I know attempted to get into the rock thing, and they goofed badly because this is a thing that you gotta have a feel for. I didn't feel it, so I just decided to cool it."

Lutcher has largely been inactive as a performer since the 1960s, instead tending to her real estate investments. She also served for eight years on the board of directors of the Los Angeles local of the American Federation of Musicians. Sporadic appearances during the 1980s included engagements at Disneyland, Barney Josephson's Cookery in New York City, and the Marin County Blues Festival in northern California.

FRANKIE LYMON
AND THE TEENAGERS

The Teenagers, featuring boy soprano Frankie Lymon (b. Sept. 30, 1942, New York), were not the first child stars of rhythm and blues. Precedents were set in 1948 by 11-year-old vocalist Toni Harper with the number 15 R&B, number 22 pop "Candy Store Blues" on Columbia; in 1949 by 9-year-old pianist Sugar Chile Robinson with the number four R&B "Numbers Boogie" on Capitol; and in 1950 by 14-year-old singer Little Esther Phillips with the Number One R&B "Double Crossing Blues" on Savoy. Thirteen-year-old Lymon and his four slightly older New York–born cohorts—first tenor Herman Santiago, second tenor Jimmy Merchant, baritone Joe Negroni, and basso Sherman Garnes—were, however, the first pubescent R&B act to achieve massive pop appeal on an international basis.

If the Teenagers' success served as a model for such subsequent young singing groups as the Jackson 5 and New Edition, their quick rise to stardom also stands as an example of what can go wrong when inexperienced kids are thrust into the middle of the cut-throat music business. The doo wop quintet's recording career lasted a mere 18 months, ending with Lymon splitting from the others due to a combination of ego conflicts and managerial manipulation. Neither he nor the Teenagers were able to reclaim their previous status. And for decades following their first hit, 1956's "Why Do Fools Fall in Love," legal battles raged over the ownership of Lymon's half of the songwriters' royalties.

Frankie grew up harmonizing with his brothers Louis (later leader of his own doo wop group, the Teenchords) and Howie in the Harlemaires Juniors, a gospel group fashioned after the Harlemaires in which their father Howard sang. When he was 10, Frankie told *Ebony* magazine years later, "I made a good living hustling prostitutes for white men who would come up to Harlem looking for Negro girls." By age 12, he had found a more legitimate job—delivering groceries—and had hooked up with four singers called the Premiers. Their repertoire consisted of songs by other groups, including "Lily Maebelle" by the Harlem-based Valentines, until a neighbor suggested they put music to some poems his girlfriend had written. One was titled "Why Do Birds Sing So Gay."

Richard Barrett, a member of the Valentines who doubled as a talent scout and producer for the Tico-

---

TOP ALBUM

THE TEENAGERS FEATURING FRANKIE LYMON (The Teenagers featuring Frankie Lymon, Gee, '56, *19*)

TOP SONGS

WHY DO FOOLS FALL IN LOVE (The Teenagers featuring Frankie Lymon, Gee, '56, *1 R&B, 6 Pop*)

I WANT YOU TO BE MY GIRL (Gee, '56, *3 R&B, 13 Pop*)

I PROMISE TO REMEMBER (Gee, '56, *10 R&B*)

WHO CAN EXPLAIN? (Gee, '56, *7 R&B*)

THE ABC'S OF LOVE (Gee, '56, *8 R&B*)

OUT IN THE COLD AGAIN (Gee, '57, *10 R&B*)

GOODY GOODY (Gee, '57, *20 Pop*)

Frankie Lymon and the Teenagers

Rama-Gee group of record labels, brought the Premiers to the attention of company owner George Goldner in 1955. That November, they cut their first record, backed by Jimmy Wright's band. The saxophonist came up with the idea to change their name to the Teenagers, and Goldner suggested that they change "Why Do Birds Sing So Gay" to "Why Do Fools Fall in Love" and that Lymon, instead of Santiago, sing lead. For his contributions, Goldner received a piece of the songwriter's credit. Early pressings of the single, released on Gee in January 1956, listed Lymon, Santiago, and Goldner as the composers, though Santiago's name was soon dropped. In later years, Morris Levy of Roulette Records, which had acquired Goldner's catalog, claimed full writer's credit.

"Why Do Fools Fall in Love" shot to Number One R&B and number six pop in *Billboard*. It also went to Number One in England—the first British hit by an American R&B or rock act. The Teenagers' next three singles—"I Want You to Be My Girl," the double-sided "I Promise to Remember"/"Who Can Explain?," and "The ABC's of Love"—also made the R&B top 10. Their fifth release, "I'm Not a Juvenile Delinquent" b/w "Baby, Baby," failed to dent the U.S. charts, despite being featured in the Alan Freed motion picture *Rock, Rock, Rock*. In England,

however, the A side charted at number 12 and the flip at number four.

While the group was on tour in England in early 1957, Gee Records began recording Lymon as a solo artist without telling the other members. By the summer of that year, when their single "Out in the Cold Again" hit number 10 R&B, he was no longer with the group. His final hit, "Goody Goody," entered the pop chart in August 1957 and peaked at number 20. Although credited on the label to Frankie Lymon and the Teenagers, it was actually a solo effort on which he was supported vocally by a white chorus.

The Teenagers, using a series of different leads, went on to record for Roulette, End, and Columbia through 1961, all with little success. Garnes died in 1977, followed the next year by Negroni. In 1981, Santiago and Merchant organized a new set of Teenagers, with a woman, Pearl McKinnon, singing Lymon's old parts. They've been working the oldies circuit ever since.

Lymon himself had little luck with solo recordings on Roulette, TCF, Columbia, and Big Apple. His gloriously soaring voice had deepened and he'd become a heroin addict. Reflecting on the past, not long before his death from an overdose on February 20, 1968, Lymon told writer Gene Lees, "I was merely a pawn in a big chess game."

THE MANHATTANS

Legend has it that George "Smitty" Smith, Edward "Sonny" Bivins, Kenneth Kelly, Richard Taylor, and Winfred "Blue" Lovett came to call themselves the Manhattans because, as teenage singers in Jersey City, New Jersey, they'd dream about the big time while gazing across the Hudson River at the Manhattan skyline. It's a nice story, but, unfortunately, it isn't true. In fact, the quintet took its name from a cocktail known as the Manhattan that's made from whiskey, vermouth, and bitters. Still, the name suggested class, something the Manhattans have epitomized throughout their long career.

Although they began making records in 1963, the Manhattans didn't strike it big until the mid-1970s, when they successfully bucked the disco trend with a series of romantic ballads for Columbia Records. Eight of these songs—"There's No Me Without You," "Don't Take Your Love," "Hurt," "Kiss and Say Goodbye," "I Kinda Miss You," "It Feels So Good to Be Loved So Bad," "We Never Danced to a Love Song," and "Am I Losing You"—made the R&B top 10 between 1973 and 1978, with the country-tinged Lovett composition "Kiss and Say Good Bye" going to Number One on both the R&B and pop charts in 1976 and placing in the top five in England and Australia. All featured the lilting, Sam Cooke–inspired lead tenor of Gerald Alston—who joined in 1970 following the death from spinal meningitis of original lead singer Smith—wrapped in a full, warm harmony blanket anchored by Lovett's billowing bass.

Lovett (b. Nov. 16, 1943, Macon, Georgia), who characterizes the group's elegant style as "progressive doo wop," first got together with first tenor Bivins and baritone singer Taylor in a group called the Statesmen while they were serving with the Air Force in Germany during the late 1950s. Following their discharge, Lovett and Taylor organized the Dulcets with Smith and Ethel Sanders and, in 1961, recorded one single, "Pork Chops," for the obscure New York City–based Asnes label. The record got little bite at the time, but is today much coveted by record collectors. After the Dulcets disbanded, Lovett, Bivins, Taylor, Smith, and second tenor Kelly formed the Manhattans.

The quintet came in third at an Apollo Theater amateur night in 1964, but the audience reception was so strong that word filtered to Joe Evans, an alto saxophonist who was running Carnival Records out of Newark. Two 1964 Manhattans singles failed to click, but the next year's New Orleans–styled "I Wanna Be (Your Everything)" placed at number 12 on the *Billboard* R&B chart. Seven more Carnival releases—"Searchin' for My Baby," "Follow Your Heart," "Baby I Need You," "Can I," "I Bet'cha (Couldn't Love Me)," "When We Were Made as One," and "I Call It Love"—made the R&B top 40 through 1967. Most were penned by Lovett and/or Bivins, although 1967's "We Were Made as One," a haunting neo–doo wop ballad that the group later rerecorded for Columbia, was by Smith and producer Evans.

A move to the Nashville-based Deluxe label, a subsidiary of King, resulted in four top 40 R&B charters between 1970 and 1973, the biggest being 1972's number three "One Life to Live." By that time, Gerald Alston (b. Nov. 8, 1942), a former gospel quartet singer from North Carolina and nephew of Johnny Fields of the Five Blind Boys of Alabama, had taken over for the late George Smith. "Alston's arrival," critic Mike Freedberg commented, "altered the group slightly, moving them away from the street cool and toward churchy soul-singing mainstream." The Manhattans switched to Columbia in 1973, scored with their first single—the

---

TOP ALBUM

THE MANHATTANS (Columbia, '76, *16*)

Additional Top 40 Albums: 1

TOP SONGS

ONE LIFE TO LIVE (Deluxe, '72, *3 R&B*)

THERE'S NO ME WITHOUT YOU (Columbia, '73, *3 R&B*)

DON'T TAKE YOUR LOVE (Columbia, '74, *7 R&B, 37 Pop*)

KISS AND SAY GOODBYE (Columbia, '76, *1 R&B, 1 Pop*)

I KINDA MISS YOU (Columbia, '76, *7 R&B*)

IT FEELS SO GOOD TO BE LOVED (Columbia, '77, *6 R&B*)

AM I LOSING YOU (Columbia, '78, *6 R&B*)

SHINING STAR (Columbia, '80, *4 R&B, 5 Pop*)

CRAZY (Columbia, '83, *4 R&B*)

Additional Top 40 R&B Songs: 24

Bivins-penned "There's No Me Without You"—and remained with the company for 14 years. Their 1970s hits were produced in Philadelphia or New York by arranger Bobby Martin, after which they recorded in Chicago with producer Leo Graham (1980's number four R&B, number five pop "Shining Star") and in New York with Morrie Brown (1984's uncharacteristic uptempo "Crazy," which was their last top 10 R&B hit, placing at number four.)

Taylor left the fold in 1976 to become a Muslim minister and was not replaced. In 1985 and '86, vocalist Regina Belle toured and recorded with the Manhattans before launching a successful solo career at Columbia. Alston quit in 1988 to record as a soloist for Motown, where he had three top 10 R&B charters—"Take Me Where You Want To," "Slow Motion," and "Getting Back into Love"—between 1988 and '91. Roger Harris became the new lead singer and appeared on the group's modestly successful *We're Back* album in 1989 on the Valley Vue label. By 1993, Lovett was the only original member left, but the Manhattans were again a quintet, comprising Lovett, Al Pazant, Harsey Hemphill, Charles Handy, and lead Lee Williams.

THE
MARVELETTES

Five teenagers from the Detroit suburb of Inkster, Michigan—Gladys Horton, Katherine Anderson, Juanita Cowart, Georgeanna Tillman, and Wanda Young—were the first artists to give Berry Gordy, Jr.'s fledgling Motown operation a Number One hit. All born in 1944, they called themselves the Casinyets, but Gordy felt "Marvelettes" had a better ring. The record, "Please Mr. Postman," was issued on the Tamla label in August 1961 and took its time climbing the charts. By year's end, it had become the top R&B and pop song in the land. While the young women never had another chart-topper and were soon eclipsed by two other Motown "girl groups"—the Supremes and Martha and the Vandellas—they continued making hits through 1968.

Horton, whose coarse alto voice gave the Marvelettes' early sides much of their youthful appeal,

was born to West Indian parents in Gainesville, Florida, but raised in a series of foster homes in the Detroit area after being orphaned at the age of nine months. She sang in a church choir before joining the glee club at Inkster High School. When an announcement was made about an upcoming talent contest at the school, she recruited other members of the chorus to compete. The three winning acts would be given auditions at Motown. Singing hits of the day by the Shirelles and the Chantels, Horton, Anderson, Cowart, Tillman, and their friend Georgia Dobbins came in fourth. One of their teachers was so impressed with the Casinyets' performance that a chance for them to be heard by Motown was arranged nevertheless.

At the April 1961 audition, the group was told to come back with some original material. They returned with "Please Mr. Postman," a blues song by Dobbins's friend William Garrett that she had rearranged. Before the session was held, however, Dobbins opted out of the group and was replaced by Inkster High classmate Wanda Young. Producers Robert Bateman and Brian Holland further polished the tune, and at the session, drummer Marvin Gaye gave it a bouncing, Latin-flavored "twist" beat.

Horton remained the Marvelettes' primary soloist through 1965, fronting such hits as "Playboy" (composed by herself and producer William Stevenson), "Beechwood 4-5789" (written by Stevenson, Gaye, and George Gordy), "Someday Someway" and "Strange I Know" (both by Brian

TOP SONGS

PLEASE MR. POSTMAN (Tamla, '61, *1 R&B, 1 Pop*)
PLAYBOY (Tamla, '62, *4 R&B, 7 Pop*)
BEECHWOOD 4-5789 (Tamla, '62, *7 R&B, 17 Pop*)
SOMEDAY SOMEWAY (Tamla, '62, *8 R&B*)
STRANGE I KNOW (Tamla, '62, *10 R&B*)
I'LL KEEP HOLDING ON (Tamla, '65, *11 R&B, 34 Pop*)
DON'T MESS WITH BILL (Tamla, '66, *3 R&B, 7 Pop*)
THE HUNTER GETS CAPTURED BY THE GAME (Tamla, '67, *2 R&B, 13 Pop*)
WHEN YOU'RE YOUNG AND IN LOVE (Tamla, '67, *9 R&B, 23 Pop*)
MY BABY MUST BE A MAGICIAN (Tamla, '67, *8 R&B, 17 Pop*)

Additional Top 40 R&B Songs: 8

Holland and Lamont Dozier) and splitting leads with the higher, smoother Young on "Locking Up My Heart" (the first-ever Holland, Dozier, and Eddie Holland writing credit) and "Too Many Fish in the Sea" (produced by Norman Whitfield). Cowart left the group in 1962, followed three years later by Tillman, who was married to Billy Gordon of the Contours. (Tillman died of lupus and sickle-cell anemia in 1980.)

Young, who'd married Bobby Rogers of the Miracles, made her debut as the Marvelettes' sole lead on "You're My Remedy," a minor 1964 hit penned and produced by Smokey Robinson. With the following year's Stevenson-produced "I'll Keep Holding On," she became the group's main soloist and was heard in the role on "Don't Mess with Bill," "The Hunter Gets Captured by the Game," "My Baby Must Be a Magician" (all written and produced by Robinson), and "When You're Young and in Love" (produced by James Dean and William Witherspoon and composed, originally for Ruby and the Romantics, by Van McCoy). "When You're Young and in Love" became the group's only British hit, peaking there at number 13 in 1967.

Horton, who'd married a trumpet player in Joe Tex's band, left the group that year to give birth to her first child and was replaced by Anne Bogan. The post-Horton Marvelettes had two minor hits in 1968—"Here I Am Baby" (by Robinson) and "Destination: Anywhere" (by Ashford and Simpson)—then disappeared from the charts. They stuck it out at Motown with fluctuating personnel (former Supreme Florence Ballard briefly substituted for a pregnant Young) through 1971 and then disbanded.

Various bogus editions of the Marvelettes worked the oldies circuit before Horton, who'd been living in Los Angeles, organized her own set with two other women in the mid-1980s. This trio traveled to Detroit in 1989 to record "Holding On with Both Hands" with British producer Ian Levine. Young contributed to the session, through she was not a member of the new group. She'd fallen apart emotionally years earlier, after witnessing her sister being shot to death, then having her brother left an invalid from another shooting, and finally losing custody of her two children to Rogers following a divorce. Her performance was tentative, but Levine managed to piece together her vocals on the tape line by line. Issued in England on the Motorcity label, it was the Marvelettes' first record in 18 years.

Curtis Mayfield

CURTIS MAYFIELD

As a performer and record producer, and especially as a songwriter and businessman, Curtis Mayfield (b. June 3, 1942) was ahead of his time. As the leader of the Impressions during the 1960s, he wrote and sang gospel-tinged tunes like "Keep on Pushing," "People Get Ready," "We're a Winner," and "Choice of Colors" that were more in sync with the civil rights movement than those of any other musical group of the era.

"My songs were not only personal to me but they were personal to a movement," he said in 1989. "They were inspiring to a mass of people, not only black people but all people. The country was ripe for something different, and the statements had morals to them."

Having taught himself to play guitar in an unusual open–F-sharp tuning, Mayfield grew up singing and picking at Chicago's Traveling Soul Spiritualist Church, a storefront congregation headed by his grandmother, the Reverend A. B. Mayfield. He performed gospel music with friend Jerry Butler in the Northern Jubilee Singers before they joined forces in 1957 with members of the Roosters, a doo wop group that had relocated to Chicago from Chattanooga. Changing their name to the Impressions, the quintet scored a number three R&B, number 11 pop smash the next year with "For Your Precious Love," written by Butler and group members Arthur

---

TOP ALBUMS

KEEP ON PUSHING (The Impressions, ABC-Paramount, '64, 8)
SUPERFLY (Curtom, '72, 1)

Additional Top 40 Albums: 7

TOP SONGS

The Impressions:
GYPSY WOMAN (ABC-Paramount, '61, 2 R&B, 20 Pop)
IT'S ALL RIGHT (ABC-Paramount, '63, 1 R&B, 4 Pop)
PEOPLE GET READY (ABC-Paramount, '65, 3 R&B, 14 Pop)
WE'RE A WINNER (ABC, '68, 1 R&B, 14 Pop)
FOOL FOR YOU (Curtom, '68, 3 R&B, 22 Pop)
CHOICE OF COLORS (Curtom, '69, 1 R&B, 21 Pop)

Curtis Mayfield:
(DON'T WORRY) IF THERE'S A HELL BELOW WE'RE ALL
    GOING TO GO (Curtom, '70, 3 R&B, 29 Pop)
FREDDIE'S DEAD (Curtom, '72, 2 R&B, 4 Pop)

Additional Top 40 R&B Songs: 39

---

and Richard Brooks. The ballad featured the deep-voiced Butler, who left the group within a year to sing solo, taking Mayfield with him as guitarist and songwriter. Mayfield also continued recording with the Impressions, but releases on Abner (including "At the Country Fair," the first to spotlight Mayfield's high, reedy voice), Swirl, and Bandera made little impression in the marketplace.

Mayfield had his first hit as a songwriter in 1960 with Butler's "He Will Break Your Heart," followed the next year by "Find Another Girl." Soon other Chicago soul singers turned to Mayfield's pen. "Rainbow" and "Just Be True" by Gene Chandler, "Mama Don't Lie" by Jan Bradley, and "The Monkey Time" and "Um, Um, Um, Um, Um, Um" by Major Lance also became hits.

The Impressions, comprising Mayfield, Fred Cash (an ex-Rooster who had replaced Butler), Sam Gooden, and the Brooks brothers, signed with ABC-Paramount in 1961, and their first release for the company, the flamenco-flavored Mayfield composition "Gypsy Woman," became a number two R&B, number 20 pop charter. The group, which became a trio upon the 1962 departure of the Brooks brothers, had 11 additional top 10 R&B hits through 1970, all featuring high, Mayfield-led harmonies and the brassy horn arrangements of Johnny Pate.

Mayfield realized early on the benefits of having financial control of his songs and, while still in his teens, formed the Curtom Publishing Company with then-manager Eddie Thomas. "The first time I ever ventured into Washington, D.C., was to find out where the Library of Congress copyright office was," Mayfield recalled. "My way of thinking…was to own as much of myself as possible, rather than just give it away."

He also dreamed of owning his own record company. A couple of early labels, Windy C and Mayfield, were short-lived, although they yielded a few moderate hits, including the Five Stairsteps' 1966 "World of Fantasy" on Windy C and the Fascinations' 1967 "Girls Are Out to Get You" on Mayfield. When the Impressions' contract with ABC expired in 1968, he formed Curtom Records and continued to produce the group and others for the label, even after launching his solo career in 1970.

The first three Mayfield solo albums—*Curtis, Curtis/Live!* and *Roots*—made the top 40. The fourth, his 1972 soundtrack for the motion picture *Superfly*, went all the way to Number One and spawned the hit singles "Freddie's Dead" and "Superfly." Its massive success led to other Mayfield film scores: 1974's *Claudine* (featuring Gladys Knight and the Pips), 1975's *Let's Do It Again* (the Staple Singers), 1976's *Sparkle* (Aretha Franklin), and 1977's *Short Eyes* (in which Mayfield made his acting debut). The number eight R&B "Only You Babe," a 1976 Curtom single, was Mayfield's final top 10 entry. Later releases on RSO, Boardwalk, CRC, and a revived Curtom label had minimal impact. He moved his recording studio from Chicago to Atlanta in 1980 and three years later reunited with Butler and the Impressions for a national tour.

On August 13, 1990, while Mayfield was performing at an outdoor concert in Brooklyn, a sudden burst of wind sent a 500-pound lighting bank crashing down on him. He was left paralyzed from the neck down. In 1994, he was honored by the release of *All Men Are Brothers: A Tribute to Curtis Mayfield,* a Warner Bros. collection of his songs as rendered by such artists as Gladys Knight, Whitney Houston, Bruce Springsteen, Eric Clapton, the Isley Brothers, Aretha Franklin, B.B. King, and Stevie Wonder, as well as by a similar all-star salute at the Grammy Awards.

PERCY MAYFIELD

"I fell in love with sadness because there's more truth in it," blues singer Percy Mayfield (b. Aug. 12, 1920, Minden, Louisiana) once stated. Indeed, a deep, often doomed melancholy ran through many of Mayfield's best-known compositions, including "Two Years of Torture," "Life Is Suicide," "Lost Love" (also known as "Baby Please"), "River's Invitation," and "Memory Pain."

"Every man that has really lived has had pain," he explained. "If you've loved and lost, that's pain. If you bust your finger, that's pain, but that heals. The other pain grows and develops, and it ages you and sharpens your mind. So I ventured over into the world of sadness."

There was, however, a message of hope in Mayfield's biggest hit, the 1950 blues ballad "Please Send Me Someone to Love," which he sang in his trademark dry, drawling baritone. "I wrote that as a prayer for peace between the black man and the white man—that hate that goes on in the world," he said. The song, perhaps the first of the rhythm and blues era to address racism, became a standard that was recorded by numerous others, among them Dale Evans, the Moonglows, B.B. King, Nancy Wilson, Lou Rawls, Brook Benton, Esther Phillips, and Linda Hopkins. Mayfield, however, felt that most singers incorrectly interpreted it as a romantic ballad. "You don't find me mentioning a woman nowhere in there," he pointed out.

Mayfield was raised 30 miles east of Shreveport, Louisiana. "We had a big farm," he recalled. "We didn't have to go to the store to get anything but matches, because we raised everything." As a boy, he wrote poems and set them to music but, because his mother didn't approve of the blues, sang only in church. Leaving home at age 15, he hoboed around

the country on freight trains before settling in Los Angeles in 1942. He pressed pants for a local dry cleaner and worked as a cook and as a Pullman porter at various times, but he earned most of his income from hustling pool.

In 1949, hoping to break into the music business as a songwriter, Mayfield took one of his compositions, "Two Years of Torture," to the Los Angeles–based Supreme Records in the hope that Jimmy Witherspoon would record it. Impressed with the writer's distinctive vocal style, somewhat influenced by that of Al Hibbler, the company insisted he cut it himself. A year later, he signed with Hollywood's larger Specialty label and hit Number One on the *Billboard* R&B chart with "Please Send Me Someone to Love," his first release for the company. Six additional top 10 R&B hits followed through 1952, when a near-fatal auto accident near Las Vegas left him in a coma for three weeks and with a deep, permanent cleft in the forehead of his once-handsome

Percy Mayfield

face. "Ain't nobody in show business looks like me but me," he would often quip.

Leaving Specialty in 1954, Mayfield had little luck with subsequent singles on Chess, Cash, 7 Arts, and Imperial. His greatest success came as a staff writer for Ray Charles in the early 1960s. In 1961 and '62, Charles turned four Mayfield tunes into top 10 hits: the Number One R&B and pop "Hit the Road, Jack," the number 10 R&B "But on the Other Hand Baby," the number seven R&B "Hide Nor Hair," and the number seven R&B "At the Club." Also while under contract to Charles, Mayfield recorded two albums of his own for the star's Tangerine label on which he was accompanied by Charles and his orchestra. The first, *My Jug and I,* included an inspired Charles arrangement of "River's Invitation," a song about suicide that Mayfield had done earlier for Specialty. Placing at number 25 on the R&B chart in 1963, it was the singer's first top 40 chart entry in 11 years. It also proved to be his last.

He continued recording sporadically, doing one album for Brunswick, three for RCA Victor, a single for Atlantic (the brilliant 1974 Johnny "Guitar" Watson–produced "I Don't Want to Be President"), and one album apiece for Timeless and Winner, and he also made a guest appearance on a live 1970 album by Bobby Womack. A 30-minute video titled *Percy Mayfield: Poet Laureate of the Blues,* featuring the songwriter performing and talking with pianist Mark Naftalin, as well as on-camera comments by Ray Charles and B.B. King, premiered in 1983. He died of a heart attack the following year, on August 11, a day shy of his 64th birthday.

TOP ALBUM

MY JUG AND I (Tangerine, '63)

TOP SONGS

PLEASE SEND ME SOMEONE TO LOVE (Specialty, '50, 1 *R&B*, 26 *Pop*)
STRANGE THINGS HAPPENING (Specialty, '51, 7 *R&B*)
LOST LOVE (Specialty, '51, 2 *R&B*)
WHAT A FOOL I AM (Specialty, '51, 8 *R&B*)
PRAYIN' FOR YOUR RETURN (Specialty, '51, 9 *R&B*)
CRY BABY (Specialty, '52, 9 *R&B*)
BIG QUESTION (Specialty, '52, 6 *R&B*)
RIVER'S INVITATION (Tangerine, '63, 25 *R&B*)

MAZE FEATURING FRANKIE BEVERLY

Much like the prospectors of 1849, singer, songwriter, and rhythm guitarist Frankie Beverly and his Philadelphia-based band, originally known as Raw Soul, came to California in 1972 in search of gold. It took them several years of struggle on the San Francisco Bay Area club circuit and a name change to Maze, but they eventually struck gold six times, with the Capitol albums *Maze featuring Frankie Beverly* (1977), *Golden Time of the Day* (1978), *Inspiration* (1979), *Joy and Pain* (1981), *Live in New Orleans* (1981), and *Can't Stop the Love* (1985), all without the aid of any significant pop crossover singles. Curiously, the group's highest charting album, 1983's number 25 *We Are One,* fell short of the 500,000 sales needed to attain gold certification.

Beverly began his career in Philadelphia with a group called the Blenders and then became lead singer of the Butlers, a Temptations-style stand-up vocal group. Beginning in 1963, the Butlers recorded a series of singles for such local labels as Guyden, Liberty Bell, Fairmount, and Gamble. In 1968, inspired by Sly and the Family Stone, the first major soul group to break the traditional mold of vocalists with a backup band, some of the Butlers learned to play their own instruments and changed their name to Raw Soul. Three Raw Soul singles appeared on the RCA-distributed Gregar label, but only Beverly's voice was featured, because the producers insisted on using studio musicians instead of the band itself.

Frustrated, Raw Soul purchased a broken-down 1946 bus and drove to San Francisco, " 'cause that's where Sly and Santana and those self-contained bands were coming from," Beverly explained. Work was scarce in the Bay Area. Within a year, half the band had gone back to Philadelphia. Beverly, keyboardist Sam Porter, and singing percussionists Ronald "Roame" Lowry and McKinley "Bug" Williams stayed, forming a core that remained constant through 1986, when Porter departed. Early California recruits were guitarist Wayne Thomas, bassist Robin Duhe, and drummer Joe Provost. Later members included keyboardists Phillip Woo, Wayne "Ziggy" Lindsey, James "Kimo" Cornwell, and William Bryant; guitarists Ron Smith and Vernon "Ice" Black; and drummers Ahaguna G. Sun, Billy

"Shoes" Johnson, and Michael White. By 1993, Maze consisted of Beverly, Lowry, Williams, Duhe, Woo, Bryant, Smith, and Johnson.

Consistency has been a hallmark of Maze. Ever since the group signed with Capitol in 1976, at the recommendation of Marvin Gaye, Beverly has had complete artistic control of the band's music, writing, arranging, and producing all the material himself. He has refused to bow to pressure to use horns, strings, drum machines, or—except on a few occasions—players and singers from outside the group.

Drawing on vocal techniques from Gaye and Sam Cooke, Beverly is an extremely relaxed, rhythmically inventive singer. His songs, most of which treat male-female relationships with mature sensitivity, tend to be long, thus allowing him plenty of room to stretch out and improvise around and against Lowry's and Williams's smooth harmonies and the rhythm section's laid-back yet funky grooves. A subtle master of tension-release, he'd sing a syncopated phrase of quarter-note triplets (three beats against two) or chant a hypnotic string of percussive "ah" after-beats (a device derived from reggae) and then break into a clear sustained note or a stream of gospel melismas, all rendered pitch-perfect in round, glowing tenor tones.

In 1986, a year after scoring its first R&B chart-topping single with "Back in Stride," Maze left Capitol and disbanded, regrouping in 1989 to join the

---

TOP ALBUM

WE ARE ONE (Capitol, '83, 25)

Additional Top 40 Albums: 6

TOP SONGS

WORKIN' TOGETHER (Capitol, '78, 9 *R&B*)
FEEL THAT YOU'RE FEELIN' (Capitol, '79, 7 *R&B*)
SOUTHERN GIRL (Capitol, '80, 9 *R&B*)
RUNNING AWAY (Capitol, '81, 7 *R&B*)
LOVE IS THE KEY (Capitol, '83, 5 *R&B*)
BACK IN STRIDE (Capitol, '85, 1 *R&B*)
TOO MANY GAMES (Capitol, '85, 5 *R&B*)
CAN'T GET OVER YOU (Warner Bros., '89, 1 *R&B*)
SILKY SOUL (Warner Bros., '89, 4 *R&B*)

Additional Top 40 R&B Songs: 16

Warner Bros. roster. *Silky Soul,* the first album for the label, spawned the Number One R&B single "Can't Get Over You." Capitol then issued *Lifelines Volume 1,* a greatest hits collection that included several tracks doctored with new mixes and rap overdubs. Beverly was livid. "Our old fans want to hear those songs the way we made them," he complained to Larry Kelp of the *Oakland Tribune.* "They're going to think that's our idea, and it's

Maze

wrong." And to add insult to injury, rapper Rob Base transformed the 1980 Maze song "Joy and Pain" into a number 11 R&B hit, even sampling the original rhythm track, without giving credit.

Beverly, a laid-back kinda guy, took it in stride and continued making a brand of sweet, sophisticated soul music that critic Nelson George has dubbed "retronuevo." A second Warner Bros. album, 1993's *Back to Basics*, was, like the previous ones, unbending to fad. And if, like the others, it generated minimal crossover interest, it was warmly received by an adoring, decidedly adult African-American audience that had been Beverly and company's main constituency since the first Capitol album 16 years earlier.

VAN McCOY

Sweetness rippled through the symphonic soul of songwriter, producer, arranger, pianist, and occasional vocalist Van McCoy (b. Jan. 6, 1940, Washington, D.C.), with the frequent use of orchestra bells heightening the music's ethereal lilt. In 1975, the year of McCoy's greatest commercial success, British critic Tony Cummings commented, "With apparently obsessional care, McCoy created a billowing multi-layered cocoon of strings, harp and woodwind into which his delicate voiced singers could effortlessly slide, while often he'd evolve complex brass and violin figures which swirled in and out of sustained chords or haunting counter-melodies."

While he was best known to the general public for a basically instrumental 1975 disco smash with his 30-piece Soul City Symphony, the Number One R&B and pop "The Hustle," it was as a key behind-the-scenes figure throughout the 1960s and '70s that McCoy made his major contributions. Among his outstanding credits as a composer and/or producer were songs performed by Gladys Knight and the Pips ("Giving Up"); Barbara Lewis ("Baby, I'm Yours"); Peaches and Herb ("Close Your Eyes"); the Marvelettes ("When You're Young and in Love"); Jackie Wilson ("I Got the Sweetest Feeling"); Chris Bartley ("The Sweetest Thing This Side of Heaven"); the Presidents ("5-10-15-20-25-30 Years of Love"); Brenda and the Tabulations ("Right on the Tip of My Tongue"); Faith, Hope and Charity ("To Each His Own"); David Ruffin ("Walk Away from Love"); Melba Moore ("This Is It"); and Aretha Franklin ("Sweet Bitter Love").

McCoy, who studied psychology at Howard University for two years, began his recording career at End Records in 1958 as a vocalist with the Starlighters, a doo wop group that also included his brother Norman. Two years later, McCoy emerged as a solo singer with "Mr. D.J." on his own Philadelphia-based Rock'n label. The ballad, on which a chiming celesta presaged his later use of orchestra bells, was a hit on the East Coast and attracted the attention of Scepter Records, which picked it up for national distribution. The New York company then brought him to New York to serve as an assistant to producer Luther Dixon on sessions by the Shirelles, Chuck Jackson, and Maxine Brown. McCoy continued apprenticing during the 1960s, developing his skills as a producer and arranger under such masters as Jerry Leiber and Mike Stoller, Bert Berns, Teacho Wilshire, and Gary Sherman.

After a mid-1960s attempt by Columbia Records producer Mitch Miller to groom him as a middle-of-the-road Johnny Mathis–type pop crooner failed, McCoy put singing on hold to focus on writing and producing for others. He placed songs with such artists as Chad and Jeremy, Bobby Vee, Bobby Vinton, and Nancy Wilson and scored his first chart entry as a writer-producer in 1964 with Gladys Knight and the Pips' number 38 pop "Giving Up" on the Maxx label. A year later, he made the top 10 for the first time as the composer of (and background singer on) Barbara Lewis's number five R&B "Baby, I'm Yours" on Atlantic.

McCoy continued having hits as a producer for a variety of companies, including his own short-lived Vando and Share labels, finally reemerging as a vocalist with the commercially unsuccessful 1971 Buddah album *Soul Improvisations*. Working as an arranger for producers Hugo Peretti and Luigi Creatore at their Avco label on a series of Stylistics hits,

---

TOP ALBUM

Disco Baby (Avco, '75, 12)

TOP SONGS

The Hustle (Avco, '75, 1 R&B, 1 Pop)
Change with the Times (Avco, '75, 6 R&B)
Party (H&L, '76, 20 R&B)

including "Heavy Fallin' Down," led to *Disco Baby,* the first in a string of dance-oriented instrumental McCoy albums for the company. It yielded the international hit "The Hustle," inspired by a dance craze of the same name. McCoy was on a roll, hitting the top of the R&B chart twice again over the next six months—as the writer and producer of Faith, Hope and Charity's "To Each His Own" on RCA and as the producer of David Ruffin's "Walk Away from Love" on Motown.

In 1978, McCoy expanded his horizons to film. He composed the music for the NBC-TV movie *A Woman Called Moses* starring Cicely Tyson and scored and acted in the offbeat Mae West comedy *Sextette.* He also recorded a vocal album for MCA titled *My Favorite Fantasy,* its title track becoming a minor R&B hit. It was his last. A workaholic, McCoy died of a heart attack on July 6, 1979.

CLYDE McPHATTER

Clyde Lensley McPhatter (b. Nov. 15, 1933, Durham, North Carolina) was, along with blues shouter Roy Brown, one of the first singers to infuse rhythm and blues with an intense gospel-derived fervor, thus laying the groundwork for soul music. His dramatic tenor style, filled with effortlessly soaring glides, fluttering sobs, cascading melismas, and great rhythmic invention, had a pronounced influence on such others as Jackie Wilson (his 1953 replacement in Billy Ward's Dominoes), Dee Clark, Donnie Elbert, Smokey Robinson, and Ben E. King. "It all came together in Clyde," stated King, who first made his mark in the Drifters, the group McPhatter had founded after leaving the Dominoes.

Yet for McPhatter, the product of a stern Baptist upbringing, the act of applying gospel phrasing to secular songs played heavily on his mind. "Religion was nothing but another word for discipline—you know, 'God don't like this,' 'God don't like that'— so one day I said, 'God damn it,' and my father beat the hell out of me," the singer said on January 28, 1972, less than five months before his death. "It was really based on fear—hocus-pocus. If you sang the blues, it was 'devil's music.' You weren't supposed to sing with sincerity unless it was to God. My older brother said to my father, 'Bishop'—we always referred to my father as the Bishop—'if God is a just

God, I can't really see how you can hold it against him if he wants to sing this type of music.' "

The fourth of the seven children of George and Eva McPhatter, Clyde grew up singing in a church where his father was pastor and his mother the choir mistress. The family moved from North Carolina to Teaneck, New Jersey, when Clyde was 12, and two years later he formed the Mount Lebanon Singers, a gospel quartet that included David and Wilbur Baldwin, brothers of author James Baldwin.

McPhatter made his secular singing debut at the Apollo Theater's legendary amateur night, winning second prize with a rendition of the Lonnie Johnson hit "Tomorrow Night." He competed again in mid-1950, as a member of pianist-arranger Billy Ward's new group, the Dominoes, this time taking first prize. In October of that year, the Dominoes appeared on Arthur Godfrey's "Talent Scouts" radio show and won, which led to a contract with Federal Records.

The Dominoes' first disc, the McPhatter-led "Do Something for Me," became a number six R&B hit in early 1951. McPhatter remained with the group through June 1953 and was featured on the top 10 R&B hits "I Am with You," "That's What You're Doing for Me," "Have Mercy Baby," "I'd Be Satisfied," "The Bells," and "These Foolish Things Remind Me of You." He then organized the Drifters and signed with Atlantic. Receiving star billing with the group, he waxed the top 10 R&B hits "Money Honey," "Such a Night," "Lucille," "Honey Love," "Bip Bam," "White Christmas," and "What'Cha Gonna Do" through early 1955.

TOP SONGS

LOVE HAS JOINED US TOGETHER (Ruth Brown and Clyde McPhatter, Atlantic, '55, 8 R&B)
SEVEN DAYS (Atlantic, '56, 2 R&B)
TREASURE OF LOVE (Atlantic, '56, 1 R&B, 16 Pop)
WITHOUT LOVE (THERE IS NOTHING) (Atlantic, '57, 4 R&B, 19 Pop)
JUST TO HOLD MY HAND (Atlantic, '57, 6 R&B, 26 Pop)
LONG LONELY NIGHTS (Atlantic, '57, 1 R&B)
COME WHAT MAY (Atlantic, '58, 3 R&B)
A LOVER'S QUESTION (Atlantic, '58, 1 R&B, 6 Pop)
TA TA (Mercury, '60, 7 R&B, 23 Pop)

Additional Top 40 R&B Songs: 5

McPhatter was already contemplating a solo career when drafted into the Army in 1954. Placed with the Special Services and stationed not far from New York City, he was able to continue recording for Atlantic during his two-year stint. After scoring a number eight R&B duet hit with Ruth Brown titled "Love Has Joined Us Together," he had his first solo hit, 1956's number two R&B "Seven Days." It was followed by the Number One R&B "Treasure of Love," and he hit the top of the *Billboard* R&B chart again in 1958 with "A Lover's Question."

If McPhatter's Atlantic sides were more pop-oriented than those he'd made with the Dominoes and the Drifters, he headed straight down the middle of the road after joining MGM Records in 1959. His one-year association with the label resulted in only one hit, 1960's number 13 R&B "Let's Try Again," after which he was signed to Mercury by producer Clyde Otis. The singer hit number seven R&B with his first Mercury single, 1960's "Ta Ta," but it proved to be his final top 10 R&B entry. He scored again a year and a half later with the number seven pop "Lover Please," but it didn't register on the R&B chart.

By the time McPhatter left Mercury in 1965, alcoholism had begun to take its toll. He had no luck at Amy Records in 1966 and '67 and in 1968 moved to England, where singles on the Deram and B&C labels fell on deaf ears. Returning to the U.S. in 1970, he was reunited the following year with Clyde Otis for the little-noticed Decca album *Welcome Home.* A broken and bitter man, McPhatter died of a heart attack on June 13, 1972. He was 38.

AMOS MILBURN

Named top R&B artist in both 1949 and 1950 by *Billboard* magazine, singer-pianist Amos Milburn (b. Apr. 1, 1927, Houston, Texas) fused three of the main strains of African-American popular music—the jump blues of Louis Jordan, the smooth "cocktail" blues of Charles Brown, and the boogie woogie of Albert Ammons and Pete Johnson—into a delightfully infectious approach of his own. The sound of Milburn and his six-piece combo, the Aladdin Chickenscratchers, influenced such artists as Fats Domino and Floyd Dixon and helped pave the way for rock and roll, although Milburn himself was unable to adjust to the new style.

"I really didn't dig that rock music," Milburn explained to Norbert Hess of *Living Blues* magazine. "It was too extravagant, a whole lot of electronics instead of actual playing."

One of 12 children of a poor Texas family, Milburn started playing at age five. His parents had rented a piano for his oldest sister's wedding. The next morning he sat down at it and plucked out "Jingle Bells." Impressed by this early display of talent, his folks decided to keep the instrument and find a piano teacher. Dropping out of school after the seventh grade, Milburn played at after-hours house parties around Houston before joining the navy at age 15. He spent three years in the service during World War II, entertaining officers in the Pacific much of the time. He formed a band upon his return to Houston.

While appearing at trumpeter Don Albert's club in San Antonio, Milburn came to the attention of Lula Ann Cullum, a doctor's wife and a music lover. She became his manager, cut a crude demo at her home and, in 1947, traveled with him to Los Angeles. After turning down an offer from Modern Records, they tried Aladdin. Legend has it that the company's president, Eddie Mesner, was in the hospital at the time, so Cullum took the demo and a tiny record player to his bedside. Milburn became an Aladdin recording artist and remained with the label for nine years.

Milburn's first release, 1947's "After Midnite," on which he was accompanied only by piano and drums, sold respectably. Things opened up for him considerably, however, late the next year, when he had a smash with "Chicken Shack Boogie." The rollicking number, aided by a hard-riffing band under the leadership of saxophonist-arranger Maxwell Davis, topped the *Billboard* R&B chart for five weeks. Both "After Midnite" and "Chicken Shack" were penned by Milburn (with co-credit to Cullum), but subsequent hits were written by others. "With that," *Variety* pointed out in its 1980 obituary of the musician, "Milburn represented a step away from the traditional singer-songwriter bluesman of the day and a move closer to the commercial interpreter role of contemporary R&B."

His next release, "Bewildered," a melancholy blues ballad performed in the style of Charles Brown, also went to Number One R&B. Milburn hit the chart peak twice again, in 1949 with "Roomin' House Boogie" and in 1950 with "Bad, Bad Whiskey." The latter kicked off a series of successful drinking songs by Milburn, including "Thinking and Drinking," "Let Me Go Home Whiskey," "One Scotch, One Bourbon, One Beer," and his last chart entry, 1954's number five R&B "Good Good Whiskey." Attempts by Aladdin to adapt the artist's style to rock and roll were not well received, and the company dropped him in 1956.

Milburn disbanded the Chickenscratchers in 1954 and began working as a single, soon forming a close professional and personal alliance with Charles Brown, whose career was also on the wane. In 1958, they recorded as a duo in New Orleans for Ace Records and enjoyed some regional interest with the ballad "I Want to Go Home," a Brown-Milburn composition that served as a prototype for the later Sam Cooke hit "Bring It on Home to Me." They then headed for King Records in Cincinnati and individually cut two perennial favorites—"Please Come Home for Christmas" by Brown and "Christmas (Comes But Once a Year)" by Milburn—both in 1960.

In 1963, Milburn turned up at, of all places, Motown Records, where he recorded the album *The Return of Amos Milburn: The Blues Boss,* which received scant notice. A decade later, he did another for Johnny Otis's Blues Spectrum label. Milburn played only the right-hand piano parts, Otis the left, as Milburn's left side had been paralyzed by strokes suffered in 1969 and '70. He spent his final years in a wheelchair, living alone in Houston, and died on January 3, 1980, not long after the amputation of his left leg.

Stephanie Mills

TOP SONGS

CHICKEN SHACK BOOGIE (Aladdin, '48, *1 R&B*)

BEWILDERED (Aladdin, '48, *1 R&B*)

HOLD ME, BABY (Aladdin, '49, *2 R&B*)

IN THE MIDDLE OF THE NIGHT (Aladdin, '49, *3 R&B*)

ROOMIN' HOUSE BOOGIE (Aladdin, '49, *1 R&B*)

LET'S MAKE CHRISTMAS MERRY, BABY (Aladdin, '49, *3 R&B*)

BAD, BAD WHISKEY (Aladdin, '50, *1 R&B*)

LET'S ROCK A WHILE (Aladdin, '51, *3 R&B*)

LET ME GO HOME WHISKEY (Aladdin, '53, *3 R&B*)

ONE SCOTCH, ONE BOURBON, ONE BEER (Aladdin, '53, *2 R&B*)

Additional Top 40 R&B Songs: 9

STEPHANIE MILLS

It's sometimes said that you can't go home again. For Stephanie Mills (b. Mar. 22, 1957, New York), "Home" was a sentimental ballad written by Charlie Smalls for *The Wiz,* an all-black musical theater adaptation of *The Wizard of Oz,* that thrust her into the limelight at age 14. But after five years of singing it on Broadway, Mills had grown tired of the song and dropped it from her concert repertoire. Audiences, however, kept demanding "Home." In

1989, the pint-sized (4'11") singer rerecorded it as a tribute to Smalls and Wiz producer Ken Harper, both of whom had recently died. It became her fifth Number One R&B hit.

Mills made her public singing debut at age three at Cornerstone Baptist Church in her native Brooklyn and her Broadway stage debut at nine in the cast of *Maggie Flynn*, starring Shirley Jones and Jack Cassidy. Two years later, she won six Apollo amateur shows in a row with her melisma-dripping renditions of Smokey Robinson's "Who's Lovin' You" and the Stevie Wonder hit "For Once in My Life," leading to a paid engagement at the Harlem theater as an opener for the Isley Brothers. She later joined the Negro Ensemble Company Workshop, where she appeared with Ben Vereen in a production of *A Piece of the Action*.

Her first record, 1974's "Movin' in the Right Direction" for the Paramount label, attracted little notice, except from Ken Harper, who sought out Mills and cast her in the leading role of Dorothy in *The Wiz*. After a trial run in Baltimore, the show hit Broadway in January 1975 and garnered eight Tony Awards. The young star won none for herself, however, and was further insulted when Diana Ross was handed the role for the 1978 motion picture version.

Invited to join the Motown roster by Jermaine Jackson and his wife Hazel, Mills cut an album for the company in 1975. Titled *For the First Time*, and produced by Burt Bacharach and Hal David, the disc flopped. It was "too sophisticated," the singer admitted later. A second Motown album, produced in part by Earth, Wind and Fire's Philip Bailey, was kept in the can.

Mills's recording career took off after she signed with 20th Century Fox Records in 1979. Working with the production team of James Mtume and Reggie Lucas, she scored several disco-styled hits over the next two years, including "What Cha Gonna Do with My Lovin'," "Sweet Sensation," and "Never Knew Love Like This Before." The latter tune, taken from the Sweet Sensation album, rose to number six on the *Billboard* pop chart and to number four in England, but only as high as number 12 on the domestic R&B list. It proved to be her only top 10 pop charter.

After a marriage to Shalimar's Jeffrey Daniel in 1980 that ended in divorce 14 months later, Mills reemerged with a svelte figure, streamlined nose, and sexy persona. Having finally shed the little-girl trappings associated with Dorothy, the vocalist acted out her new image with love-man Teddy Pendergrass on the hit 1981 duet "Two Hearts" and a tour that followed. She switched to Casablanca Records in 1982 and had several hits, including a 1983 rendition of the sizzling, gospel-imbued Prince ballad "How Come U Don't Call Me Anymore?" (number 12 R&B) and the following year's uptempo, quite erotic "The Medicine Song" (number eight R&B).

"Home" kept calling, however, and in 1984 Mills starred in a revival of *The Wiz*. She signed with MCA the next year. The new association, under which she and her sister-in-law manager Cassandra Mills served as executive producers, proved highly fruitful. Each of the first three albums spawned Number One R&B singles: the Ron Kersey–produced "I Have Learned to Respect the Power of Love" from 1985's *Stephanie Mills*, the Nick Martinelli–produced "I Feel Good All Over" and the Paul Laurence–produced "(You're Puttin') A Rush on Me" from 1987's *If I Were Your Woman*, and the Angela Winbush–produced "Something in the Way (You Make Me Feel)" and the Martinelli-produced title track (with distinctive background vocals by Take 6) from 1989's *Home*. All, with the exception of "(You're Puttin') A Rush on Me," were ballads that showcased Mills's roof-raising gospel-

---

TOP ALBUM

SWEET SENSATION (20th Century Fox, '80, *16*)

Additional Top 40 Albums: 3

TOP SONGS

WHAT CHA GONNA DO WITH MY LOVIN' (20th Century Fox, '79, *8 R&B, 22 Pop*)

SWEET SENSATION (20th Century Fox, '80, *3 R&B*)

TWO HEARTS (Stephanie Mills featuring Teddy Pendergrass, 20th Century Fox, '81, *3 R&B, 40 Pop*)

I HAVE LEARNED TO RESPECT THE POWER OF LOVE (MCA, '86, *1 R&B*)

I FEEL GOOD ALL OVER (MCA, '87, *1 R&B*)

(YOU'RE PUTTIN') A RUSH ON ME (MCA, '87, *1 R&B*)

SECRET LADY (MCA, '87, *7 R&B*)

SOMETHING IN THE WAY (YOU MAKE ME FEEL) (MCA, '89, *1 R&B*)

HOME (MCA, '89, *1 R&B*)

Additional Top 40 R&B Songs: 14

Roy Milton and His Solid Senders

flavored delivery. Her later MCA albums—1991's *Christmas* and the following year's *Something Real* —were less successful.

ROY MILTON

A rt Rupe, owner of the Hollywood-based Specialty record label, once described singing drummer Roy Milton (b. July 31, 1907, Wynnewood, Oklahoma) as the "West Coast counterpart" of Louis Jordan. While Jordan and His Tympany Five reigned as the "race" music kings of the 1940s, Milton and His Solid Senders began giving them some serious competition in 1946 when "R. M. Blues" entered the *Billboard* chart, where it

remained for 25 weeks and peaked at number two. And if the Jordan sextet's compacted big-band jazz style, infused with a heavy dose of boogie woogie, provided the primary blueprint for what would become known as rhythm and blues, Milton's sextet placed even more emphasis on the evolving genre's boogie, blues, and riffing-horn content.

Raised outside of Tulsa, Milton sang in church as a child and played in his high school's marching band. After attending college in Austin on a football scholarship, he made his professional debut in 1931 as vocalist with Ernie Fields's orchestra. During one tour, when the band's drummer was in jail, Milton was asked to fill in and thereafter sang and played simultaneously. He left Fields in 1933 and settled in southern California two years later.

The Solid Senders, formed in 1938, were one of

TOP SONGS

R. M. Blues (Juke Box, '46, *2 R&B, 20 Pop*)

Milton's Boogie (Juke Box, '46, *4 R&B*)

True Blues (Specialty, '47, *4 R&B*)

Thrill Me (Specialty, '47, *5 R&B*)

Everything I Do Is Wrong (Specialty, '48, *5 R&B*)

Hop, Skip and Jump (Specialty, '48, *3 R&B*)

Hucklebuck (Specialty, '49, *5 R&B*)

Information Blues (Specialty, '50, *2 R&B*)

Oh Babe (Specialty, '50, *5 R&B*)

Best Wishes (Specialty, '51, *2 R&B*)

Additional Top 40 R&B Songs: 11

the most popular combos in the Los Angeles area during World War II. They entertained white Hollywood audiences with pop tunes during early evenings and then traveled to black after-hours clubs in south central L.A., where their repertoire changed to blues and boogies. With Milton singing in a rhythmically assured tenor over a band that sported the two-fisted yet elegant piano of Camille Howard and a three-man horn section, the sextet made its first recording, "I'll Always Be in Love with You," in September 1945 for Lionel and Gladys Hampton's Hamp-Tone label. It wasn't issued until the following year, however, by which time the Milton composition "R. M. Blues," cut in December 1945 for Rupe's Juke Box label, had become a smash. (Buddy Floyd's buzz-toned, legato tenor saxophone solo on "R. M. Blues" would serve as a model for such tenor men as Don Wilkerson with Little Willie Littlefield's group, Herb Hardesty and Lee Allen with Fats Domino, and Dr. Wild Willie Moore with Jimmy McCracklin.)

When Milton's next Juke Box release, 1946's "Milton's Boogie" (an adaptation of Count Basie's "I May Be Wrong"), hit the charts, he had already left the label to form his own Roy Milton Record Company, for which he rerecorded the two hits. He remained active in the record business through 1949 with several other labels, including Miltone, which issued over 50 78s by such R&B, jazz, and gospel artists as Little Miss Cornshucks, Dorothy Donegan, and J. Earle Hines. Although none of the Roy Milton or Milton label sides made the charts, they are nonetheless remembered today for their unique label artwork by African-American cartoonist William Alexander.

Rupe parted company with his partners in Juke Box later in 1946. He then established Specialty Records and signed Milton to an exclusive contract in 1947. Milton's Specialty recordings made regular appearances in the R&B top 10 through 1953. Among them were such original Milton numbers as "True Blues," "Everything I Do Is Wrong," "Hop, Skip and Jump," "Information Blues," and "Early in the Morning" as well as covers of Paul Williams's "Hucklebuck" and Louis Prima's "Oh Babe." Camille Howard was featured as the vocalist on her own composition, 1947's "Thrill Me," and went on to cut a series of instrumental and vocal numbers under her own name (with Milton on drums) for Specialty, the most successful being the 1948 double-sided hit "X-Temporaneous Boogie"/"You Don't Love Me."

After leaving Specialty in 1953, Milton had little luck with releases on Dootone and King. A contract with Warwick Records in 1960 brought renewed, though temporary, interest in his music. A brilliant rearrangement of "Early in the Morning," featuring Howard's rippling piano and Papa John Creach's bluesy violin, enjoyed regional success, while the next year's "Red Light" made it to number 27 on the national R&B chart. This prompted Specialty to issue the 1953 Milton recording "Baby You Don't Know," which went to number 23 R&B later in 1961, but it proved to be the final chapter in his 15-year chart history.

Milton continued recording sporadically, for such labels as Cenco, Lou Wa, Movin', Kent, and Blues Spectrum, and took part in Johnny Otis's all-star revue at the 1970 Monterey Jazz Festival that was captured for disc by Epic Records. The jump-blues drummer died of a stroke on September 18, 1983.

THE MOMENTS

The early hits of New Jersey's Moments, including the 1970 R&B chart-topper "Love on a Two-Way Street," sounded as if they'd been recorded inside a garbage can. The drums had so much treble and echo that they reminded British critic Tony Cummings of "a stick hitting a biscuit tin full of dry peas." And, he added, the strings "seemed to originate from warped tapes, eerily sighing in wobbly waves of sound."

"Nobody knew how to work the boards," group

member Al Goodman admitted to Cummings. "The production was a shambles, yet it seemed to work."

Work it did, especially on the young women who comprised the Moments' core audience. The cheesy sound quality served to heighten the teen appeal of the high-harmony trio's songs, nearly all of them romantic ballads featuring quavering falsetto leads. But improved fidelity by the mid-1970s didn't stop the hits from coming. Between 1968 and 1979, the Moments scored 25 top 40 R&B hits on Joe and Sylvia Robinson's Englewood, New Jersey–based Stang label. ("Girls," a 1975 meeting of the Moments and the Whatnauts, reached only as high as number 25 R&B in the U.S. but rose to number three pop in the U.K., while two other Moments singles that didn't even chart domestically—1975's "Dolly My Love" and 1977's "Jack in the Box"— also became top 10 hits in England.) After leaving Stang and changing its name to Ray, Goodman and Brown in 1979, the group had seven more top 40 R&B chart entries over the next eight years.

The original Moments were Mark Greene, Richie Horsley, and John Morgan. Green sang lead falsetto on the group's first recording, 1968's number 13 R&B "Not on the Outside," written and produced by Sylvia Robinson. (Formerly half of Mickey and Sylvia, which had a Number One R&B, number 11 pop smash with 1956's "Love Is Strange," she later ushered in the hip-hop era as the producer in 1979 of the first rap hit, the Sugarhill Gang's number four R&B, number 36 pop "Rapper's Delight.")

The Moments' second hit, 1969's number 13 R&B "Sunday," featured a different lineup: Green and Horsley were gone, replaced by new lead Billy Brown (b. June 30, 1946, Perth Amboy, New Jersey) and baritone-basso Al Goodman (b. Mar. 31, 1947, Jackson, Mississippi). Other hits by this edition followed, culminating in the forlorn "Love on a Two-Way Street," produced by Sylvia and written by her and arranger Bert Keyes. Not long after the song finished its five-week run atop the R&B chart, Morgan too was gone, hastily replaced by Harry Ray (b. Dec. 15, 1946, Hackensack, New Jersey) three days before the Moments left on their first cross-country tour.

"Love on a Two-Way Street" also reached number three on the *Billboard* pop chart, but it was the only Moments song to crack the pop top 10. The

The Moments

trio, featuring the alternating leads of Brown and Ray, maintained a steady presence on the R&B charts, however, with 1973's number three "Sexy Mama" (written and produced by Ray, Goodman, and Sylvia) and 1975's "Look at Me (I'm in Love)" (written and produced by Ray, Goodman, and the group's guitarist, Walter Lee Morris) being the strongest sellers.

The Moments left Stang in 1977, but the company held onto their name. After a two-and-a-half-year hiatus from recording, they reemerged on Polydor as Ray, Goodman and Brown. "Special Lady," taken from their eponymous 1979 debut album for the company, featured a fuller harmony sound emphasized by a haunting a cappella introduction. Produced by former Stang engineer Vincent Castellano and composed by Ray, Goodman, and Morris, the song went to Number One R&B and number five pop. Three subsequent Polydor albums were less successful, and in 1982, Ray left the group to join Mr. and Mrs. Robinson at their new Sugar Hill label, for which he recorded a lovely but overlooked solo album titled *It's Good to Be Home* that yielded one minor hit, the number 37 R&B "Sweet Baby."

Ray was replaced by Kevin Ray Owens but returned to the group by the time of its modest-selling 1985 sides for the Panoramic label. The threesome signed with EMI America the following year and scored with the number eight R&B "Take It to the Limit" from an album of the same name. The group's last album, 1988's *Mood for Lovin'* on EMI Manhattan, spawned no top 40 R&B hits but is notable for its closing track, "Don't Make Me Wait," a duet by Ray and former Labelle member Sarah Dash. Ray's death in 1992 marked the final moment in the trio's history.

THE MOONGLOWS

Alan "Moondog" Freed, the disc jockey who coined the term *rock and roll*, played an important role in the careers of a number of rhythm and blues artists, including Chuck Berry and Frankie Lymon, but perhaps none more so than in that of the Moonglows. The vocal group, featuring Harvey Fuqua (b. July 27, 1928, Louisville, Kentucky) and Bobby Lester (b. Robert Dallas, Jan. 13, 1930, Louisville), and originally known as the Crazy Sounds, was appearing in 1952 at the Chesterfield Lounge in Cleveland, Ohio. In attendance was vocalist Al "Fats" Thomas, who was so taken with the quartet that he called Freed at local radio station WJW and had him listen to the performance over the phone. The deejay was also impressed and decided to start his own company to record the Crazy Sounds, renaming them the Moonglows.

The group's first and only release on Freed's short-lived Champagne Records was a Fuqua-Lester composition titled "I Couldn't Tell a Lie." The label lied, however, crediting "Al Lance," a Freed pseudonym, as the sole writer. The single sold well in the Cleveland area, but 1953–54 releases on the Chicago-based Chance label did better, and the group exploded nationally after moving to the Windy City's larger Chess outfit later in 1954. Many of the Moonglows' records, including their biggest, "Sincerely," listed Freed (now using his real name) as co-writer. Fuqua, the author of most of them, has always insisted that the group's benefactor suggested a word here and there, but such a minor contribution hardly merited half the royalties. For his part, however, Freed did give heavy exposure to the Moonglows' records, especially after he took a nationally influential position at WINS in New York City, and featured them in his 1956 motion picture *Rock, Rock, Rock*.

Fuqua (nephew of the Ink Spots' Charlie Fuqua)

TOP ALBUM

RAY, GOODMAN & BROWN (Ray, Goodman and Brown, Polydor, '80, *17*)

TOP SONGS

NOT ON THE OUTSIDE (Stang, '68, *13 R&B*)

I DO (Stang, '69, *10 R&B*)

LOVE ON A TWO-WAY STREET (Stang, '70, *1 R&B, 3 Pop*)

IF I DIDN'T CARE (Stang, '70, *7 R&B*)

ALL I HAVE (Stang, '70, *9 R&B*)

SEXY MAMA (Stang, '73, *3 R&B, 17 Pop*)

LOOK AT ME (I'M IN LOVE) (Stang, '75, *1 R&B, 39 Pop*)

Ray, Goodman and Brown:

SPECIAL LADY (Polydor, '79, *1 R&B, 5 Pop*)

TAKE IT TO THE LIMIT (EMI America, '86, *8 R&B*)

Additional Top 40 R&B Songs: 21

The Moonglows

and Lester began singing together in Louisville around 1950 and briefly toured with tenor saxophonist Ed Wiley's Rhythm Rockers. After a fire killed Fuqua's two children and badly injured his wife, he relocated to Cleveland, got a job as a truck driver for a coal company, and formed the Crazy Sounds with Danny Coggins and Prentiss Barnes. By the time Freed heard the group, it consisted of Lester (lead tenor), Fuqua (lead baritone), Alexander "Pete" Graves (harmony tenor), and Barnes (basso). Guitarist Billy Johnson was soon added.

After recording a mixture of bluesy ballads and jump tunes for Chance, the Moonglows took their distinctive style of "blow harmony" to Chess and had an immediate hit with the Lester-led ballad "Sincerely," which spent 20 weeks on the *Billboard* R&B chart, two of them at Number One. A cover version by the McGuire Sisters undercut theirs on the pop chart, however, staying at the top for 10 weeks.

The Moonglows, who also cut a couple of Checker singles as Bobby Lester and the Moonlighters, gave Chess seven more top 10 R&B hits through 1958, when Lester's drug addiction forced him to leave the group. A second set of Moonglows, com-

TOP SONGS

SINCERELY (Chess, '54, *1 R&B, 20 Pop*)
MOST OF ALL (Chess, '55, *5 R&B*)
WE GO TOGETHER (Chess, '56, *9 R&B*)
SEE SAW (Chess, '56, *6 R&B, 25 Pop*)
WHEN I'M WITH YOU (Chess, '56, *15 R&B*)
PLEASE SEND ME SOMEONE TO LOVE (Chess, '57, *5 R&B*)
TEN COMMANDMENTS OF LOVE (Harvey and the Moonglows, Chess, '58, *9 R&B, 22 Pop*)

prising Fuqua, bass singer Chuck Barksdale of the Dells, and a young Washington, D.C., quartet called the Marquees that included Marvin Gaye, made two unsuccessful singles for Chess in 1959 before disbanding, with Fuqua and Gaye heading to Detroit in search of new opportunities.

The Moonglows' sophisticated "blow harmony" approach, in which they crooned with mouths closed to create a mooing sound, had a major impact on such other groups as the Spinners (whose career Fuqua launched in 1961 at his own Tri-Phi label) and the Dells. In a 1981 interview with Larry Kelp of the Oakland Tribune, Fuqua described the Moonglows' style as "a wailing tenor with an unusual harmony chord structure. See, everyone else then and now sings in triads, the different singers hitting the 1-3-5 notes. We were four voices singing major sevenths, 1-3-5-7."

Fuqua went on to produce hits for the Spinners and Jr. Walker at the Tri-Phi and Harvey labels in the early 1960s; for Walker, Marvin Gaye and Tammi Terrell, David Ruffin, Stevie Wonder, and the Supremes at Motown from the mid-to-late 1970s; for New Birth and the Nite-Liters at RCA in the early 1980s; and for Sylvester at Fantasy in the late 1970s. Shades of the Moonglows' trademark sound could be heard on the 1982 Gaye smash "Sexual Healing," to which Fuqua contributed harmonies.

Graves formed his own group of Moonglows in 1964, but their releases on Lana, Times Square, and Crimson were little noticed. In 1972, Fuqua, Lester, and Graves were briefly reunited in another set that cut an album for RCA Victor titled Return of the Moonglows. Lester sporadically fronted other editions of the group from 1971 until his death from cancer on October 15, 1980.

MELBA MOORE

Melba Moore's show-stopping rendition of "I Got Love" in Purlie, the hit 1971 Broadway musical in which she co-starred with Cleavon Little, led critics to dub her "the black Streisand." Yet unlike Barbra Streisand, the petite, saucer-eyed singer-actress did not immediately make the transition from musical theater star to successful recording artist. Her recorded output during the 1970s, for Mercury, Buddah, and Epic, resulted in only three

top 20 R&B hits. A switch to EMI America in 1981, then to the affiliated Capitol label, finally established Moore as a viable record seller, though she never was able to penetrate the pop top 40 in the U.S. She did, however, reach Number One on the Billboard R&B chart twice, with singles taken from the 1986 album A Lot of Love.

"I think that a lot of record people and even producers tended to think of me as an actress, and that held me back as a recording artist," she told Blues and Soul magazine editor John Abbey in 1981. "They put me in this…'class' bag, I guess. But I explained that I have to be marketed as a black R&B female artist first and foremost. I may sing a song like 'Memories' ["The Way We Were"]…but I'm not Barbra Streisand! If she were to sing R&B, she'd have a lot of trouble selling records, too."

Born in New York City during the mid-1940s and raised in Harlem and Newark, Moore was encouraged to study classical voice and piano by her mother and father. But unlike her parents, both of whom were professional musicians, she decided on a career as a school teacher. After graduating New Jersey's Montclair College with a bachelor's degree in music education, she taught music at Preshine Avenue School in Newark during the 1964–65 term. She quickly became bored with the job, however, and launched a career as a vocalist, first in local clubs, then at resorts in the Catskills.

By 1968, Moore had done background sessions for such artists as Harry Belafonte, Jerry Butler, Aretha Franklin, Johnny Mathis, Dionne Warwick, and Andy Williams as well as recorded a little-noticed single of her own for the Musicor label. At one of the sessions, she met Galt McDermott, who recruited her for a musical he was producing and co-writing called Hair. During her two-year stay with the smash Broadway production, Moore progressed from being a semi-nude member of the chorus to taking over the leading role. From Hair, she moved to Purlie and won prestigious Tony, New York Critics, Variety, and Drama Desk awards. Her stage notoriety led to a contract with Mercury Records in addition to a 1972 CBS-TV summer variety series (co-hosted with Clifton Davis) and acting roles in such motion pictures as Pigeons (1971) and Lost in the Stars (1974).

Her Mercury albums were geared to a middle-of-the-road audience and generated little interest. In 1976, a year after signing with Buddah, she was paired with producer-songwriter Van McCoy for the album *This Is It,* which spawned the disco-styled title track (number 18 R&B in the U.S. and number nine pop in England) and the number 17 R&B ballad "Lean on Me" (originally recorded by Vivian Reed). A 1978–80 association with Epic resulted in three albums but only one hit, her 1979 number 17 R&B rendition of the Bee Gees' "You Stepped into My Life," produced by Gene McFadden and John Whitehead, who had worked on one of her earlier Buddah albums.

Moore broke into the R&B top 10 at number five with 1982's "Love's Comin' at Ya,' an EMI America single written and produced by Paul Laurence Jones III. She scored seven more top 10 R&B entries through 1990. Two hit the top—"A Little Bit More" (a duet with Freddie Jackson, whom she previously had discovered and signed to a production company run by her husband) and "Falling"—both produced and co-written by McFadden. For her last album, 1990's *Soul Exposed,* Moore pulled out the stops by inviting an all-star cast to join her for a reading of James Weldon Johnson and J. Rosamond Johnson's "Negro national anthem," "Lift Every Voice and Sing." Produced by gospel artist BeBe Winans, the track featured guest appearances by Anita Baker, Bobby Brown, the Clark Sisters, Freddie Jackson, Stephanie Mills, Jeffrey Osborne, Take 6, Dionne Warwick, and Stevie Wonder, among others.

Throughout her recording career, Moore remained active as an actress. Besides returning to the stage for 1978's *Timbuktu* and 1981's *Inacent*

TOP SONGS

LOVE'S COMIN' AT YA (EMI America, '82, *5 R&B*)

LIVIN' FOR YOUR LOVE (Capitol, '84, *6 R&B*)

READ MY LIPS (Capitol, '85, *12 R&B*)

LOVE THE ONE I'M WITH (A LOT OF LOVE) (Melba and Kashif, Capitol, '86, *5 R&B*)

A LITTLE BIT MORE (Melba Moore with Freddie Jackson, Capitol, '86, *1 R&B*)

FALLING (Capitol, '86, *1 R&B*)

IT'S BEEN SO LONG (Capitol, '87, *6 R&B*)

I CAN'T COMPLAIN (Melba Moore with Freddie Jackson, Capitol, '88, *12 R&B*)

LIFT EVERY VOICE AND SING (Capitol, '90, *9 R&B*)

DO YOU REALLY WANT MY LOVE (Capitol, '90, *10 R&B*)

Additional Top 40 R&B Songs: 13

Black, she appeared in motion picture adaptations of *Hair* and *Purlie.* Her television acting credits include guest roles on "Love Boat" and "Captain Kangaroo," a part in the 1985 CBS mini-series "Ellis Island," and her own 1986 CBS sitcom series "Melba."

THE NEVILLE BROTHERS

While widely acclaimed as the first family of New Orleans rhythm and blues, the Neville Brothers—Art (b. Dec. 17, 1938), Charles (b. Dec. 28, 1939), Aaron (b. Jan. 24, 1941), and Cyril (b. Jan. 10, 1950)—never managed to crack the R&B top 40 as a unit. Their recordings, which mix syncopated second-line Crescent City funk and sweet soul ballads, are largely unknown to African Americans but have won them a devoted following of rock critics, roots-music fans, and such fellow artists as Keith Richards, Bette Midler, and Linda Ronstadt. Prior to coming together in the group in 1977, however, vocalist Aaron enjoyed massive though fleeting success with the Number One R&B, number two pop 1966 ballad "Tell It Like It Is," and keyboardist Art scored a string of R&B charters during the late 1960s and early '70s as leader of the Meters.

Art was the first to record, in 1954 as a member of the Hawkettes, a teenage band he'd recently joined. The Professor Longhair–inspired "Mardi Gras Mambo" was issued on the Chess label and, although it didn't chart nationally, became a perennial local favorite at carnival time. Art recorded as a solo artist and session musician for Specialty between 1956 and '58 and for a period took the Hawkettes on the road as a backup band for more-successful labelmate Larry Williams. Drafted into the Navy in 1959, Art turned leadership of the band over to brother Aaron.

Signing with Joe Banashak's Minit label, Aaron became the first in the family to make the national charts, in 1960 with the number 21 R&B Allen Toussaint–penned-and-produced "Over You." Following his discharge, Art recorded the ballad "All These Things," a 1962 Toussaint production for Banashak's Instant label that enjoyed great regional success. The haunting "Tell It Like It Is," produced and

The Neville Brothers

co-written by former Hawkettes saxophonist George Davis for the tiny Par-Lo label, took Aaron to the top of the R&B chart in 1967 and on a national tour, but within a year he was back at his day job as a longshoreman. He continued performing at local clubs as a member of Art Neville and the Neville Sounds, which also included younger brother Cyril on percussion.

The Neville Sounds, minus Aaron and Cyril, became the house rhythm section for Toussaint and Marshall Sehorn's Sansu Productions in 1968. Changing their name to the Meters, organist Art, guitarist Leo Nocentelli, bassist George Porter, and drummer Joseph "Zigaboo" Modeliste supplied riveting, contemporized second-line grooves for such vocalists as Lee Dorsey, Dr. John, Robert Palmer, Labelle, King Biscuit Boy, and Paul McCartney over

the next seven years. As a basically instrumental combo, the Meters cut a series of distinctive dance-oriented sides for the Josie label between 1969 and '71, hitting the R&B top 40 eight times. A move to Reprise, for which they cut five albums between 1972 and '77, resulted in greater mainstream notoriety but fewer hits. Cyril joined the band in 1975 prior to a tour of the U.S. and Europe with the Rolling Stones.

Saxophonist Charles, who'd left New Orleans at age 15 and worked for a while in New York with Joey Dee and the Starlighters, was reunited with his brothers in 1976 for a Toussaint-produced Island album by the Wild Tchoupitoulas, a group of ceremonial black New Orleans "Indians" led by the Nevilles' uncle George "Big Chief Jolly" Landry.

By 1978, the Meters had dissolved, and the four

siblings reemerged as the Neville Brothers with an eponymous album for Capitol. With seven subsequent albums for A&M, Black Top, and EMI through 1994, the Neville Brothers built a devoted cult following but never penetrated the R&B market, despite a concerted effort by A&M to get black radio play for "Sister Rosa," a rap-style tribute to civil rights movement pioneer Rosa Parks from the much-heralded 1989 album *Yellow Moon*.

Aaron, whose post–"Tell It Like It Is" Toussaint-produced singles for such labels as Bell, Mercury, and Palm Tree had fallen on deaf ears, saw his solo career begin to skyrocket in 1989 with "Don't Know Much," a duet with Linda Ronstadt that reached number two on the pop chart. His lilting, vibrato-rich, melisma-spewing tenor became one of the most widely heard voices in America through television commercial jingles and duets with country singers like Kathy Mattea, Tammy Wynette, and Trisha Yearwood as well as such solo hits for A&M as his 1991 number eight pop version of the Main Ingredient's "Everybody Plays the Fool" and his 1993 number 37 country rendition of the George Jones classic "The Grand Tour." He remained a member of the Neville Brothers. In 1994, they toured as the opening act for country star Wynonna Judd, and director Oliver Stone delivered the first draft of a screenplay for a motion picture based on the family group.

TOP ALBUMS

THE GRAND TOUR (Aaron Neville, A&M, '93, 37)
AARON NEVILLE'S SOULFUL CHRISTMAS (Aaron
  Neville, A&M, '93, 36)

TOP SONGS

Aaron Neville:
OVER YOU (Minit, '60, 21 R&B)
TELL IT LIKE IT IS (Par-Lo, '86, 1 R&B, 2 Pop)

The Meters:
SOPHISTICATED CISSY (Josie, '69, 7 R&B, 34 Pop)
CISSY STRUT (Josie, '69, 4 R&B, 23 Pop)
EASE BACK (Josie, '69, 20 R&B)
LOOK-KA PY PY (Josie, '69, 11 R&B)
CHICKEN STRUT (Josie, '70, 11 R&B)
A MESSAGE FROM THE METERS (Josie, '70, 21 R&B)

Additional Top 40 R&B Songs: 3

NEW EDITION

O f the countless youthful African-American singing acts that attempted to repeat the success enjoyed by the Jackson 5 during the 1970s, New Edition came closest. Adopting an updated variant on the Jacksons' early bubblegum soul sound, the Boston group, originally comprising Bobby Brown (b. Feb. 5, 1969), Ralph Tresvant (b. May 16, 1968), Ricky Bell (b. Sept. 18, 1967), Michael Bivins (b. Oct. 10, 1968), and Ronald DeVoe (b. Nov. 17, 1967), scored 14 top 10 R&B hit singles between 1983 and '89, including the chart-toppers "Candy Girl," "Cool It Now," "Mr. Telephone Man," and "Can You Stand the Rain." Their legion of fans included Michael Jackson, who sometimes attended New Edition concerts in disguise.

Although his pinched nasal tenor was no match for Jackson's fuller tones, principal New Edition lead Tresvant recalled the young Jackson with his tortured vocal delivery and slinky, knee-wiggling dance routines. The other members backgrounded him in full, high harmonies and, during the group's elaborately staged arena concerts, performed snake, worm, and popping movements; cartwheels; and mildy suggestive pelvic bumps and grinds to the delight of their adoring pre- and post-pubescent followers.

Raised in the Orchard Park projects of Boston's Roxbury district, the five singers began harmonizing together in 1981. Entering a local talent contest in which they performed a medley of Jackson 5 hits, they came in second but so impressed show promoter Maurice Starr that he took them under his wing. "Candy Girl," their Starr-produced debut single, was issued on the Streetwise label in early 1983 and shot to the top of the *Billboard* R&B chart, where it remained for one week before being bumped by Michael Jackson's "Beat It." Two more Streetwise singles followed—the number eight R&B "Is This the End" and the number 25 R&B "Popcorn Girl"—after which the group parted company with Starr and Streetwise. Starr then proceeded to organize New Kids on the Block, a white version of New Edition that eventually enjoyed more success on the pop charts than his old, black edition ever would.

New Edition, however, did have tremendous R&B and occasional crossover success after joining MCA Records in 1984. The quintet's eponymous debut album for the company yielded two Number One R&B hits: "Cool It Now" (written and pro-

TOP ALBUMS

NEW EDITION (MCA, '84, 6)
HEART BREAK (MCA, '88, 12)

Additional Top 40 Albums: 1

TOP SONGS

CANDY GIRL (Streetwise, '83, *1 R&B*)
COOL IT NOW (MCA, '84, *1 R&B, 4 Pop*)
MR. TELEPHONE MAN (MCA, '84, *1 R&B, 12 Pop*)
COUNT ME OUT (MCA, '85, *2 R&B*)
A LITTLE BIT OF LOVE (IS ALL IT TAKES) (MCA, '86, *3 R&B, 38 Pop*)
EARTH ANGEL (MCA, '86, *3 R&B, 21 Pop*)
IF IT ISN'T LOVE (MCA, '88, *2 R&B, 7 Pop*)
CAN YOU STAND THE RAIN (MCA, '88, *1 R&B*)

Additional Top 40 R&B Songs: 10

duced by Vincent Brantley and Rick Timas) and "Mr. Telephone Man" (written and produced by Ray Parker, Jr.). Brown left the group in 1985 for a solo career and emerged as a major star three years later with the massive success of the MCA album *Don't Be Cruel.* New Edition continued as a quartet until 1988, when 22-year-old Washington, D.C., veteran Johnny Gill (who'd had several moderate solo hits on Cotillion) was added.

Their 1985 album *All for Love* spawned the top 10 R&B hits "Count Me Out," "A Little Bit of Love (Is All It Takes)," and "With You All the Way," while the next year's *Under the Blue Moon* found them reprising such doo wop classics as the Penguins' "Earth Angel" and Little Anthony and the Imperials' "Tears on My Pillow" (on which they were joined by Little Anthony himself). With the addition of second lead singer Gill and the employment of Minneapolis producers Jimmy Jam and Terry Lewis, New Edition adopted a more contemporary and somewhat more mature approach for 1988's *Heart Break.* The album, containing the hits "If It Isn't Love," "You're Not My Kind of Girl," "Can You Stand the Rain," and "Crucial" (all of which made the R&B top five), was the group's last, aside from a greatest hits collection issued in 1993.

After the group disbanded, all five members of the final New Edition had considerable success. Gill signed with Motown, where he scored four Number

New Edition

One R&B hits—"Where Do We Go from Here" (a duet with Stacy Lattisaw), "Rub You the Right Way," "My, My, My," and "Wrap My Body Tight"—through 1991. Bell, Bivins, and DeVoe formed the singing-rapping group Bell Biv DeVoe and hit Number One R&B twice in 1990 with the MCA singles "Poison" and "B.B.D. (I Thought It Was Me)?" Tresvant also remained at MCA, where he had the Number One R&B 1990 hit "Sensitivity." And Bivins formed his own Biv Entertainment management and production company, which shepherded the career of, among others, Boyz II Men, a young Philadelphia vocal group which took its name from a track on New Edition's *Heart Break* album.

THE OHIO PLAYERS

The raw, syncopated street funk that placed the Ohio Players on the top of the R&B charts five times during the mid-1970s—and twice at Number One pop—had its roots in an earlier era of rhythm and blues. The Dayton-based band was formed around 1960 by Georgia-born singer-guitarist Robert Ward, whose distinctive style was influenced by gospel artist Sister Rosetta Tharpe. The trio, comprising Ward, bassist Levar Fredrick, and drummer Cornelius Johnson, called itself the Ohio Untouchables, drawing the name from the television series "The Untouchables" that starred Robert Stack. Trumpeter Ralph "Pee Wee" Middlebrook and saxophonist Clarence "Satch" Satchell were soon added.

The Ohio Untouchables had little luck with their own singles on the Thelma and Lupine labels, but they backed the Falcons (featuring Wilson Pickett) on the vocal group's number six R&B hit "I Found a Love" on Lupine in 1962. Ward left the Untouchables two years later to record as a solo artist for Lupine and Groove City before drifting into obscurity, only to reemerge in 1991 as a blues guitar hero with a critically acclaimed album on Black Top. He was replaced by disciple Leroy "Sugarfoot" Bonner (b. circa 1944, Henderson, Ohio), although Bonner wouldn't become the primary focus of the band until a decade later.

Bonner started out as a teenager playing in roadhouses around Dayton with a band led by guitarist Lonnie Mack, another Ward disciple. "I used to play harmonica with them," Bonner recalled. "Then Lon-

nie would take all the women home. I said, 'The hell with that. I'm playing guitar from now on.' "

By 1967, the Ohio Untouchables had become the Ohio Players and included Bonner, Middlebrook, Satchell, and drummer Greg Webster. Joe Harris, later of Undisputed Truth, was the group's first vocalist. The Ohio Players' debut single, "Trespassin'," appeared in 1968 on Dayton's Compass label and became a minor national hit. *Observations in Time,* a Capitol album issued later that year, featured the lineup of Bonner, Middlebrook, Satchell, Webster, bassist Marshall Jones, keyboardist-vocalist Dutch Robinson, and singer Bobby Fears, but it yielded no hits. Trumpeter-trombonist Marvin Pierce joined not long thereafter, and the two singers were dropped.

"Pain," a 1971 single on the local Top Hit label, was picked up by Detroit's Westbound Records and went to number 35 on the *Billboard* R&B chart. An album of the same title sported a cover with a baldheaded, scantily clad, whip-wielding dominatrix, the first in a series of controversial S&M-related art concepts (the brainchild of leader Satchell) that continued through the albums *Pleasure, Ecstasy, Climax* (all on Westbound) and *Skin Tight* (the group's first for Mercury). Only one major hit emerged from the Ohio Players' two-year association with Westbound, 1973's Number One R&B "Funky Worm," featuring the wacky vocals and synthesizer of Walter "Junie" Morrison, who later became a key member of Parliament-Funkadelic.

TOP ALBUMS

FIRE (Mercury, '74, *1*)
HONEY (Mercury, '75, *2*)

Additional Top 40 Albums: 3

TOP SONGS

FUNKY WORM (Westbound, '73, *1 R&B, 15 Pop*)
JIVE TURKEY (PART 1) (Mercury, '74, *6 R&B*)
SKIN TIGHT (Mercury, '74, *2 R&B, 13 Pop*)
FIRE (Mercury, '74, *1 R&B, 1 Pop*)
I WANT TO BE FREE (Mercury, '75, *6 R&B*)
SWEET STICKY THING (Mercury, '75, *1 R&B, 33 Pop*)
LOVE ROLLERCOASTER (Mercury, '75, *1 R&B, 1 Pop*)
WHO'D SHE COO? (Mercury, '76, *1 R&B, 18 Pop*)

Additional Top 40 R&B Songs: 11

Signed to Mercury in 1974 with keyboardist Billy Beck in place of Morrison and new drummer Jimmy "Diamond" Williams, the Ohio Players launched a two-and-a-half-year assault on the charts that included the top 10 R&B singles "Jive Turkey," "Skin Tight," "Fire," "I Want to Be Free," "Sweet Sticky Thing," "Love Rollercoaster," "Fopp," "Who'd She Coo?" and "O-H-I-O." All featured the vocals and fast-fingered, blues-bitten guitar of Bonner, whose snarling, nasal singing style had a huge influence on such others as Lionel Richie of the Commodores, Michael Cooper of Con Funk Shun, and Larry Blackmon of Cameo. Five of the group's Mercury albums—*Skin Tight, Fire, Honey, Contradiction*, and the aptly titled *Gold* (a greatest hits collection)—went gold.

After 1977, the Ohio Players never again penetrated the R&B top 10. They cut an unsuccessful album for Arista the next year, then broke into rival camps, with Bonner, Middlebrooks, Jones, and Pierce remaining with the Players and Beck and Williams forming a group called Shadow that recorded an album for Elektra. *Ouch!*, a 1981 Ohio Players album on Boardwalk Records produced by Richard "Dimples" Fields (previous albums had been group productions) spawned two minor top 40 R&B hits, but a single two years later on the Air City label was less successful.

Working with producer Roger Troutman of Zapp, Bonner cut the brilliant but little-noticed album *Sugar Kiss* for Warner Bros. in 1985 under the name "Sugarfoot." It featured the key Ohio Players of the period—Bonner, Beck, Williams, second guitarist Clarence Willis (formerly of Shadow), and bassist Darwin Dortch—but they were prevented for legal reasons from using the group identification. *Back*, a self-produced 1988 album for the Track label, found the band (with Ronald Nooks added on keyboards) reclaiming its name but not its earlier star status.

THE O'JAYS

"**A**cts come and go every year," Eddie Levert (b. June 16, 1942) has stated, "but the O'Jays were here yesterday, we're here today, and we'll be here for years to come."

Levert and Walter Williams (b. Aug. 25, 1942), his co-lead in the Canton, Ohio, vocal group, had known each other since elementary school and sang

---

TOP ALBUMS

FAMILY REUNION (Philadelphia International, '75, 7)
SO FULL OF LOVE (Philadelphia International, '78, 6)

Additional Top 40 Albums: 8

TOP SONGS

BACK STABBERS (Philadelphia International, '72,
    1 R&B, 3 Pop)
LOVE TRAIN (Philadelphia International, '73,
    1 R&B, 1 Pop)
GIVE THE PEOPLE WHAT THEY WANT (Philadelphia
    International, '75, *1 R&B*)
I LOVE MUSIC (PART 1) (Philadelphia International,
    '75, *1 R&B, 5 Pop*)
LIVIN' FOR THE WEEKEND (Philadelphia
    International, '76, *1 R&B, 20 Pop*)
MESSAGE IN OUR MUSIC (Philadelphia International,
    '76, *1 R&B*)
DARLIN' DARLIN' BABY (SWEET, TENDER, LOVE)
    (Philadelphia International, '76, *1 R&B*)
USE TA BE MY GIRL (Philadelphia International, '78,
    1 R&B, 4 Pop)

Additional Top 40 R&B Songs: 37

---

as a gospel duo known as the Levert Brothers on a local radio station. In 1958, while attending McKinley High School, they hooked up with William Powell, Bobby Massey, and Bill Isles to form the Triumphs. After briefly using the name the Mascots, the doo wop quintet became the O'Jays. The other original members eventually fell by the wayside, but Levert and Williams kept the group going throughout a recording career that yielded 10 Number One R&B hit singles and nine gold albums, three of which—1975's *Family Reunion*, 1978's *So Full of Love*, and 1979's *Identify Yourself*—also went platinum.

Major success was a long time in coming, and the O'Jays considered calling it quits more than once. As the Mascots, they recorded for King Records in Cincinnati in 1959, but the results weren't released at the time. Later in 1959, having changed their name again due to their sponsorship by Cleveland disc jockey Eddie O'Jay, they cut "Miracles" for the obscure Daco label. The Don Davis–produced single generated enough interest around Ohio to be picked up by Apollo Records in New York and to prompt King to issue two 45s from the Mascots' debut session.

The O'Jays

The O'Jays spent the mid-1960s in Los Angeles, working as background singers for producer-arranger H. B. Barnum on sessions by such artists as Jimmy Norman, Nat "King" Cole, and Lou Rawls. As artists in their own right, they recorded for Barnum's Little Star label and then signed with Imperial, where they had four moderate hits—"Lonely Drifter," "Lipstick Traces (On a Cigarette)," "Let It All Out," and "Stand in for Love"—between 1963 and '66. After being transferred to the Minit label and having even less luck, the quartet (Isles had dropped out in 1965) returned to Cleveland and contemplated throwing in the towel.

The group's fortunes improved temporarily while working with producer George Kerr at Bell Records. They scored two ballad hits: 1967's number eight R&B "I'll Be Sweeter Tomorrow (Than I Was Today)" and the next year's number 27 R&B "Look Over Your Shoulder." The O'Jays next recorded for songwriter-producers Kenny Gamble and Leon Huff's Chess-distributed Neptune label. The brilliant 1969 album *The O'Jays in Philadelphia*, containing the top 20 R&B singles "One Night Affair" and

"Looky Looky (Look at Me Girl)," was a harbinger of bigger things to come.

When Neptune collapsed, the O'Jays reunited with Barnum, but singles on Saru and Little Star were flops. Then, in 1971, Gamble and Huff called with an offer for the quartet to rejoin them at their new Columbia-distributed Philadelphia International label. All agreed, except Massey, who felt the group should be writing and producing its own records. He quit and produced one modest hit, a 1971 version of "You Send Me" by the Ponderosa Twins + One that peaked at number 12 on the R&B chart. The O'Jays went on to score nine Number One R&B songs at Philadelphia International, beginning with 1972's "Back Stabbers" and ending with 1987's "Lovin' You," all produced by Gamble and Huff. Many of the group's hits, including "Back Stabbers," "Love Train," "Give the People What They Want," and "Message in Our Music," reflected their producers' deep concern with social issues.

The trio—Sammy Strain (formerly of Little Anthony and the Imperials) took over in 1976 for an ailing Powell (who died a year later), and Nathaniel

Best replaced Strain in 1993—augmented its harmonies on records with session singers and in person with two of its band members, all of whom contributed anonymously. The focus, however, remained on Levert's shouting, gravel-toned low tenor and on Williams's lighter, yet more flexible tenor, which often dropped to bass-baritone or soared into falsetto wails.

After experiencing a relative dry spell during the early 1980s, the O'Jays returned with strength in 1987 with "Lovin' You," their last Number One R&B hit with Gamble and Huff. The group was becoming increasingly involved in the production end and was often employing the services of Levert's son Gerald and his partner Marc Gordon, both of the highly successful group LeVert. While maintaining their trademark vocal style, the O'Jays updated their instrumental backgrounds and, for 1989's R&B chart-topping "Have You Had Your Love Today" on the EMI label, featured an interlude by a rapper known as the JAZ. They continued scoring top 10 R&B hits into the 1990s, including a 1991 rendition of Bob Dylan's "Emotionally Yours," which led to participation in the following year's all-star Dylan tribute concert at Madison Square Garden.

THE ORIOLES

The Orioles, led by the mellow tenor voice of Sonny Til (b. Earlington Carl Tilghman, circa 1930), served as the prototype for many of the street-corner doo wop groups of the 1950s. Singing in a romantic ballad style that lacked some of the show-biz polish of such earlier units as the Mills Brothers, the Ink Spots, and the Ravens but had immense youth appeal, the Baltimore quartet chocked up 10 R&B hits between 1948 and '53, with two—"It's Too Soon to Know" and "Crying in the Chapel"—making significant inroads into the pop market.

Adopting the nickname Sonny at an early age because he hated his real first name and because he admired Al Jolson's recording of "Sonny Boy," Til grew up in Baltimore and sang with a group in high school. After serving in the Army's chemical corps during World War II, he returned home and began participating as a solo vocalist in amateur contests at the Avenue Club. His influences at the time included the Cats and a Fiddle, the Ink Spots, the Mills Broth-

TOP SONGS

IT'S TOO SOON TO KNOW (Natural, '48, *1 R&B, 13 Pop*)

TELL ME SO (Jubilee, '49, *1 R&B*)

A KISS AND A ROSE (Jubilee, '49, *12 R&B*)

I CHALLENGE YOUR KISS (Jubilee, '49, *11 R&B*)

FORGIVE AND FORGET (Jubilee, '49, *5 R&B*)

WHAT ARE YOU DOING NEW YEAR'S EVE (Jubilee, '49, *9 R&B*)

(IT'S GONNA BE A) LONELY CHRISTMAS (Jubilee, '49, *5 R&B*)

BABY, PLEASE DON'T GO (Jubilee, '52, *8 R&B*)

CRYING IN THE CHAPEL (Jubilee, '53, *1 R&B, 11 Pop*)

IN THE MISSION OF ST. AUGUSTINE (Jubilee, '53, *7 R&B*)

ers, Nat Cole, and Charles Brown. He joined forces at the club with first tenor Alexander Sharp, baritone George Nelson, and bass singer–bass player Johnny Reed to form the Vibra-Naires in 1947. Local songwriter Deborah Chessler became their manager, and guitarist Tommy Gaither was soon added. Because their original name was difficult to spell, it was changed to that of the Maryland state bird, the oriole.

Driving with Chessler to New York City in a second-hand Ford, the Orioles auditioned for Frank Schiffman at the Apollo Theater and were hired. His son Jack Schiffman later noted Til's aphrodisiac-like effect on women in the audience, who screamed, "Ride my alley, Sonny!" as he crooned while "sensuously gyrating his shoulders and caressing the air with his hands." Chessler also got the Orioles booked on Arthur Godfrey's weekly CBS radio program "Talent Scouts," where they came in second to British jazz pianist George Shearing. They were called back to sing on Godfrey's daily morning broadcast and caught the ear of record distibutor Jerry Blaine, who signed them to his Natural label. (The label logo read: "It's a Natural.")

At their first session, held in the spring of 1948, the Orioles cut "It's Too Soon to Know," a ballad written by Chessler. Despite its primitive quality— Til's lead and the other singers' harmonies were tentatively pitched and the instrumental accompaniment consisted of only guitar, piano, and bass— their original version of the song rose to Number One on the R&B chart and crossed to number 13 pop, outdistancing numerous more-polished cover renditions, including ones by Dinah Washington,

Ella Fitzgerald, and the Ravens that also made the R&B list. Natural then changed its name to Jubilee, and the group remained with the label through 1955.

The Orioles hit the top of the R&B chart again in 1949 with "Tell Me So," another Chessler ballad. Guitarist Gaither was killed in an auto accident in 1950 and was replaced by Ralph Williams. Nelson, who'd sung the bridges on many of the group's records, developed a drinking problem and began missing some of the sessions. (He died of an asthma attack around 1959.) Williams filled in the baritone harmony parts until Gregory Carroll, formerly of the Four Buddies, was recruited in 1953. That year the group scored its biggest hit with the Number One R&B, number 11 pop "Crying in the Chapel," a quasi-religious ballad written by Artie Glenn, recorded first by his son Darrell Glenn, then by the Orioles and June Valli, and years later by Elvis Presley. A string of other "inspirational" Orioles songs followed, including "In the Mission of St. Augustine" (their last chart entry), "Robe of Calvary," "In the Chapel in the Moonlight," and "Count Your Blessings Instead of Sheep."

The original Orioles disbanded in late 1954, and Til quickly replaced them with members of the Regals, a modern harmony group he'd spotted at the Apollo. This edition filled out the remainder of the Orioles' Jubilee contract and then cut three singles for Vee-Jay before breaking up in 1958. Til continued recording as both a soloist and with later permutations of the Orioles for such labels as Roulette, Jubilee, Charlie Parker, RCA Victor, Clown, Dobre, and Ivory until his death from a heart attack on December 9, 1981.

JEFFREY OSBORNE

Clarence "Legs" Osborne was reputedly a great jazz trumpet player who received offers to go on the road with Count Basie, Duke Ellington, and Lionel Hampton. He turned down all of them, choosing to stay home in Providence, Rhode Island, with his wife and 12 kids. He was idolized by his youngest son, Jeffrey Osborne (b. March 9, 1948, Providence), who took up trumpet in elememtary school. Jeffrey put aside the trumpet at age 13 when his dad died and taught himself to play drums.

Unlike his father, Jeffrey jumped at the chance to leave the coastal island. It happened in 1969 when a band called Love Men Ltd. passed through town. He attended one of the group's gigs, and when the drummer was carted off to jail for fighting outside the club during intermission, he offered to fill in. Thus began an 11-year association with the band, later to be rechristened L.T.D., that would find him leaving the drum seat to become the star vocalist before finally launching a successful solo career.

The band was born in 1968 when four members of Sam and Dave's Miami-based horn section—trumpeter Carle Vickers, trombonist Jake Riley, Jr., and saxophonists Arthur Lorenzo Carnegie and Abraham Joseph "Onion" Miller—hooked up with keyboardist Jimmie "J. D." Miller in Greensboro, North Carolina. After a few local engagements, they headed to New York City in a '57 Chevy in search of a recording contract. None was forthcoming, and they survived by playing at top 40 bars up and down the East Coast.

After picking up Jeffrey, they drove to Los Angeles and became Love Ltd., then simply L.T.D. The group accompanied a female impersonator at an after-hours joint for a period, served as the house band at the Southern Christian Leadership Conference's local Operation Breadbasket headquarters, and, in late 1970, made its first recording, backing Rufus Thomas on his live Stax album *Doing the Push & Pull at P.J.'s.* A year later, with Jeffrey's older brother Billy having been added as a multi-purpose keyboardist, guitarist, percussionist, and vocalist, L.T.D. accompanied singer Merry Clayton at the Monterey Pop Festival. Bassist Henry E. Davis soon joined the aggregation. (The first permanent guitarist, Johnny "J. T." Davis, was drafted in 1976.)

Though a connection with Jerry Butler, L.T.D. signed with A&M Records in 1973. The group's first two albums—*Love, Togetherness & Devotion* and *Gittin' Down*—were jazzy, self-produced affairs that failed to generate any hits. For the third, 1976's *Love to the World,* Philadelphia producer Bobby Martin was brought in to assist, giving the group a more commercial direction and a solid hit, the Number One R&B, number 20 pop, Skip Scarborough–penned "Love Ballad." Previous recordings had sported group vocal efforts, but "Love Ballad" thrust Jeffrey's silky tenor into the spotlight. In order to allow him to stand up front, drummer Melvin Webb was hired in 1977 and contributed his driving backbeat to that year's Number One R&B, number four pop "(Every Time I Turn Around) Back in Love Again," the group's biggest hit. Webb died shortly thereafter and was replaced by Alvino Bennett.

Jeffrey began developing not only as a singer but also as a songwriter, and he co-wrote (with McGhee) L.T.D.'s third and last Number One R&B single, 1978's "Holding On (When Love Is Gone)" from the album *Togetherness*. Musical differences between the Osbornes and the other eight members led to the brothers' resignation in 1980. "I wanted to sing pop ballads," Jeffrey explained to Dennis Hunt of the *Los Angeles Times*. "They wanted to stick to straight R&B."

Remaining with A&M, Jeffrey released five solo albums between 1982 and '88, the first three produced by George Duke. Hit R&B singles, many co-authored by Jeffrey, were drawn from each: "I Really Don't Need No Light" (number three) and "On the Wings of Love" (number 13) from 1982's *Jeffrey Osborne;* "Don't You Get So Mad" (number three), "Stay with Me Tonight" (number 10), and "Plane Love" (number 10) from 1983's *Stay with Me Tonight;* "Don't Stop" (number six) and "The Borderlines" from 1984's *Don't Stop;* "You Should Be Mine (The Woo Woo Song)" (number two) from 1986's *Emotional;* and the Robert Brookins–Jeffrey

---

TOP ALBUM

TOGETHERNESS (L.T.D., A&M, '78, *18*)

Additional Top 40 Albums: 6

TOP SONGS

LOVE BALLAD (L.T.D., A&M, '76, *1 R&B, 20 Pop*)

(EVERY TIME I TURN AROUND) BACK IN LOVE AGAIN (L.T.D., A&M, '77, *1 R&B, 4 Pop*)

HOLDING ON (WHEN LOVE IS GONE) (L.T.D., A&M, '78, *1 R&B*)

I REALLY DON'T NEED NO LIGHT (A&M, '82, *3 R&B, 39 Pop*)

DON'T YOU GET SO MAD (A&M, '83, *3 R&B, 25 Pop*)

THE LAST TIME I MADE LOVE (Joyce Kennedy and Jeffrey Osborne, A&M, '84, *2 R&B, 40 Pop*)

YOU SHOULD BE MINE (THE WOO WOO SONG) (A&M, '86, *2 R&B, 13 Pop*)

SHE'S ON THE LEFT (A&M, '88, *1 R&B*)

ONLY HUMAN (Arista, '90, *3 R&B*)

Additional Top 40 R&B Songs: 19

Osborne–produced "She's on the Left" (his first and only R&B chart-topper after leaving L.T.D.) from 1988's *One Love—One Dream.* He also scored with two duets: 1984's "The Last Time I Made Love" (number two R&B) with Joyce Kennedy and 1987's "Love Power" (number five R&B, number 12 pop) with Dionne Warwick.

"Love Power," Jeffrey's greatest crossover success of the 1980s, was issued on Arista. In hopes of expanding his pop horizons, he switched to that label in 1990. The title track of that year's album, *Only Human,* gave him a number three R&B charter, but it didn't cross over.

JOHNNY OTIS

Once known as "the Duke Ellington of Watts" and later as "Reverend Hand Jive," Johnny Otis (b. John Veliotes, Dec. 28, 1921, Vallejo, California) is an American original. During a career that spans over half a century, he has distinguished himself, often simultaneously, as a drummer, vibraharpist, pianist, vocalist, bandleader, songwriter, record producer, disc jockey, television show host, political functionary, preacher, cartoonist, painter, sculptor, and organic farmer. He is best known as one of the pioneering figures of rhythm and blues, the creator of such hits as "Double Crossing Blues," "Mistreatin' Blues," "Cupid's Boogie," and "Willie and the Hand Jive."

As a drummer, he led his own jazz orchestra from 1945 to '48, backed Lester Young and Illinois Jacquet on record dates, and played on singer-pianist Charles Brown's first hit, 1946's "Drifting Blues," with Johnny Moore's Three Blazers. As a talent scout and leader of the Johnny Otis Show, originally called the California Rhythm and Blues Caravan, he discovered such singers as Esther Phillips, Linda Hopkins, Willie Mae "Big Mama" Thornton, the Royals (later known as the Midnighters), Jackie Wilson, Little Willie John, Etta James, Sugar Pie DeSanto, and Marie Adams. As a producer, he cut Thornton's original rendition of "Hound Dog," Johnny Ace's "Pledging My Love," and James's "The Wallflower (Roll with Me Henry)," in addition to sides by Little Richard, Johnny "Guitar" Watson, and many others. His songwriting credits include "Every Beat of My Heart," "So Fine," "The Wallflower," and "Willie and the Hand Jive."

The oldest of three children (the youngest, Nicholas, would become American ambassador to Egypt) born to Greek immigrant parents, Otis was raised in Berkeley among African Americans. As a teenager, he made a conscious break with white society and has considered himself black ever since. Having taken up snare drum in junior high school, he made his professional debut in 1939 with a combo called the West Oakland Houserockers before going on the road with midwestern territory bands led by George Morrison and Lloyd Hunter. At the recommendation of Nat Cole, the drummer moved to Los Angeles in 1943 to join Harlan Leonard's jazz orchestra. Otis formed his own big band there two years later and recorded the Ellington-styled instrumental "Harlem Nocturne" for the Excelsior label. Although it didn't make the national charts, the record was a strong enough seller to get the band bookings across the country, including a stint at the Apollo Theater.

Post–World War II economics forced Otis to disband his orchestra, after which he began performing with a smaller unit. "I had noticed in the years with my big band that the people loved jazz, but they really came to life when we played 'After Hours' or boogie woogies and jumps," he said in 1987. "We began a synthesis of bringing together big-band flavors, country blues, a touch of gospel and even a little bebop. That's how rhythm and blues was born."

Otis had his best year in 1950, when he scored a total of 10 top 10 R&B hits on Savoy Records, all featuring his Lionel Hampton–inspired vibraharp work and the vocals of Little Esther, the Robins, Mel Walker, and/or Lee Graves. After Savoy, he record-

ed for Peacock, Mercury, his own Dig label, and then Capitol, where he hit as a vocalist with 1958's number three R&B, number nine pop "Willie and the Hand Jive," his only crossover hit in the U.S. ("Ma He's Making Eyes at Me," a Capitol single featuring Marie Adams and the Three Tons of Joy, had gone to number two in England the previous year.)

During the 1960s, Otis turned his attention to politics and served for a decade as deputy chief of staff to Mervin Dymally, whose career he followed from the state assembly, state senate, and lieutenant governorship of California to the U.S. Congress. Otis also became an ordained minister and in 1978 opened his own nondenominational Landmark Community Church in south central Los Angeles. He continued to record and perform with the Johnny Otis Show, frequently featuring his son Shuggie on guitar, and made a triumphant appearance at the 1970 Monterey Jazz Festival with an all-star cast that included such luminaries as Ivory Joe Hunter, Roy Milton, Esther Phillips, Joe Turner, and Eddie "Cleanhead" Vinson.

After five decades in southern California, Otis and his wife, Phyllis, moved back to the northern part of the state in the early 1990s. Based in Sebastopol, he remained busy creating distinctive paintings and sculptures based on African-American themes; hosting a weekly radio program; marketing his own brand of organic apple juice; operating a combination grocery store, café, and nightclub; and touring the country with his 13-member blues, jazz, soul, and rock and roll revue.

RAY PARKER, JR.

By early 1976, Ray Parker, Jr. (b. May 1, 1954) had been a professional musician for eight of his 21 years. He was hired at age 13 as the Spinners' guitarist and soon graduated to studio work, playing on hits by such artists as Chairmen of the Board, Freda Payne, Honey Cone, Laura Lee, Stevie Wonder, and Barry White. Having established himself as one of the most in-demand session pickers in the business—raking in the bucks (at triple union scale) by doing as many as four record dates a day, sometimes six days a week—Parker branched into songwriting. He penned the 1974 Number One R&B hit "You Got the Love" for Rufus as well as material for White, Nancy Wilson, Bobby Womack, Labelle, and Herbie Hancock.

When "Doin' It," a number he'd written for Hancock, was nominated for a Grammy in 1976 and Parker wasn't even invited to the awards ceremony, his ego got the best of him. "That was the straw that broke the camel's back," he stated in a 1978 interview with Geoff Brown of England's *Black Music* magazine. Tired of the anonymity of being in the background, Parker decided to cut his own album. He recorded a demo at his home studio and took it to Arista Records head Clive Davis, who offered the young veteran a deal that included complete creative control. Parker produced and engineered and played most of the instruments—guitar, bass, drums, keyboards—himself, adding vocalists later and calling the yet-to-be-organized group Raydio. "Jack and Jill," the debut 1977 single, became a top 10 hit on both the R&B and pop charts, the first of five double-chart crossover smashes for Parker through 1984's Number One R&B and pop "Ghostbusters."

The son of a Ford crane operator, Parker took up clarinet at age six and played in a trio that entertained at PTA meetings. After seeing the Lovin' Spoonful playing electric guitars on TV when he was 12, he got one himself, practiced 10 hours a day, and was working with the Spinners within a year. He

then joined drummer Hamilton Bohannon's band at Detroit's Twenty Grand club, backing such Motown acts as Gladys Knight and the Pips, the Temptations, and Stevie Wonder. Parker played on only one Motown session—a Marvin Gaye date—before being hired at age 15 as the house guitarist for Holland, Dozier, and Holland's new Invictus and Hot Wax labels, with which he remained for three years.

A call from Wonder, who was opening the Rolling Stones' 1972 tour, took Parker on the road, and he contributed to Wonder's *Talking Book* and *Innervisions* albums. The guitarist moved to Los Angeles the following year, but having played on so many hits in Detroit seemed to count for nothing in the new environment. Work was scarce at first, until Parker bluffed his way into a session by arranger Gene Page. That led to an association with Barry White and eventually so many sessions that Parker could barely fit sleep into his schedule.

Raydio started as a studio concept. When "Jack and Jill" broke, Parker formed a band—keyboardists Arnell Carmichael and Vincent Bonham, second guitarist Charles Fearing, and bassist Jerry Knight—to become Raydio. Knight left in 1978 to pursue a solo career and was replaced by Carmichael's younger brother Darren. A permanent drummer, Larry Tolbert, was also hired. By 1981's *A Woman Needs Love*, the group's fourth and final album, membership was down to Parker, Tolbert, and Arnell Carmichael.

A Woman Needs Love marked a change in direction for Raydio, as well as signaled the group's demise. Parker, unhappy with the sound of his own voice, had previously left the singing to the others, especially lead vocalist Carmichael. For the album's title track, however, his cohorts talked him into featuring his own thin yet warm tenor pipes, and the single became an R&B chart-topper. Parker emerged as a solo artist with the next album, 1982's *The Other Woman*, its title song going to number two R&B.

He scored his biggest record with the silly, hastily written theme song from the 1984 motion picture comedy *Ghostbusters*. It was penned in such a hurry that Huey Lewis was able to win an out-of-court settlement to a suit charging that Parker had plagiarized "I Want a New Drug," the rock singer's hit of earlier that year. Parker never fully regained his momentum. He scored two final top 10 R&B entries—the number five "I Don't Think That Man Should Sleep Alone" and the number 10 "Over You" (a duet with Natalie Cole)—after moving to Geffen Records in

TOP ALBUM

THE OTHER WOMAN (Arista, '82, *11*)

Additional Top 40 Albums: 3

TOP SONGS

JACK AND JILL (Raydio, Arista, '77, *5 R&B, 8 Pop*)
YOU CAN'T CHANGE THAT (Raydio, Arista, '79, *3 R&B, 9 Pop*)
TWO PLACES AT THE SAME TIME (Ray Parker, Jr., and Raydio, Arista, '80, *6 R&B, 30 Pop*)
A WOMAN NEEDS LOVE (JUST LIKE YOU DO) (Ray Parker, Jr., and Raydio, Arista, '81, *1 R&B, 4 Pop*)
THE OTHER WOMAN (Arista, '82, *2 R&B, 4 Pop*)
LET ME GO (Arista, '82, *3 R&B, 38 Pop*)
BAD BOY (Arista, '82, *6 R&B, 35 Pop*)
GHOSTBUSTERS (Arista, '84, *1 R&B, 1 Pop*)
I DON'T THINK THAT MAN SHOULD SLEEP ALONE (Geffen, '87, *5 R&B*)

Additional Top 40 R&B Songs: 9

1987. Neither single crossed to the pop top 40. He had less luck at MCA in 1991 and back at Arista in 1993.

Parker also produced records for a number of other artists at his Ameraycan Studios in North Hollywood, his greatest successes being Cheryl Lynn's number five R&B "Shake It Up Tonight" in 1981 and New Edition's Number One R&B "Mr. Telephone Man" three years later.

PEACHES AND HERB

All five main characters in the saga of Peaches and Herb, "the Sweethearts of Soul," hailed from the nation's capitol. Singer Herb Fame (b. Herb Feemster, 1942) was working in a Washington record shop in 1966 when D.C.-born producer Van McCoy came in to promote a single by the Sweet Things, a local female vocal trio he'd cut for Columbia's Date label. Fame auditioned for McCoy and was signed to Date. At the recording session, McCoy and partner David Kapralik came up with the idea of pairing Fame with the Sweet Things' lead, Francine Barker (b. Francine Hurd, 1947), who'd been dubbed Peaches as a child due to her pleasant disposition. The duo of Peaches and Herb was thus born and became one of the hottest dates in pop music, scoring 10 top 40 R&B hits between 1966 and '69. At the time of Fame and McCoy's meeting, future hitmaking songwriter-producer Freddie Perren was working at another record store around the corner, but he didn't become involved until 13 years later, when he rejuvenated the career of Peaches and Herb, by then comprising Fame and a new Peaches, the D.C.-born Linda Green.

Both Fame and Barker grew up singing in church. He made his secular debut at age 11, winning a talent contest at Washington's Carver Theater with a rendition of Ivory Joe Hunter's "I Almost Lost My Mind." Later influences included Clyde McPhatter and Little Anthony Gourdine. Barker sang in high school with a group called the Keystones before organizing the Darlettes, who became the Sweet Things after signing with Date.

Peaches and Herb's first single, a McCoy arrangement of the Harold Arlen–Ted Koehler chestnut "Let's Fall in Love," rose to number 11 on the *Billboard* R&B chart and to number 21 pop, setting a romantic, soft-soul course for the duo, as well as greatly influencing the direction Marvin Gaye and Tammi Terrell would soon take at Motown. Fame

Peaches and Herb

and Barker had their biggest hit in 1967 with the Chuck Willis ballad "Close Your Eyes," originally a number five R&B charter in 1955 for the Five Keys. The Peaches and Herb rendition went to number four R&B and number eight pop and was followed by successful covers of Ed Townsend's "For Your Love" and Mickey and Sylvia's "Love Is Strange." Before 1967 was out, however, Barker had retired from making public appearances, although she continued to sing on the duo's records, including the Kenny Gamble and Leon Huff composition and production "United" (first recorded by the Intruders) and the country song "When He Touches Me (Nothing Else Matters)." For live engagements, she was replaced by Marlene Mack.

Fame became a cop on the D.C. force in 1970, but he made a few more recordings with Peaches and Herb, including a 1971 version of Simon and Garfunkel's "The Sound of Silence" for Columbia, before throwing in the towel. "At the time I left the business in 1972, I felt it would be for good," he said five years later, "but as time went on I found that every time I went to a concert or show, I wanted to be on the stage." McCoy got back in touch with Fame in 1975 to discuss reviving the act. A new Peaches had to be recruited.

Linda Green, who'd studied classical piano as a child, lived only a few blocks from Fame, but he found her at a club in Virginia Beach, singing with Bill Deal and the Rondells. McCoy cut an album by the new duo for Atlantic that wasn't released. One was issued in 1977 on MCA, but it flopped. Instead of finding new fame and fortune, Fame and Green made their living on the Holiday Inn circuit.

Enter Freddie Perren, who, since his record-selling days in D.C., had gone on to create hit records for such artists as the Jackson 5, the Sylvers, Tavares, and Yvonne Elliman. He signed the pair to his Grand Slam Productions in Studio City, California, and proceeded to record the album *2 Hot!*. Released in 1978 on Polydor, the Peaches and Herb disc went platinum on the strength of two smash singles. The number four R&B, number five pop "Shake Your Groove Thing" found the pair riding the disco wave, while "Reunited," a Perren–Dino Fekkaris ballad inspired by the old Peaches and Herb hit "United," took them back to the old love mold and to the top of both the R&B and pop charts.

In 1979, Peaches and Herb became the first African-American artists to appear in the People's Republic of China, performing on the steps of the Sacred Temple of Heaven as part of a Bob Hope show. That year's *Twice the Fire*, their second Polydor album, went gold but spawned no major hit singles. Two more Perren-produced Polydor albums were less successful, after which Peaches and Herb returned to Columbia for their final chart entry, 1983's number 35 R&B "Remember."

TOP ALBUMS

LET'S FALL IN LOVE (Date, '67, 30)
2 HOT! (Polydor, '79, 2)

Additional Top 40 Albums: 1

TOP SONGS

LET'S FALL IN LOVE (Date, '66, 11 R&B, 21 Pop)
CLOSE YOUR EYES (Date, '67, 4 R&B, 8 Pop)
FOR YOUR LOVE (Date, '67, 10 R&B, 20 Pop)
LOVE IS STRANGE (Date, '67, 16 R&B, 13 Pop)
UNITED (Date, '68, 11 R&B)
WHEN HE TOUCHES ME (NOTHING ELSE MATTERS)
    (Date, '69, 10 R&B)
SHAKE YOUR GROOVE THING (Polydor, '78, 4 R&B,
    5 Pop)
REUNITED (Polydor, '79, 1 R&B, 1 Pop)

Additional Top 40 Songs: 10

ANN PEEBLES

Ann Peebles (b. Apr. 27, 1947, St. Louis), who waxed a string of intense, blues-bitten southern soul classics with Memphis producer Willie Mitchell during the early 1970s, is a tiny woman. "I'm only 99 pounds, 5'3"," she stated in a 1974 interview with Tony Cummings of *Black Music* magazine. "I suppose that's why I project a lot. I'm so small I've gotta wail loud to make up for it."

Mitchell may have had bigger hits with Al Green, but Peebles was his leading lady at Hi Records, where her brittle, emotion-searing alto tones served as an ideal foil for the chugging backbeats of his crack rhythm section and the punching riffs of the Memphis Horns. "She has always been one of the subtlest of soul singers, bending and twisting notes only when it makes sense in the context of the song and using crowd-pleasing octave jumps and gospel melisma with restraint," critic Robert Palmer commented in a 1992 *Rolling Stone* review. "If she alters a song, chances are she'll alter the melody line, like a superior jazz singer, or convey shifts in meaning with changes in vocal texture."

One of the 11 children of Perry and Eula Peebles, Ann learned her craft at the First Baptist Church in Kinloch, Missouri, a small town outside St. Louis. Her dad directed the chorus, known as the Peebles Choir, which had been part of the family for four generations. Mahalia Jackson, who the choir accompanied on a few occasions, was a major inspiration. Later influences included Aretha Franklin and Otis Redding.

Peebles began performing at clubs in East St. Louis, Illinois, after graduating Kinloch High School. In 1968, while visiting Memphis, she and a brother stopped at the Rainbow Club, where veteran trumpeter Gene "Bowlegs" Miller was appearing with his band. She asked to sit in and was told to come back the next night. Peebles returned with a rendition of the Jimmy Hughes song "Steal Away." Another trumpet player, Willie Mitchell, was in the audience and invited her to record for Hi. He had vocalist Don Bryant help her work up some tunes, and the partnership blossomed, with Bryant and Peebles marrying in 1973.

Peebles' debut release, the Oliver Sain–penned ballad "Walk Away," entered the *Billboard* R&B chart in April 1969 (predating Al Green's first Hi label chart single by 10 months) and rose to number 22. She scored stronger the next year, at number seven R&B, with a gripping mid-tempo rearrangement of

Ann Peebles

the blues tune "Part Time Love," a Number One R&B hit for Little Johnny Taylor in 1963. Peebles and Mitchell continued mining the soul-blues vein with the moderate R&B hits "I Pity the Fool" (the Bobby Bland classic), "Slipped, Tripped and Fell in Love" (also recorded by Clarence Carter), "Breaking Up Somebody's Home" (covered by Albert King), "Somebody's on Your Case," and "I'm Gonna Tear Your Playhouse Down." While none penetrated the pop top 40, such rock and pop artists as Ringo Starr, Bonnie Raitt, Bette Midler, and Humble Pie's Steve Marriott had become Peebles fans.

Her greatest hit, 1973's number six R&B, number 38 pop "I Can't Stand the Rain," written by the singer with Bryant and disc jockey Bernard Miller and featuring electric bongos to simulate the sound of raindrops, was not a major crossover success. It did, however, expand her cult of notable admirers. John Lennon stated that it was the "best record since

TOP ALBUMS

PART TIME LOVE (Hi, '70)
I CAN'T STAND THE RAIN (Hi, '73)

TOP SONGS

WALK AWAY (Hi, '69, 22 *R&B*)
PART TIME LOVE (Hi, '70, 7 *R&B*)
I PITY THE FOOL (Hi, '71, 18 *R&B*)
BREAKING UP SOMEBODY'S HOME (Hi, '72, 13 *R&B*)
SOMEBODY'S ON YOUR CASE (Hi, '72, 32 *R&B*)
I'M GONNA TEAR YOUR PLAYHOUSE DOWN (Hi, '73, 31 *R&B*)
I CAN'T STAND THE RAIN (Hi, '73, 6 *R&B*, 38 *Pop*)
(YOU KEEP ME) HANGIN' ON (Hi, '74, 37 *R&B*)

[the O'Jays'] 'Love Train,'" while Freda Payne called Peebles "the most haunting singer on the music scene today." The tune was quickly covered by Humble Pie and later by Graham Central Station, Eruption, Tina Turner, and Tease.

The follow-up, a version of the country song "(You Keep Me) Hangin' On" that had been given an earlier soul treatment by Joe Simon, placed only as high as number 37 R&B. Peebles never again cracked the R&B top 40, though she kept recording for Hi through 1981. She then retired from the business to raise her son and run a day-care center in Memphis, finally returning in 1989 to cut the album *Call Me* for Mitchell's new Wayco label. It received little notice. A 1992 album for Bullseye Blues, *Full Time Love,* produced by Ron Levy and sporting a batch of new Peebles-Bryant compositions and three-fourths of the old Hi rhythm section, met with critical acclaim and led to renewed touring.

TEDDY PENDERGRASS
....

By 1972, the Blue Notes, a Philadelphia doo-wop-group-turned-slick-cabaret-act, had been making records for 16 years with limited success. Of their dozen or so singles, only two—1960's number 19 R&B "My Hero" on the Val-ue label and 1965's number 38 R&B "Get Out" on Landa—had charted, but that didn't seem to bother leader Harold Melvin. Nightclubs, not records, were the Blue Notes' bread and butter.

"My objective was to build an act that would keep me in show business," he recalled in a 1977 interview with Frederick Douglas Murphy of *Black Stars* magazine. "I didn't concentrate on making hit records. I just wanted to have enough money to take care of my family, buy some clothes and have some extra change. I enjoyed what I was doing, and my goal was to clear $500 a week."

Melvin and the Blue Notes' fortunes changed radically in 1972 when they signed with Kenny Gamble and Leon Huff's Philadelphia International Records and began featuring the raspy, often growling baritone voice of Theodore Pendergrass (b. Mar. 26, 1950, Philadelphia). He had joined the group in the mid-1960s as a drummer but took over the lead vocal role in 1970 upon the departure of longtime

member John Atkins. Pendergrass had sung gospel music since age three and had become an ordained minister at 10. He brought to the Blue Notes an intense vocal style strongly influenced by that of Marvin Junior of the Dells, as well as a rhythmic inventiveness drawn from his experience as a percussionist.

The 1972 edition of the Blue Notes comprised Melvin, Pendergrass, Lawrence Brown, Bernard Wilson, and Lloyd Parks (who was soon replaced by Jerry Cummings). This group's first two hits—the number seven R&B Bobby Martin–arranged "I Miss You" and the Number One R&B, number three pop Thom Bell–arranged "If You Don't Know Me by Now"—had been written by Gamble and Huff for the Dells. Indeed, the interplay between Pendergrass's hoarse baritone and Parks's floating falsetto on the former song recalled that of Marvin Junior and Johnny Carter in the famous Chicago group. Of the latter song, Tony Cummings noted in his book *The Sound of Philadelphia,* "By giving [Pendergrass] full scope to roar and moan and sob across the group's ethereal harmonies and bursts of falsetto, [Gamble, Huff, and Bell] had the perfect vocal sound over which to introduce massive dramatic orchestrations, with violins, harps, French horns and crashing timpani."

Gamble and Huff, working with arrangers Martin and Norman Harris, gave the Pendergrass-led Blues Notes seven additional top 10 R&B hits— "The Love I Lost," "Satisfaction Guaranteed (Or Take Your Love Back)," "Where Are All My Friends," "Bad Luck," "Hope That We Can Be Together Soon" (a Pendergrass duet with Melvin discovery Sharon Paige), "Wake Up Everybody," and "Tell the World How I Feel About 'Cha Baby"— through 1976, when Pendergrass, Brown, and Wilson broke away and joined with former member Parks to form a rival set of Blue Notes. This group lasted only a few months, after which Pendergrass went solo and the others cut an unsuccessful album for Glades before disappearing. Melvin formed a new set of Blue Notes with Cummings, Dwight Johnson, Bill Spratley, and Pendergrass clone David Ebo, which scored one last top 10 R&B charter with 1977's number six "Reaching for the World." Later recordings by Melvin's Blue Notes for Source, ABC, and Philly World were less successful.

Pendergrass, nicknamed "Teddy Bear," rejoined Philadelphia International in 1977 and became the soul sex symbol of the late 1970s and early '80s with the top 10 R&B solo hits "I Don't Love You Anymore," "Close the Door," "Turn Off the Lights," "Can't We Try," "Love T.K.O.," "Two Hearts" (a duet with Stephanie Mills), "I Can't Live Without Your Love," and "You're My Latest, My Greatest Inspiration." His impassioned readings of such blatantly sensual songs as "Close the Door" and "Turn Off the Lights" were matched by a macho stage act that found him rolling his hips and posturing like a body builder.

On March 18, 1982, his car smashed into a highway divider near his home in Philadelphia, leaving him paralyzed from the neck down. Singing from a wheelchair, Pendergrass reemerged two years later at Elektra-Asylum Records. He has remained with the company ever since, scoring the top 10 R&B hits "Hold Me" (a 1984 duet with a then-little-known Whitney Houston), "Love 4/2," "Joy," "2 A.M.," and "It Should've Been You."

Melvin continues to lead the Blue Notes. As of 1994, they consisted of himself, Johnson, Spratley, Rufus Thorne, and lead singer Gilbert Samuels.

TOP ALBUMS

WAKE UP EVERYBODY (Harold Melvin and the Blue Notes, Philadelphia International, '75, 9)

TEDDY (Philadelphia International, '79, 5)

Additional Top 40 Albums: 7

TOP SONGS

Harold Melvin and the Blue Notes:

IF YOU DON'T KNOW ME BY NOW (Philadelphia International, '72, 1 R&B, 3 Pop)

THE LOVE I LOST (PART 1) (Philadelphia International, '73, 1 R&B, 7 Pop)

HOPE THAT WE CAN BE TOGETHER SOON (Sharon Paige and Harold Melvin and the Blue Notes, Philadelphia International, '75, 1 R&B)

WAKE UP EVERYBODY (PART 1) (Philadelphia International, '75, 1 R&B, 12 Pop)

Teddy Pendergrass:

CLOSE THE DOOR (Philadelphia International, '78, 1 R&B, 25 Pop)

LOVE T.K.O. (Philadelphia International, '80, 2 R&B)

JOY (Asylum, '88, 1 R&B)

IT SHOULD'VE BEEN YOU (Elektra, '91, 1 R&B)

Additional Top 40 R&B Songs: 29

ESTHER PHILLIPS

When Little Esther (b. Esther Mae Jones, Dec. 23, 1935, Galveston, Texas) made her Apollo Theater debut in 1950 with the Johnny Otis band on the strength of "Double Crossing Blues," a comic duet with bass singer Bobby Nunn of the Robins that was inspired by a vaudeville routine, she neither looked nor sounded her age. Although short, she was quite bosomy for her 14 years, and her scratchy, melisma-dripping alto voice was also mature, a cross between those of Little Miss Cornshucks and Esther's main idol, Dinah Washington.

For the occasion, however, Otis dressed his young singing star in bobby socks, her hair in ribbons. Washington, who was in attendance, protested. The blues queen confronted the bandleader backstage, telling him, "You take them bobby socks off that girl and little ribbons off them plaits...Put some curls in her hair and some stockings on her." Washington then took Esther to a dressing room, curled her hair, and sent someone out to purchase hose.

Esther Phillips, as she was known later in her career, grew up fast and died relatively young, at age 48, on August 7, 1984, from cirrhosis of the liver and bacterial endocarditis. But between 1949 and 1984, with several breaks due to recurring addiction to heroin, she recorded a remarkable body of music, from straight blues and jumpin' R&B to country, soul, jazz, and disco material, delivered with a wide vibrato and marked by clipped phrases, staccato bursts, breathy hums, gutteral inflections, and a unique sense of timing.

Her parents, Arthur Jones and Lucille Washington, divorced when Esther was young (they remarried years later), and she divided her time between her dad's home in Houston and her mom's in the Watts district of Los Angeles. Having sung in church as a child, she entered a talent contest at the Largo Theater in Los Angeles when she was 13. Performing the Dinah Washington hit "Baby, Get Lost" with Big Jay McNeely's band, she caught the ears of Johnny Otis, who was in the audience. He invited her to join him at the Barrelhouse Club and soon produced her first two singles, "I Gotta Guy" and "Mean Ole Gal," for the Modern label.

Esther hadn't yet turned 14 when she cut "Double Crossing Blues" for Savoy. The record shot to the top of the *Billboard* R&B chart in early 1950 and remained in that position for nine weeks. Otis then hit the road with his California Rhythm and Blues Caravan featuring Esther and Mel Walker, a vocalist whom she was paired with on such subsequent hits as "Mistrustin' Blues," "Deceivin' Blues," "Wedding Blues," "Faraway Blues," and "Ring-A-Ding-Doo" after the Robins (who'd sung on "Double Crossing Blues") decided to remain in L.A. She moved to producer Ralph Bass's new Federal label in 1951 but continued recording with the Otis band (its leadership credited to Earle Warren or Preston Love for contractual reasons) as well as with Little Willie Littlefield and the Dominoes. Esther left Otis and Federal in 1954 and worked for a period with Slide Hampton's band, but she had little luck with recordings for Decca, Savoy, and Warwick through the late 1950s.

By 1962, Esther was back in Houston, living with her father and appearing at local clubs. At one, she shared the bill with the Bobby Dolye Trio, a group that included then-unknown singer Kenny Rogers. He recommended her to his brother, producer Lelan Rogers, who formed the Lenox label and recorded her doing a soul version of the 1954 Ray Price country hit "Release Me." Taking the name "Phillips" from a Phillips 66 gasoline sign, Esther found herself with a Number One R&B, number eight pop hit, her first chart record in over a decade. Lenox soon folded, and her contract was acquired by Atlantic, for whom she did a 1965 treatment of the Beatles' "And I Love Her" (retitled "And I Love Him") that rose to

number 11 R&B and caused the Fab Four to invite her to join them on the BBC-TV program "Ready Steady Go."

Esther spent the years 1967–69 in the Synanon drug rehabilitation program in California. She then reemerged on Roulette Records with a brilliant though little-noticed rendition of King Pleasure's "Moody's Mood for Love" before rejoining Atlantic in 1970 and cutting the live jazz album *Burnin'*. She signed with Creed Taylor's Kudu label two years later and recorded *From a Whisper to a Scream*, an album containing the moving Gil Scott-Heron anti-drug ode "Home Is Where the Hatred Is." The album garnered a Grammy nomination, but when Aretha Franklin won instead, the soul queen declared, "She deserves it," and handed the trophy to Esther. The singer's third comeback was capped by 1975's number 10 R&B, number 20 pop disco treatment of "What a Diff'rence a Day Makes," the old Dinah Washington hit. Later recordings for Mercury, Winning, and Muse were less successful.

WILSON PICKETT

"God, you sure are wicked," a miniskirted secretary screamed at soul singer Wilson Pickett (b. Mar. 18, 1941, Prattville, Alabama) after he pinched her thigh during a 1966 visit to the New York headquarters of Atlantic Records.

Company vice president Jerry Wexler ran out of his office, exclaiming, "That's his next album—'The Wicked Pickett'!" The name stuck, befitting a vocalist whose fierce, leather-lunged approach matched an often-combustible offstage personality that some found downright evil.

Pickett, who scored 17 top 10 R&B hits during his 1964–72 association with Atlantic, began picking cotton when he was four to help support his mother and her 11 other children. He worked in the field three days a week and attended school only two. Moving to Detroit at age 16 to join his father, an auto worker, Pickett found himself so far behind in his education that he dropped out of school in the 10th grade.

Back in Alabama, he'd sung gospel with a quartet called the Songs of Zion. In Detroit, he joined the Violinaires and made one record with them in 1957 for the Gotham label, although he didn't solo. He

---

TOP ALBUM

WHAT A DIFF'RENCE A DAY MAKES (Kudu, '75, 32)

TOP SONGS

Little Esther with the Johnny Otis Orchestra:
DOUBLE CROSSING BLUES (Savoy, '50, 1 R&B)
MISTRUSTIN' BLUES (Savoy, '50, 1 R&B)
CUPID'S BOOGIE (Savoy, '50, 1 R&B)
DECEIVIN' BLUES (Savoy, '50, 4 R&B)
WEDDING BOOGIE (Savoy, '50, 6 R&B)
FARAWAY BLUES (Savoy, '50, 6 R&B)

Esther Phillips:
RING-A-DING-DOO (Little Esther, Federal, '52, 8 R&B)
RELEASE ME (Lenox, '62, 1 R&B, 8 Pop)
WHAT A DIFF'RENCE A DAY MAKES (Kudu, '75, 10 R&B, 20 Pop)

Additional Top 40 R&B Songs: 8

did lead, however, on "Call Him Up" b/w "Christ's Blood," an obscure 1963 Peacock release by the Spiritual Five.

Early influences on Pickett's intense vocal style and flamboyant stage manner were Archie Brownlee of the Five Blind Boys of Mississippi, Clarence Fountain of the Five Blind Boys of Alabama, and especially Julius Cheeks of the Sensational Nightingales. "I learned from him how to capture the house and hold it," Pickett said of Cheeks. "When you get the audience at a point, you gotta take 'em on over."

By the time of Pickett's session with the Spiritual Five, he'd already been doubling on the secular side as a member of the Falcons, a gospel-styled R&B group from Detroit that also included Eddie Floyd and Mack Rice. Pickett made his debut as the Falcons' lead on the 1960 United Artists single "Pow! You're in Love." While it flopped, the group's 1962 Atlantic-distributed Lupine recording of "I Found a Love," written by and featuring Pickett, became a number six R&B hit. His first solo single, "Let Me Be Your Boy," appeared later in 1962 on the Correc-Tone label. He signed the following year with Lloyd Price's Double L label in New York, only to find his first release for the company, "If You Need Me" (penned by Pickett and producer Robert Bateman) covered by Atlantic artist Solomon Burke. Burke's version shot to number two

Wilson Pickett

TOP ALBUM

THE EXCITING WILSON PICKETT (Atlantic, '66, 21)

Additional Top 40 Albums: 1

TOP SONGS

IN THE MIDNIGHT HOUR (Atlantic, '65, *1 R&B, 21 Pop*)

634-5789 (SOULSVILLE, U.S.A.) (Atlantic, '66, *1 R&B, 13 Pop*)

LAND OF 1,000 DANCES (Atlantic, '66, *1 R&B, 6 Pop*)

FUNKY BROADWAY (Atlantic, '67, *1 R&B, 8 Pop*)

SUGAR SUGAR (Atlantic, '70, *4 R&B, 25 Pop*)

ENGINE NUMBER 9 (Atlantic, '70, *3 R&B, 14 Pop*)

DON'T LET THE GREEN GRASS FOOL YOU (Atlantic, '71, *2 R&B, 17 Pop*)

DON'T KNOCK MY LOVE—PT. 1 (Atlantic, '71, *1 R&B, 13 Pop*)

FIRE AND WATER (Atlantic, '72, *2 R&B, 24 Pop*)

Additional Top 40 R&B Songs: 30

on the R&B chart, while Pickett's stalled at number 30. His follow-up, "It's Too Late," fared better, reaching number seven R&B.

Atlantic purchased the vocalist's contract from Double L in 1964, but his first two New York–made singles for the firm bombed. Impressed by Otis Redding's recordings for Stax-Volt, Pickett suggested to Wexler that he be given the Memphis treatment. "In the Midnight Hour," a composition by Pickett and guitarist Steve Cropper from the singer's initial Memphis session, became the first of his five R&B chart-toppers. Other fruits of the Stax connection were "Don't Fight It," "634-5789 (Soulsville, U.S.A)" (written by Cropper and Eddie Floyd), and "Ninety-Nine and a Half Won't Do."

Pickett turned up next at Rick Hall's Fame studio in Muscle Shoals, Alabama, where he recorded the hits "Land of 1,000 Dances" (originally recorded by Chris Kenner), "Mustang Sally" (a cover of a tune first recorded by its composer, Mack Rice), "Everybody Needs Somebody to Love" (originally done by Solomon Burke), a new version of "I Found a Love," and a reworking of Dyke and the Blazers' "Funky Broadway." Returning to Memphis in 1967 to work at Chips Moman's studio, Pickett scored with "I'm in Love" and "I'm a Midnight Mover," both written by Bobby Womack, as well as with a cover of Rodger Collins's "She's Lookin' Good." Back at Fame, the vocalist cut an incendiary version of the Beatles' "Hey Jude," which featured the searing guitar of Duane Allman, before going to Miami in 1970 to transform the Archies' bubblegum ditty "Sugar Sugar" into a believable burst of soul.

A 1970–71 association with Philadelphia producers Kenny Gamble and Leon Huff resulted in two top 10 R&B hits—"Engine Number 9" and "Don't Let the Green Grass Fool You"—after which Pickett went back to Muscle Shoals to cut "Don't Knock My Love," "Call My Name, I'll Be There," and his last top 10 R&B charter, "Fire and Water." He signed a lucrative contract with RCA Victor in 1973, but the new deal proved disappointing, with only three singles, all from that year—"Mr. Magic Man," "Take a Closer Look at the Woman You're With," and "Soft Soul Boogie Woogie"—managing to crack the R&B top 20. Later sides for his own T.K.-distributed Wicked Records (1975–76), the Atlantic-distributed Big Tree label (1978), EMI America (1979–80), and Motown (1987) were even less successful.

THE PLATTERS

Samuel "Buck" Ram was a successful pop tunesmith during the 1940s, having co-written such hits as Bing Crosby's "I'll Be Home for Christmas" and the Three Suns' "Twilight Time." He was also a shrewd businessman, who, by the the early 1950s, had his finger on the pulse of the nascent Los Angeles rhythm and blues scene as manager of such artists as Linda Hayes, the Flairs, Shirley Gunter and the Queens, the Penguins, and the Platters. Ram had gotten the Platters a deal with Federal Records in 1953, but none of their sides attracted notice beyond southern California. Then, in early 1955, the Penguins had a Number One R&B, number eight pop smash with "Earth Angel" on the tiny DooTone label. Mercury Records wanted the Penguins bad, and Ram offered their services—but on the condition that the Chicago company also take the Platters. Mercury agreed reluctantly, only to

watch the Penguins sink into obscurity, while the Platters became the biggest vocal group of the 1950s.

The Platters evolved from a group originally consisting of Cornell Gunter, Joe Jefferson, Herbert Reed, and brothers Alex and Gaynel Hodge. Gunter soon left to join the Flairs and Jefferson to become a member of the Turks. By 1953, the Platters—a name Reed had come up with—comprised Reed, Alex Hodge, David Lynch, and Tony Williams (b. Apr. 15, 1928, Elizabeth, New Jersey), a singer who'd come to Los Angeles to join his sister Linda Hayes following the success of her number two R&B 1953 recording of "Yes I Know (What You're Putting Down)" on the Recorded in Hollywood label. Through Hayes's connection to Ram, the Platters signed with his management firm and began recording for Federal.

The quartet's early sides for the Cincinnati-based label were crude, so in 1954 Ram recruited Zola Taylor from Shirley Gunter's Queens to smooth out the harmonies. Hodge was soon replaced by Paul Robi, whose skills as an arranger added further polish. The lineup of Williams (lead), Taylor (alto), Lynch (second tenor), Robi (baritone), and Reed (bass) would take the Platters to international stardom.

The group's first Mercury recordings were made in Los Angeles in April 1955 at the end of a Penguins session produced by Bob Shad. Four songs were cut in three hours, the last being "Only You (And You Alone)," a Ram composition that the Platters had recorded earlier for Federal. Whereas the Federal performance of the romantic ballad was so awful that it wasn't released until after the group had attained fame, the Mercury version was decidedly professional and found Williams's high, hiccuping tenor soaring with new confidence. Although slow in taking off, "Only You" eventually rose to Number One R&B and remained on that chart for 30 weeks. It also crossed to number five on the pop chart, outdistancing a white cover version by the Hilltoppers, which peaked at number eight.

After "Only You," no other white group dared to cover a Platters tune. The quintet had a pop appeal that exceeded that of any other black harmony group of the era. Their next single, "The Great Pretender" (another number credited to Ram), topped both the R&B and pop charts, a feat that would be repeated in 1956 by "My Prayer" (written by Jimmy Kennedy and Georges Boulanger and first recorded in 1939 by the Ink Spots) and in 1958 with "Twilight Time" (a vocal version of Ram's old instrumental hit for the Three Suns). Under Ram's supervision, the productions became increasingly lavish, with the use of sweeping strings on "Twilight Time" and a haunting 1958 reworking of Jerome Kern and Otto Harback's "Smoke Gets in Your Eyes" serving to heighten the drama of Williams's remarkable octave-leaping leads.

The Platters' six-year run on the top 10 ended with 1960's number 15 R&B, number eight pop "Harbor Lights" (another Jimmy Kennedy tune). Williams, who'd recorded several solo sessions for Mercury, left the group that year to sign with Reprise, but he had little luck on his own. He was replaced by Charles "Sonny" Turner, but Mercury had so little faith in the new singer that it kept issuing previously recorded sides featuring Williams until finally letting Turner lead on "It's Magic," a minor 1962 hit.

In 1966, the Platters, consisting of Turner, Reed, Sandra Dawn, and former Flamingo Nate Nelson, reemerged on the Musicor label with a more contemporary soul sound under the direction of producer Luther Dixon. Three hits resulted: "I Love You 1000 Times" (number six R&B, number 31 pop), "With This Ring" (number 12 R&B, number 14 pop), and "Washed Ashore (On a Lonely Island in the Sea)" (number 29 R&B).

TOP ALBUMS

THE PLATTERS (Mercury, '56, 7)

ENCORE OF GOLDEN HITS (Mercury, '60, 6)

Additional Top 40 Albums: 3

TOP SONGS

ONLY YOU (AND YOU ALONE) (Mercury, '55, *1 R&B, 5 Pop*)

THE GREAT PRETENDER (Mercury, '55, *1 R&B, 1 Pop*)

(YOU'VE GOT) THE MAGIC TOUCH (Mercury, '56, *4 R&B, 4 Pop*)

MY PRAYER (Mercury, '56, *1 R&B, 1 Pop*)

HE'S MINE (Mercury, '57, *5 R&B, 16 Pop*)

TWILIGHT TIME (Mercury, '58, *1 R&B, 1 Pop*)

SMOKE GETS IN YOUR EYES (Mercury, '58, *3 R&B, 1 Pop*)

I LOVE YOU 1000 TIMES (Musicor, '66, *6 R&B, 31 Pop*)

Additional Top 40 R&B Songs: 13

Various sets of Platters, some containing one or more former members, worked the oldies circuit after the group's heyday. Ram, who owned the name, fought them all in court and even formed a new group billed as "the Buck Ram Platters." Lynch died in 1981, Robi in 1989, Ram in 1991, and Williams in 1992. Reed and Taylor continue to perform.

THE POINTER SISTERS

Early in 1973, a week after the release of the Pointer Sisters' eponymous David Rubinson–produced debut album, Blue Thumb took out a full-page ad in *Billboard*. It read: "Congratulations to the Pointer Sisters on their first week in show business." The four Oakland-born daughters of Church of God ministers Elton and Sarah Elizabeth Pointer—Ruth (b. 1946), Anita (b. 1948), Bonnie (b. 1950), and June (b. 1954)—were destined for stardom. They knew it, and the smart money knew it. It would be only a matter of time. "I know we can make it if we try," they sang prophetically on the Allen Toussaint song "Yes We Can Can," a single from the album that became a top 20 R&B and pop hit.

It took more than a decade of ups and downs, experimenting with soul, rock, bebop, blues, country, and pop nostalgia, before the Pointers finally hit platinum. In 1984, the sisters—minus Bonnie, who left in 1977 to pursue a semi-successful solo career at Motown—sold three million copies of the Richard Perry–produced techno-pop album *Break Out* on Planet Records. The disc spawned four top 10 pop hits—the number five "Automatic," the number three "Jump (For My Love)," the number nine "I'm So Excited," and the number six "Neutron Dance" —with the first two both placing at number three on the R&B charts.

The sisters grew up singing in church and were briefly members of Edwin Hawkins's pioneering progressive gospel Northern California State Youth Choir. In 1969, the two youngest—Bonnie and June—became the first two to break with their strict religious upbringing and perform in San Francisco clubs, billing themselves as the Pointers, a Pair. Anita soon joined them, and they began doing background vocals for Rubinson on sessions by such artists as Elvin Bishop, Cold Blood, and Tower of Power.

The Pointer Sisters

The producer introduced the Pointers to jazz, and together they worked up arrangements of Lambert, Hendricks, and Ross jazz tunes as well as composed original material in a similar style. But before Rubinson could record the sisters, Jerry Wexler signed them to Atlantic and sent them to Malaco Studios in Jackson, Mississippi, to work with veteran New Orleans producer-arranger Wardell Quezergue. Two singles—"Don't Try to Take the Fifth" and "Destination No More Heartaches"—were released in 1971 and '72, but neither managed to repeat the magic Quezergue had worked earlier with King Floyd ("Groove Me") and Jean Knight ("Mr. Big Stuff").

Adding eldest sister Ruth to the lineup, the Pointers returned to Rubinson and signed with Blue Thumb. They created a sensation, not only with their wildly eclectic repertoire but also with their campy secondhand-store garb. "They are dressed in funky mid-calf florals, sporting paper camellias and gift-package ribbons in their marcelled hair, clunky Deco beads, spoon rings and dangling earrings (the bonus kind you get from a gum machine), platform shoes and seamed opaque stockings," Karin Winner observed in *Women's Wear Daily.*

While the Pointers hit the top of the R&B chart with 1975's funky "How Long (Betcha' Got a Chick on the Side)," written by the four sisters with Rubinson, they'd also made a splash in country music a year earlier with the Anita and Bonnie composition "Fairytale," which landed them a spot on the Grand Ole Opry and a Grammy for Best Country Vocal Performance by a Duo or Group. June dropped out in 1975 due to a nervous breakdown, but she returned to replace Bonnie by the time they joined Richard Perry's Planet label in late 1978.

Under Perry's guidance, the trio developed a new style that, while still rooted in the gospel tradition, imaginatively combined a 1960s girl-group sound with a contemporary pop-rock snap. Besides the four singles from *Break Out,* the Pointers' greatest hits during their seven-year association with Planet were 1979's number 14 R&B, number two pop version of Bruce Springsteen's "Fire" (famous for its pregnant mid-song pause); 1980's number 10 R&B, number three pop "He's So Shy"; and 1981's number seven R&B, number two pop "Slow Hand" (later a Number One country hit for Conway Twitty).

After Planet folded, the sisters continued working with Perry at RCA, where they scored in 1985 with the number six R&B, number 11 pop "Dare Me" from the million-selling album *Contact.* Subsequent recordings for RCA (through 1988), Motown (1990–91), and SBK/ERG(1993) were less successful. While still members of the group, June made solo albums for Planet in 1983 and Columbia in 1989, and Anita did one for RCA in 1987.

TOP ALBUM

BREAK OUT (Planet, '83, *8*)

Additional Top 40 Albums: 6

TOP SONGS

YES WE CAN CAN (Blue Thumb, '73, *12 R&B, 11 Pop*)
HOW LONG (BETCHA' GOT A CHICK ON THE SIDE) (Blue Thumb, '75, *1 R&B, 20 Pop*)
HE'S SO SHY (Planet, '80, *10 R&B, 3 Pop*)
SLOW HAND (Planet, '81, *7 R&B, 2 Pop*)
I NEED YOU (Planet, '83, *13 R&B*)
AUTOMATIC (Planet, '84, *2 R&B, 5 Pop*)
JUMP (FOR MY LOVE) (Planet, '84, *3 R&B, 3 Pop*)
NEUTRON DANCE (Planet, '84, *13 R&B, 6 Pop*)
DARE ME (RCA, '85, *6 R&B, 11 Pop*)

Additional Top 40 R&B Songs: 12

BILLY PRESTON

The close association of Billy Preston (b. Sept. 9, 1946, Houston, Texas) with major figures in three distinct musical genres should, in itself, merit him a special place in history. In gospel, he worked with choir kingpin James Cleveland and was a member of the COGICS (Church of God in Christ Singers), Andrae Crouch's ground-breaking progressive gospel group. In R&B and soul, Preston lent his fat organ sound to Little Richard, Sam Cooke, and Ray Charles. And in rock, he made important keyboard contributions to both the Beatles and the Rolling Stones. As an artist in his own right, Preston had a brief though impressive run of hits in the early 1970s, including two R&B chart-toppers and two Number One pop songs.

A Los Angeles resident since age one, Preston followed his mother, pianist and choir director Robbie Preston Williams, into the gospel world, taking up

Billy Preston

a 1962 trip to England and Germany. Richard had thought he'd been booked to do gospel, but when the British crowds clamored for his old hits, he obliged. While they were in Hamburg, Preston struck up a friendship with the then-little-known Beatles. Also on the tour was Sam Cooke, and upon their return to the U.S., Preston played organ on the singer's 1963 hit "Little Red Rooster" and made an album for Cooke's Derby label. Other all-instrumental albums followed on Vee-Jay and on Capitol; he cut 1966's *The Wildest Organ in Town* on Capitol, arranged by the soon-to-be-famous Sly Stone.

A one-year stint as a band member and featured artist on the television series "Shindig" led Preston to a three-year association with Ray Charles, for whom he played on the 1966 hit "Let's Go Get Stoned." Two years later, while in England with Charles, Preston became reacquainted with the Beatles and began playing on their sessions, receiving label credit on 1969's Number One pop "Get Back." Signed to the group's Apple label, he emerged as a keyboardist and vocalist and scored in the U.K. with 1969's number 11 "That's the Way God Planned It" and in the U.S. two years later with the number 23 R&B "My Sweet Lord." Both were produced by Beatle George Harrison.

Preston's solo career mushroomed when he joined A&M Records in 1972 and began producing himself. He hit the top of the R&B chart that year with the funky clavinet instrumental "Outa-Space," went to the pop summit in 1973 with the vocal "Will

piano himself at three and organ at six. His introduction to show business came at 10, when executives from Paramount Pictures came to his church, Grace Memorial Church of God in Christ, to hear guest soloist Mahalia Jackson in hopes of hiring her for a film biography of songwriter W. C. Handy. Jackson not only got a role in *St. Louis Blues,* but Preston was cast as the young Handy.

The organist remained steeped in gospel music, and he traveled during the early 1960s with Rev. A. A. Allen, performing at the barnstorming evangelist's tent revivals and recording for his Miracle label. Preston then joined singer-songwriter James Cleveland and was featured on a series of Savoy albums by Cleveland and the Angelic Choir, including 1962's near-million-selling *Peace Be Still,* that were pivotal in launching the modern gospel choir movement. In the mid-1960s, Preston recorded for Vee-Jay and Exodus with the COGICS, led by Andrae Crouch, a singer-songwriter who would soon usher in gospel's next era.

Preston's introduction to playing secular music came by accident. Little Richard, the rocker who had turned singing evangelist, hired him as a sideman for

TOP ALBUMS

I WROTE A SIMPLE SONG (A&M, '72, 32)
MUSIC IS MY LIFE (A&M, '73, 32)
THE KIDS & ME (A&M, '74, 17)

TOP SONGS

OUTA-SPACE (A&M, '72, 1 R&B, 2 Pop)
SLAUGHTER (A&M, '72, 17 R&B)
WILL IT GO ROUND IN CIRCLES (A&M, '73, 10 R&B, 1 Pop)
SPACE RACE (A&M, '73, 1 R&B, 4 Pop)
YOU'RE SO UNIQUE (A&M, '74, 11 R&B)
NOTHING FROM NOTHING (A&M, '74, 8 R&B, 1 Pop)
STRUTTIN' (A&M, '74, 11 R&B, 22 Pop)

Additional Top 40 R&B Songs: 3

It Go Round in Circles," followed it with the Number One R&B instrumental "Space Race," then repeated his previous pop triumph with the 1974 vocal "Nothing from Nothing." The latter tune was part of the album *The Kids & Me*, which also contained a Preston-penned ballad titled "You Are So Beautiful" that Joe Cocker turned into a number five pop hit in 1975.

During his six-year relationship with A&M, Preston also recorded as a sideman with such artists as Aretha Franklin, the Rolling Stones (with whom he toured in 1973 as both an opening act and sideman), Sly and the Family Stone, Quincy Jones, and Barbra Streisand and produced the Stairsteps' number 10 R&B hit "From Us to You" in 1976 for Harrison's Dark Horse label.

In 1978, Preston entered into a then-unique arrangement that allowed him to record gospel music for Myrrh Records and secular sides for Motown. At Motown, however, he had only one significant hit, the romantic love ballad "With You I'm Born Again," a duet with Stevie Wonder's former wife Syreeta Wright that rose to number four on the pop chart in 1980 but failed to dent the R&B top 40.

Dropped by Motown in 1982, Preston had little luck with subsequent recordings for Megatone, ERC, and Motorcity. He continued to crop up from time to time on sessions by such artists as Luther Vandross and Al Green and made occasional gospel albums with his mother and his sister Rodena Preston, as well as with a new edition of the COGICS.

LLOYD PRICE

In March 1952, Art Rupe of Specialty Records in Hollywood flew to New Orleans in search of fresh sounds. Imperial, another southern California label, had a virtual lock on New Orleans rhythm and blues talent, but Rupe somehow managed to secure the services of the rival company's ace A&R man, Dave Bartholomew, and its top R&B artist, Fats Domino, for the debut session by Lloyd Price (b. Mar. 9, 1933, Kenner, Louisiana). The then-unknown 18-year-old singer had written an engaging eight-bar blues titled "Lawdy Miss Clawdy" that was inspired by an expression used by disc jockey James "Okey Dokey" Smith of local radio station WBOK.

Price's wailing vocals, combined with Barthol-

TOP SONGS

LAWDY MISS CLAWDY (Specialty, '52, 1 R&B)

OOOH, OOOH, OOOH (Specialty, '52, 4 R&B)

AIN'T IT A SHAME (Specialty, '53, 4 R&B)

JUST BECAUSE (ABC-Paramount, '57, 3 R&B, 29 Pop)

STAGGER LEE (ABC-Paramount, '58, 1 R&B, 1 Pop)

WHERE WERE YOU (ON OUR WEDDING DAY)? (ABC-Paramount, '59, 4 R&B, 23 Pop)

PERSONALITY (ABC-Paramount, '59, 1 R&B, 2 Pop)

I'M GONNA GET MARRIED (ABC-Paramount, '59, 1 R&B, 3 Pop)

COME INTO MY HEART (ABC-Paramount), '59, 2 R&B, 20 Pop)

LADY LUCK (ABC-Paramount, '60, 3 R&B, 14 Pop)

Additional Top 40 R&B Songs: 11

omew's slow-dragging horn arrangement, Domino's rolling piano, Ernest McLean's loping rhythm guitar, and Herb Hardesty's smooth tenor saxophone solo, took "Lawdy Miss Clawdy" to the top of the *Billboard* R&B chart, where it remained for seven weeks. (It was named R&B Record of the Year in the trade publication's year-end tabulation.) The record didn't cross over to the pop chart, but Rupe's research indicated that whites, especially in the South, were buying it in significant numbers. True pop stardom for Price, however, was still a few years up the road.

The eighth of 11 children, Price grew up singing in church. He began writing songs in grade school and learned to play trumpet and piano, organizing a combo while in his early teens with his brother Leo on drums. Prior to recording "Lawdy Miss Clawdy," he was a construction worker and led a band called the Blue Boys at the Top of the Town club in New Orleans.

While initially unable to recapture the mammoth success of his first record, Price scored double-sided top 10 R&B hits with two follow-ups: "Ooh, Ooh, Ooh" b/w "Restless Heart" and "Tell Me Pretty Baby" b/w "Ain't It a Shame." His career was ceremoniously interrupted at the beginning of 1954 when he was drafted into the Army, in which he served for two years in the Special Services entertaining troops in Korea and Japan. Upon his discharge in 1956, he recorded again for Specialty, this time in Hollywood, but the results, including a ditty titled "I Yi Yi Gomen-A-Sai" inspired by his tour of duty in Asia, drew little interest.

The vocalist then settled in Washington, D.C., where he launched the KRC label with partners William Boskent and Harold Logan and recorded the self-penned blues ballad "Just Because." As Price's record was beginning to take off, Larry Williams, his second cousin and former valet, cut a faithful cover version for Specialty. To head off the competition, Price leased his record to ABC-Paramount. In the end, Price's went to number seven R&B and number 29 pop, while Williams's made it as far as number 11 R&B. Later Price sides for KRC didn't fare as well, and in late 1958 he became an official ABC-Paramount recording artist.

Teamed with pop producer Don Costa, Price hit the top of both the R&B and pop charts with "Stagger Lee," based on a folk song about a game of craps that ends in murder. ABC-TV network censors objected when Dick Clark wanted to feature the record on "American Bandstand," so Price recut the tune with less-violent lyrics.

The singer continued to bask in the national limelight through 1960 with such pop-styled crossover hits as "Personality," "I'm Gonna Get Married," and "Lady Luck." He formed an 18-piece jazz orchestra that featured the arrangements of Gil Askey and Slide Hampton and frequently appeared on the television programs of Clark, Ed Sullivan, and Perry Como.

When the big hits stopped, Price and partner Logan invested their money in real estate, including New York City's famous Birdland club, which they purchased from Morris Levy and renamed Lloyd Price's Turntable. They also launched Double L Records. The label's roster included Wilson Pickett, former Spaniels lead Pookie Hudson, and New Orleans keyboardist (and Price sideman) James Booker, in addition to Price himself, who scored moderate hits with 1963's "Misty" (its swing arrangement borrowed by jazz organist Richard "Groove" Holmes's for his hit 1966 instrumental version) and the following year's "Billy Boy." The singer continued to record sporadically in the years that followed, for such labels as Turntable, GSF, and LPG, but increasingly turned his attention to other concerns, including a business venture with boxing promoter Don King that found Price running an office in Lagos, Nigeria, for several years during the 1970s.

PRINCE

Singer, songwriter, multi-instrumentalist, producer, actor, and record mogul Prince (b. Prince Roger Nelson, June 7, 1958, Minneapolis, Minnesota) has been perhaps the most prolific recording artist since James Brown in his heyday. Since his debut at age 19, the ingenious, unpredictable performer has released 15 albums (three of which went to Number One), recorded some 500 additional songs that have not been released, and written and/or produced records for numerous others. When he's not on tour, he reportedly puts in 15 hours a day at his 65,000-square-foot multimedia Paisley Park production facility in Minneapolis, which would leave little time for sleep, let alone the sexual activity he so often celebrates in his songs.

The culmination of a tradition of performing artists—James Brown, Mick Jagger, Liberace, Little Richard, and Elvis Presley among them—who've had the nerve to publicly expose their egos and the talent to attract mass audiences for their self-indulgence, Prince has created a dizzyingly eclectic body of music that encompasses funk, sweet soul, hard rock, and jazz. Singing in squealing falsetto to macho baritone tones with wondrous elasticity, he's broken down sexual and racial taboos in the process. "He's driven like an artist," admirer Joni Mitchell has stated. "His motivation is growth and experiment as opposed to formula and hits."

Prince was named after the Prince Rogers Trio, a Minneapolis jazz group led by his pianist father, John Nelson, and featuring his vocalist mother, the former Mattie Shaw. Growing up in an integrated neighborhood on the Minnesota city's North Side, he taught himself to play piano at age seven and soon mastered some 20 other instruments, including guitar. While still in his early teens, he formed a band called Grand Central with bassist Andre Anderson (later known as Andre Cymone), whose family had taken Prince in after he'd fallen out with his parents. At 18, armed with a demo he'd cut at a local studio, Prince headed for New York in hopes of securing a contract. Three labels turned him down due to his insistence that he produce himself, but Warner Bros. finally bit and signed him to a three-album deal.

He played all the instruments on *For You*, his 1978 debut album, as would be the rule through 1982. One track, the scintillating "Soft and Wet," gave him a number 12 R&B hit but attracted little

Prince

the *Cherry Moon, Sign "O" the Times,* and *Graffiti Bridge* were less well received. *Under the Cherry Moon,* however, did contain the Number One R&B and pop 1986 hit "Kiss," and 1987's Number One R&B, number three pop "Sign 'O' the Times" emerged from the concert film of the same name.

Prince's musical contributions to the 1989 motion picture *Batman* (Danny Elfman composed the main score) resulted in a Number One album and the Number One R&B and pop single "Batdance." The 1991 album *Diamonds and Pearls* spawned two smash singles: the Number One pop "Cream" (which failed to crack the R&B chart) and the Number One R&B, number three pop title cut. The next Prince album, issued in 1992, had an unpronounceable, unspellable symbol as its title, which Prince began insisting was also his new name. The album, although it rose to number five, produced no major hit singles. *The Hits/The B-Sides,* a three-CD career retrospective, was issued in 1993 and quickly went gold.

Prince had launched the Warner Bros.-distributed Paisley Park label in 1985 and scored hits with his

pop interest. (*For You* was the only Prince album not to be certified gold; most struck platinum.) The next year's *Prince* yielded the Number One R&B, number 11 pop "I Wanna Be Your Lover," while the 1980 album *Dirty Mind* contained the number five R&B hit "Uptown." The frank sexuality of many of the disc's tunes, in addition to Prince's flamboyant stage act, stirred much controversy, which became the title of the next album. *Controversy,* issued in 1981, spawned two hits, the number three R&B title track and the number nine R&B "Let's Work."

The double-disc *1999,* released in 1982, marked the beginning of Prince's ascent to major crossover success, with the rock-styled "Little Red Corvette" (his first hit to feature members of his band) becoming a pop top 10 charter, reaching number six, although it made only number 15 on the R&B list. Superstardom was cemented with 1984's *Purple Rain,* containing the atmospheric "When Doves Cry" and the driving "Let's Go Crazy," both of which topped the R&B and pop charts. He also starred in the motion picture *Purple Rain,* a box-office smash, although the subsequent films *Under*

TOP ALBUMS

Prince and the Revolution:
PURPLE RAIN (Warner Bros., '84, *1*)
AROUND THE WORLD IN A DAY (Paisley Park, '85, *1*)

Prince:
BATMAN (WARNER BROS., '89, *1*)

Additional Top 40 Albums: 9

TOP SONGS

Prince and the Revolution:
WHEN DOVES CRY (Warner Bros., '84, *1 R&B, 1 Pop*)
LET'S GO CRAZY (Warner Bros., '84, *1 R&B, 1 Pop*)
KISS (Paisley Park, '86, *1 R&B, 1 Pop*)

Prince:
SIGN 'O' THE TIMES (Paisley Park, '87, *1 R&B, 3 Pop*)
BATDANCE (Warner Bros, '89, *1 R&B, 1 Pop*)

Prince and the New Power Generation:
DIAMONDS AND PEARLS (Paisley Park, '91, *1 R&B, 3 Pop*)

Additional Top 40 R&B Songs: 31

productions of singing percussionist Sheila E. (Earlier Prince productions for the Time and Vanity 6 had appeared on Warner Bros.) Records by such later Paisley Park artists as Taja Sevelle, Ingrid Chavez, Mavis Staples, Good Question, T. C. Ellis, and George Clinton were not strong sellers, however, and in January 1994 Warner Bros. dropped the label. Shortly thereafter, Prince emerged with the single "The Most Beautiful Girl in the World" on his own NPG label (distributed by the tiny Bellmark Records), although the label read that what's-his-name appeared "courtesy of Warner Bros. Records."

THE RAVENS

The Ravens, featuring the astonishingly deep bass voice of Jimmy Ricks (b. 1924, Jacksonville, Florida), did much more than inspire the names of a string of "bird" groups, among them the Orioles, the Robins, the Cardinals, the Flamingos, and the Penguins. While the Orioles had a more direct impact on the course black secular harmony would take during the 1950s, the Ravens were the first to achieve wide popularity by breaking with the pop-oriented sounds of the Mills Brothers, the Ink Spots, and the Delta Rhythm Boys and introducing a bluesier yet handsomely polished approach that influenced such later groups as the Dominoes, the Drifters, and the Temptations. The Harlem-based quartet was also the first to incorporate choreography into its act.

Ricks, who greatly admired Delta Rhythm Boys basso Lee Gaines, initially planned on being a solo artist but, while working at Harlem's Four Hundred Tavern, struck up a friendship with baritone Warren Suttles, a fellow waiter. Singing along with records on the jukebox while tending tables, they decided to organize a group and recruited tenors Leonard Puzey and Ollie Jones from a talent agency. The Ravens, formed in 1945, cut their first records the next year for their manager Ben Bart's Hub label. Six sides were released simultaneously, but none created much of a stir. After replacing Jones with Maithe Marshall, they rerecorded the Hub songs for King Records, but those remained in the can until after the Ravens had achieved fame at another label. "Bye Bye Baby

Blues," made in 1946, became a hit two years later.

Signing with Albert Green's National Records in 1947, the quartet scored with its third release, "Write Me a Letter," a ballad written by the group's pianist-arranger, Howard Biggs. It broke first on the pop chart, peaking at number 24, then crossed to the R&B list, rising to number five. The song's success led to the Ravens' second single, "Old Man River," also becoming a hit. The group's swinging arrangement of the Jerome Kern–Oscar Hammerstein II standard, first popularized by bass-baritone Paul Robeson in the 1927 Broadway musical *Show Boat*,

The Ravens

later served as a feature for Temptations basso Melvin Franklin. The Ravens had seven more R&B chart hits at National through 1950, including a 1948 cover of the Orioles' first smash, "It's Too Soon to Know," and a 1949 treatment of Irving Berlin's "White Christmas" that was borrowed in 1954 by Clyde McPhatter's Drifters. Most of the Ravens' National 78s spotlighted Ricks on the A sides and falsetto tenor Marshall on the flips.

Ricks left the Ravens briefly in 1950 to tour with Benny Goodman, with whose orchestra he waxed "Oh Babe!" in duet with Nancy Reed for Columbia. The Goodman version of the infectious Louis Prima jump blues placed at number 25 on the pop chart, while renditions by Larry Darnell, Roy Milton, Jimmy Preston, and Wynonie Harris all made the R&B top 10. The bassman then returned to the group, which signed with Columbia later in 1950. Releases on the major label and its Okeh subsidiary were unsuccessful. A reconstituted Ravens, comprising Ricks, baritone Louis Frazier, tenor Jimmy Stewart, and falsetto specialist Joe Van Loan, joined the Mercury roster in 1951, charting their last hit the following year with the number four R&B "Rock Me All Night Long." Also while at Mercury, Ricks recorded several solo sides, as well as a duet treatment of the Hank Williams country hit "Hey Good Lookin' " with Dinah Washington.

Leaving Mercury in 1954, the Ravens moved on to Jubilee, where they made a remarkable version of the old Jimmy Dorsey hit "Green Eyes." Ricks left in 1956, with a new Ravens consisting of brothers Joe, Paul, and James Van Loan and basso David Bowers

---

TOP SONGS

WRITE ME A LETTER (National, '48, *5 R&B, 24 Pop*)

OLD MAN RIVER (National, '48, *10 R&B*)

SEND FOR ME IF YOU NEED ME (National, '48, *5 R&B*)

BYE BYE BABY BLUES (King, '48, *8 R&B*)

IT'S TOO SOON TO KNOW (National, '48, *11 R&B*)

SILENT NIGHT (National, '48, *8 R&B*)

WHITE CHRISTMAS (National, '49, *9 R&B*)

RICKY'S BLUES (National, '49, *8 R&B*)

DON'T HAVE TO RIDE NO MORE (National, '50, *9 R&B*)

ROCK ME ALL NIGHT LONG (Mercury, '52, *4 R&B*)

Additional Top 40 R&B Songs: 1

---

having little luck with releases on Argo, 1957's remake of the Scarlets' "Dear One" being their last.

All of the original members went on to sing with other groups and occasionally reunited in various editions of the Ravens. Ricks had a prolific solo career, recording for Josie, Atlantic (including duets with LaVern Baker and Esther Phillips and a haunting reading of the blues "Trouble in Mind"), Felsted, Mainstream, and Jubilee, although none of his sides charted. Just prior to his death from a heart attack on July 2, 1974, Ricks was touring as Count Basie's band vocalist. Also deceased are Louis Frazier and Joe and James Van Loan.

LOU RAWLS

T hroughout a secular recording career that yielded two R&B chart-toppers—1966's "Love Is a Hurtin' Thing" and 1976's "You'll Never Find Another Love Like Mine"—Lou Rawls (b. Dec. 1, 1935, Chicago) has applied his velvet baritone voice with effortless elasticity to blues, jazz, soul, and middle-of-the-road pop material. His deep roots in gospel quartet music, however, were never far from the surface.

Raised by his grandmother on Chicago's South Side—a fact he often reminds audiences of in his hipster monologues on the songs "Dead End Street" and "Tobacco Road"—Rawls began singing at age seven at Mount Olive Baptist Church. By 1950, he was a member of the Holy Wonders and with them made his first recording, "Move in the Room," an ultra-rare 78 on the Premium label. After a stint with the Highway QC's, in which his friend Sam Cooke had sung earlier, he joined the Los Angeles–based Chosen Gospel Singers in 1953.

"My grandmother had passed about a year or two before that," he recalled, "so there was no need for me to stay in Chicago, as far as I was concerned. As a kid, [I had] always aspired to become what they call a professional traveling on the road...It was great, 'cause, hey, you're coming out of Chicago, you haven't been nowhere really, and all of a sudden you're out on the road and packing auditoriums and stuff like that."

Rawls recorded with the Chosen Gospel Singers for Specialty in 1954 and, after two years in the Army, again for Nashboro in 1957. He switched to the more-established Pilgrim Travelers later that year and recorded with them for Andex, including some pop songs credited to "the Travelers," among them "Teenage Machine Age," a tune forgettable except for its title. In 1958, while the Travelers were on tour with Cooke (who'd left gospel for pop the previous year), Rawls was seriously injured in an auto accident that left him incapacitated for nearly a year.

"Love Love Love" on the Shardee label, his 1959 solo debut, flopped, as did later releases on Candix. In 1962, he harmonized with Cooke on that singer's number two R&B hit "Bring It on Home to Me." Rawls's nightclub repertoire of blues and jazz had attracted the attention of Capitol Records, which paired him that year with jazz pianist Les McCann's trio for the album *Stormy Monday*. The company soon began grooming Rawls as an easy-listening crooner along the lines of Nat "King" Cole, a strategy that established him as a successful adult-oriented album artist. During his eight-year stay at the label, however, the vocalist did manage to score three top 10 R&B singles: "Love Is a Hurtin' Thing," the Grammy-winning "Dead End Street," and a cover of the Mabel John hit "Your Good Thing (Is About to End)," penned by Isaac Hayes and David Porter.

A two-year association with MGM Records

resulted in the number 17 R&B and pop "A Natural Man," which won Rawls a Grammy for Best Rhythm and Blues Vocal Performance, Male, over higher-charting competition from nominees Marvin Gaye, Isaac Hayes, and Stevie Wonder. A shorter service at Bell was less fruitful. The singer's recording career was rejuvenated in 1976 at Philadelphia International, where songwriter-producers Kenny Gamble and Leon Huff brought him closer to the soul mainstream with the rhumba-flavored "You'll Never Find Another Love Like Mine" and such subsequent hits as "See You When I Git There," "Lady Love," "Let Me Be Good to You," and "Sit Down and Talk to Me."

Singles on Epic between 1982 and '85 failed to crack the R&B top 40, after which Rawls turned up on the Gamble and Huff label for 1987's number 28 R&B "I Wish You Belonged to Me," his last R&B chart entry. He signed with Blue Note in 1989 and cut *At Last*. The first of three Blue Note albums, produced by Michael Cuscuna and Billy Vera, that found Rawls going back to his earlier blues and jazz stylings, it featured guest appearances by Ray Charles, George Benson, Dianne Reeves, David "Fathead" Newman, and Bobby Hutcherson, among others. Singing commericals for Budweiser beer and hosting "Lou Rawls' Parade of Stars" (the annual telethon, begun in 1980, raised over $70 million for the United Negro College Fund within a decade) also helped to maintain the vocalist's high media profile.

TOP ALBUMS

Lou Rawls Live! (Capitol, '66, 4)

Lou Rawls Soulin' (Capitol, '66, 7)

All Things in Time (Philadelphia International, '76, 7)

Additional Top 40 Albums: 3

TOP SONGS

Love Is a Hurtin' Thing (Capitol, '66, 1 R&B, 13 Pop)

Dead End Street (Capitol, '67, 3 R&B, 29 Pop)

Your Good Thing (Is About to End) (Capitol, '69, 3 R&B, 18 Pop)

A Natural Man (MGM, '71, 17 R&B, 17 Pop)

You'll Never Find Another Love Like Mine (Philadelphia International, '76, 1 R&B, 2 Pop)

See You When I Git There (Philadelphia International, '77, 8 R&B)

Let Me Be Good to You (Philadelphia International, '79, 11 R&B)

Additional Top 40 R&B Songs: 11

OTIS REDDING

Otis Redding (b. Sept. 9, 1941, Dawson, Georgia) was the quintessential southern soul singer. Not only did his emotion-gripping, Georgia-hewn style come to epitomize the Stax-Volt Memphis sound of the 1960s but as a vocalist, songwriter, and arranger, he played a key role in shaping it.

The son of Otis and Fanny Redding, Otis, Jr., was raised in the Bellevue section of Macon. The city was a hotbed of rhythm and blues activity during the 1950s, and the huge success of two Macon-based singers—Little Richard and James Brown—gave impetus to young Redding's desire to become a professional entertainer. He began doing Little Richard and Elvis Presley songs at talent shows in the area and, in 1958, briefly toured with the Upsetters, the very band Richard had just abandoned due to a reli-

Otis Redding

gious calling. (Later vocal influences included Sam Cooke and Solomon Burke.)

A visit to a sister in Los Angeles during the summer of 1960 found Redding making his first recording, "She's All Right" for the Trans World label, but it went nowhere. "Shout Bamalama," a Little Richard–inspired rave-up that he cut not long thereafter for the Confederate label in Athens, Georgia, caused a minor stir in the South, but real success continued to elude him. Redding performed mostly around Macon with extrovert guitarist Johnny Jenkins's Pinetoppers, a band managed by Phil Walden, a white teenager who would soon shepherd Redding's rise to stardom.

The singer made his first trip to Memphis in October 1962 as Jenkins's driver. At the tail end of the guitarist's Stax session, Redding was given the opportunity to record two songs, both of his own composition. The uptempo "Hey Hey Baby" was yet another Little Richard takeoff, but the pleading, highly distinctive ballad "These Arms of Mine" so impressed Stax co-owner Jim Stewart that Redding was signed to the company, where his recordings were issued on the Volt label. Released in October 1962, "These Arms of Mine" reached number 20 on the *Billboard* R&B chart by March of the following year.

Bigger hits followed over the next four years, including "Pain in My Heart" (based on the Irma Thomas recording of Allen Toussaint's "Ruler of My Heart"), "That's How Strong My Love Is" (written by Roosevelt Jamison), "Mr. Pitiful" (the singer's first successful songwriting collaboration with guitarist Steve Cropper), "I've Been Loving You Too Long (To Stop Now)," (penned by Redding and Jerry Butler), "Respect" (a Redding composition revived by Aretha Franklin in 1967), "Satisfaction" (a loose rendition of the Rolling Stones' hit), "Try a Little Tenderness" (an old Bing Crosby favorite), and "Tramp" (a duet with Stax labelmate Carla Thomas on a Jimmy McCracklin–Lowell Fulson tune initially recorded by Fulson).

Redding proved an ideal collaborator with the crack Stax rhythm section, consisting of Cropper, bassist Donald "Duck" Dunn, drummer Al Jackson, Jr., and keyboardists Booker T. Jones and/or Isaac Hayes. The singer's unique major-key chord progressions, as well as the riveting riffs he dictated to the Mar-Keys horns, greatly influenced the direction the musicians took with other Stax artists. He also produced records for several non-Stax artists, the most important being vocalist Arthur Conley's number two R&B and pop "Sweet Soul Music" in 1967 on Atco.

A sensation in the African-American community from the onset of his tenure at Stax, Redding was in the process of a crossover to white audiences—having appeared at the trendy Whisky a Go Go rock club in Los Angeles in 1966 (the results eventually issued on the albums *Otis Redding in Person at the Whisky A Go Go* and *Good to Me*), toured Europe as part of the 1967 Stax-Volt Revue, and later that year taken part in the ground-breaking Monterey International Pop Festival (his triumphant set cap-

tured on the album *Otis Redding/The Jimi Hendrix Experience: Historic Performances Recorded at the Monterey International Pop Festival*)—when he and four members of his road band, the Bar-Kays, perished in a Wisconsin plane crash on December 10, 1967.

Full crossover appeal was achieved posthumously, when the innovative "(Sittin' on the) Dock of the Bay," a Redding-Cropper tune recorded several days before the accident, topped both the R&B and pop charts in early 1968. Nine additional Redding titles made the R&B top 40 following his death, the biggest being "I've Got Dreams to Remember," a haunting ballad written by Redding, his wife, Zelma, and Joe Rock.

Redding was 26 at the time of his tragic demise. He left behind three children: Dexter, Karla, and Otis III. With their cousin Mark Locket, Dexter and Otis III formed a band called Father's Pride. Changing their billing to the Reddings, they scored several R&B chart singles, including 1980's number six "Remote Control" and 1982's number 21 reworking of "(Sittin' on the) Dock of the Bay," both on the Believe label.

TOP ALBUMS

HISTORY OF OTIS REDDING (Volt, '68, 9)
THE DOCK OF THE BAY (Volt, '68, 4)

Additional Top 40 Albums: 3

TOP SONGS

I'VE BEEN LOVING YOU TOO LONG (TO STOP NOW)
    (Volt, '65, 2 R&B, 21 Pop)
RESPECT (Volt, '65, 4 R&B, 35 Pop)
SATISFACTION (Volt, '66, 4 R&B, 31 Pop)
TRY A LITTLE TENDERNESS (Volt, '66, 4 R&B, 25 Pop)
TRAMP (Otis and Carla, Volt, '67, 2 R&B, 26 Pop)
KNOCK ON WOOD (Otis and Carla, Volt, '67,
    8 R&B, 30 Pop)
(SITTIN' ON) THE DOCK OF THE BAY (Volt, '68,
    1 R&B, 1 Pop)
I'VE GOT DREAMS TO REMEMBER (Atco, '68, 6 R&B)

Additional Top 40 R&B Songs: 18

MARTHA REEVES AND THE VANDELLAS

"**M**artha and the Vandellas had a rowdiness about them. Rowdy the way youth is rowdy. We'd go out and cause the perspiration. Not like the syrupy baby-dolls that didn't get down."

The "syrupy baby-dolls" that Martha Reeves (b. July 18, 1941, Eufaula, Alabama) was referring to in her 1974 talk with John Calendo of *Interview* magazine were the Supremes, the Vandellas' distaff rivals at Motown during the 1960s. The feisty Reeves was resentful of the fact that the record company gave more attention (and often better songs) to Diana Ross and the Supremes than it did to her group. The two trios were a study in contrasts: the Supremes presented an image of vulnerability, while the Vandellas, fronted by Reeves's harsh yet flexible alto voice, took a more aggressive stance. "The Supremes were pretty to look at, sure," Reeves added, "but you didn't exactly dance in the streets."

One of the twelve children of Elijah and Ruby

Reeves, both of whom sang and played guitar, Martha grew up singing at her grandfather's Metropolitan A.M.E. Church in Detroit. While attending North Eastern High School for Women, she formed the Fascinations with three other young women but quit before the group moved to Chicago and began recording for producer Curtis Mayfield on the ABC-Paramount and Mayfield labels. Reeves then joined the Del-Phis, which already comprised Gloria Jean Williams, Rosalind Ashford, and Annette Beard Sterling. With Williams singing lead, the Del-Phis cut their first record, "I'll Let You Know," in 1961 for Check-mate, a subsidiary of Chess. The single flopped, and the group disbanded.

Reeves performed for a period as a single under the name Martha LaVaille and was spotted at the Twenty Grand club by Motown producer William "Mickey" Stevenson," who invited her to the company for an audition. But instead of getting an audition, she was hired as a secretary in the A&R department. "I'd be maybe sitting at the typewriter," she told Calendo, "and someone would say, 'Hey, we got this session going. Come and do some hand claps,' or, 'We need some vocal backing.' " She was paid $5 for hand claps, $7.50 for foot stomps, $10 for singing.

Her big break came when Mary Wells failed to appear for a session. Reeves hastily recruited Williams,

Martha Reeves

TOP SONGS

Martha and the Vandellas:
COME AND GET THESE MEMORIES (Gordy, '63, 6 R&B, 29 Pop)
(LOVE IS LIKE A) HEAT WAVE (Gordy, '63, 1 R&B, 4 Pop)
NOWHERE TO RUN (Gordy, '65, 5 R&B, 8 Pop)
LOVE (MAKES ME DO FOOLISH THINGS) (Gordy, '65, 22 R&B)
MY BABY LOVES ME (Gordy, '66, 3 R&B, 22 Pop)
I'M READY FOR LOVE (Gordy, '66, 2 R&B, 9 Pop)
JIMMY MACK (Gordy, '67, 1 R&B, 10 Pop)
LOVE BUG LEAVE MY HEART ALONE (Gordy, '67, 14 R&B, 25 Pop)

Martha Reeves and the Vandellas:
HONEY CHILE (Gordy, '67, 5 R&B, 11 Pop)
IN AND OUT OF MY LIFE (Gordy, '72, 22 R&B)

Additional Top 40 R&B Songs: 6

Ashford, and Sterling for the date. The result, a Stevenson song titled "There He Is (At My Door)," appeared on Motown's Mel-O-Dy label in late 1962, credited to the Vells (Chess owned the Del-Phis' name). The group also did background vocals on such early Marvin Gaye hits as "Stubborn Kind of Fellow," "Pride and Joy," and "Hitch Hike." Lead singer Williams soon dropped out, leaving Reeves at the helm.

Renamed the Vandellas, after Van Dyke Street (near Reeves's home) and Detroit vocalist Della Reese, the trio scored with its second single, 1963's number six R&B "Come and Get These Memories." Issued on the Tamla label, it was one of their first songs written by Eddie Holland, Lamont Dozier, and Brian Holland. Martha and the Vandellas scored six more top 10 R&B hits through 1967, two of which, 1963's "(Love Is Like a) Heat Wave" and 1967's "Jimmy Mack" (both by H-D-H), struck Number One. Their biggest hit, 1964's number two pop "Dancing in the Streets" (penned by Stevenson and Gaye), didn't register R&B, as *Billboard* was not publishing an R&B chart during that period. All of the Vandellas' hits were uptempo, gospel-flavored tunes, with the exeption of the lovely 1965 H-D-H ballad "Love (Makes Me Do Foolish Things)."

Sterling quit the trio in 1964 and was replaced by Betty King. Personnel changed again in 1968, with Martha's sister Lois Reeves taking over for King and Sandra Tilley for Ashford. By that time, however, the group's records were no longer hitting even the R&B top 20, and the new members didn't sing on many later releases, Reeves instead being backed by the Andantes, a studio group. She suffered a nervous breakdown in 1969 and, after recovering, kept the Vandellas going until a farewell performance in Detroit on December 21, 1972.

Reeves resurfaced two years later at MCA as a solo artist with a lavish album produced by Richard Perry. While critically acclaimed, it spawned only two minor hits: covers of Joe Simon's "Power of Love" and Van Morrison's "Wild Night." Subsequent solo albums, for Arista in 1975 and for Fantasy in 1979 and '81, were even less successful. The singer continued touring and, in 1989, got back together with Sterling and Ashford to dance in the streets once more.

LIONEL RICHIE

"I think I can pretty much have my cake and eat it too," Lionel Richie, Jr. (b. June 20, 1949, Tuskegee, Alabama) stated in 1981, denying widespread rumors that he planned to leave the Commodores, the hugely popular band of which he'd been a member for 13 years. It was a watershed year for the mild-mannered singer-songwriter. The Commodores' then-current album *In the Pocket* went platinum, as had two earlier albums by the sextet. But other Richie projects away from the group brought him even greater notoriety. "Endless Love," his self-penned-and-produced duet with Diana Ross from the motion picture of the same title, became the biggest single in the history of Motown Records, topping the *Billboard* R&B chart for seven weeks and the pop list for nine. And Richie wrote and produced two Number One pop hits for Kenny Rogers, 1980's "Lady" and the next year's "I Don't Need You," as well as produced the country-pop singer's 1981 platinum album *Share Your Love*.

Whereas the Commodores' recordings had been

joint productions by the band and arranger James Anthony Carmichael, working with Rogers gave Richie greater artistic freedom. "With the Commodores, you've got six perfectionists," he explained. "You've got to go through six different opinions to get one answer. I was pretty much in seventh heaven with Kenny because every decision I came up with was the final decision."

Before 1981 was up, Richie had decided to leave the cake out in the rain and bolt the Commodores. The move resulted in three multi-platinum solo albums—*Lionel Richie* (1982), *Can't Slow Down* (1983), and *Dancing on the Ceiling* (1986)—and three singles—"All Night Long (All Night)" (1983), "Hello" (1984), and "Say You, Say Me" (1985)—that topped both the R&B and pop charts. (All were co-produced by Richie and Carmichael.) Richie's sweet songs, sung in a honey-glazed if slightly nasal tenor, cut to the core of middle American pop and made him a crossover superstar. Then, after 1986, he stopped recording. Finally returning in 1992, he cut the Number One R&B "Do It to Me" (one of three new tunes on the career retrospective album *Back to Front*), but the single rose only as high as number 19 on the pop chart. Richie then ended his 21-year association with Motown and signed a multi-million-dollar contract with Mercury in hopes of rekindling his crossover flame.

A self-taught saxophonist and pianist, Richie became a full-time musician in 1968 after two groups—the Mystics and the Jades—merged on the campus of the Tuskegee Institute. Richie, trumpeter William King, and guitarist Thomas McClary had been members of the Mystics, while keyboardist Milan Williams and bassist Ronald LaPread were with the Jades. Having picked "commodore" at random from the dictionary and added drummer Walter "Clyde" Orange, the new band began gigging around the South on weekends. During the 1969 summer break from college they traveled to New York City to appear at Small's Paradise and the Cheetah.

The Commodores' debut single, the Jerry "Swamp Dogg" Williams–produced "Keep on Dancing," appeared on Atlantic in 1970. They signed with Motown the following year, but early sides on the company's MoWest label sank with little trace. Valuable experience was gained, however, during two and a half years spent on the road as the opening act for the Jackson 5. Transferred to the Motown label proper, the band finally scored in 1974 with the number seven R&B "Machine Gun," a funk instrumental feature for the synthesizer work of composer Williams. The Commodores had 19 additional top 40 R&B hits over the next seven years. Many, such as 1977's number four R&B, number five pop "Brick House" and the same year's Number One R&B, number 24 pop "Too Hot to Trot," were funk numbers co-written by the members and featuring the lead vocals of drummer Orange. Beginning with 1975's number two R&B, number five pop "Sweet Love," however, Richie's more pop-oriented singing and songs became the group's main drawing card.

The Commodores' two greatest crossover hits, 1978's "Three Times a Lady" and the next year's "Still," were country-tinged ballads, written and led by Richie, that topped both the R&B and pop charts and attracted the interest of Kenny Rogers, thus leading to the original sextet's demise. They struggled on at Motown without Richie and Carmichael and with McClary departing in 1974 for an uneventful solo career. In 1985, the Commodores were back at the top of the R&B chart with "Nightshift," a haunting Dennis Lambert–produced tribute to Marvin Gaye and Jackie Wilson featuring Orange and new co-lead singer, J. D. Nicholas, formerly of Heatwave. Switch-

ing to Polydor the next year, the group returned to funk and scored with the number two R&B "Goin' to the Back" before fading into obscurity.

SMOKEY ROBINSON

William "Smokey" Robinson, Jr. (b. Feb. 19, 1940, Detroit) first noticed he had a knack for rhyme at age five and composed his first song while in the first grade, for a play at Detroit's Dwyer Elementary School in which he starred as Uncle Remus. Bitten by the pop bug, he was soon spending his allowance on *Hit Parader* magazine in order to study the lyrics of the top tunes of the day.

Before he was out of his teens, Robinson was recording his songs with the Miracles, a vocal group, originally known as the Matadors, that he formed at Northern High School. His prolific pen produced such hits for the Miracles as "Shop Around," "You've Really Got a Hold on Me," "Ooo Baby Baby," "The Tracks of My Tears," "My Girl Has Gone," "Going to a Go-Go," "More Love," "I Second That Emotion," "If You Can Wait," "Special Occasion," "Baby, Baby Don't Cry," "Point It Out," and "The Tears of a Clown" (all placing in the top five on the *Billboard* R&B chart). He also penned huge hits for Mary Wells ("The One Who Really Loves You," "You Beat Me to the Punch," "Two Lovers," "Laughing Boy," "Your Old Stand By," "What's Easy for Two Is So Hard for One," "My Guy"), the Temptations ("The Way You Do the Things You Do," "My Girl," "Since I Lost You Baby," "My Baby," "Get Ready," "Ain't Too Proud to Beg," "Beauty Is Only Skin Deep," "You're My Everything"), Marvin Gaye ("I'll Be Doggone," "Ain't That Peculiar," "One More Heartache"), and the Marvelettes ("Don't Mess with Bill," "The Hunter Gets Captured by the Game," "My Baby Must Be a Magician"). Some were written in collaboration with others, including Berry Gordy, Jr., Al Cleveland, Miracles Warren "Pete" Moore and Bobby Rogers, Miracles guitarist Marvin Tarplin, and, in the case of the group's biggest hit, 1970's Number One R&B and pop "The Tears of a Clown," Henry Cosby and Stevie Wonder.

Robinson had been singing with Moore and Ronnie White since he was 11. In 1955, they organized a group called the Five Chimes that evolved into the

TOP ALBUMS

CAN'T SLOW DOWN (Motown, '83, *1*)
DANCING ON THE CEILING (Motown, '86, *1*)

Additional Top 40 Albums: 13

TOP SONGS

The Commodores:
JUST TO BE CLOSE TO YOU (Motown, '76, *1 R&B, 7 Pop*)
EASY (Motown, '77, *1 R&B, 4 Pop*)
THREE TIMES A LADY (Motown, '78, *1 R&B, 1 Pop*)
STILL (Motown, '79, *1 R&B, 1 Pop*)

Lionel Richie:
ENDLESS LOVE (Diana Ross and Lionel Richie, Motown, '81, *1 R&B, 1 Pop*)
ALL NIGHT LONG (ALL NIGHT) (Motown, '83, *1 R&B, 1 Pop*)
HELLO (Motown, '84, *1 R&B, 1 Pop*)
SAY YOU, SAY ME (Motown, '85, *1 R&B, 1 Pop*)

Additional Top 40 R&B Songs: 27

Matadors. Two years later, the quintet—Robinson, basso Moore, baritone White, and tenor Rogers and his cousin (and Robinson's future bride) Claudette Rogers—auditioned for Nat Tarnapol, manager of Robinson's idol, Jackie Wilson. (Other vocal influences on Robinson were Clyde McPhatter, Nolan Strong, Frankie Lymon, and Sam Cooke.) The quintet failed to impress Tarnapol, but Berry Gordy, Jr. (Wilson's chief songwriter at the time) was quite taken with the group, especially with its leader's lilting high tenor voice and his tunes.

Gordy became Robinson's mentor and helped him to polish his songs. "He was the one who taught me how to write a song and make it mean something," Robinson recalled in 1983. "I had a bunch of songs, and I was a great rhymer, but they had no continuity. He taught me how to make my songs be a story and have a beginning, a middle, and an end and a theme."

The young singer-songwriter became a key player in Gordy's fledgling record production operation, soon to be christened Motown, and remained with the company until 1990. The Miracles' first record,

Smokey Robinson

TOP ALBUM

GREATEST HITS, VOL. 2 (Smokey Robinson and the Miracles, Tamla, '68, 7)

Additional Top 40 Albums: 11

TOP SONGS

The Miracles:
SHOP AROUND (Tamla, '60, 1 R&B, 2 Pop)
YOU'VE REALLY GOT A HOLD ON ME (Tamla, '62, 1 R&B, 8 Pop)
THE TRACKS OF MY TEARS (Tamla, '65, 2 R&B, 16 Pop)
GOING TO A GO-GO (Tamla, '66, 2 R&B, 11 Pop)

Smokey Robinson and the Miracles:
I SECOND THAT EMOTION (Tamla, '67, 1 R&B, 4 Pop)
THE TEARS OF A CLOWN (Tamla, '70, 1 R&B, 1 Pop)

Smokey Robinson:
BABY THAT'S A BACKATCHA (Tamla, '74, 1 R&B, 26 Pop)
BEING WITH YOU (Tamla, '81, 1 R&B, 2 Pop)
JUST TO SEE HER (Motown, '87, 2 R&B, 8 Pop)

Additional Top 40 R&B Songs: 59

---

the Gordy-produced "Get a Job," was issued in 1958 by End Records in New York. After one other for that label, they recorded "Bad Girl" in 1959 for the newly launched Motown Records, but it was issued nationally on Chess. Robinson then persuaded Gordy to go national himself, and the Tamla label was created. The Miracles' second Tamla single, 1960's "Shop Around," became the company's first hit, soaring to the top of the R&B chart and to number two pop. It was the first of 20 top 10 R&B singles for the Miracles through Robinson's departure from the group twelve years later.

While producing the Miracles' records and touring with the group, Robinson also found time to produce such other Motown artists as Wells, the Temptations, Gaye, the Marvelettes, the Supremes, the Contours, Jimmy Ruffin, and Brenda Holloway. He became a vice president of Motown in 1964, but his productions for others decreased by the mid-1960s as the Miracles' own career mushroomed.

Tired of touring and wanting to spend more time with his two children, Berry and Tamla, Robinson left the group in 1972. He was replaced by Billy Griffin, and the new Miracles went on to score three more top 10 R&B hits, including 1975's number five R&B, Number One pop "Love Machine," before disbanding in the late 1970s.

After a year's break, Robinson emerged in 1973 as a solo artist and went on to have 13 top 10 R&B charters through 1990. The biggest, 1981's Number One R&B, number two pop "Being with You," was written by Robinson but produced by George Tobin. Later recordings found the increased use of outside writers and producers. As if signing his farewell, the singer's final Motown album was titled *Love, Smokey.* Issued in 1990, it spawned the number four R&B single "Everything You Touch," written by Pam Reswick and Steve Werfel and produced by Dennis Lambert. A year later, Robinson appeared on the SBK label, where he recorded *Double Good Everything,* his first self-produced album in seven years. The title track went to number 23 on the R&B chart.

ROSE ROYCE

In 1975, after 16 years at Motown Records as the writer and producer of hits for such artists as Marvin Gaye, Gladys Knight and the Pips, Edwin Starr, Rare Earth, Undisputed Truth, and especially the Temptations, Norman Whitfield decided to leave the company and launch his own label. Whitfield Records would feature such former Motown acts as Willie Hutch, Undisputed Truth, and Jr. Walker, but its cornerstone turned out to be a previously unknown group called Rose Royce.

Whitfield was in the process of cutting Rose Royce's debut album for his new label when he received an offer too good to refuse. Director Michael Schultz approached him about scoring the music for a motion picture comedy about the odd, yet appealing subject of life in a car wash. Rather than use an established group to perform the music, Whitfield chose Rose Royce.

Car Wash was a box-office smash, as was the MCA soundtrack album, which went gold and earned Whitfield a Grammy for Best Original Score Written for a Motion Picture or Television Special. It also launched the career of Rose Royce in a big way.

The title track, the first single released, shot to the top of both the R&B and pop charts in December of 1976, while the next two—"I Wanna Get Next to You" and "I'm Going Down"—also became hits. *Rose Royce II/In Full Bloom,* the album that was put on the back burner at the time Schultz called, was finally issued in 1977 on the Warner Bros.-distributed Whitfield label. It went platinum and yielded the top 10 R&B hits "Do Your Dance" and "Ooh Boy." The following year's *Rose Royce III/Strikes Again!,* containing the top 10 R&B hits "I'm in Love (And I Love the Feeling)" and "Love Don't Live Here Anymore," struck gold.

The core of Rose Royce—trumpeters Kenny Copeland and Freddie Dunn, saxophonist Michael Moore, keyboardist Victor Nix (replaced in 1976 by Michael Nash), guitarist Kenji Chiba Brown, bassist Lequeint "Duke" Jobe, drummer Henry Garner, and percussionist Terral Santiel—came together around 1970. All had known each other from different bands in the Los Angeles area, where they provided support for various vocal groups. Tired of backing others, they decided to form a self-contained unit and do all the singing and playing themselves. They called it Total Concept Unlimited. It would be several years, however, until the group emerged as more than a backup band.

Edwin Starr hired Total Concept Unlimited in

TOP ALBUMS

CAR WASH (Soundtrack, MCA, '76, *14*)
ROSE ROYCE II/IN FULL BLOOM (Whitfield, '77, *9*)
ROSE ROYCE III/STRIKES AGAIN! (Whitfield, '78, *28*)

TOP SONGS

CAR WASH (MCA, '76, *1 R&B, 1 Pop*)
I WANNA GET NEXT TO YOU (MCA, '77, *3 R&B, 10 Pop*)
I'M GOING DOWN (MCA, '77, *10 R&B*)
DO YOUR DANCE—PART 1 (Whitfield, '77, *4 R&B, 39 Pop*)
OOH BOY (Whitfield, '77, *3 R&B*)
I'M IN LOVE (AND I LOVE THE FEELING) (Whitfield, '78, *5 R&B*)
LOVE DON'T LIVE HERE ANYMORE (Whitfield, '78, *5 R&B, 32 Pop*)

Additional Top 40 R&B Songs: 2

Rose Royce

1973 to tour England and Japan as his band. Through Starr, the octet was introduced to Whitfield and made its studio debut playing on the producer's final project for the Temptations, 1973's Number One R&B, number 28 pop "Let Your Hair Down." Studio and road work followed with Yvonne Fair and Undisputed Truth, two other Whitifield-produced Motown acts.

Total Concept Unlimited became Rose Royce with the addition of vocalist Gwen Dickey, who was initially billed as Rose Norwalt. Formerly with a Miami group known as the Jewels, she came into the fold in a roundabout way, having been flown to Los Angeles to try out for Undisputed Truth, only to end up auditioning for Total Concept Unlimited. Her sensual, flexible voice would be featured on such Rose Royce songs as the uptempo disco-styled "Car Wash" and "Do Your Dance" and the ballads "I'm Going Down," "Ooh Boy," and "Love Don't Live Here Anymore." Trumpeter Copeland handled

the leads on the ballads "I Wanna Get Next to You" and "I'm in Love (And I Love the Feeling)," his high, gossamer falsetto recalling that of Eddie Kendricks on earlier Whitfield productions for the Temptations.

While making hits of its own, Rose Royce also did studio work for Whitfield label artists Willie Hutch and Undisputed Truth as well as played on the female vocal trio Stargard's Number One R&B, number 21 pop Whitfield-penned "Theme Song from 'Which Way Is Up' " in 1977.

Rose Royce had no more top 10 records after 1978. Dickey and Brown left two years later and were replaced by Ricci Benson and Walter McKinney. A final Whitfield-produced album, 1972's *Stronger Than Ever* on Epic, failed to live up to its title. "Doesn't Have to Be This Way," a 1986 single on the Omni label, went to number 22 R&B, giving the group its first top 40 entry in seven years. It also proved to be the last.

DIANA ROSS
• • • • • • • • • • • • • • • • • •

As lead singer of the Supremes during the 1960s, then as a solo artist, Diana Ross (b. Diane Ross, Mar. 26, 1944, Detroit, Michigan) achieved a level of crossover success most other soul singers only dream of. She was not the Supremes' only featured vocalist in the beginning, but Motown boss Berry Gordy, Jr., quickly recognized something special in her sensually cooing voice and fashion-model looks and began grooming her for superstardom. With the Supremes and on her own, she scored 10 Number One R&B hit singles and 18 that topped the pop charts. She had three pop chart-topping albums with the Supremes and one, 1972's *Lady Sings the Blues,* of her own. She was nominated for Grammy Awards 10 times but, surprisingly, never won one.

The second of the six children of Fred Earl Ross and his wife, Ernestine, Diana was greatly inspired by Etta James's 1955 hit "The Wallflower." "The shock of hearing a voice so powerful and so deep made me marvel that one young woman could claim such power and passion!" Ross recalled in her 1993 book *Secrets of a Sparrow.* The Ross family was living in Detroit's Brewster projects when Diana met Florence Ballard and Mary Wilson. In 1959, Milton Jenkins, manager of a local doo wop group called the Primes that included future Temptations Eddie Kendricks and Paul Williams, asked Ballard to form a "sister" group to be known as the Primettes. Wilson, Ross, and Betty Travis were recruited, with Travis soon being replaced by Barbara Martin.

The Primettes cut their first record, the Wilson-led "Pretty Baby" b/w the Ross-led "Tears of Sorrow," in 1960 for the local Lupine Records and also sang backgrounds for such label artists as Eddie Floyd and Al Garner. When the single failed to spark, the four women began hanging out at Motown and picking up a few dollars doing handclaps on early Marvin Gaye sessions and providing harmony for Mabel John. Gordy signed them in 1961 and, at Ballard's suggestion, they changed their name to the Supremes. After two unsuccessful releases on Tamla and one on Motown and the departure of Martin, the group finally clicked with 1962's number 26 R&B "Let Me Go the Right Way," penned and produced by Gordy.

Three flops later, the Supremes were back on the R&B chart at number 23 with "When the Love Light Starts Shining Through His Eyes," written and produced by Holland, Dozier, and Holland.

With Ross at the helm and H-D-H at the creative controls, the trio broke big in 1964 with the Number One pop "Where Did Our Love Go." (*Billboard* published no R&B chart that year.) It was the first of the Ross-era Supremes' 12 Number One pop hits, all written and produced by H-D-H, with the exception of 1968's "Love Child" (produced by Gordy, Frank Wilson, Henry Cosby, Deke Richards, and R. Dean Taylor) and the next year's "Someday We'll Be Together" (by Johnny Bristol). In 1967, Ballard was fired (she died nine years later), replaced by Cindy Birdsong of Patti LaBelle and the Blue Belles. Also that year, Gordy changed the group's billing to "Diana Ross and the Supremes."

No one was surprised when Ross left the trio in 1969. The new Supremes, at first featuring Jean Terrell, had a Number One R&B hit the next year with "Stone Love," went through several personnel changes, and disbanded in the late 1970s. Ross hit

---

TOP ALBUM
• • • • • • • • • • • • • •

DIANA ROSS AND THE SUPREMES GREATEST HITS (Diana Ross and the Supremes, Motown, '70, *1*)

Additional Top 40 Albums: 35

TOP SONGS
• • • • • • • • • • • • • •

The Supremes:
BACK IN MY ARMS AGAIN (Motown, '65, *1 R&B, 1 Pop*)
YOU CAN'T HURRY LOVE (Motown, '66, *1 R&B, 1 Pop*)
YOU KEEP ME HANGIN' ON (Motown, '66, *1 R&B, 1 Pop*)
LOVE IS HERE AND NOW YOU'RE GONE (Motown, '67, *1 R&B, 1 Pop*)
SOMEDAY WE'LL BE TOGETHER (Diana Ross and the Supremes, Motown, '69, *1 R&B, 1 Pop*)

Diana Ross:
AIN'T NO MOUNTAIN HIGH ENOUGH (Motown, '70, *1 R&B, 1 Pop*)
LOVE HANGOVER (Motown, '75, *1 R&B, 1 Pop*)
UPSIDE DOWN (Motown, '80, *1 R&B, 1 Pop*)
ENDLESS LOVE (Diana Ross and Lionel Richie, Motown, '81, *1 R&B, 1 Pop*)

Additional Top 40 R&B Songs: 54

Diana Ross

the top of both the R&B and pop charts with her second post-Supremes single, "Ain't No Mountain High Enough," written and produced by Ashford and Simpson and previously recorded by Marvin Gaye and Tammi Terrell. Although she was unable to maintain the chart consistency of her last six years with the group, Ross had five more pop chart-toppers through 1981, three of which—1975's "Love Hangover" (produced by Hal Davis), 1980's "Upside Down" (written and produced by Bernard Edwards and Nile Rodgers of Chic), and 1981's "Endless Love" (a duet with its writer and producer, Lionel Richie)—also reached the R&B peak.

"Endless Love" was the biggest selling single in the history of Motown, but by the end of 1981, the 20-year relationship between Ross and the company was also history (at least for the time being). She jumped ship to RCA, making her debut at the company with a self-produced remake of Frankie Lymon and the Teenagers' "Why Do Fools Fall in Love" that went to number six R&B and number seven pop. But she managed only one chart-topper during her seven-year association with the label, 1984's Number One R&B, number 10 pop "Missing You," a tribute to Marvin Gaye written and produced by Lionel Richie. Ross returned to Motown in 1989 and scored at number three R&B with the Nile Rodgers–produced "Workin' Overtime."

The vocalist made her acting debut as Billie Holiday in the 1972 motion picture *Lady Sings the Blues,* for which received an Oscar nomination as Best Actress. She also starred in the 1975 Gordy-produced film *Mahogany* and three years later in the screen adaptation of *The Wiz.*

SADE
· · · · · · ·

A cool, airy sophistication permeates the artful jazz- and Latin-tinged pop music of singer-songwriter Sade (b. Helen Folasade Adu, Jan. 16, 1959, Ibadan, Nigeria). Caressing her thoughtful lyrics and warm melodies in a silky, vibratoless alto that recalls the bittersweet tone of Miles Davis' trumpet, the Anglo-African chateuse became an international sensation upon the 1984 release of her debut *Diamond Life* LP and maintained her multi-platinum success with the subsequent albums *Promise, Stronger Than Pride,* and *Love Deluxe.*

"I consider myself to be a soul singer," Sade

(pronounced "**Sha**-day") stated in a 1984 interview with England's *Blues and Soul* magazine. "I know most people call me a jazz singer, but I think the real jazz enthusiasts would object to that." Her eclectic range of influences includes Ray Charles, Miles Davis, Gil Evans, Aretha Franklin, Marvin Gaye, Al Green, Billie Holiday, Rahsaan Roland Kirk, Teddy Pendergrass, Gil Scott-Heron, Nina Simone, Sly Stone, Tom Waits, Bill Withers, and the tropical '70s soul sounds of Miami's T.K. Records.

Basi and Anne Adu met in England while he was working on a master's degree at the London School of Economics. After the birth of son Banji, the family moved to Nigeria, where Mr. Adu took a position as a university lecturer. Sade, the Adu's second child, was born in Ibadan, a village 50 miles from the capital of Lagos. Following her parents' divorce, when she was four, Sade settled in the Essex village of Great Hawkesley with her brother, mother, and grandparents. Her passion for American soul music developed during her teen years in Holland-on-Sea.

At 17, Sade moved to London to enroll at St. Martin's College of Art, where she studied fashion and design for three years. She then began designing and selling her own line of men's clothing (some of which was worn by the group Spandau Ballet for its first U.S. appearance) as well as working as a fashion model.

In 1980, she joined the local Latin-funk band Arriva, which mutated into another group called Pride, in which she evolved from being one of the group's background vocalists into a soloist and songwriter. She formed a close musical relationship with three members of Pride—saxophonist-guitarist Stuart Matthewman, keyboardist Andrew Hale, and bassist Paul S. Denman—and cut a demo. Sade, the name of this quartet as well as of its vocalist, was signed to Epic Records in late 1983. Sade, Matthewman, Hale, and Denman have remained a unit ever since.

"Your Love Is King," Sade's debut single, was issued on February 8, 1984, and rose to number six on the British chart. A second single, "When Am I Going to Make a Living," was less successful. Then, on July 16, the Robin Millar–produced debut album *Diamond Life* was issued. It entered the British chart a week later—at number two—and sold over a million copies in England alone. In Holland, France, Germany, and New Zealand, it went to Number One.

Sade entered the U.S. market later that year with

"Hang on to Your Love," a single on the Portrait label that peaked at number 14 R&B but failed to dent the pop top 40. *Diamond Love,* which had been selling briskly as an import, was finally issued domestically in early 1985 and yielded the number five R&B and pop single "Smooth Operator" (written with former Arriva guitarist Ray St. John). The sophomore effort, *Promise,* largely produced by Millar, hit the stores in November of that year, rose to Number One on the *Billboard* album chart and spawned the singles "The Sweetest Taboo" (number three R&B, number five pop) and "Never As Good As the First Time" (number eight R&B, number 20 pop). Sade received a Grammy for Best New Artist of 1985.

The third album, 1988's group-produced *Stronger Than Pride,* was recorded in the Bahamas and in the south of France. It contained Sade's biggest R&B hit, the Number One "Paradise" (number 16 pop), as well as the number three R&B "Nothing Can Come Between Us" and the number 12 R&B "Turn My Back on You."

After taking a four-year break, part of which she spent living in Madrid, Sade and company returned in 1992 with the self-produced album *Love Deluxe,* made in Venice, Italy. Drawn from it were the singles "No Ordinary Love" (number nine R&B, number 28 pop) and "Kiss of Life" (number 10 R&B). Like Sade's previous works, *Love Deluxe* was an international favorite and a top 10 album in the U.S.

TOP ALBUMS

DIAMOND LIFE (Portrait, '85, 5)
PROMISE (Portrait, '85, 1)
STRONGER THAN PRIDE (Epic, '88, 7)
LOVE DELUXE (Epic, '92, 3)

TOP SONGS

SMOOTH OPERATOR (Portrait, '85, 5 R&B, 5 Pop)
THE SWEETEST TABOO (Portrait, '85, 3 R&B, 5 Pop)
NEVER AS GOOD AS THE FIRST TIME (Portrait, '86, 8 R&B, 20 Pop)
PARADISE (Epic, '88, 1 R&B, 16 Pop)
NOTHING CAN COME BETWEEN US (Epic, '88, 3 R&B)
NO ORDINARY LOVE (Epic, '92, 9 R&B, 28 Pop)

Additional Top 40 R&B Songs: 4

SAM AND DAVE

The beads of sweat that dripped like badly leaking faucets from the chins of Sam Moore (b. Oct. 12, 1935, Miami, Florida) and Dave Prater (b. May 9, 1937, Ocilla, Georgia) during their live performances practically oozed through the grooves of their Stax records. Both came from gospel quartet backgrounds, a tradition in which the lead singer s role is to work the congregation into spiritual delirium. Sam and Dave operated on the secular side like two preachers in tandem, trading intense leads, urging each other on verbally between phrases and joining together in chilling harmony to bring their listeners to a state of catharsis.

The Miami-based duo scored seven top 10 R&B hits for the Memphis-based Stax label over a period of little more than two years (1966–68). Two— "Hold On! I'm a Comin' " and "Soul Man"—went to Number One. All were written by Isaac Hayes and David Porter.

Sam, who grew up singing in church, made his first record, "Nitey Nite," in 1954 with a vocal group called the Majestics for Henry Stone's Marlin label in Miami. The doo wop group eventually reverted to gospel and became known as the Gales, a name inspired by the famous Sensational Nightingales. In 1959, he joined the Melionaires. It was while performing in church with one of those groups that Sam first met Dave, then with the Sensational Hummingbirds, another fledgling quartet that borrowed its moniker from an established gospel unit.

After seeing a Jackie Wilson show, Sam decided to return to R&B and landed a job as an emcee and warm-up singer at the King of Hearts, a Miami club owned by Fort Lauderdale mayor John Lomello. Dave, who also was pursuing a secular career, came by the club one night in 1961 to participate in a talent contest and ended up improvising a rendition of the Wilson hit "Doggin' Around" with Sam. The audience reception was so strong that Lomello booked them as a duo and recommended them to Henry Stone.

Sam and Dave's first single appeared in 1961 on Stone's Alston label, followed by another on Marlin. Both were produced by Steve Alaimo and Brad Shapiro. They generated enough local interest to be leased to Roulette Records. Five additional Sam and Dave singles were issued through 1963 by the New York company, some produced in that city by the veteran Henry Glover. None of the duo's early efforts made the national charts.

Jerry Wexler signed them to Atlantic in 1965, but in an unusual business arrangement, he sent them to Memphis to record for the Atlantic-distributed Stax label. The duo's first single, the Porter-penned, Prater-led "A Place Nobody Can Find," found little reception. The second, "I Take What I Want," fared little better but established the pattern for Sam and Dave's future Stax hits. Inspired by the title of an article in the "confessional" magazine *Bronze Thrills*, the hard-socking number was written by Hayes and Porter (with guitarist Mabon "Teenie" Hodges) and was the first Sam and Dave side to feature the two singers tossing lines back and forth with frenzied abandon.

Their third release, 1966's "You Don't Know Like I Know," became their first chart hit, peaking at number seven R&B. The next, "Hold On! I'm a Comin'," went all the way to Number One and crossed to number 21 on the pop chart. After three more top 10 R&B singles—"Said I Wasn't Gonna Tell Nobody," "You Got Me Hummin'," and the slow-dragging ballad "When Something Is Wrong with My Baby," Sam and Dave broke through to the pop top 10 with the number two (Number One R&B) "Soul Man" in 1967 and the number nine (number four R&B) "I Thank You" early the next year.

Sam and Dave's newfound fortunes began to decline when Stax ended its distribution deal with Atlantic in May 1968. The duo's records then began appearing on Atlantic. Four Hayes-Porter–produced leftovers from the Stax period, including 1969's "Soul Sister, Brown Sugar," were moderate R&B chart hits, but the crossover momentum had died.

By the time of their final Atlantic release, 1971's "Don't Pull Your Love," produced by Brad Shapiro and Dave Crawford, Sam and Dave had broken up. Sam recorded as a solo artist for Atlantic and Dave for Alston, neither with much success. They were reunited in 1974 at United Artists for a Steve Cropper–produced United Artists album that quickly wound up in the cutout bins, after which they recorded for Contempo in England before splitting up again.

The Blues Brothers' 1979 hit parody of "Soul Man" prompted the pair to perform again, but the reunion lasted only two years and yielded no records. Sam himself revived "Soul Man" in duet with Lou Reed for the soundtack of the 1986 motion picture of the same title, and teamed with Jr. Walker for the 1988 film *Tapeheads* and with Bruce Springsteen for the rock star's 1992 album *Human Touch*. Dave was killed in a car crash on April 9, 1988, near Sycamore, Georgia.

SHALAMAR

"**U**ptown Festival," a disco collage of old Motown songs by a group billed as Shalamar, appeared in early 1977 on Soul Train Records, a label formed two years earlier by concert promoter Dick Griffey and TV dance-show host Don Cornelius. Initially a dance club hit, the single rose to number 10 on the *Billboard* R&B chart and to number 25 pop. Requests for live appearances created a dilemma, however, as there was no such group as Shalamar. The medley had been performed by a bunch of studio singers, including Gary Mumford.

Cornelius solved the problem by recruiting two of the most popular dancers from "Soul Train"—Jody Watley (b. Jan. 30, 1961, Chicago) and Jeffrey Daniel (b. Aug. 24, 1957, Los Angeles)—to join Mumford in forming a real group. Watley, the daughter of a radio evangelist and his piano-playing wife, and former gospel singer Daniel had been creating a sensation on the syndicated program since 1974 with their imaginatively choreographed routines.

"It was a serious thing," Watley said in 1982. "We worked hard to become the most creative couple on the dance floor. I started dancing with Oriental

TOP SONGS

You Don't Know Like I Know (Stax, '66, 7 *R&B*)

Hold On! I'm a Comin' (Stax, '66, 1 *R&B, 21 Pop*)

Said I Wasn't Gonna Tell Nobody (Stax, '66, 8 *R&B*)

You Got Me Hummin' (Stax, '66, 7 *R&B*)

When Something Is Wrong with My Baby (Stax, '67, 2 *R&B*)

Soothe Me (Stax, '67, 16 *R&B*)

Soul Man (Stax, '67, 1 *R&B, 2 Pop*)

I Thank You (Stax, '68, 4 *R&B, 9 Pop*)

Can't You Find Another Way (Of Doing It) (Atlantic, '68, 19 *R&B*)

Soul Sister, Brown Sugar (Atlantic, '69, 18 *R&B*)

Additional Top 40 R&B Songs: 3

fans. Jeffrey brought in mannequins. We roller-skated. Basically, we did things the other dancers didn't have the nerve to do."

Watley and Daniel brought their voices, as well as their visual flair, to Shalamar. Lead singer Mumford soon dropped out and was replaced by Gerald Brown by the time of the trio's second significant hit, 1978's number 11 R&B "Take That to the Bank" on Griffey's new Solar (Sound of Los Angeles Records) label. It was co-written and co-produced by Leon Sylvers III, who would remain the primary creative force behind Shalamar's recordings through the mid-1980s. When Brown quit in the middle of a 1979 tour, Griffey quickly auditioned another ex-gospel singer, Howard Hewitt (b. Oct. 1, 1957, Akron, Ohio), and gave him a plane ticket to join the group in New Jersey.

With Hewitt's emotively ringing tenor at the helm, Shalamar hit the top of the R&B chart with 1979's "The Second Time Around," a distinctively loping Sylvers and William Shelby dance tune from the album *Big Fun*. The trio's popularity spread to England, where in 1982 three singles from the album *Friends*—"I Can Make You Feel Good," "A Night to Remember," and "There It Is"—placed in the top 10. Daniel (whose short-lived 1980 marriage to Stephanie Mills had created much fodder for the teen magazines) and Watley (who'd co-led with Hewitt on the ballad "A Night to Remember") were beginning to feel creatively stifled within the group. Both left in 1983 and moved to England, Daniel to host the British edition of "Soul Train," Watley for a vacation that turned into a two-and-a-half-year stay and career as a fashion model.

A new Shalamar—Hewitt, Micki Free (a former associate of Prince bassist Brown Mark), and Delia Davis (a onetime Miss Teenage Georgia and Miss Tennessee State)—emerged in 1985 with a more

Shalamar

rock-oriented sound on the album *Heart Break*, containing the number 18 R&B, number 17 hit "Dancing in the Sheets" from the soundtrack of the motion picture *Footloose* and the Grammy-winning "Don't Get Stopped in Beverly Hills" from *Beverly Hills Cop*. Hewitt left in 1985 to pursue a solo career and was replaced by New Orleans–born singer Sidney Justin, a defensive back with both the Los Angeles Rams and the Baltimore Colts before an injury ended his football career.

The Justin-Free-Davis edition of Shalamar scored with two singles—the number 30 R&B "Circumstantial Evidence" and the number 11 "Games"—from a 1987 Solar album. The next, 1990's *Wake Up* on Epic, left radio programmers snoozing and generated no hits.

As Shalamar drifted into oblivion, Hewitt's and Watley's solo careers soared. Signed to Elektra, he enjoyed four top 10 R&B hits, including 1986's "I'm for Real" and 1990's "Show Me," both of which peaked at number two. She was even more successful. The 1987 MCA album *Jody Watley* yielded four top 10 R&B and pop hits, including the Number One R&B, number two pop "Looking for a New Love." She repeated that statistical feat in 1989 with "Real Love" from the album *Larger Than Life*. Both hits were co-written by Watley and her boyfriend, early Prince associate Andre Cymone.

TOP ALBUM

BIG FUN (Solar, '80, 23)

Additional Top 40 Albums: 3

TOP SONGS

UPTOWN FESTIVAL (Soul Train, '77, *10 R&B, 25 Pop*)

TAKE THAT TO THE BANK (Solar, '78, *11 R&B*)

THE SECOND TIME AROUND (Solar, '79, *1 R&B, 8 Pop*)

MAKE THAT MOVE (Solar, '81, *6 R&B*)

THIS IS FOR THE LOVER IN YOU (Solar, '81, *17 R&B*)

A NIGHT TO REMEMBER (Solar, '82, *8 R&B*)

DEAD GIVEAWAY (Solar, '83, *10 R&B, 22 Pop*)

DANCING IN THE SHEETS (Columbia, '84, *18 R&B, 17 Pop*)

GAMES (Solar, '87, *11 R&B*)

Additional Top 40 R&B Songs: 8

THE SHIRELLES

The Shirelles were the most popular "girl group" of the early 1960s and paved the way for such others as the Chiffons, the Crystals, the Marvelettes, the Orlons, and the Ronettes. Comprising four natives of Passaic, New Jersey—Shirley Owens Alston (b. June 10, 1941), Doris Kenner Jackson (b. Aug. 2, 1941), Addie "Micki" Harris (b. Jan. 22, 1940), and Beverly Lee (b. Aug. 3, 1941)—they scored 11 top 40 R&B hits between 1960 and 1963, seven of which made the top 10. They did even better on the pop charts, with two singles—1960's "Will You Love Me Tomorrow" and 1962's "Soldier Boy"—going to Number One.

"We were considered pop," Alston said in a 1984 interview with Randy Russi of *Goldmine* magazine. "We never were considered an R&B act."

Alston and Harris had known each other since elementary school and met Jackson and Lee in junior high. Inspired by the Chantels and the Bobbettes, among others, they began singing together for fun and named themselves the Poquellos (Spanish for "little birds"). During their sophomore year in high school, they wrote a tune titled "I Met Him on Sunday" and performed it at a talent show at the school. Classmate Mary Jane Greenberg was so impressed with their sound that she began insisting they audition for her mother, Florence, who was running a little record company called Tiara. After much coaxing, the four teenagers finally auditioned in Mrs. Greenberg's living room and were signed to a five-year contract. She didn't like their name and suggested "Honeytones." They balked at the idea and instead came up with something along the lines of "Chantels": "Shirelles."

With Stan Green, the company owner's son, handling the band, the Shirelles cut "I Met Him on Sunday" on February 7, 1958. It appeared on Tiara before being picked up by Decca and becoming a minor national pop hit. Two subsequent Decca releases were less successful, after which Greenberg formed a new company, Scepter Records, and employed the services of songwriter-producer Luther Dixon, a onetime member of the Four Buddies who'd proven his penchant for pop as the composer of tunes for such artists as Pat Boone, Nat "King" Cole, Perry Como, and the Crests.

The teenage singers had heard the Five Royales do an original blues ballad titled "Dedicated to the

TOP ALBUM

THE SHIRELLES GREATEST HITS (Scepter, '63, *19*)

TOP SONGS

TONIGHT'S THE NIGHT (Scepter, '60, *14 R&B, 39 Pop*)

WILL YOU LOVE ME TOMORROW (Scepter, '60, *2 R&B, 1 Pop*)

DEDICATED TO THE ONE I LOVE (Scepter, '61, *2 R&B, 3 Pop*)

MAMA SAID (Scepter, '61, *2 R&B, 4 Pop*)

BIG JOHN (Scepter, '61, *2 R&B, 21 Pop*)

BABY IT'S YOU (Scepter, '62, *3 R&B, 8 Pop*)

SOLDIER BOY (Scepter, '62, *3 R&B, 1 Pop*)

EVERYBODY LOVES A LOVER (Scepter, '62, *15 R&B, 19 Pop*)

FOOLISH LITTLE GIRL (Scepter, '63, *9 R&B, 4 Pop*)

Additional Top 40 R&B Songs: 2

a half later when reissued in the wake of "Will You Love Me Tomorrow."

The quartet had its first substantial hit in 1960 with the Alston-led "Tonight's the Night," a number penned by Dixon and Alston that rose to number 14 on the *Billboard* R&B chart and to number 39 pop. Dixon gave the tune a Caribbean beat because, he told author Bruce Pollock, "we knew there was a West Indian market in New York City, and they're the ones who bought the record first." Strings were used to give it more pop appeal.

With Dixon's market-wise productions and Alston's declarative alto leads, the Shirelles went on to have massive R&B and pop impact with such hits as "Will You Love Me Tomorrow" (written by Carole King and Gerry Goffin), "Mama Said" (co-written by Dixon), "Baby It's You" (by Burt Bacharach, Hal David, and Barney Williams), and "Soldier Boy" (by Dixon and Greenberg). Dixon's departure from Scepter for a position at Capitol Records signaled the end of the group's hit streak, after which they had only two more top 40 entries, the number nine R&B, number four pop "Foolish Little Girl" and the number 26 pop "Don't Say Goodnight and Mean Goodbye," both in 1963.

One I Love" at the Howard Theater in Washington, D.C., and offered it for their debut Scepter session. The Shirelles' version, featuring Jackson's plaintive lead, became a minor pop charter in 1959 but rose to number two R&B and number three pop a year and

The Shirelles

A suit against Scepter, in which the women charged the company with having failed to turn over monies that were supposedly being held in trust until they reached 21, kept the Shirelles off the recording scene during the mid-1960s. They briefly returned to the label in 1967, then moved to Black Rock in '68, to Bell in '69, to United Artists in '70, and to RCA Victor in '71, all without much notice.

Jackson retired from the Shirelles in 1968 but rejoined seven years later to replace Alston, who'd left to pursue a a solo career. Harris died of a heart attack following a performance with the group in Atlanta on June 10, 1982. A year later, Alston was reunited with Jackson and Lee to sing on former Scepter labelmate Dionne Warwick's Luther Van-dross–produced Arista recording of "Will You Love Me Tomorrow."

JOE SIMON

Like Roy Hamilton and Jackie Wilson before him, Joe Simon (b. Sept. 2, 1943, Simmesport, Louisiana) effectively combined the seemingly opposing traditions of European opera and African-American gospel music. The soul star didn't attempt to sing serious opera, although his live performances sometimes included a hilarious lampoon of Italian opera in which he would do both the baritone and soprano parts in a duet with himself. Inspired by Arthur Prysock, as well as by the Five Blind Boys of Mississippi and the Soul Stirrers, Simon used his booming, remarkably elastic baritone voice to evoke great emotion—as he did when he brought tears to the eyes of mourners with a spiritual at Otis Redding's funeral—on both tender country ballads and driving disco tunes.

Apart from his connection to opera, the vocalist's major contribution to American music was in the field of soul-country fusion. Ray Charles had popularized the process earlier, but with his own band, and Joe Tex had been recording his own soul songs with Nashville studio musicians, but Simon was the first soul man to cut country tunes with Nashville country pickers and score a string of hits, beginning in 1969 with "The Chokin' Kind." The Harlan Howard composition had previously been recorded by Waylon Jennings, but in Simon's hands it didn't sound like a country record, nor like any other soul record before it. Produced by his manager, John

Richbourg (a disc jockey better known to listeners of Nashville's WLAC as "John R"), "The Chokin' Kind" became the first of the singer's three chart-topping R&B hits.

The idea of recording country songs did not appeal to Simon at first. "I didn't know how to pick songs, but by workin' with John R., I learned how to appreciate lyrics," he said in 1981. "For that reason, I now like country songs. Country, gospel, and R&B are very close. There's a thin line between the three of them."

Simon began his singing career with the Golden West Gospel Singers in the late 1950s, shortly after moving to Richmond, California. With members of that quartet, he organized a doo wop group called the Golden Tones, with whom he made his first record, "Little Island Girl," in 1959 for local producer Gary Thompson's Hush label. By the next year, Simon had gone solo and scored another hit in the San Francisco–Oakland area with "It's a Miracle," also on Hush. In 1964, his recording of "My Adorable One" for Thompson's Irral label began to attract national attention, prompting Vee-Jay Records in Chicago to purchase his contract. Simon saw his first national chart entry the following year with the number 13 R&B Rick Hall–produced "Let's Do It Over."

After the collapse of Vee-Jay, the vocalist signed in 1966 with Richbourg's Monument-distributed Sound Stage 7 label and had such moderate R&B hits as "Teenager's Prayer," "My Special Prayer," "Nine

---

TOP SONGS

THE CHOKIN' KIND (Sound Stage 7, '69, *1 R&B, 13 Pop*)

YOUR TIME TO CRY (Spring, '70, *3 R&B, 40 Pop*)

DROWNING IN THE SEA OF LOVE (Spring, '71, *3 R&B, 11 Pop*)

POWER OF LOVE (Spring, '72, *1 R&B, 11 Pop*)

TROUBLE IN MY HOME (Spring, '72, *5 R&B*)

STEP BY STEP (Spring, '73, *6 R&B, 37 Pop*)

THEME FROM CLEOPATRA JONES (Spring, '73, *3 R&B, 18 Pop*)

RIVER (Spring, '73, *6 R&B*)

GET DOWN, GET DOWN (GET ON THE FLOOR) (Spring, '75, *1 R&B, 8 Pop*)

I NEED YOU, YOU NEED ME (Spring, '76, *5 R&B*)

Additional Top 40 R&B Songs: 29

Pound Steel," and "(You Keep Me) Hangin' On" before reaching the chart summit with "The Chokin' Kind." Later Nashville-made R&B charters included "Baby, Don't Be Looking in My Mind," "Farther On Down the Road," "Yours Love," "Help Me Make It Through the Night," and "Misty Blue."

In 1970, Richbourg took Simon to the Polydor-distributed Spring label, where he stayed for the rest of the decade. The singer was soon working in Philadelphia with producer-songwriters Kenny Gamble and Leon Huff, an association yielding the number three R&B "Drowning in the Sea of Love" in 1971 and the next year's Number One R&B "Power of Love." Simon remained a fixture on the R&B top 10 and hit Number One again in 1975 with "Get Down, Get Down (Get on the Floor)," a disco stomper he wrote and produced with Raeford Gerald.

By the late 1980s, Simon's sales were slipping badly and he started donning bouffant wigs and dangling earrings in an attempt to attract publicity. The ploy backfired, drawing decidedly negative response from his fans, after which he reverted to a more masculine image, even growing a beard for the first time. He signed with Posse Records in 1980 and recorded an album in Nashville produced by country singer Porter Wagoner. It generated little attention, as did 1986 sessions with producer Skip Scarborough for the Compleat label. At the end of the decade, Simon moved back to his native Louisiana and became a traveling evangelist, still singing, although "Amazing Grace" had replaced "The Chokin' Kind" in his repertoire.

SISTER SLEDGE

Philadelphia's Sledge sisters—Debbie (b. 1955), Joni (b. 1957), Kim (b. 1958), and Kathy (b. 1959)—gave themselves a decade to make it in the music business. Known collectively as Sister Sledge, they spent eight years on the fringe of stardom and were getting close to throwing in the towel when, in 1979, they scored two back-to-back R&B chart-toppers, "He's the Greatest Dancer" and "We Are Family," both written and produced by Bernard Edwards and Nile Rodgers of Chic.

The four sisters began singing as children at Philadelphia's Second Macedonia Church and were greatly encouraged by mother Flo, older sister Carol,

---

TOP ALBUMS

WE ARE FAMILY (Cotillion, '79, 3)
LOVE SOMEBODY TODAY (Cotillion, '80, 31)

TOP SONGS

HE'S THE GREATEST DANCER (Cotillion, '79, 1 R&B, 9 Pop)
WE ARE FAMILY (Cotillion, '79, 1 R&B, 2 Pop)
GOT TO LOVE SOMEBODY (Cotillion, '80, 6 R&B)
REACH YOUR PEAK (Cotillion, '80, 21 R&B)
ALL AMERICAN GIRLS (Cotillion, '81, 3 R&B)
NEXT TIME YOU'LL KNOW (Cotillion, '81, 28 R&B)
MY GUY (Cotillion, '82, 14 R&B, 23 Pop)
B.Y.O.B. (BRING YOUR OWN BABY) (Cotillion, '83, 22 R&B)

Additional Top 40 R&B Songs: 4

---

and grandmother Viola Hairston Williams, an operatic soprano. Originally known as Mrs. Williams' Grandchildren, then as Brand New Generation, A Group Called Sledge, and the Sledge Sisters, they became Sister Sledge as the result of an emcee's error. They took a liking to the singular name, because it symbolized, according to Joni, "oneness and togetherness in mind and body."

Carol Sledge, a music teacher, was friendly with a member of the Stylistics, which led her siblings to the local Money Back label, where in 1971 they cut their first record, a girl-group ballad titled "Time Will Tell." It was produced by Marty Brown and featured the band Slim and the Boys, the same team behind the Stylistics' debut single "You're a Big Girl Now." The young women began doing session work at Sigma Sound Studios before being signed to Atlantic Records by executive Henry Allen.

Two singles, "Weatherman" and "Mama Never Told Me," produced in Philadelphia by the Young Professionals, appeared on the Atco label in 1973. Neither made the charts at the time, although the Jackson Five–inspired "Mama Never Told Me" showed up two years later in England at number 20. Also in 1973, the Young Professionals used the sisters to back non-relative Percy Sledge on "Sunshine," a minor R&B hit on Atlantic.

Sister Sledge broke into the R&B top 40 in early 1975 with the number 31 "Love Don't You Go Through No Changes on Me," produced by Tony Sylvester and Bert DeCoteaux. It would be their only

Sister Sledge

R&B top 40 single until 1979. Transferred to the Cotillion label, they were shuffled among such producers as Brad Shapiro, Bobby Eli, and Munich disco-meisters Michael Kunze and Sylvester Levay before landing in the Chic camp. Even without hits, however, the quartet maintained a busy schedule that included tours with the Spinners, an appearance at the Muhammad Ali–George Foreman heavyweight championship fight in Zaire, and a win at the fourth annual Tokyo Music International Contest.

When Atlantic offered Edwards and Rodgers the opportunity to produce any act on the its roster, including the Rolling Stones and Bette Midler, they selected Sister Sledge. The result was the album *We Are Family*, containing the international crossover smashes "He's the Greatest Dancer" and the title song, both featuring Kathy's husky alto leads. The infectious "We Are Family" was quickly adopted as an anthem by both the feminist and gay rights movements, as well as by the 1979 World Series–winning Pittsburgh Pirates. For their first tour as headliners, however, Debbie was on maternity leave, her place in the group filled by sister Carol.

The sisters' success came at a time in which a

backlash against disco was brewing in the U.S. A second album with Edwards and Rodgers, 1980's *Love Somebody Today*, fared less well, yielding the number six R&B "Got to Love Somebody" and the number 21 R&B "Reach Your Peak," but no top 40 pop singles. The group scored its last major hit the next year with the number three R&B "All American Girls," to which producer Narada Michael Walden applied a dance-oriented, Chic-like sheen.

After 1983's number 14 R&B "My Guy," a group-produced remake of the old Mary Wells hit, and the following year's George Duke–produced number 22 R&B "B.Y.O.B. (Bring Your Own Baby)," the women cut the 1985 Rodgers-produced Atlantic album *When the Boys Meet the Girls*. "Frankie," a perky, reggae-imbued single from the disc, went only as high as number 32 R&B and became the sisters' last top 40 R&B entry. In England, however, it rose all the way to Number One.

Kathy left the group in 1989 for a solo career but managed only one moderate hit, 1992's number 24 R&B "Take Me Back to Love Again" on Epic. Debbie, Joni, and Kim continued on as a trio, spending much of their time performing overseas.

Percy Sledge

PERCY SLEDGE

The heart-wrenching, country-tinged soul ballad "When a Man Loves a Woman" has had a life that outdistanced the notoriety of Percy Sledge (b. Nov. 15, 1940, Leighton, Alabama), the singer who made it a smash in 1966. The unadorned, hauntingly plaintive performance marked the singer's debut in a studio and became the first southern soul record to hit the top of the *Billboard* pop chart. As Sledge faded from the spotlight, scoring only three more top 10 R&B chart entries over the next two years, the song remained a popular oldie, the background for countless make-out sessions and marriages.

In England, it reached number four in 1966 then returned 19 years later at number two in the wake of a Levi's 501 commercial in which it was featured. Michael Bolton's version became a U.S. pop chart-topper in 1991 and earned him a Grammy, while the Sledge original emerged the next year on the soundtrack of the hit film *The Crying Game*. In 1993, BMI named it Song of the Year. And in 1994, the Sledge recording served as the theme song for a Luis Mandoki motion picture titled—of all things—*When a Man Loves a Woman*.

"It's kind of mind-boggling to me that the song is still doing what it's doing," Calvin Lewis (the song's co-author with Andrew Wright) later told Harry Weinger of *BMI Music World*. "At the time we wrote it, it didn't hit me what having an 'A' side release meant until the song was well on its way to number one."

Sledge was working as an orderly at Colbert County Hospital at the time of the recording. He was then singing at night with the Esquires, a four-piece band that appeared at clubs and fraternity parties throughout Alabama, Mississippi, and Tennessee. He had taken over the vocal chores in the group from his cousin Jimmy Hughes of "Steal Away" fame, with whom he earlier had performed gospel in a quartet called the Singing Clouds.

At one of the Esquires' engagements, Sledge was in an especially desolate mood and began improvising lyrics to some gospel chord changes by organist Wright. The song, originally titled "Why Did You Leave Me," found its way to Quin Ivy, a disc jockey and record store owner in Sheffield, Alabama, who was trying to get his primitive recording studio off the ground. Ivy had Lewis, the Esquires' bassist, come up with some new lyrics. Working with co-producer and guitarist Marlin Greene and using musicians borrowed from his friend Rick Hall's Fame Studio in nearby Muscle Shoals, Ivy cut "When a Man Loves a Woman" around Christmas of 1965.

"Percy was so out of tune we thought his voice might break a window," engineer Jimmy Johnson later told author Peter Guralnick. The three-man horn section was also off-pitch. Yet those qualities

---

TOP SONGS

WHEN A MAN LOVES A WOMAN (Atlantic, '66, 1 *R&B, 1 Pop*)

WARM AND TENDER LOVE (Atlantic, '66, *5 R&B, 17 Pop*)

IT TEARS ME UP (Atlantic, '66, *7 R&B, 20 Pop*)

OUT OF LEFT FIELD (Atlantic, '67, *25 R&B*)

LOVE ME TENDER (Atlantic, '67, *35 R&B, 40 Pop*)

COVER ME (Atlantic, '67, *39 R&B*)

TAKE TIME TO KNOW HER (Atlantic, '68, *6 R&B, 11 Pop*)

ANY DAY NOW (Atlantic, '69, *35 R&B*)

I'LL BE YOUR EVERYTHING (Capricorn, '74, *15 R&B*)

only seemed to heighten the song's tear-jerking ambience. Hall felt it could be a Number One record and phoned Jerry Wexler, who agreed and issued it on Atlantic, warts and all.

"When a Man Loves a Woman" topped both the R&B and pop charts and launched Muscle Shoals as a major recording center. Sledge remained on the Atlantic roster for eight years. With Ivy and Green producing, he scored later in 1966 with the number five R&B, number 17 pop "Warm and Tender Love" and the number seven R&B, number 20 pop "It Tears Me Up" and again in 1968 with the number six R&B, number 11 pop "Take Time to Know Her," all of which were country-soul ballads in the mold of his first.

While the domestic hits dried up after 1969, Sledge became a top-seller in South Africa, and an early 1970s tour of that racially segregated country generated some controversy back home. In 1973, hoping to modernize the vocalist's by-then-dated southern soul sound, Atlantic sent him to Philadelphia to work with producers LeBaron Taylor, Phil Hurtt, and Bunny Sigler. The resulting single, "Sunshine," to which non-relatives Sister Sledge contributed background vocals, flopped and Sledge was dropped by the company. (The song became a moderate R&B hit for the O'Jays a year later.)

Signing with Capricorn Records in 1974, Sledge had his first top 40 R&B charter in five years with the number 15 Ivy-produced "I'll Be Your Everything." It was also his last, and few additional recordings followed. He surfaced in Nashville in 1980 with an album on Gusto of new versions of his old songs. Having settled in Louisiana, Sledge returned to Sheffield in 1986 and '87 to cut an all-country album with producer David Johnson that was issued as *Wanted Again* in 1989 by England's Demon Records.

SLY AND THE FAMILY STONE

The innovations that Sly Stone (b. Sylvester Stewart, Mar. 15, 1943, Denton, Texas) unleashed on the world in 1968 had a permanent effect on the direction of African-American popular music. With his multi-racial, mixed-sex band, the Family Stone, the singer, multi-instrumen-

Sly Stone

talist, songwriter, and producer ushered in the era of the self-contained band by freeing the music from its vocalists-with-backup-band mold, and the popping bass style of original member Larry Graham set the pulse for what became known as funk. Sly's genre-crossing mix of soul and rock not only influenced future stars like the Jackson Five, George Clinton's Parliament-Funkadelic, the Bar-Kays, the Ohio Players, Rick James, and Prince but also changed the course for such already established artists as the Temptations and Stevie Wonder.

Sly reigned for a little less than four years, after which his creations became sporadic and less profound. His downhill slide began almost as soon as he had reached the mountaintop. Following his triumphant 1969 appearance at Woodstock, he started showing up late or not at all for engagements. His music turned from the joyous celebration of 1968's

"Dance to the Music" to the dark cynicism of 1971's *There's a Riot Goin' On,* an album containing the hit "Family Affair." The man who had wanted to take everyone higher took himself so high on cocaine that he was never able to come down for long, and when he did, he appeared a burned-out shadow of his former self.

His career began as a religious family affair in Vallejo, California, near San Francisco. His mother, Alpha Stewart, sang and played guitar at a local Church of God in Christ, and his father, K. C. Stewart, served as a deacon. With older sister Loretta on piano, Sly sang with younger siblings Rose, Freddie, and Vaetta in the Stewart Four. The gospel group appeared at churches throughout the state and cut a 78, "On the Battlefield," for the Church of God in Christ Northern California Sunday School Dept. label.

Sly taught himself to play guitar and soon mastered organ, harmonica, and other instruments. He became lead vocalist of the Viscaynes, a doo wop group with which he cut two singles—"Stop What You're Doing" on the Tropo label and "Yellow Moon" (a pop top 10 hit in the Bay Area) on VPM—in 1960 and '61. After studying musical theory and composition for three years at Vallejo Junior College, he hooked up with Tom Donahue's Autumn Records and produced Bobby Freeman's national

number five pop hit "C'mon and Swim" in 1964 and the Beau Brummels' number eight "Just a Little Love" the next year, as well as his own instrumental single "Buttermilk." Other early Sly productions include the Mojo Men and the Great Society for Autumn and Gloria Scott for Warner Bros.

Sly maintained a hectic schedule during the mid-1960s, also leading his own band, the Stoners, and working as a disc jockey at KSOL in San Francisco, then at KDIA in Oakland. His mix of records by Bob Dylan, the Beatles, and other rock artists into the Motown and Stax fare reflected a daring eclecticism that would further reveal itself in Sly and the Family Stone.

The band was born in 1966 when the Stoners merged with guitarist Freddie Stewart's Stone Souls. The original Family Stone consisted of Sly, Freddie, Graham, trumpeter Cynthia Robinson, saxophonist Jerry Martini, and drummer Greg Errico. Sister Rose joined after the release of the group's little-noticed debut album, 1967's *A Whole New Thing* on Epic. Their career took off in early 1968 with "Dance to the Music." Three subsequent singles—1968's "Everyday People," 1970's "Thank You (Falettinme Be Mice Elf Agin)," and 1971's "Family Affair"—topped both the R&B and pop charts. And, in 1970, Sly launched his own short-lived, Atlantic-distributed Stone Flower label, for which he wrote and produced two hits—the number four R&B "You're the One" and the number eight R&B "Somebody's Watching You"—by Little Sister, a female vocal trio that included sister Vaetta.

The leader's increasingly erratic behavior led band members to become disaffected. Graham left in 1972 and soon formed Graham Central Station. By the 1976 release of the group's final Epic album, *Heard Ya Missed Me, Well I'm Back,* only Robinson remained. It, like 1979 and 1983 albums for Warner Bros., generated minimal interest.

Sly surfaced from time to time during the 1980s. He briefly joined the P-Funk camp, performing on George Clinton's 1981 album *Electric Spanking of War Babies* and on the next year's single "Hydrolic Pump" by the P-Funk All-Stars; sang a duet with Martha Davis on "Love and Affection" from the soundtrack of the 1986 motion picture *Soul Man;* and contributed to albums by Bobby Womack, the Bar-Kays, and Jesse Johnson. The troubled musician made his last chart appearance at number two R&B on former Time member Johnson's 1986 A&M single "Crazay."

TOP ALBUM

THERE'S A RIOT GOIN' ON (Epic, '71, *1*)

Additional Top 40 Albums: 4

TOP SONGS

DANCE TO THE MUSIC (Epic, '68, *9 R&B, 8 Pop*)

EVERYDAY PEOPLE (Epic, '68, *1 R&B, 1 Pop*)

HOT FUN IN THE SUMMERTIME (Epic, '69, *3 R&B, 2 Pop*)

THANK YOU (FALETTINME BE MICE ELF AGIN) (Epic, '70, *1 R&B, 1 Pop*)

FAMILY AFFAIR (Epic, '71, *1 R&B, 1 Pop*)

IF YOU WANT ME TO STAY (Epic, '73, *3 R&B, 12 Pop*)

TIME FOR LIVIN' (Epic, '74, *10 R&B, 32 Pop*)

I GET HIGH ON YOU (Sly Stone, Epic, '75, *3 R&B*)

CRAZAY (Jesse Johnson featuring Sly Stone, A&M, '86, *2 R&B*)

Additional Top 40 R&B Songs: 8

The Spinners

THE SPINNERS

Although the Spinners' chart history spans from 1961 to 1984, it was during a briefer period—1972 to 1977—that the Detroit-based vocal group enjoyed its greatest popularity, scoring a total of 14 entries in the top 10 of the *Billboard* R&B singles chart. Six of them—"I'll Be Around," "Could It Be I'm Falling in Love," "One of a Kind (Love Affair)," "Mighty Love," "They Just Can't Stop It the (Games People Play)," and "The Rubberband Man"—went to Number One. All were produced and arranged by Thom Bell for Atlantic Records. And all featured lead vocals by Philippe Wynne (b. Apr. 3, 1941, Cincinnati, Ohio).

The group had only three top 10 R&B charters prior to Wynne's recruitment in 1971 and only two following his departure less than six years later. The bespectacled vocalist was the Spinners' spark plug, an inspired, spontaneous stylist who fashioned a highly distinctive approach, inspired by Sam Cooke, Otis Redding, and Billy Stewart, that was filled with gospel yodels, melismatic warbles, and sputtering scats. If Wynne sang like a man possessed, he matched his buoyant improvisations with an effervescent stage manner that found him skipping through the aisles or standing still with his arms outstretched, hands waving, fingers wiggling.

Pervis Jackson, Billy Henderson, and Henry Fambrough began singing together while in elementary school in Ferndale, Michigan. In 1955, while attending Ferndale High, they were joined by George Dixon to become the Domingoes and performed their first engagement at the Idlewild Resort outside Detroit singing a cappella on a bill with the Four Aims. "They were dancing then," Fambrough said of the Aims, later known as the Four Tops. "That's when we first thought of putting routines to our act."

Bobbie Smith, who joined the Domingoes around 1957, suggested a name change. "Back in the '50s," he explained, "all the kids had the hot rod cars with big wide skirts and great big Cadillac hubcaps that they called 'spinners.' "

TOP ALBUM

PICK OF THE LITTER (Atlantic, '75, 8)

Additional Top 40 Albums: 7

TOP SONGS

IT'S A SHAME (V.I.P., '70, 4 R&B, 14 Pop)
I'LL BE AROUND (Atlantic, '72, 1 R&B, 3 Pop)
COULD IT BE I'M FALLING IN LOVE (Atlantic, '72, 1 R&B, 4 Pop)
ONE OF A KIND (LOVE AFFAIR) (Atlantic, '73, 1 R&B, 11 Pop)
MIGHTY LOVE—PART 1 (Atlantic, '74, 1 R&B, 20 Pop)
I'M COMING HOME (Atlantic, '74, 3 R&B, 18 Pop)
THEN CAME YOU (Dionne Warwicke and the Spinners, Atlantic, '74, 2 R&B, 1 Pop)
THEY JUST CAN'T STOP IT THE (GAMES PEOPLE PLAY) (Atlantic, '75, 1 R&B, 5 Pop)
THE RUBBERBAND MAN (Atlantic, '76, 1 R&B, 2 Pop)

Additional Top 40 R&B Songs: 24

During their formative years—and as part of their stage act ever since—the Spinners specialized in imitating other groups. Their favorite was the Moonglows, led by Harvey Fuqua. It was perhaps ironic that, in 1961, after Fuqua had disbanded the Moonglows and moved to Detroit to start his own record company with wife Gwen Gordy, he would take the Spinners under his wing. That year, the group cut its first single, the Fuqua-Gordy ballad "That's What Girls Are Made For," for the couple's Tri-Phi label. The song, on which Smith's plaintive lead tenor sounded so much like Fuqua's that many have mistakenly assumed that it was that of the former Moonglow, became a number eight R&B hit and sent the Spinners on the road playing major theaters across the country, including the Uptown in Philadelphia, where the house band included pianist Thom Bell.

After the release of five more singles on Tri-Phi, the label was swallowed up in 1964 by Motown, where the Spinners became lost in the shuffle through 1971. Only two singles—1965's number eight "I'll Always Love You" (written by William Stevenson and Ivy Hunter) on Motown and 1970's number four "It's a Shame" (produced and co-written by Stevie Wonder) on the V.I.P. label—made the R&B top 10 during the quintet's association with the Detroit firm. Featured on "It's a Shame" was G. C.

Cameron, who'd joined the group in 1967. (Earlier leads were George Dixon, Edgar "Chico" Edwards, and Crathman Spencer.) When the Spinners finally left Motown, Cameron opted to stay as a solo artist, but he put them in touch with Philippe Wynne, who'd sung previously in Cincinatti with the Pacesetters, a band led by bassist Bootsy Collins.

Wynne gave the Spinners a five-year string of smashes and then launched a solo career that yielded only two R&B top 40 charters: 1977's number 17 "Hats Off to Mama" on Cotillion and 1983's number 33 "Wait 'Til Tomorrow/Bye Bye Love" on Fantasy. He also hooked up with George Clinton for a period and was featured on Funkadelic's Number One R&B 1979 hit "(Not Just) Knee Deep" on Warner Bros. On July 13, 1984, as he was jumping off the stage into the audience at a club in Oakland, Wynne was stricken with a heart attack and died.

St. Louis–born singer John Edwards, a Sam Cooke–inspired tenor who'd recorded earlier as a solo artist for such labels as Twin Stacks, Weis, Bell, Aware, and Cotillion, had replaced Wynne in the group. Attempts by Thom Bell to repeat the Spinners' Wynne-led successes were commercial failures, but a 1979–80 association with producer Michael Zager took them back to the upper reaches of the charts with the medleys "Working My Way Back to You/Forgive Me, Girl" (number six R&B, number two pop) and "Cupid/I've Loved You for a Long Time" (number five R&B, number four pop). A year after their last R&B top 40 entry—1984's "Right or Wrong"—the Spinners were dropped by Atlantic. They reemerged in 1989 with a little-noticed album on Volt.

THE STAPLE SINGERS

In their more than four decades of performing as a group, Chicago's Staple Singers traveled a long, artistically rich road from their beginnings as a gospel quartet through the folk-rock era into the mainstream of American popular music. The quartet, featuring the breathy, vibrato-less tenor voice and bluesy, reverberating guitar picking of leader Roebuck "Pops" Staples (b. Dec. 28, 1915, Winona, Mississippi) and the throaty, emotion-gripping contralto of daughter Mavis Staples (b. 1940, Chicago), twice struck the top of both the R&B charts, in 1972 with "I'll Take You There" and three years later with "Let's Do It Again."

The Staple Singers

TOP ALBUMS

BEALTITUDE: RESPECT YOURSELF (Stax, '72, *19*)
LET'S DO IT AGAIN (Soundtrack, Curtom, '75, *20*)

TOP SONGS

RESPECT YOURSELF (Stax, '71, *2 R&B, 12 Pop*)
I'LL TAKE YOU THERE (Stax, '72, *1 R&B, 1 Pop*)
OH LA DE DA (Stax, '73, *4 R&B, 33 Pop*)
IF YOU'RE READY (COME GO WITH ME) (Stax, '73, *1 R&B, 9 Pop*)
TOUCH A HAND, MAKE A FRIEND (Stax, '74, *3 R&B, 23 Pop*)
CITY IN THE SKY (Stax, '74, *4 R&B*)
LET'S DO IT AGAIN (Curtom, '75, *1 R&B, 1 Pop*)
NEW ORLEANS (Curtom, '76, *4 R&B*)

Additional Top 40 Songs: 10

Raised on Will Dockery's plantation in Drew, Mississippi, Roebuck Staples dropped out of school after the eighth grade to pick cotton, potatoes, and other crops for 10 cents a day. He fell under the spell of the blues and was inspired by Charley Patton (also a Dockery plantation resident), Howlin' Wolf, and Muddy Waters. Roebuck's financial situation improved when he began earning $5 a night as a teenager entertaining dancers and gamblers at a local juke joint.

He put the blues behind him after moving to Chicago in 1935. "I was a Christian man," he explained. "I figured blues wasn't the right field for me." Forbidden to play guitar at the Baptist church he'd joined in Chicago, he abandoned the instrument for a period, only to buy another in order to teach gospel songs to his children Cleotha (b. 1934, Drew), Pervis (b. 1935, Drew), Yvonne (b. 1939, Chicago), and Mavis. "I sung in a church down south, and I knew the four parts of music," he said. "I knew how to get harmony, and I taught each one. I'd hit the guitar string where they were supposed to sing, and they caught on."

Roebuck, Cleo, Pervis, and Mavis began appearing at local churches in 1948 and four years later cut their first record, "These Are They" b/w "Faith and Grace," for their own Royal label. Following sides for the nationally distributed United label, they signed with Vee-Jay in 1955. Their plaintive 1957 recording of "Uncloudy Day" sold "like a rock and roll record," according to Roebuck, establishing the group as a major attraction on the gospel circuit, as well as drawing attention in folk and blues circles.

The Staples signed with the Riverside jazz label in 1962 when the folk music boom was in full force and began picking up college bookings, in addition to their religious dates. While at Riverside, they were the first African-American group to record material by then-emerging songwriter Bob Dylan. Their secular following continued to expand in the mid-1960s at Epic Records, where they became identified with social protest songs like "Freedom Highway" and "Why? (Am I Treated So Bad)," both penned by

Roebuck, and Stephen Stills's "For What It's Worth."

By the time the Staples joined Stax Records in 1968, they were performing on bills with major rock acts at such venues as Fillmore West and East. Their first two albums for the company, produced by Steve Cropper, were still very much in the folk-rock and civil rights vein, but the third, 1970's Al Bell–produced *The Staple Swingers*, offered a bold new direction that was neither sacred nor entirely secular. The next, *Bealtitude: Respect Yourself*, produced by Bell in Muscle Shoals, Alabama, broke the group wide open in 1971, with the Mack Rice–Luther Ingram song "Respect Yourself" rising to number two on the *Billboard* R&B chart and the reggae-spiced Bell composition "I'll Take You There" becoming a double chart-topper.

The group, in which Yvonne had replaced Pervis in 1970, had more hits at Stax, including 1973's Number One R&B "If You're Ready (Come Go with Me)," before moving to Curtom Records and scoring another double Number One smash with 1975's "Let's Do It Again" (penned and produced by Curtis Mayfield) from the motion picture of the same title. The sexually suggestive number was a departure for the group, which dropped "Singers" from its name after being transferred to Warner Bros. the next year. The group had no more major hits, however, 1975's number four "New Orleans" (also from *Let's Do it Again*) being the last.

The quartet reverted to the "Staple Singers" billing in the early 1980s but had little luck with recordings for the 20th Century Fox and Private I labels. Although the group still performs on occasion as a unit, Mavis and Roebuck began making appearances on their own during the late 1980s. Mavis, who'd earlier cut solo albums for Volt, Curtom, and Warner Bros., was signed in 1989 to Paisley Park, where some of her material was produced by Prince. Roebuck, who'd done two singles at Stax, recorded two gospel albums, for the I Am label in 1987 and for Pointblank/Charisma in 1992.

EDWIN STARR

Singer-songwriter Edwin Starr (b. Charles Edwin Hatcher, Jan. 21, 1942, Nashville) found success with his very first solo recording, "Agent Double-O-Soul," an original composi-

TOP SONGS

AGENT DOUBLE-O-SOUL (Ric-Tic, '65, 8 R&B, 21 Pop)
STOP HER ON SIGHT (S.O.S.) (Ric-Tic, '66, 9 R&B)
TWENTY-FIVE MILES (Gordy, '69, 6 R&B, 6 Pop)
WAR (Gordy, '70, 3 R&B, 1 Pop)
STOP THE WAR NOW (Gordy, '70, 5 R&B, 26 Pop)
FUNKY MUSIC SHO NUFF TURNS ME ON (Gordy, '71, 6 R&B)
THERE YOU GO (Soul, '73, 12 R&B)
PAIN (Granite, '75, 25 R&B)
ABYSSINIA JONES (Granite, '75, 25 R&B)
CONTACT (20th Century, '79, 13 R&B)

Additional Top 40 R&B Songs: 5

tion inspired by James Bond movies. Issued in 1965 on Ed Wingate's tiny Detroit-based Ric-Tic label, it went to number eight on the *Billboard* R&B chart and crossed to number 21 pop. Starr's fame soon spread across the Atlantic, his 1966 number nine R&B recording "Stop Her on Sight (S.O.S)" going to number 35 in England when issued there on Polydor. His next release, "Headline News," didn't make the U.S. top 40 but charted at number 39 in the U.K.

The fact that Starr's hits sounded much like Motown productions of the period didn't escape Berry Gordy, Jr. Doing some detective work of his own, the Motown boss discovered that his studio musicians had played on the Ric-Tic sides. He fined them $1,000 each for the indiscretion, but when that didn't stop them from moonlighting, he simply purchased the upstart label and its artist roster.

Upon returning home in 1967 from his third British tour, Starr learned that he was a Motown recording artist. As had been the case of others, including the Spinners, who'd come to the firm through label acquisition, he became lost in the shuffle at Motown. He has stated that the company felt he lacked crossover potential, but he would eventually prove that assessment wrong. A succession of producers and songwriters failed to give him a significant hit until he teamed up with Harvey Fuqua and Johnny Bristol to write "25 Miles." Released in 1969 on the Gordy label, it went to number six on both the R&B and pop lists. The title of Starr's Bristol-produced follow-up, "I'm Still a Struggling Man," seemed to sum up his career situation at the time, as it stalled at number 27 on the R&B chart.

The vocalist's star ascended in 1970 with the release of "War." The tune, composed by Norman Whitfield and Barrett Strong, had been a track on the Temptations' *Psychedelic Shack* album. Although Vietnam was not mentioned in the lyric, anti-war protesters flooded Motown with requests to have it issued as a single. The company instead had Whitfield redo it with Starr, albeit with a much tougher rhythm track than the Temps' original. Singing in a gruff low tenor, broken with grunts and screams, Starr drove the message home with galvanizing urgency. "War" not only became an unofficial anthem of the peace movement but climbed to number three on the R&B chart and to Number One pop, as well as to number three in England. It was Starr's biggest hit, earning him a Grammy nomination, and was successfully revived in later years by both Frankie Goes to Hollywood and Bruce Springsteen.

Raised in Cleveland, Starr was a member of a teenage doo wop group called the Futuretones that in 1957 cut a single titled "Roll On" for the Tress label. After military service in Germany, he spent two and a half years on the road as featured vocalist with organist Bill Doggett's combo. A Detroit disc jockey put the singer in touch with Ed Wingate. Besides co-writing his own three Ric-Tic hits, Starr penned and produced the number 16 R&B, number 12 pop "Oh So Happy" for the white group Shades of Blue on the Impact label and sang lead on the number seven R&B "I'll Love You Forever" by the Holidays (a studio group consisting of Starr, J. J. Barnes, and Steve Mancha) on Golden World, both in 1966.

Starr continued working with Whitfield after "War" and scored two more top 10 R&B charters: "Stop the War Now" and "Funky Music Sho Nuff Turns Me On." He then got lost in the shuffle again and was transferred to the Motown label in 1973, the year he recorded the soundtrack for the low-budget film *Hell Up in Harlem,* starring Fred Williamson. The singer recorded with moderate success for Granite Records in 1975 and reemerged four years later at the RCA-distributed 20th Century Fox label with the self-produced disco hits "Contact" and "H.A.P.P.Y. Radio." The first went to number 13 R&B and the second to number 28 R&B, while in England they placed at number six and number nine respectively.

Starr, who'd been touring the U.K. and Western Europe an average of three months a year, settled in Warwickshire, England, during the mid-1980s. He recorded in that country for Streetwave, Hippodrome, Avatar, and Motorcity, as well as in Germany for WEA.

CANDI STATON

Singing in a raspy alto that ached with emotion, Candi Staton (b. Canzetta Staton, 1943, Hanceville, Alabama) reigned as the queen of southern soul music between 1969 and 1975 with 14 top 10 R&B hits, all produced in Muscle Shoals, Alabama, by Rick Hall. Her greatest success, however, came in 1976 in Los Angeles, where she hooked up with producer-songwriter Dave Crawford for the disco-styled "Young Hearts Run Free," her first and only R&B chart-topper.

Coming from a strict religious background and having begun her career as a child gospel singer, Staton was never entirely comfortable in the secular music world. Two failed marriages, which left her with five children to raise alone, led to heavy drinking and an eventual return to gospel.

As a youngster in rural Alabama, Candi was exposed to gospel and country music. After her parents divorced, her mother took her and her two sisters and three brothers to Cleveland, Ohio, where they met Bishop M. L. Jewel, a woman preacher. At age 10, Candi became a member of the Jewel Gospel Trio, a group that also included her older sister Maggie. The trio traveled the gospel circuit to raise money for Bishop Jewel's school in Nashville and recorded five singles for Nashboro during the late 1950s. Candi was the group's firebrand. "One of these new dances you call the Stroll, but when Jesus comes, He's gonna destroy rock and roll," she wailed in the song "Too Late."

After attending nursing school for a period, Staton found herself singing and playing piano at a church in Birmingham. In 1968, her brother persuaded her to enter a talent contest at the local 27-28 Club, where she sang the Aretha Franklin hit "Do Right Woman—Do Right Man," the only secular song she knew at the time. She was soon booked at the club and caught the attention of Clarence Carter, who hired her to be part of his show. Staton recorded "You've Got the Upper Hand," an obscure single for the Unity label, before being recommended by Carter to Rick Hall.

Candi Staton

"The first time I heard her," Hall told *Soul* newspaper, "I said, 'Whew! What a voice.' It was a blues voice, a gospel voice and a pop voice, all at once."

Staton scored at number nine R&B in 1969 with the Carter–George Jackson–Raymond Moore tune "I'd Rather Be an Old Man's Sweetheart (Than a Young Man's Fool)," her first release on Hall's Capitol-distributed Fame label. More hits followed, including the number 13 R&B "I'm Just a Prisoner (Of Your Good Lovin')," the number 13 R&B "Sweet Feeling," the number four R&B "Stand by Your Man" (a soul treatment of the Tammy Wynette country chart-topper), the number nine R&B "He Called Me Baby" (an old Patsy Cline hit), and the number 12 R&B "In the Ghetto," through 1972. When, in 1973, "In the Ghetto" earned Staton the second of her four Grammy nominations, Elvis Presley, who'd originally recorded the Mac Davis song, sent her a congratulatory note. She and Carter, having married three years earlier, recorded a duet for Atlantic titled "If You Can't Beat 'Em" before breaking up.

After several less-successful singles for Fame under a new distribution alliance with United Artists, Staton signed with Warner Bros. in 1974 and returned to the R&B top 10 with the number six "As Long As He Takes Care of Me," her last hit to be produced by Hall. Dave Crawford, whom she had known since her gospel days when he was the pianist for the Caravans, gave the singer's music a more contemporary direction with the Number One R&B "Young Hearts Run Free," which also went to number 20 on the pop chart and to number two in England. She continued to tread the disco current with her number 16 R&B (number six in the U.K.) Bob Monaco–produced version of the Bee Gees' "Nights on Broadway" in 1977, the semi-autobiographical Crawford-produced number 17 R&B "Victim" in 1978, and the number 13 R&B "When You Wake Up Tomorrow" in 1979, produced by Staton and Jimmy Simpson. Later work with Crawford for the LA and Sugar Hill labels ignited few sparks.

The singer's course changed in 1982 when she and her new husband, drummer John Sussewell, embraced Christianity and became ordained ministers. With backing from Jim Bakker's PTL Club, they launched Beracah Records. Staton's debut gospel album, 1983's *Make Me an Instrument*, peaked at number seven on *Billboard*'s spiritual chart. She continued recording for Beracah while scoring a minor R&B hit in 1986 with the quasi-religious "You Got

TOP SONGS

I'D RATHER BE AN OLD MAN'S SWEETHEART (THAN A
    YOUNG MAN'S FOOL) (Fame, '69, 9 *R&B*)
I'M JUST A PRISONER (OF YOUR GOOD LOVIN')
    (Fame, '70, 13 *R&B*)
SWEET FEELING (Fame, '70, 5 *R&B*)
STAND BY YOUR MAN (Fame, '70, 4 *R&B*, 24 Pop)
HE CALLED ME BABY (Fame, '71, 9 *R&B*)
IN THE GHETTO (Fame, '72, 12 *R&B*)
AS LONG AS HE TAKES CARE OF HOME (Warner
    Bros., '74, 6 *R&B*)
YOUNG HEARTS RUN FREE (Warner Bros, '76,
    1 *R&B*, 20 Pop)
WHEN YOU WAKE UP TOMORROW (Warner Bros.,
    '79, 13 *R&B*)

Additional Top 40 R&B Songs: 10

the Love" as a guest with a group called the Source on the Source label. Staton never fully penetrated the African-American gospel market, however, and instead focused on evangelistic crusades and appearances with such controversial white television preachers as Bakker, Pat Robertson, and Robert Tilton.

THE STYLISTICS

Because of Russell Thompkins, Jr.'s 6'1" stature, many of his friends assumed he'd become a professional basketball player, but instead of going for the hoops, the young Philadelphian reached for some of the highest notes in the annals of sweet soul music, particularly on "You're a Big Girl Now," the debut recording by his group, the Stylistics. A hit in the City of Brotherly Love when issued in 1970 on the tiny Sebring label, it became a number seven R&B charter nationally the following year after being picked up by Avco Embassy Records, the first of 13 Top 10 R&B hits (five of which crossed to the pop top 10) for the quintet through 1975.

The Stylistics were formed in 1968 when members of two rival groups from north Philadelphia—Thompkins, Airrion Love, and James Smith of the Monarchs and Herb Murrell and James Dunn, Jr., of the Percussions—joined forces. They toured around Pennsylvania with a band called Slim and the Boys, whose guitarist, Robert Douglas, got together with the Stylistics' road manager, ex-Monarch Marty Bryant, to compose the ballad "You're a Big Girl Now." In spite of its crude production quality and bass singer Smith's rather laughable mid-song monologue, the recording worked on the strength of Thompkins's soaring, if somewhat nasal, Eddie Kendricks–inspired falsetto.

Avco Embassy (soon to become simply Avco) purchased both the record master and the group's contract from Sebring. The company hired producer-arranger-songwriter Thom Bell to polish the group's sound. Working with lyricist Linda Creed, Bell created the symphonic soul masterpieces "Stop, Look, Listen (To Your Heart)," "You Are Everything," "Betcha by Golly, Wow," and "People Make the World Go Round" (notable for its social commentary and shifting time signatures) for the Stylistics' eponymous debut album. All four ballads became hit

singles. Bell also convinced Thompkins to lower his range a bit in order to make the enunciation clearer.

"Thompkins had a voice of such unique tonal pitch and sweet, almost effeminate purity that an accompaniment of just strings and woodwinds would have produced a sound of cloying slickness," Tony Cummings observed in his book *The Sound of Philadelphia*. "So Bell, in addition to orchestral instrumentation, utilized electric pianos, more emphatic bass and drums....The result was captivating: soul music that neither excited the listener with deep intensity, nor left him marvelling at his mellow coolness, but soul music which came from a remote ethereal world of love, sadness and purity."

Bell supplied the group with an unbroken string of additional hits—"I'm Stone in Love with You," "Break Up to Make Up," "You'll Never Get to Heaven (If You Break My Heart)" (the old Dionne Warwick hit), "Rockin' Roll Baby" (the Stylistics' first uptempo hit), and "You Make Me Feel Brand New" (the group's biggest pop record in the U.S.)—through early 1974, when his schedule became too full (especially with sessions for the Spinners) to allow him to continue working with the Stylistics. Avco executives Hugo Perretti and Luigi Creatore then decided to produce the group themselves and

---

TOP ALBUM

LET'S PUT IT ALL TOGETHER (Avco, '74, 14)

Additional Top 40 Albums: 2

TOP SONGS

YOU'RE A BIG GIRL NOW (Avco Embassy, '71, 7 R&B)

STOP, LOOK, LISTEN (TO YOUR HEART) (Avco Embassy, '71, 6 R&B, 39 Pop)

BETCHA BY GOLLY, WOW (Avco, '72, 2 R&B, 3 Pop)

PEOPLE MAKE THE WORLD GO ROUND (Avco, '72, 6 R&B, 25 Pop)

I'M STONE IN LOVE WITH YOU (Avco, '72, 4 R&B, 10 Pop)

BREAK UP TO MAKE UP (Avco, '73, 5 R&B, 5 Pop)

ROCKIN' ROLL BABY (Avco, '73, 3 R&B, 14 Pop)

YOU MAKE ME FEEL BRAND NEW (Avco, '74, 5 R&B, 2 Pop)

HEAVY FALLIN' OUT (Avco, '74, 4 R&B)

Additional Top 40 R&B Songs: 10

brought in songwriting associate George David Weiss and arranger Van McCoy to help. But their lyrics lacked Creed's earlier depth, and McCoy's candy-coated charts combined with the quintet's sweet vocal blend to create a sticky syrup. Only three top 10 R&B singles—1974's "Let's Put It All Together" and "Heavy Fallin' Out" and 1975's "Thank You Baby"—emerged from this goo.

While the Stylistics' fortunes declined in the U.S., they soared in other parts of the world. PolyGram, which distributed Avco internationally, launched a major British television ad campaign in 1975 for the *Best of the Stylistics* album, which shot to Number One and sold over a million copies there. Later that year, the group's disco single "Can't Give You Anything (But My Love)" (a number 18 R&B charter in the U.S.) hit the top of the English chart. The next year's disco version of the Perretti-Creatore-Weiss song "Can't Help Falling in Love" (originally a hit for Elvis Presley) failed to penetrate the domestic top 40, but it went to number four in the U.K. The group became a major concert attraction in England and Western Europe, as well as in Japan, the Philippines, Australia, and New Zealand.

The Stylistics had minor R&B hits at Hugo and Luigi's H&L label in 1976 and '77, at Mercury (with producer Teddy Randazzo) in 1978 and '79, at TSOP (with Dexter Wansel and others) in 1980 and '81, at Streetwise (with Maurice Starr and Arthur Baker) from 1984 to '86, and at Amherst (with Randy Waldman and Jeff Tyzik) in 1991 and '92. *Love Talk*, a 1991 Amherst album, contained two songs composed and produced especially for the group by Burt Bacharach and Carol Bayer Sager, but neither charted.

The trio—Dunn left the group in the late 1970s and was soon followed by Smith—continues to tour internationally.

DONNA SUMMER

When singer-songwriter Donna Summer (b. LaDonna Andrea Gaines, Dec. 31, 1948) emerged on the international music scene in 1975 with "Love to Love You Baby," a 16-minute, 50-second disco tour de force of orgasmic panting and moaning, she was immediately dubbed a sex kitten. The song, written by Summer with her Munich producers Giorgio Moroder and Pete Bel-

lotte, was denounced by Rev. Jesse Jackson and banned from the BBC.

Moroder and Bellotte gradually allowed her to really sing, however, exposing a powerful voice, not unlike that of Martha Reeves, that is at once sweet and harsh—qualities that enabled her to evoke both innocence and all-knowing worldliness. They also encouraged her to expand her stylistic horizons, bringing in elements of rock and pop, thus allowing the reigning disco diva to sustain her career after the genre had become moribund.

Summer had 11 gold albums between 1976 and 1983 and 11 gold singles between 1976 and 1989. Three of the albums (1978's *Live and More*, 1978's *Bad Girls*, and 1979's *On the Radio/Greatest Hits Volumes I and II* [all double-disc sets]) and two of the singles ("Hot Stuff" and "Bad Girls" [both from *Bad Girls*]) also went platinum, all of which were produced by Moroder and Bellotte.

One of seven children of a butcher and his school-teaching wife, Donna was inspired to sing at age 10 by the recordings of Mahalia Jackson and began performing with gospel groups and choirs at Grant A.M.E. Church and other congregations in the Boston area. Later influences included Janis Joplin and Lou Reed. At 18, after having performed for a period with a rock band at Boston's Psychedelic Supermarket, she moved to New York City, did background sessions for Three Dog Night and others, and auditioned for the lead role in *The Wiz*, which was being vacated by Melba Moore. Donna was instead offered a part in the road production of *Hair* and sent to Munich, where she married a member of the cast, Austrian actor Helmut Sommer. They eventually divorced, but she kept the surname, the spelling of which was later changed by Neil Bogart.

Staying in Germany after the musical closed, Summer appeared in Vienna Folk Opera productions of *Porgy and Bess* and *Showboat* and started doing commercial jingles and demos at Munich's MusicLand studio, where she met Moroder and Bellotte and was signed to their Oasis label. Her first two singles, "Hostage" and "Ladies of the Night," were continental hits. The third, the Summer-Moroder-Bellotte composition "Love to Love You Baby," became an international smash after being picked up by Bogart's Casablanca company in Los Angeles.

Subsequent singles failed to reach the mark of "Love to Love You Baby," but after nearly two years as a disco cult favorite, Summer broke back into the R&B and pop top 10 with 1977's number nine

R&B, number six pop "I Feel Love" from the album *I Remember Yesterday*. She scored big the following year with "Let's Dance," from the disco motion picture comedy *Thank God, It's Friday* (in which she starred) and with a disco treatment of Jimmy Webb's "MacArthur Park" (her first Number One pop single) from *Live and More*.

Summer's popularity swelled in 1979 as her Euro-disco sound grew more diversified. The rock-imbued "Hot Stuff" became her first R&B chart-topper, while the similarly styled follow-up, "Bad Girls" (co-written by future husband Bruce Sudano), reached the summit on both the R&B and pop lists. And a duet with Barbra Streisand, "No More Tears (Enough Is Enough)," gave Summer her fourth Number One pop hit.

After one last major hit for Casablanca, 1980's "On the Radio," the singer sued the company and signed with Geffen Records. Sales of 1980's rockish *The Wanderer*, her final Moroder-Bellotte–produced album, were disappointing. Quincy Jones was then brought in for 1983's *Donna Summer*, which spawned the hit "Love Is in Control (Finger on the Trigger)." Owing Polygram (which had acquired Casablanca) one more album, Summer teamed with producer Michael Omartian for 1983's *She Works Hard for the Money* on Mercury, the title track giving her the second R&B chart-topper of her career.

TOP ALBUMS

LIVE AND MORE (Casablanca, '78, *1*)
BAD GIRLS (Casablanca, '79, *1*)
ON THE RADIO/GREATEST HITS VOLUMES I AND II
 (Casablanca, '79, *1*)

Additional Top 40 Albums: 9

TOP SONGS

LOVE TO LOVE YOU BABY (Oasis, '75, *3 R&B, 2 Pop*)
LAST DANCE (Casablanca, '78, *5 R&B, 3 Pop*)
MACARTHUR PARK (Casablanca, '78, *8 R&B, 1 Pop*)
HOT STUFF (Casablanca, '79, *3 R&B, 1 Pop*)
BAD GIRLS (Casablanca, '79, *1 R&B, 1 Pop*)
LOVE IS IN CONTROL (FINGER ON THE TRIGGER)
 (Geffen, '82, *4 R&B, 10 Pop*)
SHE WORKS HARD FOR THE MONEY (Mercury, '83,
 1 R&B, 3 Pop)

Additional Top 40 R&B Songs: 21

Later hits included 1987's number 10 R&B Richard Perry–produced "Dinner with Gershwin" on Geffen and 1989's number seven pop "This Time I Know It's for Real," produced by British hitmakers Stock, Aitken, and Waterman for Atlantic Records.

THE SYLVERS

The four oldest of Shirley Sylvers's children—Olympia Ann (b. Oct. 13, 1951), Leon Frank III (b. Mar. 5, 1953), Charmaine Elaine (b. Mar. 3, 1954), and James Jonathan (b. June 8, 1955)—made their mark in show business well before they reached puberty and years prior to their recording debut. Originally based in Memphis, then in Harlem, they began singing publicly in 1958. Billed as the Little Angels, the quartet made its television debut on Art Linkletter's network program. Appearances followed on "The Dinah Shore Show," "The Spike Jones Show," "The Groucho Marx Show," and Danny Thomas's "Make Room for Daddy." And during summer vacations there were tours with Ray Charles and Johnny Mathis.

Then, in the mid-1960s, their world came crashing down. Shirley and her husband divorced. They'd had ten kids by that time, but she was no longer financially able to care for all of them. The five eldest were sent to live with various relatives, thus ending the Little Angels' career. She eventually brought the entire brood back together to live on welfare in a cramped two-bedroom apartment in the Watts section of Los Angeles.

The Sylvers children had put singing behind them when Leon, who'd set his sights on becoming a professional basketball player, noticed an announcement of an upcoming talent contest at Verbum Dei High School. He rehearsed the original Little Angels, plus Edmund Theodore (b. Jan. 25, 1957) and Joseph Richard (Ricky) (b. Oct. 15, 1958), on harmony and choreography. They entered and won, then began cutting demos. After being rejected by several companies, they were signed by Mike Curb of MGM Records.

The Sylvers' first single, "Fool's Paradise," issued in 1972 on MGM's Pride label, became a number 14 R&B chart hit and was followed by the number 10 R&B "Wish That I Could Talk to You." Before the year was out, they had appeared on "The Bill Cosby Show" and toured Japan twice. The opening act on their second Japanese trip was a younger trio of Sylvers kids comprising Angela Marie (b. Apr. 11, 1960), Patricia Lynn (b. Mar. 25, 1961), and Foster Emerson (b. Feb. 25, 1962).

Eleven-year-old Foster bested his siblings by scoring a number seven R&B, number 22 pop hit in 1973 with "Misdemeanor," a brilliant burst of Jackson Five–inspired bubblegum soul written by brother Leon. By 1974, when the Sylvers were transferred to the main MGM label, Angie, Pat, and Foster had joined the group. The nonet switched to Capitol the following year and hit the top of both the R&B and pop charts with the perky proto-disco Edmund Sylvers–led "Boogie Fever," produced and co-written by Freddie Perren in his first assignment after a six-year association with Motown that had included working on many of the Jackson Five's greatest hits. Two more Perren-produced crossover hits followed: 1976's number three R&B, number five pop "Hot Line," and 1977's number six R&B, number 17 pop "High School Dance."

Longing to produce themselves in order to shed their bubblegum image, the Sylvers moved to Casablanca Records in 1978 and had a number 15 R&B charter with the disco-styled "Don't Stop, Get Off," which proved to be their last top 40 entry. An album the next year with Euro-disco hitmaker Giorgio Moroder attracted little attention. The group had become a septet by that time, Olympia and Charmaine having left. Leon was soon gone also and became a creative force at Dick Griffey's Solar label, where he wrote and produced hits for Shalamar (1979's Number One R&B "The Second Time Around"), the Whispers (1980's Number One R&B "And the Beat Goes On"), and others, including Dynasty, a group he officially joined in 1981.

TOP SONGS

FOOL'S PARADISE (Pride, '72, 14 R&B)
WISH THAT I COULD TALK TO YOU (Pride, '72, 10 R&B)
STAY AWAY FROM ME (Pride, '73, 33 R&B)
BOOGIE FEVER (Capitol, '75, 1 R&B, 1 Pop)
COTTON CANDY (Capitol, '76, 19 R&B)
HOT LINE (Capitol, '76, 3 R&B, 5 Pop)
HIGH SCHOOL DANCE (Capitol, '77, 6 R&B, 17 Pop)
ANY WAY YOU WANT ME (Capitol, '77, 12 R&B)
DON'T STOP, GET OFF (Casablanca, '78, 15 R&B)

Edmund launched a solo career at Casablanca in 1980 but had only moderate success with that year's number 38 R&B "That Burning Love."

The 1980s were not especially kind to the Sylvers, although Leon stayed active as a writer and producer and contributed to Janet Jackson's 1982 debut album, among other projects. The remaining members joined the Solar roster early in the decade, but no hits resulted. A new lineup—Charmaine, James, Ricky, Angie, Pat, and Foster—emerged at Geffen Records in 1984, but the single "In One Love and Out the Other," produced by Leon, James, and Foster, fell short of cracking the R&B top 40. A solo album by Leon appeared on Motown five years later, receiving scant notice.

JOHNNIE TAYLOR

The roots of vocalist Johnnie Harrison Taylor (b. May 5, 1938, Crawfordsville, Arkansas) reach back to the beginnings of soul music. During a prolific recording career of more than four decades, he went through a number of phases—doo wopper, gospel crooner, blues wailer, and soul philosopher—before emerging in 1976 as an across-the-board star with the Number One R&B and pop smash "Disco Lady."

Taylor has referred to himself as a "salesman" of songs. "In gospel you start off with a cold audience and work them into an emotional state," he said in 1972. "People feel what you do, and they automatically get with you. A song is a song. If you sing 'Jesus' or if you say 'baby,' it's basically melodically the same. I think that anything that makes people happy is good, anything that takes people's minds off their problems."

Inspired by R. H. Harris and Sam Cooke of the Soul Stirrers and Archie Brownlee of the Five Blind Boys of Mississippi, Taylor spent his early teens with the Melody Masters, a Kansas City gospel quartet. Later, in Chicago, he alternated between the secular and sacred music worlds, doing doo wop with the Five Echoes and gospel with the Highway Q.C.'s. His first record, 1953's "A Lonely Mood," was with the Echoes on the Sabre label. In 1955, he recorded for Vee-Jay, both with the Echoes and with the Q.C.'s, who featured his low-tenor tones on such numbers as "Somewhere to Lay My Head" and "I Dreamed Heaven Was Like This." The effortless elasticity of

TOP ALBUM

EARGASM (Columbia, '76, 5)

TOP SONGS

WHO'S MAKING LOVE (Stax, '68, *1 R&B, 5 Pop*)
TAKE CARE OF YOUR HOMEWORK (Stax, '69,
  2 R&B, 20 Pop)
TESTIFY (I WONNA) (Stax, '69, *4 R&B, 36 Pop*)
STEAL AWAY (Stax, '70, *3 R&B, 37 Pop*)
JODY'S GOT YOUR GIRL AND GONE (Stax, '71,
  1 R&B, 28 Pop)
I BELIEVE IN YOU (YOU BELIEVE IN ME) (Stax, '73,
  1 R&B, 11 Pop)
CHEAPER TO KEEP HER (Stax, '73, *2 R&B, 15 Pop*)
DISCO LADY (Columbia, '76, *1 R&B, 1 Pop*)
LOVE IS BETTER IN THE A.M. (PART 1) (Columbia,
  '77, *3 R&B*)

Additional Top 40 R&B Songs: 2

Taylor's leads with the Q.C's brought Cooke to mind, as did his yodels, yet his timbre had a grittier edge and his rhythmic placement a harder drive.

In 1957, Taylor replaced Cooke in the Soul Stirrers. During his early months on the road with the group, he was featured on singing parts associated with Cooke. Audiences, Taylor recalled in 1993, "were kind to me, but it took them a minute to kinda get with me. Once I started recording [with the Soul Stirrers], people started to accept me." He remained with the group until 1960, cutting such songs as "The Love of God" for Specialty and "Stand by Me Father" for SAR.

After a brief period as a Baptist minister, Taylor returned to Cooke's SAR Records in 1961 as an R&B artist. Six singles appeared on SAR and its affiliated Derby label, of which the Cooke-penned soul tunes "Rome (Wasn't Built in a Day)," "Dance What You Wanna," and "Baby, We've Got Love" were hits on the West Coast. He also recorded some slow blues for Cooke's companies, including his own "I Need Lots of Love" on Derby. It was stylistically similar to 1963's Number One R&B hit "Part Time Love" by Little Johnny Taylor (no relation) and created confusion with the public, a situation that Johnnie capitalized on by adding "Part Time Love" to his club repertoire. (He cut his own version of the song on the 1968 album *Raw Blues*.)

Taylor continued with the blues at Stax Records in Memphis, making his R&B chart debut at number 19 in 1966 with "I Had a Dream," the first in a series of David Porter–Isaac Hayes blues compositions that also included that year's number 15 R&B "I Got to Love Somebody's Baby." His direction changed two years later when he teamed up with Don Davis, a Detroit producer who'd come south to join the Stax crew and gave the singer's gritty southern soul style a Motown-like gloss. The hard-socking "Who's Making Love" gave the vocalist a Number One R&B, number five pop hit. Dubbed "the Soul Philosopher" by Stax, Taylor maintained his hit streak with Davis and scored such subsequent top 10 R&B singles as "Take Care of Your Homework," "Testify (I Wonna)" (first recorded by George Clinton's Parliaments), "Love Bones," "Steal Away" (originally a hit for Jimmy Hughes), "I Am Somebody," "Jody's Got Your Girl and Gone," "I Believe in You (You Believe in Me)," "Cheaper to Keep Her," and "We're Getting Careless with Our Love."

Jumping to Columbia in 1976, Taylor and Davis hit their career peak with their first release for the label, "Disco Lady." Written by Davis with Harvey Scales and Al Vance and recorded in Detroit with the Parliament-Funkadelic rhythm section, it sold in excess of two million copies, becoming the first-ever single in record industry history to be certified platinum. After two more top five R&B entries—1976's "Somebody's Gettin' It" and the next year's "Love Is Better in the A.M."—Taylor never again cracked the top 10. He remained with Columbia until 1980, moved to Beverly Glen two years later, and, since 1984, has recorded for Malaco in Jackson, Mississippi, where his albums have contained a mixture of soul ballads, gospel-tinged funk, and blues.

THE TEMPTATIONS

The Temptations stand tall as the top vocal group in the history of rhythm and blues. Between 1965 and 1989, the Detroit quintet chocked up a total of 43 top 10 singles on the *Billboard* R&B chart, 14 of which placed at Number One. Although the group went through numerous personnel changes over the years, it is best remembered for the classic 1963–68 lineup of Eddie Kendricks (b. Dec. 17, 1939, Birmingham, Alabama), David Ruffin (b. Jan. 18, 1941, Whyknot, Mississippi), Otis Williams (b. Otis Miles, Oct. 30, 1949, Texarkana, Texas), Paul Williams (b. July 2, 1939, Birmingham), and Melvin Franklin (b. David English, Oct. 12, 1942, Montgomery, Alabama). Charter members Otis Williams and Melvin Franklin remain with the group.

While growing up in Birmingham, Kendricks and friend Paul Williams were drawn to the doo wop sounds of Clyde McPhatter's Drifters. The two dropped out of high school and moved to Cleveland, where they organized a group called the Cavaliers with Cal Osborne and Wiley Waller. At the suggestion of manager Milton Jenkins, they relocated to Detroit in 1956, sans Waller, who remained behind. The trio became known as the Primes and recruited a female group, naming it the Primettes, to share local engagements. The Primettes later emerged as the Supremes, while Kendricks and Paul Williams joined with Otis Williams, Melvin Franklin, and Elbridge Bryant (members of another Jenkins-managed group, the Distants) to form the Elgins (not be confused with the later Motown group of the same name). The Elgins signed with Motown in 1960 and were rechristened the Temptations. Bryant left in 1963 and was replaced by Ruffin, who had sung gospel with the Dixie Nightingales during the mid-1950s before moving to Detroit and recording as an R&B solo singer for the Anna, Checkmate, and Miracle labels.

The Temptations' first two singles were issued on Miracle, a Motown subsidiary, after which they were transferred to the Gordy label. They broke big with their seventh single, "The Way You Do the Things You Do," penned and produced by Smokey Robinson and a number 11 pop charter in 1964. (*Billboard* published no R&B charts during that period.) It was the first in a series of Kendricks-led hits for the Temptations, including "Girl (Why You Wanna Make Me Cry)," "Get Ready," "You're My Everything," "Please Return Your Love to Me," and "Just My Imagination (Running Away with Me)." The gossamer falsetto specialist shared leads with Ruffin on "You're My Everything"; with Dennis Edwards (Ruffin's 1968 replacement) on "Cloud Nine," "Don't Let the Joneses Get You Down," "I Can't Get Next to You," and "Psychedelic Shack"; and with Diana Ross on "I'm Gonna Make You Love Me," a 1968 Supremes-Temptations summit meeting. Ruffin, whose intense, remarkably elastic tenor-baritone delivery reflected his gospel quartet roots, sang lead on such hits as "My Girl," "It's Growing," "Since I Met My Baby," "My Baby," "Ain't Too Proud to Beg," "Beauty Is Only Skin Deep," "(I Know) I'm Losing You," "(Loneliness Made Me Realize) It's You That I Need," "I Wish It Would Rain," and "I Could Never Love Another (After Loving You)" before leaving in 1968 for what would be a spotty solo career.

Robinson served as the Temptations' main producer through 1966's "Get Ready," after which Norman Whitfield was put behind the creative driving wheel. The arrival of former Contours lead Dennis Edwards (b. Feb. 3, 1943) coincided with a change of stylistic course. Having come under the spell of Sly Stone's psychedelic soul sound, Whitfield fashioned a more complex vocal web for the group and, in collaboration with Barrett Strong, composed such hits as "Cloud Nine," "Runaway Child, Running Wild," "Don't Let the Joneses Get You Down," "I Can't Get Next to You," "Psychedelic Shack," "Ball of Confusion," and "Papa Was a Rolling Stone." Whitfield's departure from Motown in 1975 signaled that an end was nearing for the Temptations' steady chart run, although they hit Number One R&B twice later that year with the Jeffrey Bowen–Berry Gordy, Jr., productions "Happy People" and "Shakey Ground."

TOP ALBUM

TCB (Diana Ross and the Supremes with the Temptations, Motown, '69, *1*)

Additional Top 40 Albums: 27

TOP SONGS

MY GIRL (Gordy, '65, *1 R&B, 1 Pop*)
AIN'T TOO PROUD TO BEG (Gordy, '66, *1 R&B, 13 Pop*)
BEAUTY IS ONLY SKIN DEEP (Gordy, '66, *1 R&B, 3 Pop*)
(I KNOW) I'M LOSING YOU (Gordy, '66, *1 R&B, 8 Pop*)
I WISH IT WOULD RAIN (Gordy, '68, *1 R&B, 4 Pop*)
RUN AWAY CHILD, RUNNING WILD (Gordy, '69, *1 R&B, 6 Pop*)
I CAN'T GET NEXT TO YOU (Gordy, '69, *1 R&B, 1 Pop*)
JUST MY IMAGINATION (RUNNING AWAY WITH ME) (Gordy, '71, *1 R&B, 1 Pop*)
MASTERPIECE (Gordy, '73, *1 R&B, 7 Pop*)

Additional Top 40 R&B Songs: 55

By 1972, Kendricks had become displeased with the direction in which Whitfield had taken the Temptations' music—"I don't dig those weird, freaky sounds," he stated—and left after leading on the lovely ballad "Just My Imagination (Running Away with Me)." He went on to score three Number One solo hits—"Keep on Truckin'," "Boogie Down," and "Shoeshine Boy"—between 1973 and '75 before fading into relative obscurity and dying of lung cancer on October 5, 1992. Ruffin, who'd had a long history of drug abuse, died on June 1, 1991, under mysterious circumstances; his biggest solo successes were 1969's number two R&B "My Whole World Ended (The Moment You Left Me)" and 1975's Number One R&B "Walk Away from Love." Paul Williams left the group in 1971 and committed suicide two years later.

Kendricks's place was taken by Damon Harris and later by Glenn Leonard, then Ron Tyson. Paul Williams was replaced by former Distants member Richard Street. Edwards was in and out of the group during the 1980s and had a solo hit with 1984's number two R&B "Don't Look Any Further." Lou Price was his initial replacement, then Ali-Ollie Woodson. Amid all this fluctuation, the Temptations managed to score occasional top 10 R&B entries, including "Standing on the Top" (1982), "Treat Her Like a Lady" (1984), "Lady Soul" (1986), "I Wonder Who She's Seeing Now" (1987), and "Special" (1989).

TAMMI TERRELL

Tammi Terrell (b. Thomasina Montgomery, Apr. 29, 1945, Philadelphia) had been making records with modest success for six years when, in 1967, producers Harvey Fuqua and Johnny Bristol decided to team her with their in-law, vocalist Marvin Gaye. The result was "Ain't No Mountain High Enough," a Nickolas Ashford–Valerie Simpson composition that gave soul music's new lovebirds their first of 10 R&B chart hits. Unfortunately, Terrell was unable to fully savor her sudden fame. Later that year, at the conclusion of a performance of their follow-up hit "Your Precious Love" (also by Ashford and Simpson) during a concert at Hamden-Sidney College in Virginia, she collapsed into her singing partner's arms. Diagnosed with a brain tumor, she underwent six operations over the next two years. Although she was able to return to the studio a few more times, she never again performed in public and died at Philadelphia's Graduate Hospital on March 16, 1970. She was not quite 25.

The singer had been complaining of blinding migraine headaches in the months prior to her collapse and was taking Darvon in an attempt to relieve the pain. It was widely rumored that her condition was the result of beatings allegedly suffered at the hands of the Temptations' David Ruffin, her boyfriend at the time. However, in February 1968, following Terrell's second operation, Graduate Hospital's chief of neurology Dr. Richard Harner told Soul newspaper, "There was no evidence that she had been hit. She could have been hit, but it had nothing to do with the operations."

Encouraged by her mother, a former actress, Tammi began participating in talent contests at Philadelphia's Earle Theater at age 11. She was discovered four years later by producer Luther Dixon and signed to Scepter Records in New York. Her first record, "If You See Bill" b/w "It's Mine," appeared in 1961 on Scepter and was followed the next year by "Voice of Experience" b/w "I Wancha to Be Sure" on the affiliated Wand label. Both were issued under the name Tammi Montgomery.

Spotted at the Uptown Theater in her hometown by James Brown, Tammi became part of the singer's revue and recorded one single, the Brown-produced "I Cried" b/w "If You Don't Think," in 1963 for his Try Me label. According to Brown, he and Tammi became romantically involved, but the affair—and her tenure with his show—was cut short due to the objections of her family. The last Tammi Montgomery single, the Bert Berns–produced "If I Would Marry You" b/w "This Time Tomorrow," came out on Checker in 1964 but generated little more interest than had the first three. During this period, she spent two years as a pre-med student at the University of Pennsylvania and was married briefly.

Tammi was appearing with Jerry Butler at Detroit's Twenty Grand club in 1965 when Berry Gordy, Jr., heard her and offered a Motown contract. Only four solo singles and one album, 1969's *Irresistable Tammi Terrell*, were issued during her tenure with the company. Three of the singles—the number 27 R&B "I Can't Believe You Love Me," the number 25 R&B "Come On and See Me" (both 1965–66 productions by Fuqua and Bristol), and the number 31 R&B "This Old Heart of Mine (Is Weak for You)" (a 1969 revival of the Isley Brothers' Hol-

Tammi Terrell

land-Dozier-Holland–penned hit of three years earlier)—proved moderately successful. Her duets with Gaye were a another story.

Gaye, who'd recorded earlier with Mary Wells and Kim Weston and later with Diana Ross, found his ideal match in Terrell. Their voices blended in a creamy harmony, and their interacting leads displayed such a sensual repartee that many listeners became convinced they were lovers. Their first four hits—"Ain't No Mountain High Enough," "Your Precious Love," "If I Could Build My World Around You" (written by Fuqua, Bristol, and Vernon Bullock), and "If This World Were Mine" (written by Gaye)—were produced by Fuqua and Bristol, after which Ashford and Simpson assumed full writing-and-producing control of the the duo's recordings.

Terrell had recovered sufficiently to perform on the 1968 sessions that yielded the back-to-back R&B chart-toppers "Ain't Nothing Like the Real Thing" and "You're All I Need to Get By." By the next year, however, she had become so debilitated that Simpson had to sing many of her parts. The female voice on the three final hits credited to Marvin and Tammi—"Good Lovin' Ain't Easy to Come By," "What You Gave Me," and the posthumous "The Onion Song"—was that of Valerie Simpson.

TOP SONGS

Tammi Terrell:
COME ON AND SEE ME (Motown, '66, 25 R&B)

Marvin Gaye and Tammi Terrell:
AIN'T NO MOUNTAIN HIGH ENOUGH (Tamla, '67, 3 R&B, 19 Pop)
YOUR PRECIOUS LOVE (Tamla, '67, 2 R&B, 5 Pop)
IF I COULD BUILD MY WHOLE WORLD AROUND YOU (Tamla, '67, 2 R&B, 10 Pop)
AIN'T NOTHING LIKE THE REAL THING (Tamla, '68, 1 R&B, 8 Pop)
YOU'RE ALL I NEED TO GET BY (Tamla, '68, 1 R&B, 7 Pop)
KEEP ON LOVIN' ME HONEY (Tamla, '68, 11 R&B, 24 Pop)
GOOD LOVIN' AIN'T EASY TO COME BY (Tamla, '69, 11 R&B, 30 Pop)
WHAT YOU GAVE ME (Tamla, '69, 6 R&B)
THE ONION SONG (Tamla, '70, 18 R&B)

Additional Top 40 R&B Songs: 3

JOE TEX

Alternating between gospel-tinged soul ballads filled with homiletic back-porch philosophy—like "Hold What You've Got," "I Want To (Do Everything for You)," and "A Sweet Woman Like You"—and such humor-laced dance ditties as "Skinny Legs and All," "I Gotcha," and "Ain't Gonna Bump No More (With No Big Fat Woman)," singer-songwriter Joe Tex (b. Joseph Arrington, Jr., Aug. 8, 1935, Rogers, Texas) scored a dozen top 10 R&B hits in a dozen years (1965–77). All were written by Tex and produced by prominent Nashville country music publisher Buddy Killen.

"We sort of combined the blues with country and came across with a pop sound," Tex stated in 1972. "All of the things that I write are from personal experiences. I just can't make up a fictitious story and really put myself into it. It has to be something that has happened to me or to somebody that I know. This way I can sing it with feeling. And I think people can relate better to everyday-life things."

Tex was not a virtuoso singer. His range was rather limited and his low-tenor tone scratchy, and he once stated that, in the studio, he'd sing until he got hoarse in order to duplicate the way he sounded in person. Live appearances were his forte, and he was an entertainer whose shows came close to those of James Brown in excitement. (Tex and Brown maintained a public, not-always-friendly rivalry from 1957 to 1967.) Tex's specialty was kicking a microphone stand toward the audience, then falling to his knees and catching it on the rebound with one hand, a trick borrowed by both Brown and Mick Jagger.

Joe Arrington, Jr.'s abilities as a performer were his ticket out of the poverty of his sharecropping youth in Baytown, Texas. As a teenager, he took part in talent shows at clubs in Houston, where one of the owners gave him his stage last name. At a city-wide contest at Phyllis Wheatly High School, he slew the competition, which included future stars Hubert Laws, Johnny Nash, and Johnny "Guitar" Watson. The prize was a round trip to New York City and an audition for Arthur Godfrey's "Talent Scouts." While he never made it to the CBS-TV show, Tex ended up at the Apollo Theater and won the amateur show there four weeks in a row. Vocalist Arthur Prysock attended the fouth show and recommended the teenager to producer Henry Glover of King

Records. Tex went back home for a year to finish high school and, in 1955, returned to New York to record for King.

His debut recording, "Davy You Upset My Home," a self-penned send-up of the period's Davy Crockett craze, failed to make the charts, as did his other King sides through 1957. He recorded for Ace Records in New Orleans (imitating Little Richard) in 1958 and '59 and for Anna Records in Detroit the following year. His first two Anna singles, "All I Could Do Was Cry" and "I'll Never Break Your Heart," were answers to hits by Etta James and Jerry Butler respectively and featured his soon-to-become-trademark monologues, while the third, "Baby, You're Right," gave him his first taste of success as a songwriter when it was covered by James Brown, who took the tune to number two on the R&B chart in 1961.

Buddy Killen brought Tex under his wing that year and launched the Dial label to release the singer's records. The early Dial sides, recorded in Nashville and distributed by London Records, were unsuccessful. Dial switched its distribution to Atlantic in 1964, and Killen took his charge to Muscle Shoals, Alabama, to record with a band that included country star Roger Miller on gutstring guitar. The session yielded the number two R&B, number five pop song "Hold What You've Got," Tex's first national hit. Most subsequent recordings were made in Memphis with Chips Moman's studio band

Joe Tex

(sometimes including guitarist Bobby Womack) or in Nashville with a combination of the singer's sidemen and some of the city's top country pickers.

Dial moved its distribution to Mercury in 1971, and the next year Tex had the biggest hit of his career, the Number One R&B, number two pop "I Gotcha." Within months of its success, however, he quit show business, changed his name to Joseph Hazziez, and began traveling the country as a spokesman for the Nation of Islam. He did so at the behest of Elijah Muhammad, leader of the controversial separatist sect.

"The Messenger [Muhammad]," Tex explained in a 1977 interview with Bob Lucas of *Black Stars* magazine, "said leaving while my record was on top was necessary because people listen to you when you're on top and later they couldn't say I left the business because I wasn't selling any records."

Following Muhammad's death in 1975, Tex returned to performing and recording for Dial. Through Killen, he signed with Epic and had his last major hit, 1977's disco-styled "Ain't Gonna Bump No More (With No Big Fat Woman)." Tex died of a heart attack five years later, on August 13, 1982, at his home in Navasota, Texas.

TOP ALBUM

I Gotcha (Dial, '72, *17*)

TOP SONGS

Hold What You've Got (Dial, '65, *2 R&B, 5 Pop*)

I Want To (Do Everything for You) (Dial, '65, *1 R&B, 23 Pop*)

A Sweet Woman Like You (Dial, '65, *1 R&B, 29 Pop*)

The Love You Save (May Be Your Own) (Dial, '66, *2 R&B*)

I Believe I'm Gonna Make It (Dial, '66, *8 R&B*)

Skinny Legs And All (Dial, '67, *2 R&B, 10 Pop*)

Men Are Gettin' Scarce (Dial, '68, *7 R&B, 33 Pop*)

I Gotcha (Dial, '72, *1 R&B, 2 Pop*)

Ain't Gonna Bump No More (With No Big Fat Woman) (Epic, '77, *7 R&B, 12 Pop*)

Additional Top 40 R&B Songs: 18

CARLA THOMAS
••••••••••••••••••••••

The recording career of Memphis soul queen Carla Thomas (b. Dec. 21, 1942, Memphis, Tennessee) coincided with the rise and fall of Stax Records. The daughter of veteran R&B vocalist Rufus Thomas, she was the first artist to give the company, originally known as Satellite, a national hit—1961's number five R&B, number 10 pop "Gee Whiz (Look at His Eyes)"—and remained on the label's roster until it finally went out of business 15 years later, after which she made no futher recordings.

Carla was surrounded as a child by several types of music. "I feel the gutsy warmth of the blues, the sweet melodies of country music, and the emotional release from the blues," she wrote in a 1974 article for *Phonograph Record* magazine. She often attended shows at the Palace Theater on Beale Street, where her father worked as a comedian, dancer, singer, and emcee. While going to Hamilton High School, she was a member of the Teen Town Singers, a group selected from black schools from throughout the city, and at age 16 composed "Gee Whiz (Look at His Eyes)," a plaintive teen love ballad that reflected the influence of New York–based R&B singer Jeanette "Baby" Washington.

Hoping to launch his daughter's career, Rufus Thomas sent a home demo of "Gee Whiz" to Vee-Jay Records in Chicago, but it was rejected. In 1960, he took Carla to Satellite, a fledgling Memphis label run by country fiddler Jim Stewart and his sister Estelle Axton, and father and daughter recorded "Cause I Love You" as a duet at the company's new studio in an old movie theater on East McLemore Avenue. The record, a New Orleans–style Rufus Thomas composition that featured his son Marvell on piano and 16-year-old Booker T. Jones on baritone sax, became a hit in parts of the South and in northern California, attracting the attention of Atlantic Records in New York.

The follow-up was Carla's solo recording of "Gee Whiz," produced by Chips Moman and sporting a string arrangement by Stewart and the Memphis Symphony's Noel Gilbert. It was issued locally on Satellite, then nationally on Atlantic. Its success led to an album, but as Carla was by that time attending Tennessee Agricultural and Industrial State University in Nashville, Moman traveled to Nashville to complete the sessions. Over the next few years, Carla juggled her time between her studies, recording, and occasional live performances.

Although signed to Stax, her records, including the hits "I'll Bring It on Home to You" (an answer to Sam Cooke's "Bring It on Home to Me") and "I've Got No Time to Lose," appeared on Atlantic until 1965. Working with songwriter-producers Isaac Hayes and David Porter, she scored in 1966 with the singles "Let Me Be Good to You" and "B-A-B-Y." The next year, while working on her master's degree at Howard University, she was teamed with Otis Redding to cut the album *King & Queen*, which yielded hits with cover versions of Lowell Fulson's "Tramp" and Eddie Floyd's "Knock on Wood."

After finishing college, Carla toured more frequently, but her success on records began to slip. "I Like What You're Doing (To Me)," a 1969 Don Davis production, rose to number nine on the R&B chart, but proved to be her final top 40 entry. The company kept trying her with different producers, but none of their efforts generated much spark in the marketplace, including a lilting 1970 Moman production of the Toni Wine–Irwin Levine–Phil Spector song "I Loved You Like I Love My Very Life." Nevertheless, Carla stuck by the company until the bankruptcy court closed it down in January 1976.

TOP ALBUM
••••••••••••

KING & QUEEN (Otis Redding and Carla Thomas, Stax, '67, 36)

TOP SONGS
•••••••••••

GEE WHIZ (LOOK AT HIS EYES) (Atlantic, '61, 5 R&B, 10 Pop)

I'LL BRING IT HOME TO YOU (Atlantic, '62, 9 R&B)

LET ME BE GOOD TO YOU (Stax, '66, 11 R&B)

B-A-B-Y (Stax, '66, 3 R&B, 14 Pop)

TRAMP (Otis and Carla, Stax, '67, 2 R&B, 26 Pop)

I'LL ALWAYS HAVE FAITH IN YOU (Stax, '67, 11 R&B)

KNOCK ON WOOD (Otis and Carla, Stax, '67, 8 R&B, 30 Pop)

PICK UP THE PIECES (Stax, '68, 16 R&B)

I LIKE WHAT YOU'RE DOING (TO ME) (Stax, '69, 9 R&B)

Additional Top 40 R&B Songs: 8

Carla Thomas

"I have been personally depressed over the Stax thing," she told the *San Francisco Chronicle*'s Joel Selvin in 1991. "You lose self-esteem and you didn't even know you had any until you lost it. All I knew was I was working, I had records, everything was great. But, in this business, people only want to know what is it now. And that can be a stressful thing, worrying about that now. At least I'm working. I got some money. I can see the spiritual side."

After a period in Los Angeles, where she wrote commercial jingles and ad copy, Carla returned to Memphis in the early 1980s to teach performance to preteens in the public school system. She tours on occasion, still singing her old Stax hits.

RUFUS THOMAS

Singer, songwriter, dancer, and comedian Rufus Thomas (b. Mar. 26, 1917, Cayce, Mississippi) was not the biggest star at 1972's Watts Summer Festival, held on a hot Sunday afternoon at the Los Angeles Memorial Coliseum. Headliner Isaac Hayes, "the Black Moses," was. Thomas, then in his mid-50s, was enjoying his third decade of R&B chart success with such infectious, ultra-funky dance ditties as "Do the Funky Chicken," "(Do the) Push and Pull," and "The Breakdown." Yet the old man, dressed in his trademark hot pink shorts and cape and white boots, ended up as the day's clear crowd-pleaser.

While the Memphis-based entertainer flapped his arms and kicked his legs to his band's driving "Do the Funky Chicken" beat, something extraordinary occurred. Many in the throng began vaulting the barbed wire barriers that separated them from the empty football field. It quickly filled with ecstatic, dancing fans doing the Funky Chicken, or variations thereof. Security became alarmed, but all it took was a guard's whisper in Thomas's ear and the singer proceeded to talk the revelers, numbering in the tens of thousands, back into the bleachers. Having restored order, the old vaudevillian went on with the show.

Two years earlier, at a swank Hollywood nitery, Thomas was elated when Sammy Davis, Jr., came to see him perform. It was their first meeting. Both men had much in common, being among the last of the old-school entertainers who did it all: song, dance, and comedy. Thomas, of course, never reached

Davis's level of mainstream superstardom, but on the other hand, Davis never had as many hit records as did the slightly older showman.

It was during the mid-1930s, while working as a comedian at the Palace Theater on Beale Street in Memphis, that Thomas first learned how to handle audiences. His early inspirations were Fats Waller, Louis Armstrong, and Memphis blues singer Gatemouth Moore, artists who, he told writer Peter Guralnick, "were very, very versatile, always able to do more than one thing." Thomas went on the road with the Rabbit Foot Minstrels, telling jokes, tap dancing, and singing the blues, until 1940, when he married and returned to the Palace as emcee of the Wednesday night amateur shows. He cut his first record in 1950 for the Star Talent label and, the next year, became a disc jockey at Memphis station WDIA, where he remains on the air. After three singles for Chess, produced by Sam Phillips, Thomas scored his first hit, 1953's number three R&B "Bear Cat," an answer to Willie Mae Thornton's original Number One R&B recording of "Hound Dog," issued on Phillips's own Sun label.

After another release on Sun and one on Meteor, Thomas and his teenage daughter Carla recorded a duet of a Rufus composition titled "Cause I Love You" for Satellite Records, soon to become known as Stax. Released in 1960, it was a hit in some regions but didn't chart nationally. Carla had a major hit the next year with her solo "Gee Whiz (Look at His Eyes)." Dad broke through in 1963 with the number 22 R&B "The Dog," the first of a series of self-penned dance-oriented novelty numbers that included the even bigger (number five R&B, number 10 pop) "Walking the Dog" and the minor

Rufus Thomas

hits "Can Your Monkey Do the Dog" and "Somebody Stole My Dog."

After a six-year absence from the R&B top 10, Thomas returned with his first Stax release of the 1970s, the number five "Do the Funky Chicken." Later in 1970, he reached the R&B chart summit for the only time in his career with "(Do the) Push and Pull." After the number two R&B "The Breakdown" and the number 11 R&B "Do the Funky Penguin," the funky R&B grandfather had no more top 40 chart entries, although he remained at Stax until it went out of business at the beginning of 1976.

Thomas later recorded sporadically for such labels as Artists of America and Alligator but with little success. In 1994, he returned to disc with "Do the Funky Something," a track from an all-star album titled *Godchildren of Soul: Anyone Can Join* on the Forward label. Besides Carla, Rufus's two other children did well in the business: keyboardist Marvell has been a key Memphis session man since the 1960s, while Vaneese emerged during the 1980s as a background singer in New York and had a number 12 R&B hit of her own with 1987's "(I Wanna Get) Close to You."

TOP SONGS

BEAR CAT (Rufus Hound Dog Thomas, Jr., Sun, '53, *3 R&B*)

THE DOG (Stax, '63, *22 R&B*)

WALKING THE DOG (Stax, '63, *5 R&B, 10 Pop*)

DO THE FUNKY CHICKEN (Stax, '70, *5 R&B, 28 Pop*)

(DO THE) PUSH AND PULL, PART 1 (Stax, '70, *1 R&B, 25 Pop*)

THE WORLD IS ROUND (Stax, '71, *34 R&B*)

THE BREAKDOWN (PART 1) (Stax, '71, *2 R&B, 31 Pop*)

DO THE FUNKY PENGUIN PART 1 (Stax, '71, *11 R&B*)

THE THREE DEGREES

"I 'll make you into stars," songwriter-producer Richard Barrett told the Three Degrees upon hearing them in 1964. Linda Turner, Shirley Porter, and Fayette Pinkney believed him, as his track record included discovering Frankie Lymon and the Teenagers and producing and writing hits for Little Anthony and the Imperials and the proto-typical "girl group," the Chantels. Barrett, a Philadelphia native who'd begun his career in the mid-1950s as the lead singer of New York's doo-wopping Valentines, became their manager. Reaching stardom, however, was not an overnight process.

The Philadelphia trio's debut single, "Gee Baby (I'm Sorry)," issued in early 1965 on the Swan label, became a local hit, but it wasn't enough to sustain the singers. Personnel fluctuated over the next year, and Porter and Turner quit. Sheila Ferguson, who'd earlier sung with the Royalettes in Baltimore and recorded as a solo artist for Jamie and Swan, was brought in as lead singer in 1966. Helen Scott sang with the group briefly, and Valerie Holiday became a permanent member. The Three Degrees continued recording for Swan (where they cut remakes of the Chantels' "Look in Your Eyes" and "Maybe," both penned by Barrett) and then for Warner Bros., Metromedia, and Kenny Gamble and Leon Huff's short-lived Neptune label through 1969, but none of their sides made the national charts.

Barrett had other ideas and began grooming his three charges as a slick, sexy supper-club act. "Richard took us to Boston to create and build up our stage work so that, if and when we did get a hit record, we had an act," Pinkney said in a 1974 interview with Tony Cummings of *Black Music* magazine. "Because a lot of groups get a hit and they don't know the front from the back of the stage, we thought it would really be a feather in our cap to be able to perform and entertain people as well as just singing on the record." Bookings in Las Vegas and at New York City's prestigious Copacabana followed.

Signing with Roulette Records, the trio finally had a hit in 1970 with a second revival of "Maybe," which went to number four R&B and number 29 pop on the *Billboard* charts. Over four minutes in length, the Barrett production opened with an extended heartthrob monologue by Ferguson. After an abrupt horn flourish, the women came in singing with intense gospel passion as Bernard Purdie's dra-

matic drum fills pushed Ferguson's emotive lead vocals to a fever-pitched conclusion. Atypical of their polished, pop-oriented style, the record stands as the Three Degree's greatest soul performance.

Later Roulette recordings included the number seven R&B "I Do Take You" (written by Myra March) and the number 19 R&B "You're the One" (a cover of a Sly Stone song originally done by Little Sister). Joining Gamble and Huff's Philadelphia International roster in 1973, the Three Degrees sang the following year on the studio band MFSB's Number One R&B and pop charter "TSOP (The Sound of Philadelphia)," but their contributions to this basically instrumental song were largely incidental. Later in 1974, they made the R&B top 10 for the fourth and final time with "When Will I See You Again," a soft-harmony number penned and produced by Gamble and Huff. The tune did better on the pop chart, rising to number two, while it went to Number One in England, where Princess Anne presented them with a gold record and Prince Charles stated that they were his favorite group.

While later sides for Epic (composers Marvin Hamlisch and Ed Kleban said that the trio's 1976 Brad Shapiro–produced "What I Did for Love" was the finest version of their song) and Ariola (with Munich-based disco-meister Giorgio Moroder) made little noise stateside, the three women remained a

---

TOP ALBUM

THE THREE DEGREES (Philadelphia International, '75, 28)

TOP SONGS

MAYBE (Roulette, '70, *4 R&B, 29 Pop*)

I DO TAKE YOU (Roulette, '70, *7 R&B*)

YOU'RE THE ONE (Roulette, '71, *19 R&B*)

THERE'S SO MUCH LOVE ALL AROUND ME (Roulette, '71, *33 R&B*)

TSOP (THE SOUND OF PHILADELPHIA) (MFSB featuring the Three Degrees, Philadelphia International, '74, *1 R&B, 1 Pop*)

WHEN WILL I SEE YOU AGAIN (Philadelphia International, '74, *4 R&B, 2 Pop*)

I DIDN'T KNOW (Philadelphia International, '75, *18 R&B*)

GIVING UP, GIVING IN (Ariola, '78, *39 R&B*)

WOMAN IN LOVE (Ariola, '79, *27 R&B*)

favorite in England, where they scored five top 10 charters between 1974 and '79. They spent much of their time abroad, performing to capacity houses in Britain, Europe, South Africa, and Japan.

Fayette Pinkney left the Three Degrees in 1976 and was replaced by early member Helen Scott. Sheila Ferguson dropped out during the 1980s, with her slot being filled by Victoria Wallace. In 1989, Ferguson published a soul food cookbook.

THE TIME

The Time was, in the words of Prince biographer Dave Hill, "the definitive post-disco, postmodernist '80s funk band." Initially comprising lead vocalist Morris Day, guitarist Jesse Johnson, keyboardists Monte Moir and James "Jimmy Jam" Harris III, bassist Terry Lewis, and drummer Jellybean Johnson, the group was created by Prince in 1981. Sporting a retro-gangster look, a refreshingly tongue-in-cheek arrogance, and a propulsive techno-funk sound, the group's popularity, as well as Harris and Lewis's moonlighting production work for others, led to friction with Prince. Following two hit albums, 1981's *The Time* and the next year's *What Time Is It?*, Harris and Lewis were fired by their mentor, after which Moir and Jesse Johnson quit. Johnson returned for 1984's *Ice Cream Castle,* two tracks of which were featured in *Purple Rain.* Day won acclaim for his role as Prince's comic foil in the motion picture, but he had broken with the Minneapolis maestro by the time of its premiere.

Day, who mixed zany choreography into his singing act like a modern-day Cab Calloway, began his career as a teenage drummer with Grand Central, a trio led by Prince. The Day composition "Partyup" was used on Prince's third album, 1980's *Dirty Mind,* but credited to Prince. To pay back his friend, Prince took Day into the studio and produced *The Time,* playing most of the instruments and writing all the songs, with the exception of "Cool" (by Prince and guitarist Dez Dickerson) and "After Hi School" (by Dickerson alone). A band was then assembled to back Day. Rock guitarist Jesse Johnson was recruited from Enterprise, a struggling Minneapolis group in which Day had also been a member. The others were drawn from Flyte Tyme. Named after the Charlie Parker tune "Bird in Flight," Flyte Tyme had been playing local clubs for a decade.

The Time's debut Warner Bros. album yielded the hit singles "Get It Up" and "Cool," while the follow-up contained the ingeniously syncopated "777-9311" (Dickerson's phone number, but not for long) and "The Walk." On tour with Prince, the ultra-tight group often threatened to upstage him. "That was the only band that ever really scared me," he stated in 1986.

But what particularly perturbed Prince was Harris and Lewis's outside production work, which began in 1982 with "Wild Girls" by Klymaxx. The next year, when a plane flight cancellation following a session with the S.O.S. Band caused the two to miss a concert date, Prince filled for Harris from the wings, while Jerome Benton (the group's onstage valet, famous for holding a mirror in front of which Day primped) pretended to play his half-brother Lewis's bass. Harris and Lewis were fined $900 apiece then fired a few days later. "He's like dad," Harris said of Prince in a 1984 interview with Leo Sacks of *Rock & Soul* magazine, "and we were like the kids who stayed out too late, so he threw us out of the house."

With help from Prince, Day, Jesse, and Jellybean Johnson (no relation), Benton, bassist Jerry Hubbard, and keyboardists Paul Peterson and Mark Cardeas recorded the 1984 album *Ice Cream Castle* and performed two songs from it—"Jungle Love" and "The Bird"—in *Purple Rain.* Following Day's departure, the group attempted to stay together but broke up in 1985.

Day moved to California and became a solo artist

TOP ALBUMS

WHAT TIME IS IT? (Warner Bros., '82, *26*)
ICE CREAM CASTLE (Warner Bros., '84, *24*)
PANDEMONIUM (Paisley Park, '90, *18*)

TOP SONGS

GET IT UP (Warner Bros., '81, *6 R&B*)
COOL (PART 1) (Warner Bros., '81, *7 R&B*)
777-9311 (Warner Bros., '82, *2 R&B*)
THE WALK (Warner Bros., '82, *24 R&B*)
ICE CREAM CASTLES (Warner Bros., '84, *11 R&B*)
JUNGLE LOVE (Warner Bros., '84, *6 R&B, 20 Pop*)
JERK OUT (Paisley Park, '90, *1 R&B, 9 Pop*)

Additional Top 40 R&B Songs: 1

at Warner Bros., scoring at number three R&B with 1985's "The Oak Tree" and at Number One R&B with 1988's "Fishnet," produced by Harris and Lewis. The Time's guitarist formed the Jesse Johnson Revue and signed with A&M, for whom he had five top 10 R&B hits, including 1986's "Crazay" featuring Sly Stone. Moir produced Janet Jackson's 1987 Number One R&B hit "The Pleasure Principal," while Jellybean Johnson produced her 1980 Number One pop "Black Cat."

After leaving the Time, Harris and Lewis were able to focus on their Minneapolis-based Flyte Tyme production company, writing and producing R&B chart-toppers for Cheryl Lynn, Alexander O'Neal (the Flyte Tyme band's old vocalist), Herb Alpert, Day, Cherrelle, New Edition, Johnny Gill, and Ralph Tresvant. They formed their own A&M-distributed Perspective label in 1991 and the following year produced the soundtrack for the motion picture comedy *Mo' Money,* which contained the Number One R&B hit "The Best Things in Life Are Free" by Luther Vandross and Janet Jackson with Bell Biv DeVoe and Tresvant. Their greatest successes, however, were as producers of Jackson's multi-platinum *Control, Janet Jackson's Rhythm Nation 1814,* and *janet.* albums.

With blessings from Prince, who owned the group name, the six charter members of the Time, plus Benton, temporarily re-formed for the 1990 Paisley Park album *Pandemonium.* It gave the group its first Number One R&B hit, "Jerk Out," composed in part by Prince.

TONY TONI TONÉ

No one in the Oakland-based group Tony Toni Toné is named Tony. Inspired by the 1983 motion picture *Scarface,* in which Al Pacino portayed a drug dealer named Tony, it started as an in-joke among the group's three principals. Raphael Wiggins (lead vocals and bass), his older brother D'Wayne Wiggins (guitar), and their cousin Timothy Christian Riley (drums and keyboards) would primp in front of a mirror. "Tony! Tony! Tony!" they'd proclaim in self-mocking arrogance. (The group's name originally had exclamation marks in it, but they were dropped by the third album.) The adjective *tony* means "stylish" or "cool."

The Wiggins brothers and Riley scored five Number One R&B hits

Tony Toni Toné

TOP ALBUMS

THE REVIVAL (Wing, '90, 34)
SONS OF SOUL (Wing, '93, 24)

TOP SONGS

LITTLE WALTER (Wing, '88, 1 R&B)
BORN TO KNOW (Wing, '88, 4 R&B)
BABY DOLL (Wing, '88, 5 R&B)
THE BLUES (Wing, '90, 1 R&B)
FEELS GOOD (Wing, '90, 1 R&B, 9 Pop)
IT NEVER RAINS (IN SOUTHERN CALIFORNIA)
    (Wing, '90, 1 R&B, 34 Pop)
WHATEVER YOU WANT (Wing, '91, 1 R&B)
ANNIVERSARY (Wing, '93, 2 R&B, 10 Pop)

Additional Top 40 R&B Songs: 3

R&B chart. A tale of a drug dealer whose fast living catches up with him, its familiar melody based in part on that of the spiritual "Wade in the Water," the tune was co-written (with Tony Toni Toné) and produced by Thomas McElroy and Denzil Foster, both formerly of the group Club Nouveau.

"I had a concept to do a song about drug dealers 'cause I always see them around here," the Oakland-based McElroy said in 1988. "They have all this money and never have jobs."

"Little Walter" was included on the album *Who?*, which yielded the additional top 10 R&B hits "Born to Know," "Baby Doll," and "For the Love of You." For their sophomore album, 1990's *The Revival*, the Wiggins brothers and Riley decided to produce most of the tracks themselves. They hit the jackpot, scoring four Number One R&B hits in a row—"The Blues," "Feels Good," "It Never Rains (In Southern California)," and "Whatever You Want"—with "Feels Good" becoming their first single to make the pop top 10.

"We didn't even know how to approach producing," D'Wayne admitted in a 1991 interview with Paul Freeman of the *San Francisco Chronicle*. "So we just went in and started jammin', comin' up with a nice drum groove and bass lines. We built from there. It was easier than we thought."

Although sampling from old records remained a component of the group's recorded music, Tony Toni Toné abandoned drum machines, employing live drums, as well as a horn section, in order to create more of a "live" feel for their third album, 1993's *Sons of Soul*. It spawned the top 10 R&B and pop hits "If I Had the Loot" and "Anniversary."

between 1988 and 1993, making significant inroads into the pop charts in the process, with their cool combination of traditional R&B and hip-hop elements. "We see ourselves as the bridge between the generations," Riley said in a 1994 interview with Greg Rule of *Drum!* magazine. "We pay homage to the tradition of R&B because we're a self-contained band that really plays, appreciates, and understands the rootsiness of the music. But we are of the hip-hop generation, so it's just a natural part of our mentality to create much the way rappers do."

Raphael and D'Wayne's respect for tradition came from their father, amateur blues guitarist Charlie Wiggins. They were surrounded by blues, soul, and gospel music as children and later played in church and with various teenage bands, as well as sang in the choir at Castlemont High School. By 1985, D'Wayne was working with gospel diva Tramaine Hawkins, while Raphael, Timothy, and keyboardist Carl Wheeler (soon to become a key Tony Toni Toné sideman) toured with Sheila E. After more than a year as part of the singing percussionist's rhythm section, Raphael, Timothy, and Carl returned home in 1986 and hooked up with D'Wayne to form their own band with bassist Elijah Baker and keyboardist Antron Haile.

Tony Toni Toné's first single, "One Night Stand," was issued in 1987 on the Macola label, but it drew scant notice. Their second, the next year's "Little Walter" on the newly launched Mercury subsidiary Wing, shot to Number One on the *Billboard*

JOE TURNER

During a prolific recording career that lasted nearly half a century, blues shouter Joe Turner (b. Joseph Vernon Turner, May 18, 1911, Kansas City, Missouri) performed with a wide variety of instrumental accompanists—from such sophisticated jazzmen as Coleman Hawkins and Art Tatum to intuitive blues players like Fats Domino and Elmore James—but never bent his brassy, rhythmically assured style to match theirs. He was "the Boss of the Blues," and they followed his lead. From his 1938 debut recording of "Roll 'Em Pete" with boogie woogie piano titan Pete Johnson to his breakthrough in the early 1950s as a past-40-year-old idol of the nascent rock and roll genre with such hits as "Honey Hush" and "Shake, Rattle, and Roll," Turner's iron-like vocal delivery never changed, only his musical environments.

One of two children, Turner grew up singing spirituals in church and blues on street corners. After his father's death in 1926, Joe began working as a cook, waiter, and bartender at Kansas City clubs. He often sang along with bands as he worked and attracted the attention of musicians, including Pete Johnson, with whom he formed a professional relationship around 1929 that lasted on and off for two decades. During the 1930s, Turner also sang in the Kansas City area with the bands of Bennie Moten, George E. Lee, Andy Kirk, and Count Basie.

Turner and Johnson had little luck on their first visit to New York City, in 1936, to appear at the Apollo Theater and the Famous Door, but they returned two years later to take part in producer John Hammond's now-legendary "From Spirituals to Swing" concert at Carnegie Hall. They then guested on Benny Goodman's "Camel Caravan" CBS radio show, were signed to Vocalion Records, and began engagements at Barney Josephson's two prestigious Cafe Society clubs (often teamed with pianists Albert Ammons and Meade Lux Lewis as "the Boogie Woogie Boys") that lasted for over four years. With all-star jazz accompaniment, Turner recorded for Vocalion until 1940, then for Decca through 1944, and in 1945 and '46 for National Records. "My Gal's a Jockey," a 1946 National 78 with Wild Bill Moore's combo, gave the vocalist his first chart hit. The next five years were spent jumping from label to label—Stag, Aladdin, National (again), RPM, Downbeat, MGM, Dootone, Excelsior, Freedom (for which he scored a second R&B hit, 1949's "Still in the Dark)," and Imperial—before landing at Atlantic Records.

In 1950, Turner was working again with the Basie orchestra and having trouble adapting to arrangements that had been written for his predecessor, Jimmy Rushing. At an Apollo engagement, the singer became so confused that the audience jeered him. Atlantic co-owner Ahmet Ertegun, who was in attendance, found Turner at a neighborhood bar after the ill-fated show. "I walked over to him and told him to pay no mind," the producer recalled in 1986, "that he really wasn't a band singer anyway, but a great singer in his own right, and that I was going to record him and things would pick up for all of us."

They did indeed. Between 1951 and 1956, Turner had 14 top 10 R&B hits for the company, two of which—1953's "Honey Hush" and the next year's "Shake, Rattle, and Roll"—went to Number One R&B and made significant inroads onto the pop charts at a time when few rhythm and blues records were getting play on white-oriented stations. "Chains of Love" and "Sweet Sixteen" were written by Ertegun under the pseudonym "A. Nugetre." "Honey Hush" and "TV Mama" were Turner originals that he credited to wife Lou Willie Turner. "Shake, Rattle, and Roll" was by "Charles E. Calhoun," really Jesse Stone, the Kansas City jazz veteran who arranged many of Turner's Atlantic sessions. The singer appeared in two motion pictures—1955's *Rhythm and Blues Revue* and the next year's *Shake, Rattle, and Roll*—and toured for a period as part of Alan Freed's all-star rock and roll package shows.

Turner stayed with Atlantic until 1961, though he had no more hits after 1958's number 15 R&B "(I'm Gonna) Jump for Joy." He continued recording for such labels as Jewel, Blues Spectrum, Pablo, and Muse, but even as his health declined in later years, his booming baritone voice remained majestic. "Sometimes [his lyrics] are intelligible and the passions harbored in his words stare through," *New Yorker* critic Whitney Balliett wrote of a 1976 Turner engagement at Barney Josephson's Cookery, "and sometimes he pushes words together, lopping off the consonants and flattening the vowels so that whole lines go past as pure melody, as pure horn playing."

The Boss of the Blues died of a heart attack on November 24, 1985.

TOP SONGS

My Gal's a Jockey (National, '46, 6 *R&B*)

Chains of Love (Atlantic, '51, 2 *R&B*, 30 *Pop*)

Chill Is On (Atlantic, '51, 3 *R&B*)

Sweet Sixteen (Atlantic, '52, 3 *R&B*)

Don't You Cry (Atlantic, '52, 5 *R&B*)

Honey Hush (Atlantic, '53, 1 *R&B*, 23 *Pop*)

Shake, Rattle, and Roll (Atlantic, '54, 1 *R&B*, 22 *Pop*)

Flip Flop and Fly (Atlantic, '55, 2 *R&B*)

Hide and Seek (Atlantic, '55, 3 *R&B*)

Corrine Corrina (Atlantic, '56, 2 *R&B*)

Additional Top 40 R&B Songs: 10

Ike and Tina Turner

TINA TURNER

Tina Turner (b. Annie Mae Bullock, Nov. 26, 1938, Brownsville, Tennessee) is more than a soul music survivor. In 1984, after a decade without a hit and eight years without mentor and former husband Ike (b. Ikear Luster Turner, Nov. 5, 1931, Clarksdale, Mississippi), she made a stunning comeback. At age 46, she was bigger than ever, riding the crest of her five-million-selling *Private Dancer* album containing "What's Love Got to Do with It," the first Number One pop single of her long career.

Raised in Nut Bush, Tennessee, where she sang at Woodlawn Baptist Church, Annie Mae moved to St. Louis in 1956. A year later, she encountered pianist-guitarist Ike Turner, a rhythm and blues bandleader who had earlier been instrumental in bringing such blues artists as Howlin' Wolf, Little Junior Parker, and Little Milton to record. Ike and his Kings of Rhythm band also backed vocalist Jackie Brenston on the Number One R&B hit "Rocket '88,' " a 1951 Chess single that some critics feel was seminal in the development of rock and roll.

Wailing B.B. King's "You Know I Love You" in a rough, sandpaper-like contralto, Annie Mae sat in with the Kings of Rhythm at the Club Manhattan in East St. Louis, Illinois, and soon became one of the band's vocalists. She made her first appearance on record in 1958, singing a tune titled "Box Top" as "Little Ann" with Ike's band on the local Tune Town label. Romance ensued between Annie and Ike, and he dubbed her "Tina Turner," though they weren't married until 1962. Her next recording came as an accident. While in New York in 1960 to do a session for the Sue label, Ike asked Tina to fill in at the last minute for a singer who'd failed to show up. The tune, "A Fool in Love," became a number two R&B, number 27 pop hit. More hits for Sue followed—"I Idolize You," "It's Gonna Work Out Fine," "Poor Fool," and "Tra La La La La"—establishing Ike and Tina Turner as a viable recording act through the beginning of 1962, after which they had no more top 10 R&B hits for nine years.

The next phase in Ike's plan was to establish the Ike and Tina Turner Revue as one of the country's hottest performing acts, and that he quickly did by tranforming her into a sexy tigress flanked by three clones known as the Ikettes. She was billed as "the human bombshell." The raw energy and frenzied motions of Tina and the Ikettes, coupled with the precision musicianship of Ike's band, were rivaled in excitement only by James Brown and the Famous Flames.

By the mid-1960s, the revue had become one of the most popular spectacles on the so-called chitlin circuit, but things weren't faring so well on records as the duo jumped from label to label, among them Kent, Modern, Sonja, Innis, Loma,

TOP ALBUMS

PRIVATE DANCER (Capitol, '84, 3)
BREAK EVERY RULE (Capitol, '86, 4)

Additional Top 40 Albums: 4

TOP SONGS

Ike and Tina Turner:
A FOOL IN LOVE (Sue, '60, 2 R&B, 27 Pop)
IT'S GONNA WORK OUT FINE (Sue, '61, 2 R&B, 14 Pop)
POOR FOOL (Sue, '61, 4 R&B, 38 Pop)

Tina Turner:
LET'S STAY TOGETHER (Capitol, '84, 3 R&B, 26 Pop)
WHAT'S LOVE GOT TO DO WITH IT (Capitol, '84, 2 R&B, 1 Pop)
PRIVATE DANCER (Capitol, '85, 3 R&B, 7 Pop)
WE DON'T NEED ANOTHER HERO (THUNDERDOME) (Capitol, '85, 3 R&B, 2 Pop)
TYPICAL MALE (Capitol, '86, 3 R&B, 2 Pop)

Additional Top 40 R&B Songs: 16

and Warner Bros. Phil Spector's grandiose 1966 production of "River Deep, Mountain High" (Tina's first record without Ike, though he received co-billing on the label) failed to crack the U.S. charts, but it rose to number three in England. On the home front, however, they began moving into the show business mainstream with appearances on "The Ed Sullivan Show" and other national television programs that spread their following beyond the black community.

Signed to Minit Records in 1969 (and soon transferred to Liberty, then to United Artists), Ike and Tina scored their biggest hit two years later with a rousing rendition of Creedence Clearwater Revival's "Proud Mary" that reached number five on the R&B chart and number four pop. An international star by that time, Tina was becoming increasingly frustrated by Ike's iron-fisted control of her career and personal life. In 1976, prior to a scheduled performance in Dallas, she walked out with only her clothes, a gasoline credit card, and 35 cents in her pocket. She lived on welfare for a period before launching a solo performing career in 1977, but was without a recording contract for a time. Tina toured Europe and England frequently, and it was in England that she cut the Capitol album *Private Dancer* that resulted in her triumphant comeback.

Private Dancer, which included the crossover hits "Let's Stay Together," "What's Love Got to Do with It," "Better Be Good to Me," and the title track, employed some of Britain's brightest young talent, including members of Dire Straits, Heaven 17, and the Fixx. Their songs, productions, and musicianship gave her raspy voice a contemporary pop sheen. Synthesizer underpinnings and computerized percussion grooves helped to transform her career, almost overnight, from the Vegas circuit to the top of the pop music world.

Tina, who'd made her major motion picture debut in 1975 as the Acid Queen in Ken Russell's adaptation of the Who's *Tommy*, returned to the screen 10 years later as co-star of *Mad Max Beyond Thunderdome*, from which the hit single "We Don't Need Another Hero (Thunderdome)" came. *I, Tina*, an autobiography written with Kurt Loder, was published in 1986. Her life story became the subject of the critically acclaimed 1993 film *What's Love Got to Do with It*. Angela Bassett starred as Tina, with the singer supplying her own vocal parts. A soundtrack album on Virgin Records yielded the number nine pop hit "I Don't Wanna Fight."

LUTHER VANDROSS

Luther Vandross

Singer, songwriter, and producer Luther Ronzoni Vandross, Jr. (b. Apr. 20, 1951, New York), dubbed "the Pavarotti of pop" by *People* magazine, grew up on Manhattan's Lower East Side idolizing female vocalists. "The female voice to me is just special, and women's interpretive values seem wider, less restricted," he said in a 1983 interview with David McGee of *The Record*. "The peaks and valleys are much wider than what men choose to do—not what men are capable of doing, but what they choose to do."

His favorites were the Shirelles—until, when he was 14, he went to see them at one of Murray the K's Brooklyn Fox shows and heard Dionne Warwick, who was on the same bill. "It was like wearing rhinestones all your life and not knowing what diamonds could be like," he said of the experience. Warwick, along with her aunt Cissy Houston, Aretha Franklin, and Diana Ross, became Vandross's main divas. Years later, he would compose and produce records for Warwick, Franklin, and Ross, and use Houston as a background vocalist on some of his own chart-topping R&B hits.

Although he is largely self-taught as a vocalist, arranger, and pianist and never sang gospel music, Vandross was raised in a musical family. His father, who died when Luther was eight, was a big band and gospel vocalist. His older sister Patricia was a charter member of the doo wop group the Crests. He began singing with neighborhood friends in apartment building stairwells and in the hallways of Taft High School. He was later a member of a group called Shades of Jade and of the 16-member ensemble Listen My Brother, with which he sang the alphabet on the premier episode of "Sesame Street." After high school, Vandross studied electrical engineering and music at Western Michigan University for a year before returning to New York to live with his mother and work a variety of humdrum jobs, including filing defective merchandise forms for the S&H Green Stamp company.

The singer's big break came in 1974 when guitarist Carlos Alomar, formerly of Shades of Jade, invited him to hang out at a David Bowie session in Philadelphia. While recording his *Young Americans* album, the British rock star overheard Vandross singing and hired him on the spot to sing and arrange background vocals on the record. Vandross then organized a vocal group and spent a year on the road with Bowie. Also in 1974, a Vandross composition titled "Everybody Rejoice (A Brand New Day)" became part of the hit Broadway show *The Wiz*.

Through Bowie, Vandross met Bette Midler and, through Midler, producer Arif Mardin. The vocalist quickly became one of the country's most in-demand background singers, contributing to countless sessions by the likes of Midler, Carly Simon, the Average White Band, Ringo Starr, Judy Collins, Chaka Khan, Roberta Flack, Todd Rundgren, Cat Stevens, Quincy Jones, Z. Z. Hill, Lou Rawls, Chic, and Sister Sledge, in addition to handling the vocal arrangements for Barbra Streisand and Donna Summer's Number One pop hit "No More Tears (Enough Is Enough)." He also broke into even more lucrative commercial jingle work, lending his ringing tenor to spots for Kentucky Fried Chicken, G.E., AT&T, Juicy Fruit, Pepsi Cola, Miller Beer, Burger King, the Army, Navy, Air Force, Marines, and many others.

With G. Diane Sumler, Anthony Hinton, Theresa V. Reed, and Christine Whitshire, Vandross formed the group Luther and cut two albums for Cotillion in 1976 and '77. The first single, "It's Good for Your Soul," placed at number 28 on the *Billboard* R&B

chart, but neither album was commercially successful and the group disbanded. In 1979, he began shopping for a contract as a solo artist, with the stipulation that he be allowed to produce himself. No company seemed interested in taking that risk, but his lead vocals on the studio group Change's number 23 R&B hit "Searching" in 1980 attracted new interest, leading Epic Records to give him a chance.

His debut solo single, "Never Too Much," sung, composed, and produced by Vandross, rose to Number One on the R&B chart in 1981, becoming the first of his seven R&B chart-toppers through 1992. (Most of his later hits were co-productions with bassist Marcus Miller.) Then Aretha Franklin called, and he produced and co-wrote 1982's "Jump to It" (her first Number One R&B hit in over five years), as well as the next year's Number One R&B "Get It Right." And, in 1983, he produced an album for Dionne Warwick that included the number seven R&B Warwick-Vandross duet "How Many Times Can We Say Goodbye." "It's Hard for Me to Say," a 1987 production for Diana Ross, was less successful.

Famous for his syllable-splitting curlicues, ascending and descending slides, deep moans, and breathy shivers, Vandross has been the most widely admired male soul singer of the post-disco era. His

---

TOP ALBUMS

ANY LOVE (Epic, '88, 9)
POWER OF LOVE (Epic, '91, 7)
NEVER LET ME GO (Epic, '93, 6)

Additional Top 40 Albums: 6

TOP SONGS

NEVER TOO MUCH (Epic, '81, *1 R&B, 33 Pop*)
STOP TO LOVE (Epic, '86, *1 R&B, 15 Pop*)
THERE'S NOTHING BETTER THAN LOVE (Luther
    Vandross with Gregory Hines, Epic, '87,
    1 R&B)
ANY LOVE (Epic, '88, *1 R&B*)
HERE AND NOW (Epic, '89, *1 R&B, 6 Pop*)
POWER OF LOVE/LOVE POWER (Epic, '91, *1 R&B,
    4 Pop*)
THE BEST THINGS IN LIFE ARE FREE (Luther Vandross
    and Janet Jackson with BBD and Ralph
    Tresvant, Perspective, '92, *1 R&B, 10 Pop*)

Additional Top 40 R&B Songs: 24

---

singing, Barney Hoskyns commented in the book *From a Whisper to a Scream: The Great Voices of Popular Music,* "is not about passion or libido as such, but about grace and beauty, control and restraint, finesse and craftsmanship."

JR. WALKER AND THE ALL STARS

The good-time mid-1960s party sounds of such Jr. Walker and the All Stars hits as "Shotgun," "Do the Boomerang," "Shake and Finger-pop," "Cleo's Back," "(I'm a) Road Runner," "How Sweet It Is (To Be Loved by You)," and "Pucker Up Buttercup" were different from other Motown recordings of the period. Unique among the company's roster of solo singers and stand-up vocal groups —who relied on hired rhythm sections and pickup orchestras to replicate their records for live performances—the Walker combo was a self-contained unit that shook and finger-popped in person much as it did on disc.

Walker (b. Autry DeWalt, 1938 or '42, Blytheville, Arkansas) first sunk his teeth into a saxophone mouthpiece in South Bend, Indiana, where he'd settled with his mother at age 14. He started on alto sax, then switched to the larger, deeper tenor. Illinois Jacquet, Lester Young, Gene Ammons, and Boots Randolph were early inspirations. From Jacquet, he learned how to honk and to soar into high "freak" tones, while Young and Ammons influenced his graceful melodic flow. And he found a way to apply country saxman Randolph's tricky staccato patterns to rhythm and blues.

After playing in his high school's marching band, then with dance bands at parties, he turned professional at 16 with the Jumping Jacks, a combo led by drummer Billy "Sticks" Nicks. By the time the band had settled in Battle Creek, Michigan, leadership had fallen in the hands of its saxophonist. In 1962, Walker and the All Stars (organist Vic Thomas, guitarist Willie Woods, and drummer James Graves) were performing at the El Grotto Club in Battle Creek with Johnny (Bristol) and Jackey (Beavers), a singing duo that had recorded the original version of "Someday We'll Be Together" (later a hit for the Supremes) for Detroit's Tri-Phi label, operated by Harvey Fuqua and his wife, Gwen Gordy. Bristol suggested to Walker that he and his group make records. "If there's some money in it," the saxophonist replied, "yeah, let's make it."

The quartet cut three singles for the Fuquas' Harvey label in 1962, of which the laid-back blues instrumental "Cleo's Mood" received substantial airplay in some regions of the country (and rose to number 14 on the *Billboard* R&B chart when reissued by Motown three years later). When Tri-Phi and Harvey were absorbed by Motown, Walker and the All Stars made a separate deal with Berry Gordy, Jr.'s corporation and were placed on the Soul subsidiary label. Their debut single, 1964's "Monkey Jump," flopped, but the second, the following year's Number One R&B, number four pop "Shotgun," triggered the combo's rapid ascent from bar band to international stardom.

"Shotgun," an original Walker composition, signaled two other significant changes for the All Stars. While they originally had been an instrumental group, the record marked the leader's debut as a vocalist. And to fatten the band's sound, producers Berry Gordy, Jr., and Lawrence Horn added bassist James Jamerson (organist Thomas had initially carried the bass lines) and other studio players.

Drummer Graves was killed in a 1967 auto accident, and the other original All Stars left not long after. At the behest of producers Bristol and Fuqua, Walker adopted a softer, more pop-oriented approach, beginning with 1969's "What Does It Take (To Win Your Love)." The midtempo ballad

became his second crossover smash and achieved the exact R&B and pop chart positions as had "Shotgun." The singing saxman continued having hits, including a 1971 number 24 R&B vocal version of the Crusaders' instrumental "Way Back Home," with lyrics by Bristol and Gladys Knight. The next year's number 10 R&B instrumental "Walk in the Night" was Walker's final top 40 entry, though he remained with Motown through 1976.

Walker reemerged in 1979 with a little-noticed album on the Whitfield label, contributed his searing sax to Foreigner's 1981 number four pop hit "Urgent," returned to Motown for the 1983 album *Blow the House Down,* and sang, played, and acted (with Sam Moore of Sam and Dave) in a 1988 motion picture parody of rock videos titled *Tapeheads.* Even without new hit records of their own, Walker and later editions of the All Stars (for a time including son Autry DeWalt, Jr., on drums) toured incessantly.

"I am a road runner," he stated in 1991. "Ever since Berry Gordy told me to scare up a truck and git—he had some dates lined up for me—I got the truck and lit out. Same now. I travel. I blow some. People dance. And I like it."

WAR

War's distinctively loping mixture of funk, jazz, and Latin influences, combined with lyrics that stressed peace and universal brotherhood, made it a favorite of black, white, and Latino audiences during the pre-disco period. "Why Can't We Be Friends?" the southern California septet asked in 1975.

The band—percussionist Thomas Sylvester "Papa Dee" Allen (b. July 18, 1931, Wilmington, Delaware), drummer Harold Brown (b. Mar. 17, 1946, Long Beach, California), bassist Morris DeWayne "B. B." Dickerson (b. Aug. 3, 1949, Torrance, California), organist-pianist Leroy "Lonnie" Jordan (b. Nov. 21, 1948, San Diego, California), tenor saxophonist–flutist Charles William Miller (b. June 2, 1946, Olathe, Kansas), harmonica player Lee Oskar (b. Oskar Levetin Hansen, Mar. 24, 1946 or '48, Copenhagen, Denmark), and guitarist Howard E. Scott (b. Mar. 15, 1946, San Pedro, California)— scored a string of group-penned crossover smashes between 1972 and '77. Seven singles placed in both

---

TOP SONGS

SHOTGUN (Soul, '65, 1 *R&B*, 4 Pop)

SHAKE AND FINGERPOP (Soul, '65, 7 *R&B*, 29 Pop)

CLEO'S BACK (Soul, '65, 7 *R&B*)

(I'M A) ROAD RUNNER (Soul, '66, 4 *R&B*, 20 Pop)

HOW SWEET IT IS (TO BE LOVED BY YOU) (Soul, '66, 3 *R&B*, 18 Pop)

HIP CITY—PART 2 (Soul, '68, 7 *R&B*, 31 Pop)

WHAT DOES IT TAKE (TO WIN YOUR LOVE) (Soul, '69, 1 *R&B*, 4 Pop)

THESE EYES (Soul, '69, 3 *R&B*, 16 Pop)

GOTTA HOLD ON TO THIS FEELING (Soul, '70, 2 *R&B*, 21 Pop)

DO YOU SEE MY LOVE (FOR YOU GROWING) (Soul, '70, 3 *R&B*, 32 Pop)

Additional Top 40 R&B Songs: 11

War

TOP ALBUM

THE WORLD IS A GHETTO (United Artists, '72, *1*)

Additional Top 40 Albums: 8

TOP SONGS

SLIPPIN' INTO DARKNESS (United Artists, '72,
   12 R&B, 16 Pop)

THE WORLD IS A GHETTO (United Artists, '72,
   3 R&B, 7 Pop)

THE CISCO KID (United Artists, '73, *5 R&B, 2 Pop*)

GYPSY MAN (United Artists, '73, *6 R&B, 8 Pop*)

WHY CAN'T WE BE FRIENDS? (United Artists, '75,
   9 R&B, 6 Pop)

LOW RIDER (United Artists, '75, *1 R&B, 7 Pop*)

SUMMER (United Artists, '76, *4 R&B, 7 Pop*)

L.A. SUNSHINE (Blue Note, '77, *2 R&B*)

GALAXY (MCA, '77, *5 R&B, 39 Pop*)

Additional Top 40 R&B Songs: 9

the R&B and pop top 10, and nine of the group's albums struck gold, with 1976's *Greatest Hits* also hitting platinum.

The nucleus of War came from the Creators, formed in 1962 by Brown and Scott. By 1965, when the group was signed to Dore Records and cut such singles as "Burn, Baby, Burn" (the theme song of Los Angeles disc jockey Magnificent Montague, its title became the rallying cry for that year's Watts uprising) and "Lonely Feelin'," Dickerson, Jordan, and Miller had joined. Initially an R&B cover band, the Creators began incorporating salsa, ska, and organ-jazz elements into their repertoire. Later recordings were made as "the Romeos" for Montague's Mark II label, with guitarist Bobby Womack filling in for Scott, who'd been drafted into the military. Dickerson left in 1967 and was replaced by Peter Rosen.

Scott was back by 1969, playing with Brown, Jordan, Miller, Rosen, and Delaware transplant Allen in a large band called the Nightshift. They were backing vocalist and ex–football player Deacon Jones at the Rag Doll club in North Hollywood when, at Rosen's invitation, British rock singer Eric Burdon (formerly of the Animals), producer Jerry Goldstein (whose past credits included co-producing the Number One pop hits "My Boyfriend's Back" by the Angels and "Hang On Sloopy" by the McCoys), and struggling Danish harmonica virtuoso Oskar came to check them out. The Nightshift, plus Oskar but minus a couple of horn players, became Burdon's new band and joined Goldstein and partner Steve Gold's Far Out Productions as War.

"There was a big peace movement going on," Goldstein explained to writer Barry Alfonso. "We thought if we chose a name like 'War,' nobody would just pass us by."

War spent nearly a year on the road with Burdon (during which time Rosen died of a drug overdose and was replaced by Dickerson) before joining him in the studio to record the 1970 MGM album *Eric Burdon Declares "War."* It yielded the number three pop hit "Spill the Wine," a Latin-spiced tune that was written in the studio after Jordan had destroyed an expensive console with an accidentally spilled bottle of wine. Following a second album with Burdon and a debut United Artists album by the band alone, both commercially unsuccessful, the vocalist dropped his cohorts during a European tour.

With Goldstein editing the band's open-ended studio jams, as well as sometimes lending a hand with the lyrics, War came up with a winning formula for the next album, *All Day Music.* Issued in late 1971, it contained the number 12 R&B, number 16 pop hit "Slippin' into Darkness." Greater crossover action followed over the next five years, with 1973's number five R&B, number two pop "The Cisco Kid" and 1975's Number One R&B, number seven pop "Low Rider" becoming the band's biggest hits.

War scored its last significant hit with 1977's number five R&B, number 39 pop "Galaxy" on MCA. Personnel began to change over the next two years. Pat Rizzo replaced Miller (who later was stabbed to death, in 1980), and Luther Rabb replaced Dickerson. Vocalist Alice Tweed Smith was added, and Ronnie Hammon became second drummer (sole stickman after Brown's 1984 departure.) Allen died of a heart attack during a 1988 club date with the band.

While sides made during the 1980s for MCA, LAX, RCA, Coco Plum, and Priority generated infrequent radio interest, the band's reputation had become enhanced by the end of the decade through samples of its old grooves on rap records. In 1992, Jordan, Scott, Oskar, and Hammon responded with the Avenue Records album *Rap Declares War*, featuring an all-star cast of hip-hop artists. As of 1994, War consisted of Brown (back after a 10-year break), Jordan, Scott, Hammon, harmonica player Tetsuya Nakamura, percussionist Sal Rodriguez, keyboardist Rae Valentine, and saxophonists Kerry Campbell and Charles Green.

BILLY WARD AND HIS DOMINOES

Billy Ward (b. Sept. 19, 1921, Los Angeles) not only played a role in the naming of rock and roll but was attendant at its christening—or so he has claimed. While the non-singing leader of the Dominoes was on a promotional visit to Alan Freed at Cleveland radio station WJW, the disc jockey played "Sixty-Minute Man," the rhythm and blues vocal group's then-recent smash. This rollicking boast of male sexual prowess, penned by Ward and his agent Rose Marks, was the biggest R&B record of 1951. It stayed at the top of the *Billboard* R&B chart for 14 weeks and crossed to the pop chart, peaking at number 17. As the deejay was spinning the disc, his ears zeroed in on a line sung by basso Bill Brown: "I rock 'em, roll 'em, all night long."

"Freed leaped to his feet," Ward recalled in an interview of unknown origin. " 'That's it!' he cried hoarsely. 'Rock and Roll! That's what it is.' Immediately he broadcast his name for our sound. And all the trade publications fell in line with his thinking."

The Dominoes were, Nick Toshes stated in his book *The Unsung Heroes of Rock 'n' Roll*, "the most brilliant, and the classiest, of the rock-'n'-roll vocal groups....Their mastery of rhythm and meter, their subtle interweaving of the coarse and the sublime, their lyrics which never seemed to rhyme for the sake of rhyme alone—these are qualities so rare and so close to poetry's edge that one is almost tempted to bring that inescapable little gray mouse of a word, 'art,' into play."

The son of a minister and his choir-directing wife, Ward was raised on gospel and classical music in Philadelphia. He played organ at Wayland Baptist Church and, at age 14, won a city-wide competition for his composition "Dejection," which was performed by a symphony orchestra under the baton of

TOP SONGS

The Dominoes:
DO SOMETHING FOR ME (Federal, '51, 6 R&B)
SIXTY-MINUTE MAN (Federal, '51, 1 R&B, 17 Pop)
THAT'S WHAT YOU'RE DOING FOR ME (Federal, '52, 7 R&B)
HAVE MERCY BABY (Federal, '52, 1 R&B)

Billy Ward and His Dominoes:
I'D BE SATISFIED (Federal, '52, 8 R&B)
THE BELLS (Federal, '53, 3 R&B)
PEDAL PUSHIN' PAPA (Federal, '53, 4 R&B)
THESE FOOLISH THINGS REMIND ME OF YOU (Federal, '53, 5 R&B)
RAGS TO RICHES (King, '53, 2 R&B)
STAR DUST (Liberty, '57, 5 R&B, 12 Pop)

Additional Top 40 R&B Songs: 2

Walter Damrosch. Ward served during World War II as a commissioned officer at Fort Eustis, Virginia, where he directed the Coast Artillery Choir. After his discharge, he studied at the Chicago Art Institute and at the Juilliard School of Music and began working in New York City as a vocal coach.

In 1950, at the suggestion of songwriter Rose Marks, Ward formed a vocal group comprising Clyde McPhatter (lead), Charlie White (tenor), Joe Lamont (baritone), and Bill Brown (bass). Ward functioned as arranger and pianist. After winning an amateur show at the Apollo Theater, the Ques, as they were originally known, took top prize on Arthur Godfrey's "Talent Scouts" CBS radio program with a Ward arrangement of "Goodnight Irene," the Weavers' then-current hit. This attracted the attention of producer Ralph Bass, then forming his own Federal label as a subsidiary of King Records in Cincinnati. The Ques became the Dominoes.

The group's first release, the Ward-Marks ballad "Do Something for Me," featured the chilling, churchy tenor of McPhatter, who Ward began billing as his younger brother, "Clyde Ward." It went to number six on the R&B chart, becoming the first of the Dominoes' dozen top 10 R&B hits. "Sixty-Minute Man," their third release, cemented the group's success. Ward is said to have run the quartet like a drill sergeant, causing members to defect. Gone by the time of the Dominoes' second R&B chart-topper, 1952's McPhatter-led jump blues "Have Mercy

Baby," were White and Brown, who were replaced by James Van Loan and David McNeil.

The last Dominoes hit to feature McPhatter was 1953's "These Foolish Things Remind Me of You." He left the group in April of that year to form his own group, the Drifters, with whom he quickly found greater fame at Atlantic Records. He was replaced by Detroit vocalist Jackie Wilson, whose soaring McPhatter-inspired tenor was featured on the 1953 hits "You Can't Keep a Good Man Down" and "Rags to Riches," which, like "These Foolish Things," were drawn from the pop repertoire as opposed to being original R&B compositions.

Ward continued taking his men down the pop path at Jubilee Records in 1954 and '55 (where they had no hits) and at Decca in 1956 and '57 (their first release, the Wilson-led "St. Theresa of the Roses," became a number 13 pop charter). Wilson soon launched a successful solo career at Brunswick Records. When the Dominoes signed with Liberty Records later in 1957, they consisted of lead Eugene Mumford (formerly of the Larks, the Golden Gate Quartet, and the Serenaders), tenor Milton Grayson, baritone Milton Merle, and basso Clifford Givens. The first two Liberty singles, the number five R&B, number 12 pop "Star Dust" and the number 20 pop "Deep Purple," were both Ward arrangements of pop standards, complete with strings and far removed stylistically from the group's early sound. Later recordings for Liberty, ABC-Paramount, and Ro Zan failed to chart.

DIONNE WARWICK

Dionne Warwick (b. Marie Dionne Warrick, Dec. 12, 1940, East Orange, New Jersey) first encountered Burt Bacharach in 1961. She was singing backgrounds with younger sister Dee Dee, aunt Cissy Houston, and friend Doris Troy on a Drifters session for Atlantic Records. He was conducting his arrangement of "Mexican Divorce," a tune he'd penned with lyricist Bob Hillard. The meeting led to one of the most memorable musical marriages in the annals of pop music, with Bacharach and lyricist Hal David writing and producing a string of hits for the vocalist between 1963 and 1970. Eight—"Anyone Who Had a Heart," "Walk on By," "Message to Michael," "I Say a Little Prayer," "(Theme from) Valley of the Dolls,"

Dionne Warwick

began having Warwick cut demos of tunes for—as well as sing on sessions by—Maxine Brown, Tommy Hunt, Chuck Jackson, and the Shirelles, all of whom recorded for Florence Greenberg's Scepter Records. This led to Warwick's solo debut for the label, "Don't Make Me Over," which placed in early 1963 at number five on the R&B chart and at number 21 on the pop list. Within a year, she was a full-fledged crossover star, hitting the pop top 10 with "Anyone Who Had a Heart" and "Walk on By." (*Billboard* ran no R&B tabulations during 1964.) Warwick made the R&B top 10 three more times during the decade—with "Message to Michael" (originally recorded by Lou Johnson as "Message to Martha"), "Alfie," and "This Girl's in Love with You" (first done by Herb Alpert as "This Guy's in Love with You")—even as the music she and her producers were creating moved away from the R&B into the pop mainstream.

Warwick, Bacharach, and David left Scepter for Warner Bros. in 1971, but *Dionne,* their first album for the label, flopped. The songwriting partners then parted company, and the singer slapped them with a suit for not fulfilling their contractual obligations to

"Do You Know the Way to San Jose," "This Girl's in Love with You," and "I'll Never Fall in Love Again"—placed in the pop top 10.

Warwick's alternately poised and impassioned vocal style, which proved ideally suited to Bacharach and David's sophisticated compositions and brilliant Bacharach arrangements filled with tension and release, is rooted in gospel music. Her father served as director of gospel promotion for Chess Records, while her mother managed the Drinkard Singers, a gospel group that recorded for Savoy, Verve, and RCA Victor during the 1950s. Dionne often played piano or organ for the Drinkards and sometimes joined them vocally. She also studied formally at the Hartt College of Music in Hartford, Connecticut. With Dee Dee, she formed a trio called the Gospelaires that began doing secular session work during the late 1950s with such artists as Sam "The Man" Taylor, Nappy Brown, and Bobby Darin.

After the "Mexican Divorce" session, Bacharach

TOP ALBUM

VALLEY OF THE DOLLS (Scepter, '68, 6)

Additional Top 40 Albums: 13

TOP SONGS

DON'T MAKE ME OVER (Scepter, '63, *5 R&B, 21 Pop*)
MESSAGE TO MICHAEL (Scepter, '66, *5 R&B, 8 Pop*)
ALFIE (Scepter, '67, *5 R&B, 15 Pop*)
THIS GIRL'S IN LOVE WITH YOU (Scepter, '69, *7 R&B, 7 Pop*)
THEN CAME YOU (Dionne Warwicke and Spinners, Atlantic, '74, *2 R&B, 1 Pop*)
ONCE YOU HIT THE ROAD (Warner Bros., '75, *5 R&B*)
HOW MANY TIMES CAN WE SAY GOODBYE (Dionne Warwick and Luther Vandross, Arista, '83, *7 R&B, 27 Pop*)
THAT'S WHAT FRIENDS ARE FOR (Dionne and Friends, Arista, '85, *1 R&B, 1 Pop*)
LOVE POWER (Dionne Warwick and Jeffrey Osborne, Arista, '87, *5 R&B, 12 Pop*)

Additional Top 40 R&B Songs: 15

her. On the advice of a numerologist, she had an "e" appended legally to her last name in hopes of improving her luck, but Ms. Warwicke had little luck during her five years at Warner Bros., where she moved from producer to producer, including Holland, Dozier, and Holland; Thom Bell; Jerry Ragavoy; and Michael Omartian. She surfaced in the top 10 only twice during the entire period, in 1974 with "Then Came You," a number two R&B, Number One pop Bell-produced duet with the Spinners, and the next year (by which time she'd dropped the "e") with the number five R&B Ragavoy-produced "Once You Hit the Road."

After making a duet album with Isaac Hayes for ABC in 1977, Warwick signed with Arista in 1979 and saw her fortunes improve. Producer Barry Manilow put her back on the charts that year with the number 18 R&B, number five pop "I'll Never Love This Way Again." "Heartbreaker," a number written and produced in part by Barry Gibb of the Bee Gees, became a number 14 R&B, number 10 pop hit in 1982, while the next year's "How Many Times Can We Say Goodbye," a duet with producer Luther Vandross, went to number seven on the R&B chart. In 1984, besides singing with Stevie Wonder on the soundtrack of the motion picture *The Woman in Red,* Warwick was reunited with Bacharach (working with new partner Carol Bayer Sager) for the album *Finder of Lost Loves.* Bacharach and Sager went on to produce 1985's R&B and pop chart-topping "That's What Friends Are For" (on which Warwick was joined by Wonder, Elton John, and Gladys Knight) and 1987's number five R&B, number 12 pop "Love Power" (a duet with Jeffrey Osborne).

By the early 1990s, Warwick was again dabbling in the occult, this time as host of the controversial late-night television "infomercial" series "The Psychic Friends Network." She remained with Arista, but her recordings, including a duet with cousin Whitney Houston from the 1993 Warwick album *Friends Can Be Lovers,* generated little attention.

DINAH
WASHINGTON

Music trade publications dubbed Dinah Washington (b. Ruth Lee Jones, Aug. 29, 1924, Tuscaloosa, Alabama) "Queen of the Juke Boxes," while she referred to herself as "Queen of the Blues." There was a regalness in the way she sang—with crystalline diction in assertive, trumpet-like tones—as well as in how she carried herself both on and off stage. During a prolific recording career that spanned from 1943 until shortly before her death twenty years later from an accidental overdose of alcohol and diet pills, she tackled all manner of material—blues, jazz, pop ballads, country tunes, rock and roll—and in the process scored a total of 38 top 10 R&B chart entries, counting her three seminal hits with Lionel Hampton.

When Ruth Jones was three, she settled on Chicago's South Side with her mother, father, brother, and two sisters and was soon singing at St. Luke's Baptist Church. Following her mother's lead, she took up piano at age 11 and performed with her family at St. Luke's and other congregations in the area. Pioneering Chicago gospel singer-pianist Roberta Martin was an important early influence, as was local blues singer Georgia White. At 15, Ruth won an amateur contest at the Regal Theater and began appearing in nightclubs before returning to gospel as lead singer and pianist with the Sallie Martin Colored Ladies Quartet from 1940 to 1942. "She could really sing but, shoot, she'd catch the eye of some man and she'd be out the church before the minister finished off the doxology," Martin told author Anthony Heilbut years later.

Ruth's decision to leave gospel and return to club work led to a lifelong rift with her mother, which some cite as the source of the singer's soon-to-become-infamous Jekyll-and-Hyde personality and series of short-lived marriages—eight or nine, by most estimates. She was performing in 1942 at Garrick's Show Bar, a Chicago club managed by Joe Sherman, when agent Joe Glaser heard her and recommended her to Lionel Hampton, who was in town appearing at the Regal. She was invited to join the orchestra for a matinee show. "She could make herself heard, even with my blazing band in the background, and she had that gutty style that they would later call rhythm and blues," the vibraharpist recalled in his autobiography. She was hired on the spot and remained with the band for over three years, billed as "Dinah Washington," a name that Sherman, Glaser, and Hampton have all claimed credit for.

Until her first recording session, on December 29, 1943, blues had not been a part of the singer's repertoire, but critic Leonard Feather felt she had a good blues voice and arranged for her to cut two of his tunes, "Evil Gal Blues" and "Salty Papa Blues," for the Keynote label backed by Hampton and a combo of his bandsmen. Both were hits in 1944. By the time of her next, as featured vocalist with the entire Hampton band on the Decca recording of Feather's "Blow Top Blues," which made both the R&B and pop charts in 1947, Washington had already struck out on her own. After making a dozen non-charting sides in 1945 for Apollo Records with an all-star Los Angeles jazz group, Washington signed with Mercury Records in Chicago and began her 13-year run as a solo artist on the R&B charts and jukeboxes with a 1948 rendition of Fats Waller's "Ain't Misbehavin'." During her long stay at Mercury, she recorded pop tunes, covers of R&B hits (the Orioles' "It's Too Soon to Know") and country hits (Hank Williams's "Cold, Cold Heart"), such double-entendre blues as "Long John Blues" (about a dentist who "thrills me when he drills me") and "TV Is the Thing (This Year)," and a series of jazz albums with all-star accompaniment.

The Queen's domain spread to the pop charts in 1959 with her Clyde Otis–produced, Belford Hendricks–orchestrated rendition of the standard "What a Diff'rence a Day Makes," which went to number eight pop and number four R&B. Otis teamed her with Brook Benton the next year for the spunky duets "Baby (You've Got What It Takes)" and "A Rockin' Good Way (To Mess Around and Fall in Love)," both topping the R&B charts and making the pop top 10.

After two final hits at Mercury—1960's "This Bitter Earth" (her fifth R&B chart-topper) and the next year's "September in the Rain"—Washington jumped ship to Roulette. Although she recorded eight albums for the company, none of her singles charted. She remained a popular supper club attraction, however, until her demise at age 39 on December 14, 1963.

MARY WELLS

Mary Esther Wells (b. May 13, 1943, Detroit) was Motown's first superstar, as well as the first major artist to bolt the company. Between 1960 and 1964, the teenage vocalist scored nine top 10 R&B hits and four top 10 pop charters, the majority written and produced by Smokey Robinson. While riding atop the pop chart in the spring of 1964 with the song "My Guy," Wells turned 21 and declared her Motown contract invalid. The court agreed, but the career move proved disastrous for the emancipated singer.

Although she'd been singing at her uncle's Baptist church since age three, Wells wanted to be a songwriter, not a singer. While attending Detroit's Northwestern High School, she penned a gospel-flavored tune entitled "Bye Bye Baby." She idolized Jackie Wilson, a local artist who'd become a national star, and was looking for a way to get her song to him. Through Robert Bateman, a member of a vocal group called the Satintones, she met Berry Gordy, Jr., who'd written Wilson's seminal hits. When Gordy heard Wells sing her composition, he immediately decided he wanted it—and her—for his fledgling Motown operation.

Issued in late 1960, the eighth single to appear on the Motown label, the Gordy-produced "Bye Bye Baby" rose to number eight on the *Billboard* R&B chart. Unlike Wells's later work, in which her voice was soft and fragile, the record featured a rough, assertive stylist, the result of her becoming hoarse after 22 takes of the tune. It also marked an end, for the time being, to her songwriting career. There were other priorities. "I had to start learning to perform in

---

TOP ALBUM

Unforgettable (Mercury, '61, *10*)

Additional Top 40 Albums: 2

TOP SONGS

Am I Asking Too Much (Mercury, '48, *1 R&B*)

It's Too Soon to Know (Mercury, '48, *2 R&B*)

Baby, Get Lost (Mercury, '49, *1 R&B*)

I Only Know (Mercury, '50, *3 R&B*)

Cold, Cold Heart (Mercury, '51, *3 R&B*)

Wheel of Fortune (Mercury, '52, *3 R&B*)

Baby (You've Got What It Takes) (Dinah Washington and Brook Benton, Mercury, '60, *1 R&B, 5 Pop*)

A Rockin' Good Way (To Mess Around and Fall in Love) (Dinah Washington and Brook Benton, Mercury, '60, *1 R&B, 7 Pop*)

This Bitter Earth (Mercury, '60, *1 R&B, 24 Pop*)

Additional Top 40 R&B Songs: 36

Mary Wells

board published no R&B charts during that period.) Her biggest record, it also proved to be her last major pop hit. By the time her double-sided duet single with Marvin Gaye, "Once Upon a Time" b/w "What's the Matter with You Baby," entered the pop top 20, Wells was tangled in a bitter legal battle with Motown.

At the urging of husband Herman Griffin (also an early Motown artist), Wells accepted a lucrative offer from 20th Century Fox Records. Without Robinson's guidance, however, she was only able to score as high as number 13 R&B, number 34 pop with 1965's "Use Your Head." Her fortunes improved somewhat a year later at Atco, for whom she placed at number six R&B with "Dear Lover," but the song failed to penetrate the pop top 40.

Divorcing Griffin, she married singer-guitarist Cecil Womack in 1967. The two also formed a songwriting partnership. A series of Wells-Womack productions for the Jubilee label gave the singer three minor hits, with 1969's number 35 "Dig the Way I Feel" being her final R&B top 40 entry. She reemerged during the early 1980s at Reprise, but work with producers Rick Hall, Sonny Limbo, and brother-in-law Bobby Womack generated little attention, as did later Wells recordings for Epic, Allegiance, Nightmare, and Motorcity.

The vocalist divorced Cecil in 1977 and later married his brother Curtis. Cecil wed Linda Cooke

front of an audience and get my nerves together," she stated in 1977.

After a second hit single, 1961's number nine R&B "I Don't Want to Take a Chance," co-written by William "Mickey" Stevenson with producer Gordy, Wells was placed in the creative hands of the Miracles' Smokey Robinson. This association gave Motown its first important artistic marriage between a singer and a songwriter-producer. Robinson focused on the gentle side of Wells's voice to garner a cotton-candy tone not unlike that of his own. "Smokey popped her up," Harvey Fuqua told writer David Ritz. "He turned her from straight R&B to a new kind of pop never really heard before."

Beginning with 1962's calypso-imbued "You Beat Me to the Punch," Wells became an R&B-to-pop crossover success, and the formula continued with "The One Who Really Loves You" and "Two Lovers," both of which topped the R&B charts that year. After such other brilliant Robinson creations as "Laughing Boy," "Your Old Stand By," and "What's Easy for Two Is So Hard for One," she hit Number One pop in 1964 with his "My Guy." (*Bill-*

TOP ALBUM

GREATEST HITS (Motown, '64, *18*)

TOP SONGS

BYE BYE BABY (Motown, '60, *8 R&B*)
I DON'T WANT TO TAKE A CHANCE (Motown, '61, *9 R&B, 33 Pop*)
THE ONE WHO REALLY LOVES YOU (Motown, '62, *2 R&B, 8 Pop*)
YOU BEAT ME TO THE PUNCH (Motown, '62, *1 R&B, 9 Pop*)
TWO LOVERS (Motown, '62, *1 R&B, 7 Pop*)
LAUGHING BOY (Motown, '63, *6 R&B, 15 Pop*)
YOUR OLD STAND BY (Motown, '63, *8 R&B, 40 Pop*)
WHAT'S EASY FOR TWO IS SO HARD FOR ONE (Motown, '63, *8 R&B, 29 Pop*)
DEAR LOVER (Atco, '66, *6 R&B*)

Additional Top 40 R&B Songs: 6

(Sam Cooke's daughter, as well as Bobby's former stepdaughter), with whom he formed the singing-songwriting duo Womack and Womack. This seemingly incestuous situation remained friendly, however, with Mary, Curtis, and Bobby all contributing background vocals to Cecil and Linda's 1983 Elektra album *Love Wars*.

Wells continued performing her old Motown hits on the oldies circuit until diagnosed with throat cancer in 1991. Rather than lose her voice to a laryngectomy that doctors felt would remove virtually all the cancer, she opted for riskier radiation therapy. It didn't work. Wells succumbed on July 26, 1992.

THE WHISPERS

Persistence paid off for the Whispers, featuring the like-sounding tenor leads of identical twins Wallace and Walter Scott (b. Sept. 3, 1943, Fort Worth, Texas). Formed at Jordan High School in the Watts district of Los Angeles during the early 1960s, the jazz- and doo wop–influenced soul vocal group recorded for 16 years before finally hitting it big in 1980 with the Number One R&B single "And the Beat Goes On."

Raised in Hawthorne, Nevada, and Los Angeles, the Scott brothers made their performing debut at age five singing the vaudeville standard "Me and My Shadow." Greatly inspired by the Trenier twins, they continued appearing as an amateur duo until hooking up with the Eden Trio, a group comprising tenors Nicholas Caldwell (b. Apr. 5, 1944, Loma Linda, California) and Gordy Harmon and baritone Marcus Hutson (b. Jan. 8, 1943, St. Louis, Missouri). In 1964, the quintet signed with Dore Records in Hollywood and was christened the Whispers by label owner Lou Bedell.

"The name came because we basically have a soft sound," songwriter and group choreographer Caldwell explained in 1974. "We used to enjoy the sounds of the Four Freshmen and the Hi-Lo's. In our early stages we were singing these kinds of tunes, so when we were introduced to rhythm and blues, this came along with us."

Although none charted nationally, such Dore singles as "The Dip," "As I Sit Here," and "You Got a Man on Your Hands" sold well in southern California and especially in the San Francisco/Oakland Bay

The Whispers

TOP ALBUM

THE WHISPERS (Solar, '80, 6)

Additional Top 40 Albums: 4

TOP SONGS

SEEMS LIKE I GOTTA DO WRONG (Soul Clock, '70, 6 *R&B*)

AND THE BEAT GOES ON (Solar, '80, *1 R&B, 19 Pop*)

LADY (Solar, '80, *3 R&B, 28 Pop*)

IT'S A LOVE THING (Solar, '81, *2 R&B, 28 Pop*)

TONIGHT (Solar, '83, *4 R&B*)

KEEP ON LOVIN' ME (Solar, '83, *4 R&B*)

ROCK STEADY (Solar, '87, *1 R&B, 7 Pop*)

INNOCENT (Capitol, '90, *3 R&B*)

IS IT GOOD TO YOU (Capitol, '90, *4 R&B*)

Additional Top 40 R&B Songs: 24

Area, where the group (minus Walter, who'd been drafted and saw service in Vietnam) relocated in 1966 at the behest of Sly Stone, then a disc jockey at KDIA in Oakland. The Whispers began recording for the local Soul Clock label in 1969, scoring regionally with "Great Day" and making their first *Billboard* chart appearance at number 17 R&B with the follow-up, a ballad titled "Time Will Come," penned by Caldwell and Harmon and produced by Ron Carson. They broke into the top 10 with 1970's number six R&B "Seems Like I Gotta Do Wrong," their biggest hit until 1980. Subsequent singles for Janus, some produced in Philadelphia by Norman Harris and Bunny Sigler, were less successful.

The Whispers were managed by Lewis Chinn, owner of the Dragon a Go-Go club in San Francisco's Chinatown. In the early 1970s, he opened the larger Soul Train club in partnership with concert promoter Dick Griffey and television host Don Cornelius. Griffey took over as the Whispers' manager, featuring them as an opening act on many of his shows, and they also became frequent guests on Cornelius's syndicated "Soul Train" program. The group, with Leaveil Degree (b. July 31, 1948, New Orleans) in the place of Harmon, who'd ruptured his larynx in a 1973 auto accident, joined the roster at Griffey and Cornelius's Soul Train label in 1975. Two Soul Train singles— 1976's Norman Harris–produced "One for the Money" and the next year's cover of Bread's "Make It with You"—made it to number 10 on the R&B chart.

After Griffey ended his partnership with Cornelius, the group was transferred to Griffey's new Solar label, for which they scored again at number 10 R&B with the 1978 ballad "(Let's Go) All the Way." The quintet's profile mushroomed with 1980's uncharacteristically uptempo "And the Beat Goes On," produced by the Whispers with Griffey and Leon Sylvers III. "I still pinch myself every now and then to make sure that this is real," Wallace (better known as "Scotty") said just after the tune had reached the R&B chart summit.

The Whispers maintained a strong presence in the R&B top five during the early 1980s with the hits "Lady," "It's a Love Thing," "Tonight," and "Keep On Lovin' Me." They returned to the top of the R&B list and crossed into the pop top 10 for the first time with 1987's upbeat "Rock Steady." It was the first major hit to be produced by Antonio "L.A." Reid and Kenny "Babyface" Edmonds, then recording for Solar as members of the Deele.

Following a bitter legal battle between the group and Griffey, the Whispers reemerged in 1990 at Capitol with *More of the Night,* an album containing the top 10 R&B hits "Innocent," "My Heart Your Heart," and "Is It Good to You." While the group remained a unit, the Scott twins cut a duet album for the company three years later that included a version of the Intruders classic "I Want to Know Your Name."

BARRY WHITE

Crooning and rapping in a raspy bedroom bass-baritone over billowing orchestral cushions and meticulously crafted rhythm tracks, singer-pianist-songwriter-producer Barry White (b. Sept. 12, 1944, Galveston, Texas) was the ultimate soul loveman of the 1970s. His sensuous songs treated male-female relationships with great sensitivity, while his fusion of symphonic sounds with Latin-tinged funk greatly influenced disco music as well as the later British soul of Lisa Stansfield and Soul II Soul.

As a vocalist, White had 14 top 10 R&B hits, six of which rose to Number One, with one—1974's "Can't Get Enough of Your Love, Babe"—also cresting the pop chart. As leader of the Love Unlimited Orchestra, he reached the pop summit with the 1973 instrumental "Love's Theme." And as mentor-

Barry White

(Nelson) and played on their minor 1963 pop hit "Harlem Shuffle" and on Nelson's major 1965 solo hit "The Duck" (issued under the name "Jackie Lee"). While heading the A&R department at Bob Keene's Bronco-Mustang company, White formed a lasting relationship with arranger Gene Page and scored twice in 1967 as producer and writer for Diana Ross clone Felice Taylor—in the U.S. with the minor R&B and pop hit "It May Be Winter Outside (But in My Heart It's Spring)" and in England with the number 11 "I Feel Love Comin' On." He also recorded as a vocalist—as "Lee Barry" for Downey and under his own name for Bronco—but without success. White, his first wife, and their four children survived for five years on public assistance.

If the seeds of White's '70s style were found on his productions for Taylor and on 1971's "Oh Love (Well We Finally Made It)" by Smoke (a group that included Bob Relf) on the Mo-Soul label, they were fully realized on Love Unlimited's debut single, 1972's "Walkin' in the Rain with the One I Love"

producer of Love Unlimited, a San Pedro, California, vocal trio comprising his wife Glodean, her sister Linda James, and Diane Taylor, he created the 1974 R&B chart-topper "I Belong to You."

The portly producer's mammoth success came after years of struggle on the Los Angeles music scene. He settled in California with his mother and brother when he was six months old, began singing in a Baptist choir at age eight, became its organist two years later, and was soon serving as assistant director. He made his recording debut at age 11, playing piano on Jesse Belvin's 1956 hit "Goodnight My Love," one of the first L.A. doo wop records to employ strings. After a scrape with the law that found him spending four months in juvenile hall for tire theft, White resolved to straighten up and joined the Upfronts as bass singer. The vocal group cut six singles for the obscure Lummetone label.

White spent the 1960s as a sideman, songwriter, and arranger for a variety of small southern California labels, including Ebb, Class, Rampart, Marc, Mirwood, Bronco, and Mustang. He worked for a period as road manager for duo Bob (Relf) and Earl

---

TOP ALBUM

CAN'T GET ENOUGH (20th Century, '74, *1*)

Additional Top 40 Albums: 6

TOP SONGS

I'M GONNA LOVE YOU JUST A LITTLE BIT MORE BABY (20th Century, '73, *1 R&B, 3 Pop*)

NEVER, NEVER GONNA GIVE YA UP (20th Century, '73, *2 R&B, 7 Pop*)

CAN'T GET ENOUGH OF YOUR LOVE, BABE (20th Century, '74, *1 R&B, 1 Pop*)

YOU'RE THE FIRST, THE LAST, MY EVERYTHING (20th Century, '74, *1 R&B, 2 Pop*)

WHAT AM I GONNA DO WITH YOU (20th Century, '75, *1 R&B, 8 Pop*)

IT'S ECSTASY WHEN YOU LAY DOWN NEXT TO ME (20th Century, '77, *1 R&B, 4 Pop*)

YOUR SWEETNESS IS MY WEAKNESS (20th Century, '78, *2 R&B*)

THE SECRET GARDEN (SWEET SEDUCTION SUITE) (Quincy Jones featuring Al B. Sure!, James Ingram, El DeBarge and Barry White, Qwest, '90, *1 R&B, 31 Pop*)

PUT ME IN YOUR MIX (A&M, '91, *2 R&B*)

Additional Top 40 R&B Songs: 19

on MCA. The moody number, featuring rain effects, footsteps, White's deep voice over a telephone, and Page's lavish orchestration of White's arrangement, went to number six on the *Billboard* R&B chart and to number 16 pop. The trio, which White had been grooming since 1969, then signed with 20th Century Records, where the producer quickly emerged as a solo vocalist, beginning with the hypnotic "I'm Gonna Love You Just a Little More Baby," a Number One R&B, number three pop hit in 1973.

White continued making hits for 20th Century through 1978's bluesy number two R&B "Your Sweetness Is My Weakness," scored the 1974 soundtrack for the suspense thriller *Together Brothers,* and starred in the following year's controversial film *Coonskin.* Besides Love Unlimited and the Love Unlimited Orchestra, he produced Gloria Scott's number 14 R&B "Just As Long As We're Together (In My Life There Will Never Be Another)" in 1975 and Danny Pearson's number 16 R&B "What's Your Sign Girl?" in 1978. From 1979 to 1982, White had less luck as an artist on his own Columbia-distributed Unlimited Gold label, and even an inspired 1981 version of "Louie Louie," a tune by his early idol Richard Berry, fell on deaf ears.

After a five-year hiatus, White reemerged with a 1987 A&M album titled *The Man Is Back.* His first top 10 charter of the post-disco era came in 1990 as a participant on Quincy Jones's Number One R&B "The Secret Garden (Sweet Seduction Suite)." The next year, he collaborated with rapper Big Daddy Kane for the number 14 R&B "All of Me," as well as vaulted to number two R&B with the A&M single "Put Me in Your Mix," his first major solo hit in 13 years.

DENIECE WILLIAMS

At the beginning of her career, Deniece Williams (b. June Deniece Chandler, June 3, 1951, Gary, Indiana) found herself torn between her strong religious principles and her work as a soul singer. "I kept trying to get out of music," she said in a 1990 interview with *Christian Activities Calendar.* "However, I saw that the Lord kept putting me back in....I know the only reason that happened was because of God's divine plan for my life."

Delivering wholesome musical messages that matched the purity of her lilting coloratura soprano,

Williams scored seven top 10 R&B hits between 1976 and 1987, two of which—1978's "Too Much, Too Little, Too Late" (a duet with Johnny Mathis) and 1984's "Let's Hear It for the Boy"—topped both the R&B and pop charts. She often had to fight to include gospel songs on her albums but managed to get one on the majority of her 10 pop LPs. In 1986, she recorded the first of three all-gospel albums.

Williams began singing at age five at Faith Temple Church of God in Christ in Gary. Secular music also had an early pull, and her favorite artists included Nancy Wilson, Johnny Mathis, Tony Bennett, Gladys Knight, Aretha Franklin, Roy Hamilton, and the Jackie Gleason Orchestra. While attending Tolleston High School, she got a part-time job in a record store. In 1968, the owner of the shop heard her singing along with current hits and recommended her to Toodlin' Town, a small Chicago record label.

Three Toodlin' Town singles, including "Yes I'm Ready" and "Love Is Tears," were issued under her maiden name of Deniece Chandler. They sold respectably around Gary but caused her to get kicked out of the church choir. Williams was more interested in becoming a nurse, however. She spent a year and a half at Morgan State College in Baltimore, where she appeared in local clubs to help pay her tuition. Dropping out, she returned to Gary, married, and had two sons. Then, in 1971, Stevie Wonder called.

Williams toured on and off with Wonder between 1972 and '76 as a member of the vocal trio Wonderlove and sang on his albums *Talking Book, Innervisions, Fulfillingness' First Finale,* and *Songs in the Key of Life.* Her religious scruples caused her to quit several times, and she worked for a period as a technician at a Chicago hospital. Finally settling on a musical career that brought an end to her marriage, she moved to southern California with her children and became active as both a session singer and a songwriter. She sang on sessions by such artists as Roberta Flack, Linda Lewis, Minnie Riperton, D. J. Rogers, and the Tubes and had tunes recorded by Merry Clayton, the Emotions, the Soul Train Gang, and Frankie Valli.

In 1976, Williams tried to place some of her songs with Earth, Wind and Fire, but ended up being signed as an artist to leader Maurice White's Kalimba Productions. *This Is Neicy,* her debut Columbia album, was produced by White and Charles Stepney. All of the songs were penned in whole or in part by

Williams, including her first hit single, the number two R&B "Free."

In 1978, producer Jack Gold teamed her with Johnny Mathis for the single "Too Much, Too Little, Too Late." It not only became Williams's first Number One record but also gave Mathis his first R&B top 40 entry in 15 years and his first pop chart-topper in over 20. *That's What Friends Are For*, an album of Mathis-Williams duets, followed and featured a remake of the old Marvin Gaye–Tammi Terrell favorite "You're All I Need to Get By."

Recording for White's Columbia-distributed ARC label between 1979 and 1982, Williams hit the top of the R&B chart for the second time with "It's Gonna Take a Miracle," a 1982 revamp (produced by the singer and Thom Bell) of a moderate pop hit by the Royalettes from 17 years earlier. Back on the parent label, she enjoyed her second double chart-topper with 1984's perky George Duke–produced "Let's Hear It for the Boy" from the motion picture *Footloose*. Williams's final top 10 R&B single came in 1988 with the number eight Duke-produced "I Can't Wait."

The vocalist won her first Grammy Award for her participation in the 1982 all-star children's recording

---

TOP ALBUMS

THAT'S WHAT FRIENDS ARE FOR (Johnny Mathis and Deniece Williams, Columbia, '78, *19*)

NIECY (ARC, '82, *20*)

Additional Top 40 Albums: 2

TOP SONGS

FREE (Columbia, '76, *2 R&B, 25 Pop*)

TOO MUCH, TOO LITTLE, TOO LATE (Johnny Mathis/Deniece Williams, Columbia, '78, *1 R&B, 1 Pop*)

YOU'RE ALL I NEED TO GET BY (Johnny Mathis/ Deniece Williams, Columbia, '78, *10 R&B*)

IT'S GONNA TAKE A MIRACLE (ARC, '82, *1 R&B, 10 Pop*)

DO WHAT YOU FEEL (Columbia, '83, *9 R&B*)

LET'S HEAR IT FOR THE BOY (Columbia, '84, *1 R&B, 1 Pop*)

NEVER SAY NEVER (Columbia, '87, *6 R&B*)

I CAN'T WAIT (Columbia, '88, *8 R&B*)

Additional Top 40 R&B Songs: 11

In Harmony II. She took home two for tunes from her 1986 gospel album debut, *So Glad I Know* (produced by new husband Brad Westering and issued on the Sparrow label), and one for a gospel song from 1987's *Water Under the Bridge*, her second to last secular LP. Her sophomore all-religious disc, 1989's *Special Love*, included a duet with Natalie Cole, while the next year's Sparrow release, *From the Beginning*, compiled gospel selections from Williams's earlier Columbia/ARC albums.

CHUCK WILLIS

Turban-topped blues balladeer Chuck Willis (b. Harold Willis, Jan. 31, 1928, Atlanta, Georgia) was known as "Sheik of the Blues" during his career as an R&B hitmaker in the early and mid-1950s. Crossover success came in 1957 with his Number One R&B, number 12 pop Atlantic recording of "C. C. Rider." Dancers on "American Bandstand" found the medium-tempo shuffle beat of the singer's treatment of the Ma Rainey blues classic ideally suited to doing the Stroll. Host Dick Clark described the dance as "a cool, modern-day version of the Virginia Reel—two lines were formed, boys on one side, girls on the other, then the end couple would stroll in a wiggle-wobble fashion down the corridor between the two lines, separate, and become the end boy and girl at the other end of the line."

When Willis appeared on the popular ABC-TV show early the next year to promote his follow-up record, the number 15 R&B, number 33 pop "Betty and Dupree" (another song of folk-blues origin), Clark dubbed him "King of the Stroll." The title stuck, but the vocalist wasn't able to stick around long enough to enjoy his newfound royalty. He succumbed to a perforated ulcer on April 10, 1958, at Hugh Spalding Hospital in his hometown of Atlanta. The posthumously issued "What Am I Living For" became his biggest hit, reaching Number One R&B and number eight pop. Its flip, the self-penned "Hang Up My Rock and Roll Shoes," also charted, making the single a haunting double-sided epitaph.

Breaking into the business at teen talent contests in Atlanta, Willis turned professional around 1946 and appeared at local clubs and theaters with the bands of Ron Mays, Red McAllister, and Austell Adams. Many of the shows were promoted by Zenas

"Daddy" Sears, a white disc jockey who played black music over radio station WGST. Sears also functioned as a talent scout for major record companies in the North and arranged contracts for Piano Red and Little Richard with RCA Victor. In 1950, he introduced Willis to Danny Kessler of Columbia.

After making his recording debut in 1951 with the Columbia single "It Ain't Right to Treat Me Wrong," Willis was transferred to the firm's reactivated Okeh subsidiary. He became the label's first nationally successful R&B artist, beginning in 1952 with the number three R&B "My Story," an original blues ballad that reflected the influence of Charles Brown. Willis scored four more top 10 R&B hits through 1954, all of his own composition with the exception of a 1953 cover of Fats Domino's "Goin' to the River." The Latin-tinged 12-bar blues "I Feel So Bad" became a blues standard and was revived in later years by Elvis Presley (number 15 R&B, number five pop in 1961) and Little Milton (number seven R&B in 1967). At the suggestion of Okeh labelmate Screamin' Jay Hawkins, Willis took to wearing a turban and eventually owned 54.

After a two-year absence from the charts, the singer reemerged at Atlantic in 1956 with the number three R&B blues ballad "It's Too Late," arranged by Jesse Stone and featuring vocal backing by the Cookies (later to become the Raeletts.) Although Willis's Atlantic sessions used many of the same New York studio musicians who'd played on his Okeh sides, they had crisper fidelity, courtesy of ace engineer Tom Dowd, and ultimately more pop appeal. With "C. C. Rider," arranged by Stone and sporting the tenor saxophone of Gene Barge, his

transition from urban bluesman to rock and roll star was complete.

Besides penning much of his own material, the prolific songwriter tailored tunes for other artists, the most successful being Ruth Brown's Number One R&B "Oh What a Dream" in 1954, the Cardinals' number four R&B "The Door Is Still Open" in 1955, and the Five Keys' number five R&B "Close Your Eyes," also in 1955. (The latter went to number four R&B and number eight pop when revamped by Peaches and Herb in 1967.) Other artists who recorded Willis compositions over the years include the Band, Solomon Burke, the Cadillacs, Don Cornell, the Drifters, Foghat, Eydie Gorme, Buddy Holly, Wanda Jackson, Jerry Lee Lewis, Little Richard, Dean Martin, Delbert McClinton, Otis Redding, Charlie Rich, Ike and Tina Turner, and Conway Twitty.

JACKIE WILSON

Musicologist Robert Pruter called Jackie Wilson (b. Jack Leroy Wilson, June 9, 1934, Detroit, Michigan) "the most tragic figure in rhythm and blues." The most obvious tragedy was that the onetime star spent the last eight years of his life as a virtual vegetable, a largely forgotten man whose contorted, brain-damaged body was shuffled from one nursing home to another while the IRS pursued him for $234,000 in back taxes and two women, each claiming to be his wife, fought over his estate. The other was that Wilson's association with Berry Gordy, Jr., co-author of his first five solo hits, was so brief. Had the singer been brought into Gordy's creative stable at Motown, instead of being kept in servitude at Brunswick Records for his entire 18-year solo career, he might have been spared the schlock that marred much of his post-Gordy output.

Wilson was one of the most glorious entertainers ever to command a stage, a vocal and physical gymnast who executed graceful spins, slides, and splits as his powerful, ringing tenor soared, driving female fans to a frenzy in the process. He was greatly inspired by blues shouter Roy Brown and by the man Wilson replaced in Billy Ward's Dominoes—Clyde McPhatter. Wilson, critic Barney Hoskyns has observed, "took the sob that had begun with Roy Brown in the late '40s and developed through Clyde McPhatter to a new and delirious extreme. The

TOP SONGS

My Story (Okeh, '52, 2 R&B)
Goin' to the River (Okeh, '53, 4 R&B)
Don't Deceive Me (Okeh, '53, 6 R&B)
You're Still My Baby (Okeh, '54, 4 R&B)
I Feel So Bad (Okeh, '54, 8 R&B)
It's Too Late (Atlantic, '56, 3 R&B)
Juanita (Atlantic, '56, 7 R&B)
C. C. Rider (Atlantic, '57, 1 R&B, 12 Pop)
What Am I Living For (Atlantic, '58, 1 R&B, 9 Pop)
Hang Up My Rock and Roll Shoes (Atlantic, '58, 9 R&B, 24 Pop)

Additional Top 40 R&B Songs: 4

range of the voice was slightly lower than Clyde's, but if anything the melisma was even more elastic and intoxicating." Other influences were vaudevillian Al Jolson and opera star Mario Lanza.

Known as "Sonny" to his family and friends, Wilson grew up singing at Detroit's Russell Street Baptist Church, boxed for a brief period, and, during the late 1940s, was a member of the local Ever Ready Gospel Singers. He made his recording debut in 1951 with two singles for Dizzy Gillespie's Dee Gee label, one being his first version of "Danny Boy," an old Irish song that became a staple of his supper club act. In 1953, having learned that McPhatter was about to quit the Dominoes, Wilson showed up at an audition claiming he could out-sing McPhatter. After hearing the teenager, Ward took him on the road, with McPhatter showing him the ropes for a few weeks before leaving to form the Drifters. Wilson spent three years as the Dominoes' lead tenor and was featured on the 1953 R&B hits "You Can't Keep a Good Man Down" (on Federal) and "Rags to Riches" (King) and on the 1956 pop hit "St. Theresa of the Roses" (Decca).

Al Greene, owner of Detroit's Flame Show Bar, had become Wilson's manager and, in 1957, pulled him out of the Dominoes and got him a contract with Brunswick Records, then a Decca subsidiary. "Reet Petite," Wilson's debut for the label, was penned by two struggling local songwriters, Berry Gordy, Jr., and (under the pseudonym "Tyran Carlo") Roquel "Billy" Davis. Cut in New York with arranger Dick Jacobs, the infectious uptempo tune found Wilson parodying Elvis Presley. It became a minor pop hit but didn't dent *Billboard*'s R&B chart. In England, however, it rose to number six (and to Number One when reissued in 1987).

The next four Wilson releases—"To Be Loved," "Lonely Teardrops," "That's Why (I Love You So)," and "I'll Be Satisfied"—were written by Gordy and Davis (with Gordy's sister Gwen) and became crossover hits in the U.S. The Number One R&B "Lonely Teardrops" was the only Wilson record that Gordy actually produced. By 1959, Greene was dead and Wilson's management had been taken over by Nat Tarnapol, the club owner's former assistant. Gordy parted company with Tarnapol in a dispute over royalties and launched his own company. Wilson maintained a strong chart presence through 1960, hitting Number One R&B with "You Better Know It," "Doggin' Around," and "A Woman, A Lover, A Friend." Tarnapol then began grooming

him as a middle-of-the-road crooner, and the singer's material became increasingly conservative.

Wilson spent the 1960s vacillating between soul and pop and managed to score only six top 10 R&B hits between 1961 and 1970, as compared to his 10 from 1958 to 1960. He hit Number One twice during the latter period, in 1963 with "Baby Work Out" (written by Wilson and former Midnighters guitarist Alonzo Tucker) and in 1967 with "(Your Love Keeps Lifting Me) Higher and Higher." Produced in Chicago by Carl Davis, "Higher and Higher" became the vocalist's biggest hit since "Lonely Teardrops" and, ironically, was co-written by Roquel "Billy" Davis and utilized a moonlighting Motown rhythm section.

Wilson and Tarnapol had a falling out around that time, the result being that Wilson continued recording for Brunswick (which Tarnapol had come to control) while the company stopped promoting his releases. By the early 1970s, the singer was working the oldies circuit. While wailing "Lonely Teardrops" during a Dick Clark package show at the Latin Casino in Cherry Hill, New Jersey, on September 29, 1975, Wilson was hit with a massive heart attack. After coming out of a three-month coma, he showed little response to therapy and finally died on January 21, 1984.

TOP ALBUM

BABY WORKOUT (Brunswick, '63, 36)

TOP SONGS

LONELY TEARDROPS (Brunswick, '58, 1 R&B, 7 Pop)

THAT'S WHY (I LOVE YOU SO) (Brunswick, '59, 2 R&B, 13 Pop)

YOU BETTER KNOW IT (Brunswick, '59, 1 R&B, 37 Pop)

TALK THAT TALK (Brunswick, '59, 3 R&B, 34 Pop)

DOGGIN' AROUND (Brunswick, '60, 1 R&B, 15 Pop)

NIGHT (Brunswick, '60, 3 R&B, 4 Pop)

A WOMAN, A LOVER, A FRIEND (Brunswick, '60, 1 R&B, 15 Pop)

BABY WORKOUT (Brunswick, '63, 1 R&B, 5 Pop)

WHISPERS (GETTIN' LOUDER) (Brunswick, '66, 5 R&B, 11 Pop)

(YOUR LOVE KEEPS LIFTING ME) HIGHER AND HIGHER (Brunswick, '67, 1 R&B, 6 Pop)

Additional Top 40 R&B Songs: 30

BILL WITHERS

Bill Withers (b. July 4, 1938, Slab Fork, West Virginia) was a late musical bloomer. He hadn't given much thought to music while growing up, the youngest of six children, in coal-mining country nor during his nine years in the Navy. After his discharge, he moved to San Jose, California, and got a job as a mechanic at Lockheed. His specialty was installing toilet seats in airplanes. He spent his weekends at nightclubs in San Francisco and Oakland. He befriended up-and-coming singer Al Jarreau at one. At another, he saw Lou Rawls.

"He [Rawls] was late coming and I overheard the bartender—probably the owner—complaining," Withers recalled in a 1993 interview with Wayne Jancik of *DISCoveries* magazine. " 'I'm paying this guy $2,000 a week,' he said, 'and he can't even be on time.' It stopped me cold. I thought, 'Wait a minute. That's two grand just to sing some songs.' "

Withers purchased a cheap guitar, taught himself some chords, and started writing songs. He moved to Los Angeles, continued installing commodes (for Hughes), and saved his money to cut demos. One of his tapes wound up in the hands of Clarence Avant of the fledgling Sussex label. "Ain't No Sunshine," the then-33-year-old Withers' Booker T. Jones–produced debut for the company, became a crossover hit, placing at number six on the *Billboard* R&B chart and at number three on the pop list. It also received a Grammy as the year's Best Rhythm and Blues Song.

If Withers had gotten into the music business as a means of making money—which he did—his warm, scratchy tenor voice and sensitive, highly literate songs betrayed an artist with much more on his mind than simply being commercial. Indeed, the singer-songwriter's intimate creations (dubbed "folk-soul" by some) cut against the grain of African-American pop music of the period. "Ain't No Sunshine" and such other tunes from his debut *Just As I Am* album as "Grandma's Hands" and "Harlem" came from a deeply personal place.

"It's not a style or nothin'," he told Jancik. "It's all just my personality coming through whatever sounds I've heard on the radio or comin' outta somebody's window. It's no secret, no magic, just me."

Withers put together a band composed of keyboardist Ray Jackson, guitarist Benorce Blackman, bassist Melvin Dunlap, and drummer James Gadson, all formerly of Charles Wright's Watts 103rd Street Rhythm Band. The rhythm section gave a distinctively syncopated underpinning to the vocalist's self-produced sophomore album, 1972's *Still Bill,* which spawned the biggest hits of his career: the Number One R&B and pop "Lean on Me" and the number two R&B and pop "Use Me." (The oft-covered "Lean on Me" garnered a Grammy for Best Rhythm and Blues Song in 1987 in the wake of Club Nouveau's number two R&B, Number One pop version and inspired a motion picture of the same title two years later.)

A disastrous one-year marriage to actress Denise Nicholas, combined with a bitter legal dispute with Avant, began to affect Withers' music during 1973. The battle with Avant was the hardest. "That was certainly more difficult than the divorce," he said in a 1976 interview with Walter Price Burrell of *Players* magazine, "because there are a hell of a lot more pretty girls for me to look up than there are successful black businessmen."

Withers reemerged at Columbia Records in 1975 but never fully regained his footing in the marketplace. He cut five albums for the company through 1985, though only two singles—1975's "Make Love to Your Mind" and 1977's "Lovely Day"—made the R&B top 10, neither becoming significant

---

TOP ALBUM

STILL BILL (Sussex, '72, 4)

Additional Top 40 Albums: 2

TOP SONGS

AIN'T NO SUNSHINE (Sussex, '71, 6 *R&B, 3 Pop*)

LEAN ON ME (Sussex, '72, 1 *R&B, 1 Pop*)

USE ME (Sussex, '72, 2 *R&B, 2 Pop*)

KISSING MY LOVE (Sussex, '73, 12 *R&B, 31 Pop*)

THE SAME LOVE THAT MADE ME LAUGH (Sussex, '74, 10 *R&B*)

MAKE LOVE TO YOUR MIND (Columbia, '75, 10 *R&B*)

LOVELY DAY (Columbia, '77, 6 *R&B, 30 Pop*)

JUST THE TWO OF US (Grover Washington, Jr., with Bill Withers, Elektra, '81, 3 *R&B, 2 Pop*)

IN THE NAME OF LOVE (Ralph MacDonald with Bill Withers, Polydor, '84, 13 *R&B*)

Additional Top 40 R&B Songs: 7

crossover hits. His greatest post-Sussex success was as guest vocalist on saxophonist Grover Washington, Jr.'s 1981 single "Just the Two of Us," a number three R&B, number two pop hit that earned Withers and co-writers William Salter and Ralph McDonald a Grammy for Best Rhythm and Blues Song. Withers also contributed vocals to the Crusaders' "Soul Shadows" in 1980 and to percussionist McDonald's "In the Name of Love" four years later.

The singer-songwriter has not recorded since 1985, although his tunes remain in the repertoires of countless other artists. Among those who've done his material are Creative Source, Aretha Franklin, Joel Grey, the Isley Brothers, Michael Jackson, Tom Jones, Gladys Knight and the Pips, Johnny Mathis, Liza Minnelli, Mud, Esther Phillips, Diana Ross, the Temptations, Tina Turner, and the Winans.

BOBBY WOMACK

Bobby Womack

Like his friend and mentor Sam Cooke, singer-guitarist-songwriter Bobby Womack (b. Mar. 4, 1944, Cleveland, Ohio) parlayed a background in gospel quartet music into a distinctive soul style. Singing in a raspy low tenor that was somewhat of a cross between the intensity of the Five Blind Boys of Mississippi's Archie Brownlee and Cooke's gentler approach, Womack scored 11 top 10 R&B hits, not counting his first chart entry, 1962's number eight R&B "Lookin' for a Love," as lead vocalist of the Valentinos. Two of them—1972's uniquely loping "Woman's Gotta Have It" and a 1974 solo remake of "Lookin' for a Love"—hit Number One.

His father, Friendly Womack, Sr., worked in a Cleveland steel mill and sang and played guitar with a quartet called the Voices of Love. When his young sons Bobby, Cecil, Curtis, Harry, and Friendly, Jr., began imitating the quartet, Friendly, Sr., quit the group and formed the Womack Brothers. In 1953, the Womacks opened a local gospel program for the Soul Stirrers (then featuring Sam Cooke) and were soon performing around the Midwest with such gospel stars as the Caravans and the Staples Singers.

By watching his father, who played like Roebuck Staples, Bobby taught himself guitar, left-handed and upside down. Other guitar influences included George Scott of the Five Blind Boys of Alabama, Jo Wallace of the Sensational Nightingales, Howard Carroll of the Dixie Hummingbirds, Curtis Mayfield, and country pianist Floyd Cramer. ("He played such pretty stuff," Womack said of Cramer. "I wanted to duplicate what he does playing grace notes...to put a little more funk in it and execute it through the guitar.") Besides Cooke and Brownlee, Womack was influenced vocally by his second cousin, Solomon Womack of the Swan Silvertones.

The Womack Brothers were signed in 1961 to Cooke and J. W. Alexander's SAR label, for which they recorded the single "Somebody's Wrong" b/w "Yield Not to Temptation." At Cooke's urging, they went secular the following year, as the Valentinos, and were kicked out of the house by their disapproving father. "Lookin' for a Love," originally an Alexander-penned gospel song titled "Couldn't Hear Nobody Pray" that Zelda Samuels set new lyrics to, established the brothers on the soul circuit. In addition to having them open shows for him, Cooke recruited Bobby as his bassist, then as his guitarist. The group's fourth single, "It's All Over Now," was written by Bobby and became a minor pop hit in 1964. The Rolling Stones fared better with a cover version, which went to number 26 on the pop chart that year.

Shortly after Cooke's 1964 death, Bobby married his widow Barbara. (Years later, brother Cecil would wed Sam and Barbara's daughter Linda.) The Valentinos stuck together for about a year, recording unsuccessfully for Checker, but Bobby's career as a guitar player and songwriter was beginning to take off. From 1966 through 1968, he toured with Ray Charles, Wilson Pickett, and Aretha Franklin and played on sessions, mostly held in Memphis, for Pickett, Franklin, Joe Tex, the Box Tops, Dusty Springfield, King Curtis, and others. He also composed the Pickett hits "I'm in Love" and "I'm a Midnight Mover." Womack recorded unsuccessfully as a solo artist during this period for Him, Checker, Atlantic, and Keymen.

His own career finally began to take off after he signed with Minit Records in 1968. Working in Memphis with producer Chips Moman, he had moderate R&B chart success with soul versions of pop tunes like "Fly Me to the Moon" and "California Dreamin' " as well as with such songwriting collaborations with Darryl Carter as "How I Miss You Baby" and "More Than I Can Stand." His fortunes improved greatly in 1971 when, inspired by Sly Stone, to whose album *There's a Riot Goin' On* he

had contributed, he decided to produce himself and proceeded to cut the United Artists album *Communication* in Muscle Shoals and Memphis. It yielded the hits "That's the Way I Feel About Cha" and "Woman's Gotta Have It."

Womack maintained a fairly steady chart presence through 1976, when he signed with Columbia and experienced a severe career slump. After another unsuccessful association, with Arista, he reemerged in 1981 on the Beverly Glen label with an album titled *The Poet,* from which came the hit "If You Think You're Lonely Now." The follow-up, 1984's *The Poet II,* spawned "Love Has Finally Come at Last," a duet with Patti LaBelle. Womack then signed with MCA and in 1985 scored with "I Wish He Didn't Trust Me So Much," which proved to be his final top 40 R&B entry. He was reunited the next year with Moman for the brilliant MCA album *Womagic,* but it fell on deaf ears, as did 1989's self-produced *Save the Children* on Solar.

STEVIE WONDER

Singer, multi-instrumentalist, songwriter, and producer Stevie Wonder (b. Steveland Morris, May 13, 1950, Saginaw, Michigan) stands as the all-time R&B chart-topping champ, having reached the peak of *Billboard*'s R&B bestseller list a total of 18 times. Three of his albums— 1963's *Little Stevie Wonder/The 12 Year Old Genius,* 1974's *Fulfillingness' First Finale,* and 1976's *Songs in the Key of Life*—went to Number One pop. By 1981, he had garnered 17 Grammy Awards, an achievement topped only by Sir George Solti, Quincy Jones, Vladimir Horowitz, and Henry Mancini. Wonder accomplished all of this while recording for just one company—Motown— throughout his entire career.

Born blind, the third oldest of Lulu Hardaway's six children, Stevie grew up in Detroit and attended Whitestone Baptist Church, where he sang in the choir, served as a junior deacon, and thought about one day becoming a minister. By age 11 he was playing harmonica, piano, and drums. He formed a duo with his friend John Glover, who was a cousin of Ronnie White of the Miracles. After White heard Stevie, he had the boy audition for Motown staffer Brian Holland. Signed to the company and placed on the Tamla label, Stevie was christened "Stevie Won-

---

TOP ALBUM

THE POET (Beverly Glen, '82, 29)

Additional Top 40 Albums: 1

TOP SONGS

THAT'S THE WAY I FEEL ABOUT CHA (United Artists, '71, 2 R&B, 27 Pop)

WOMAN'S GOTTA HAVE IT (United Artists, '72, 1 R&B)

NOBODY WANTS YOU WHEN YOU'RE DOWN AND OUT (United Artists, '73, 2 R&B, 29 Pop)

LOOKIN' FOR A LOVE (United Artists, '74, 1 R&B, 10 Pop)

YOU'RE WELCOME, STOP ON BY (United Artists, '74, 5 R&B)

DAYLIGHT (United Artists, '76, 5 R&B)

IF YOU THINK YOU'RE LONELY NOW (Beverly Glen, '81, 3 R&B)

LOVE HAS FINALLY COME AT LAST (Bobby Womack and Patti LaBelle, Beverly Glen, '84, 3 R&B)

I WISH HE DIDN'T TRUST ME SO MUCH (MCA, '85, 2 R&B)

Additional Top 40 R&B Songs: 16

TOP ALBUM

Songs in the Key of Life (Tamla, '76, *1*)

Additional Top 40 Albums: 16

TOP SONGS

Fingertips - Pt 2 (Little Stevie Wonder, Tamla, '63, *1 R&B, 1 Pop*)

Uptight (Everything's Alright) (Tamla, '66, *1 R&B, 3 Pop*)

I Was Made to Love Her (Tamla, '67, *1 R&B, 2 Pop*)

Signed, Sealed, Delivered I'm Yours (Tamla, '70, *1 R&B, 3 Pop*)

I Wish (Tamla, '76, *1 R&B, 1 Pop*)

Master Blaster (Jammin') (Tamla, '80, *1 R&B, 5 Pop*)

That Girl (Tamla, '82, *1 R&B, 4 Pop*)

I Just Called to Say I Love You (Tamla, '84, *1 R&B, 1 Pop*)

Part-Time Lover (Tamla, '85, *1 R&B, 1 Pop*)

Additional Top 40 R&B Songs: 52

in 1970 as a producer, both of his own Number One R&B "Signed, Sealed, Delivered I'm Yours" and of the Spinners' number four R&B "It's a Shame." In 1971, upon turning 21, he broke with the entire Motown assembly-line process, negotiating for his own publishing rights and higher royalties and setting up Taurus Productions to produce his own records and lease them to Motown. "Wonder's goal was to shatter the limitations Motown had imposed on its artists, whose albums were rarely more than one or two hits and 10 tracks of filler," *Newsday* critic Wayne Robbins observed in 1991. "Like the progressive rockers, Wonder wanted to make fully conceived albums that reflected his political, spiritual, and romantic philosophy.

He spent a year working on synthesizer music with Malcolm Cecil and Robert Margouleff and, playing virtually all the instruments himself, created the 1972 tour de force album *Music of My Mind*.

Stevie Wonder

der" and, in an attempt to compare him to Ray Charles, the blind superstar who was then being billed as "the genius," advertised him as a "12-year-old genius."

Wonder's first single, 1962's "I Call It Pretty Music But the Old People Call It the Blues," failed to click, as did the next two, but the fourth, 1963's "Fingertips—Pt 2," shot to the top of the *Billboard* R&B and pop charts. Penned by Henry Cosby and Clarence Paul, it was the first recording of a live performance ever to become a Number One hit. Cut at Chicago's Regal Theater, where Wonder was appearing as part of the Motortown Revue, it captured the excitement generated in the crowd by his exuberant vocals and harmonica blowing, as well as the chaos of the moment, including bassist Larry Moses' shouts of "What key? What key?" at the beginning of the reprise.

"Little" was dropped from Stevie's name the following year, but he didn't have another sizeable hit until 1966's Number One R&B, number three pop "Uptight (Everything's Alright)," written by Wonder with Cosby and Sylvia Moy. He hit the R&B summit again that year with a rendition of Bob Dylan's "Blowin' in the Wind," revealing for the first time a sociopolitical consciousness that would become a major factor in his later music.

Having matured as a performer and composer with such subsequent hits as "I'm Wondering," "Shoo-Be-Doo-Be-Doo-Da-Day," "You Met Your Match," and "My Cherie Amour," Wonder emerged

Although it spawned only two moderate hits, the number 13 R&B "Superwoman (Where Were You When I Needed You)" and the number 36 R&B "Keep on Running," it served notice that Wonder was a major innovative force. This was borne out by the huge success of his next four albums: *Talking Book* (containing the hits "Superstition" and "You Are the Sunshine of My Life"), *Innervisions* ("Higher Ground," "Living for the City"), *Fulfillingness' Final Finale* ("You Haven't Done Nothin'," "Boogie Down Reggae Woman"), and *Songs in the Key of Life*. A two-record set (with a supplementary single), the 1976 release marked his career pinnacle, topping the *Billboard* pop album chart for 14 weeks and yielding the Number One R&B and pop hits "I Wish" and "Sir Duke."

After a three-year break, Wonder reemerged in 1979 with the esoteric, largely instrumental album *Journey Through the Secret Life of Plants*. The next year's *Hotter Than July* was better received and yielded the reggae-imbued Number One R&B hit "Master Blaster (Jammin')." During the 1980s, Wonder hit the top of both the R&B and pop charts twice, in 1984 with "I Just Called to Say I Love You" and the next year with "Part-Time Lover."

He composed soundtracks for the films *The Woman in Red* (1984) and *Jungle Fever* (1991). Besides lending jazz-tinged harmonica solos to recordings by numerous other artists, Wonder produced the Supremes' unjustly overlooked "Bad Weather" (1973) and Minnie Riperton's number three R&B, Number One pop "Lovin' You" (1975), and he wrote Jermaine Jackson's Number One R&B, number nine pop "Let's Get Serious" (1980).

BETTY WRIGHT

B etty Wright (b. Dec. 21, 1954, Miami, Florida) was only 13 when she had her first taste of national success with the 1968 hit "Girls Can't Do What the Guys Do." "It can be quite strange when you have your first hit at a young age because people typecast you as this little girl who sings these songs that she couldn't possibly know anything about," she stated in 1986. "Then years later, they imagine you're a lot older than you really are because they've been hearing you for so many years."

The seventh of seven children, Wright began

Betty Wright

TOP ALBUM

BETTY WRIGHT LIVE (Alston, '78, 26)

TOP SONGS

GIRLS CAN'T DO WHAT THE GUYS DO (Alston, '68, *15 R&B, 33 Pop*)

CLEAN UP WOMAN (Alston, '71, *2 R&B, 6 Pop*)

BABY SITTER (Alston, '72, *6 R&B*)

IT'S HARD TO STOP (DOING SOMETHING WHEN IT'S GOOD TO YOU) (Alston, '73, *11 R&B*)

LET ME BE YOUR LOVEMAKER (Alston, '73, *10 R&B*)

SECRETARY (Alston, '74, *12 R&B*)

WHERE IS THE LOVE (Alston, '75, *15 R&B*)

TONIGHT IS THE NIGHT PT. 1 (RAP) (Alston, '78, *11 R&B*)

NO PAIN, NO GAIN (Ms. B, '88, *14 R&B*)

Additional Top 40 R&B Songs: 12

singing at age three with her family's gospel group, the Echoes of Joy (in which her mother played guitar), and was soon performing at talent shows around Miami. At 11, she was discovered singing Billy Stewart's tongue-twisting arrangement of "Summertime" by the songwriting-producing team of Willie Clarke and Clarence Reid. She did background vocals on some of the pair's productions for their Deep City label and, at 12, cut her first single, "Paralyzed," for the company.

The local success of "Paralyzed" and other Deep City releases brought Clarke and Reid to the attention of record distributor Henry Stone, who wanted them on his team at Alston Records. They brought their young discovery to their first meeting with Stone. "I was turned down because he said I sang in a monotone," she recalled. "I think it had more to do with the fact that I had one pants leg rolled up and one down and clay on my legs. I had just come from winning a baseball championship. I didn't look like I could do anything but play ball."

Two weeks later, however, Stone signed her, and she recorded "Girls Can't Do What the Guys Do," a Clarke-Reid composition that became the first hit on Alston, reaching number 15 on the R&B chart and number 33 pop. Three years later, before she had graduated high school, she scored a million-seller with Clarke and Reid's "Clean Up Woman," which went to number two R&B and number six pop. Driven by the guitar syncopations of Willie "Little Beaver" Hale, the catchy Caribbean-flavored number epitomized the rapidly emerging Miami sound.

"It has to do with the climate," Wright said of Miami soul. "People tend to dance apart when the weather's hot, so it a different kind of music. It's more of a salad bowl than a melting pot. Miami people tend to keep their heritage when they move here. You've got a little Cuba, a little Jamaica, and a little Haiti. You've got a large Jewish culture. You've got calypso, that island influence from the Bahamas. We've got a large Puerto Rican and Panamanian population. Then you've got people who were born here or came from South Carolina where they've got a heavy African culture too. It's a very rhythmic roots music. Even the white acts that come out of Miami tend to be very soulful. We've got that serious, serious conga rhythm."

Besides being the first successful artist on Alston, which soon gave birth to T.K. Productions, Wright introduced such artists as H. W. Casey (of KC and the Sunshine Band), George and Gwen McCrae,

Jimmy "Bo" Horne, and Peter Brown to the company. After scoring more hit singles, including "Baby Sitter, "Let Me Be Your Lovemaker," "Shoorah! Shoorah!," and "Where Is the Love," and a well-received 1978 live album that featured her sassy monologues and impressions of other singers, she signed with Epic for two LPs. The first, 1981's *Betty Wright,* included a cut written and produced by Stevie Wonder. Neither was successful.

Wright moved to Connecticut in 1982 and recorded two disco-style singles for the New York–based Jamaica label. She soon became disenchanted with what she later described as "faceless music," as well as with the New England climate. "There's a difference between snow, sleet, rain, and bricks and the atmosphere that water, palm trees, and sunshine give you," she explained. Moving back to Miami, she launched her own Ms. B label in 1985 and scored moderate R&B chart hits with such self-penned songs as "Pain," "No Pain, No Gain," and "From Pain to Joy."

While her alternately sweet and gritty multi-octave voice grew in elasticity, her later lyrics reflected strong Christian values. "God wants you to tell the truth," Wright explained. "I talk to people in words they can understand." The mother of four children and stepmother of 16, she is married to Jamaican singer Noel "King Sporty" Williams, who wrote "Buffalo Soldier" for Bob Marley.

ZAPP AND ROGER

Singer, multi-instrumentalist, songwriter, producer, and leader of the Dayton, Ohio, band Zapp, Roger Troutman (b. Hamilton, Ohio) is the clown prince of funk. He cuts up constantly in live performance, mugging and rolling his eyes as he creates comic, Darth Vader–like tones through a plastic tube that runs from the corner of his mouth to his electric organ or guitar—sounds inspired by Stevie Wonder and Peter Frampton that became the trademark of Roger's R&B chart-topping hits "I Heard It Through the Grapevine," "Dance Floor," and "I Want to Be Your Man." He also does Chuck Berry duckwalks across the stage while picking brittle blues guitar lines and often drops his drawers to expose his bare posterior.

"I've always been wild and crazy," Roger, who uses only his first name professionally and refuses to give his age, stated in 1986. "I was a gentle trouble-maker in school. I could really take over the whole classroom with shenanigans. The teacher would have to cover her mouth because she didn't want the students to see her laughing at me. The principal told me to steer my energy in a positive direction."

Encouraged by his parents, Roger learned to play guitar, bass, violin, flute, French horn, tuba, keyboards, harmonica, and comb and, in 1962, formed his first band. It went through several name changes, among them Roger and the Veils and Roger and the Hungry People, before becoming Roger and the

Zapp

Human Body. The Human Body, which included brothers Larry Troutman (percussion), Lester Troutman (drums), and Terry "Zapp" Troutman (bass), cut its first record, *Introducing Roger,* in 1975 for the Troutman Brothers label. The album was a regional success and led to opening slots on Ohio-area shows starring George Clinton's Parliament-Funkadelic.

Through the group's connection with Clinton, the Human Body signed with Warner Bros. Records and changed its name to Zapp, borrowing a nickname that had been given to Terry Troutman as a child because of the way he mispronounced the name of his older brothers' elementary school principal, Elza Sapp. *Zapp,* the band's 1980 debut album for the company, was co-produced by Roger and his long-time friend, Clinton associate Bootsy Collins, and yielded the number two R&B hit "More Bounce to the Ounce."

Over the next 12 years, Roger would release three more albums under the group name, four under his own, and one, 1993's *All Time Greatest Hits,* as by "Zapp and Roger," scoring a dozen top 20 R&B hit singles in the process. None crossed into the pop top 40, with the exception of 1987's Number One R&B, number three pop "I Want to Be Your Man." He also produced three hit singles for sometime Zapp vocalist Shirley Murdock—"As We Lay," "Go On Without You," and "Husband"—each of which placed at number five on the *Billboard* R&B chart between 1986 and 1988.

Although Roger's cutting-edge funk makes use of synthesizers and other electronic instruments, blues roots run deep through it, especially when he plays guitar or blows harmonica. He was first drawn to the blues by Ohio Players guitarist Leroy "Sugarfoot" Bonner (whose 1985 solo album for Warner Bros. was co-produced by Roger) and by his parents' record collection.

"Through the week, my parents would be a little mean and down to business," Roger recalled, "but on weekends, they'd get something to drink and loosen up and play their favorite records. I always liked them on weekends, and I thought that the music made them feel like that. Now I know that the music was only part of it, but then I said that if my parents are gonna act like that because of the music, I'm gonna learn how to do it so I can make everybody feel like that all the time."

TOP ALBUM

ZAPP (Zapp, Warner Bros., '80, 19)

Additional Top 40 R&B Albums: 5

TOP SONGS

MORE BOUNCE TO THE OUNCE PART I (Zapp, Warner Bros., '80, 2 R&B)

I HEARD IT THROUGH THE GRAPEVINE (Roger, Warner Bros., '81, 1 R&B)

DANCE FLOOR (PART I) (Zapp, Warner Bros., '82, 1 R&B)

DOO WA DITTY (BLOW THAT THING) (Zapp, Warner Bros., '83, 10 R&B)

I CAN MAKE YOU DANCE (PART I) (Zapp, Warner Bros., '83, 4 R&B)

HEARTBREAKER (PART I) (Zapp, Warner Bros., '83, 15 R&B)

IN THE MIX (Roger, Warner Bros., '84, 10 R&B)

COMPUTER LOVE PART I (Zapp, Warner Bros., '86, 8 R&B)

I WANT TO BE YOUR MAN (Roger, Reprise, '87, 1 R&B, 3 Pop)

Additional Top 40 R&B Songs: 9

By the late 1980s, Larry, Lester, and Terry had left the group to help their non-playing brother Rufus, Jr., at Troutman Enterprises, a diversified Dayton firm that operates a record production facility, a limousine service, and a construction and real estate branch that renovates dilapidated houses for low-income tenants. Zapp remained a family affair, however, with "Little" Roger Troutman, Jr. (guitar and keyboards) and Rufus Troutman III (keyboards and trumpet) joining the lineup. Former Parliament-Funkadelic bass singer "Sting" Ray Davis also became a member.

The frequent use of Roger and Zapp samples in hip-hop records led to a revival of interest in the group in 1992. "Mega Medley Mix," a remix of snippets of old Roger and Zapp songs, was issued the following year on Reprise and rose to number 30 R&B. It was included on *All Time Greatest Hits,* which went to number 39 on the *Billboard* album chart and spawned a number 18 R&B hit with the newly recorded "Slow and Easy."

INDEX

Aaron Neville's Soulful Christmas (Neville), 163
Abbey, John, 160
ABC (Jackson 5), 111
"ABC" (Jackson 5), 111
"ABC's of Love, The" (Lymon), 141
Abner, Ewart, 33, 34, 61
Abramson, Herb, 29, 30, 47
"Abyssinia Jones" (Starr), 216
Ace, Johnny, 1–2, 19
Ackerman, Paul, 32
Acklin, Barbara, 43
Adams, Berle, 119
"Addicted to Your Love" (LeVert), 134
"Adorable" (Drifters), 67
Adu, Helen Folasade, 201
Afanadieff, Walter, 37, 38
"After the Dance" (DeBarge), 58
"Agent Double-O-Soul" (Starr), 216
"Ain't Gonna Bump No More (With No Big Fat Woman)" (Tex), 228
"Ain't It a Shame" (Domino), 63
"Ain't It a Shame" (Price), 185
Ain't No 'Bout-a-Doubt It (Graham), 87
"Ain't No Mountain High Enough" (Ross), 199
"Ain't No Mountain High Enough" (Terrell), 227
"Ain't No Sunshine" (Withers), 256
"Ain't No Woman (Like the One I've Got)" (Four Tops), 81
"Ain't Nobody Here But Us Chickens" (Jordan), 119
"Ain't Nobody" (Khan), 122
"Ain't Nothing Gonna Change Me" (Everett), 74
"Ain't Nothing Like the Real Thing" (Terrell), 227
"Ain't Nothing You Can Do" (Hill), 96
"Ain't That Peculiar" (Gaye), 86
"Ain't Too Proud to Beg" (Temptations), 224
"Ain't Understanding Mellow" (Butler), 34
Aladdin Chickenscratchers, 152
Alaimo, Steve, 202
Ales, Barney, 58
Alexander, J. W., 53, 257
Alexander, James, 9, 10
Alexander, John Marshall, Jr., 1
Alexander, Margie, 39
Alexander, William, 156
"Alexander's Ragtime Band" (Lutcher), 140
"Alfie" (Warwick), 245
Alfonso, Barry, 243
All American Girls (Sister Sledge), 207
"All Around the World" (John), 115
"All by Myself" (Domino), 63
"All I Could Do Was Cry" (James), 113
"All I Have" (Moments), 158
"All I Want Is Forever" (Belle), 14
"All the Man That I Wanted" (Houston), 98
"All My Love Belongs to You" (Jackson), 104
"All My Love" (Bryson), 31
"All of My Love" (Gap Band), 84
All in the Name of Love (Atlantic Starr), 4
"All Night Long (All Night)" (Richie) 195
"All Nite Long" (Otis), 171
"All Season" (LeVert), 134
"All She Wants to Do Is Rock" (Harris), 91
All Things in Time (Rawls), 190
All This Love (DeBarge), 58
"All the Way Lover" (Jackson), 109
Allen, Carl, 9, 10
Allen, Henry, 208
Allen, Lee, 63, 138, 156
Allen, Rev. A. A., 184
Allen, Thomas Sylvester "Papa Dee," 241

Allison, Verne, 59, 60
Allman, Duane, 180
"Almost Grown" (Berry), 18
Alomat, Carlos, 239
Alston, Gerald, 13, 143
Alston, Shirley Owens, 205–7
Altairs, 14
"Always" (Atlantic Starr), 4
"Always Together" (Dells), 61
"Am I Asking Too Much" (Washington), 247
"Am I Losing You" (Manhattans), 143
American Breed, 121
"Amor" (King), 123
"And the Beat Goes On" (Whispers), 250
Andantes, 194
Anderson, Alfa, 44
Anderson, Andre, 186
Anderson, Katherine, 144
"Angel" (Baker), 5
"Annie Had a Baby" (Ballard), 8
"Anniversary" (Tony Toni Toné), 235
"Another Saturday Night" (Cooke), 53
"Any Day Now" (Sledge), 210
Any Love (Vandross), 240
"Any Love" (Vandross), 240
"Any Way You Want Me" (Sylvers), 222
"Anymore" (Ace), 1
"Aqua Boogie (A Psychoalphadiscobeta-bioaquadoloop)" (Clinton), 45
Archer, Cliff, 3
"Are You Serious" (Davis), 56
Armstead, Joshie Jo, 3
Arnold, Billy Boy, 61
Around the World in a Day (Prince/Revolution), 187
Arrington, Joseph, Jr., 227
Arriva, 201
As the Band Turns (Atlantic Starr), 4
"As Long As It Takes Care of Home" (Staton), 218
Ashford, Nickolas, 2–3, 104, 201, 227
Ashford, Rosalind, 193, 194
"Ask Me What You Want" (Jackson), 109
Askey, Gil, 186
"At Last" (James), 113
"At Midnight (My Love Will Lift You Up)" (Khan), 122
Atkins, John, 176
Atkins, Mickey, 45
Atlantic Starr, 3–4
"Atomic Dog" (Clinton), 45
"Attack Me" (Cameo), 36
Austell, Leo, 74
Austin, Dallas, 22
"Automatic" (Pointer Sisters), 183
Avant, Clarence, 256
Axton, Estelle, 12, 51–52, 229

"B-A-B-Y" (Thomas), 229
"Baby Come to Me" (Belle), 14
"Baby Doll" (Tony Toni Toné), 235
"Baby, Don't Do It" (5 Royales), 75
"Baby Don't You Cry" (Johnson), 116
"Baby Get Lost" (Washington), 247
"Baby, I Love You" (Little Milton), 137
"Baby, I'm Hooked (Right into Your Love)" (Con Funk Shun), 51
"Baby I'm Ready" (LeVert), 134
"Baby It's You" (Shirelles), 206
"Baby, Please Don't Go" (Orioles), 168
"Baby Sitter" (Wright), 260
"Baby That's a Backatcha" (Robinson), 196
Baby Workout (Wilson), 255
"Baby Workout" (Wilson), 255
"Baby (You've Got What It Takes)" (Benton), 16
"Baby (You've Got What It Takes)" (Washington), 247

Bacharach, Burt, 154, 244–45, 246
Back on the Block (Jones), 118
"Back and Forth" (Cameo), 36
"Back in My Arms Again" (Ross/Supremes), 199
"Back Stabbers" (O'Jays), 166
"Back in Stride" (Maze), 149
"Back Together Again" (Flack/Hathaway), 93
Bad (Jackson), 108
"Bad" (Jackson), 108
"Bad, Bad Whiskey" (Milburn), 153
"Bad Boy" (Parker), 172
Bad Girls (Summer), 221
"Bad Girls" (Summer), 221
Bailey, John "Buddy," 47, 48
Bailey, Philip, 68, 69, 154
Baker, Anita, 4–6
Baker, Elija, 235
Baker, LaVern, 6–7, 123
Baldwin, David, 151
Baldwin, Wilbur, 151
Ballard, Clint, Jr., 74
Ballard, Florence, 145, 199
Ballard, Hank, 7–8, 115
Balliett, Whitney, 140, 236
Banashak, Joe, 161
Banks, Patryce "Chocolate," 87, 88
Banks, Ron, 65, 66
Bar-Kays, 8–10, 192
"Bar Room Blues" (Brown), 29
Barge, Gene, 138, 254
Barker, Francine, 173–74
Barksdale, Chuck, 59, 60, 160
Barnes, Prentiss, 159
Barnum, H. B., 167
Barrett, Richard, 101, 136, 141–42, 232
Barri, Steve, 19, 81
Bart, Ben, 188
Bartholomew, Dave, 29, 62, 63, 185
Bass, Fontella, 138
Bass, Ralph, 7, 26, 75, 178, 244
Bateman, Robert, 144, 247
Bates, Ellas, 61
Batman (Prince), 187
Baughan, David, 67
Baxter, Les, 90
Bayyan, Khalis, 128–29
"Be My Girl" (Dramatics), 65
Beale Streeters, 1, 18
Bealtitude: Respect Yourself (Staple Singers), 215
"Bear Cat" (Thomas), 231
Beard, Michael, 9, 10
Beatles, 17, 42, 45, 89, 102, 178, 184
"Beauty Is Only Skin Deep" (Temptations), 224
Beavers, Jackey, 240
"Because, Pts. 1 & 2" (Johnson), 116
Beck, Billy, 166
Beckett, Barry, 113
Bedell, Lou, 249
"Beechwood 4-5789" (Marvelettes), 144
"Beep a Freak" (Gap Band), 84
"Being With You" (Robinson), 196
Belfield, Denny, 121
Bell, Al, 19, 79, 216
Bell, Archie, 10–12
Bell, Lee, 11
Bell, Ricky, 23, 163, 165
Bell, Robert "Kool," 128–29
Bell, Ronald, 128
Bell, Thom, 44, 58, 136, 176, 213, 214, 219, 253
Bell, William, 9, 12–13, 20, 79, 115
Bell Biv DeVoe, 21, 24
Belle, Regina, 13–14, 31, 32, 129, 144
Bellotte, Pete, 220, 221

"Bells, The" (Ward), 244
Belushi, John, 54
Belvin, Jesse, 251
Bennett, Alvino, 170
Benny and Us (King), 123
Benson, Al, 78
Benson, George, 14–15, 92, 122, 123, 190
Benson, Renaldo "Obie," 80
Benson, Ricci, 198
Benton, Brook, 15–17, 80, 94, 125, 147, 247
Benton, Jerome, 233, 234
Berns, Bert, 31, 33, 67, 90, 101, 150, 225
Berns, Ilene, 31
Berry, Chuck, 17–18, 25, 48, 54, 68, 118
Berry, Richard, 49, 112–13, 252
"Best of My Love" (Emotions), 71
Best, Nathaniel, 167–68
"Best Thing That Ever Happened to Me" (Knight/Pips), 126
"Best Things in Life Are Free" (Vandross), 240
"Best Wishes" (Milton), 156
"Best Years of My Life, The" (Floyd), 79
"Betcha by Golly, Wow" (Stylistics), 219
Betty Wright Live (Wright), 260
Beverly, Frankie, 148–50
"Bewildered" (Milburn), 153
Big Fun (Shalamar), 205
"Big John" (Shirelles), 206
"Big Question" (Mayfield), 148
Big Throwdown, The (LeVert), 134
Biggs, Howard, 90, 188
Bihari, Lester, 12
Birch, Gaylord, 88
Birdsong, Cindy, 130, 199
Bivens, Michael, 21, 22, 23, 163, 165
Bivins, Edward "Sonny," 143
Black Moses (Hayes), 94
"Black Night" (Brown), 26
Black, Vernon "Ice," 148
Blackman, Benorce, 256
Blackmon, Larry, 10, 23, 35–36, 166
Blackwell, Bumps, 53, 117, 138
Blaine, Jerry, 168
Bland, Bobby, 1, 18–19, 28, 54, 56, 95, 137
"Bloodshot Eyes" (Harris), 91
"Blow Mr. Jackson" (Liggins), 135
Blue Belles, 130
Blue Boys, 185
"Blue Light Boogie" (Jordan), 119
"Blue Monday" (Domino), 63
Blue Notes, 22, 100, 176–77
"Blueberry Hill" (Domino), 63
Bluebirds, 48
"Blues, The" (Tony Toni Toné), 235
"Blues at Sunrise" (Hunter), 100
Blues Brothers, 54, 203
Blues Brothers Band, 79
"Bo Diddley" (Diddley), 62
Board, Johnny, 1
Bob and Earl, 251
Body Heat (Jones), 118
Bodyguard, The (Houston), 98
Bogan, Anne, 145
Bogart, Neil, 220
Bohannon, Hamilton, 172
"Boll Weevil Song, The" (Benton), 16
Bonham, Vincent, 172
Bonnefond, Jim, 129
Bonner, Leroy "Sugarfoot," 10, 165, 166, 263
"Boogaloo Party, The" (Flamingos), 78
"Boogie at Midnight" (Brown), 29
"Boogie Body Land" (Bar-Kays), 10
"Boogie Fever" (Sylvers), 222
"Boogie Wonderland" (Earth, Wind and Fire/Emotions), 71

INDEX

"Boogie Woogie Blue Plate" (Jordan), 119
Boogie Woogie Boys, 236
Booker T and the MGs, 8, 12, 94
Boone, Pat, 47, 63, 78, 100, 138, 205
"Boot-Leg" (Booker T), 21
Booth, Henry, 7
"Bop-Ting-A-Ling" (Baker), 7
"Born to Know" (Tony Toni Toné), 235
Born to Love (Bryson/Flack), 31
Born to Sing (En Vogue), 73
Boskent, William, 186
"Bottom's Up" (Chi-Lites), 43
Bowen, Jeffrey, 224
Bowie, David, 44, 123, 239
Boyd, Steve, 66
Boyz II Men, 21–23, 165
Bracey, William, 136
Braun, Jules, 245
Break Every Rule (Turner), 238
Break Out (Pointer Sisters), 183
"Break Up to Make Up" (Stylistics), 219
"Break Your Promise" (Delfonics), 59
"Breakdown" (Thomas), 231
"Breaking Up Somebody's Home" (Peebles), 175
Breezin' (Benson), 15
Breston, Jackie, 237
Brewer, Theresa, 1, 99
Bright, Jeryl, 36
Brilliance (Atlantic Starr), 4
"Bring It on Home to Me" (Cooke), 53
"Bring It on Home to Me" (Floyd), 79
"Bring It Home to Me" (Johnson), 116
Bristol, Johnny, 216, 225, 240–41
Bromberg, Bruce, 54
Bronco, 251
Brook Benton Today (Benton), 16
Brooks, Arthur, 33, 146
Brooks, Richard, 33, 146
Brown, Bill, 243, 244
Brown, Billie, 157–58
Brown, Bobby, 23–24, 99, 161, 163, 164
Brown, Charles, 1, 17, 25–26,41, 62, 99, 125, 153, 170, 254
Brown, Erroll, 96, 97
Brown, Geoff, 44, 172
Brown, George, 128, 190
Brown, Gerald, 204
Brown, Harold, 241, 242
Brown, James, 8, 26–27, 47, 66, 76, 101, 115, 118, 190, 225, 227
Brown, Kenji Chiba, 197, 198
Brown, Lawrence, 176
Brown, Marty, 208
Brown, Morrie, 144
Brown, Roy, 18, 28–29, 91, 151, 254
Brown, Ruth, 29–31, 99, 152
Brown, Sam "Little Sonny," 100, 101
Brown, Tommy, 126
Brownleee, Archie, 179, 222, 257
Broyles, Ben, 39
Bryant, Don, 175
Bryant, Elbridge, 224
Bryant, Ray, 82
Bryant, Sharon, 3, 4
Bryant, William, 148, 149
Bryson, Peabo, 14, 31–32, 77, 92
"Buffalo Soldier" (Flamingos), 78
Bullock, Annie Mae, 237
Burch, Vernon, 9
Burdon, Eric, 242–43
Burke, Solomon, 32–33, 90, 99, 123, 179, 191
"Burn Rubber (Why You Wanna Hurt Me)" (Gap Band), 84
"Burnin' Love" (Con Funk Shun), 51
Burrage, Harold, 55
Burrell, Walter Price, 256
Busby, Tanny, 10
Butler, Huey "Billy," 10
Butler, Jerry, 33–34, 40, 74, 92, 100, 146, 161, 225
Butlers, 148
"Buzz Me" (Jordan), 119
"Bye Bye Baby" (Wells), 248
"Bye Bye Baby Blues" (Ravens), 189

Bynum, Mark, 10
"B.Y.O.B. (Bring Your Own Baby)" (Sister Sledge), 207
Byrd, Bobby, 26

Cain, Randy, 59
"Caldonia" (Jordan), 119
Caldwell, Nicholas, 249, 250
Caldwell, Ronnie, 9
Calendo, John, 192
"California Girl" (Floyd), 79
Call on Me (Bland), 19
"Call Operator 210" (Otis), 171
Calloway, Blanche, 29
Camden Jubilee Singers, 16
Cameo, 10, 23, 34–36, 131
Cameron, G. C., 22, 214
Campbell, Barbara, 53. *See also* Cooke, Barbara
Campbell, Little Milton, 137–38
Campbell, Thomas, 36
"Can I Change My Mind" (Davis), 56
"Can You Handle It?" (Graham/Central Station), 87
"Can You Stand the Rain" (New Edition), 164
"Can You Stop the Rain" (Bryson), 31
"Candy" (Cameo), 36
"Candy Girl" (New Edition), 164
Can't Get Enough (White), 251
"Can't Get Enough of Your Love, Babe" (White), 251
"Can't Get Over You" (Maze), 149
"Can't Let Go" (Carey), 36
Can't Slow Down (Richie), 195
"Can't You Find Another Way (Of Doing It)" (Sam and Dave), 203
Capone, Ron, 52
Car Wash (Rose Royce), 197
"Car Wash" (Rose Royce), 197
Cardeas, Mark, 233
Cardinals, 188
Carey, Ezekiel "Zeke," 77, 78
Carey, Jacob "Jake," 77, 78
Carey, Mariah, 36–38
Carmichael, Arnell, 172
Carmichael, Darren, 172
Carmichael, James Anthony, 4, 194, 195
Carnegie, Arthur Lorenzo, 169
Carroll, Earl "Speedo," 49
Carroll, Gregory, 169
Carroll, Porter, Jr., 3
Carson, Ron, 250
Carter, Billy, 17
Carter, Calvin, 33, 34, 74, 138
Carter, Clarence, 38–39, 113, 217
Carter, Darryl, 258
Carter, Johnny, 59, 60, 77, 78
Carter, Obadiah, 75
"Casanova" (LeVert), 134
Casey, Al, 125
Casey, Harry Wayne "KC," 120–21
Cash, Fred, 146
Castellano, Vincent, 158
Caught Up (Jackson), 109
Cauley, Ben, 9
Cavaliers, 224
"C.C. Rider" (Willis), 254
Cecil, Malcolm, 259
Celebrate! (Kool and the Gang), 128
"Celebration" (Kool and the Gang), 128
"Chain of Fools" (Franklin), 83
"Chain Gang" (Cooke), 53
"Chains of Love" (Turner), 236
Chandler, Gene, 39–40, 146
Chandler, June Deniece, 252
"Change with the Times" (McCoy), 150
Chapter 8, 5
Charles, Ray, 3, 25, 33, 38, 40–42, 48, 54, 59, 64, 117, 118, 123, 148, 184, 190, 259
"Charlie Brown" (Coasters), 49
"Chase Me" (Con Funk Shun), 51
"Cheaper to Keep Her" (Taylor), 223
"Cheating in the Next Room" (Hill), 96
Checker, Chubby, 7, 8

Cheeks, Julius, 26, 179
Chenier, Clifton, 113
"Cherish" (Kool and the Gang), 128
Chess, Leonard, 17, 61, 138
Chess, Phil, 61
Chessler, Deborah, 168
Chesters, 136
Chi-Lites, 42–43
Chic, 43–44
Chic (Chic), 44
"Chicken Shack Boogie" (Milburn), 153
"Chicken Strut" (Neville), 163
"Chill It On" (Turner), 236
"Choice of Colors" (Mayfield), 146
"Chokin' Kind" (Hill), 96
"Chokin' Kind, The" (Simon), 207
"Choo Choo Ch'Boogie" (Jordan), 119
Chosen Gospel Singers, 189
Christgau, Georgia, 97
Christmas Interpretations (Boyz II Men), 23
Christmas Singers, 189
Chudd, Lew, 62
Ciner, Al, 121
"Circles" (Atlantic Starr), 4
"Cisco Kid, The" (War), 242
"Cissy Strut" (Neville), 163
"City in the Sky" (Staple Singers), 215
Clark, Dick, 8, 17, 64, 186, 253, 255
Clark, James "Poppa," 67
Clarke, Willie, 261
Clayton, Merry, 169
"Clean Up Woman" (Wright), 260
"Cleo's Back" (Walker), 241
Cleveland, James, 41, 184
Clinton, George, 45–47, 65, 177, 214, 263
"Clock, The" (Ace), 1
"Close the Door" (Pendergrass), 177
"Close Your Eyes" (Peaches and Herb), 174
"Closer I Get to You, The" (Flack/Hathaway), 77, 93
Clovers, 47–48
Coasters, 48–50,124
Cobb, Arnett, 99
Coday, Bill, 131, 132
Coggins, Danny, 159
COGICS, 183, 184, 185
"Cold Blooded" (James), 114
"Cold, Cold Heart" (Washington), 247
"Cold Sweat (Part 1)" (Brown/Famous Flames), 27
Cole, Nat "King," 16, 28, 41, 49, 99, 125, 126, 136, 140, 167–68, 171, 205
Cole, Natalie, 32, 49–50, 172, 253
Coleman, Cornelius, 63
Coles, Earl S., Jr., 4
Collier, Mitty, 13
Collins, Bootsy, 47, 263
Collins, Clarence, 136
"Come and Get It Honey" (Lutcher), 140
"Come and Get These Memories" (Reeves/Vandellas), 193
"Come Into My Heart" (Price), 185
"Come On and See Me" (Terrell), 227
"Come What May" (McPhatter), 151
Commodores, 10, 194–95
Compositions (Baker), 5
"Computer Love Part 1" (Zapp), 263
Con Funk Shun, 50–52
Condon, Eddie, 29
Conley, Arthur, 192
Conner, Tony, 96
Conover, Willis, 29
Conquest, June, 92
"Contact" (Starr), 216
Control (Jackson), 106
Cook, Bill, 90
Cook, Roger, 68
Cooke, Barbara, 257
Cooke, L. C., 52, 53, 109
Cooke, Linda, 248–49, 258
Cooke, Sam, 15, 31, 32, 52–53, 54, 79, 81, 90, 95, 115, 123, 139–140, 143, 149, 153, 184, 189, 190, 222, 257
Cookies, 254
"Cool It Now" (New Edition), 164

"Cool (Part 1)" (Time), 233
"Cool Water" (Lutcher), 140
Cooleyhighharmony (Boyz II Men), 23
Cooper, Barry Michael, 23
Cooper, Michael, 50, 51
Cooper, Wayne, 35
Copeland, Kenny, 197, 198
Cordell, Denny, 83
Cornelius, Don, 203, 250
Cornwell, James "Kimo," 148
"Corrine Corrina" (Turner), 236
Costa, Don, 136, 186
"Could It Be I'm Falling in Love" (Spinners), 214
"Count Me Out" (New Edition), 164
"Count Your Blessings" (Ashford and Simpson), 3
"Court Room, The" (Carter), 39
Cousins, Richard, 54
"Cover Me" (Sledge), 210
Coward, Juanita, 144
"Cowboys to Girls" (Intruders), 101
"Crackin' Up" (Diddley), 62
Cramer, Floyd, 12, 257
Crawford, Dave, 203, 217, 218
"Crawlin'" (Clovers), 48
Cray, Robert, 18, 54
"Crazy" (Sly/Family Stone), 212
"Crazy" (Manhattans), 143
"Crazy, Crazy, Crazy" (5 Royales), 75
Creatore, Luigi, 53, 101, 150, 219
Creators, 242
Creed, Linda, 15, 214, 219
Crewe, Bob, 124
Cropper, Steve, 8, 20, 21, 75, 78, 79, 179, 191, 192, 203
Crosby, Bing, 26, 28, 180, 192
Crosby, Henry, 259
Cross, Joe, 11
"Cross My Heart" (Ace), 1
Crouch, Andrae, 183, 184
Crouch, Stanley, 85
Crumwell, Martha, 92
"Cry Baby" (Mayfield), 148
"Cry to Me" (Burke), 33
"Crying in the Chapel" (Orioles), 168
Cullum, Lula Ann, 152
Cully, Frank "Cole Slaw," 47
Cummings, Jerry, 176
Cummings, Tony, 58, 100, 150, 156–57, 174, 176, 214, 232
Cunningham, Carl, 9
"Cupid's Boogie" (Otis), 171
"Cupid's Boogie" (Phillips), 178
Curb, Mike, 221
Cuscuna, Michael, 190
Cymone, Andre, 186, 205

"Daddy Daddy" (Brown), 30
Dallas, Robert, 158
Damrosch, Walter, 244
"Dance, Dance, Dance" (Chic), 44
"Dance Floor (Part 1)" (Zapp), 263
"Dance to the Music" (Sly/Family Stone), 212
"Dance with Me" (Drifters), 67
"Dance Wit' Me—Part 1" (James), 114
"Dancing Machine" (Jackson 5), 111
"Dancing in the Sheets" (Shalamar), 205
"Dancing to Your Music" (Bell), 11
Dangerous (Jackson), 108
Daniel, Jeffrey, 154, 203–4
Daniel, Reggie, 154
Daniels, Richard, 58
"Dare Me" (Pointer Sisters), 183
"Darktown Strutters' Ball" (Liggins), 135
"Darlin' Darlin' Baby (Sweet Tender Love)" (O'Jays), 166
Dash, Sarah, 130, 131, 158
Daughtery, Eugene "Bird," 100
David, Hal, 34, 94, 154, 206, 244–45
Davis, Carl, 39, 40, 42, 55, 61, 123, 128, 201, 254
Davis, Clive, 97, 172

Davis, Delia, 204, 205
Davis, Don, 60, 65, 138, 166, 223, 229
Davis, Eddie "Lockjaw," 100
Davis, George, 161
Davis, Henry E., 169
Davis, Johnny "J. T.," 169
Davis, Maxwell, 95, 152
Davis, Miles, 36, 116
Davis, Raymond, 45, 263
Davis, Roderick, 65
Davis, Roquel "Billy," 137, 255
Davis, Sammy, Jr., 230
Davis, Theresa, 71
Davis, Tyrone, 55–56
Dawn, Sandra, 180
Day, Morris, 233
"Daylight" (Womack), 258
De Jesus, Luchi, 34
"Dead End Street" (Rawls), 189
"Dead Giveaway" (Shalamar), 205
Deadato, Eumir, 52, 129
"Dear Lover" (Wells), 248
DeBarge, 56–58
DeBarge, Bobby, 56, 58
DeBarge, Chico, 57–58
DeBarge, Eldra "El," 56, 57, 58
DeBarge, Etterlene "Bunny," 56
DeBarge, James, 56, 58, 106
DeBarge, Mark, 56, 57, 58
DeBarge, Randy, 57, 58
DeBarge, Tommy, 56
"Deceivin' Blues" (Otis), 171
"Deceivin' Blues" (Phillips), 178
DeCoteaux, Bert, 96, 208
"Dedicated to the One I Love" (Shirelles), 206
Degree, Leavell, 250
Delfonics, 58–59
Del-Phis, 193
Delk, William, 136
Dells, 59–61, 78
Demps, Larry "Squirrel," 65, 66
Denman, Paul S., 201
Deodato, Eumir, 52, 129
DeSanto, Sugar Pie, 112, 170
DeSario, Teri, 121
"Devil or Angel" (Clovers), 48
DeVoe, Ronnie, 23, 163, 165
DeWalt, Autry, 240
Diamond Life (Sade), 202
"Diamonds and Pearls" (Prince/New Power Generation), 187
Diana Ross and the Supremes Greatest Hits (Ross/Supremes), 199
Dickerson, Morris DeWayne "B. B.," 241–43
Dickey, Gwen, 198
Diddley, Bo, 61–62, 85, 118
"Diddley Daddy" (Diddley), 62
"Didn't I (Blow Your Mind This Time)" (Delfonics), 59
Dillard, Varetta, 1
Dion, Celine, 32
Disco Baby (McCoy), 150
"Disco Lady" (Taylor), 223
"Disco Queen" (Hot Chocolate), 97
Distants, 224
Dixie Hummingbirds, 18, 257
Dixie Nightingales, 224
Dixon, Eugene, 39
Dixon, George, 213
Dixon, Luther, 150, 205, 206, 225
Dixon, Willie, 16, 62, 74
"Do-Re-Mi" (Dorsey), 64
"Do the Choo Choo" (Bell), 11
"Do the Funky Chicken" (Thomas), 231
"Do the Funky Penguin Part 1" (Thomas), 231
"Do It (Let Me See You Shake)" (Bar-Kays), 10
"Do It in the Name of Love" (King), 123
"Do Me Again" (Jackson), 105
"Do Something for Me" (Ward), 244
"(Do the) Push and Pull, Part 1" (Thomas), 231
"Do What You Feel" (Williams), 253

"Do You or Don't You Love Me" (Lutcher), 140
"Do You Love What You Feel" (Khan), 122
"Do You Really Want My Love" (Moore), 161
"Do You See My Love (For You Growing)" (Walker), 241
"Do You Wanna Party" (KC/Sunshine Band), 121
"Do Your Dance—Part 1" (Rose Royce), 197
"Do Your Thing" (Hayes), 94
Dock of the Bay, The (Redding), 192
Dockey, William, 136
Dodson, Larry, 9, 10
"Dog, The" (Thomas), 231
Doggett, Bill, 217
"Doggin' Around" (Wilson), 255
"Doin' Our Thing" (Carter), 39
Domingoes, 213
Domino, Fats, 25, 29, 62–63, 64, 118, 152, 156, 185
Dominoes, 7, 48, 67, 151, 243–44, 255
Donahue, Tom, 212
Donny Hathaway Live (Hathaway), 93
"Don't Ask Me Why" (Jackson), 104
"Don't Ask My Neighbors" (Emotions), 71
Don't Be Afraid of the Dark (Cray), 54
"Don't Be Cruel" (Brown), 24
Don't Be Cruel (Brown), 24
"Don't Cry, Baby" (James), 113
"Don't Cry No More" (Bland), 19
"Don't Deceive Me" (Willis), 254
"Don't Go" (En Vogue), 73
"Don't Have to Ride No More" (Ravens), 189
"Don't Knock My Love" (Pickett), 179
"Don't Let Go" (Hamilton), 90
"Don't Let the Green Grass Fool You" (Pickett), 179
"Don't Make Me Over" (Warwick), 245
"Don't Make Me Pay for His Mistakes" (Hill), 96
"Don't Mess with Bill" (Marvelettes), 144
"Don't Play That Song (You Lied)" (King), 123
"Don't Say Goodnight (It's Time for Love)" (Isley Brothers), 102
"Don't Stop, Get Off" (Sylvers), 222
"Don't Stop 'Til You Get Enough" (Jackson), 108
"Don't Take Your Love" (Manhattans), 143
"Don't Tell Your Mama (Where You've Been) (Floyd), 79
"(Don't Worry) If There's a Hell Below We're All Going to Go" (Mayfield), 146
"Don't You Cry" (Turner), 236
"Don't You Get So Mad" (Osborne), 170
"Don't You Know I Love You" (Clovers), 48
"Doo Wa Ditty (Blow That Thing)" (Zapp), 263
Dorn, Joel, 76
Dorsey, Lee, 63–65, 162
Dortch, Darwin, 166
Douglas, Robert, 219
Dow, Gary, 35, 36
Dowd, Tom, 254
"Down in Mexico" (Coasters), 49
Dozier, Lamont, 80–81, 96, 102, 124, 145, 193
Dramatics, 65–66
"Dreamlover" (Carey), 36
Drells (Archie Bell and the), 10–12
Drifters, 67–68, 123, 151, 244
"Drifting Blues" (Brown), 26
Drinkard Singers, 245
"Drinkin' Wine Spo-Dee-O-Dee" (Harris), 91
"Drown in My Own Tears" (Charles), 42
"Drowning in the Sea of Love" (Simon), 207

Dubin, Al, 78
Dude, The (Jones), 118
Duhe, Robin, 148, 149
Dukays, 39
"Duke of Earl" (Chandler), 40
Duke, George, 5, 170
Dunlap, Melvin, 256
Dunn, Donald "Duck," 9, 20, 21, 79, 191, 192
Dunn, Freddie, 197
Dunn, James, Jr., 219, 220
Dunn, Larry, 68
DuPonts, 67
Dupree, Cornell, 17, 126
Duram, Eric, 35, 36
Dylan, Bob, 21, 52, 82, 168, 215
Dynasty, 272

Eargasm (Taylor), 223
"Early in the Morning" (Gap Band), 84
"Earth Angel" (New Edition), 164
Earth, Wind and Fire, 68–69, 71
"Ease Back" (Neville), 163
"Easy Lovin' Out" (Bell), 13
"Easy" (Richie/Commodores), 195
"Ebb Tide" (Hamilton), 90
Echoes, 222
Echoes of Joy, 261
Eden Trio, 249
Edmonds, Kenneth "Babyface," 22, 23, 99, 250
Edwards, Bernard, 43–44, 209
Edwards, Dennis, 224
Edwards, Earl, 39
Edwards, John, 214
Edwards, Robert "Big Sonny," 100
El DeBarge (DeBarge), 58
El-Rays, 60
"Electric Lady" (Con Funk Shun), 51
Elgins, 224
Eli, Bobby, 4
Elizondo, Rene, 107
Ellington, Duke, 29, 78, 99, 115, 116, 135
Ellington, Robert, 65
Ellis, Terry, 71
"Emma" (Hot Chocolate), 97
Emotions, 70–71
"Emotions" (Carey), 36
Emotions (Carey), 36
"Empty Arms" (Hunter), 100
En Vogue, 71–73
Encore of Golden Hits (Platters), 181
"End of the Road" (Boyz II Men), 23
"Endless Love" (Richie), 195
"Endless Love" (Ross), 199
"Engine Number 9" (Pickett), 179
English, David, 224
Enterprise, 233
Errico, Greg, 212
Ertegun, Ahmet, 29, 47, 48, 124, 236
"Escapade" (Jackson), 106
Eurythmics, 85
Evans, Joe, 143
Evans, Richard, 31
Evans, Walter, 115
Ever Ready Gospel Singers, 255
Everett, Betty, 34, 43, 68, 73–74
"Every 1's a Winner" (Hot Chocolate), 97
Every 1's a Winner (Hot Chocolate), 97
"Every Beat of My Heart" (Knight/Pips), 126
"Every Little Step" (Brown), 24
"(Every Time I Turn Around) Back in Love Again" (Osborne), 170
"Everybody Dance" (Chic), 44
"Everybody Loves a Lover" (Shirelles), 206
"Everybody Loves a Winner" (Bell), 13
"Everyday People" (Sly/Family Stone), 212
"Everything I Do Gohn Be Funky (From Now On)" (Dorsey), 64
"Everything I Do is Wrong" (Milton), 156
Exciting Wilson Pickett, The (Pickett), 179

Facts of Life, 109–10
Fakir, Abdul "Duke," 80
Falcons, 79, 165, 179

"Falling" (Moore), 161
Fambrough, Henry, 213
Fame, Herb, 173–74
"Family Affair" (Sly/Family Stone), 212
Family Reunion (O'Jays), 166
Famous Flames, 8, 26, 75
"Faraway Blues" (Phillips), 178
"Farther Up the Road" (Bland), 19
Fascinations, 193
Father's Pride, 192
Fears, Bobby, 165
Feather, Leonard, 116, 246–47
"Feel Like Makin' Love" (Flack), 77
"Feel That Your Feelin' " (Maze), 149
Feelin' Bitchy (Jackson), 109
"Feeling Is Right, The" (Carter), 39
"Feels Good" (Tony Toni Toné), 235
"Feels Like Another One" (LaBelle), 131
"Feel So Bad" (Little Milton), 137
Feemster, Herb, 173
Feld, Irving, 103
Ferbie, Willie, 67
Ferguson, Larry, 96
Ferguson, Sheila, 232, 233
"Fever" (John), 115
"Ffun" (Con Funk Shun), 51
Fields, Ernie, 155
"Fight the Power Part 1" (Isley Brothers), 102
Finch, Richard, 120
"Fine Brown Frame" (Lutcher), 140
"Finger Poppin' Time" (Ballard), 8
"Fingertips—Pt 2" (Wonder), 259
Fire (Ohio Players), 165
"Fire" (Ohio Players), 165
"Fire and Water" (Pickett), 179
First Take (Flack), 77
"First Time Ever I Saw Your Face, The" (Flack), 77
Fisher, Andre, 50, 121
Five Blind Boys of Alabama, 179, 257
Five Blind Boys of Mississippi, 54, 179, 207, 222, 257
Five Chimes, 195
5 Royales, 7, 26, 74–76
"5-10-15 Hours" (Brown), 30
Flack, Roberta, 32, 76–77, 92, 93, 126
Flairs, 180
Flamingos, 59, 77–78, 136, 188
"Flash Light" (Clinton), 45
"Flip Flop and Fly" (Turner), 236
"Flowers" (Emotions), 71
Floyd, Eddie, 13, 20, 54, 78–79, 115, 199
Flyte Tyme, 233
"Fool, Fool, Fool" (Clovers), 48
"Fool in Love, A" (Turner), 238
"Fool for You" (Mayfield), 146
"Foolish Little Girl" (Shirelles), 206
"Fool's Paradise" (Sylvers), 222
"(For God's Sake) Give More Power to the People" (Chi-Lites), 43
(For God's Sake) Give More Power to the People (Chi-Lites), 43
"For You, My Love" (Lutcher), 140
"For Your Precious Love" (Butler/Impressions), 34
Ford, Willie, 65
"Fore Day in the Morning" (Brown), 29
"Forgive and Forget" (Orioles), 168
"Forgive This Fool" (Hamilton), 90
Foster, David, 50, 99
Foster, Denzil, 71, 73, 235
"Found a Cure" (Ashford and Simpson), 3
Four B's, 123
Four Tops, 7, 77, 80–81, 213
Four Tops Greatest Hits, The (Four Tops), 81
Franklin, Aretha, 1, 26, 36, 49, 80, 81–83, 88, 93, 98, 115, 124, 125, 146, 147, 150, 160, 178, 192, 240
Franklin, Rev. C. L., 81, 115
Franklin, Carolyn, 81
Franklin, Erma, 81
Franklin, Melvin, 224
Franklin, Sammy, 134
Frazier, Louis, 189

"Freakshow on the Dance Floor" (Bar-Kays), 10
"Freaky Dancin' " (Cameo), 36
"Freddie's Dead" (Mayfield), 146
Fredericks, Bill, 68
Fredrick, Levar, 165
Free, Micki, 204, 205
"Free" (Williams), 253
Freed, Alan, 7, 17, 135, 142, 158, 236, 243
Freedberg, Mike, 44, 55, 143
Freedman, Samuel G., 54
Freeman, Paul, 235
"Freeway of Love" (Franklin), 83
French, Don, 109
"Fresh" (Kool and the Gang), 128
"Full of Fire" (Green), 89
Fuller, Johnny, 1
Fuller, Karl, 51
Fulson, Lowell, 41, 87, 192, 229
Fulwood, Ramon "Tiki," 45
Funches, Johnny, 60
Funkadelic, 45, 47, 263
Funkentelechy vs. the Placebo Syndrome (Clinton), 45
"Funky Broadway" (Pickett), 179
Funky Divas (En Vogue), 73
"Funky Music Sho Nuff Turns Me On" (Starr), 216
"Funky Worm" (Ohio Players), 165
Fuqua, Harvey, 85, 86, 113, 158–60, 214, 216, 225, 240–41, 248
Futuretones, 217

Gabler, Milt, 120
Gadson, James, 256
Gaines, LaDonna Andrea, 220
Gaither, Tommy, 168, 169
"Galaxy" (War), 242
Gamble, Kenny, 11, 33, 34, 59, 61, 100, 101, 111, 131, 167, 168, 174, 176, 180, 190, 208, 232
"Games" (Shalamar), 205
Gant, Cecil, 28
Gap Band, 83–85
Gap Band IV (Gap Band), 84
Gardner, Carl, 49
Garner, Henry, 197
Garnes, Sherman, 141
Garrel, Milt, 41
Garrett, William, 144
Gastel, Carlos, 140
Gaye, Marvin, 2, 4, 79, 85–86, 105, 144, 149, 160, 193, 225, 227, 248
Gayten, Paul, 116
"Gee Baby" (Otis), 171
"Gee Whiz (Look at His Eyes)" (Thomas), 229
George, Lanston, 126, 127
George, Nelson, 95, 150
Gerald, Raeford, 109
"Get Down" (Chandler), 40
"Get Down Get Down" (Simon), 207
"Get Down Tonight" (KC/Sunshine Band), 121
"Get on the Good Foot (Part 1)" (Brown), 27
"Get It" (Ballard), 8
"Get It Up" (Time), 233
"Get Out of My Life, Woman" (Dorsey), 64
"Get Yourself Another Fool" (Brown), 26
"Getaway" (Earth, Wind and Fire), 69
"Ghostbusters" (Parker), 172
"G.I. Jive" (Jordan), 119
Gibb, Barry, 246
Gibbs, Georgia, 6, 7, 47, 113
Gibson, Andy, 26
Gill, Johnny, 164
Gillespie, Dizzy, 115, 117, 123
"Gimme Some Time" (Cole/Bryson), 31
"Girl You're Too Young" (Bell), 11
"Girls Can't Do What the Guys Do" (Wright), 260
"Give It to Me Baby" (James), 114
"Give It Up (Turn It Loose)" (Davis), 56
"Give It Up, Turn It Loose" (En Vogue), 73

"Give Me the Night" (Benson), 15
Give Me the Night (Benson), 15
"Give the People What They Want" (O'Jays), 166
"Give Your Baby a Standing Ovation" (Dells), 61
"Giving Him Something He Can Feel" (En Vogue), 73
"Giving Up, Giving In" (Three Degrees), 232
"Giving You the Best That I Got" (Baker), 5
Giving You the Best That I Got (Baker), 5
Glaser, Joe, 246
Glenn, Artie, 169
Glover, Henry, 103, 115, 203, 227–28
Glover, John, 258
"Glow" (James), 114
"Go-Go Girl" (Dorsey), 64
Godfrey, Arthur, 151, 168, 244
"Goin' Home" (Domino), 63
"Goin' Out of My Head" (Little Anthony), 136
"Goin' to the River" (Willis), 254
"Going in Circles" (Gap Band), 84
"Going to a Go-Go" (Robinson/Miracles), 196
Gold, Jack, 253
Gold, Steve, 243
Golden Gate Quartet, 16, 75
Golden Tones, 207
Golden West Gospel Singers, 207
Goldner, George, 78, 101, 136,
Goldstein, Jerry, 243
"Good Golly, Miss Molly" (Little Richard), 138
"Good Lovin'," (Clovers), 48
"Good Lovin' Ain't Easy to Come By" (Terrell), 227
"Good Morning Judge" (Harris), 91
"Good Rockin' Daddy" (James), 113
"Good Rockin' Tonight" (Harris), 91
"Good Times" (Chic), 44
Gooden, Sam, 33, 146
Goodman, Al, 157–58
Goodman, Benny, 189, 236
"Goody Goody" (Lymon), 141
Gordine, Anthony, 135–37, 173
Gordine, Elizabeth, 136
Gordine, Thomas, 136
Gordon, Bobby, 145
Gordon, Marc, 133–34, 168
Gordon, Ronnie, 9
Gordon, Rosco, 9
Gordy, Anna, 85, 86
Gordy, Berry, Jr., 56, 80, 85, 86, 110, 111, 144, 196, 199, 216, 224, 225, 240, 247, 248, 254, 255
Gordy, Gwen, 85, 86, 214, 240, 255
Gordy, Hazel, 111
Gordy, Iris, 58
Gore, Lesley, 117
Gospel Starlighters, 26
Gospelaires, 245
"Got a Right to Cry" (Liggins), 135
"Got to Be Enough" (Con Funk Shun), 51
"Got to Get You into My Life" (Earth, Wind and Fire), 69
"Got to Get You Off My Mind" (Burke), 33
"Got to Give It Up (Part 1)" (Gaye), 86
"Got to Love Somebody" (Sister Sledge), 207
"Gotta Hold On to This Feeling" (Walker), 241
Goytisolo, Fermin, 120
Graham Central Station, 86, 87, 212
Graham, Dell, 87
Graham, Larry, Jr., 86–88, 211
Graham, Leo, 56, 144
Graham, Tina, 144
Grand Central, 186, 233
Grand Tour, The (Neville), 163
Gratitude (Earth, Wind and Fire), 69
Graves, Alexander "Pete," 159, 160
Graves, James, 240, 241

Grayson, Milton, 244
"Great Pretender, The" (Platters), 181
Greatest Hits (Wells), 248
Greatest Hits, Vol. 2 (Robinson/Miracles), 196
"Greatest Love of All, The" (Benson), 15
Green, Al, 6, 9, 21, 53, 54, 97, 185, 188
Green Brothers, 88
Green, Cal, 8
Green, Doc, 67
Green, Jerome, 61, 62
Green, Linda, 173, 174
"Green Onions" (Booker T), 21
Green, Robert, 88
Green, Stan, 205
Green, Walter, 88
Green, William, 88
Greenberg, Florence, 205
Greenberg, Mary Jane, 205
Greene, Al, 6
Greene, Eleanor, 126
Greene, Mark, 157
Greenway, Roger, 68
Griffey, Dick, 203, 204, 250
Griffin, Billy, 197
Griffin, Gene, 23
Griffin, Herman, 248
Grimes, Howard, 89
"Grits Ain't Groceries" (Little Milton), 137
"Groovin' " (Booker T), 21
"Groovy Situation" (Chandler), 40
"Guess Who" (Hunter), 100
Guest, Eleanor, 126
Guest, William, 126
Gunter, Cornell, 49, 180
Gunter, Shirley, 180
Guralnick, Peter, 210
Guy, Billy, 49
Guy, Sherman, 10
"Gypsy Man" (War), 242
"Gypsy Woman" (Mayfield), 146

Haile, Antron, 235
Hale, Andrew, 201
Hale, Willie "Little Beaver," 261
Hall, Rene, 53
Hall, Rick, 38, 39, 82, 113, 179, 217–18, 248
Hall, Willie, 9, 21
Hambly, Don, 99
Hamilton, Roy, 32, 89–91
Hamlisch, Marvin, 82
Hammer, M. C., 22, 43, 52, 69, 114
Hammon, Ronnie, 243
Hammond, John, 15, 82, 236
Hampton, Gladys, 156
Hampton, Lionel, 78, 91, 117, 125, 156, 171, 246, 247
Hampton, Slide, 186
"Hang 'Em High" (Booker T), 21
"Hang Up My Rock and Roll Shoes" (Willis), 254
Hankerson, Barry, 127
"Hard Luck Blues" (Brown), 29
Hardaway, Lulu, 258
Hardesty, Herb, 63, 156, 185
Harding, Ebby, 17
Harlemaires Juniors, 141
Harmon, Gordy, 249, 250
Harper, Ken, 154
Harper, Toni, 141
Harper, Vaughn, 13
Harrell, Paul, 51
Harris, Addie "Micki," 205, 207
Harris, Adrianne, 71
Harris, Bill, 47
Harris, Damon, 225
Harris, James "Jimmy Jam" III, 106, 107, 164, 233
Harris, Joe, 165
Harris, Major, 59
Harris, Martin, 176
Harris, Norman, 59, 176, 250
Harris, R. H., 52, 53, 222
Harris, Roger, 144
Harris, Wynonie, 28, 91–92, 103, 125
Harrison, George, 184

Hart, Clarence, 140
Hart, Wilbert, 58
Hart, William, 58, 59, 136
Hartman, Dan, 27
Haskins, Clarence "Fuzzy," 45
Hatcher, Charles Edwin, 216
Hathaway, Donny, 14, 15, 31, 32, 74, 76, 77, 92–93, 125, 126
Hathaway, Lalah, 93
"Have Mercy Baby" (Ward), 244
"Have You Ever Loved Somebody" (Jackson), 105
"Have You Seen Her" (Chi-Lites), 43
Hawkettes, 161
Hawkins, Edwin, 181
Hawkins, Jamesetta, 111
Hawkins, Roger, 82
Hawkins, Screamin' Jay, 254
Hayes, Isaac, 8, 20–21, 71, 93–95, 100, 192, 229, 246
Hayes, Linda, 180
Hazel, Eddie, 45
Hazziez, Joseph, 228
"He Called Me Baby" (Staton), 218
"He Will Break Your Heart" (Butler), 34
Heart Break (New Edition), 164
"Heartbreak Hotel" (Jackson 5), 111
"Heartbreak (It's Hurtin' Me)" (John), 115
"Heartbreaker (Part 1)" (Zapp), 263
Heat Is On, The (Isley Brothers), 102
"Heavy Fallin' Out" (Stylistics), 219
Heilbut, Anthony, 246
"Hello" (Richie), 195
"Help Me Find a Way (To Say I Love You)" (Little Anthony), 136
"Help Me Somebody" (5 Royales), 75
Henderson, Billy, 213
Henderson, Fletcher, 6, 116
Henderson, Harvey, 9, 10
Henderson, Willie, 55
Hendricks, Belford, 16, 247
Hendricks, Bobby, 49, 67
Hendryx, Nona, 130–31
Hentoff, Nat, 125
"Here I Am (Come and Take Me)" (Green), 89
"Here and Now" (Vandross), 240
Here's Little Richard (Little Richard)
Herron, Cindy, 71
Hersey, John, 65
"He's the Greatest Dancer" (Sister Sledge), 207
"He's Mine" (Platters), 181
"He's a Real Gone Guy" (Lutcher), 140
"He's So Shy" (Pointer Sisters), 183
Hess, Norbert, 152
Hester, Tony, 66
Hewitt, Howard, 204, 205
"Hey Lover" (Jackson), 105
"Hey, Miss Fannie" (Clovers), 48
"Hey, Western Union Man" (Butler), 34
"Hey You! Get Off My Mountain" (Dramatics), 65
Hi-Lites, 42
Hi Rhythm Section, 132
Hibbler, Al, 90
Hickey, Patricia, 36
"Hide and Seek" (Turner), 236
Higgins, Monk, 19
"High School Dance" (Sylvers), 222
"Higher Plane" (Kool and the Gang), 128
Highway Q.C.'s, 52, 189, 222, 223
Hill, Dave, 233
Hill, Matt, 95, 96
Hill, Z. Z., 95–96, 132
Hinckley, David, 62
Hinsley, Harvey, 96, 97
Hinton, Anthony, 239
"Hip City—Part 2" (Walker), 241
"Hip Hug-Her" (Booker T), 21
Hirshey, Gerri, 52
History of Otis Redding (Redding), 192
"Hit the Road Jack" (Charles), 42
"Hit and Run" (Bar-Kays), 10
"Hittin' on Me" (Johnson), 116
Hobbs, Elsbury, 67

Hodge, Alex, 180
Hodge, Gaynel, 180
Hodges, Charles, 89
Hodges, Leroy, 89
Hodges, Teenie, 89
"Hold Me Baby" (Milburn), 153
"Hold On" (En Vogue), 73
"Hold On! I'm a Comin' " (Sam and Dave), 203
"Hold What You've Got" (Tex), 228
"Holding On (When Love Is Gone)" (Osborne), 170
Holiday, Valerie, 232
Holland, Brian, 80–81, 102, 144, 193, 258
Holland, Eddie, 80–81, 102, 145, 193
"Hollywood Swinging" (Kool and the Gang), 128
Holmes, Johnny, 75
Holt, Patricia Louise, 130
"Holy Cow" (Dorsey), 64
"Holy Ghost" (Bar-Kays), 10
Holy Wonders, 189
"Home" (Mills), 154
"Home at Last" (John), 115
"Homely Girl" (Chi-Lites), 43
"Honey Chile" (Reeves/Vandellas), 193
"Honey Hush" (Turner), 236
Honey (Ohio Players), 165
"Honey Love" (Drifters/McPhatter), 67
"Honeydripper, The" (Liggins), 135
Honeydrippers, 44, 134–35
"Hoochie Coochie Coo, The" (Ballard), 8
"Hop, Skip, and Jump" (Milton), 156
"Hope That We Can Be Together Soon" (Pendergrass), 177
Hopkin, Mary, 96
Horn, Lawrence, 240
Horsley, Richie, 157
Horton, Gladys, 144, 145
Hoskyns, Barney, 5, 88, 104, 115, 136, 240, 254
Hot Buttered Soul (Hayes), 94
Hot Chocolate (Bay Area–based), 87
Hot Chocolate (London–based), 96–97
"Hot Fun in the Summertime" (Sly/Family Stone), 212
"Hot Line" (Sylvers), 222
"Hot Stuff" (Summer), 221
"Hot! Wild! Unrestricted Crazy Love" (Jackson), 109
"Hotel Happiness" (Benton), 16
Houston, Emily "Cissy," 97, 98, 239, 244
Houston, John, 98
Houston, Whitney, 2, 15, 24, 97–99, 123, 147, 177, 246
"How Do You Feel the Morning After" (Jackson), 109
"How Long (Betcha' Got a Chick on the Side)" (Pointer Sisters), 183
"How Many Times Can We Say Goodbye" (Warwick), 245
"How Sweet It Is (To Be Loved by You)" (Walker), 241
"How Will I Know" (Houston), 98
Howard, Camille, 155
Howard, William "Weegee," 65, 66
Hubbard, Jerry, 233
"Hucklebuck" (Milton), 156
Huff, Leon, 11, 33, 34, 59, 61, 100, 101, 111, 167, 168, 174, 176, 180, 190, 208, 232
Hughes, Jimmy, 210
Hughes, Leon, 49
Human Body, Roger and the, 263
"Humpin' Around" (Brown), 24
Humpin' Around (Brown), 24
Hunt, Dennis, 83, 170
Hunt, Tommy, 78
Hunter, Alvin, 9
Hunter, Clifford, 126
Hunter, Ivory Joe, 25, 99–100, 171, 173
"Hunter Gets Captured by the Game, The" (Marvelettes), 144
Hurd, Francine, 173
"Hurry on Down" (Lutcher), 140
"Hurt" (Hamilton), 90

"Hurt So Bad" (Little Anthony), 136
"Hurts So Good" (Jackson), 109
Hurtt, Phil, 211
"Hustle, The" (McCoy), 150
Hutchinson, Jeanette, 70–71
Hutchinson, Joe, Jr., 70, 71
Hutchinson, Pamela, 71
Hutchinson, Sheila, 70–71
Hutchinson Sunbeams, 70
Hutchinson, Wanda, 70–71
Hutson, Marcus, 249

"I Almost Lost My Mind" (Hunter), 100
"I Believe I'm Gonna Make It" (Tex), 228
"I Believe in You (You Believe in Me)" (Taylor), 223
"I Can Make You Dance" (Zapp), 263
"I Can Sing a Rainbow/Love is Blue" (Dells), 61
"I Can't Complain" (Moore), 161
"I Can't Get Next to You" (Temptations), 224
"I Can't Get Over You" (Dramatics), 65
"I Can't Go On Without You" (Jackson), 104
"I Can't Help Myself" (Four Tops), 81
"I Can't Leave Your Love Alone" (Carter), 39
"I Can't Love You Enough" (Baker), 7
"I Can't Say No to You" (Everett), 74
I Can't Stand the Rain (Peebles), 175
"I Can't Stand the Rain" (Peebles), 175
"I Can't Stop Dancing" (Bell), 11
"I Can't Stop Loving You" (Charles), 42
"I Can't Wait" (Williams), 253
"I Challenge Your Kiss" (Orioles), 168
"I Created a Monster" (Hill), 96
"I Cried a Tear" (Baker), 7
"I Didn't Know" (Three Degrees), 232
"I Do" (5 Royales), 75
"I Do" (Moments), 158
"I Do Take You" (Three Degrees), 232
"I Don't Care Who Knows" (Johnson), 116
"I Don't Think That Man Should Sleep Alone" (Parker), 172
"I Don't Wanna Cry" (Carey), 36
"I Don't Want to Lose Your Love" (Emotions), 71
"I Don't Want to Take a Chance" (Wells), 248
"I Feel Good All Over" (Mills), 154
"I Feel Like a Song (In My Heart)" (Knight/Pips), 126
"I Feel So Bad" (Willis), 254
"I Feel for You" (Khan), 122
"I Fooled You This Time" (Chandler), 40
"I Forgot to Be Your Lover" (Bell), 13
"I Get High on You" (Sly/Family Stone), 212
"I Got the Feelin' " (Brown/Famous Flames), 27
"I Got to Tell Somebody" (Everett), 74
"I Got You (I Feel Good)" (Brown/Famous Flames), 27
I Gotcha (Tex), 228
"I Gotcha" (Tex), 228
"I Had It All the Time" (Davis), 56
"I Have Learned to Respect the Power of Love" (Mills), 154
"I Heard It Through the Grapevine" (Gaye), 86
"I Heard It Through the Grapevine" (Knight/Pips), 126
"I Heard It Through the Grapevine" (Zapp), 263
"I Just Called to Say I Love You" (Wonder), 259
"I Just Want to Be" (Cameo), 36
"I Keep on Lovin' You" (Hill), 96
"I Kinda Miss You" (Manhattans), 143
"(I Know) I'm Losing You" (Temptations), 224
"I Know Who Threw the Whiskey in the Well" (Jackson), 104
"I Like It" (DeBarge), 58
"I Like My Baby's Pudding" (Harris), 91

"I Like to Do It" (KC/Sunshine Band), 121
"I Like What You're Doing" (Thomas), 229
"I Live for Your Love" (Cole), 50
"I Love the Music (Part 1)" (O'Jays), 166
"I Love You 1000 Times" (Platters), 181
"I Love You More Than You'll Ever Know" (Hathaway), 93
"I Love You, Yes I Do" Jackson), 104
"I Love You Yes I Do" (Jackson), 104
"I Miss You" (Dells), 61
"I Miss You So" (Little Anthony), 136
"I Need Someone (To Love Me)" (Hill), 96
"I Need You" (Pointer Sisters), 183
"I Need You So" (Hunter), 100
"I Need You, You Need Me" (Simon), 207
"I Need Your Lovin' " (Hamilton), 90
I Never Loved a Man The Way I Loved You (Franklin), 83
"I Never Loved a Man The Way I Loved You" (Franklin), 83
"I Only Have Eyes for You" (Flamingos), 78
"I Only Know" (Washington), 247
"I Pity the Fool" (Peebles), 175
"I Pity The Fool" (Bland), 19
"I Played the Fool" (Clovers), 48
"I Promise to Remember" (Lymon), 141
"I Quit My Pretty Mama" (Hunter), 100
"I Really Don't Need No Light" (Osborne), 170
"I Second That Emotion" (Robinson/Miracles), 196
"I Thank You" (Sam and Dave), 203
"I Waited Too Long" (Baker), 7
"I Wanna Be With You (Part 1)" (Isley Brothers), 102
"I Wanna Do More" (Brown), 30
"I Wanna Get Next to You" (Rose Royce), 197
"I Wanna Know Your Name" (Intruders), 101
"(I Wanna) Testify" (Clinton), 45
"I Want a Bowlegged Woman" (Jackson), 104
"I Want to Be Free" (Ohio Players), 165
"I Want To Be Your Man" (Zapp), 263
"I Want To (Do Everything for You)" (Tex), 228
"I Want to Walk You Home" (Domino), 63
"I Want You Back" (Jackson 5), 111
"I Want You to Be My Girl" (Lymon), 141
"I Want Your Love" (Chic), 44
"I Was Made to Love Her" (Wonder), 259
"I (Who Have Nothing)" (King), 123
"I Will Always Love You" (Houston), 98
"I Wish He Didn't Trust Me So Much" (Womack), 258
"I Wish It Would Rain" (Temptations), 224
"I Wish" (Wonder), 259
"I Wouldn't Treat a Dog (The Way You Treated Me)" (Bland), 19
I Wrote a Simple Song (Preston), 184
Ice Cream Castle (Time), 233
"Ice Cream Castles" (Time), 233
Ice Man Cometh, The (Butler), 34
"I'd Be Satisfied" (Ward), 244
"I'd Rather Be an Old Man's Sweetheart (Than a Young Man's Fool)" (Staton), 218
"If Ever You're in My Arms Again" (Bryson), 31
"If I Can't Have You" (James), 113
"If I Could" (Belle), 14
"If I Could Build My Whole World Around You" (Terrell), 227
"If I Didn't Care" (Moments), 158
"If I Loved You" (Hamilton), 90
"If I Were Your Woman" (Knight/Pips), 126
"If It Isn't Love" (New Edition), 164
"If Only You Knew" (LaBelle), 131
"If Walls Could Talk" (Little Milton), 137
"If You Don't Know Me By Now" (Pendergrass), 177

"If You Need Me" (Burke), 33
"If You Think You're Lonely Now" (Womack), 258
"If You Want Me to Stay" (Sly/Family Stone), 212
"If Your Heart Isn't in It" (Atlantic Starr), 4
"If You're Not Back in Love by Monday" (Jackson), 109
"If You're Ready (Come Go With Me)" (Staple Singers), 215
"Ike's Rap" (Hayes), 94
Ikettes, 237
"I'll Always Have Faith in You" (Thomas), 229
"I'll Always Love My Mama" (Intruders), 101
"I'll Be Around" (Spinners), 214
"I'll Be Good to You" (Charles), 42
"I'll Be Good to You" (Jones), 118
"I'll Be Good to You" (Khan), 122
"I'll Be Home" (Flamingos), 78
"I'll Be There" (Jackson 5), 111
"I'll Be There for You" (Ashford and Simpson), 3
"I'll Be Your Everything" (Sledge), 210
"I'll Bring It Home to You" (Thomas), 229
"I'll Come Running Back to You" (Cooke), 53
"I'll Keep Holding On" (Marvelettes), 144
"I'll Take Care of You" (Bland), 19
"I'll Take You There" (Staple Singers), 215
"I'll Wait for You" (Brown), 30
"(I'm a) Road Runner" (Walker), 241
"I'm Coming Home" (Spinners), 214
"I'm Every Woman" (Khan), 122
"I'm Falling in Love With You" (Little Anthony), 136
"I'm Going Down" (Rose Royce), 197
"I'm Gonna Get Married" (Price), 185
"I'm Gonna Love You Just a Little Bit More Baby" (White), 251
"I'm Gonna Tear Your Playhouse Down" (Peebles), 175
"I'm Just a Prisoner (Of Your Good Lovin')" (Staton), 218
"I'm Just Your Fool" (Johnson), 116
"I'm in Love Again" (Domino), 63
"I'm in Love (And I Love the Feeling)" (Rose Royce), 197
"I'm the Midnight Special" (Carter), 39
"I'm Ready for Love" (Reeves/Vandellas), 193
"I'm So into You" (Bryson), 31
"I'm Sorry" (Diddley), 62
"I'm Still in Love with You" (Green), 89
I'm Still in Love with You (Green), 89
"I'm Stone in Love with You" (Stylistics), 219
"I'm Walkin' " (Domino), 63
I'm Your Baby Tonight (Houston), 98
"I'm Your Baby Tonight" (Houston), 98
"I'm Your Boogie Man" (KC/Sunshine Band), 121
Imagination (Knight/Pips), 126
Imperial Jazz Band, 140
Imperials, Little Anthony and the, 135–37
Impressions, 1, 11, 68, 92, 146
"In the Evening When the Sun Goes Down" (Brown), 26
In Flight (Benson), 15
"In the Ghetto" (Staton), 218
"In the Middle of the Night" (Milburn), 153
"In the Midnight Hour" (Pickett), 179
"In the Mission of St. Augustine" (Orioles), 168
"In the Mix" (Zapp), 263
"In the Mood" (Davis), 56
"In the Name of Love" (Withers), 256
"In and Out of My Life" (Reeves/Vandellas), 193
"In the Rain" (Dramatics), 65
"In the Still of the Night (I'll Remember)" (Boyz II Men), 23
"Information Blues" (Milton), 156
Injoy (Bar-Kays), 10

"Inner City Blues (Make Me Wanna Holler)" (Gaye), 86
"Innocent" (Whispers), 250
"Inseparable" (Cole), 50
"Instant Groove" (Curtis), 125
Intruders, 100–101
"Is It Good to You" (Whispers), 250
"Is It Something You've Got" (Davis), 56
Is It Still Good to Ya (Ashford and Simpson), 3
Isaac Hayes Movement, The (Hayes), 94
Isles, Bill, 166
Isley Brothers, 101–3
Isley, Ernie, 101, 103
Isley, Marvin, 101, 103
Isley, O'Kelley, 101–3
Isley, Ronald, 101–3
Isley, Rudolph, 101–3
"It Ain't No Use" (Hill), 96
"It Feels So Good to Be Loved" (Manhattans), 143
"It Never Rains (In Southern California)" (Tony Toni Toné), 235
"It Seems to Hang On" (Ashford and Simpson), 3
"It Should've Been You" (Pendergrass), 177
"It Tears Me Up" (Sledge), 210
"It's All Right" (Mayfield), 146
"It's All in Your Mind" (Carter), 39
"It's Been a Long Time" (Everett), 74
"It's Been So Long" (Moore), 161
"It's Ecstasy When You Lay Down Next To Me" (White), 251
"(It's Gonna Be a) Lonely Christmas" (Orioles), 168
"It's Gonna Take a Miracle" (Williams), 253
"It's Gonna Work Out Fine" (Turner), 238
"It's Hard to Stop (Doing Something When It's Good to You)" (Wright), 260
"It's Just a Matter of Time" (Benton), 16
"It's a Love Thing" (Whispers), 250
"It's a Man's Man's World" (Brown/Famous Flames), 27
"It's the Same Old Song" (Four Tops), 81
"It's a Shame" (Spinners), 214
"It's So Hard to Say Goodbye" (Boyz II Men), 23
"It's Too Late" (Willis), 254
"It's Too Soon to Know" (Orioles), 168
"It's Too Soon to Know" (Ravens), 189
"It's Too Soon to Know" (Washington), 247
"It's Your Thing" (Isley Brothers), 102
"I've Been Loving You Too Long" (Redding), 192
"I've Got Dreams to Remember" (Redding), 192
"I've Got Love on My Mind" (Cole), 50
"I've Got to Use My Imagination" (Knight/Pips), 126
"I've Never Found a Girl (To Love Me Like You Do)" (Floyd), 79

"Jack and Jill" (Parker), 172
"Jack, You're Dead" (Jordan), 119
Jackson, Al, Jr., 8, 20, 21, 89, 192
Jackson, Bernard, 14
Jackson, Bull Moose, 103–4
Jackson, Charles, 34, 50, 61
Jackson, Doris Kenner, 205–7
Jackson, Freddie, 104–5, 161
Jackson, George, 95
Jackson, Janet Dameta, 58, 105–7, 110, 111
Jackson, Jermaine La Jaune, 56, 98, 110, 111, 154, 260
Jackson, Jesse, 93, 220
Jackson, Joseph, 105, 106, 107, 110
Jackson, La Toya Yvonne, 110, 111
Jackson, Little Willie, 135
Jackson, Mahalia, 5, 30, 70, 175, 184
Jackson, Marlon David, 110, 111
Jackson, Maureen Reilette "Rebbie," 110, 111
Jackson, Michael Joseph, 107–8, 110, 111, 117–18, 122, 163

Jackson, Millie, 108–10
Jackson, Pervis, 213
Jackson, Ray, 256
Jackson, Roosevelt, 61
Jackson, Sigmund Esco "Jackie," 110, 111
Jackson, Steven Randall "Randy," 110, 111
Jackson, Toriano Adaryal "Tito," 110
Jackson, Wayne, 54
Jackson 5, 105, 107, 110, 111
Jacksons, 110–11
Jacobs, Adolph, 49
Jacquet, Illinois, 91, 99, 170, 240
Jades, 194
Jagger, Mick, 32, 44, 62, 227
Jam, Jimmy. *See* Harris, James
"Jam, The" (Graham/Central Station), 87
"Jam Tonight" (Jackson), 105
Jamerson, James, 44, 241
James, Etta, 7, 18, 38, 68, 111–13, 170, 199
James, Linda, 251
James, Rick, 113–14
Jancik, Wayne, 256
janet. (Jackson), 106
Janet Jackson's Rhythm Nation (Jackson), 106
Jasper, Chris, 101, 103
Jasper, Vernon, 101
"Jealous" (Hunter), 100
Jefferson, Joe, 180
Jeffries, Otto, 75
Jenkins, Johnny, 191
Jenkins, Milton, 199, 224
Jenkins, Tomi, 35, 36
"Jenny, Jenny" (Little Richard), 138
"Jerk Out" (Time), 233
Jerusalem Stars, 16
Jessie Johnson Revue, 234
Jessie, Obie, 49
Jeter, Claude, 59, 88
Jewel, Bishop M. L., 217
Jewel Gospel Trio, 217
Jewels, 198
"Jim Dandy" (Baker), 7
"Jim Dandy Got Married" (Baker), 7
"Jimmy Mack" (Reeves/Vandellas), 193
"Jive Turkey (Part 1)" (Ohio Players), 165
"Joanna" (Kool and the Gang), 128
Jobe, Lequeint "Duke," 197
"Jody's Got Your Girl and Gone" (Taylor), 223
John, Little Willie, 18, 114–15, 170
John, Mabel, 94, 115, 190, 199
"Johnny B. Goode" (Berry), 18
Johnny and Jackey, 240
Johnson, Billy, 159
Johnson, Billy "Shoes," 148–49
Johnson, Buddy, 116–17, 140
Johnson, Clarence, 42
Johnson, Cornelius, 165
Johnson, David, 211
Johnson, Dwight, 176
Johnson, Ella, 116, 117
Johnson, Gregory, 35, 36
Johnson, J. Rosamond, 161
Johnson, James Ambrose, Jr., 113
Johnson, James Weldon, 161
Johnson, Jellybean, 107, 233
Johnson, Jesse, 233, 234
Johnson, Jimmy, 82, 210
Johnson, Johnnie, 17
Johnson, Keg, 133
Johnson, Mabel Gladden, 113
Johnson, Merline, 6
Johnson, Pete, 235–36
Johnson, Ricky, 58
Johnson, Robert, 120
Johnson, Terry, 78
Jolson, Al, 168, 255
Jones, Allen, 10
Jones, Bill, 132
Jones, Booker T., 8, 9, 12, 13, 20–21, 79, 94, 192, 229, 256
Jones, Craig, 66
Jones, Creadel "Red," 42
Jones, Ester Mae, 177

Jones, Johnny, 13
Jones, Marshall, 165
Jones, Maxine, 71, 73
Jones, Ollie, 188
Jones, Paul Laurence, III, 104, 105, 154, 161
Jones, Phalon, 9
Jones, Quincy, 2, 15, 42, 58, 82, 107, 108, 117–18, 122, 221
Jones, Ruth Lee, 246
Jones, Shirley, 39
Jones, Will "Dub," 49
Jordan, Leroy "Lonnie," 241–43
Jordan, Louis, 17, 26, 117, 118–20, 125, 135, 140, 152, 155
Joseph, Quinton, 43
Josephson, Barney, 236
"Joy" (Pendergrass), 177
"Joy—Part 1" (Hayes), 94
Jr. Walker and the All Stars, 160, 240–41
"Juanita" (Willis), 254
"Jump (For My Love)" (Pointer Sisters), 183
"Jump Start" (Cole), 50
"Jump to It" (Franklin), 83
Jumping Jacks, 240
"Jungle Love" (Time), 233
Junior, Marvin, 59, 60
"Just A Little Bit" (Little Milton), 137
"Just Be My Lady" (Graham), 87
"Just Because" (Baker), 5
"Just Because" (Price), 185
"Just Coolin' " (LeVert/Heavy D.), 134
"Just My Imagination (Running Away with Me)" (Temptations), 224
"Just Out of Reach (Of My Two Open Arms)" (Burke), 33
"Just to Be Close to You" (Richie/Commodores), 195
"Just to Hold My Hand" (McPhatter), 151
"Just to See Her" (Robinson), 196
"Just the Two of Us" (Withers), 256
Justin, Sidney, 205

Kane, Big Daddy, 251
Kapralik, David, 173
KC and the Sunshine Band, 120–21
KC and the Sunshine Band (KC/Sunshine Band), 121
Keeler, Ruby, 78
Keene, Bob, 251
"Keep It Comin' Love" (KC/Sunshine Band), 121
"Keep a Knockin' " (Little Richard), 138
"Keep on Lovin' Me" (Whispers), 250
"Keep on Lovin' Me Honey" (Terrell), 227
Keep on Pushing (Mayfield), 146
Kelly, Kenneth, 143
Kelp, Larry, 149, 160
Kendricks, Eddie, 199, 223–25
Kendricks, Kevin, 36
Kennedy, Hershall, 87
Kent, Bob, 125
Kerr, George, 167
Kershaw, Doug, 63
Kessler, Danny, 254
Keyes, Bert, 157
Khan, Chaka, 2, 4, 42, 98, 117, 118, 121–23
"Kiddio" (Benton), 16
Kids & Me, The (Preston), 184
Killen, Buddy, 227, 228
Killing Me Softly (Flack), 77
"Killing Me Softly with His Song" (Flack), 77
King & Queen (Thomas), 229
King, Albert, 9, 20, 175
King, B.B., 1, 18, 19, 28, 54, 99, 118, 137, 147
King, Ben E., 67, 76, 123–24, 126, 151
King, Betty, 194
King, Carole, 38, 74, 206
King Curtis, 124–26
King Curtis Plays the Great Memphis Hits (Curtis), 125
King, Don, 186

King, Ian, 96
King, Maurice, 6, 126
King, William, 194
Kings of Rhythm, 237
"Kiss from Your Lips, A" (Flamingos), 78
"Kiss" (Prince/Revolution), 187
"Kiss and a Rose, A" (Orioles), 168
"Kiss and Say Goodbye" (Manhattans), 143
"Kissing My Love" (Withers), 256
Kitchings, Grant, 68
Knight, Brenda, 126
Knight, Gladys, 2, 5, 7, 109, 110, 126–28, 147, 150, 241
Knight, Jean, 132, 183
Knight, Jerry, 172
Knight, Merald "Bubba," 126
"Knock on Wood" (Floyd), 79
"Knock on Wood" (Redding), 192
"Knock on Wood" (Thomas), 229
Kool and the Gang, 128–29
Krefetz, Lou, 47

"L-O-V-E (Love)" (Green), 89
"La-La-Means I Love You" (Delfonics), 59
"L.A. Sunshine" (War), 242
LaBelle, Patti, 130–31, 162, 258
Lady In the Street, A (LaSalle), 132
"Ladies Night" (Kool and the Gang), 128
"Lady" (Whispers), 250
"Lady Luck" (Price), 185
"Lady Marmalade" (LaBelle), 131
La'Face, 23, 24
Lambert, Dennis, 50, 81, 195
Lamont, Joe, 244
"Land of 1,000 Dances" (Pickett), 179
Langford, Bill, 16
Langfordaires, 16
LaPread, Ronald, 194
LaSalle, Denise, 108, 131–32
"Last Dance" (Summer), 221
"Last Time I Made Love, The" (Osborne), 170
Lauderdale, Jack, 41
"Laughing Boy" (Wells), 248
Laurence Jones Ensemble, 104
Laurie, Annie, 116
LaVaille, Martha, 193
"Lawdy Miss Clawdy" (Price), 185
Lawrence, Rhett, 37
"Le Freak" (Chic), 44
Leake, Butch, 68
"Lean on Me" (Withers), 256
Lear, Norman, 30–31, 105
Leavill, Otis, 43
LeBow, Carl, 75
Lee, Beverly, 205, 207
Lees, Gene, 142
"Left a Good Deal in Mobile" (Liggins), 135
Leftenant, Arnett, 35
Leftenant, Nathan, 35, 36
Leiber, Jerry, 7, 30, 48, 49, 67, 90, 123, 124, 150
Lennon, John, 1, 65, 96, 108, 124, 125, 175–76
Lennox, Annie, 89
Leonard, Glenn, 225
Leonard, Harlan, 171
Lester, Bobby, 158–60
Lester, Robert "Squirrel," 42
"Let the Feeling Flow" (Bryson), 31
"Let the Four Winds Blow" (Brown), 29
"Let It Be Me" (Everett/Butler), 74
"Let Me Be Good to You" (Rawls), 190
"Let Me Be Good to You" (Thomas), 229
"Let Me Be Your Lovemaker" (Wright), 260
"Let Me Go" (Parker), 172
"Let Me Go Home Whiskey" (Milburn), 153
"Let Me into Love" (Baker), 5
"Let Them Talk" (John), 115
"Let's Beat Out Some Love" (Johnson), 116
"Let's Do It Again" (Staple Singers), 215
Let's Do It Again (Staple Singers), 215

Let's Fall in Love (Peaches and Herb), 174
"Let's Get It On" (Gaye), 86
Let's Get It On (Gaye), 86
"Let's Get Together" (Little Milton), 137
"Let's Go Crazy" (Prince/Revolution), 187
"Let's Go Get Stoned" (Charles), 42
"Let's Go, Let's Go, Let's Go" (Ballard), 8
"Let's Groove" (Earth, Wind and Fire), 69
"Let's Groove (Part 1)" (Bell), 11
"Let's Hear It for the Boy" (Williams), 253
"Let's Make Christmas Merry, Baby"
   (Milburn), 153
Let's Put It All Together (Stylistics), 219
"Let's Rock a While" (Milburn), 153
"Let's Stay Together" (Green), 89
"Let's Stay Together" (Turner), 238
"Let's Wait Awhile" (Jackson), 106
"Letter from My Darling" (John), 115
"Letter to Myself, A" (Chi-Lites), 43
LeVert, 132–34, 166
Levert, Eddie, 132, 133, 166
Levert, Gerald, 132 132–34, 168
Levert, Sean, 132
Levine, Ian, 145
Levy, Morris, 142, 186
Levy, Ron, 176
Lewis, Barbara, 59, 150
Lewis, David, 3–4
Lewis, Earl, 77
Lewis, Huey, 171
Lewis, Jonathan, 3–4
Lewis, Ramsey, 68, 69
Lewis, Rudy, 67, 68
Lewis, Terry, 106, 107, 164, 233
Lewis, Wayne, 3–4
"Lies" (En Vogue), 73
"Lift Every Voice and Sing" (Moore), 161
Liggins, Joe, 134–35
Light, Alan, 22
Limbo, Sonny, 248
Lindsey, Wayne "Ziggy," 148
LiPuma, Tommy, 15
Listen My Brother, 239
Little Angels, 221
Little Anthony and the Imperials, 135–37,
   164
"Little Bit of Love, A (Is All It Takes)"
   (New Edition), 164
"Little Bit More, A" (Moore), 161
"Little Egypt (Ying-Yang)" (Coasters), 49
"Little Girl, Don't Cry" (Jackson), 104
"Little Joe's Boogie" (Liggins), 135
Little Milton, 54, 115, 137–38, 237, 254
Little Miss Cornshucks, 6, 156, 177
Little Richard, 32, 47, 108, 118, 138–40,
   170, 184, 190, 191
Little Sister, 212
"Little Walter" (Tony Toni Toné), 235
Littlefield, Little Willie, 62, 156, 178
Live at the Apollo (Brown), 27
Live at Fillmore West (Curtis), 125
Live and More (Summer), 221
Livin' Inside Your Love (Benson), 15
"Livin' for the Weekend" (O'Jays), 166
"Livin' for You" (Green), 89
"Livin' for Your Love" (Moore), 161
Locket, Mark, 192
Lockett, Anthony, 36
Loder, Kurt, 238
Logan, Harold, 186
Lomax, Alan, 99
Lomax, Michele, 19
Lomello, John, 202
Lonely Man, A (Chi-Lites), 43
"Lonely Teardrops" (Wilson), 255
"Long About Midnight" (Brown), 29
"Long Lonely Nights" (McPhatter), 151
"Long Tall Sally" (Little Richard), 138
"Look at Me (I'm in Love)" (Moments),
   158
"Look What You Done for Me" (Green),
   89
"Look-Ka Py Py" (Neville), 163
"Lookin' for a Love" (Womack), 258
"Loosey's Rap" (James/Shante), 114
"Lost Love" (Mayfield), 148

Lou Rawls Live! (Rawls), 190
Love, Airrion, 219
Love, Andrew, 54
"Love" (Graham/Central Station), 87
"Love Ballad" (Osborne), 170
"Love Bug Leave My Heart Alone"
   (Reeves/Vandellas), 193
Love Deluxe (Sade), 202
"Love Doesn't Make It Right" (Ashford and
   Simpson), 3
"Love Don't Live Here Anymore" (Rose
   Royce), 197
"Love Don't Love Nobody" (Brown), 29
"Love Hangover" (Ross), 199
"Love Has Finally Come at Last" (LaBelle),
   131
"Love Has Finally Come at Last"
   (Womack), 258
"Love Has Joined Us Together"
   (McPhatter), 151
"Love Is Better in the A.M." (Taylor), 223
"Love Is in Control (Finger on the Trigger)"
   (Summer), 221
"Love Is a Dangerous Game" (Jackson),
   109
"Love Is a Doggone Good Thing" (Floyd),
   79
"Love Is Here and Now You're Gone"
   (Ross/Supremes), 199
"Love Is a Hurtin' Thing" (Rawls), 189
"Love Is the Key" (Maze), 149
"(Love Is Like a) Baseball Game"
   (Intruders), 101
"(Love Is Like a) Heat Wave"
   (Reeves/Vandellas), 193
"Love Is So Good When You're Stealing It"
   (Hill), 96
"Love Is Strange" (Peaches and Herb), 174
"Love I Lost, The (Part 1)" (Pendergrass),
   177
"Love, Love, Love" (Hathaway), 93
"Love (Makes Me Do Foolish Things)"
   (Reeves/Vandellas), 193
"Love Me Down" (Jackson), 105
"Love Me Right" (LaSalle), 132
"Love Me Tender" (Sledge), 210
Love Men Ltd., 169
"Love the One I'm With (A Lot of Love)"
   (Moore), 161
"Love the One You're With" (Isley
   Brothers), 102
"Love Overboard" (Knight/Pips), 126
"Love Power" (Warwick), 245
"Love Rollercoaster" (Ohio Players), 165
Love Somebody Today (Sister Sledge), 207
"Love Takes Time" (Carey), 36
"Love T.K.O." (Pendergrass), 177
"Love to Love You Baby" (Summer), 221
"Love Train" (O'Jays), 166
"Love on a Two-Way Street" (Moments),
   158
"Love We Had, The (Stays on My Mind)
   (Dells), 61
"Love You Save, The" (Jackson 5), 111
"Love You Save, The (May Be Your Own)"
   (Tex), 228
"Lovely Day" (Withers), 256
"Lovers Never Say Goodbye" (Flamingos),
   78
"Lover's Question, A" (McPhatter), 151
"Love's Comin' at Ya" (Moore), 161
"Love's Street and Fool's Road" (Burke), 33
Loveshine (Con Funk Shun), 51
Lovett, Leroy, 100
Lovett, Winfred "Blue," 143
"Lovey Dovey" (Clovers), 48
"Lovin' on Borrowed Time" (Bell), 13
"Lovin' Machine" (Harris), 91
"Low Rider" (War), 242
Lowe, James, 39
Lowry, Bill, 38
Lowry, Ronald "Roame," 148, 149
L.T.D., 169
Lucas, Bob, 228
Lucas, Harold, 47, 48
Lucas, Reggie, 77

Lucas, Reginald, 154
"Lucille" (Little Richard), 138
Lumet, Sidney, 107, 117
Lunceford, Jimmie, 135
Lutcher, Nellie, 140–41
Luther, 239–40
Lymon, Frankie, and the Teenagers, 141–42
Lymon, Howie, 141
Lymon, Louis, 141
Lynch, David, 180
Lynn, Cheryl, 172

"MacArthur Park" (Summer), 221
McCall, Louis, 51
McCann, Les, 76, 190
McCartney, Paul, 107, 108, 162
McCary, Michael "Bass," 21, 22
McClary, Thomas, 194, 195
McCoy, Norman, 150
McCoy, Van, 127, 150–51, 160–61, 173,
   174, 220
McCracklin, Jimmy, 156, 192
McCrae, George, 120
McCrae, Gwen, 120
McDaniels, Eugene, 77
McDermott, Galt, 160
McDonald, Ralph, 76, 257
McDuff, Jack, 14–15
McElroy, Sollie, 77
McElroy, Thomas, 71, 73, 235
McFadden, Gene, 105, 161
McGee, David, 239
McGee, Gosady, 41
McGill, Lucius, 60
McGill, Michael, 59, 60
McJohn, Goldy, 114
Mack, Lonnie, 165
Mack, Marlene, 174
McKay, Al, 68
McKenny, Stan, 43
McKinney, Walter, 198
McKinnon, Pearl, 142
McLean, Ernest, 63, 185
McNeely, Big Jay, 177
McNeil, David, 244
McPhatter, Clyde, 7–8, 16, 67, 124, 136,
   151–52, 173, 244, 254, 255
McQuater, Matthew, 47
McSon Trio, 41
Maiden, Tony, 122
Majestics, 202
"Make It Like It Was" (Belle), 14
"Make That Move" (Shalamar), 205
"Make Your Love to Your Mind"
   (Withers), 256
"(Mama) He Treats Your Daughter Mean"
   (Brown), 30
"Mama Said" (Shirelles), 206
"Mambo Boogie" (Otis), 171
"Man Sized Job" (LaSalle), 132
Manchester, Melissa, 32
Mandaro, Bob, 79
Manhattan, 14
Manhattans, 13, 143–44
Manhattans, The (Manhattans), 143
Manilow, Barry, 246
Manuel, Bobby, 21
Mar-Keys, 9, 20
Mardin, Arif, 17, 122, 239
Margouleff, Robert, 259
Margulies, Ben, 36
Mariah Carey (Carey), 38
Marie, Teena, 114
Marks, Rose, 243, 244
Marquees, 85, 160
"Married, But Not to Each Other"
   (LaSalle), 132
Marsh, Dave, 48
Marshall, Maithe, 188–89
Martha and the Vandellas, 192–94
Martin, Barbara, 199
Martin, Bobby, 144, 169, 176
Martin, Cedric, 51
Martin, Porscha, 3, 4
Martinelli, Nick, 14, 154
Martini, Jerry, 212

Marvelettes, 144–45, 150, 196
"Mary Jane" (James), 114
Mary Jane Girls, 114
Mascots, 166
Masser, Michael, 15, 50, 98
Massey, Bobby, 166, 167
"Master Blaster (Jammin')" (Wonder), 259
"Masterpiece" (Atlantic Starr), 4
"Masterpiece" (Temptations), 224
Matadors, 195, 196
Mathis, Johnny, 117, 160, 253
Matthewman, Stuart, 201
Matthews, Ricky James, 113
Mattis, David James, 1, 19
Maxwell, Larry, 124
"Maybe" (Three Degrees), 232
"Maybelline" (Berry), 18
Mayes, Lenny, 66
Mayfield, Curtis, 33–34, 40, 82, 92, 93,
   127, 145–46, 147, 193, 216, 257
Mayfield, Percy, 42, 147–48
Maze featuring Frankie Beverly, 148–50
"Me and Mrs. Jones" (Dramatics), 65
Melionaires, 202
"Mellow Madness" (Jones), 118
Melody Masters, 222
"Melting Pot" (Booker T), 21
Melvin, Harold, 176
Memphis Horns, 9, 54, 174
"Memphis Soul Stew" (Curtis), 125
"Men Are Gettin' Scarce" (Tex), 228
Mendes, Damon, 36
Merchant, Jimmy, 141
"Mercy Mercy Me" (Gaye), 86
Merle, Milton, 244
"Merry Christmas Baby" (Brown), 26
Mesner, Eddie, 152
"Message From the Meters, A" (Neville),
   163
"Message in Our Music" (O'Jays), 166
"Message to Michael" (Warwick), 245
Meters, 65, 162
MG's (Booker T. and the), 20–21
Michael, George, 83
Mickens, Robert, 128
Middlebrook, Ralph "Pee Wee," 165
"Midnight Train to Georgia" (Knight/Pips),
   126
"Midnight and You" (Burke), 33
Midnighters (Hand Ballard and the), 8, 26,
   48, 75, 115
"Mighty Love—Part 1" (Spinners), 214
Milburn, Amos, 25, 62, 125, 152–53
Miles, Otis, 224
Millar, Robin, 201, 202
Miller, Abraham Joseph "Onion," 169
Miller, Bobby, 60
Miller, Charles William, 241, 242
Miller, Gene "Bowlegs," 12, 132, 174
Miller, Jimmie "J. D.," 169
Miller, Marcus, 77
Miller, Mitch, 150
Miller, Roger, 228
Millinder, Lucky, 29, 91, 103
Mills, Aaron, 36
Mills, Cassandra, 154
Mills, Stephanie, 2, 134, 153–55, 161, 204
Milton, Roy, 135, 155–56, 171
"Milton's Boogie" (Milton), 156
"Mio Amore" (Flamingos), 78
Miracles, 195–97
"Miss You Like Crazy" (Cole), 50
"Miss You Much" (Jackson), 106
"Mistreatin' Blues" (Otis), 171
"Mistrustin' Blues" (Phillips), 178
Mitchell, Billy, 48
Mitchell, Joni, 123, 186
Mitchell, Paul, 13
Mitchell, Phillip, 109
Mitchell, Willie, 12, 19, 21, 29, 74, 88, 89,
   97, 132, 174, 175
Mizell, Fonze, 111
Modeliste, Joseph "Zigaboo," 162
*Modern Sounds in Country and Western
   Music* (Charles), 42
Moir, Monte, 233

Moman, Chips, 12, 90, 94, 180, 228, 229, 258
Moments, 156–58
Monaco, Bob, 121
Monarchs, 219
"Money Honey" (McPhatter/Drifters), 67
Montague, Magnificent, 242
Montana, Vince, 58, 100
Montgomery, Tammi, 225
Montgomery, Wes, 15
"Moody Woman" (Butler), 34
Moon Band, 31
Moonglows, 85, 158–60, 62, 147, 214
Moore, Felicia, 120
Moore, Jackie, 13
Moore, Jimmy, 75
Moore, Johnny (Drifters), 67–68
Moore, Johnny (Three Blazers), 1, 25, 41, 99, 170
Moore, Melba, 105, 160–61
Moore, Michael, 197
Moore, Oscar, 25, 41
Moore, Sam, 94, 126, 202–3, 241
Moore, Stephen, 36
Moore, Warren "Pete," 195–96
Moore, Dr. Wild Willie, 156
"More Bounce to the Ounce Part 1" (Zapp), 263
Morgan, John, 157
Moroder, Giorgio, 220, 221, 222
Morris, Nathan "Alex Vanderpool," 21, 22
Morris, Steveland, 258
Morris, Wanya "Squirt," 21, 22
Morrison, Walton "Junie," 165
Moses, Larry, 259
Most, Mickie, 96
"Most of All" (Moonglows), 159
"Mother Popcorn (You Got to Have a Mother for Me)" (Brown), 27
Mothership Connection (Clinton), 45
"Motownhill" (Boyz II Men), 23
Mottola, Tommy, 37
Mount Lebanon Singers, 67
"Move Your Boogie" (Bar-Kays), 10
Moy, Sylvia, 259
"Mr. Telephone Man" (New Edition), 164
Mtume, James, 77, 154
MTV Unplugged (Carey), 36
Muhammad, Elijah, 228
Muldrow, Gail, 88
Mumford, Eugene, 244
Mumford, Gary, 203, 204
Murdock, Shirley, 263
Murphy, Frederick Douglas, 49, 86, 108, 176
Murphy, Kevin, 121
Murrell, Herb, 219
Music Box (Carey), 36
Music Is My Life (Preston), 184
"My Baby Loves Me" (Reeves/Vandellas), 193
"My Baby Must Be a Magician" (Marvelettes), 144
"My Dearest Darling" (James), 113
"My First Love" (Atlantic Starr), 4
"My Forever" (LeVert), 134
"My Gal's A Jockey" (Turner), 236
"My Girl" (Temptations), 224
"My Guy" (Sister Sledge), 207
My Jug and I (Mayfield), 148
"My Lovin' (You're Never Gonna Get It)" (En Vogue), 73
"My Man, A Sweet Man" (Jackson), 109
"My Prayer" (Platters), 181
"My Prerogative" (Brown), 24
"My Song" (Ace), 1
"My Story" (Willis), 254
"My Sweet Potato" (Booker T), 21
Mynah Birds, 113, 114
Myrick, Don, 68
Mystic Merlin, 104, 105
Mystics, 194

"Nasty" (Jackson), 106
Nathan, Syd, 29, 103, 104, 115
"Natural Man, A" (Rawls), 190

"Need Your Love So Bad" (John), 115
Negroni, Joe, 141
"Neither One of Us (Wants to be the First to Say Goodbye)" (Knight/Pips), 126
Nelson, Benjamin Earl, 123
Nelson, Billy, 45
Nelson, Earl, 251
Nelson, George, 168
Nelson, John, 186
Nelson, Nate, 77, 78, 180
Nelson, Prince Roger, 186
Nelson, Walter "Papoose," 63
Nelson, Willie, 21
"Neutron Dance" (Pointer Sisters), 183
"Never As Good As the First Time" (Sade), 202
"Never Can Say Goodbye" (Hayes), 94
"Never Can Say Goodbye" (Jackson 5), 111
"Never Give Up" (Butler), 34
"Never Let Me Go" (Ace), 1
Never Let Me Go (Vandross), 240
"Never Like This Before" (Bell), 13
"Never, Never Gonna Give Ya Up" (White), 251
"Never Say Never" (Williams), 253
"Never Too Much" (Vandross), 240
Neville, Aaron, 161–63
Neville, Art, 161–63
Neville, Charles, 161–63
Neville, Cyril, 161–63
Neville Brothers, 161–63
"New Attitude" (LaBelle), 131
New Edition, 23, 136, 163–65, 173
New Edition (New Edition), 164
New Kids on the Block, 163
"New Orleans Blues" (Brown), 26
"New Orleans" (Staple Singers), 215
Newman, David "Fathead," 41, 190
"Next Time You'll Know" (Sister Sledge), 207
Nicholas, Denise, 256
Nichols, J. D., 195
Nicks, Billy "Sticks," 240
Niecy (Williams), 253
"Night to Remember, A" (Shalamar), 205
"Night" (Wilson), 255
Nightbirds (LaBelle), 131
Nightshift, 242
Nix, Victor, 197
"No One in the World" (Baker), 5
"No Ordinary Love" (Sade), 202
"No Pain, No Gain" (Wright), 260
"Nobody Loves Me Like You" (Flamingos), 78
"Nobody Wants You When You're Down and Out" (Womack), 258
Nocentelli, Leo, 162
Nooks, Ronald, 166
Norman, Gene, 49
North, Alex, 90
Northern Jubilee Gospel Singers, 33
"(Not Just) Knee Deep" (Clinton), 45
"Not on the Outside" (Moments), 158
"Nothing Can Change This Love" (Cooke), 53
"Nothing Can Come Between Us" (Sade)., 202
"Nothing Can Stop Me" (Chandler), 40
"Nothing from Nothing" (Preston), 184
"Now Do-U-Wanta Dance" (Graham/Central Station), 87
"Now Run and Tell That" (LaSalle), 132
"Nowhere to Run" (Reeves/Vandellas), 193
Nunn, Bobby, 48, 177

"Oasis" (Flack), 77
"Ode to Billie Joe" (Curtis), 125
Off the Wall (Jackson), 108
"Oh Babe" (Milton), 156
"Oh Baby" (Diddley), 62
"Oh Girl" (Chi-Lites), 43
"Oh La De Da" (Staple Singers), 215
"Oh What A Dream" (Brown), 30
"Oh What a Nite" (Dells), 61
"Oh, What a Night" (Dells), 61

Ohio Players, 165–66
Ohio Untouchables, 165
O'Jay, Eddie, 166
O'Jays, 22, 35, 100, 133, 134, 136, 166–68
"Old Man River" (Ravens), 189
Oldham, Spooner, 82
Olive, Patrick, 96, 97
Oliver, Rachel, 3, 4
Olson, Dave, 54
Omartian, Michael, 221
"On Broadway" (Benson), 15
"On My Own" (LaBelle/McDonald), 131
"On Our Own" (Brown), 24
On the Radio/Greatest Hits Volumes I and II (Summer), 221
"On a Saturday Night" (Floyd), 79
"Once You Hit the Road" (Warwick), 245
"One Chain Don't Make No Prison" (Four Tops), 81
"One Hundred Ways" (Jones), 118
"One of a Kind (Love Affair)" (Spinners), 214
"One Kiss Led to Another" (Coasters), 49
"One Life to Live" (Manhattans), 143
"One in a Million You" (Graham), 87
One in a Million You (Graham), 87
"One Mint Julep" (Charles), 42
"One Mint Julep" (Clovers), 48
"One Nation Under A Groove—Part 1" (Clinton), 45
One Nation Under a Groove (Clinton), 45
"One Night Affair" (Butler), 34
"One Scotch, One Bourbon, One Beer" (Milburn), 153
"One Who Really Loves You, The" (Wells), 248
"Onion Song, The" (Terrell), 227
"Only Human" (Osborne), 170
"Only the Strong Survive" (Butler), 34
"Only You (And You Alone)" (Platters), 181
"Ooh Boy" (Rose Royce), 197
"Oooh, Oooh, Oooh" (Price), 185
"Open Your Heart" (Dells), 61
Orange, Walter "Clyde," 194, 195
Orioles, 168–69, 188
Orphonics, 58
Osborne, Cal, 224
Osborne, Clarence "Legs," 169
Osborne, Jeffrey, 92, 161, 169–70
Oskar, Lee, 241, 243
Other Woman, The (Parker), 172
"Other Woman, The" (Parker), 172
Otis, Clyde, 15, 16, 17, 50, 152, 247
Otis, Johnny, 1, 7, 25, 29, 48, 62, 91, 100, 112, 115, 126, 139, 153, 156, 170–71, 177, 178
Otis, Shuggie, 171
"Our Love" (Cole), 50
Ousley, Curtis, 124
"Out in the Cold Again" (Lymon), 141
"Out of Left Field" (Sledge), 210
"Out of Sight, Out of Mind" (Little Anthony), 136
"Outa-Space" (Preston), 184
"Outstanding" (Gap Band), 84
"Outta the World" (Ashford and Simpson), 3
"Over You" (Neville), 163
Owens, Kevin Ray, 158

Page, Gene, 172, 251, 252
"Pain" (Starr), 216
Palmer, Bruce, 114
Palmer, Earl, 63
Pandemonium (Time), 233
"Papa Got a Brand New Bag" (Brown/Famous Flames), 27
"Paradise" (Sade), 202
Parker, Little Junior, 1, 19, 237
Parker, Ray, Jr., 164, 171–73
Parks, Lloyd, 176
Parliaments, 45, 47, 65, 263
Parnell, Willie, 10
"Part-Time Lover" (Wonder), 259
Part 3 (KC/Sunshine Band), 121

Part Time Love (Peebles), 175
"Part Time Love" (Peebles), 175
"Party" (McCoy), 150
"Party Train" (Gap Band), 84
Patten, Edward, 126
Patterson, Lover, 123
Paul, Clarence. See Pauling, Clarence
Pauling, Clarence, 75, 259
Pauling, Curtis, 75
Pauling, Lowman, Jr., 75, 76
Payne, Freda, 176
Payton, Lawrence, 80
Peaches and Herb, 150, 173–74
Peay, Benjamin Franklin, 15–16
"Pedal Pushin' Papa" (Ward), 244
Peebles, Ann, 174–76
Pendergrass, Teddy, 55, 98, 154, 176–77
Penguins, 180, 188
Peniger, Eddie "Sugarman," 6
Penniman, Richard Wayne, 138
"People Get Ready" (Mayfield), 146
"People Make the World Go Round" (Stylistics), 219
Percussions, 219
Peretti, Hugo, 53, 101, 150, 219
Perren, Freddie, 22, 111, 173, 174, 222
Perry, Richard, 57, 63, 181, 183, 194
"Personality" (Price), 185
Peterson, Paul, 233
Phillips, Arthur, 65
Phillips, Esther, 15, 48, 125, 141, 147, 170, 171, 177–78, 189
Phillips, Joseph, 3, 4
Phillips, Sam, 19, 137, 231
Pick of the Litter (Spinners), 214
"Pick Up the Pieces" (Thomas), 229
Pickett, Wilson, 20, 79, 98, 125, 178–80, 186
Pierce, Marvin, 165
Pilate, Felton II, 50–52
Pilgrim Travelers, 18, 53, 189
Pimettes, 224
Pinetoppers, 191
"Pink Champagne" (Liggins), 135
Pinkney, Bill, 67
Pinkney, Fayette, 232, 233
Pips, Gladys Knight and the, 2, 7, 126–28, 146, 150
Pitts, Leonard, Jr., 113
Plant, Robert, 44, 134
Platters, 180–81
Platters, The (Platters), 181
"Play It Fair" (Baker), 7
"Playboy" (Marvelettes), 144
"Playful Baby" (Harris), 91
"Please Don't Go" (Boyz II Men), 23
"Please Forgive Me" (Ace), 1
"Please Mr. Postman" (Marvelettes), 144
"Please Send Me Someone to Love" (Mayfield), 148
"Please Send Me Someone to Love" (Moonglows), 159
"Pledging My Love" (Ace), 1
Poet, The (Womack), 258
Pointer, Anita, 181–83
Pointer, Bonnie, 181–83
Pointer, June, 181–83
Pointer, Ruth, 181–83
Pointer Sisters, 181–83
"Poison Ivy" (Coasters), 49
Pollock, Bruce, 206
"Poor Fool" (Turner), 238
"Poor Me" (Domino), 63
"(Pop, Pop, Pop) Goes My Mind" (LeVert), 134
Porter, Arthur, 8
Porter, Brian, 81
Porter, David, 71, 94, 229
Porter, George, 162
Porter, Sam, 148
Porter, Shirley, 232
Poulson-Bryant, Scott, 24
Powell, Dick, 78
Powell, Michael J., 6, 14
Powell, Ric, 92
Powell, William, 166, 167

"Power of Love" (Simon), 207
Power of Love (Vandross), 240
"Power of Love/Love Power" (Vandross), 240
Power Station, 44
Prater, David, 94, 202–3
"Prayin' for Your Return" (Mayfield), 148
Premiers, 141
Presley, Elvis, 17, 22, 28, 47, 62, 90, 99, 169, 190, 218, 235, 254
Preston, Billy, 53, 83, 140, 183–85
Preston, Rodena, 185
"Pretty Mama" (Hunter), 100
"Pretty Thing" (Diddley), 62
Price, Lloyd, 49, 179, 185–86
Pride, 201
"Pride, The (Part 1)" (Isley Brothers), 102
Primes, 199, 224
Primettes, 79, 199
Prince, 10, 123, 154, 186–88, 233, 234
Prince Rogers Trio, 186
Private Dancer (Turner), 238
"Private Dancer" (Turner), 238
"Private Number" (Bell), 13
Promise (Sade), 202
"Proud Mary" (Burke), 33
Provost, Joe, 148
Prutor, Robert, 254
Prysock, Arthur, 116, 207, 227
"Pull Over" (LeVert), 134
Purdie, Bernard, 126, 232
Purple Rain (Prince/Revolution), 187
"Put Me in Your Mix" (White), 251
Puzey, Leonard, 188

Rabb, Luther, 243
Raeletts, 42, 115, 254
"Rag Mop" (Liggins), 135
Rags to Rufus (Khan), 122
"Rainbow" (Chandler), 40
"Rainbow '65 (Part 1)" (Chandler), 40
Rainbows, 85
"Rainy Night in Georgia" (Benton), 16
"Rainy Weather Blues" (Brown), 29
"Raise Your Hand" (Floyd), 79
Raitt, Bonnie, 26
Ram, Samuel "Buck," 180
Ramsey Lewis Trio, 68
Randazzo, Teddy, 136
Ranglin, Wilmer, 133
Rapture (Baker), 5
Ravens, 188–89
Raw Soul, 148
Rawls, Lou, 98,147, 166, 189–90
Ray, Goodman and Brown, 158
Ray, Harry, 157–58
Ray, Johnnie, 6
Ray, Goodman, & Brown (Moments/Ray, Goodman, & Brown), 158
Raydio, 172
"Reach Out, I'll Be There" (Four Tops), 81
"Reach Your Peak" (Sister Sledge), 207
"Reaching for the Sky" (Bryson), 31
"Read My Lips" (Moore), 161
"Rebels Are We" (Chic), 44
Record, Eugene, 42, 61, 74
Redd, Gene, 129
Redding, Dexter, 192
Redding, Otis, 8, 9, 12, 20, 33, 34, 53, 54, 79, 94, 95, 109, 190–92, 229
Redding, Otis III, 192
Reed, Herbert, 180
Reed, Isaac, 66
Reed, Jimmy, 38, 95
Reed, Johnny, 168
Reed, Larry, 65
Reed, Theresa V., 239
Reeves, Lois, 194
Reeves, Martha, 192–94
Regals, 169
Reid, Antonio "L. A.," 22, 23, 99, 250
Reid, Clarence, 120, 261
Rejoice (Emotions), 71
"Release Me" (Phillips), 178
Relf, Bob, 251

"Remember the Time" (Jackson), 108
Rene, Leon, 99
"Respect" (Franklin), 83
"Respect" (Redding), 192
"Respect Yourself" (Staple Singers), 215
"Reunited" (Peaches and Herb), 174
Revival, The (Tony Toni Toné), 235
Reynolds, L. J., 66
Rhodes, Todd, 6
"Rhythm Nation" (Jackson), 106
Rhythm of the Night (DeBarge), 58
Richards, Billy, 48
Richards, Deke, 111
Richards, Reynauld, 64
Richards, Roy, 48
Richardson, Marcel, 64
Richbourg, John "John R," 207–8
Richie, Lionel, Jr., 194–95
Ricks, Jimmy, 188–89
"Ricky's Blues" (Ravens), 189
"Ride Your Pony" (Dorsey), 64
Riley, Jake, Jr., 169
Riley, Teddy, 23, 24, 108
Riley, Timothy Christian, 234–35
"Ring-A-Ding-Doo" (Phillips), 178
"Rip It Up" (Little Richard), 138
Riperton, Minnie, 36, 252, 260
Risque (Chic), 44
Ritz, David, 248
"River" (Simon), 207
"River's Invitation" (Mayfield), 148
Rizzo, Pat, 243
"R.M. Blues" (Milton), 156
"Road Runner" (Diddley), 62
Robbins, Wayne, 259
Roberta Flack & Donny Hathaway (Flack/Hathaway), 77, 93
Robey, Don, 1, 19, 38
Robi, Paul, 180
Robins, 48, 49, 171, 178, 188
Robinson, Bobby, 64, 126
Robinson, Cynthia, 212
Robinson, Dawn, 71
Robinson, Dutch, 165
Robinson, Joe, 157
Robinson, John, 122
Robinson, Ray Charles, 40
Robinson, Smokey, 15, 145, 151, 154, 195–97, 224, 247, 248
Robinson, Sugar Chile, 141
Robinson, Sylvia, 157
"Rock Me All Night Long" (Ravens), 189
Rock Me Tonight (Jackson), 105
"Rock Me Tonight (For Old Times' Sake)" (Jackson), 105
"Rock and Roll Music" (Berry), 18
Rock and Rollin' with Fats Domino (Domino), 63
"Rock Steady" (Whispers), 250
"Rock Wit'cha" (Brown), 24
"Rock With You" (Jackson), 108
"Rockin' at Midnight" (Brown), 29
"Rockin' Blues" (Otis), 171
"Rockin' Good Way, A (To Mess Around and Fall in Love)" (Benton), 16
"Rockin' Good Way, A (To Mess Around and Fall in Love)" (Washington), 247
"Rockin' Roll Baby" (Stylistics), 219
Rodgers, Nile, Jr., 43–44, 209
Rogers, Bobby, 145, 195, 196
Rogers, Charles E., 104
Rogers, Claudette, 196
Rogers, D. J., 83
Rogers, Glouster "Nate," 136
Rogers, Kenny, 178, 194
Rogers, Lelan, 83
"Roll Over Beethoven" (Berry), 18
Rolling Stones, 17, 32, 62, 83, 162, 183, 192
"Roni" (Brown), 24
Ronstadt, Linda, 163
"Roomin' House Boogie" (Milburn), 153
Rose Royce, 197–98
Rose Royce II/In Full Bloom (Rose Royce), 197

Rose Royce III/Strikes Again! (Rose Royce), 197
Rosen, Peter, 242, 243
Ross, Diana, 2, 44, 73, 81, 86, 107, 110, 117, 154, 194, 199–201, 224
Ross, Jerry, 34
Ross, Lucius Tawl, 45
Royal Sons Quintet, 75
Royals, 7, 75, 115, 170
"Rubberband Man" (Spinners), 214
Rubinson, David, 181, 183
Ruffin, David, 150, 151, 160, 223–25
Rufus, 117, 121–22, 172
Rule, Greg, 235
"Run Away Child, Running Wild" (Temptations), 224
"Runaway Love" (En Vogue), 73
"Running Away" (Maze), 149
Rupe, Art, 53, 155, 185
Rushing, Jimmy, 91
Russell, Ken, 238
Russell, Leon, 15, 83
Russi, Randy, 205

Sacks, Leo, 233
"Sad Girl" (Intruders), 101
Sade, 201–2
Safice, 79
Sager, Carol Bayer, 57, 82, 131, 246
"Said I Wasn't Gonna Tell Nobody" (Sam and Dave), 203
Salgado, Curtis, 54
Sallie Martin Colored Ladies Quartert, 246
Salonga, Leah, 31, 32
Salter, William, 257
Sam, Robert, 87
Sam Cooke (Cooke), 53
Sam and Dave, 94, 169, 202–3
"Same Love That Made Me Laugh, The" (Withers), 256
Samuels, William, 75, 76
Samuels, Zelda, 257
Sanders, Ethel, 143
Sandmen, 16
Santiago, Herman, 141, 142
Santiel, Terral, 197
Satchell, Clarence "Satch," 165
"Satisfaction" (Redding), 192
Satterfield, Louis, 68
"Saturday Night Fish Fry (Part 1)" (Jordan), 119
"Save the Last Dance for Me" (Drifters), 67
"Saving All My Love for You" (Houston), 98
"Saving My Love for You" (Ace), 1
"Say It Loud—I'm Black and I'm Proud (Part 1)" (Brown), 27
"Say Man, Back Again" (Diddley), 62
"Say Man" (Diddley), 62
"Say You, Say Me" (Richie), 195
Scarborough, Skip, 52, 208
Schiffman, Frank, 168
Schiffman, Jack, 168
"School Day" (Berry), 18
Schultz, Michael, 22, 197
Scott, Calvin, 38
Scott, Helen, 232, 233
Scott, Howard E., 241, 242
Scott, Joe, 19
Scott, Wallace, 249–50
Scott, Walter, 249–50
"Searchin' " (Coasters), 49
Sears, Zenas "Daddy," 139, 253–54
"Second Chance" (Hill), 96
"Second Time Around, The" (Shalamar), 205
"Secret Garden, The" (DeBarge), 58
"Secret Garden, The (Sweet Seduction Suite)" (Jones), 118
"Secret Garden, The (Sweet Seduction Suite)" (White), 251
"Secret Lady" (Mills), 154
"Secret Lovers" (Atlantic Starr), 4
"Secretary" (Wright), 260
"See Saw" (Moonglows), 159
"See You When I Get There" (Rawls), 190

"Seems Like I Gotta Do Wrong" (Whispers), 250
Sehorn, Marshall, 64, 65, 126, 162
Selvin, Joel, 230
"Send for Me If You Need Me" (Ravens), 189
"Send Me Some Lovin'" (Little Richard), 138
Sensational Nightingales, 26, 179, 202
"September" (Earth, Wind and Fire), 69
Sequins, 131, 132
"Serpentine Fire" (Earth, Wind and Fire), 69
"Seven Days" (McPhatter), 151
"Seven Letters" (King), 123
"Seven Long Days" (Brown), 26
"Sexual Healing" (Gaye), 86
"Sexy Mama" (Moments), 158
"Sexy Ways" (Ballard), 8
"Sha-La-La (Make Me Happy)" (Green), 89
Shad, Bob, 180
Shades of Jade, 239
Shadow, 166
Shaft (Hayes), 94
"Shake" (Cooke), 53
"Shake" (Gap Band), 84
"Shake and Dance with Me" (Con Funk Shun), 51
"Shake and Fingerpop" (Walker), 241
"Shake, Rattle and Roll" (Turner), 236
"(Shake, Shake, Shake) Shake Your Booty" (KC/Sunshine Band), 121
"Shake Your Groove Thing" (Peaches and Herb), 174
"Shake Your Rump to the Funk" (Bar-Kays), 10
Shalamar, 203–5
Shannon, Ronnie, 82
Shapiro, Brad, 109, 202, 203
"Share What You Got" (Bell), 13
"Share Your Love With Me" (Franklin), 83
Sharp, Alexander, 168, 169
Shaw, Arnold, 48
Shaw, Mattie, 186
"She Works Hard for the Money" (Summer), 221
Shelby, William, 204
Sheridan, Art, 77
"She's On the Left" (Osborne), 170
"She's Strange" (Cameo), 36
Shewey, Don, 97
"Shimmy, Shimmy, Ko-Ko-Bop" (Little Anthony), 136
Shindler, Merrill, 104
"Shining Star" (Earth, Wind and Fire), 69
"Shining Star" (Manhattans), 143
Shirelles, 2, 76, 125, 150, 205–7, 239
Shirelles Greatest Hits, The (Shirelles), 206
"Shoop Shoop Song, The (It's in His Kiss)" (Everett), 74
"Shop Around" (Robinson/Miracles), 196
"Shotgun" (Walker), 241
"Show Me How" (Emotions), 71
"Show Me the Way" (Belle), 14
"Show and Tell" (Bryson), 31
Sigler, Bunny, 211, 250
"Sign 'O' the Times" (Prince), 187
"Signed, Sealed, Delivered I'm Yours" (Wonder), 259
"Silent Night" (Ravens), 189
"Silky Soul" (Maze), 149
Silver, Horace, 125, 128
Simmons, Chester, 79
Simmons, Daryl, 22, 24
Simmons, Lonnie, 83
Simon, Calvin, 45
Simon, Joe, 207–8
Simpson, Jimmy, 218
Simpson, Valerie, 2–3, 74, 104, 201, 227
Sims, Dupree, 66
"Since I Met You Baby" (Hunter), 100
"Sincerely" (Moonglows), 159
"Sing a Song" (Earth, Wind and Fire), 69
Singing Clouds, 210
"Single Life" (Cameo), 36
Singleton, Charlie, 36

Singleton, Shelby, 16
Sister Rose, 212
Sister Sledge, 44, 208–9, 211
"Sittin' on It All the Time" (Harris), 91
"(Sittin' On) the Dock of the Bay, The"
  (Redding), 192
"634–5789" (Pickett), 179
"Sixty-Minute Man" (Ward), 244
"Skin Tight" (Ohio Players), 165
"Skinny Legs and All" (Tex), 228
Slater, William, 76
"Slaughter" (Preston), 184
Sledge, Carol, 208–9
Sledge, Debbie, 208–9
Sledge, Joni, 208–9
Sledge, Kathy, 208–9
Sledge, Kim, 208–9
Sledge, Percy, 208
"Sleep" (John), 115
Slim and the Boys, 208, 219
"Slip Away" (Carter), 39
"Slippin' into Darkness" (War), 242
Sloven, Larry, 54
"Slow Drag" (Intruders), 101
"Slow Hand" (Pointer Sisters), 183
Sly and the Family Stone, 3, 10, 51, 86, 87,
  211–12
Smalls, Charles, 153–54
Smallwood, David, 16
"Smile" (Emotions), 71
Smith, Alice Tweed, 243
Smith, Bobbie, 213–14
Smith, Claydes, 128
Smith, George "Smitty," 143
Smith, James, 219, 220
Smith, Jerome, 120
Smith, Lawson, 7, 8
Smith, Lloyd, 9, 10
Smith, Otis, 5, 6
Smith, Ron, 148, 149
Smoke, 251
"Smoke Gets in Your Eyes" (Platters), 181
"Smooth Operator" (Sade), 202
"Snatching It Back" (Carter), 39
"Sneaky Pete" (Jackson), 104
Snoop Doggy Dog, 66
So Full of Love (O'Jays), 166
"So I Can Love You" (Emotions), 71
"So Long" (Charles Brown), 26
"So Long" (Ruth Brown), 30
"So Long" (Hamilton), 90
"So Many Tears" (Belle), 14
"So Many Ways" (Benton), 16
"So Mean To Me" (Little Milton), 137
"So Much" (Little Anthony), 136
"So You Win Again" (Hot Chocolate), 97
"Soldier Boy" (Shirelles), 206
Solid (Ashford and Simpson), 3
Solid Senders, 155–56
"Somebody Loves You Baby (You Know
  Who It Is)" (LaBelle), 131
"Somebody's on Your Case" (Peebles), 175
"Someday Someway" (Marvelletes), 144
"Someday We'll Be Together"
  (Ross/Supremes), 199
"Something He Can Feel" (Franklin), 83
"Something in the Way" (Mills), 154
"Something on Your Mind" (Curtis), 125
"Something's Got a Hold on Me" (James),
  113
"Song is Ended, The (But the Melody
  Lingers On)" (Lutcher), 140
Songs in the Key of Life (Wonder), 259
Sons of Soul (Tony Toni Toné), 235
"Soothe Me" (Sam and Dave), 203
"Sophisticated Cissy" (Neville), 163
"Sophisticated Lady (She's a Different
  Lady)" (Cole), 50
"Soul-Limbo" (Booker T), 21
Soul Children, 51
Soul City Symphony, 150
"Soul Finger" (Bar-Kays), 10
"Soul Man" (Sam and Dave), 203
"Soul Sister, Brown Sugar" (Sam and Dave),
  203
Soul Stirrers, 52–53, 54, 223, 257

"Soul Twist" (Curtis/Noble Knights), 125
"Sound Your Funky Horn" (KC/Sunshine
  Band), 121
Sounds...and Stuff Like That!! (Jones), 118
"Soup for One" (Chic), 44
"Southern Girl" (Maze), 149
"Space Race" (Preston), 184
Spandau Ballet, 201
"Spanish Harlem" (Franklin), 83
"Spanish Harlem" (King), 123
Sparks, Willie, 87, 88
"Special Lady" (Moments), 158
Spector, Phil, 67, 229
Spinners, 85, 160, 171, 172, 213–14, 246
"Spirit of the Boogie" (Kool and the Gang),
  128
Spirit of Love (Con Funk Shun), 51
Spratley, Bill, 176
"Stagger Lee" (Price), 185
"Stand By Me" (King), 123
"Stand By Your Man" (Staton), 218
"Standing in the Shadows of Love" (Four
  Tops), 81
"Standing on the Top—Part 1"
  (James/Temptations), 114
Staple Singers, 9, 70, 146, 214–16
Staples, Cleotha, 215
Staples, Mavis, 5, 188, 214–16
Staples, Pervis, 70, 215, 216
Staples, Roebuck "Pops," 214–16, 257
Staples, Yvonne, 215, 216
"Star Dust" (Ward), 244
Starlets, 130

Starr, Bobby, 101
Starr, Brenda K., 37
Starr, Edwin, 197–98, 216–17
Starr, Maurice, 23, 51, 163
Staton, Candi, 38–39, 217–19
Staton, Maggie, 217
"Stay Away from Me" (Sylvers), 222
Stay Free (Ashford and Simpson), 3
"Stay in My Corner" (Dells), 61
"Steal Away" (Taylor), 223
Steinberg, Lewis, 20
"Step by Step" (Simon), 207
Stephenson, Wolf, 96, 138
Stepney, Charles, 60, 68, 252
Sterling, Annette Beard, 193, 194
Stevens, Yvette Marie, 121
Stevenson, William "Mickey," 85, 144, 193,
  248
Stewart, Alpha, 212
Stewart, Curtis, 212
Stewart, Floyd, 79
Stewart Four, 212
Stewart, Freddie, 212
Stewart, Jim, 12, 191, 229
Stewart, Jimmy, 189
Stewart, K. C., 212
Stewart, Loretta, 212
Stewart, Sylvester, 211
Stewart, Vaetta, 212
Stewart, Winston, 9, 10
"Still" (Baker), 7
"Still" (Richie/Commodores), 195
Still Bill (Withers), 256
Still Trapped (LaSalle), 132
Stockert, Ron, 121
Stockman, Shawn, 22
Stoller, Mike, 7, 30, 48, 49, 67, 90, 123,
  124, 150
Stone, Henry, 12, 120, 202, 261
Stone, Jesse, 48, 90, 124, 236, 2054
Stone, Sly, 9, 10, 47, 87, 184, 211–12, 250,
  258
"Stone Cold Dead in the Market (He Had It
  Coming)" (Jordan), 119
"Stoned Out of My Mind" (Chi-Lites), 43
Stoners, 212
"Stop Her on Sight (S.O.S.)" (Starr), 216
"Stop, Look, Listen (To Your Heart)"
  (Stylistics), 219
"Stop to Love" (Vandross), 240
"Stop the War Now" (Starr), 216
"Stop the Wedding" (James), 113

Stories, 97
Strain, Sammy, 136, 167
"Strange I Know" (Marvelletes), 144
"Strange Things Happening" (Mayfield),
  148
"Street Corner" (Ashford and Simpson), 3
Street, Richard, 225
Street Songs (James), 114
Streisand, Barbra, 69, 160, 185, 220, 239
Strong, Barrett, 217, 224
Strong Persuader (Cray), 54
Stronger than Pride (Sade), 202
"Struttin' " (Preston), 184
Stubbs, Joe, 79
Stubbs, Levi, 7, 80, 81
"Stuff Like That" (Jones), 118
Stylistics, 59, 150, 219–20
"Such a Night" (McPhatter/Drifters), 67
Sudderth, Bill III, 3
"Sugar Sugar" (Pickett), 179
Sumler, G. Diane, 239
Summer, Donna, 220–2, 239
"Summer" (War), 242
Sun, Ahaguna G., 148
"Sunbeam" (Emotions), 71
"Sunny Road" (Brown), 26
"Super Bad (Part 1 & Part 2) (Brown), 27
"Super Freak (Part 1)" (James), 114
Superfly (Mayfield), 146
Supernatural (King), 123
"Supernatural Thing—Part 1" (King), 123
Supremes, 73, 80, 81, 130, 160, 192, 199,
  224, 260
Sussewell, John, 218
Suttles, Warren, 188
Sutton, Charles, 7
Swallows, 77
Swan Silvertones, 59, 88, 257
"Sweet Dan" (Everett), 74
"Sweet Feeling" (Staton), 218
"Sweet Georgia Brown" (Liggins), 135
Sweet Inspirations, 98
"Sweet Little Sixteen" (Berry), 18
"Sweet Love" (Baker), 5
Sweet Sensation (Mills), 154
"Sweet Sensation" (LeVert), 134
"Sweet Sensation" (Mills), 154
"Sweet Sixteen" (Turner), 236
"Sweet Sticky Thing" (Ohio Players), 165
"(Sweet Sweet Baby) Since You've Been
  Gone" (Franklin), 83
"Sweet Thing" (Khan), 122
Sweet Things, 173
"Sweet Woman Like You, A" (Tex), 228
"Sweetest Taboo, The" (Sade), 202
Switch, 56
"Switch-A-Roo, The" (Ballard), 8
Sykes, Roosevelt, 135
Sylvers, 221–22
Sylvers, Angela Marie, 222
Sylvers, Charmaine Elaine, 221, 222
Sylvers, Edmund Theodore, 221, 222
Sylvers, Foster Emerson, 222
Sylvers, James Jonathan, 221, 222
Sylvers, Leon Frank, III, 221, 222
Sylvers, Leon, III, 204, 250
Sylvers, Olympia Ann, 221, 222
Sylvers, Patricia Lynn, 222
Sylvers, Shirley, 221
Sylvester, Tony, 208
"System of Survival" (Earth, Wind and
  Fire), 69

"Ta Ta" (McPhatter), 151
Take 6, 21, 154, 161
"Take Care of Your Homework" (Taylor),
  223
"Take It to the Limit" (Moments), 158
"Take Me Back" (Little Anthony), 136
"Take Me (Just As I Am)" (Burke), 33
"Take Me to the Next Phase" (Isley
  Brothers), 102
"Take My Heart (You Can Have It If You
  Want It)" (Kool and the Gang), 128
"Take My Love (I Want to Give It All to
  You)" (John), 115

"Take Time to Know Her" (Sledge), 210
"Talk That Talk" (Wilson), 255
"Talk to Me, Talk to Me" (John), 115
"Talk to Me" (Baker), 5
Tanner, Eugene, 75
Tanner, John, 75
"Tanya" (Liggins), 135
Tarnapol, Nat, 196, 255
"Tasty Love" (Jackson), 105
Taylor, Creed, 15, 178
Taylor, Dallas, 60
Taylor, Diane, 251
Taylor, Felice, 251
Taylor, James "J. T.," 14, 128, 129
Taylor, Johnnie, 9, 19, 20, 55, 94, 95,
  222–23
Taylor, LaBaron, 211
Taylor, Little Johnny, 95, 223
Taylor, Richard, 143
Taylor, Sam "the Man," 124
TCB (Temptations), 224
"Teardrops from My Eyes" (Brown), 30
"Teardrops on Your Letter" (Ballard), 8
"Tears of a Clown, The"
  (Robinson/Miracles), 196
"Tears of Joy" (5 Royales), 75
"Tears on My Pillow" (Little Anthony), 136
Teddy (Pendergrass), 177
Teenagers Featuring Frankie Lymon, The
  (Lymon), 141
Teenagers, Frankie Lymon and the, 141–42
"Tell It Like It Is" (Neville), 163
"Tell Me So" (Orioles), 168
Tempo Toppers, 139
Temptations, 13, 21, 43, 77, 89, 114, 189,
  195, 223–25
"Ten Commandments of Love"
  (Moonglows), 159
10 Greatest Hits (Hot Chocolate), 97
Terrell, Jean, 199
Terrell, Tammi, 2, 86, 160, 225–27
Terrell, Ty, 48
Terry, Phil, 100
"Testify (I Wonna)" (Taylor), 223
Tex, Joe, 6, 115, 227–28
"Thank You (Falettinme Be Mice Elf Agin)"
  (Sly/Family Stone), 212
"Thank You Pretty Baby" (Benton), 16
Tharpe, Sister Rosetta, 165
"That Girl" (Wonder), 259
"That Lady (Part 1)" (Isley Brothers), 102
"That's the Stuff You Gotta Watch"
  (Johnson), 116
"That's the Way (I Like It)" (KC/Sunshine
  Band), 121
"That's the Way Love Is" (Bland), 19
"That's the Way I Feel About Cha"
  (Womack), 258
"That's the Way Love Is" (Jackson), 106
That's the Way of the World (Earth, Wind
  and Fire), 69
That's What Friends Are For (Williams),
  253
"That's What Friends Are For" (Warwick),
  245
"That's What Love Will Make You Do"
  (Little Milton), 137
"That's What You're Doing for Me"
  (Ward), 244
"That's Why (I Love You So)" (Wilson),
  255
"Theme from Cleopatra Jones" (Simon), 207
"Theme from Shaft" (Hayes), 94
"Then Came You" (Spinners), 214
"Then Came You" (Warwick), 245
"There Goes My Baby" (Drifters), 67
There Is (Dells), 61
"There You Go" (Starr), 216
"There'll Come A Time" (Everett), 74
"There's Gonna Be a Showdown" (Bell), 11
"There's No Me Without You"
  (Manhattans), 143
"There's Nothing Better Than Love"
  (Vandross), 240
There's a Riot Goin' On (Sly/Family Stone),
  212

"There's So Much Love Around Me" (Three Degrees), 232
"These Eyes" (Walker), 241
"These Foolish Things Remind Me of You" (Ward), 244
"These Hands (Small But Mighty)" (Bland), 19
"They All Say I'm the Biggest Fool" (Johnson), 116
"They Just Can't Stop It (The Games People Play)" (Spinners), 214
"Think" (5 Royales), 75
Third Album (Jackson 5), 111
"Thirty Days" (Berry), 18
"This Bitter Earth" (Washington), 247
"This Girl's in Love with You" (Warwick), 245
"This I Swear" (Davis), 56
"This Is Love" (Belle), 14
"This Is for the Lover in You" (Shalamar), 205
"This Masquerade" (Benson), 15
"This Time I'm Gone For Good" (Bland), 19
"This Will Be" (Cole), 50
Thomas, Carla, 9, 12, 20, 78, 92, 94, 102, 229–30, 231
Thomas, Charlie, 67, 68
Thomas, Dennis, 128
Thomas, Eddie, 146
Thomas, Grady, 45
Thomas, Marvell, 229, 231
Thomas, Rufus, 12, 20, 51, 94, 169, 229, 230–31
Thomas, Vaneese, 231
Thomas, Vic, 240
Thomas, Wayne, 148
Thomas, Will, 10
Thompkins, Russell, Jr., 136, 219
Thompson, Frank, 10
Thompson, Gary, 207
Thompson, Jerry, 40
Thompson, Marshall, Jr., 42
Thompson, Tony, 43
Thornton, Willie Mae "Big Mama," 1, 48–49, 170
Thrasher, Andrew, 67
Thrasher, Gerhart, 67
Thrasher, Norman, 8
Three Blazers, 25, 99, 170
Three Degrees, 232–33
Three Degrees, The (Three Degrees), 232
"Three Times a Lady" (Richie/Commodores), 195
"Thrill Me" (Milton), 156
Thriller (Jackson), 108
"Tighten Up" (Bell), 11
Til, Sonny, 7, 168–69
Tilghman, Earlington Carl, 168
Tilley, Sandra, 194
Tillman, Georgeanna, 144, 145
Time, 233–34
"Time Is Tight" (Booker T.), 21
"Time for Livin'" (Sly/Family Stone), 212
"Time Will Reveal" (DeBarge), 58
"Ting-A-Ling" (Clovers), 48
To Be Continued (Hayes), 94
"To Be a Lover" (Chandler), 40
Tobin, Geroge, 197
"Toby" (Chi-Lites), 101
"Together" (Intruders), 101
Togetherness (Osborne), 170
Tolbert, Larry, 172
Toles, Michael, 9
"Tomorrow (A Better You, A Better Me)" (Jones), 118
Tompkins, J. H., 10
"Tonight" (Whispers), 250
"Tonight, I Celebrate My Love" (Bryson/Flack), 31, 77
"Tonight Is the Night Pt. 1" (Wright), 260
"Tonight's the Night" (Burke), 33
"Tonight's the Night" (Shirelles), 206
Tony Toni Toné, 234–35
"Too Busy Thinking About My Baby" (Gaye), 86

"Too Hot to Stop (Pt. 1)" (Bar-Kays), 10
"Too Many Games" (Maze), 149
"Too Much Lovin' " (5 Royales), 75
"Too Much Monkey Business" (Berry), 18
"Too Much, Too Little, Too Late" (Williams), 253
"Too Tight" (Con Funk Shun), 51
"Too Weak to Fight" (Carter), 39
Toshes, Nick, 243
Total Concept Unlimited, 197–98
"Touch a Four Leaf Clover" (Atlantic Starr), 4
"Touch a Hand, Make a Friend" (Staple Singers), 215
Toussaint, Allen, 63, 64, 65,95, 113, 121, 161, 162, 181, 191
"Tracks of My Tears, The" (Robinson/Miracles), 196
"Tramp" (Redding), 192
"Tramp" (Thomas), 229
Trapped By a Thing Called Love (LaSalle), 132
"Trapped By a Thing Called Love" (LaSalle), 132
Travis, Betty, 199
Treadwell, George, 67, 123
"Treasure of Love" (McPhatter), 151
Tresvant, Ralph, 23, 163–65
"Tribute to a King, A" (Bell), 13
"Trouble Blues" (Brown), 26
"Trouble in My Home" (Simon), 207
Troutman, Larry, 263
Troutman, Lester, 263
Troutman, "Little" Roger, Jr., 263
Troutman, Roger, 166, 261–63
Troutman, Rufus, Jr., 263
Troutman, Rufus, III, 263
Troutman, Terry "Zapp," 263
"True Blues" (Milton), 156
"Trust in Me" (James), 113
"Try a Little Tenderness" (Redding), 192
"Tryin' to Love Two" (Bell), 13
"Trying to Make a Fool of Me" (Delfonics), 59
"TSOP (The Sound of Philadelphia)" (Three Degrees), 232
TSU Tornadoes, 10
Tucker, Alonzo, 7, 255
Tucker, Ira, 18
Turks, 180
"Turn Back the Hands of Time" (Davis), 56
"Turn Your Love Around" (Benson), 15
"Turn on Your Love Light" (Bland), 19
Turner, Charles "Sonny," 180
Turner, Ike, 19, 74, 83, 137, 237–38
Turner, Joe, 91, 140, 171, 235–36
Turner, Linda, 232
Turner, Lou Willie, 236
Turner, Tina, 54, 176, 236–37
"Turning Point" (Davis), 56
"Tutti-Frutti" (Little Richard), 138
"Tweedlee Dee" (Baker), 7
"Twenty-Five Miles" (Starr), 216
"Twilight Time" (Platters), 181
"Twist and Shout" (Isley Brothers), 102
"Twist, The" (Ballard), 8
"Twistin' the Night Away" (Cooke), 53
"Two Hearts" (Mills), 154
2 Hot! (Peaches and Herb), 174
"Two Lovers" (Wells), 248
"Two Places at the Same Time" (Parker), 172
Tyler, Alvin "Red," 63
Tympany Five, 118
"Typical Male" (Turner), 238
Tyson, Ron, 225

U-4, 71
"Uhh Ahh" (Boyz II Men), 23
"Unchain My Heart" (Charles), 42
"Unchained Melody" (Hamilton), 90
Uncle Jam Wants You (Clinton), 45
Undisputed Truth, 165
Unforgettable (Washington), 247
Unforgettable with Love (Cole), 50
"United" (Peaches and Herb), 174

United Four, 115
Unpredictable (Cole), 50
Upsetters, 139, 190–91
"Upside Down" (Ross), 199
"Uptight (Everything's Alright)" (Wonder), 259
"Uptown Festival" (Shalamar), 205
"Use Me" (Withers), 256
"Use Ta Be My Girl" (O'Jays), 166

Valentines, 141
Valentinos, 53, 257–58
Valley of the Dolls (Warwick), 245
Van Loan, James, 189, 244
Vandellas, Martha Reeves and the, 192–94
Vandross, Luther, 1, 83, 92, 104, 105, 185, 239–40
Vandross, Patricia, 239
Vega, David, 87
Veliotes, John, 170
Vera, Billy, 190
Verrett, Harrison, 62, 63
Vickers, Carle, 169
Victory (Jacksons), 111
Vinson, Eddie "Cleanhead," 99, 113, 171
Violinaires, 178
Viscaynes, 212
"Vision of Love" (Carey), 36
Vogue, 71
Voices of Love, 257

"Waiting in Vain" (Hunter), 100
"Wake Me, Shake Me" (Coasters), 49
Wake Up Everybody (Pendergrass), 177
"Wake Up Everybody (Part 1)" (Pendergrass), 177
Walden, Narada Michael, 14, 37, 83, 98, 208
Walden, Phil, 191
"Walk, The" (Time), 233
"Walk Away" (Peebles), 175
"Walk Right Up to the Sun" (Delfonics), 59
Walker, Dennis, 54
Walker, Esther, 178
Walker, Jr., and the All Stars, 160, 240–41
Walker, Mel, 178
Walker, T-Bone, 17, 19, 91
"Walking the Dog" (Thomas), 231
Wallace, Victoria, 232
Waller, Wiley, 224
"Wallflower, The" (James), 113
Wansel, Dexter, 133
War, 241–43
"War" (Starr), 216
Ward, Billy, 67, 151, 243–44
Ward, Robert, 165
"Warm and Tender Love" (Sledge), 210
Warren, Harry, 78
Warwick, Dionne, 59, 97, 99, 128, 160, 170, 207, 239, 240, 244–46
Washington, Dinah, 16, 29, 60, 105, 117, 168, 177, 246–47
Washington, Grover, Jr., 257
Waters, Muddy, 17, 61, 68, 73
Watley, Jody, 44, 203–4, 205
Watson, Anthony, 43
Watson, Bobby, 122
Watson, Johnny "Guitar," 74, 112, 148, 170, 227
Watson, Stan, 58
Watts 103rd Street Rhythm Band, 256
"Way You Make Me Feel, The" (Jackson), 108
We Are Family (Sister Sledge), 207
"We Are Family" (Sister Sledge), 207
We Are One (Maze), 149
"We Don't Need Another Hero" (Turner), 238
"We Go Together" (Moonglows), 159
Weathers, Barbara, 3, 4
Webb, Jim, 94
Webb, Melvin, 169–70
Webster, Greg, 165
"Wedding Boogie" (Phillips), 178
Weekend in L.A. (Benson), 15
Weiger, Harry, 210

Weiss, George David, 220
"Welcome Home" (Dramatics), 65
"(We'll Be) United" (Intruders), 101
Wells, Mary, 39, 86, 247–49, 195
"We're a Winner" (Mayfield), 146
"We're Gonna Make It" (Little Milton), 137
West, Robert, 79
Westfield, Rickey, 128
Weston, Ruth, 29
Wexler, Jerry, 32, 48, 52, 82, 93, 113, 178, 179, 183, 203, 211
"What Am I Gonna Do with You" (White), 251
"What Am I Living For" (Willis), 254
"What Are You Doing New Year's Eve" (Orioles), 168
"What 'Cha Gonna Do" (Drifters/McPhatter), 67
"What 'Cha Gonna Do for Me" (Khan), 122
"What Cha Gonna Do with My Lovin' " (Mills), 154
What a Difference a Day Makes (Phillips), 178
"What a Difference a Day Makes" (Phillips), 178
"What Does It Take (To Win Your Love)" (Walker), 241
"What a Fool I Am" (Mayfield), 148
"What Goes Around" (Belle), 14
"What Have You Done for Me Lately" (Jackson), 106
"What It Takes to Get a Good Woman (That's What It's Gonna Take to Keep Her)" (LaSalle), 132
What Time Is It? (Time), 233
"What You Gave Me" (Terrell), 227
"Whatcha See Is Whatcha Get" (Dramatics), 65
Whatcha See Is Whatcha Get (Dramatics), 65
"What'd I Say (Part 1)" (Charles), 42
"Whatever You Want" (Tony Toni Toné), 235
"What's Easy for Two Is So Hard for One" (Wells), 248
"What's Going On" (Gaye), 86
"What's Love Got to Do with It" (Turner), 238
"What's the Use of Breaking Up" (Butler), 34
"Wheel of Fortune" (Washington), 247
Wheeler, Carl, 235
"When the Doves Cry" (Prince/Revolution), 187
"When He Touches Me (Nothing Else Matters)" (Peaches and Herb), 174
"When I'm with You" (Moonglows), 159
"When a Man Loves a Woman" (Sledge), 210
"When My Man Comes Home" (Johnson), 116
"When She Was My Girl" (Four Tops), 81
"When Something is Wrong with My Baby" (Sam and Dave), 203
"When We Get Married" (Graham), 87
"When We Get Married" (Intruders), 101
"When Will I See You Again" (Three Degrees), 232
"When You Get Right Down to It" (Delfonics), 59
"When You Wake Up Tomorrow" (Staton), 218
"When You're Young and in Love" (Marvelettes), 144
"When You've Been Blessed (Feels Like Heaven)" (LaBelle), 131
"Where Is the Love" (Flack), 77
"Where Is the Love" (Flack/Hathaway), 93
"Where Is the Love" (Wright), 260
"Where Were You (On Our Wedding Day)" (Price), 185
Whispers, 93, 249–50
Whispers, The (Whispers), 250
"Whispers (Gettin' Louder)" (Wilson), 255

White, Barry, 58, 95, 172, 250–52
White, Charlie, 244
White, Fred, 68
White, Maurice, 58, 68, 71, 252
White, Michael, 149
White, Ronnie, 195–96, 258
White, Verdine, 68
White Cane, 114
"White Christmas" (Drifters/McPhatter), 67
"White Christmas" (Ravens), 67
Whitfield, Norman, 86, 93, 145, 197, 217, 224, 225
Whitehead, John, 161
Whitney (Houston), 98
Whitney Houston (Houston), 98
Whitsett, Carson, 21
Whitshire, Christine, 239
"Who Can Explain?" (Lymon), 141
"Who's Cheating Who?" (Little Milton), 137
"Who'd She Coo?" (Ohio Players), 165
"Whole New World, A" (Belle), 14
"Who's Holding Donna Now" (DeBarge), 58
"Who's Johnny" (DeBarge), 58
"Who's Making Love" (Taylor), 223
"Why Can't We Be Friends?" (War), 242
"Why Do Fools Fall in Love" (Lymon), 141
"Why Don't You Haul Off and Love Me" (Jackson), 104
"Why Is the Wine Sweeter (On the Other Side)" (Floyd), 79
Wickman, Vicki, 130
Wiggins, Charlie, 235
Wiggins, D'Wayne, 234–35
Wiggins, Raphael, 234–35
Wilburn, Vince, 36
"Wild Wild Young Men" (Brown), 30
Wilkerson, Don, 156
Wilkins, Barry, 9
Wilkins, Elbert, 65, 66
"Will It Go Round in Circles" (Preston), 184
"Will You Love Me Tomorrow" (Shirelles), 206
Williams, Deniece, 69, 252–53
Williams, Eddie, 99
Williams, Gloria Jean, 193
Williams, Jimmy "Diamond," 166
Williams, Keith, 136
Williams, Larry, 140, 161, 186
Williams, McKinley "Bug," 148, 149
Wiliams, Milan, 194
Williams, Noel "King Sporty," 261
Williams, Otis, 224
Williams, Paul, 199, 224, 225
Williams, Ralph, 169
Williams, Robbie Preston, 183

Williams, Tony, 180, 181
Williams, Viola Hairston, 208
Williams, Walter, 166, 168
"Willie and the Hand Jive" (Otis), 171
Willis, Chuck, 16, 79, 117, 136, 150, 151, 170, 196, 253–54
Willis, Clarence, 166
Willis, Harold, 253
Wilson, Bernard, 176
Wilson, Charlie, 83–85
Wilson, Jackie, 7, 15, 31, 68, 102, 107, 115, 136, 150, 151, 170, 196, 244, 247, 254–55
Wilson, Mary, 199
Wilson, Paul, 77
Wilson, Robert, 83–85
Wilson, Ronnie, 83–85
Wilson, Tony, 96
"(Win, Place or Show) She's a Winner" (Intruders), 101
Winans, 6
Winans, BeBe, 99, 161
Winans, Carvin, 14
Winans, CeCe, 99
Wingate, Ed, 2160, 217
Winley, Harold, 47
Winner, Karin, 183
Winner in You (LaBelle), 131
"Wish That I Could Talk to You" (Sylvers), 222
Withers, Bill, 21, 256–57
"Without Love" (McPhatter), 151
"Without You" (Belle), 14
"Without You in My Life" (Davis), 56
Wolf, James, 132
Wolf, Peter, 57
Wolinski, David "Hawk," 122
Womack, Bobby, 13, 15, 148, 172, 228, 242, 248–49, 257–58
Womack, Cecil, 248–49, 257
Womack, Curtis, 248–49, 257
Womack, Friendly, Jr., 257
Womack, Harry, 257
"Woman, A Lover, A Friend, A" (Wilson), 255
"Woman in Love" (Three Degrees), 232
"Woman Needs Love, A (Just Like You Do)" (Parker), 172
"Woman's Gotta Have It" (Womack), 258
Wonder, Stevie, 5, 15, 26, 36, 75, 84, 92, 111, 121–22, 147, 160, 161, 172, 195, 246, 252, 258–60, 993
"Wonderful World" (Cooke), 53
Woo, Phillip, 148, 149
Woods, James "Pip," 126
Woods, Sonny, 7

Woods, Willie, 240
Woodson, Ali–Ollie, 225
Woolfolk, Andrew, 68
Word (Cameo), 36
"Word Up" (Cameo), 36
"Work with Me Annie" (Ballard), 8
"Workin' Together" (Maze), 149
"Working in a Coal Mine" (Dorsey), 64
World Is a Ghetto, The (War), 242
"World Is a Ghetto, The" (War), 242
"World Is Round, The" (Thomas), 231
Worrell, Bernie, 45
Worsham, Doris, 51
Wright, Betty, 120, 260–61
Wright, Charles, 256
Wright, Ernest, Jr., 136
Wright, George, 45
Wright, Norma Jean, 44
Wright, Syreeta, 185
"Write Me a Letter" (Ravens), 189
Wynne, Philippe, 213, 214
"Wynonie's Blues" (Harris), 91

"Ya Ya" (Dorsey), 64
"Yakety Yak" (Coasters), 49
Yancey, Jimmy, 47
Yancy, Rev. Marvin, 34, 50, 61
Yarborough, William, 12
Yarian, Christine, 22
"Yes We Can" (Pointer Sisters), 183
"You Are My Heaven" (Flack/Hathaway), 93
"You are My Lady" (Jackson), 105
"You Are My Sunshine" (Charles), 42
"You Beat Me to the Punch" (Wells), 248
"You Better Know It" (Wilson), 255
"You Can Have Her" (Hamilton), 90
"You Can't Change That" (Parker), 172
"You Can't Hurry Love" (Ross/Supremes), 199
"You Can't Judge a Book by Its Cover" (Diddley), 62
"You Don't Have to Worry" (En Vogue), 73
"You Don't Know Like I Know" (Sam and Dave), 203
"You Dropped a Bomb on Me" (Gap Band), 84
"You Give Good Love" (Houston), 98
"You Got the Love" (Khan), 122
"You Got Me Hummin' " (Sam and Dave), 203
"You Got Yours and I'll Get Mine" (Delfonics), 59
"You and I" (James), 114
"(You Keep Me) Hangin' On" (Peebles), 175

"You Keep Me Hangin' On" (Ross/Supremes), 199
"You Make Me Feel Brand New" (Stylistics), 219
"You Make Me Work" (Cameo), 36
"You Ought to be with Me" (Green), 89
"You Send Me" (Cooke), 53
"You Sexy Thing" (Hot Chocolate), 97
"You Should Be Mine" (Osborne), 170
"You Were Meant for Me" (Hathaway), 93
"You'll Never Find Another Love Like Mine" (Rawls), 190
"You'll Never Walk Alone" (Hamilton), 90
Young, Earl, 58, 100, 101
Young, Neil, 21, 113, 114
Young, Paul, 43
Young, Wanda, 144, 145
"Young Blood" (Coasters), 49
"Young Hearts Run Free" (Staton), 218
"Your Good Thing (Is About to End)" (Rawls), 190
"Your Love" (Graham/Central Station), 87
"(Your Love Keeps Lifting Me) Higher and Higher" (Wilson), 255
"Your Old Stand By" (Wells), 248
"Your Precious Love" (Terrell), 227
"Your Sweetness Is My Weakness" (White), 251
"Your Time to Cry" (Simon), 207
"You're a Big Girl Now" (Stylistics), 219
"You're All I Need to Get By" (Terrell), 227
"You're All I Need to Get By" (Williams), 253
"You're the First, the Last, My Everything" (White), 251
"You're Fooling You" (Dramatics), 65
"You're Good for Me" (Burke), 33
"You're a Lady" (Chandler), 40
"You're the One" (Three Degrees), 232
"(You're' Puttin') A Rush on Me" (Mills), 154
"You're So Unique" (Preston), 184
"You're Still My Baby" (Willis), 254
"You're Welcome, Stop on By" (Womack), 258
"You've Got a Friend" (Flack/Hathaway), 93
"(You've Got) the Magic Touch" (Platters), 181
"You've Really Got a Hold on Me" (Robinson/Miracles), 196

Zager, Michael, 31, 214
Zapp (Zapp), 263
Zaret, Hy, 90

PHOTO CREDITS

Images in this book were obtained courtesy of the following sources: ABC Records: Ray Charles, Lee Dorsey. A&M Records: Billy Preston. Arista Records: Whitney Houston. Associate Booking Corp.: Bobby Bland. Atco Records: Donnie Hathaway. Atlantic Records: Ruth Brown, LeVert, the Spinners. Blue Thumb Records: the Pointer Sisters. Camil Production Inc.: Little Milton. Capitol Records: Maze, Ike and Tina Turner. Casablanca Records: George Clinton. Cotillion Records: Sister Sledge. Curton Records: Curtis Mayfield. De-Lite Records: Kool and the Gang. Dial Records: Joe Tex. EastWest Records America: En Vogue. Elektra Entertainment: Anita Baker. Enterprise Records: Isaac Hayes. Epic Records: the Jacksons, LaBelle, Luther Vandross, Mary Wells, Betty Wright. Hervey & Company: Mariah Carey. Hi Records: Al Green, Ann Peebles. Ichiban Records: Tyrone Davis, Ben E. King. Island Records: Etta James. Janus Records: The Whispers. Louis Jordan: Louis Jordan. MCA Records: Bobby Brown, the Dramatics, the Flamingoes, the Moonglows, New Edition. Motown Records: Boyz II Men, Marvin Gaye, Diana Ross, Stevie Wonder. Neville Productions, Inc.: the Neville Brothers. Philadelphia International Records: Archie Bell, the O'Jays. PolyGram Records: the Bar-Kays, Cameo, Con Funk Shun, the Four Tops, Millie Jackson, Stephanie Mills, Peaches and Herb. RCA Records: Sam Cooke, King Curtis. Rhino Records: Solomon Burke, Aretha Franklin, Wilson Pickett, Percy Sledge. Rounder Records: Charles Brown. Shaw Artists Corporation: Gladys Knight, the Shirelles. Showtime: Martha Reeves. Solar Records: Shalimar. Specialty Records, Inc.: Joe Liggins, Little Richard, Percy Mayfield, Little Milton. Stax Records: Booker T. and the MG's, Carla Thomas, Rufus Thomas. Striped Horse Records: DeBarge. Tamla Records: Smokey Robinson. Total Experience Records: the Gap Band. 20th Century Records: Barry White. United Artist Records: War, Bobby Womack. Universal Attractions: Roy Brown, the 5 Royales, the Ravens, Tammi Terrell. Virgin Records: Janet Jackson. Volt Records: the Emotions, Otis Redding. Wand Records: the Isley Brothers. Warner Bros. Records: Ashford & Simpson, Larry Graham, Chaka Khan, Prince, the Staple Singers, Candi Staton, Sly Stone, Dionne Warwick, Zapp. Whitfield Records: Rose Royce. Wilbe Recording Company: William Bell. Wing Records: Tony Toni Tone. Edward Windsor Wright Corporation: Earth, Wind & Fire.

ABOUT THE AUTHOR

Oakland, California, resident **Lee Hildebrand** has written about soul, blues, jazz, and gospel music since 1968. His articles and reviews have appeared in such publications as the *San Francisco Chronicle,* the *Oakland Tribune,* the *Los Angeles Times, Blues Unlimited, Living Blues,* and the *Express,* a Berkeley weekly where he serves as an associate editor. He is also co-producer of the "Legends of Gospel" reissue series on Specialty Records.